THE HISTORY AND THEORY OF INTERNATIONAL LAW

System, Order, and International Law

THE HISTORY AND THEORY OF INTERNATIONAL LAW

General Editors

NEHAL BHUTA

Professor of Public International Law, European University Institute

ANTHONY PAGDEN

Distinguished Professor, University of California Los Angeles

BENJAMIN STRAUMANN

Alberico Gentili Senior Fellow, New York University School of Law

In the past few decades the understanding of the relationship between nations has undergone a radical transformation. The role of the traditional nation-state is diminishing, along with many of the traditional vocabularies which were once used to describe what has been called, ever since Jeremy Bentham coined the phrase in 1780, 'international law'. The older boundaries between states are growing ever more fluid, and new conceptions and new languages have emerged which are slowly coming to replace the image of a world of sovereign independent nation-states which has dominated the study of international relations since the early nineteenth century. This redefinition of the international arena demands a new understanding of classical and contemporary questions in international and legal theory. It is the editors' conviction that the best way to achieve this is by bridging the traditional divide between international legal theory, intellectual history, and legal and political history. The aim of the series, therefore, is to provide a forum for historical studies, from classical antiquity to the twenty-first century, that are theoretically-informed and for philosophical work that is historically conscious, in the hope that a new vision of the rapidly evolving international world, its past, and its possible future, may emerge.

PREVIOUSLY PUBLISHED IN THIS SERIES

The Law of Nations in Global History

C. H. Alexandrowicz

Edited by David Armitage and Jennifer Pitts

To Reform the World

International Organizations and the Making of Modern States

Guy Fiti Sinclair

International Law and Empire

Historical Explorations

Edited by Martti Koskenniemi, Walter Rech, and Manuel Jiménez Fonseca

Formalizing Displacement

International Law and Population Transfers

Umut Özsu

The Project of Positivism in International Law

Mónica García-Salmones Rovira

System, Order, and International Law

The Early History of International Legal Thought from Machiavelli to Hegel

Edited by
STEFAN KADELBACH
THOMAS KLEINLEIN
and
DAVID ROTH-ISIGKEIT

OXFORD
UNIVERSITY PRESS

OXFORD
UNIVERSITY PRESS

Great Clarendon Street, Oxford, OX2 6DP,
United Kingdom

Oxford University Press is a department of the University of Oxford.
It furthers the University's objective of excellence in research, scholarship,
and education by publishing worldwide. Oxford is a registered trade mark of
Oxford University Press in the UK and in certain other countries

First Edition published in 2017

Published in the United States of America by Oxford University Press
198 Madison Avenue, New York, NY 10016, United States of America

British Library Cataloguing in Publication Data
Data available

Library of Congress Control Number: 2017934725

ISBN 978-0-19-876858-6

In memory of Merio Scattola

Series Editors' Preface

Long before international law became an institutionalized academic discipline in the nineteenth century, prominent thinkers engaged in debates about the reach of legal norms. As the idea of sovereign statehood emerged in early modern Europe, and as European empire-states competed with each other and with non-European polities in their imperial endeavours, questions concerning moral and legal norms capable of reaching beyond these emerging states became especially salient. Could there be any role for specifically legal norms in creating order outside the state? And if so, what were the sources of these norms, what their grounds of validity?

The present volume provides a broad perspective on these questions and on the sophisticated answers that have been given to them over the centuries. It aims successfully at walking the fine line between a potentially parochial contextualism on the one hand and a too-exclusive attention to ideas, without consideration of the historical problems that gave rise to the ideas in the first place, on the other. The guiding concern that lends unity to this collection of essays is the place of international law in the development of a secular international order.

The unconventional choice of Machiavelli and Hegel as starting and ending points of the analysis presented here is as startling as it is illuminating. Machiavelli, not usually discussed in the context of international legal thought, marks the beginning of the analysis because he can be interpreted as the first thinker to have given expression to an idea of international order, however rudimentary, after the independence of the Italian communes from the Holy Roman Empire became a late medieval reality. The French invasion of Italy in the late fifteenth century was one of the key factors prompting early modern state formation and forced Machiavelli to consider the viability of Italian city-states in this novel international structure. His inclusion in a discussion of international political and legal thought helps considerably in clarifying what it was that later international legal thinkers were trying to achieve, what kind of order they sought to remake in light of their normative systems.

Jean Bodin, another author who is not usually included in discussions of international legal thought, is a further example of the important insights that can be gained once one is willing to cast a wider net and enlarge the canon of those writing about international order. The idea of state sovereignty, as developed most influentially by Bodin, created interesting problems concerning the legal rights and duties of sovereigns, both inside and outside of the state. Other authors discussed in the first part of the present collection who are not conventionally discussed as international legal thinkers include Althusius, Spinoza, Montesquieu, Rousseau, and Hegel. Hegel marks the end of international law understood in its expansive prepositive sense as a philosophical and historical endeavour before the establishment of a specialized academic curriculum. The volume therefore redirects our attention to the fundamentals of international order by offering a broad understanding of international legal thought not confined to the disciplinary borders of nineteenth century positivism.

The subtle and original interpretations of these authors put forward here prove how much sustained reflection on international law can gain from ideas that were developed outside the narrow province of the canon of what is today commonly accepted as constituting international legal theory. The volume gives us what the editors call a 'creative reading of history', which, while attentive to the historical problem situations within which these ideas took shape, does not insulate itself from the texts analysed. As the editors emphasize, the volume pursues a 'moderate anachronism' in search of a conception of legal order outside the state that makes sense 'beyond its contingent existence conditions'.

Moderate anachronism thus really turns out to be an ambitious programme that allows us to put the historical material to the test and to evaluate it comparatively. In its second, systematic part the volume draws on the insights gained from the first, historical part. Some of the ideas treated in the first part are here considered in a critical way that seeks to provide a sense of long-term orientation. In this second part, causal historical explanations for the current state of international law and international legal thinking are given, all the while attending to the reasoning contained in the historical material. The second part builds on the first in showing how our point of view was reached, but it goes beyond that and attempts to formulate historically literate answers to some of the problems touched upon by the cast of historical thinkers.

By adopting a deep, historical view, the authors of this collection provide an antidote to an ahistorical worldview that is blind to its own limitations. By offering a long-term historical picture of international legal ideas and the problems they were designed to answer, the approaches to the challenges of global order portrayed in this book provide a refreshing and original sense of available alternatives. No longer the slaves of some defunct political or legal theorists, international lawyers and international legal thinkers are now in a position to make up their own minds.

Benjamin Straumann
New York City
December 2016

Avant-Propos

Like a pair of Herculean pillars, System and Order are presiding over the present expedition into three centuries of nascent international legal thought. The field that is being explored is the early history of a philosophical perspective of international law, the *Ideengeschichte* of its genesis. In recent years the historical aspects of international law have aroused considerable interest among wider circles of jurists and neighbouring disciplines. This historical turn (as it has been dubbed) was fairly unexpected to those who have dwelt upon that field earlier on. Those were essentially internationalists who felt themselves, and would appear to their colleagues, as a few *aficionados* cultivating their secret garden, without being taken very seriously. As in other legal disciplines, the history of international law usually has at best an ornamental value, except when it can be instrumentalized for practical purposes. Of course there are professional legal historians, but these would hardly ever care for international law. The traditional historians of international law, starting with their remote ancestor, Robert Ward, were rather seen as marginal amateurs. Genuine internationalists (just as other jurists) deal with current law, which means actual practice rather than detached theoretical considerations.

And yet such a sharp division between supposedly positive law and the halo of ideas surrounding it, while it may work in most fields of municipal law, is untenable in international law. By ignoring its roots, which lie in history and philosophy, one loses sight as it were of its very matrix and soul. This seemed already obvious, at the height of legal positivism toward the end of the nineteenth century, to one of its outstanding representatives, Alphonse Rivier. A staunch positivist, Rivier was the Swiss consul in Belgium and professor of Roman and international law at the Université Libre de Bruxelles (with Ernest Nys, the most eminent historian of international law of his time, as his colleague). Rivier considered what he still called the law of nations—'Principes du droit des gens' is the title of his main work—as 'an eminently historical discipline': history is more than just an auxiliary science, he asserted, 'it is its main basis, its foremost source being the usage of nations' (*Völkerbrauch*). Almost in the same breath he added that philosophy is quite as indispensable in its critical and theoretical function, striving to integrate the existing materials and practices into 'a harmonious and logically articulated whole' (*Lehrbuch des Völkerrechts*, Stuttgart, 1889). He also recognized the crucial part played by abstract philosophical constructions in the origins of international law (though he judged them irrelevant for the present).

In fact, international law in its beginnings appears to a large extent as an offshoot of early modern political and moral philosophy at grips with the Romanistic and Canonistic *jus commune*; and philosophy has ever since had an important share in its development. The reason for this philosophical bias lies in the very nature and structure of the discipline. 'There is no praetor', as was famously stated by Hegel, the last of the authors examined in this volume. At best there are arbitrations and mediators, he says, but these are mere expedients depending on the states' individual wills. There is no common power constituted above them, which entails a general precariousness of whatever they may have stipulated by treaty (Hegel, *Grundlinien der Philosophie des Rechts,* 1821). In line with Hobbes, Spinoza, Rousseau, and Kant, Hegel considered the states as remaining side by side in a state of nature, and hence in a basically lawless condition. In spite of lofty pseudo-constitutional devices like Wolff's *civitas maxima,* this Vattelian horizontality remains the essential structural feature of international law, although Hegel's divinization of the state and its sovereign will is nowadays considered as past and of another age. In spite of considerable developments in international organization, international law remains fundamentally 'anarchical'. Kant's sneer at the 'sorry comforters' could easily be redirected to the present. In fact, no legal discipline is confronted with equal scepticism on the part of other jurists as to its soundness. It constantly has to explain and justify its legal foundations and its very legal nature, precisely on account of the lack of a 'praetor' endowed with true public authority over the states.

This situation was even more obvious at a time when the discipline of international law did not yet exist as such, that is, roughly up to the middle of the seventeenth century. The European state was by then still taking shape, either in its princely or its republican shape. Intense reflection and theorizing was devoted to it by political thinkers such as Machiavelli, Bodin, Althusius, or Hobbes, for whom conversely international aspects were at best a marginal preoccupation. On the other hand, the relationship between states was a central concern to the so-called classics (or 'founders') of international law during that period, from Vitoria to Grotius. What they had in mind, however, when they mentioned *jus gentium* was not yet international law in our sense, as would clearly be the case a century thereafter with Leibniz, Textor, Bynkershoek, or Wolff; at most they had at times a vague intuition of such an overarching legal order, of which Vitoria's *totus orbis* as the legislator of *jus gentium* governing the whole world 'in peace and in war' is an outstanding (and rare) example (*Relectio de potestate civili,* 1527–58). What they were usually writing about was the law of war, not as part of a wider international law, but as a self-contained legal subject-matter which reached back for its formative stages to the medieval *jus belli.* This is eloquently shown by the very titles of their works: *De indis et de jure belli* (Vitoria, 1538–9), *De re militari et bello* (Belli, 1563), *De jure et officiis bellicis* et *disciplina militari* (Ayala, 1582), *De jure belli* (Gentili, 1588–9/1598), and *De jure belli ac pacis* (Grotius, 1625). With the rise of the state, war was by then increasingly becoming an exclusively inter-state relationship, as was much later famously to be proclaimed by Rousseau. Already Gentili defined it as 'a just and public contest of arms' (*publicorum armorum justa contentio*) in which only 'princes', that is, sovereign powers in Bodin's style could take part. Though limited to belligerency, this was of course precisely the kind of relationship that raised the question of a possible legal order above those powers (much more drastically than the law of embassies, which also formed an autonomous legal tradition partly related to *jus gentium* since Roman times). Here then lies the spring of what the editors of this volume postulate as 'international legal thought' (a somewhat ethereal concept which could remind one, if a bit of mischief be allowed, of the mythical 'phlogiston' that was supposed to account for the inflammability of substances in eighteenth century chemistry).

All the sixteenth and early seventeenth century authors just mentioned felt the need to tackle this basic problem of a law among belligerents when they undertook to writing on the law of war. This is the main object of the Prolegomena to Grotius' *magnum opus* of 1625 on the law of war and the return to peace: the celebrated diatribe against Carneades seeks to discard *a limine* the 'realist' denial of any normative order beyond the states by affirming, in the steps of Cicero and the Spanish scholastics, the reality of a natural law inherent in human nature and valid 'even if God did not exist'. Gentili in 1598 had given a similar demonstration to the same effect by adding in the final version of his treatise a substantial introductory chapter 'on the law of nations relating to war' (*De jure gentium bellico*). War was obviously the main catalyst of international legal thought during the first part of the period examined in this volume.

A more general apprehension of *jus gentium* as an all-embracing system of international law became common only after the middle of the seventeenth century. What has been termed the first textbook of international law was indeed published exactly in 1650 by Richard Zouche, the successor of Gentili in the Regius Chair of civil law at Oxford. His relatively slender manual was named after the Roman *jus fetiale*, the law governing Rome's foreign relations, and it did indeed encompass the whole of the relationships between nations in peace and in war (significantly in this order, the law of war being henceforth integrated into a wider framework). Zouche also called it *jus inter gentes* (instead of the traditional and ambiguous *jus gentium*) as applying specifically to the *communio inter gentes*, that is, between nations confronting each other as personified Hobbesian polities. The expression conveys a clear sense of international legal thought. International law was here for the first time articulated as a complete and autonomous legal field, prefiguring classical international law as delineated a century later in Wolff's *Jus Gentium* (1749) and Vattel's *Droit des Gens* (1758). International law is presented in both these works as a fully systematized and independent 'science' rationally deduced from natural law principles. About the same time, Johann Jacob Moser published two booklets in a very different vein rejecting the very idea of a universal system. They set out dryly, without more ado, the actual practice prevailing among European nations in time of peace (1750) and war (1752). Moser is the archpositivist and stands in stark contrast to Wolff and the natural law of tradition of Pufendorf. Both Moser and Wolff could, for all that, have claimed Zouche as their patron. The Oxford professor himself considered Gentili and Grotius as his main inspiration, the one for *Jus*, the other for *Ratio*, acknowledging thereby the equal relevance of both practice and principle.

While the two approaches were obviously complementary for Zouche, they were clearly drifting apart a century later with Moser and Wolff. Three and a half decades later this discrepancy was noted and regretted by Dietrich von Ompteda in his *Litteratur des Völkerrechts* of 1785. This repertory of the literature on the law of nations was intended as a preliminary study to a truly thorough and complete *system* of the law of the nations, natural as well as positive, which would duly take into account the principles (*Grundregeln*) and their practical application (*Anwendung*) by custom and treaties. The first step to be taken in this regard was 'to put the various objects of the law of nations into an adequate *order* and mutual relationship' (*Litteratur des gesamten sowohl natürlichen als positiven Völkerrechts*, 1785) (emphasis added). This is indeed what Ompteda did in the detailed plan he drew of the treatise he had in mind (with some trepidation). He never wrote the book, but the sketch he left is a signal token of mature international legal thought. To the participants in this expedition returning from their bountiful venture Ompteda's outline could surely appear as a safe haven, with System and Order watching like two towers over its entrance.

Peter Haggenmacher

Acknowledgements

This volume is the result of a research project that has stretched over three years. We owe thanks to many people involved in its course. We would like to thank Normative Orders, Cluster of Excellence at Goethe University Frankfurt/Main, in particular its managing director Rebecca Schmidt, for financial and organizational support and for hosting the first of two conferences of authors held in July 2014. We are equally grateful to the *Deutsche Forschungsgemeinschaft*, two anonymous reviewers, as well as Immacolata Amodeo and Christiane Liermann Traniello for the opportunity to have a second workshop at Villa Vigoni in Menaggio di Como in June 2015. For important advice and inspiration, we are indebted to Anne Peters, Michael Stolleis, Matthias Lutz-Bachmann, and Stefan Häußler. In the preparation of the manuscript, we could count on valuable support from Lea Isabelle Lang, Theresa Neumann, Marie Dickel, Jennifer Drehwald, Sascha Gourdet, Christoph Hettinger, and Raven Kirchner. We would further like to thank John Louth, Merel Alstein, Emma Endean, and Eve Ryle-Hodges from Oxford University Press for their assistance in preparing this volume for publication. Last, but not least, thanks are due to Nehal Bhuta, Anthony Pagden, and Benjamin Straumann for including this book in the *History and Theory of International Law* series.

On 23 August 2015, we had to mourn for the loss of our esteemed colleague and friend Merio Scattola. Through his scholarly expertise and his unbroken optimism, he enriched our meetings and inspired our thoughts. He was working on his contribution to this volume literally until his last days. With him, the academic community loses a great scholar of the history of political thought. This book is dedicated to his memory.

Stefan Kadelbach
Thomas Kleinlein
David Roth-Isigkeit

Frankfurt/Main, January 2017

Contents

List of Contributors

Tilmann Altwicker is a SNSF-Ambizione fellow and senior lecturer at the University of Basel.

Nehal Bhuta is professor of public international law at the European University Institute, Florence.

Armin von Bogdandy is director at the Max Planck Institute for Comparative Public Law and International Law in Heidelberg and professor for public law at Goethe University Frankfurt/Main.

Kirstin Bunge is an affiliate of the Hamburg University of Applied Sciences.

Sergio Dellavalle is professor of state theory and public law at the University of Turin and a senior research affiliate at the Max Planck Institute for Comparative Public Law and International Law in Heidelberg.

Carla De Pascale is professor of the history of philosophy at the University of Bologna.

Pierre-Marie Dupuy is emeritus professor at the University of Paris (Panthéon-Assas) and honorary professor at the Graduate Institute of International and Development Studies, Geneva.

Thomas Duve is director at the Max Planck Institute for European Legal History and professor of comparative legal history at Goethe University Frankfurt/Main.

Vanda Fiorillo is professor of political philosophy at the University of Naples.

Mónica García-Salmones is a postdoctoral research fellow at the Erik Castrén Institute of International Law and Human Rights at the University of Helsinki.

Peter Haggenmacher is honorary professor at the Graduate Institute of International and Development Studies, Geneva.

Jonas Heller is a postdoctoral research fellow at 'Normative Orders', Cluster of Excellence, and at the department of philosophy, at Goethe University Frankfurt/Main.

Gunther Hellmann is professor of political science and principal investigator at 'Normative Orders', Cluster of Excellence at Goethe University Frankfurt/Main.

Thomas O. Hueglin is professor of political science at Wilfrid Laurier University, Waterloo (Ontario).

Stefan Kadelbach is professor of public international law and European constitutional law at Goethe University Frankfurt/Main.

Thomas Kleinlein is *Privatdozent* at the Institute for Public Law and associate member of 'Normative Orders', Cluster of Excellence at Goethe University Frankfurt/Main.

Martti Koskenniemi is academy professor and director of the Erik Castrén Institute of International Law and Human Rights at the University of Helsinki.

Bastian Ronge is a postdoctoral research fellow at the department of practical and social philosophy at Humboldt University Berlin.

David Roth-Isigkeit is a postdoctoral research fellow at 'Normative Orders', Cluster of Excellence at Goethe University Frankfurt/Main.

Merio Scattola† was professor of the history of political ideas at the University of Padua.

Tobias Schaffner is an attorney with Knoetzl Haugeneder Netal Rechtsanwaelte GmbH, Vienna.

Benedict Vischer is a research fellow at the Max Planck Institute for Comparative Public Law and International Law in Heidelberg and at 'Normative Orders', Cluster of Excellence at Goethe University Frankfurt/Main.

Christian Volk is professor of political science with a special focus on politics and law at the Otto-Suhr-Institute of the Free University of Berlin.

Andreas Wagner is a postdoctoral research fellow at the Academy of Science and Literature, Mainz.

Simone Zurbuchen is professor of philosophy at the University of Lausanne.

Introduction

Stefan Kadelbach, Thomas Kleinlein, and David Roth-Isigkeit

I. On the Topicality of the Past

For many centuries, thinkers have tried to understand and to conceptualize political and legal order beyond the boundaries of sovereign territories. Their theories aim at the interaction of human, social, and political communities on its highest level. While this interest in describing and designing political order beyond the state (or its preliminaries) had diverse reasons—some wanted to help their prince to stay in power, others aimed at resolving the riddles of human sociality—they share a common object of thought, the international social, political, and legal order.

The directions from which these thinkers approach their common object, however, appear intimately linked to their personal histories and contemporary contexts. Accordingly, the concepts we encounter in this discourse are deeply entangled in philosophical claims on theology,[1] state formation,[2] and human nature. Thus understood, concepts of world order are embedded in complex philosophical systems and epistemic claims. With this volume, we hope to make this framework visible and to contribute to an emerging discourse that draws its inspiration from a philosophical re-appreciation, often creative, of the history of international legal thought.

In this introduction, we will lay down our perspective on the recent trend of historical inquiry in international legal scholarship and situate international legal thought as a distinctive discursive sphere between international law, the history of political ideas, and political philosophy. This volume is dedicated to the emergence of this discursive sphere before the modern national state appeared. In this early period, international law in the modern sense had not yet been constituted as a university discipline. International legal thinking was mostly considered a reflex of other academic inquiries—theology, law, or ethics. Rudimentary as these sketches

[1] Anthony Carty, 'The Play of Medieval Ghosts and Renaissance Demons in Birth, Death and Rebirth of European International Law', in Thilo Marauhn and Heinhard Steiger (eds.), *Universality and Continuity in International Law* (2011), pp. 61–85.

[2] Annabel Brett, *Changes of State: Nature and the Limits of the City in Early Modern Natural Law* (2011).

might have been, they are inspirational in the search for answers to the challenges of a political world that appears increasingly complex.

One of the reasons for the increasing re-appreciation of the roots of international legal thought is that the questions at stake are inextricably linked with today's theoretical discourses on international law. While the world has secularized and theological arguments are replaced by ethical reasoning, old challenges such as the question of perpetual peace are a lasting topic on the philosophical agenda. Old and new questions alike seem to pervade different epochs of philosophical, political, and legal thinking: how do institutions and agreements retain their normative force in an ever-changing political world? In particular, in our days, when it is common to state that the importance of the nation-state is vanishing, the problems at issue in the classic theories do not seem too remote: is an international system without central power possible? How can a normative order come about if there is no central force to structure relations between states? In times where insecurity about the persistence of an international law of national states pervades scholarly agendas, this historically-situated form of international legal thought contains inspirational potential.

It is this inspiration and creativity of thought that appears both promising and challenging at the same time. In designing the volume, we have tried to respond to a conceptual problem to bridge the gap of up to 500 years of societal thinking. With the notions of *system* and *order*, we attempt to provide a frame of reference that makes different approaches comparable and links them to today's international legal thinking. These terms are supposed to reflect the motivation and the object of international legal thought. They are also sufficiently abstract and neutral to serve as paradigms to appreciate how the early history of international legal thought is already an indispensable part of international law as we know it and, at the same time, a valuable conceptual resource for the challenges of a changing political world.

The following sections explain the goals and the framework of this volume in four consecutive steps. Firstly, we will sketch our conceptual understanding of a history of *international legal thought* as a project that highlights the intimate relationship of philosophy and law in understanding the present models of global order. The second section sets out our frame of reference, the interplay of system and order, which serves as a reference to link historical models to today's discourse. The third section explains our particular interest in the period from Machiavelli to Hegel in a study of international legal thought. Ultimately, the fourth section illustrates some of the results of this exercise that we consider fruitful for the discourse.

II. The History of International Legal Thought

1. International legal thought: A legal project and an integrative approach

International legal thought intends to close a gap in the philosophical history of global order where little emphasis has been laid on the legal–theoretical and legal–philosophical nuances. What makes a particular normative statement one of 'law' and what distinguishes it from other kinds of normativity? Relatedly, one might ask what the relationship between a philosophical system and the legal system is, or between law and ethics. The distinction between facticity and validity, universally acknowledged in the modern concept of law, arises with this difference.

Highlighting the concept of *thought* can help us appreciate the complexity of the different roles that are connected with philosophical concepts. Such reconstruction must reflect both the role of the thinker and the object of thought, the legal norm. What are the different motivations to conceptualize International Relations as legal relations? Between self-interest and duty, and between morality and hypocrisy, we encounter a broad spectrum of different roles along the centuries.

This focus on *legal* thought, however, does not mean that we pursue a disciplinary legal project. As an inquiry into the philosophical foundations of law, it cannot conceive of its legal object without taking the perspectives of other disciplines into account. Yet, due to the diversity of perspectives one can take towards the internal structures of legality, the specificities of *legal* forms of organization tend to become blurred in the picture of politics, history, and sociology. This problem is reflected in the currently more or less separate discourses in international legal scholarship, philosophy, and International Relations, which do not necessarily take note of each other. For the purpose of understanding, our modest interdisciplinary objective is to make the traditions talk to each other, and, for this reason, bring together contributions on authors who are generally considered as relevant for the respective 'stories' of the disciplines. Yet, in its capacity to take the internal structure of legality into account, there is something distinct about international legal thought in its argumentative structure which the participating disciplines have in common and which provides for a common language.

2. The stories of the disciplines: Invented traditions?

Some of the authors discussed in this book have been of special interest in one discipline or another. In particular, international legal scholarship and International Relations have established canons or standard narratives of their own scholarly traditions. For example, international legal scholarship often refers to Gentili, Grotius, and Vattel. In turn, Machiavelli, Bodin, Hobbes, Rousseau, and Montesquieu appear primarily as political philosophers. Some authors are particularly well-known in International Relations, due to Hedley Bull's famous distinction between the Hobbesian, the Kantian, and the Grotian traditions.[3] Other authors, by contrast, such as Althusius or Spinoza, do not seem to be part of any canon.

Such reconstruction from the past applied to today's questions requires a conscious dealing with the tension between historical context and progressive

[3] Hedley Bull, *The Anarchical Society: A Study of Order in World Politics* (3rd edn, 2002), pp. 23–6.

interpretation. The historiography of political ideas is dominantly contextual.[4] Political philosophy, in turn, might necessarily imply the epistemic claim of enduring questions—and answers—beyond individual historical circumstances.[5] Here, the history of international legal thought is related to a kind of normativity that is neither purely contextual in a narrow sense nor claims to be timeless and universal. Like texts that express abstract political ideas, texts that unfold ideas of international legal order have certainly played a role as political interventions, in particular social contexts and political power struggles.[6]

By following an approach of moderate anachronism, we intend to walk the line between the inner structure of the argument, contextual research and a perspective carefully guided by today's international law. This involves thinking about questions like the author's intended audience, possible constraints, and the extent to which the theory responds to a given political context. To make sense of a use of the argument today, however, it is also important to take the theory out of its original context and reflect upon it in the light of current problems, and to ask whether its transformative value is dependent on the historical situation. This could mean, eg, to ask to what extent Vitoria's and Suárez' arguments are not only explained through colonialism, but also dependent on it. In other words, we are interested in hidden agendas, errors, and (frustrated) hopes as much as in emancipatory potentials. The ambition of international legal thought thus understood obviously reaches further than confining international law to an assemblage of concrete treaties or customary obligations. On the other hand, it cannot be reduced to natural-law thinking. It evokes a specific *form* of normativity that touches upon many of the received accounts.

Such an often creative reading of history finds its analogy in the argumentative structures that appear in legal proceedings. Arguments of legal practitioners and diplomats often reach out into the past when they cite precedents or when they aim at establishing a norm of customary international law. This includes reference to authors that this volume deals with, thus following a method Gentili, Bodin, or Grotius used themselves. Gentili, for instance, reconstructed the content of natural law using figures like overlapping customs and time tests stemming from Roman civil law doctrine.[7] Bodin obtained and extracted all rules, institutes, and customs of the 'public law of nations' from a study of examples and models preserved in ancient history. Grotius developed a new branch of legal knowledge in the early

[4] Quentin Skinner, 'Meaning and Understanding in the History of Ideas', *History and Theory* 8 (1969), 3–53; Quentin Skinner, 'Meaning and Understanding Speech Acts', in Quentin Skinner (ed.), *Visions of Politics. Volume 1 Regarding Method* (2002), pp. 57–89.

[5] Benedict Kingsbury and Benjamin Straumann, 'State of Nature versus Commercial Sociability as the Basis of International Law: Reflections on the Roman Foundations and Current Interpretations of the International Political Legal Thought of Grotius, Hobbes, and Pufendorf', in Samantha Besson and John Tasioulas (eds.), *The Philosophy of International Law* (2010), pp. 33–51, at p. 51. For a debate whether political philosophy is too ahistorical, see Jonathan Floyd and Marc Stears (eds.), *Political Philosophy versus History? Contextualism and Real Politics in Contemporary Political Thought* (2011).

[6] Skinner, 'Meaning and Understanding in the History of Ideas' (n. 4).

[7] See the contribution by Wagner in this volume.

seventeenth century on the basis of historical and literary sources. A search for the *form* of normativity thus involves a special relationship to time and history.

Thus, through the continuing self-historicization in international legal thought, this special relationship to the past reproduces itself on the reflexive level of the discipline.[8] The particular interest of international legal thought in its own idea of tradition has led us to place a specific emphasis on the reception of individual authors over the centuries and in current debates. This interest in the histories of reception is reflected in the contrast between the new popularity of theory, philosophy, and history, on the one hand, and a reference to the classics in standard discourse, on the other, which seemingly remains unaffected by these new developments. What are the reasons for the popularity of certain thinkers at a certain time? Are there stereotypes,[9] errors, or misunderstandings in reception? Are there differences in interpretation and do they follow certain patterns? Are there institutions, judgments, or arguments which are still invoked, and what are the interests behind them? What are the twists in the receptions and appropriations?

Histories of reception allow us to capture the fact that international legal thought is not a continuous conversation across time and that the migration of ideas is not a steady process.[10] In order to establish continuity and tradition, a certain degree of creativity and inventiveness is certainly needed. Today, these stories are strongly dominated by the remnants of specific cycles of reception. The way we look at Suárez, Grotius, and others today is influenced by the way in which they were portrayed in the late nineteenth and early twentieth centuries, and at times a standard account with an independent life has developed.[11] Surely, it is inevitable that any current reconstruction is influenced by today's concepts and problems. The approach to create the necessary distance to today's readers own perception is to do both, where possible: to try to place classic texts in their original context, which may be theology, philosophy, or political ethics, and to follow their reception in order to assess what can be the lessons for current notions of the international order.

3. Between construction and critique

A distanced approach also seems appropriate in a second respect, the stance taken vis-à-vis the dichotomy of construction and critique.

In today's historically interested international legal scholarship, many approaches seem to fall into one of two camps. The first type of narrative tells a story of progress,

[8] For the potential problems that this self-historization comes with, see Matthew Craven, 'Theorising the Turn to History in International Law', in Anne Orford and Florian Hoffmann (eds.), *The Oxford Handbook of the Theory of International Law* (2016), pp. 21–37.

[9] See the reading of Hobbes, Grotius, and Kant in Bull, *The Anarchical Society* (n. 3).

[10] For a very special history of reception, see Vattel's reception of Wolff and Vattel's own lasting authority in North America, as outlined in the contribution by Zurbuchen in this volume.

[11] Thomas Kleinlein, '"Wollen die leeren Worte kein Ende haben?" – Die Frühaufklärung in der heutigen Völkerrechtswissenschaft', in Tilmann Altwicker, Francis Cheneval, and Oliver Diggelmann (eds.), *Völkerrechtsphilosophie der Frühaufklärung* (2015), pp. 247–66.

the second takes a critical perspective and is interested in international law as an instrument of domination and as a product of Eurocentrism.[12]

In the first camp, we encounter the systematic use of historical arguments to underline specific claims about the normativity of international law. This strand recognizes the narrative structure of normativity and attempts to use historical ideas to underline normative judgments, be they legal or moral. This creative resort to history can be exemplified in the emergence of an ontological dimension as a foundation for the spread of human rights as the core concept of international law. Laying this foundation seems facilitated by the rediscovery of international law as a divine institution, which, in turn, is closely related to the increasing reception of the Spanish natural lawyers in the last decade.[13] The continuing interest in natural law concepts, now renewed once more, recovers arguments that are otherwise difficult to defend in secularized normative environments.[14]

In the second camp, critical scholars often engage with history for a deconstructive purpose.[15] They research how concepts and narratives of international law are related to and deeply rooted in patterns of imperialism and colonial domination over the centuries. In the 1990s, critical scholarship began to research the ways in which past texts have been drawn upon to shape new legal orders and obligations.[16] This strand of critical legal studies is paralleled by developments in critical philosophy. Critical approaches in philosophy aim at demystifying normativity by revealing the circumstances of its genesis. In revealing the contingency of metaphysical assumptions, critical philosophy erodes the narratives of universality by contrasting them with the particularities of their existence conditions.[17] In this reconstruction from the past lies a potential that allows for a reflexive conception of the discipline

[12] Ian Hunter, 'Global Justice and Regional Metaphysics: On the Critical History of the Law of Nature and Nations', in Shaunnagh Dorsett and Ian Hunter (eds.), *Law and Politics in British Colonial Thought. Transpositions of Empire* (2010), pp. 11–29, at pp. 11–12; Ian Hunter, 'The Figure of Man and the Territorialisation of Justice in "Enlightenment" Natural Law: Pufendorf and Vattel', *Intellectual History Review* 23 (2013), 289–307, at 290.

[13] See the contributions by Schaffner and Wagner in this volume.

[14] See, for related arguments, Carty, *The Play of Medieval Ghosts*, pp. 61–85 (n. 1); Oliver O'Donovan, *The Just War Revisited* (2003).

[15] Cf. Tilmann Altwicker and Oliver Diggelmann, 'What Should Remain of the Critical Approaches to International Law? International Legal Theory as Critique', *Schweizerische Zeitschrift für Internationales und Europäisches Recht* 24 (2014), 69–92, at 81.

[16] Cf. Anne Orford, 'The Past as Law or History? The Relevance of Imperialism for Modern International Law', in Mark Toufayan, Emmanuelle Tourme-Jouannet, and Hélène Ruiz Fabri (eds.), *Droit international et nouvelles approches sur le tiers-monde, entre répétition et renouveau* (2013), pp. 97–117, at p. 109; A. Anghie, *Imperialism, Sovereignty and the Making of International Law* (2005). Similarly, Orford's research points to how the concept of Responsibility to Protect reactivates just war theories and the normative foundations of authority in international law in general. See Anne Orford, *International Authority and the Responsibility to Protect* (2011).

[17] See, for further reading, Razmig Keucheyan, *The Left Hemisphere* (2013). For a discussion of 'system' in this context see pp. 79–168.

revealing 'what we study as history of international law depends on what we think "international law" is in the first place'.[18]

Acknowledging this, the present project may in itself be seen as 'organizing a system through historiography'.[19] One of the central elements of this reconstruction is the attempt to find a balance between the historical context and our perception of it. It intends to contribute to transcending this dualism and does not fall in either of these camps. Thus, the objective cannot be to approach thinkers from Machiavelli to Hegel with a common perspective, or a common critical mindset, scrutinizing their arguments and concepts in search for particular biases. Rather than to develop other linear narratives, it was intended to open up a space for reflexivity between construction and critique. A result may well be to understand the authors'—and readers'—own perception of present international law as inevitably 'European', with all good and bad associations this term might provoke.

III. System and Order

1. The concept of a system

In order to support the structure of the volume with a mediating perspective between law and philosophy, we use the concept of *system*. The term triggers certain associations: completeness, wholeness, coherence, unity, stability.[20] Not only in the legal context, but quite generally, system implies a technique used to develop concrete outcomes from general ideas by canons of methods. We find dogmatic systems in medicine, theology, and philosophy. They describe practices, actors, the interrelations between different entities and those between these entities and a common unity so that all components in their totality form a system: there can be a federal system,[21] the 'Westphalian' system,[22] a 'system of states',[23] a collective security system[24] or, most generally, the 'international' or 'world system'.[25] Thus, conceiving

[18] Martti Koskenniemi, 'A History of International Law Histories', in Bardo Fassbender and Anne Peters (eds.), *The Oxford Handbook of the History of International Law* (2012), pp. 943–71, at p. 970.

[19] Cf. Martti Koskenniemi, 'Between Coordination and Constitution: International Law as a German Discipline', *Redescriptions* 15 (2011), 45–70, at 63.

[20] 'System' is used in a different way in Luhmann's sociological theory of law. The overarching concept of 'system' here describes the interplay between societal forces, one subsystem being law itself, which, by way of functional differentiation of society, interacts with other systems. Niklas Luhmann, *A Sociological Theory of Law* (2nd edn, 2013). See also Andreas Fischer-Lescano and Gunther Teubner, 'Regime-Collisions – The Vain Search for Legal Unity in the Fragmentation of Global Law', *Mich J Int'l L* 25 (2004), 999–1046.

[21] Reinhart Koselleck, 'Bund – Bündnis, Föderalismus, Bundesstaat', in Otto Brunner et al. (eds.), *Geschichtliche Grundbegriffe*, vol. I (1972), pp. 582, 631 with further reference.

[22] Arthur Eyffinger, 'Europe in the Balance – An Appraisal of the Westphalian System', *Neth Int'l L Rev* 45 (1998), 161–87.

[23] Wilhelm Grewe, *Epochen der Völkerrechtsgeschichte* (1984), pp. 33–8.

[24] Cf. Christine Gray, 'A Crisis of Legitimacy for the UN Collective Security System?', *ICLQ* 56 (2007), 157–70.

[25] Cf. e.g. Eric Wilson, *The Savage Republic:* De Indis *of Hugo Grotius, Republicanism and Dutch Hegemony Within the Early Modern World-System (c. 1600-1619)* (2008).

International Relations in terms of a legal system entails certain demands of coherence and rationality.

On the one hand, the law has a special place in philosophical systems, so that it can be a specific trait of systematic philosophy to think of international relations as legal relations. Here, the notion of a system integrates real world and utopia in that it expresses what a polity has decided to become and what it actually wants to become. On the other hand, we might ask what this dialectic means for a conception of a legal system. In a lawyer's perspective, the notion of a system has a stronger normative meaning when it implies a context which allows one to derive obligations.[26] In that sense, it is the fitting together of institutions, rules, principles, and precedents that makes the law appear as a system. Systematic approaches provide the methodology to contextualize relationships of single norms and hence to resolve tensions between normative ideals such as peace, justice, or liberty.

Depicting international law as legal system has become a standard expression.[27] The term 'system' is found, among other places, in the works of Leibniz, Wolff, and Kant, all of which illustrate the various meanings the term may have.[28] From 1600, the concept of 'system' becomes increasingly established as a term for the external aspect of government. Grotius already refers to such a concept when he describes foreign policy as a bond between autonomous communities ('*Foedus arctissimum inter civitates*').[29] The concept becomes even more encompassing for Hobbes, who defines 'system' as 'any numbers of men joined in one interest, or one business' and dedicates a whole chapter of his *Leviathan* to its discussion.[30] Other authors refer to the meaning of system with different notions: for example, 'summa' or 'summula' refers to the same type of treatises written by Catholic scholars, which Protestant scholars would call 'system'.[31] *Fides majestas* or *civitas maxima* may also represent examples of a system of reference.

The meaning of the term 'system' has changed over the last century. In late German Idealism, the objective idea of 'system' seems to step back for a more process-oriented conception based on systematizing as the operating mode of critical reason. Since Savigny, it is also common to speak of a legal system if the particularities of different legal cultures are stressed. Today, legal systems are more often seen as a conceptual instrument for ordering and managing the law. Accordingly, reconstructing and representing positive law as a system is regarded as the specific

[26] See, in particular, Herbert Hart, *The Concept of Law* (1961), pp. 82–91.

[27] For a discussion of system-related questions, see Jean Combacau, 'Le droit international: bric-à-brac ou système?', *Archives de Philosophie du Droit* 31 (1986), 85–105; *Fragmentation of International Law: Difficulties Arising from the Diversification and Expansion of International Law*, Report of the Study Group of the International Law Commission finalized by M. Koskenniemi, 13 April 2006, in particular paras. 17, 34.

[28] See Christian Strub, 'System' II (Neuzeit), in Joachim Ritter u.a. (eds.), Historisches Wörterbuch der Philosophie, Bd. 10 (1998), pp. 825–56. See also Merio Scattola, *Krieg des Wissens – Wissen des Krieges: Konflikt, Erfahrung und System der literarischen Gattungen am Beginn der Frühen Neuzeit* (2006), pp. 87–9 and the contributions by Fiorillo, Kleinlein, and Vischer in this volume.

[29] Hugo Grotius *De Iure Belli ac Pacis Libri Tres* (1646), trans. Francis W. Kelsey (1925), Book I, Ch. 3, Section VII, 1, 3, 7.

[30] Thomas Hobbes, *Leviathan*, Oxford World Classics (2009), ch. 22.

[31] Scattola, *Krieg des Wissens*, p. 88 (n. 28).

function of legal scholarship. Legal scholarship thus creates a distinct area of discourse, which represents a sort of 'middle level' between natural law, on the one hand, and the concrete provisions of positive law, on the other. Whilst the former is primarily within the competence of philosophy and theology, the latter is in the direct grasp of politics and the courts.[32]

Thus, one distinct meaning of 'system' is epistemic. The system is man-made and represents the exercise of theorizing itself. In this regard, 'system' describes how a philosophy integrates different phenomena under one or more guiding ideas. This epistemic aspect of a system is of particular relevance for the purposes of the present volume. We will try to consider the epistemic meaning of a system, be it in the scholastic sense of theological reasoning, the philosophical sense of cognitive ordering, as found in Leibniz and Spinoza, or in the dogmatic sense of legal scholarship. Christian Wolff develops a system in which international law is one element. As opposed to natural law conceptions 'system' denotes here merely the claim to present things autonomously and 'systematically', i.e. in a consistent, non-self-contradictory way.

2. The notion of order

The concept of system as a cutting edge is supplemented with a less demanding notion of order. By *order*, we understand a pattern which social relations between human beings, groups, and states follow to provide for stability. Order appeals to facticity and is based on some form of 'authority', i.e. a force that guarantees the observance of the rules and patterns on which order rests, like power, command, or consent. Patterns of international order may be explained by 'state sociological' concepts like hegemony or balance of power. It is in this sense that order has been understood as the opposite of law.[33]

3. The relationship between system and order

In the approaches of this book, however, we will usually find both notions closely intertwined. From an international law perspective, the question is how far relations between states are thought of as normative in a sense that behaviour is stabilized and guided by legal obligations and, if so, whether these obligations form a normative whole, in the sense that they can be derived from common concepts, principles, and analogies in a consistent, self-reflective way.

The very purpose of international law as a legal 'system' might be to provide stability of expectations and thus an 'order' based on (the rule of) law. By achieving stability, a system fulfils an ordering function from which, in turn, it may derive its legitimacy. Order provided through a legal system is the utopia international

[32] Armin von Bogdandy and Sergio Dellavalle, 'Universalism and Particularism as Paradigms of International Law', *IILJ Working Paper (History and Theory of International Law Series)* 3 (2008), 7.

[33] Hersch Lauterpacht, 'The Grotian Tradition in International Law', *The British Year Book of International Law* 23 (1946), 1, at 1.

legal thought explores in its writings. 'System and order' thus retains a middle level between abstract and concrete, attempting the 'realistic utopia'[34] of international relations as law. In this function, they comprise utopian and realist aspects of international legal thought.

Through their flexibility, both terms can positively structure the inquiries of international legal thought, such as thinking about what the term 'system' might mean for different authors, and whether its definition would be fulfilled in alternative circumstances. Here, we attempt to look for and to analyse watershed marks. When can we speak about system and/or order in author A or B? What marks their difference? We believe that these terms potentially structure complex discourses and direct them in tracks, so as to contribute to a meaningful dialogue. The diversity of the use of system and order in the history of ideas puts the (also diverse, and often incoherent, and in fact problematic) use of the term *system* in current international legal scholarship in the best light. The formation of normative concepts is essentially contested, and reconstructing this contested history might contribute to today's debate.

Grotius is an example that demonstrates how researching the relationship between system and order offers intriguing insights. For Grotius, order rests on the law of nature, but the specific requirements of behaviour within that order are demonstrated by a method of civil law adapted from Roman law. In Grotian thought, it thus seems that the normative and the epistemic system often coincide, so that one may speak of 'order by system'. Different explanations as to the relationship between system and order range from Machiavelli, for whom there is little more than order, to Wolff, for whom there is apparently nothing more than a system which, characteristically, is of a purely epistemic nature, ordered by the *intellectus systematicus* alone. In Wolff, and in rationalism at large, a system is not something that is in a specific order. Rather, 'system' now means something derived from evident principles. This systematic intellect connects principles with the help of logical thinking—a doctrinal system may be a common whole of single phrases connected through the logically working mind.[35] Yet, even Wolff opened his system towards a 'strategy of reconciliation' between the universal law of nature and positive international law based on actual consent. This is the so-called voluntary law, *jus gentium voluntarium*.[36]

Authors in early modernity—with Wolff as a major exception—did not understand international law 'as a legal "system" somewhere outside statehood'.[37] Rather, they possibly understood their writings on war, treaties, and diplomacy as

[34] For the idea of a 'realistic utopia', see John Rawls, *The Law of Peoples* (1999).

[35] 'Systema enim dicitur veritatum inter se et cum principiis suis connexarum congeries.' Christian Wolff, *Philosofia rationalis sive logica* (1728) § 889.

[36] Cf. Martti Koskenniemi, *From Apology to Utopia: The Structure of International Legal Argument*, reissued with a new epilogue (2nd edn, 2006), pp. 108–12.

[37] See, for this point, Martti Koskenniemi, 'International Law and *raison d'état*: Rethinking the Prehistory of International Law', in Benedict Kingsbury and Benjamin Straumann (eds.), *The Roman Foundations of the Law of Nations: Alberico Gentili and the Justice of Empire* (2010), pp. 297, 298; Martti Koskenniemi, 'The Advantage of Treaties', *International Law in the Enlightenment* 13 (2009), 27, at 30.

contributions to the literature on state 'government'. If this was their perspective, war, treaties, and diplomacy would simply be external aspects of government and not elements of a universal normative order of international law. However, the treatises on good government did not deny the possibility of system-building as such. Rather, they located their system in a different place. Pufendorf, for example, in his '*De Systematibus Civitatum*' from 1675, referred to a particular group of states which—like the German states after the Peace of Westphalia—were sovereign and yet connected so as to form one body.[38]

In their variations according to author, time, and context the concepts 'system' and 'order' possess the necessary flexibility. They can account for the many sketches that are drawn in natural and positive laws with the help of ontological and contractual models before international law as an interstate diplomatic practice was formed in the way we know it today. Through their lasting significance in discussions on today's international law, they link the early sketches of legal thought from Machiavelli to Hegel to a present day's perspective. Seemingly old ideas and concepts might become the (re-) discovery of tomorrow. The frame of reference of system and order, in this sense, facilitates this transfer.

IV. From Machiavelli to Hegel

To embark on this rediscovery, we decided to aim at the timespan from Machiavelli to Hegel. It covers the international law of the modern world, which began, according to the received account, in the sixteenth century with Vitoria and Suárez.[39] Paradoxically at first sight, however, it was already with Machiavelli that international thought became a distinctively legal subject. If the purpose had been to find the origins of international law philosophy, one might as well have gone back to Augustine, Thomas Aquinas, or Dante, all of whom engaged in depth with the concepts stemming from antiquity.[40] One reason to start later is that, for Augustine and Thomas alike, problems that we see as falling into the realm of international law, such as the reasons for resorting to war, are from today's viewpoint questions of theology and morals, and it is only their reception in Spanish scholasticism, which translates them into the language of positive law.[41] More importantly, with

[38] See the contribution by Fiorillo in this volume.

[39] Percy E. Corbett, *Law and Society in the Relations of States* (1951); Arthur Nussbaum, *A Concise History of the Law of Nations* (1954); Nicholas G. Onuf, *The Republican Legacy in International Thought* (1998), pp. 12–13.

[40] Hans Kelsen, *Die Staatslehre des Dante Alighieri* (1905), pp. 121–35; Francis Cheneval, *Die Rezeption der Monarchia Dantes bis zur Editio princeps im Jahre 1559* (1995); Richard Tuck, *The Rights of War and Peace: Political Thought and International Order from Grotius to Kant* (1995).

[41] See the contribution by Bunge in this volume. Arguably, Thomas Aquinas already makes important distinctions on the question of just war. Importantly however, his concepts of *lex naturalis* and *lex divinae* belong to the field of morality. Yet, whether one believes that it is the more narrowly defined concept of law by Vitoria or whether it is already Thomas' *ordination rationis divinae* that qualifies as the first legal approach to the problem of just war obviously depends on the way the term law is understood. Here, however, natural and positive lawyers encounter insurmountable differences.

Machiavelli, the medieval world of order, dominated by the ideas of a *civitas Dei* and a universal monarchy, cedes to a notion of state as a commonwealth with interests vis-à-vis other entities of the same nature. Machiavelli, being one of the standard references for international relations realism, is thus the first to pronounce an idea of international order, rudimentary as it may be.

Hegel, to move to the other end of the period covered, is probably the last thinker to have dealt with international law from the standpoint of a complete philosophical system. In a paradoxical manner, Hegel's legal philosophy, which he presents as a negation of all systems of natural law, is at the same time the last and most perfect system of natural law.[42] With Hegel, the peak of systematic philosophy was reached. Afterwards, international law is no longer part of a comprehensive philosophical system. In late German idealism, the system-critical period began with Schelling and was continued by many others in the nineteenth century like Nietzsche, Kierkegaard, and Engels.

In Hegel's epoch, international law reached a turning point and began its 'gentle civilizing mission'.[43] International law became an academic discipline of its own and hence a branch of law that was distinct from natural law. Positive international law relied on treaty and state practice, as it was represented by Jeremy Bentham, Karl Gottlob Günther,[44] Johann Jakob Moser,[45] Georg Friedrich von Martens,[46] Johann Ludwig Klüber, and others.[47] In a parallel development, the economy and the common well-being in a European commercial society emancipated itself as a rationale for keeping promises between nations and accepting limitations on sovereignty.[48] Almost simultaneously, the notion of the nation-state evolved and changed the attitude to international law. The development is reflected by the nineteenth-century reception of Hegel, who stood with at least one leg in the tradition of eighteenth-century cosmopolitism, but was claimed to be the partisan to the notion of international law as external law of the state (*Außenstaatsrecht*). At the same time, Hegel's account of civil society and state foresaw important perspectives for a modern understanding of international law. He conceived the relation between

[42] Norberto Bobbio, 'Hegel und die Naturrechtslehre', in Manfred Riedel (ed.), *Materialien zu Hegels Rechtsphilosophie*, vol. 2 (1975), p. 81.

[43] Martti Koskenniemi, *The Gentle Civilizer of Nations* (2002).

[44] Karl Gottlob Günther, *Europäisches Völkerrecht in Friedenszeiten nach Vernunft, Verträgen und Herkommen mit Anwendung auf die teutschen Reichsstände*, 2 vols. (1787, 1792).

[45] Johann Jacob Moser, *Grundsätze des Völkerrechts. Versuch des neuesten Europäischen Völkerrechts in Friedens- und Kriegszeiten*, I Tl, I Bd, 1777 (1959).

[46] Georg Friedrich von Martens, *Einleitung in das positive europäische Völkerrecht auf Verträge und Herkommen gegründet* (1796).

[47] Koskenniemi, pp. 112–16 (n. 43); Martti Koskenniemi, 'Georg Friedrich von Martens (1756–1821) and the Origins of Modern International Law', in Christian Calliess et al. (eds.), *Von der Diplomatie zum kodifizierten Völkerrecht – 75 Jahre Institut für Völkerrecht der Universität Göttingen (1930-2005)* (2006), pp. 13–39.

[48] Kingsbury and Straumann, *State of Nature versus Commercial Sociability*, pp. 48–50 (n. 5).

state and international community in an innovative manner as a co-presence. Both are preserved in their respective specificity of functions and as normative orders.[49]

Therefore, we end with Hegel not primarily because the peak of systematic philosophy was reached, but also because, at his very lifetime, international law invented its own tradition[50]—thereby following a characteristic pattern of the nineteenth century[51]—and became a system of its own, detached from the philosophical system. Accordingly, we cover the timespan from the actual start of the 'invented tradition' to the time when it was 'invented' to form the basis of nineteenth century international legal scholarship.

The period from Machiavelli to Hegel covers a variety of perspectives on the relationship between state interest and obligations of a state towards the outside world. Beginning with Machiavelli raises the question of why this proto-Hobbesian author was not an international lawyer and why he did not understand international relations as legal relations.[52] Hobbes' concepts of law and right and his notion of a legal system, read together with Rousseau, may be taken as an initial point for an innovative conception of international law.[53] Another example is Spinoza who, like Hobbes, is generally perceived as a 'denier' of international law, but who provides a (weakly) normative sociological theory of international law since he outlines the sociological conditions under which international law is really 'law', i.e. the conditions under which one state is forced to comply with the will of the allied. Spinoza therefore neither simply describes international relations 'as they are', nor 'as they should be', but rather depicts international relations 'as they have the potential to be', given what law is and given the sociological conditions under which states act.[54]

V. The Plan of the Book

In the first part of this volume, thinkers from Machiavelli to Hegel are scrutinized for their answers to questions that deal with the role of law in ordering international relations, as well as the related concepts of domestic and international law. It proved difficult if not unfeasible to develop a questionnaire which would fit for all authors. However, there are eternal questions which guide the interest of a reader with an international law background. Can there be order in international relations, resting on law? How does the law of nations relate to a general concept of law?[55] Can

[49] See the contribution by Dellavalle in this volume.

[50] See Martti Koskenniemi, 'International Law and *raison d'état*: Rethinking the Prehistory of International Law', in Benedict Kingsbury and Benjamin Straumann (eds.), *The Roman Foundations of the Law of Nations: Alberico Gentili and the Justice of Empire* (2010), p. 298; David Kennedy, 'Primitive Legal Scholarship', 27 (1986) *Harv Int'l L J*, 1.

[51] Eric J. Hobsbawm and Terence Ranger (eds.), *The Invention of Tradition* (1983).

[52] See the contribution by Roth-Isigkeit in this volume.

[53] See the contribution by Heller in this volume.

[54] See the contribution by Altwicker in this volume.

[55] On Adam' Smith's sentimental approach to jurisprudence and how Smith's idea of sympathetic law might be applied to the level of international law, see the contribution by Ronge in this volume.

there be a difference between the 'is' and the 'ought', and what are the consequences? Are such tensions resolved by a distinction between different types of law? What is the force of law as compared to morals and power? Does the respective author think of his system as eternal, or is it subject to change? Are there principles or general ideas from which the system derives, such as the reason of state, the maintenance of peace, self-perfection or the satisfaction of basic needs? Is the system unitary, or does 'difference' have a role? What is the impact of confrontations of the idea of a universal system with fundamental differences in religion, culture, social patterns, or political order?[56] Does the concept start from a conception of the individual or rather from groups or states? How were these theories received in later writings, and why did later authors refer to them?

The authors discussed in the first part of the book offer a plethora of insights in this regard. Their ideas can be read as creative blueprints for social, political, and legal organization of a global society that is not confined to the concept of the state. One may think of the notion of overlapping plural rule in Althusius' federalism, compare it with Montesquieu's confederate republic,[57] and contrast it with Bodin's notion of absolute sovereignty. Fichte, to give another example for the innovatory potential that the reconstructions of the first part offer, does not examine the relations between states, but focuses on the relationship between citizens of adjacent states. It is up to the citizens of the adjacent states to decide, in consequence of a mutual 'recognition' to conclude alliances.[58]

The second part of the book is devoted to horizontal themes that open the opportunity to test old authorities against present-day approaches. Their analyses deepen the understanding of international legal thinking by pointing to often neglected elements, scrutinizing the knowledge–creation of the subject as we know it. The spatiality of law, as the contribution by Duve illustrates, cannot be adequately understood without taking the technical dimension of cartography into account. This technical dimension, in turn, relied on both traditional practices and experimental knowledge–creation.[59] García-Salmones argues in her contribution that the theological and economic spheres were closely intertwined in the genesis of the sources doctrine. In particular, the role of experts as an often highlighted and criticized source of international law can be dated back to Vitoria.[60]

The approaches of the second part are critical in a double way. On the one hand, they explain how such historical rediscoveries can re-shape a discipline's self-conception, as Hellmann's argument on the 'system of International Relations' illustrates.[61] Or, as the contribution by Bhuta demonstrates, they illustrate the methodological interdependence between concepts of the state and international

[56] With regard to Gentili, see Benedict Kingsbury, 'Confronting Difference: The Puzzling Durability of Gentili's Combination of Pragmatic Pluralism and Normative Judgment', *American Journal of International Law* 92 (1998), 713–23.

[57] See the contribution by Volk in this volume.

[58] See the contribution by De Pascale in this volume.

[59] See the contribution by Duve in this volume.

[60] See the contribution by García Salmones in this volume.

[61] See the contribution by Hellmann in this volume.

order. How we construct and imagine the state, Bhuta argues, will affect our construction of the international community and *vice versa*. In this form of critical reading, the approaches of the second part illustrate how international legal thinking is a result of and dependent on historical concepts, methods, and contingencies.

On the other hand, a different reading implicates a meta-critique of this discourse which points to the questions how contingent a history of international legal thought necessarily is, which path-dependencies there are, and what a history of international law that takes such constraints into account should be like.[62] This includes a discussion of methodological categories such as universality and particularity that, in a critical perspective, seem to be increasingly overcome.[63]

Ultimately, with this project, we try to subvert a methodological category, too. We aim to show that there is a space for theoretical argument that moves beyond the dichotomy of construction and critique. This will succeed if it manages to combine the modesty of an observer conscious of their own bias with the imaginative force of someone who is drawing on the lessons of the past in order to put the present in perspective. With this volume, we want to contribute to a growing literature that constructively tries to resolve the riddle of human sociality through imagining and theorizing legal and political order beyond the intellectual boundaries of the nation-state.

We can learn from the thinkers of the past that such an undertaking must be both responsive and explorative. It is responsive in that it must react and adapt to the factual and intellectual context of societal order that it encounters. Moreover, it is explorative in its attempt to make sense of this context beyond its contingent existence conditions. Systematizing in this way mediates rather than draws a contrast between realism and utopianism. It acknowledges that there is no ideal path of thought through the contradictions of law beyond the state, avoiding the paralysis of the perfectionist.

The philosopher Leo Singer, the protagonist in Robert Menasse's novel *Wings of Stone*, animatedly illustrates how such high hopes for an ideal path to the convergence of facts and norms may lead to frustration. He applies the systematic method to a path of thought, literally understood, trying to find an undisturbed walking path through his study:

> The floor didn't creak as loudly in some places as in others. Leo paused in irritation. He knew it. This floor was going to distract him, send his thoughts off in the wrong direction. He now walked around the room *systematically*, testing it at every step, rocking on the balls of his feet so as to determine which were the boards causing the problem, those creaking the loudest, and where the boards were firm beneath his feet and made little noise or none at all. He wanted to find the ideal path of thought through this room that he could walk up and down when he was working without being disturbed in his concentration. After a while he gave up in despair. There was no negotiable path.[64]

[62] See the contribution by Koskenniemi in this volume.

[63] See the contribution by von Bogdandy and Dellavalle in this volume.

[64] Robert Menasse, *Wings of Stone*, trans. David Bryer (2000), pp. 226, 228 (italics by the authors); original title: 'Selige Zeiten, brüchige Welt'.

Faced with these difficulties, Singer never finished his 'System of Science'.[65] In a similar vein, today's and the past's thinkers may have shied away from systematizing international legal thought because of the intimidating and frustrating task of finding an ideal path of thought on the creaking boards of the international realm. Such expectations, we submit, would unduly narrow the perspective. We aim at a history of international legal thought that takes creaking boards as an incentive for renovation, rather than despair.

[65] Menasse actually wrote the 'Phenomenology of Despiritualisation' on behalf of the hero of his novel; cf. Robert Menasse, *Phänomenologie der Entgeisterung - Geschichte des verschwindenden Wissens* (1995).

PART I

AUTHORS

1

Niccolò Machiavelli's International Legal Thought: Culture, Contingency, and Construction

David Roth-Isigkeit

Perché la cagione della disunione delle repubbliche il più delle volte è l'ozio e la pace; la cagione della unione è la paura e la guerra.[1]

There is barely any philosopher in the history of ideas who has been used in so many different fashions. From political realism to historical materialism or aesthetics, everything seems to be present in the Renaissance thinker.[2] Machiavelli seems to fit in all shoes, from a 'handbook for gangsters' (Bertrand Russell), 'le docteur de la scélératesse' (Frederick the Great), to a sincere Republican (John Pocock) or a balanced pluralist (Isaiah Berlin). In international thought, it was particularly the realist strand of International Relations scholars who appropriated his vocabulary and celebrated him as the founding father of empirical political science some hundred years before the international realm had been conceptualized in legal terms. The so-called philosopher of power and violence had not spared many words for law and peace, so that international lawyers apparently did not see much reason to engage with his writings.[3]

This chapter argues that Machiavelli plays an important role in international legal thought. Machiavelli knew a lot about things today's international lawyers are

[1] Niccolò Machiavelli, *Discorsi sopra la prima deca di Tito Livio* (1531), Book II, Chapter 25. English version: *Discourses on Livy*, trans. Harvey C. Mansfield and Nathan Tarcov (1996), 190. Here the quote reads: 'For the cause of the disunion of republics is usually idleness and peace; the cause of union is fear and war.' All references in this chapter refer to the English translation.

[2] An overview of the seemingly infinite varieties of interpretation can be found in Isaiah Berlin, 'A Special Supplement: The Question of Machiavelli', *The New York Review of Books*, November 1971, available in the article archive at <http://www.nybooks.com/articles/1971/11/04/a-special-supplement-the-question-of-machiavelli/>.

[3] One considerable exception is Anthony D'Amato, 'International Law from A Machiavellian Perspective', in Anthony D'Amato (ed.), *International Law Studies*, Collected Papers Vol.II (1997), Chs. 18 and 19, 251–78. For a recent reconsideration, see Andreas Føllesdal, 'Machiavelli at 500: From Cynic to Vigilant Supporter of International Law', *Ratio Iuris* 28(2) (2015), 242–51.

Niccolò Machiavelli's International Legal Thought – Culture, Contingency and Construction. David Roth-Isigkeit. Published 2017 by Oxford University Press.

struggling with, so that the reductionist reading of his scholarship as the counter-narrative for international law can be reasonably opposed. The argument will be that the dominant strand of reception focuses exaggeratedly on the historical context in which Machiavelli developed his methodological tools. When reconsidered in an interpretation relying on the unity of his national and international thought, Machiavelli does not turn out as the imperial thinker of war and unscrupulous violence. On the contrary, Machiavelli's progressive focus on the unification of diverse political communities through the medium of law allows for a reconceptualization of his contribution. In this light, Machiavelli can be increasingly detached from the traditional questions of the discipline on the justice or injustice of a ruler's military interventions towards a focus on law as culture and as a tool for political construction.

In order to explore Machiavelli's international legal thought, the chapter starts with a discussion of the relationship of his biographical events and his social epistemology. It proceeds with the relationship of Machiavelli's concept of law as a governance tool to the areas of morality and normativity. Ultimately, the focus lies on his understanding of imperialism and international relations in order to shape a novel picture of Machiavelli that depicts him as a reasonable historical starting point for a modern, post-critical concept of international law.

I. Niccolò Machiavelli

As with many thinkers' biographies, Machiavelli's is of particular relevance for his political thought.[4] He spent his youth in a flourishing Florence under the reign of the Medici dynasty. Cosimo de' Medici had established a system of checks and balances in the *Lega Italia* through the Peace of Lodi of 1454, a proto-Westphalian treaty system that fixed Milan, Florence, and Naples as central actors on the Italian peninsula.[5] These relatively peaceful and stable times lasted for fifty years, during which Florence dominated the political and economic landscape in Renaissance Italy. At the age of twenty-three, Machiavelli had to witness the end of this flourishing period. Lorenzo de' Medici, *Il Magnifico*, was more interested in representation and luxury and neglected to care for the maintenance of the Florentine position in the diplomatic league.[6] After the Hundred Years' War in France had ended in 1453, and after the conquest of Granada by Spain in 1492, both dynastic powers were looking for new battlefields, so that it was very welcome that, in 1494, Milan called the war-proven French to help in a political conflict with Naples. The French advanced quickly in Italy and a rebellion drove Lorenzo's successor,

[4] The literature on Machiavelli's biography is huge. See e.g. Christopher Celenza, *Machiavelli: A Portrait* (2015); Joseph Markulin, *Machiavelli: A Renaissance* Life (2013); Miles Unger, *Machiavelli: A Biography* (2012); Maurizio Viroli, *Il Sorriso di Niccolò* (1998).

[5] Kenneth R. Bartlett, *A Short History of the Italian Renaissance* (2013), pp. 225 ff.

[6] Lorenzo's most significant mistake was a dispute with the Papacy over the Romagna. This led to the loss of the Medici bank's control over the finances of the Papacy and, with that, to a considerable loss of power.

Piero de' Medici, who had taken sides with Naples, out of Florence. The French campaign ended shortly after. For the Italian city states, however, which had been substantially weakened by the invasion by foreign troops, a period of chaos, war, and revolutions began.

Machiavelli appeared on the political scene out of nowhere. In 1498, at the age of twenty-nine, he was elected into a high position in the Florentine government without having left any traces before in the political landscape. After the fall of the Medici, the Dominican Savonarola had conducted business with the help of an ascetic ideology, a dictatorship of god and a total banishment of luxury and vanity. In a city with a strong bourgeois heritage, this did not go well for long.[7] Savonarola was overturned and Machiavelli, who was also from a bourgeois, albeit poor, origin, profited from the resulting vacancies in governmental positions in the newly established Florentine Republic.

Machiavelli, as *Segretario della Repubblica*, worked in military and foreign affairs as a consultant to Piero Soderini, an important member of Florentine government at the time, who could be called his protector. In this position, which he held until 1512, the year of the breakdown of the Florentine Republic and the return of the Medici, he was sent on many diplomatic missions, where he developed his thought in reports to the *Signoria*. He learned about the advantages of the French absolutist territorial state and the problems of the Holy Roman Empire of the German Nation, about the real foundation of diplomacy (arms, money, power) and about the methods of Cesare Borgia, the unscrupulous duke whom he considered suitable to lead Italy to unity and who is often said to have inspired *The Prince*. In addition to his duties as the main diplomat for the Florentine Republic, the later part of his work was dedicated to a military reform, freeing Florence from the need of mercenaries by creating a popular army. This enterprise culminated in what Machiavelli thought of as his greatest achievement when his forces won Pisa back from Venice in 1509. Three years later, however, his army was desperately outgunned against the Spanish in Prato, a defeat that allowed the Medici to return. Machiavelli lost his job and was suspected to have partaken in a conspiracy. He was tortured in the Florentine prisons, but quickly released after it had transpired that he had nothing to hide.

After his liberation, he went into exile, beginning his writing career at his country residence *San Casciano*.[8] *Il Principe*, his first work, was written in 1513 and took him less than six months to complete. Machiavelli still hoped that he would be engaged back in government. These hopes were disappointed, however, and *The Prince* was succeeded by the more moderate *Discorsi*. Only in 1521 was he engaged as a scholar by Giulio de' Medici (later, as of 1523, Pope Clement VII),

[7] Savonarola's fate lies at the origin of Machiavelli's famous description of the 'unarmed prophet'. See e.g. Leo Strauss, *Thoughts on Machiavelli* (1958), pp. 83–4.

[8] It is not more than an anecdote that Carl Schmitt named his residence in North Rhine-Westphalia after Machiavelli's San Casciano. Schmitt sympathized with Machiavelli's life, which he interpreted as the fallen genius stuck between changing political developments and ideologies.

who requested that Machiavelli write a history of Florence and undertake minor political missions in his service.

Italy once again became witness to a number of heated battles in 1525, when conflict between the Habsburg Empire (Charles V) and the French troops escalated. This conflict revitalized Machiavelli for the last time when he put up a plan for Florentine self-defence with the help of a popular militia and even managed to convince the Papacy of his plans. However, the Florentine governor Francesco Guicciardini cancelled his plan, as the danger of a popular uprising against his government seemed to be too apparent. Instead, Machiavelli was put in charge of the construction of fortifications, which were, however, never tested, since the troops of the Empire passed by Florence and marched directly to Rome. This again weakened the Medici league—and led to a proclamation of a new Florentine Republic in May 1527. Machiavelli did not experience its fall three years later, since he died only one month after, on 21 June 1527.

II. The Political Condition

These biographical events had an important impact on his writing. Machiavelli was born in a flourishing city state, Florence, which fell into chaos. This is the analytical precondition of his thought, the internal and external dimensions of national politics in Florence and Italy. He experienced Florence in an anarchical and in a stable condition. Preferring the latter, he was convinced that the role of government is to maintain stability (*mantenere lo stato*) in the first place. Only a stable domestic government can provide for the prosperity of a nation. It is highly disputed what constituted the end of the state for Machiavelli.[9] Yet, in all these interpretations it is internal stability that provides a precondition for its realization.

Instability was thus the most pressing problem of the Italian peninsula. This is the appeal to Lorenzo in the last chapter of the Prince: 'Likewise, in order for the valour and worth of an Italian spirit (*virtù*, D.R.-I.) to be recognised, Italy has had to be reduced to the desperate straits in which it now finds itself: more enslaved than the Hebrews, more oppressed than the Persians, more scattered than the Athenians, without an acknowledged leader, and without order or stability, beaten, despoiled, lacerated, overrun, in short, utterly devastated.'[10] Consequently, embedded in the environment of a fragmented Italy after the French invasion, Machiavelli was concerned with the political conditions that lead to good, enduring government.

[9] Interpretations of the end of the state differ greatly. We find the idea of wealth and peace in Maurizio Viroli, *From Politics to Reason of State - The Acquisition and Transformation of the Language of Politics, 1250-1600* (1992); John G. A. Pocock, *The Machiavellian Moment* (1975); *Justice and Force* in Anthony J. Parel, 'Machiavelli's Notions of Justice', 18 (1990) *Political Theory*, 530–6; the end of the state is expansion for Mikael Hörnquist, *Machiavelli and Empire* (2004); and Felix Gilbert, *Machiavelli and Guicciardini* (1965).

[10] Niccolò Machiavelli, *Il Principe* (1532), Ch. 26. English version *The Prince*, trans. Quentin Skinner and Russell Price (1988), p. 88. All references in this chapter refer to the English translation.

Machiavelli operated on the basis of the anthropological assumption that human nature had not changed in the course of history. In the *Discorsi*, Machiavelli writes: 'Whoever considers present and ancient things easily knows that in all cities and in all peoples there are the same desires and same humors and have always been.'[11] For Machiavelli, human nature is a steady pursuit of self-interest that is not altered by the conditions under which man lives. Closely connected to the assumptions about human nature is the cyclical theory of history,[12] '[a]ll things of men are in motion and cannot stay ready, they must either rise or fall'.[13]

The interplay of these two main assumptions is complex. On the one hand, the task of government is to provide for stability; on the other hand, history is always in motion. The foundation of good government is thus to resist that cyclical course of history, to maintain government against its eroding forces, the place at which the famous struggle of *fortuna* and *virtù* takes place.[14] The question Machiavelli tries to answer is how to achieve a stable unity given that human nature is a steady struggle of self-interested participants. He thereby places the purpose of existence of the ruler (his normativity, so to speak) outside of himself. When Machiavelli is concerned with a government that is to endure, he does not merely conceptualize it from the limited perspective of the self-interest of the Prince, but more comprehensively from a historical situation, a certain status that is to be maintained—the stability of order.

Machiavelli's writings oscillate around the question of how to lead Italy to stability, of how to found *and* to maintain a durable state. The most important aspect in both of these is the theme of unity. It is only through a concrete unity that a durable state can be founded and maintained.[15] Firstly, this means unification in the classical, territorial sense, performed by a ruler through political action. That is the appeal to Lorenzo: 'liberate Italy from the barbarian yoke'.[16] Secondly, however, for its maintenance, the Prince has to take root in this concrete unity. He needs to transform the merely territorial unity into a unity of the people who support his rule. Only by appreciating that these two moments are conceptually divided in Machiavelli is it possible to understand the complexity of his advice.[17] The political moment of foundation would inescapably degenerate into tyranny and subsequently disintegrate again, were it not grounded in the unity it has just created.

[11] Machiavelli, *Discourses on Livy*, Book I, Ch. 39, p. 83 (n. 1).

[12] See Louis Althusser, *Machiavel et Nous*, English version *Machiavelli and Us*, trans. Gregory Elliott (1999), 36 ff., for illustration.

[13] Machiavelli, *Discourses on Livy*, Book I, Ch. 6, p. 23 (n. 1).

[14] Althusser, *Machiavelli and Us*, p. 35 (n. 12).

[15] This concrete unity is the place where political realist and materialist interpretations of Machiavelli clash. Establishing and maintaining unity requires effective power, the realist part, and this power can only be rooted in the people, the materialist (or also republican) development of his thought. This rather elegant connection between realist and materialist readings is what fascinated Antonio Gramsci the most. Unity is not only achieved by force, but needs consent, the basic pillars of his concept of hegemony. See Benedetto Fontana, *Hegemony and Power: On the Relationship Between Gramsci and Machiavelli* (1993).

[16] Machiavelli, *The Prince*, Ch. 26, p. 87 (n. 10).

[17] Instructive is Althusser, *Machiavelli and Us*, pp. 64–6 (n. 12).

A government to endure—that is his answer—needs to change its character after its foundation. 'Therefore, if you want to make a people numerous and armed so as to be able to make a great Empire, you make it of such a quality that you cannot manage it in your mode.'[18] Whereas the foundation of an order thus always carries an authoritarian and contingent moment, the political practice must be popular in order to endure, i.e. oriented towards the people. It is in this second stage where the concept of law appears explicitly, even though we might draw some interesting conclusions from the first stage as well.

The language Machiavelli speaks is the language of technique and of statecraft. He has a scientific style and it is in that regard that he is depicted as the founder of a whole discipline: empirical political science.[19] He wants to find out the technical laws of governance that allow the Prince to realize the unification of a state. In that sense, he provides a 'mirror for princes', but in a very different style than the usual piece from the genre, with a particular hostility to metaphysics.[20] The roots of his guidance lie in a particular historico-empirical method. He admires antiquity and the Roman thinkers, but not for their thought; rather, he is interested in the description of the historical events themselves, empirical practical examples. Theories are only a second-class source. 'It seems to me better to concentrate on what really happens rather than theories or speculations.'[21] Machiavelli would probably have been equally sceptical about a book project on the history of international legal thought.

This dry, secular handling of normativity (laws, religion, and ideology) as a technique makes him a very original thinker and, as he declares in the preface to the *Discorsi*, he has 'decided to take a path as yet untrodden by anyone'.[22] Because human nature is steady, there are scientific laws and techniques governing human communities. Still, Machiavelli is not neutral about the course of history. Rather, he distinguishes the normativity of unity from the task of discovering the laws of history. As Merleau-Ponty puts it, Machiavelli 'combines the most acute feeling for the contingency or irrationality in the world with a taste for the consciousness or freedom in man.'[23]

III. Techniques of Government

Techniques of government are thus always in place to *serve* the duration of a state, to establish a connection between the popular roots and stability through producing a concrete unity. Laws form part of the set of techniques, as do religion and morality, but also force and violence where necessary. All depends on the political

[18] Machiavelli, *Discourses on Livy*, Book I, Ch. 6, pp. 21–2 (n. 1).

[19] See e.g. Joseph Femia, *Machiavelli Revisited* (2004), pp. 45ff.

[20] Ibid., pp. 30–1 (n. 19). Even though Femia's interpretation of Machiavelli's scientism seems convincing, interpreting him as a positivist might go too far.

[21] Machiavelli, *The Prince*, Ch. 15, p. 54 (n. 10).

[22] Machiavelli, *Discourses on Livy*, Book I, Preface, p. 5 (n. 1).

[23] Maurice Merleau-Ponty, 'A Note On Machiavelli', in Ted Toadvine and Leonard Lawlor (eds.), *The Merleau-Ponty Reader* (2007), pp. 123, 128–9.

virtù of the Prince, who needs to maintain the concrete unity in order to provide for stability. This stability requires a set of techniques that realistically deals with the true nature of the people. 'It is necessary to whoever disposes a republic and orders laws in it to presuppose that all men are bad, and that they always have to use the malignity of their spirit whenever they have free opportunity for it.'[24] Through law and religion, which constitute the most important technical tools of the Prince, people can be linked to the polity and the political unity gains stability. 'Therefore it is said that hunger and poverty make men industrious, and the laws make them good. Where a thing works well on its own without the law, the law is not necessary; but when some good custom is lacking, at once the law is necessary.'[25] Laws thereby receive an Aristotelian connotation; they serve to educate the people.[26]

Laws contribute to this specific unity. Machiavelli does not address simply any kind of laws. Only laws originating in the political unity itself can foster stability. Returning to the difference between foundation and duration, this means the following: the founding moment, the establishment of the legal order, is a moment of solitude for the Prince. He designs the order and for that specific moment represents the common whole, the political unity. Still, this is a contingent project dependent on the political *virtù* in the act of decreeing.[27] This is the major theme in *The Prince*. Subsequently, however, the Prince has to step back from the centre by having created an order that is not merely rooted in himself, a tyranny, but to provide for something that is located in the political unity that has just arisen, the constituted people. The functioning of this (Republican) order is the theme of the *Discourses*. *The Prince* and the *Discourses* are thus not as completely unrelated or even contradictory as some scholars claim.[28] They simply address different moments in the foundation and the maintenance of a state.

It is necessary that the laws take root outside the Prince's sphere—in the sphere of the people. Laws are a tool to moderate social struggle. In this struggle, something like a melting pot, laws are the best means to overcome internal disorder by instituting societal checks and balances. 'So there is nothing that makes a republic so stable and steady as to order it in a mode so that those alternating humors that agitate it can be vented in a way ordered by the laws.'[29] One of the shortcomings of the Florentine system was an insufficient legal accountability of the public administration, because this would constitute a way of how public unrest could be moderated within the institutional system, thus reducing the danger of revolt.[30] The Prince can also govern by spreading fear or by controlling the

[24] Machiavelli, *Discourses on Livy*, Book I, Ch. 3, p. 15 (n. 1).

[25] Ibid.

[26] Aristotle, *Nicomachean Ethics*, trans. Terence Irwin (2nd edn, 1999), Book 5, pp. 67 ff. The educational function of laws is again paradoxical, given the steadiness of human nature.

[27] On this general theme, see Miguel E. Vatter, *Between Form and Event: Machiavelli's Theory of Political Freedom* (2000), in particular Part 3, pp. 219 ff.

[28] This was still the dominant interpretation for Rousseau and Spinoza, who believed that *The Prince* could not be read as anything more than a perfidious satire. See Berlin, *The Question of Machiavelli* (n. 2).

[29] Machiavelli, *Discourses on Livy*, Book I, Ch. 7, p. 24 (n. 1).

[30] Ibid., p. 25.

people through other kinds of ideology. Governance by laws involves the spreading of fear by attaching consequences to disobedience. But the distinctive feature of laws is the potential to balance the societal forces (i.e. the Prince, the nobility, the people),[31] so that these forces are not only neutralized, but also further strengthen the unity of the state altogether.[32]

How the Prince uses these different techniques is no question of moral preference, but only of political *virtù*. Everything that serves the internal unity of the state is an appropriate means to govern.[33] In that sense, Machiavelli recognizes that morals, laws, and religion are merely very specific instruments that operate through the culturally determined idea of justice. From this angle, he places the Prince completely outside the normative content of the instruments. But at this point the perspective is already more complex than simply describing laws as a tool of governance from the perspective of the ruler. The people have to internalize the content and perceive it as just in order for these instruments to be effective. And the Prince has to master different levels of law and normativity. The people will react to what he does, judging him using the culturally contingent criteria of justice. Were the Prince openly to disobey his own laws, he would endanger the internal unity of the state. The people would quickly realize that he does not live up to his promises. So Machiavelli states in the *Discorsi*: 'For I do not believe there is a thing that sets a more wicked example in a republic than to make a law and not observe it, and so much the more when it is not observed by him who made it.'[34] At the beginning of Chapter XVIII of *The Prince*, he adds: 'Everyone realizes how praiseworthy it is for a ruler to keep his promises, and live uprightly and not by trickery.'[35]

However, in the very same chapter, Machiavelli makes clear that the Prince's own laws cannot impose constraints on his capacity to act and thus potentially impede on his political *virtù*. The law is not binding on him in a moral sense. On the contrary, the Prince should 'be prepared [in other translations: "learn", D.R.-I.] to act immorally when this becomes necessary'.[36] The Prince can govern by laws, but his capacity for political action requires that he is able to break the law: 'Hence, a prudent ruler cannot and should not respect his word, when such respect works to his disadvantage and when the reasons for which he made the promise no longer exist.'[37] Later he asserts that a ruler 'is often forced to act treacherously, ruthlessly or inhumanely, and disregard the precepts of religion. Hence,

[31] Machiavelli, *Discourses on Livy*, Book I, Chs. 3 and 4, pp. 15–17 (n. 1).

[32] This is the point where the materialist interpretation becomes relevant. According to Althusser, in the conflict between nobility and the plebs, Machiavelli has a preference for the people. *Machiavelli and Us*, p. 59 (n. 12).

[33] It is here that the famous *ragione di stato* becomes clearer in light of the absence of a state as a modern political construct. *Stato* does not refer to 'the State', but rather to 'the state', in the sense of a situation that is to be maintained. See, in particular, Corrado Vivanti, *Niccolò Machiavelli: An Intellectual Biography*, trans. Simon MacMichael (2013), pp. 193–218, for an appendix that clarifies the different uses of the word *stato* in Machiavelli's language.

[34] Machiavelli, *Discourses on Livy*, Book I, Ch. 45, p. 93 (n. 1).

[35] Ibid., Book I, Ch. 18, p. 61.

[36] Machiavelli, *The Prince*, Ch. 15, p. 55 (n. 10).

[37] Machiavelli, *Discourses on Livy*, Book I, Ch. 18, p. 61 (n. 1).

he must be prepared to vary his conduct as the winds of fortune and changing circumstances constrain him'.[38]

Importantly, however, it is always necessary for the Prince seemingly to have the quality of keeping his oaths, i.e. moral virtue: 'Having and cultivating them [moral virtues, D.R.-I.] is harmful, whereas seeming to have them is useful.'[39] The Prince has to be a great liar, a hypocrite; he has to pretend to live up to that specific normativity and pretend to share the aspirations of the people. For Machiavelli, rhetoric is as important as reality. In its service to the overarching goal of stability, law, religion, and all other kinds of ideology have to be understood in instrumental terms, i.e. as what they serve. They thus represent an external perspective on normativity. If the people realize that the Prince is not part of the law, this will lead to considerable erosion of their internal perspective to law, morality, and religion. This is the Prince with a tendency for deception, the amoral ruler. However, as the next section aims to show, a reading solely from this angle is reductionist.

IV. Concept of Law

The instrumental–technical view as presented in the last section is only one dimension in which Machiavelli captures legal normativity. The claim that Machiavelli is one of the founders of the realist strand of political science relies almost exclusively on this perspective. Still, merely focusing on this dimension of Machiavelli misses out an important dimension of his thought. Machiavelli adds a complex understanding of the nature of legal obligations that relies on an internalization of the normative content on the side of the legal subjects. Machiavelli thus adds to the external understanding from the Prince's perspective—in which law is a tool for governance—a second, internal perspective that explains why the people obey the laws.

The first aspect in this explanation is one of ideology: the system of ideas that the Prince represents, which are the good customs to which the people are educated through laws, religious beliefs, and the unity created through the institutionally moderated social struggle. The unity is precisely created because the people consent to the order. So far, nothing distinguishes the Prince from Savonarola, the unarmed prophet from the Florence of Machiavelli's youth, trying (and failing) to reign simply with ideological instruments. The ideological instruments (the love of the people) are unstable since they are external to the Prince: '[W]hether men bear affection depends on themselves, but whether they are afraid will depend on what the ruler does. A wise ruler should rely on what is under his own control, not on what is under the control of others.'[40]

[38] Machiavelli, *The Prince*, Ch. 18, p. 62 (n. 10).
[39] Ibid.
[40] Ibid., pp. 60–1.

Secondly however, the Prince thus needs something originating in himself to make people obey his laws: fear. The threat that the Prince could always use violent means to render his government effective is a better back-up for power than ideology. 'Men are less hesitant about offending or harming a ruler who makes himself loved than one who inspires fear.'[41] Religion further stabilizes a reign since fearing God's punishments provides a particularly strong motive for compliance. This combination of the root of stability of an order in ideology and fear (consent backed up by force) is what inspired Antonio Gramsci in his concept of hegemony.[42] It is the combination of these elements that makes up Machiavelli's concept of legal obligation.

Focusing not on the societal structure in which it is embedded, but merely on the concept of law, some authors read the Machiavellian approach as legal positivist. Femia writes: '[F]or Machiavelli, law is an 'external' thing; it is not handed down by God to the mortals made in his immortal image, nor does it derive from moral purposes that are inherent in human nature.'[43] In terms of jurisprudence, this is very remarkable because Machiavelli's perspective on law is already more complex than a merely sanction-centred positivism as we find it in nineteenth-century jurisprudence. Normativity rests on two different pillars: force and the internalization of the normative content. Here, Machiavelli seems to foreshadow modern theories of obligation like H. L. A. Hart's concept of law.[44] Naturally, this interpretation has its limits. Machiavelli would not view law from a scientific, dogmatic angle, and even though he sometimes calls it 'system of laws', there is no clear separation from morals. This might be intended since there was no apparent necessity to distinguish between these two forms. Mansfield remarks: 'Natural law in this form contains no *summum bonum* and recommends no particular end or way of life. On the contrary, being concerned only with the necessary condition of civilization, which is security, it keeps politics impartial of ends men pursue.'[45]

Others have claimed that the duality of Machiavelli's legal thought would make up for an early theory of constitutional law.[46] One might initially be sceptical towards this interpretation, as Machiavelli would not see law as being constitutive

[41] Machiavelli, *The Prince*, Ch. 18, p. 59 (n. 10).

[42] On Gramsci's relation with Machiavelli, see Fontana, *Hegemony and Power* (n. 15). For the concept of 'hegemony', as applied to International Law, see Andreas Fischer-Lescano and Sonja Buckel, 'Gramsci Reconsidered: Hegemony in Global Law', *Leiden Journal of International Law* 22(3) (2009), 437–54.

[43] Femia, *Machiavelli Revisited*, p. 37 (n. 19).

[44] Herbert L.A. Hart, *The Concept of Law* (1961).

[45] Harvey C. Mansfield, *Machiavelli's Virtue* (1996), p. 104. 'An impartial natural law does not favour one regime over another.'

[46] Anthony D'Amato, 'The Relevance of Machiavelli to Contemporary World Politics', in Anthony Parel (ed.), *The Political Calculus* (1972), p. 209. See also Mortimer N. S. Sellers, 'Niccolò Machiavelli: Father of Modern Constitutionalism', 28(2) *Ratio Iuris* (2015), 216–25, who describes Machiavelli's methodology as a constitutional technique (217–8): 'As lawyers studied Roman civil law, and doctors studied Galen, so Machiavelli set out to draw practical lessons from the study of history to regain the liberty and virtue of the ancients. [. . .] Machiavelli turned his modern contemporaries to ancient knowledge and experience as the first step in applying reason to politics.'

for a political community.[47] Althusser notes that, in Machiavelli, 'laws postdate the beginning of society, postdate government by the most powerful'.[48] But even though the foundation of political society does not resemble a constitutional foundation, there is something important to be found in examining the relationship of the Prince to the laws. The unity that the laws create has something outside of him; it is not his unity, not his law. For example, when the Prince acquires new principalities, he must consider the option 'not to change their laws or impose new taxes'.[49] The unity that a legal system provides can also be a resistance for the new Prince which should not be easily changed when he has not acquired a stable position in the new principality. So, if the Prince wants to transform the ideology and rule in a state, he has to start by appreciating the actually existing normative structure.

The relationship of the ruler to the law is thus more complex than merely instrumental. The Prince can break the law and, since he is the ultimate instance, there is no way to prevent him from doing that. But the Prince *is* not the law; he does not amend the law by breaking it. It is a self-standing concept with an independent normativity. In that sense, it certainly differs from other tools of ideology and explains certain proximities to constitutional understandings. Religion, for example, stands completely in the service of the political. Machiavelli acknowledges an existence of legal normativity outside the ruler. But this is not necessarily desirable. Quite on the contrary, he observes that if law becomes too technical, this is equally problematic because it limits the Prince's capacity for political action, which has to be preserved at all cost. Laws as well as religion might constitute a dogmatic system. But this must not constrain the Prince.

Machiavelli thus combines internal and external perspectives to the law in his theory. The normativity of law is unavailable to the Prince; he cannot use it as he wishes. Rather, there are constraints to its usage that originate in the peculiarities of a legal perspective. Still, since the Prince must break the law in some cases, it ultimately seems subordinate to the political logic. But Machiavelli adds yet another twist to the question of political morality, which adds some additional elements to the seemingly strictly hierarchical relation of morals and politics.

V. Morality and Normativity

So far, we have discussed the normativity of political necessity, the political *virtù*, and the internal normativity of laws. Law and politics were considered as standing in a mostly instrumental perspective. Normativity, which constitutes a belief in the correctness of a practice, as well as fear, have the potential to channel the struggles of internal disorder and provide for a melting pot of concrete unity. The claims

[47] See, for the claim that Machiavelli constructs a constitutional order that unifies strategy and law, Philipp Bobbitt, *The Garments of Court and Palace – Machiavelli and the World That He Made* (2013).
[48] Althusser, *Machiavelli and Us*, p. 36 (n. 12).
[49] Machiavelli, *The Prince*, Ch. 3, p. 8 (n. 10).

that Machiavelli is the thinker of unmediated brutality, of which there are some well-known examples in *The Prince*, usually refer to this kind of instrumental relation between laws, fear, and political practice. Political *virtù* in this sense is the capacity for political action and is independent of moral virtue. The independent thinking of the political is part of Machiavelli's totalitarian and state-of-exception interpretations.

To this justificatory level of normativity as a matter of necessity, Machiavelli adds another independent level. Machiavelli is equally concerned with the moral dimension of action. He says about Romulus, who killed his brother when he founded Rome: 'for he who is violent to spoil, not he who is violent to mend, should be reproved'.[50] Violence without purpose is a negative thing. He says: '[T]here are two ways for contending: one by using laws, the other, force. The first is appropriate for man, the second for animals; but because the former is often ineffective, one must have recourse to the latter.'[51] To choose the right technique in the right moment is a question of ability, of *virtù*. It is necessity that decides which means are appropriate.

If the situation requires it, the Prince must not hesitate to be an animal. '[H]e should imitate both the fox and the lion, for the lion is liable to be trapped, whereas the fox cannot ward off wolves.'[52] Both are animal attributes which rely on violence, however different in kind they may be. The lion is simply associated with brute force. But the fox is quite another thing. The interpretation by Althusser culminates precisely in this point. The fox is associated with fraud, a very specific form of violence. Althusser remarks: 'Fraud is not a mode of government like the others; it is not on the same level. Laws exist—let us say as human institutions, recognized rules, and opinions; force exists—let us say as the army. In contrast, however, fraud possesses no objective existence: it does not exist. If fraud is a way of governing, given that it has no existence, it can be employed only when it is based on laws or force.'[53] It is thus in principle on three levels that Machiavelli's Prince operates: law/morality, force, and fraud. Althusser explains: 'Deception is counterposed to laws as immorality to morality. To engage in 'trickery' with the law is, in effect, to 'get around' people; it is 'to load the dice' by lies and deception.'[54]

This sheds light on the moral dimension of Machiavelli's scientific enterprise. The usage of these different techniques, including fraud, is dependent on concrete necessity. Political *virtù* at best overlaps with moral virtue, government by laws, since the necessity for fraud and violence does not arise. The truly virtuous Prince can avoid recurring on animal attributes by recognizing problems far in advance. Since government by laws potentially moderates social conflict, insofar as it never comes to situations of political necessity, a moral government is Machiavelli's preferred option. It is here that the Republican strand of Machiavelli interpretations comes into play.

[50] Machiavelli, *Discourses on Livy*, Book I, Ch. 9, p. 29 (n. 1).
[51] Machiavelli, *The Prince*, Ch. 18, p. 61 (n. 10).
[52] Machiavelli, *Discourses on Livy*, Book I, Ch. 18, 61 (n. 1).
[53] Althusser, *Machiavelli and Us*, p. 95 (n. 12).
[54] Ibid., p. 96.

A stable order, rooted in checks and balances between the people, avoids violent governance.

Yet, there is a remarkable antithesis to this interpretation, brought forward by Merleau-Ponty in his short *Note on Machiavelli*: 'The evil that I do I do to myself, and in struggling against others I struggle equally against myself. [...] And yet when the victim admits defeat, the cruel man perceives another life beating through those words; he finds himself before *another himself.* We are far from the relationships of sheer force that hold between objects.'[55] According to this interpretation, the transition from following animal instincts to human life involves a transformation of the character of violence. Merleau-Ponty continues: '[W]e have gone from one way of fighting to another, from 'fighting with force' to 'fighting with laws'. Human combat is different from animal combat, but it is a fight.'[56] What this brings into play is the next level of the negation. According to Merleau-Ponty, the self-reflective element of morality sheds a cynical light on the struggle of a civilization that is caught between necessity and violence against itself. It is here that one comes to understand the diversity of interpretations of Machiavelli: There are seemingly infinite opportunities to uncover further layers in his thought. What is certain is that the open structure of his texts allows for interpretations in which it is finally difficult to say where Machiavelli's part in them remains.[57]

VI. Imperialism

The focus of the argument so far has been on his domestic political philosophy in the light of laws and normativity, always based on a concrete unity to bring about the stability of a political body. Interestingly, the same considerations lead Machiavelli to argue for a completely different conception in the international realm. For Machiavelli, as Koskenniemi notes, 'the 'international' did not have any specific identity as a field of politics or as a set of problems; it was either a potential target of imperial policy or it was a source of threat—that is to say, the imperial policies of other states'.[58] Not moderate republican thought, but aggressive imperial politics are at the heart of his international thinking. The basic situation in the international realm is similar: a proto-Hobbesian view of constant conflict. But whereas in the domestic sphere it is possible to pacify this conflict via institutions of checks and balances that are ultimately rooted in a unity that is created by these institutions, we cannot find such prospects for a concrete unity between states (or kingdoms, to be precise). What Machiavelli said about the Republican organization of a unity with the help of laws is thus unthinkable in the international realm.

[55] Merleau-Ponty, *Note on Machiavelli*, pp. 123–4 (n. 23).

[56] Ibid.

[57] Bobbitt, *The Garments of Court and Palace* (n. 47), calls this the 'Machiavelli Paradox'.

[58] Martti Koskenniemi, 'Not Excepting the Iroquois Themselves... – Machiavelli, Pufendorf and the Prehistory of International Law', Max Weber Lecture No. 2007/07 at the European University Institute, Florence, available at <http://cadmus.eui.eu/handle/1814/7632?show=full>, p. 9.

Bearing in mind the necessity for stability, this leads to a series of considerations that are all interlinked and mutually conditional. (1) Aggressive imperial politics make a country less vulnerable on the outside and facilitate stability. (2) Acquired principalities enlarge the unity on which the power of the Prince is based and further ameliorate stability. (3) The use and forming of a popular army also contributes to stability on the inside and facilitates the incorporation of new principalities. (4) Domestic politics shall be conducted in order to allow for aggressive foreign politics; the organization on the inside must provide the means for external conquest. Machiavelli's international thinking is thus coherent with his domestic thinking regarding the main quest: how is it possible to stabilize an order?

In his preference for aggressive foreign policy, we find an attitude that is typical for Machiavelli: always act, never react. Aggression places the Prince on the side of action, making outcomes more predictable. When international relations are a constant struggle for survival, it is better to be a belligerent state. Additionally, with the help of conquest, the Prince might acquire territories that can be incorporated into his own empire. If it is possible (and according to Machiavelli it *must* be possible) to integrate the new principality into the concrete unity of his own Empire, this will improve its power and therefore increase stability.

Machiavelli discusses another precondition for stability as one of the most important elements in the Prince: the theory of the popular army. First, he makes clear that mercenaries are either useless, when they fight for money and are unwilling to give their lives on the battlefield, or even dangerous because they might turn against the Prince.[59] The same holds true for auxiliary troops that belong to another ruler—to rely on these groups means to relinquish one's own destiny—something one should never do.[60] His considerations here are obviously influenced by the Italian experience. A popular army, in turn, is recruited from the peasantry. In the structure of the army, infantrymen have the primacy over the cavalry.[61] In Althusser's Marxist interpretation, this 'initiates a process of social and political amalgamation that simultaneously challenges the hierarchies sanctioned by the feudal order and its military organization. Not only does the lofty reign of the cavalryman come to an end, but a new form of popular unity, hitherto non-existent, takes shape: in the army common to them, the men of the towns and countryside begin to become—learn to become—one and the same people.'[62] In that sense, the army is not only an important means to external stability. Rather, by ensuring internal societal cohesion the army constitutes also an end in itself.

In domestic politics, it is thus also important to constitute a strong state that is capable of expanding.[63] Machiavelli discusses the question of inclusiveness in the

[59] Machiavelli, *The Prince*, Ch. 17, p. 43 (n. 10).
[60] Ibid., Ch. 18, p. 48.
[61] Harvey C. Mansfield, *Machiavelli's New Modes and Orders* (1979), pp. 245–6.
[62] Althusser, *Machiavelli and Us*, p. 87 (n. 12).
[63] See also Herfried Münkler, 'Der Imperativ expansiver Selbsterhaltung', in Herfried Münkler et al. (eds.), *Demaskierung der Macht – Machiavellis Staats- und Politikverständnis* (2nd edn, 2013), p. 111.

Discourses under the heading of 'whether a state could have been ordered in Rome that would have taken away the enmities between the people and the senate'.[64] Machiavelli explains that there were two types of government in history that were able to contain that internal struggle. In Venice, the stability rested on the principle of inherited citizenship, an exclusionary form of government. Similarly, in Sparta, only a few citizens were in charge of public affairs, and no strangers were welcome in the state. So, Machiavelli continues: '[I]t was necessary for the legislators of Rome to do one of two things if they wished Rome to stay quiet like the above-mentioned republics: either not to employ the plebs in war, as did the Venetians, or not to open the door to foreigners, as did the Spartans. They did both, which gave the plebs strength and increase and infinite opportunities for tumult.'[65] In explaining why the Romans did that, Machiavelli argues that a strong Empire, an Empire that wishes to expand, needs to ground itself on an *inclusive* unity because 'if you maintain it [the people] either small or disarmed so as to be able to manage it, then if you acquire dominion, you cannot hold it or it becomes so cowardly that you are the prey of whoever assaults you.'[66] One might choose the path of government of elites, but this way of government is doomed to fail. Domestically, it is thus important that the government be as inclusive as possible to ensure the popular grounding of state power.

All these considerations point to a conception of other peoples that is not coined by respect and toleration. Still, Machiavelli's plea for imperialism can be clearly distinguished from others. That his imperialism does not have a nationalistic connotation, in the sense of superiority of its own people, is revealed when Machiavelli talks about the incorporation of conquered colonies. The people of the new colony have to accept the lead culture of its own national state because this is the only way they can be incorporated into the larger unity of the state. This cultural unity of the larger (and more powerful) entity, in turn, provides the basis for a more stable empire. In that sense, expansion is a precondition for stability. The people as a concrete foundation thus always have to consist of those people who embody the specific unity of the polity. Other people(s) are not part of Machiavelli's philosophy. What makes this conception interesting is that, even though Machiavelli does not have a conception of universal normativity based on intrinsic human value, he is not discriminating against potential members of the unity of the Empire. Normatively speaking, it is a very specific universality based on cultural facts—the acceptance of being part of a cultural (ideological) community.

VII. International Law

The role of international law in this proto-Hobbesian struggle for survival is complicated. Yet, Machiavelli had spent too many years working as a diplomat to be

[64] Machiavelli, *Discourses on Livy*, Book I, Ch. 6, p. 20 (n. 1).
[65] Ibid., p. 21.
[66] Ibid., p. 22.

able to ignore it. Diplomatic agreements constitute an important part of the intergovernmental world, but there was no way to see them as a kind of system that constrained governments from doing whatever they wished. Order was not maintained by legal checks and balances, but by two Princes who had more to lose than to gain when they put their threats into action.[67] In that sense, Koskenniemi notes that Machiavelli did not hold a 'view of the international as a single social space ("universal"), detachable from the ambition or fear of this or that ruler'.[68]

In this struggle, diplomatic agreements could potentially provide for a temporally limited stability, if your competitors believe you will stick to them. However, from the ruler's perspective, the Prince must not be constrained. Machiavelli makes that clear when he talks about the role of auxiliaries in military conflicts. With auxiliaries, another ruler's troops who aid you in conflict, you will always lose. If they are defeated, so are you, and if they win, they might turn against you.[69] 'In short, weapons and armour belonging to others fall off you or weigh you down or constrict your movements.'[70] Diplomatic agreements must not constrain the Prince's capacity for political action.

Seen from this angle, diplomatic agreements that today undoubtedly form part of international law thus did not receive the status of law as compared to the domestic realm. As explained above, domestic law, for Machiavelli, is quite a modern concept that grounds its normativity first and foremost in the concrete unity it creates—the people. Since diplomatic agreements could never be grounded in a popular unity, they did not form part of that specific, law-inherent normativity.[71] There was nothing like a moral argument to stick to treaties, no *pacta sunt servanda* in the international realm. Returning to Machiavelli's metaphor about the fox and the lion stated above, there is nothing normative that would prevent fraud and fox-like behaviour between states. Rather, in the struggle for survival, it would be smart to employ these techniques. In this sense, a highly moral domestic political theory turns into an amoral survival strategy in foreign politics.

It has been claimed—*inter alia* by Koskenniemi—that, foreshadowing discussions of later international lawyers, Machiavelli offers a certain perspective on a just war also being a matter of necessity. A just war would be war linked to the preservation and advancement of the state.[72] In fact, Machiavelli's view on the necessity of war is much more complex. Necessity depends on the underlying aims for which achieving one or the other action is deemed necessary. The problem of the necessary war thus already emerges in contrast to the question whether peace is a desirable state. This question has already been controversially debated among several authors. While Felix Gilbert argues that there is nothing in Machiavelli pointing

67 See also Koskenniemi, 'Not Excepting the Iroquois' (n. 58), who discusses Machiavelli in opposition to Guicciardini.

68 Koskenniemi, 'Not Excepting the Iroquois', pp. 9–10 (n. 58).

69 Machiavelli, *The Prince*, Ch. 13, p. 48 (n. 10).

70 Ibid., p. 50.

71 D'Amato seems to have overlooked this in qualifying diplomacy as legal in Machiavelli's sense. See D'Amato, 'The Relevance of Machiavelli' (n. 46).

72 Koskenniemi, 'Not Excepting the Iroquois', p. 11 (n. 58).

to the desirability of peace,[73] others, like Maurizio Viroli, argue that Machiavelli deals with war and international affairs just in order to replace the art of war with the 'arts of peace'.[74] Given that the latter point seems more convincing in the light of what has just been discussed, it is important how Machiavelli *uses* the concept of necessity.

Anthony Parel suggests that, for Machiavelli, necessity is a normative concept against which actions have to be measured. However, he notes that, due to its subjectivity, the concept of necessity would be unsuitable to assess a ruler's actions and promote abuse.[75] The reason for which one might be sceptical about this reading is the placement of the concept of necessity outside the ruler himself. It is against an abstract normative concept that his actions would have to be assessed. However, for Machiavelli, necessity is not a concept outside the ruler; it is closely connected with the political virtue that can be assessed only in the light of the results of the Prince's actions.

Returning to Koskenniemi's suggestion, it is no accident that Machiavelli does not talk about the question of justice in war. The reason why it might be questionable to interpret and categorize Machiavelli's view on foreign politics as inhabiting a perspective on the normativity of war leads back to the important distinction of domestic and foreign politics. The normativity of order, and with it the negative connotation of fraud, arises with the background of a concrete unity against which it can be measured. Since the international realm does not constitute a concrete unity, there is no reason—neither in Machiavelli's oeuvre nor in a teleological interpretation of his thought—that Machiavelli would even consider *applying* a notion of justice to the question of war. The necessity of justification of war does not arise against the potential opponent ruler, but only as a foreshadowing of possible effects on the own political community, the only entity against which normativity could arise.

In theoretical terms, after having rejected the purely political realist interpretation of Machiavelli in the domestic realm, we return to that strand in the international. However, we arrive there as the result of a negation, the impossibility to ground international rule in a concrete unity. Machiavelli's theory transposed to the international realm thus constitutes political realism conditioned upon the absence of (ideal, ideological) unity. While it can only be appropriately understood (and taken as potentially visionary) if it is read against his domestic political philosophy, there is no reason to whitewash his imperialism, which recognizes others (or other peoples) only as part of the cultural circle to which the concept of justice extends when they are assimilated. However, it is a different and strangely visionary cultural imperialism that provides emancipatory perspectives.

[73] Felix Gilbert, 'Machiavelli: The Renaissance of the Art of War', in Peter Paret et al. (eds.), *Makers of Modern Strategy from Machiavelli to the Nuclear Age* (1986), pp. 11–31.

[74] Viroli, *From Politics to Reason of State*, p.164 (n. 9).

[75] Parel, *Machiavelli's Notion of Justice*, p. 535 (n. 9).

VIII. Perspectives—Is Machiavelli a Part of the History of International Legal Thought?

Machiavelli was not an international lawyer. He did not believe in the traditional story of a consent-based law to provide order in the international sphere. This contribution has tried to shed light on the question why that is the case and why a thinker who is considered Republican, even a democrat, has a perspective focused on imperial foreign policy in a condition of war. In traditional readings, Machiavelli could not be a part of the history of international legal thought. Machiavelli does away with any consent-based myths—one of the reasons why he is admired by some International Relations theorists. The mere existence of laws cannot guarantee stability. But the international law Machiavelli is interested in is a different one—it is one that works with assumptions of inclusiveness and takes into account its cultural and contingent origins not merely as a blueprint for delegitimation, but as an important precondition for global peace and stability. Including Machiavelli in a history of international legal thought highlights the emancipation from theories of consensual normativity and from merely critical readings of history.

The study of Machiavelli reveals that the conditions that could potentially bring about a stable rule in the domestic realm—the possibility to ground the rule in a very concrete unity and an ideologically coherent people—are completely absent in the international field. In terms of the empirical assessment of Renaissance Italy, this is undoubtedly correct. How should a non-naturalistic normativity conception possibly arise if there was no way to connect it with a concrete unity? In his assessment of the international world at his time, Machiavelli has a point.

Thinking about perspectives, speculative as this might be, Machiavelli's thinking gives some ideas about the world as it looks today. In contrast to Renaissance Italy, the world is not in constant war anymore; one is not either aggressive or conquered. Machiavelli's historical condition might have vanished, but his theoretical contribution is recent. If we recall his central claims about stability, unity, and the people, these are precisely the discussions prevalent in normative international law scholarship today. It is quite possible to understand the concept of the international community as a combination of these claims. Machiavelli tells us that what unifies people is ideology, laws, and religion.[76] Human Rights, the secular religion of today, could potentially bring about a concrete unity in Machiavelli's sense. It might be that Machiavelli had endorsed its vocabulary, had he known it, but certainly he would have supported the enterprise of conquering the world in the name of liberty.[77]

[76] As the contribution by Christian Volk, *The Law of Nations as the Civil Law of the World*, in this volume, p. 243, shows, there are considerable similarities to the international legal thought of Montesquieu. Similarly, as Carla De Pascale, *Fichte and the Echo of his Internationalist Thinking in Romanticism*, in this volume, pp. 342–3, claims, these elements enjoy a considerable status in Fichte's thought.

[77] See also the closing words by Hörnquist, *Machiavelli and Empire*, p. 290 (n. 9).

In less concrete terms, I have discussed Machiavelli as a theorist of two distinct moments. The contingent beginning is followed by a rule that has to be grounded in the very unity it has constituted. International law thus could potentially develop into that normative concept if its ideology produces a sufficient degree of concrete unity to shift the level of political action from the national to the international realm, an organic constitutionalism somehow. Two things can make us believe that Machiavelli would have shared this idea: first, Machiavelli is a thinker of empirical assessment, who teaches the Prince the capacity to adequately react to the actual situation. Second, Machiavelli is the thinker of the beginning of a political community when its unity is yet to be achieved.[78] It is the political theory of a foundation of a community. In many ways, in international thinking, Machiavelli provides a starting point.

Selected Bibliography

Althusser, Louis, *Machiavelli and Us*, trans. Gregory Elliott (London/New York: Verso, 1999).

Bobbitt, Philipp, *The Garments of Court and Palace – Machiavelli and the World That He Made* (New York: Grove Press, 2013).

D'Amato, Anthony, 'International Law from A Machiavellian Perspective', in Anthony D'Amato (ed.), *International Law Studies*, Collected Papers Vol.II (The Hague: Kluwer Law, 1997), Chs, 18 and 19, 251–78.

Machiavelli, Niccolò, *Discourses on Livy*, trans. Harvey C. Mansfield and Nathan Tarcov (Chicago: University of Chicago Press, 1996).

Machiavelli, Niccolò, *The Prince*, trans. Quentin Skinner and Russell Price (Cambridge: Cambridge University Press, 1988).

Koskenniemi, Martti, 'Not Excepting the Iroquois Themselves . . . – Machiavelli, Pufendorf and the Prehistory of International Law', Max Weber Lecture No. 2007/07 at the European University Institute, Florence, available at <http://cadmus.eui.eu/handle/1814/7632?show=full>.

[78] This element of foundation is similarly present in the international legal thought of Rousseau. See, Jonas Heller, *Orders in Disorder – The Question of an International State of Nature in Hobbes and Rousseau*, in this volume, pp. 160–82.

2

Francisco de Vitoria

A Redesign of Global Order on the Threshold of the Middle Ages to Modern Times

Kirstin Bunge

I. Introduction: The 'School of Salamanca' and Francisco de Vitoria

In the late nineteenth century, the origin of international law was often associated with a group of Spanish and Portuguese theologians who adapted the Catholic theory of Natural Law to the altered political, economic, and pastoral conditions of the sixteenth century.* After the so-called 'discovery' and conquest of Central and South America, Europeans faced the challenge of having to revise their worldview. Part of this meant having to deal with the existence of unfamiliar yet long-standing political communities. The contours of the world as they had hitherto been known were abruptly expanded. From a western viewpoint, these geopolitical transformations resulted in a new regulation of power spheres as well as in the need to justify dominion. The prevalent concept of law, which still operated within scholastic terms of a God-given order, composed of divine, natural, and human law, had to be adapted to the altered knowledge about the world. Simultaneously, a new form of 'inter-national' law, which regulated the relationship *between* political communities, slowly emerged.

Because he had reformulated the *Institutiones*-definition of *jus gentium* from '*inter omnes homines*' to '*inter omnes gentes*'[1] the Dominican Francisco de Vitoria (1492/93–1546), professor of theology at the University of Salamanca, is known as one of the founding fathers of the so-called 'School of Salamanca'. Although he never left Europe to see America—or as the Milanese humanist Petrus Martyr called it, the 'New World'[2]—Vitoria is particularly noted for his rather critical

* I would like to thank Ursula Diewald Rodriguez for proofreading this chapter. Unless otherwise specified, translations into English by the author.

[1] Francisco de Vitoria, *De Indis*, section 3, title 1, nu. 1, in Ulrich Horst et al. (eds.), *Vorlesungen II*, (1997), p. 460. See also Section III, cycles of reception.

[2] See Anthony Pagden, *Das erfundene Amerika. Der Aufbruch des europäischen Denkens in die Neue Welt* (1996), p. 284, n. 11.

but ambivalent examinations of the Spanish Conquest and his contribution to the formation of international law. The 'School of Salamanca' cannot be considered a school in the narrow sense of a closed, cohesive theoretical system. But the representatives of this Iberian moral–theological tradition did share various consistencies and similarities. This chapter will explicate four of these similarities in order to give an impression of the methodology and the social-political context. It will subsequently concentrate on Vitoria's approach to *jus gentium* and conditions of legitimacy in the international realm.

First of all, these theologians (and later jurists) were confronted with deeply changing political and academic conditions. Medieval scholastics had already been forced to deal with the rediscovered and translated writings of Greco–Arabic philosophy and science, i.e. a comprehensive worldview based solely on human reason. This resulted in increased research activity in the field of logic, metaphysics, natural theology, and natural ethics. On these medieval groundings, the theologians of the sixteenth century had then to integrate formerly unknown foreign cultures into their conceptions of the world, i.e. into their conception of order. They thus had to reconcile their mindset, which was based on Christian revelation, with the fact that there were complex political communities in existence that had never before heard the Gospel.

Secondly, the representatives of the 'School of Salamanca' were methodologically dedicated to the medieval reception of Aristotle and conducted an inner-Catholic revision of the tradition.[3] Consequently, not only did they attempt to replicate the medieval findings but they also sought to reconstruct them with special regard to the transforming political, social, and economic conditions of their time. Closely linked with Vitoria's way of thought is Thomas Aquinas, whose work he had become acquainted with during his studies in Paris and whose *Summa Theologiae* he subsequently introduced at the University of Salamanca as the standard textbook, thereby replacing the *Sententiae* by Petrus Lombardus.[4]

During the course of this remapping and new configuration of periphery, there was, thirdly, a loosening of the strong interrelation between philosophical, theologian, and juridical approaches. As a theologian Vitoria was still dealing with questions about legitimacy of conquest, colonization, and property but only within the conceptual context of dogmatic theologian presumptions (e.g. about God's *potestas* or a post-lapsarian anthropology) as well as philosophical issues like questions of coherence, of non-contradiction, or of logical reasoning. Correspondingly, the relation between religious and secular spheres, the reliability of knowledge sources,[5]

[3] This concerned, for example, the canonistic teachings of papal supremacy and its relation to secular power. See in reference to the relationship between the 'School of Salamanca' and the Reformation Merio Scattola, 'Eine innerkonfessionelle Debatte. Wie die Spanische Spätscholastik die politische Theologie des Mittelalters mit der Hilfe des Aristoteles revidierte', in Alexander Fidora, Johannes Fried, Matthias Lutz-Bachmann, and Luise Schorn-Schütte (eds.), *Politischer Aristotelismus und Religion in Mittelalter und Früher Neuzeit* (2007), pp. 139–61.

[4] For a short overview of the methodological reasons to change, see Kurt Seelmann, 'Theologische Wurzeln des säkularen Naturrechts. Das Beispiel Salamanca', in Dietmar Willoweit (ed.), *Die Begründung des Rechts als historisches Problem* (2000), pp. 216f.

[5] Cf. probabilism and casuistry.

and instruments of power[6] were re-assessed. Furthermore, in Europe (albeit on the Iberian Peninsula to a lesser degree) the Reformation gained in importance and one could already observe early attempts at secularization.

Finally, radical and global transformations took place in the political and economic sphere. Humanism rediscovered republican values and new visions of politics in the form of early modern centralized nations competed with old ones such as the empire (*regnum/imperium*) and, in a specific way, with papacy (*sacerdotium*). On a national level, the first 'states' with a centralized use of force and fiscal system replaced the multitude of small dominions loosely associated with the feudal system of the medieval age. Under the terms of the emerging early modern states and Europe's striving for expansion, the economy expanded and the web of colonial trade and transport routes intensified. By the sixteenth century, the foundations for a conglomerate of national stakeholders or of stakeholders acting under the authority of a state (as for example Grotius' *Dutch East India Company*) came into being.[7]

II. Moral Theology and Jurisprudence

1. The Hierarchy of *leges* and the order of *jus naturale*, *jus gentium*, and *jus positivum*

Following these short introductive remarks about central similarities concerning the methodological approach of the 'School of Salamanca' to the altered conditions of the sixteenth century, the second section deals with Vitoria's conception of *leges*-order and its theological presuppositions that underlie these early beginnings of international law.[8] Which conception of order can cope, according to Vitoria, with the radical anthropological, political, social, and economic transformations?

In reference to Aristotle, Vitoria assumed a natural order which exists inherently and which can be determined by reason. Based on this idea, 'all natural things are in themselves and, vice versa, all things are necessary by themselves'.[9] Accordingly, the *jus naturale* represents 'law in and of itself'.[10] Nevertheless, enclosed in this natural fixed framework there are various degrees (*gradus*) of necessity to be distinguished. Depending on the 'quality of the object',[11] these degrees vary from logical

6 Consider, for instance, the doctrine of the Two-Swords, the teachings of papal vs. imperial world domination.

7 Cf. some of the stakeholders of the early European colonial system which had been founded between 1600 and 1786 to exploit Asian commodities: British East India Company, Dutch East India Company, Danish West India Company, Dutch West India Company, Portuguese East India Company, French East India Company, Swedish East India Company, and Swedish West India Company. See also Glenn J. Ames, *The Globe Encompassed: The Age of European Discovery, 1500–1700* (2008); and Wilhelm G. Grewe, *Epochen der Völkerrechtsgeschichte* (1984), pp. 341–53.

8 Kurt Seelmann, *Theologie und Jurisprudenz an der Schwelle zur Moderne: Die Geburt des neuzeitlichen Naturrechts in der iberischen Spätscholastik* (1997).

9 Vitoria, *De iustitia I*, q. 57, art. 2, nu. 3, Joachim Stüben ed. (2013), p. 20: 'omne naturale est de per se et econtra omne de per se est necessarium'.

10 Vitoria, *De iustitia*, q. 57, art. 2, nu. 3, p. 20: 'per se est *jus* et ex se'.

11 Vitoria, *De iustitia*, q. 57, art. 2, nu. 3, p. 20: 'qualitatem materiae'.

reasoning, like in mathematics in which 'the opposite implies a contradiction',[12] to natural things whose 'necessity is lesser'.[13] Vitoria referred to the triangle to give an example of the highest degree of necessity, in this case complying with the logical requirement for consistency. The general definition of the triangle implies that even the *potestas* of God as creator of everything could not change the nature of the triangle.

Deus enim non potest facere, quod triangulus non habeat tres angulos.[14]

Ernst-Wolfgang Böckenförde thus considers Vitoria`s approach to be between 'absolute necessity of nature and radical contingency which enables fortuity'.[15] Although Böckenförde points out certain discrepancies in the way Vitoria tried to combine Thomas Aquinas and Duns Scotus, according to Vitoria, 'on the level of God' there are no limits.

Vitoria modifies the concept of necessity. Unlike Duns Scotus, he understands it not as universal and absolute, thus also applying to God himself, but as a necessity that is inherent to creature (immanent to creation) and that does not exclude a pre-creational freedom of God. According to Vitoria, the *necessitas* thus exists (only) *de potentia dei ordinata*, as an emanation of ordering-ordered action of God, not *de potentia dei absoluta.* As a creation-inherent order (*necessitas naturalis*) it presents itself at the level of the human being, who is himself a part of that creation, as an absolute, predefined, and untangible condition. This order constitutes the point of departure for all human knowledge and action. On the level of God, however, the Creator is not necessarily bond to it.[16]

By contrast, among the realm of natural things, as for example the physical nature of humans, there is a multiplicity of variations.[17] For instance, the human being is mainly characterized by rationality (*rationalitas*), but the 'ability to laugh (*risibilitas*)' also adheres to the natural qualities of humans ('*per se homini adhaeret*'), although not to the same degree of necessity as cognition.[18]

[12] Vitoria, *De iustitia*, q. 57, art. 2, nu. 3, p. 20: 'implicat contradictionem oppositum'.

[13] Vitoria, *De iustitia*, q. 57, art. 2, nu. 3, p. 20: 'non est tanta necessitas in naturalibus'.

[14] Vitoria, *De iustitia*, q. 57, art. 2, nu. 3, p. 20.

[15] 'absoluter Naturnotwendigkeit und radikaler, der Zufälligkeit Raum gebender Kontingenz'. Böckenförde, '§ 14 Die spanische Spätscholastik, II. Francisco de Vitoria', in idem, *Geschichte der Rechts- und Staatsphilosophie. Antike und Mittelalter*, p. 348.

[16] 'Vitoria modifiziert den Begriff der *necessitas*. Er versteht ihn, anders als Duns Scotus, nicht als eine universale und absolute, also auch im Blick auf Gott selbst geltende, sondern als eine innergeschöpfliche (schöpfungsimmanente) Notwendigkeit, die eine vor-geschöpfliche Freiheit Gottes nicht ausschließt. Die *necessitas* besteht daher bei ihm (nur) *de potentia dei ordinata*, als Ausfluß des ordnend-geordneten Handelns Gottes, nicht *de potentia dei absoluta*. Als der Schöpfung eingestiftete Ordnung (*necessitas naturalis*) ist sie von der Ebene des Menschen aus, der selbst Teil dieser Schöpfung ist, eine absolute, ihm vorgegebene und für ihn nicht verfügbare. Er hat sie zum Ausgangspunkt seines Erkennens und Handelns zu machen. Auf der Ebene Gottes aber besteht für den Schöpfer nicht in jedem Fall eine Bindung daran.' Böckenförde, '§ 14 Die spanische Spätscholastik, II. Francisco de Vitoria', p. 348.

[17] Cf. Vitoria, *De iustitia*, q. 57, art. 2, nu. 3, p. 20: '(...) ut v.g. necessarium est, quod homo respiret, quod habeat duos oculos, duos pedes et quod sol oriatur cras. Et tamen Deus posset facere contrarium, scilicet quod esset homo et non respiret nec habeat oculos nec pedes et quod sol non oriatur cras.'

[18] Vitoria, *De iustitia*, q. 57, art. 2, nu. 3, p. 20.

In what way is this distinction between degrees of necessity relevant to the relation between *jus naturale* and *jus gentium*? Vitoria distinguished several degrees to which norms and principles could be derived from *jus naturale* to create positive law. *Jus naturale* is valid because it is inherently rational and not by virtue of the means of its formation. In contrast, *jus gentium* is not valid 'by itself but due to human statutes based on reason'.[19] This means that *jus gentium* results from *communis consensus omnium gentium et nationum* analogous to *jus positivum* which relies on 'private pact and agreement and (. . .) public pact'.[20] This 'consensus of all people and nations' emerges from the *pactum* of men who have formed various political and social entities. *Jus gentium* did not originate from the agreement of single humans (like in early modern theories of social contract) but 'by the authority of the whole world'.[21] Regardless of existing differences between the peoples and the nations, all are subject to *jus gentium*.

Furthermore, because it is not *jus* in the sense of *jus naturale* 'per se (. . .) et ex se',[22] the validity of *jus gentium* is measured according to the degree to which peace is (re-) established and war is restricted. Even the perpetuation of *jus naturale* depends on *jus gentium* to preserve the peace. *Jus positivum* sets standards relative to something other, standards of an *adequate* and not commensurable[23] natural order. Positive law proceeds 'adequate to another in ordination to other (*alteri adaequatum in ordine ad aliud*)'.[24]

What does this differentiation between a commensurable and an adequate order signify? It seems that Vitoria wants to add another legal order to the stable, unalterable, and commensurable natural order of *jus naturale*. This second concept of order is valid insofar as it is adequate, i.e. relative to a politically determined criterion. Because the order of natural law implies an idea of peace,[25] albeit in a general and rather undesignated manner, it is necessary to concretize it positively. In order to preserve the peace according to *jus naturale, jus gentium* mediates between the necessary order of *jus naturale* and the order of positive law with its specific arbitrariness.[26] This specific nature of *jus gentium* is reflected in several institutions such as property, the legal status of legates or ambassadors, the rules of warfare,[27] etc. It represents a concept of peace promoting trade and proselytization.

[19] Vitoria, *De iustitia*, q. 57, art. 3, nu. 1, p. 32: 'non est aequum ex se, sed ex statuto humano in ratione fixo.'

[20] Vitoria, *De iustitia*, q. 57, art. 3, nu. 3, p. 36: 'ex privato pacto et consensu et (. . .) pacto publico'.

[21] Vitoria, *De potestate civili*, nu. 21, in (ed.) Ulrich Horst et al. *Vorlesungen I*, (1995), p. 156: 'est enim latum totius orbis auctoritate'.

[22] Vitoria, *De iustitia*, q. 57, art. 2, nu. 3, p. 20.

[23] Vitoria, *De iustitia*, q. 57, art. 3, nu. 1, p. 32: 'Ius naturale est, quod ex natura sua est alteri commensuratum. (. . .) Illud, quod primo modo est adaequatum et absolute iustum, vocatur *jus* naturale, id est de iure naturali.'

[24] Vitoria, *De iustitia*, q. 57, art. 3, nu. 1, p. 32.

[25] Vitoria, *De iustitia*, q. 57, art. 3, nu. 3, p. 36: 'Est de iure naturali pax.'

[26] Vitoria, *De iustitia*, q. 57, art. 3, nu. 1, p. 32: 'ordinatur ad pacem et concordiam hominum.'

[27] See for the doctrine of 'just war', John Finnis, 'The Ethics of War and Peace in the Catholic Natural Law Tradition', and Joseph Boyle, 'Just War Thinking in Catholic Natural Law', in Terry Nardin (ed.), *The Ethics of War and Peace: Religious and Secular Perspectives* (1996), pp. 15–39 and pp. 40–53.

2. Anthropological and epistemic presumptions and the reliability of knowledge, rules, and norms

If, in the mindset of this age, there are different degrees of *jus naturale* and necessity concerning the possible range of arbitrary acts (even of God), what is the impact of this concept of order on finite, peccable, and deceivable beings, i.e. on humans? According to the doctrine of original sin, the human powers of cognition are constricted but they still have a significant part in this God-given order.[28] Likewise, according to the principle of various degrees of necessity, humans are able to recognize the rules and norms of natural law only to a certain degree. The first strict degree of necessity includes 'all which is per se known as just by natural light, and which conforms to right reason, and whose contrary is unjust'.[29] The principle 'You should not do to your neighbour what you yourself do not want to suffer!' belongs to this strict degree. The norms of the second degree are, for example, 'the Commandments of the Decalogue such as the prohibition of killing'.[30] They 'are, if concluded correctly, inferred and deduced from principles which are known by themselves'.[31] The commandments of the first and second degree are very similar to each other, so Vitoria refers to the prohibition of killing or stealing as examples for both. These degrees of deducing 'from the natural principles'[32] vary in their probability for being properly comprehended by reason (*intellectus*). But they still have in common that 'nothing (. . .) arises from natural law except that what the human being can know by nature'.[33] According to Vitoria, to know (*scire*) something signifies 'that all agree'.[34] But if it is true that what 'comes from natural law'[35] can be equated with 'what can be recognized by all',[36] how could discrepancy from *consensus* be explained?

Collective agreement and individual consent can diverge because of 'bad habit, bad dispositions, bad instructions, or ambition'.[37] Therefore dissent from general consent can be explained by deficient institutions and structures but not by a general absence of rationality. Custom and education are in good order when they impart a certain set of cognitive methods such as deductive reasoning, conclusion,

[28] Vitoria, *De iustitia*, q. 57, art. 2, nu. 4, p. 26: 'Sed quilibet nostrum potest decipi, postquam primus parens peccavit.'

[29] Vitoria, *De iustitia*, q. 57, art. 2, nu. 4, p. 22: 'Omne illud, quod lumine naturali per se notum est esse iustum ab omnibus et conforme rationi rectae et contrarium illius esse iniustum, omne tale dicitur et est *jus* naturale (. . .).'

[30] Vitoria, *De iustitia*, q. 57, art. 2, nu. 4, p. 22.

[31] Vitoria, *De iustitia*, q. 57, art. 2, nu. 4, p. 22: 'infertur et deducitur in bona consequentia ex principiis per se notis'.

[32] Vitoria, *De iustitia*, q. 57, art. 2, nu. 4., conclusion 3, p. 24: 'ex principiis naturalibus'.

[33] Vitoria, *De iustitia*, q. 57, art. 2, nu. 5, in summa, p. 30: 'nihil est de iure naturali, nisi quod naturaliter potest sciri ab homine'.

[34] Vitoria, *De iustitia*, q. 57, art. 2, nu. 4, p. 26: 'quod omnes assentiantur'.

[35] Cf. Vitoria, *De iustitia*, q. 57, art. 2, nu. 4, p. 26: 'Itaque quicumque supradicta obiiceret et quod illa, quae natura demonstrat, non sunt de iure naturali, quamvis verbo illa dicat, tamen non potest non assentire.'

[36] Vitoria, *De iustitia*, q. 57, art. 2, nu. 5, in summa, p. 30: 'quae ab omnibus possunt cognosci'.

[37] Vitoria, *De iustitia*, q. 57, art. 2, nu. 5, in summa, p. 30: 'ex mala consuetudine vel ex prava affectione vel mala doctrina vel studio'.

and dialectics.[38] Otherwise dissent could be the consequence. According to Vitoria, a person's dissent or failure to endorse something known by nature and accepted by everyone, would not be an expression of an individual act of volition, rather it would demonstrate a problem of social structure. Because *jus naturale* is a necessary law[39], independent of any act of volition, it is impossible that any singular individual or political community be excluded from it. As will be shown in the following sections, these anthropological and epistemic presumptions are integrated in Vitoria's ideas of just war and of legitimate intervention in political communities.

3. The *communitas totius orbis* and *jus gentium*

According to Vitoria, the *totus orbis* conceptualizes the physical and global space in which humans can act both as individuals (like travellers or traders) as well as a social (e.g. a religious Order) or political community (*gens* or *res publica*). Within the normative framework of natural law, the *totus orbis* is structured by *jus positivum* as well as various units, such as family, trade relations, singular political entities (*civitas*), international agreements, or the virtual republic of *totus orbis*. According to the natural law-theory, only *jus positivum* depends on volition and decisions by humans[40] whereas *jus naturale* represents fundamental moral insights. There still exist naturally binding rules between states, peoples, and mankind, to which positive law like *jus gentium* is added. In contrast to *jus naturale, jus gentium* is in principle alterable by contract (*pactum*) or mutual agreement (*consensus*), either between all parties involved or within a majority.[41] The immutability of *jus naturale* derives from the fact that it 'speaks by itself of a certain equality and justice, e.g. to return deposited goods, not to do to your next what you yourself do not want to suffer and so on'.[42] By contrast, *jus gentium* becomes morally binding only insofar that its regulations are in accordance with *jus naturale*; legally binding insofar that it conforms with positive law and thus with the majority of mankind.

Nota, quod si *jus* gentium derivatur sufficienter ex iure naturali, manifestam vim habet ad dandum *jus* et obligandum. Et dato, quod non semper derivetur ex iure naturali, sequi videtur consensus maioris partis totius orbis, maxime pro bono communi omnium.[43]

[38] Cf. Vitoria, *De iustitia*, q. 57, art. 2, nu. 5, pp. 28–31: '(. . .) quia consequentia est instrumentum dialecticae et inventa est ad hoc, ut ducat nos de notitia noti ad notitiam ignoti. (. . .) Si tamen possit sciri ab aliis, licet non ab omnibus, esset bona consequentia, et illi, qui sciunt, possunt aliis ostendere. Secundo dico, quod, quia versamur in moralibus, illa consequentia nihil valet propterea, quia si non potest sciri consequentia, nullus tenetur ad consequens, quia illa in moralibus non valet nec probat aliquid, nisi causet in nobis aliquam cognitionem. Cum ergo illa non causet cognitionem, ergo non est bona consequentia.'

[39] Cf. Vitoria, *De iustitia*, q. 57, art. 2, nu. 5, p. 28: '(. . .) *jus* naturale est idem quod *jus* necessarium'.

[40] Vitoria, *De iustitia*, q. 57, art. 2, nu. 2, p. 18: '(. . .) idem est *jus* naturale sicut *jus* necessarium, id est *jus* naturale est illud, quod est necessarium, puta quod non dependet ex voluntate aliqua. Et illud, quod dependet ex voluntate et beneplacito hominum, dicitur positivum.'

[41] This means also against a minority in case of political domination.

[42] Vitoria, *De iustitia*, q. 57, art. 3, nu. 1, p. 32: '(. . .) de se dicit aequalitatem quamdam et iustitiam, ut reddere depositum, quod tibi nos vis fieri alteri non facere etc'.

[43] Vitoria, *De Indis*, section 3, title 1, nu. 3, proposition 3, p. 466; idem, 'De iure belli', in Ulrich Horst et al. (eds.), *Vorlesungen II* (1997), p. 564.

Based on *jus naturale*, the unanimity- or majority rule, *pacta sunt servanda*, and the conception of *aequalitas* conflate in *jus gentium*. According to Vitoria, the *consensus maioris partis totius orbis* is reflected in *jus gentium*. The *jus gentium* embodies an idea of *bonum commune omnium* and is insofar 'equalised to the next in ordination to others'.[44] Although the *jus gentium* corresponds to the nature of *jus naturale*,[45] only *jus gentium* requires to be established by positive law because it does not by itself imply *aequitas*.

Ius vero gentium de se non est bonum, id est *jus* gentium dicitur, quod non habet in se aequitatem ex natura sua, sed ex condicto hominum sancitum est.[46]

Derived from natural law, and therefore under the terms of *aequalitas, jus gentium* possesses *aequitas* only when validated by becoming positive, customary, or contract law.[47] Between the requirements of natural law, the results of political legislation, and international bargaining, *jus gentium* is oriented towards *bonum commune omnium*. To ensure the common welfare of all by *jus gentium*, the protection of the legate or envoy is essential. It seems that the quasi-republic of *totus orbis* epitomizes the preconditions of legal procedures of continuous interaction and of intermediation in case of conflicts. *Jus gentium* consolidates various norms and rules commended by nature. These international norms and rules are not natural law by themselves but claim so much evidence that *jus gentium* could be found '*inter omnes gentes*'.[48] It seems that *jus gentium* refers to a law '*among* the peoples', and not any longer to a law only 'by (*apud*) the peoples' or merely in an already modern sense of 'between (*inter*) the peoples'.[49]

The mandatory nature of *jus gentium* derives from *consensus totius orbis* and from its quality to preserve *jus naturale*,[50] thus *jus gentium* cannot be abrogated.

Quia quando semel ex virtuali consensu totius orbis aliquid statuitur et admittitur, oportet, quod ad abrogationem talis iuris totus orbis conveniat, quod tamen est impossibile, quia impossibile est, quod consensus totius orbis conveniat in abrogatione iuris gentium.[51]

This leads to quite complicated and puzzling consequences, as the particular case concerning the treatment of Christian prisoners of war between Christian states shows. During Vitoria's time and in accordance to terms of the *bellum-justum*

[44] Vitoria, *De iustitia*, q. 57, art. 3,nu. 1, p. 32: 'alteri adaequatum in ordine ad aliud'.

[45] Vitoria, *De iustitia*, q. 57, art. 3, nu. 1, p. 32: 'ex natura sua est alteri commensuratum'.

[46] Vitoria, *De iustitia*, q. 57, art. 3, nu. 2, p. 34.

[47] Vitoria, *De Indis*, section 3, title 1, nu. 3, proposition 3, p. 466: 'vim habet ad dandum *jus* et obligandum'.

[48] Vitoria, *De Indis*, section 3, title 1, nu. 1, p. 460: 'Quod naturalis ratio inter omnes gentes constituit, vocatur *jus* gentium.'

[49] The ancient conception of *jus gentium* as 'law by (*apud*) the peoples or humans' understands it as rather incidentally valid, whereas the modern sense of 'law between (*inter*) the peoples' is based on an optional common agreement or arbitrary treaty. Vitoria's idea of *jus gentium* embedded in the *totus orbis* and in the overarching natural law seems to mediate between these two alternatives.

[50] Cf. Vitoria, *De iustitia*, q. 57, art. 3, nu. 3, p. 36: 'communis consensus omnium gentium et nationum'. And Vitoria, *De iustitia*, q. 57, art. 3, nu. 3, p. 38: 'facere contra *jus* gentium et illud violare est illicitum, quia de se importat iniuriam, quae infertur, et inaequalitatem quamdam'.

[51] Vitoria, *De iustitia*, q. 57, art. 3, nu. 5, p. 40.

doctrine, prisoners of war were usually taken into slavery. Christian states, however, had reached the agreement to refrain from this custom when dealing with Christian prisoners of war. But how does this exception affect the area of application of the generally admitted *jus gentium*? According to Vitoria, it is possible to partially derogate from certain elements of *jus gentium,* as for instance from enslavement. In the case of Christian states, the involved parties did not simply deviate from the law but altered the codes of conduct by agreement.[52] Nevertheless, due to the necessity of *jus naturale* and the quasi necessity of *jus gentium*, this partial derogation 'violates in part' the 'virtual consent (*virtualis consensus*) of *totius orbis*' because it alters the solid order of *jus gentium* by fractionalizing its scope.[53] Based on this ambiguous differentiation between *jus naturale* and *jus gentium,* the next section discusses Vitoria's modifications of the originally Roman idea of just war at the beginning of colonialism.

4. The doctrine of just war at the beginning of colonialism

Initiated by various reports about the brutal conquest and proselytization in Central and South America, Vitoria dealt with the scope of norms which were regarded as universal (like *jus naturale*) and others emerging from the actions of particular political communities (like *jus civile*). In some of his lectures, Vitoria investigated into how the 'New World' could be incorporated into the 'Old', using the idea of *jus gentium* which oscillates between *jus naturale* and *jus positivum.* The theory of *bellum justum* formed the traditional scholastic framework for questions about law, justice, and restored order. Originating in the context of the Roman Empire, the theory of just war was used to determine the criteria for regulating international violence and restricting the causes, methods, and purpose of war. Using the example of the conquest of America, Vitoria discussed the legitimacy and illegitimacy respectively of the exterritorial use of violence and dominion.

Vitoria retrospectively (the Spanish had already been located in America for fifty years) rejected the idea that either the emperor[54] or the pope were entitled to execute political domination (*dominium et potestas civile*) over the conquered territories.[55] At a time when the first dominant and expanding states like Spain and England gradually replaced the medieval feudal system, Vitoria studied the internal conditions of political communities. A central element of Vitoria's political theory was the conviction that there were, in principle, no differences between the political

[52] Vitoria, *De iustitia*, q. 57, art. 3, nu. 5, p. 40.

[53] Vitoria, *De iustitia*, q. 57, art. 3, nu. 5, p. 40: 'Secundo dico, quod bene potest *ex parte* abrogari *jus* gentium, licet non omnino – sicut *jus* gentium est, quod captivi in bello iusto sint servi, sed [Petrus de] Palude dicit, quod hoc non tenet inter Christianos. Si enim in bello Hispani capiant Gallos, Galli sunt captivi, sed non servi, quia possunt comparere in iudicio et alia huiusmodi, quae tamen non licerent, si essent servi. Item facta, Galli tenerent, et Christianus non posset illum omnino vendere. Ecce hic ex parte violatur *jus* gentium. Nam de iure gentium captivi in bello iusto sunt servi.'

[54] From 1530 to 1556 in personal union as Holy Roman Empire Emperor, Charles V, respectively Charles I.

[55] Vitoria, *De Indis*, section 2, title 1, pp. 410–31.

entities of the indigenous people of America and Europe. Although Vitoria took differences of cultural and technical development for granted, he did not explain them to be natural and unalterable.[56] In the sixteenth century this assumption was not as evident as it might appear today. The Humanists had reactivated Aristotle's doctrine of natural slavery which jurists of the Spanish Crown had used to legitimize the conquest and colonization of America by the Spanish.[57] According to Vitoria, differences between humans could be explained by 'bad and barbarian education'[58] as was also the case in some rural regions of Spain. The 'barbarians' of the New World were anthropologically similar to the European people as measured by established political communities (*civitas*), trade and craft, a specific order in their civil and public affairs based on property rights,[59] as well as the existence of a kind of religion.[60] As we have seen, Vitoria did not legitimize the intervention in traditional terms of empire or papacy, nor did he conceal the fact that the continent, which had hitherto merely been unknown by the Europeans, had not been 'discovered' uninhabited but brutally conquered. Nevertheless, Vitoria justified both the war against the 'barbarians' and the right of the Spanish to stay in America.

Vitoria's justification was closely related to his anthropology and his concept of peace as a specific order supported by legal ownership and dominion rights. If necessary, this order had to be restored by war. According to Vitoria, humans are characterized by rationality and freedom of choice (*liberum arbitrium*), and as political creatures living together in legal, economic, and religious structured organizations,[61] they depend on certain procedures to sustain stable conditions. Based on this anthropology and in conjunction with the concept of natural law, Vitoria postulated a 'natural society and community'[62] among the peoples which on a global scale would extend to travelling, trading, and preaching the Gospel.[63] Although, or rather precisely because this idea of an unobstructed global order implies not harming the natives, the *jus praedicandi evangelium*[64] constitutes the

[56] Vitoria, *De Indis*, section 1, pp. 384–7.

[57] At the well-known debate of Valladolid, Las Casas argued against Juan Ginés de Sepúlveda who asserted that the American natives were naturally predisposed to slavery and serfdom. See also Section III. Cycles of Reception.

[58] Vitoria, *De Indis*, p. 402. However cf. Vitoria, *De Indis*, section 3, title 1, proposition 5, p. 468: 'Sed est notandum, quod cum barbari isti sint natura meticulosi et alias stolidi et stulti, quantumcumque Hispani vellent eos demere a timore et reddere eos securos de pacifica conversatione Hispanorum, possunt adhuc merito timere videntes homines cultu extraneos et armatos et multo potentiores se.' In English: Vitoria, 'On the American Indians', q. 3, art. 1, proposition 5, in Anthony Pagden and Jeremy Lawrance (eds.), *Political Writings* (2007), p. 282: 'But I should remark that these barbarians are by nature cowardly, foolish, and ignorant besides. However much the Spaniards may wish to reassure them and convince them of their peaceful intentions, therefore, the barbarians may still be understandably fearful of men whose customs seem so strange, and who they can see are armed and much stronger than themselves.'

[59] Vitoria, *De Indis*, section 1, p. 386: 'in pacifica possessione rerum et publice et privatim'.

[60] Vitoria, *De Indis*, section 1, proposition 3, p. 402.

[61] Vitoria, *De Indis*, section 1, proposition 3, p. 402.

[62] Vitoria, *De Indis*, section 3, title 1, p. 460.

[63] Vitoria, *De Indis*, section 3, titles 1–2, pp. 460–6.

[64] Vitoria, *De Indis*, section 3, title 2, pp. 472–6.

foundations for justifying several cases of intervention causes.[65] According to Vitoria, the internal constitution of political communities authorizes an intervention to protect Christian converts[66] or 'innocent' people against tyranny or despotic laws.[67] If Christians were to build the majority in a community, he perceived it to be legitimate to remove an 'infidel' ruler and replace him with a Christian one, 'whether or not they asked him to do so'.[68] Vitoria avoided a clear assessment of whether '[(. . .) the barbarians][69] were simply children' and would therefore benefit from being placed under Spanish trusteeship.

Detached from the question concerning whether the Europeans were illegitimately or legitimately settled in America, as well as from the fact that they had unquestionably interfered with existing indigenous structures[70] to the detriment of the natives, Vitoria argued for the perpetuation of the status quo and endorsed intercontinental trade.[71] Trade was rather of mutual interest because resources and goods were not available to the same degree in any given place. It would also be obstructive to renounce trading in consideration of the serious financial damages that were to be expected. Furthermore, a conceivable political independence on the side of the 'barbarians' would not necessarily reduce Spanish profit, as the Spanish crown had discovered and still controlled the sea route. Accordingly, the Spanish could collect custom duties for exported goods. In addition to this, to protect Christian converts, it would be 'expedient (*expediret*)' and 'lawful (*liceret*)' to persist on the dependence of the American 'provinces'.[72] It is instructive to see that even in this early phase of colonialism Vitoria had conceptualized a global order based on property and domination rights, supplemented by the just war-doctrine. To ensure 'justice', trade, and proselytization the *jus gentium* creates the general framework for a stable legal order in which war could be seen as a legitimate instrument.

Pro responsione notandum, quod bellum geritur primo ad defendendum nos et nostra, secundo ad recuperandum res ablatas, tertio ad vindicandum iniuriam acceptam, quarto ad pacem et securitatem parandam.[73]

[65] By using the subjunctive in the section of the legitimate titles in *De Indis*, Vitoria still exacerbates the ambiguity of his argumentation. Cf. Stefan Kadelbach, 'Mission und Eroberung bei Vitoria. Über die Entstehung des Völkerrechts aus der Theologie', in Kirstin Bunge, Anselm Spindler, and Andreas Wagner (eds.) *Die Normativität des Rechts bei Francisco de* Vitoria (2011), pp. 300–3.

[66] Vitoria, *De Indis*, section 3, titles 3–4, p. 478.

[67] Vitoria, *De Indis*, section 3, title 5, p. 480.

[68] Vitoria, *On the American Indians*, q. 3, art. 4, p. 287. In Latin: Vitoria, *De Indis*, section 3, title 4, p. 478. Vitoria mentioned other reasons to justify a war, such as the voluntary decision to make the King of Spain the new ruler or a pact of mutual assistance between nations. Vitoria, *De Indis*, section 3, title 7, pp. 482–4.

[69] Vitoria, *On the American Indians*, q. 3, art. 8, p. 290.

[70] Cf. to the extent of the well-documented atrocities that were committed in America: 'The encounter will never again achieve such an intensity, if indeed that is the word to use: the sixteenth century perpetrated the greatest genocide in human history.' Tzvetan Todorov, *The Conquest of America. The Question of the Other* (1984), p. 5.

[71] Vitoria, *De Indis*, section 3, title 7, pp. 486–8.

[72] Vitoria, *De Indis*, section 3, title 7, p. 488.

[73] Vitoria, *De iure belli*, q. 4, part 2, dubium 5, p. 590: 'In answer to this, it is to be noticed that a war is waged firstly to defend ourselves, and our property, secondly to regain stolen goods, thirdly to vindicate received injustice, fourthly to establish peace and security.'

5. Justice and peace

As we have seen, on the one hand peace represents a conception in which *jus naturale* and *jus gentium* coalesce. On the other hand, according to the theologian Vitoria, peace is a constitutive part of justice and the just order given by God. To preserve this natural order, it is necessary to combine the natural purpose of political authority[74] with the contract–theoretical rule that those who are affected by domination should by majority be able to agree to it (*ex consensu mutuo et communi*).[75] As a reminder: while, according to Vitoria, *jus naturale* is valid by itself, *jus gentium* becomes legally binding by virtue of agreement and insofar that it politically preserves peace and concord.[76] The two are closely connected, but they are not identical. *Jus gentium* is based on *jus naturale*. But the former is also necessary to preserve the latter, as the quotation demonstrates:

> Respondeo, quod *jus* gentium non necessario sequitur ex iure naturali nec est necessarium simpliciter ad conservationem iuris naturalis; quia si necessario sequeretur ex iure naturali, iam esset *jus* naturale. (. . .) Nihilominus tamen *jus* gentium est necessarium ad conservationem iuris naturalis. Et non est omnino necessarium, sed panae necessarium, quia male posset conservari *jus* naturale sine iure gentium. Cum magna namque difficultate *jus* naturale servaretur, si non esset *jus* gentium.[77]

This capacity of *jus gentium* to conserve natural law implies assumptions about ownership and property rights. The order of natural law possesses 'by itself a certain equality and justice'[78] and operates with the conception of an original community of goods. In contrast, the arrangements of *jus gentium*, for example 'that possessions should be divided, is no question of equality and justice but is ordered to uphold peace and concord among the people'.[79] Unlike natural law, which is aimed at the fundamental relations among humans or between a person and God, the norms and rules of *jus gentium* reflect a human effort to sustain order or organization without 'equity by itself'.[80] Due to nature it is just 'to worship God, to honour the parents and to esteem the home country'.[81] Referring to 'manumissions, property of possessions, [and] conservation of kingdom,'[82] this could only be applied to *jus*

[74] That is to protect the lives of humans.

[75] Cf. the rule 'Quod omnes tangit, debet ab omnibus approbari. / What concerns everybody, has to be approved by everyone', in *Decretalium Collectiones: Liber Sextus*: 5, 13, 29 (CICan.2/1122).

[76] Cf. Vitoria, *De potestate civili*, p. 156: 'vis legis ex pacto et condicto inter homines'; and Vitoria, *De iustitia*, q. 57, art. 3, nu. 1, p. 32: 'pax et concordia hominum'.

[77] Vitoria, *De iustitia*, q. 57, art. 3, nu. 4, p. 38: 'I reply: International law does not necessarily follow from natural law and is also not necessary per se to sustain natural law; because if it necessarily followed from the natural law, it would already be natural law. (. . .) Nonetheless, international law is necessary to preserve the natural law. And it is not entirely necessary, but almost necessary because natural law could be difficultly maintained without the international law. Natural law would indeed sustain merely with great difficulty, if there were no international law.'

[78] Vitoria, *De iustitia*, q. 57, art. 3, nu. 1, p. 32: 'aequalitas quaedam et iustitia'.

[79] Vitoria, *De iustitia*, q. 57, art. 3, nu. 1, p. 32: 'quod possessiones sint divisae, non dicit aequalitatem nec iustitiam, sed ordinatur ad pacem et concordiam hominum'.

[80] Vitoria, *De iustitia*, q. 57, art. 3, nu. 2, p. 36: 'de se non habent aequitatem'.

[81] Vitoria, *De iustitia*, q. 57, art. 3, nu. 2, p. 33: 'colere Deum, honorare parentes et patriam diligere'.

[82] Vitoria, *De iustitia*, q. 57, art. 3, nu. 2, p. 36: 'manumissiones, proprietas possessionum, conservatio regni'.

gentium mediated 'by another just cause',[83] i.e. the preservation of peace and concord. According to Vitoria *jus gentium* is raised on a God-given and just order of *jus naturale* to preserve peace by law and property rights. This is based on the idea that peace could only be guaranteed by acknowledging individual property,[84] otherwise there would be 'dispute and war'.[85]

III. Cycles of Reception

The ambivalence in the way Vitoria tried to integrate Spanish transatlantic politics into the traditional theories of natural law and of just war is also reflected in the cycles of reception. After Vitoria's death in 1546, his lectures were preserved in the notes of his numerous pupils who later came to influence legislation and politics in Spain and America as advisors, confessors, or clergymen.[86] It is probably due to said ambiguity that Vitoria's work was not received in its entirety. However, the contradictory character of his work enabled later scholars to take up some of Vitoria's ideas and concepts and put them to their own use. Two famous participants of the Valladolid debate and peers of Vitoria's, Bartolomé de las Casas (1484/5–1566) and Juan Ginés de Sepúlveda (1490–1573), should illustrate this. Using the example of the conquered territories in America, the *Junta de Valladolid* (1550–1551) discussed the rights and treatment of colonized people by the settlers. For the first time in European history a moral, largely theoretical debate about colonialism and the foundations of international relations took place. Las Casas, former Spanish settler, military chaplain, and later bishop of Chiapas, relied on Vitoria in his criticism of colonization. Famous for his chronicle about the American conquest, Las Casas harshly criticized the *encomienda* system, tried to reform the policy of colonization and to introduce a peaceful way of evangelization in Guatemala. Interestingly, his opponent, the Spanish humanist Sepúlveda, although relying primarily on Aristotle's theory of natural slavery, also refers to Vitoria's writings. For Sepúlveda, the Amerindians were naturally predisposed to slavery. Waging war against them was justified by their 'barbarian' practices of idolatry and cannibalism, both of which were taken as infringing on natural law. Although the issue remained unresolved and the Spanish treatment of the Amerindians did not change substantially, the Valladolid debate was a remarkable event.

[83] Vitoria, *De iustitia*, q. 57, art. 3, nu. 1, 2. proposition, p. 32: 'ad aliud iustum'.

[84] Vitoria, *De iustitia*, q. 57, art. 3, nu. 1, p. 32: 'non potest conservari, nisi unusquisque habeat bona determinata'.

[85] Vitoria, *De iustitia*, q. 57, art. 3, nu. 4, p. 38: 'Posset quidem orbis subsistere, si possessiones essent in communi, ut est in religionibus. Tamen esset cum magna difficultate, ne homines in discordias und bella prorumperent.'

[86] For an overview of Vitoria's followers, please refer to Jörg Fisch, *Die europäische Expansion und das Völkerrecht. Die Auseinandersetzungen um den Status der überseeischen Gebiete vom 15. Jahrhundert bis zur Gegenwart* (1984), pp. 223–65.

The Dutch jurist Hugo Grotius (1583–1645) and the Italian lawyer Alberico Gentili (1552–1608) share with Vitoria, albeit within a more secular framework, not only the title of founding fathers of international law but also a conception of international order based on natural law.[87] As of the beginning of the nineteenth century, the interest in Vitoria's lectures revived particularly with the work of the Belgian legal historian Ernest Nys (1851–1920) and with that of the American jurist James Brown Scott (1866–1943) who contributed to establishing the Permanent Court of International Justice in Den Haag.[88] Both suggested that Hugo Grotius should not be considered the founder of international law but rather Vitoria and more especially the Jesuit Francisco Suárez.[89] According to Cardinal Joseph Höffner, Vitoria was considered the 'creator of the modern international law'[90] because he had reformulated the *Institutiones*-definition of *jus gentium* from '*inter omnes homines*' to '*inter omnes gentes*'.[91] But Höffner denied that there was '[e]ine klare Herausschälung des eigentlichen 'Völkerrechts' aus dem Rechtsbereich des überlieferten *Jus gentium*'[92] by Vitoria. Martti Koskenniemi points out that James Brown Scott was

> engaged during the interwar years in an effort to give shape to a new architecture of international institutions and systems of dispute-settlement and would enable the emergence of an interdependence-driven global structure of private rights and economic exchanges; a world united in search for peace through prosperity.[93]

[87] See for one Alfred Dufour, 'Les "Magni Hispani"dans l'œvre de Grotius', in Frank Grunert and Kurt Seelmann (eds.), *Die Ordnung der Praxis. Neue Studien zur Spanischen Spätscholastik* (2001), pp. 351–80.

[88] Camilo Barcia Trelles, 'Francisco de Vitoria et l'école modern du droit international', in *Recueil des Cours de l'Académie de la Haye de droit international* 17 (1927-II); Vicente Beltrán de Heredia, *Los manuscritos del Maestro Fray Francisco de Vitoria* (1928).

[89] Ernest Nys, 'Introduction', in Ernest Nys (ed.), *Francisci de Victoria, De Indis et de iure belli relectiones* (1917), pp. 9–53; in English translation pp. 55–100.

[90] 'Schöpfer der modernen Völkerrechtswissenschaft', in Joseph Höffner, *Kolonialismus und Evangelium. Spanische Kolonialethik im Goldenen Zeitalter* (1969), p. 314. According to Höffner, this was mentioned for the first time by Ernest Nys, *Les origines du droit international* (1894), p. 11; followed, for example, by James Brown Scott, *The Spanish Origin of International Law: Francisco de Vitoria and his Law of Nations* (1934), p. 139. Carl Schmitt highlights a 'ganz außerordentliche (...) Unvoreingenommenheit, Objektivität und Neutralität' ('quite extraordinary impartiality, objectivity, and neutrality') in Vitoria's *De Indis*. Based on this impression, he comes to the conclusion that '[d]ie Argumentation erscheint dadurch nicht mehr mittelalterlich, sondern "modern"' ('the argument appears to be therefore no longer medieval but "modern"'). Carl Schmitt, 'Die Rechtfertigung der Landnahme einer neuen Welt (Francisco de Vitoria)', in idem, *Der Nomos der Erde im Völkerrecht des Jus Publicum Europaeum* (1997), pp. 87–9, here p. 71.

[91] Vitoria, *De Indis*, section 3, title 1, nu. 1, p. 460: 'Quod naturalis ratio inter omnes gentes constituit, vocatur *jus* gentium.' For comparison *Institutiones*, 1. book, 2. title, nu. 1, in *Corpus Iuris Civilis*, p. 3: '[Q]uod vero naturalis ratio inter omnes homines constituit, id apud omnes populos peraeque custoditur vocaturque *jus* gentium, quasi quo iure omnes gentes utuntur.'

[92] 'no clear crystallisation of the literal "international law" from the legal domain of the traditional *jus gentium.*' Höffner, *Kolonialismus und Evangelium* (n. 90), p. 313.

[93] Martti Koskenniemi, 'Colonization of the "Indies". The Origin of International Law?', in Yolanda Gamarra Chopo (ed.), *La idea de América en el pensamiento jus internacionalista del siglo xxi* (2010), p. 44.

Today, this Iberian tradition of thought is considered less significant for the formation of international law and is discussed controversially, as the following quote should demonstrate:

> The claim of the great Spanish writers of the sixteenth and seventeenth centuries – Vitoria and Suarez in particular – to be the 'founders' of international law, a claim advanced with particular vigor by James Brown Scott in the 1930s, becomes difficult if not impossible to sustain. The Dominican Vitoria wrote expressly as a theologian concerned with matters of conscience. The Jesuit Suarez was engaged quite openly in the struggle of the Catholic church to defeat the Reformation. These men were sophisticated latter-day protagonists of the 'old' moral and religious viewpoint rather than pioneers of the 'new' secular and legal one.[94]

After the Second World War, there seemed to be the need for a new global and integrative international order which would 'complete' the Westphalian system of sovereign states. This tendency has been reinforced during the twenty-first century under the conditions of globalization, even more so in the face of the precarious status of the protection and enforcement of human rights and of provisions to prevent mass atrocities.[95]

In contrast, postnational and decolonial approaches criticize this more or less affirmative appraisal of the history of international law. In line with their alternative view of international law, authors like the Australian jurist Antony T. Anghie, Koskenniemi,[96] the Argentine-Mexican philosopher Enrique Dussel and the Argentinean professor of literature Walter D. Mignolo investigate how Vitoria and his followers had contributed not only to the 'making of international law'[97] but to imperialism and sovereignty as well.

[94] Murray Forsyth, 'The Tradition of International Law', in Terry Nardin and David R. Mapel (eds.), *Traditions of International Ethics*, (1992), p. 26. Cf. to the 'very misleading picture of the pre-Grotian ideas about the laws of war and peace' by James Brown Scott: Richard Tuck, *The Rights of War and Peace: Political Thought and the International Order from Grotius to Kant* (2009), p. 11.

[95] Cf. John Finnis, 'Boundaries', in *Human Rights and Common Good: Collected Essays* (2011), p. 132. 'It is not, perhaps, so clear that the modern *jus gentium* entirely excludes another title that Vitoria advances for the just suppression or overriding of boundaries: defence of the innocent against tyranny or other unjust attacks on human life. We hear talk of justified resort to force to prevent a humanitarian disaster – or at least, if we cannot prevent it, or perhaps unintentionally provoked it, to put an end to such radical injustice – and establish a more or less international protectorate for ensuring, so far as fairly possible, that injustice of that kind does not quickly resume.'

[96] Martti Koskenniemi, 'Colonization of the "Indies". The Origin of International Law?', (n. 93) pp. 62f. 'Spanish imperialism was constituted of the exercise of public power by the Spanish State in the form of conquest and settlement, administration and the conduct of mercantilistic policies that ultimately failed to uphold the position of Spain as the leading European power. It was followed up by Netherlands and England whose political leaders well understood the importance of the Salamancan doctrines: their imperialism was imperialism of the free trade, carried out by private companies through private transactions, if necessary protected by the public power of the State. National resources would not be wasted when private operators could be liberated to carry out the work of disciplining the natives through commerce and the extraction of resources.'

[97] Borrowed from the title of Antony Anghie's book *Imperialism, Sovereignty and the Making of International Law* (2005). Enrique Dussel, 'Eurocentrism and Modernity', *Boundary 2* (1993), 20/3 65–76: 'Modernity includes a rational 'concept' of emancipation that we affirm and subsume. But, at the same time, it develops an irrational myth, a justification for genocidal violence. The postmodernists criticize modern reason as a reason of terror; we criticize modern reason because of the irrational myth that it conceals', at 66. Walter D. Mignolo, *The Darker Side of the Renaissance. Literacy, Territoriality, and Colonization* (1995), pp. 125–69.

IV. *Dominium* and Law as Integral Parts of the Global Order

The following offers a short summary of Vitoria's conception of order and *jus gentium*: Vitoria stands in the tradition of Catholic natural law that was highly systematized by Aquinas and which arranged all parts of the world and all kinds of beings and actions in a proper order given by God. Based on Christian anthropology, Vitoria tried to integrate the foreign cultures and communities that the Spanish had encountered in America into the framework of salvation, but also in legal terms concerning international relations as well as those of trade and ownership. The close interdependency between assumptions about human nature and the world not only 'as it should be,' but also 'as it is,' is demonstrated by Vitoria's use of the term *dominium* and its conjunction with *jus gentium*. This also explains why this chapter employs the term 'order' while largely avoiding the term 'system' in terms of a conceptualizing, merely man-made practice. According to this theological worldview, 'order' does not always factually exist, but it is a presupposed idea containing the remedies to retrieve the good, stable condition originally given by God.

Because *jus gentium* depends on the law of nature, but also on the law of contract as well as on customary law, there are arbitrary, time-variant versions of order to consider (like the manner in which things were distributed in the *divisio rerum*) in order to preserve peace, for instance in trading or political domination. As law enforced among the peoples, *jus gentium* contributes to establishing and conserving political dominion and private property. According to Vitoria, *dominium* represents the necessarily given external conditions with which to enable a person and a political community to preserve them or itself and to act by choice. So in the definition of *jus gentium*, which is only valid 'as a result of human agreement (*ex condicto hominum*)',[98] theories of ownership, jurisdiction, and political domination are interconnected. According to Vitoria's anthropology, this is reflected in the term *dominium* in which three meanings were implicated, namely to have *jus*, to possess *dominium* of things, and to be *dominus* or *princeps* of things and people (including the own person). The interconnection conveyed in the idea of *dominium* seems to suggest coherence between a concept of self-determination of a person based on legal allocation of private property claims on the one hand, and the *dominium* rights of a political community on the other.

By postulating a conception of an original common ownership of the earth, the existence of particular political and private *dominium* remains foremost to be justified. After the *divisio rerum*, in which goods were distributed and the earth as such was partitioned by contract (*pactum*) or agreement (*consensus*), private ownership rights and political domination are meant to preserve the peace by regulating problems of distribution between people. However, this ownership-based conception of peace does not dissolve the unity of *totus orbis*. There still exist binding arrangements that go beyond states and peoples in that they represent a virtual consent

[98] Vitoria, *De iustitia*, q. 57, art. 3, nu. 2, p. 34.

among the people. Although these global rules and principles are more moral by nature, the doctrine of just war could confer legal force to them politically.

V. Conclusion

Departing from a conception of a natural global entity of humans, individuals as well as states can be conceived as parts of one order structured by moral, religious, political, and economic laws. This idea of order implies a peace-preserving function of *jus gentium* and its institutions that promote trade and proselytization, that is, a perpetuation of the status quo, with a view to preserve intercontinental trade.[99] In accordance with the rather ineffective condition that the natives should not be harmed, political power and *jus gentium* are meant to promote this freedom of economy and proselytization. Embedded in a concept of order pre-structured by *jus naturale, dominium* and law constitute two integral parts of the global order to maintain 'justice' and 'peace.' On the threshold of modernity, the *jus gentium* thereby created the general framework for a legal order between people and nations. Under the changing conditions of economy, theories of political domination, and relation between religious and secular spheres, the foundations of politics and law were re-assessed. At this juncture, one of the most important findings of Vitoria's political and legal philosophy was that the sphere of political practice became more autonomous although still thought of as part of a God-given order. As the political power of the pope and the emperor was fading, new stakeholders gradually appeared. The traditional conception of *totus orbis* clarifies—one hundred years before the Peace of Westphalia—the scope in which different types of stakeholders such as individuals and social or political communities can act freely and (at least theoretically) interact on equal terms, such as the political entities of the people of America and Europe.

Selected Bibliography

de Vitoria, Francisco, in Anthony Pagden and Jeremy Lawrance (eds.), *Political Writings*, (Cambridge: Cambridge University Press, 2007).

Nardin, Terry (ed.), *The Ethics of War and Peace: Religious and Secular Perspectives* (Princeton: Princeton University Press, 1996).

Nardin, Terry and David R. Mapel (eds.), *Traditions of International Ethics* (Cambridge: Cambridge University Press, 1992).

Koskenniemi, Martti, 'Colonization of the "Indies": The Origin of International Law?', in Yolanda Gamarra Chopo (ed.), *La idea de América en el pensamiento jus internacionalista*

[99] Koskenniemi, 'Colonization of the "Indies". The Origin of International Law?', (n. 93) p. 57, speaks about 'the right of the Spaniards to travel and trade in the Indies (*ius pergrinandi & jus negotiandi*) (. . ., and) portrays trade and commerce as part of the "natural partnership and communication" between humans.'

del siglo xxi (Institución 'Fernando el Católico' y Universidad de Zaragoza, 2010), pp. 43–63.

Todorov, Tzvetan, *The Conquest of America: The Question of the Other* (New York: Harper & Row, 1984).

Tuck, Richard, *The Rights of War and Peace: Political Thought and the International Order from Grotius to Kant* (Oxford: Oxford University Press, 2009).

3

Francisco Suárez S.J. on the End of Peaceful Order among States and Systematic Doctrinal Scholarship

Tobias Schaffner

I. Introduction

The introductions to most textbooks of international law convey the impression that twenty-first century lawyers can learn little of relevance from the works of Francisco Suárez (1548–1617) and other scholars, such as Francisco de Vitoria (1483–1546), Alberico Gentili (1552–1608), and Hugo Grotius (1583–1645). Such introductions mention these works, because they led to the development of a separate discipline of international law.[1] Yet this is all one needs to know about them, or so such introductions tend to make us believe.

The present chapter seeks to challenge this view. It argues that the work of Suárez, like that of other theologians and natural lawyers, offers an insightful (albeit imperfect) articulation of the values of peace and justice which continue to underpin the international legal order. Suárez reminds us that the practical reasoning of all upright statesmen, citizens, and lawyers is guided by the idea of a peaceful and just order among states. Peace and justice are potentialities which individuals and whole nations can establish and preserve, as well as fail to establish or preserve, through their co-ordinated actions. His work remains insightful precisely because most of today's accounts of international law neglect the role of peace and justice as a starting point of legal reasoning, a goal of state action, and even a source of international law.

In drawing this insight from Suárez' work, one needs to be careful, however, to avoid a common mistake. For Suárez would have been adamant that all moral values exist as potentialities even if neither he nor any of his predecessors or successors had affirmed these ideas. Given this independence of moral values (such as peace

[1] The following remarks on historical introductions apply most closely to James Crawford, *Brownlie's Principles of Public International Law* (8th edn, 2012), pp. 3–11; see also Malcolm N. Shaw, *International Law* (6th edn, 2008), pp. 14–27; Antonio Cassese, *International Law* (2nd edn, 2005), pp. 23–4.

and justice) from Suárez' work, this chapter faces a difficulty which any contribution on a theologian or natural lawyer meets: it must give *an account of Suárez' work* and at the same time convey an idea of the *lasting values* which, arguably, exist *independently of his work*. I will argue that today's textbooks ultimately suffer not from insufficient attention to the works of scholars like Suárez, but to values such as peace and justice.[2]

As indicated, international law textbooks credit the works of Suárez and his contemporaries as key for the development of a separate or new discipline of the law of nations. The textbooks tend to explain this development as a consequence of the rise of the modern state in the sixteenth century—the rise of states made lawyers *shift* from applying private law rules to rulers and peoples to applying another type of law to states: the law of nations. This (allegedly) new law was mainly gained through analogies from (Roman) private law (*jus commune*).[3] Textbook authors seem to assume that the answer to the follow-up question—why analogies from private law should be relevant for international law—is somehow obvious.[4] It will certainly seem obvious to today's law students, since international law is taught and examined as a subject distinct from private law.

Few international lawyers today seem to wonder whether the substantive overlap between private law rules and international law rules—e.g. between tort law and state responsibility—points to *ends and values shared by these branches of law*. We will see that, for Suárez, treating other citizens in conformity with the rules of private law (and criminal law)—respecting their life, bodily integrity, and property—is characteristic of the civic friendship which citizens grant each other and which constitute them as members of their political community (see Section III.2.b below). Suárez saw that citizens can only preserve the *peaceful order* of their community if (i) they treat the other members justly—i.e. if they possess constant and perpetual willingness to render each one his or her due—and, in case someone fails to show such respect, if (ii) the wrongdoer corrects the injustice by compensating his victim either willingly or as a consequence of being coerced. Suárez considered that this same civic friendship or mutual respect is due to every human being, because we are all part of the one community of mankind. Nations need to treat each other with respect in order to secure a peaceful and minimally just 'inter-national' order (see Section III.2.d below). The political community and

[2] To be fair, Crawford's *Brownlie's Principles* (n. 1) (i) refers to the idea of justice and appeals to social needs (p. 7), but the idea of justice is not explained, nor are the relevant social needs enumerated. Moreover, although the book mentions the common good (p. 11), the term appears only in a quote from John Finnis' *Natural Law and Natural Rights* (2011) and its connection to peace and justice remains unexplored.

[3] The influence of canon law principles (Church law) on the law of nations is still little explored.

[4] There are illuminating accounts of the role of private law analogies in international law. The best known is probably that of Hersch Lauterpacht. In her careful analysis of Lauterpacht's mature position, Amanda Perreau-Saussine shows that for him 'private law analogies act as one of the crucial sources or mediators between ideas of natural law or justice and international law', see her 'Lauterpacht and Vattel on the Sources of International Law: The Place of Private Law Analogies and General Principles', in Vincent Chetail and Peter Haggenmacher (eds.), *Vattel's International Law from a XXIst Century Perspective* (2011), pp. 167–85.

the 'inter-national' community thus share the same ends; it is this sharing of ends which underpins the private law analogies.

Today's international lawyers *seem* barred from such substantive engagement with Suárez' thought, because they follow the established doctrine of sources, a doctrine which *seems* to exclude consideration of Suárez' work (for an explanation why this conclusion is wrong see Section II.2 and Section V below). According to this doctrine, international law is primarily state-made law: it is law based on the will of states (on their consent) as reflected in treaties, customary law, and generally recognized principles of law (Articles 38.1 of the Statue of the International Court of Justice). To the limited extent that international lawyers and courts rely on doctrinal writings, i.e. the works of private scholars claiming no public authority for their views, they resort to 'the teachings of the most highly qualified publicists' and these teachings are only 'subsidiary means for the determination of rules of law' (Articles 38.1 lit. d ICJ Statute). Surprisingly, the International Court of Justice sometimes cites the work of Suárez (and more often, albeit still rarely, that of Grotius).[5] Still, the use made by the Court of the work of these 'founding fathers' is negligible: they do not qualify as 'most highly qualified publicists' of contemporary international law. Disputes are decided on the basis of international treaties, customary law, and case law—not by reading Suárez' work.

The topic of the present book, the ideas of order and system in international legal thought, invites us to reflect on a point which is perplexing if one subscribes to the current approach: why should international law amount to a system and guide states to co-exist in an orderly fashion, if this law is exclusively based on the will of states? We should expect constant violence and dissolution of order if states or their governments were driven by an *unqualified, arbitrary* will. Yet, for considerable stretches of history, governments have refrained from war and actively sought to preserve a peaceful order. Equally, (most) international lawyers are guided by an ideal of a peaceful and (minimally) just order.

Neither the way lawyers are trying to contribute to a peaceful order nor the approximate actualization of this ideal in the (peaceful) practice of governments can be ascribed to *arbitrary* will: something more needs to be present in the will. Yet the current approach to international law staunchly refuses to explain what this ideal is. Suárez' work is insightful because it holds out the possibility to overcome the neglect of this ideal. As we will see, especially the idea of peaceful order, including a *peaceful order among nations*, holds a commanding place in his work. Suárez, one should hasten to add, was highly aware that the realization of this ideal in practice is eminently fragile. He knew that, at any given moment, governments (e.g. a ruling party or a dictator and his lawyers) can be overcome by a will or desire for power, or wealth, or glory leading them to invade another nation. If human beings share a desire for peace and friendly co-existence, they only do so

[5] See e.g. the Separate Opinion of Judge Cançado Trindade in the case of *Ahmadou Sadio Diallo (Republic of Guinea* v. *Democratic Republic of the Congo), I.C.J. Reports* (2010) 729–811.

at times and *in an unstable way*. Most of us, that is, lack the *constant* and *perpetual* willingness to render each one his or her due.

II. Biographical, Intellectual, and Historical Background

1. Life and work

Francisco Suárez was born in Granada in 1548 and died in Lisbon in 1617.[6] He studied civil and canon law from 1561 to 1564 and, after joining the Jesuit Order, philosophy and theology (1565–1570). The Jesuit Order was founded in the sixteenth century as a reaction to the Reformation and was deeply involved in reforming the Catholic Church (the Counter-Reformation) and in defending its teachings. Suárez worked as a professor of theology and philosophy at various universities, including those at Rome, Salamanca, and Coimbra. He already enjoyed immense scholarly authority during his lifetime, as can be seen from the important tasks assigned to him, including a defence of the Catholic faith against Anglicanism.

Suárez left a vast body of work in theology, philosophy, and law. In the most easily available (yet incomplete) nineteenth-century edition it spans twenty-six volumes.[7] In philosophy, Suárez is best known for his *Metaphysical Disputations* (1597). He wrote even more extensively on almost every aspect of Christian theology, including God, the theological virtues of faith, hope, and love, grace (i.e. divine aid), and the life of Jesus.

In legal philosophy, Suárez is best known for his *On Laws and God the Lawgiver* (*De Legibus ac Deo Legislatore*) of 1612.[8] Far from being a treatment of the substance of the law of nations (*jus gentium*), the treatise is an exercise in something akin to general legal theory. It defines and clarifies the different types of law which moral theologians applied as confessors. Confessors had to be knowledgeable about law, because a good Christian is called to comply with all (just) laws. The treatise's ten books thus contain a careful discussion of the generic idea of law (*lex*), eternal law (moral truth as it is known by God), natural law (human beings' imperfect knowledge of moral truth), state law (*jus civile*), Church law (so-called canon law), customary law (i.e. unwritten law based on the custom of a people or several nations), Old Law (the positive divine law of the Old Testament, including the Ten Commandments), and the New Law promulgated by Christ.[9] Today's international

[6] For a recent biography see Sydney Penner, 'Francisco Suárez (1548–1617)', September 2015, <http://www.sydneypenner.ca/suarez.shtml>; see also P. Monnot et al., 'Suárez', *Dictionnaire de Théologie Catholique*, cols. 2638–728.

[7] Francisco Suárez, *Opera Omnia*, 26 vols, ed. Charles Berton (1856–61).

[8] A translation of extracts of *De Legibus* (as well as of *Defensio Fidei, De Fide,* and *De Bello*) can be found in Francisco Suárez, *Selection from Three Works of Francisco Suárez S.J.*, vol. 2, trans. Gwladys Williams, John Waldron, and Henry Davis (1944).

[9] For a complete list of Suárez' writings relevant for law see P. Monnot et al., 'Suárez' (n. 6); or John P. Doyle, 'Suárez on Human Rights', in V. M. Salas (ed.), *Collected Essays on Francisco Suárez, S.J. (1548–1617)* (2010, first published 2001).

lawyers who turn to the treatise are likely to be disappointed to find little of relevance to their discipline in this vast work. The following examination of Suárez' contribution to the idea of order in international legal thought therefore draws on his entire work, not just on his *De Legibus*.

2. Intellectual background: Aristotelian–Thomism

A description of Suárez' intellectual background allows us to clarify how his philosophical outlook differs from the outlook of most twenty-first century international lawyers. As mentioned, Suárez was a Jesuit university professor. The Jesuit Order's Regulation of Studies (*Ratio Studiorum*) prescribed its teachers to use the *Summa Theologiae* of the Dominican theologian Thomas Aquinas (1225–1274) as the main work to be taught and commented upon.[10] It is therefore impossible to understand Suárez' work without considering Aquinas' *Summa Theologiae*.[11]

In this vast work, Aquinas attempted to offer a complete introduction to Christian theology for students of the subject. It deals with God, his creation, and the way back to God through a moral life, as paradigmatically lived by Jesus. Apart from relying on his own intellect, Aquinas wrote the *Summa* by drawing on the Bible, the tradition of the Church fathers and later theologians, as well as on a number of pagan philosophers. Aristotle stands out among the latter. Aquinas sought to incorporate as much of Aristotle's philosophy into theology as is compatible with the Christian worldview. Accordingly, it has become customary to refer to his strand of theology as Aristotelian–Thomism.

Suárez was a follower of Aristotelian–Thomism, even if—or, more accurately, precisely because—he retained a critical stance vis-à-vis Aquinas and Aristotle. In his writings, Suárez heavily relied on Aquinas' work and the sources used by him, as well as on the works of theologians closer to Suárez' own time, including those who established Aristotelian–Thomism in Spain, such as Francisco de Victoria (1483–1546) as well as the so-called Nominalists such as Duns Scotus (1266–1308) and William of Ockham (1287–1347).

Such extensive use of Christian and pagan authorities from a distant past will make most international lawyers feel even more uneasy about the suggestion to draw substantive lessons from Suárez' work. The modern doctrine of sources seems to differ radically from Suárez' approach to legal sources. The contrast points to important differences between his philosophical outlook and the outlook from which the current doctrine of sources arose.

Suárez considered himself to be engaged in a *direct dialogue* with his predecessors, including Aquinas, who lived more than 300 years earlier, and, even more

[10] Thomas Aquinas, *Summa Theologiae*, 5 vols., trans. The Fathers of the Dominican Province (1948).

[11] For a discussion of the relationship between Suárez' work and the *Summa Theologiae*, see Monnot et al., 'Suárez' (n. 6); and my 'Is Francisco Suárez a Natural Law Ethicist?', in Kirstin Bunge et al. (eds.), *The Concept of Law (lex) in Moral, Legal, and Political Thought of the 'School of Salamanca'* (2016), pp. 150–71.

surprisingly, with Aristotle, who lived 2,000 years earlier and who, after all, was not even a Christian.[12] This direct dialogue was made possible, because Suárez conceived of philosophy and theology as a *collective* search for the *one moral truth* about the human condition and our common destiny in the vision of (the one) God. It is a search for a truth about moral values (such as peace and justice) and laws indicating ways to realize those values. For Suárez, *none* of these values depend for their existence on the authority of Aristotle or Aquinas, they simply exist as potentialities to be actualized or realized through human action.[13] Thus, peace is, for instance, a potentiality, which nations can realize through their co-ordinated actions (e.g. by abstaining from invasion). Although human beings can actualize moral values, they are perfectly actualized only in God.[14]

Suárez distinguished between three categories of values or goods: (i) distinctly moral values such as peace, justice, friendship, and love, as well as (ii) morally neutral goods such as health and survival, and (iii) apparent goods, which, if pursued for their own sake, are immoral ends such as pleasure, wealth, power, and glory.[15] For Suárez, moral values such as peace and justice held good for Aristotle and his contemporaries as much as for Aquinas and himself.

Suárez saw himself engaged in a direct dialogue with Aristotle, Aquinas, and many others about lasting moral values. For him, philosophy did not consist in a dialogue about the works of past philosophers. Nor did he rely on the authority of these works in order to prove the existence of moral values, he relied on them because they contain judgments of reason *articulating* these values and *guiding* readers (sometimes misguiding them) how to realize a particular value, for instance how to be a good friend. It is necessary to insist on these points, since the present contribution faces the difficult task to mitigate between writing *about Suárez' work* and conveying an idea of his belief in values, such as peace, which (he argues) exist as potentialities *independently of* his own work.

As noted, for Suárez values such as peace and justice held good for human beings in ancient times as much as in his own. Yet, he was not naïve: he was perfectly aware that human beings—even wise philosophers like Aristotle or Aquinas—have only imperfect knowledge of moral truth and hence sometimes err about values or about the way to realize them. Only God had perfect knowledge of moral truth (eternal law). Moreover, Suárez was also keenly aware that knowing what a given value

[12] The idea of a direct dialogue is indebted to Wilhelm Hennis, *Politik und Praktische Philosophie: Eine Studie zur Rekonstruktion der Politischen Wissenschaft* (1963), pp. 18, 26. Christians could rely on pagan reason, because for them 'faith perfects reason, it does not corrupt it', see the references in my 'The Eudaemonist Ethics of Hugo Grotius (1583–1645): Pre-Modern Moral Philosophy for the Twenty-First Century?', *Jurisprudence* 7(3) (2016), 478–522.

[13] For Suárez' moral objectivism see his *Disputationes Metaphysicae*, vol. 25, Opera Omnia, Disp. X. s. II, §§12–13 (n. 7); and *De Bonitate et Malitia Humanorum Actuum*, vol. 4, Opera Omnia, Disp. II, s. II, §12 (n. 7); for his view that moral goodness is a potential to be actualized by human beings see Suárez, *Disputationes Metaphysicae*, vol. 26, Opera Omnia, Disp. XXIII, s. VIII, §§6–8 (n. 7). For a discussion see my 'Is Francisco Suárez a Natural Law Ethicist?' (n. 11).

[14] For references see my 'Is Francisco Suárez a Natural Law Ethicist?' (n. 11).

[15] Suárez, *De Fine Hominis*, trans. Sydney Penner, September 2015, <http://www.sydneypenner.ca/translations.shtml#dfh>, Disp. V, s. I.

requires in a particular situation is never sufficient for right action: right action requires that one also *wills* the action that one's reason recognizes as right.[16]

Still, many of today's readers will consider Suárez' position implausible: changes in moral opinion and in cultural practices *seem* to indicate that all moral values are relative. Surely, then, there are no lasting moral values? This seems to open two avenues for criticism. One way is that of radical criticism: the rejection of Suárez' belief in lasting moral values and at least some lasting moral standards (or laws). The second way consists in criticizing, one by one, particular judgments of his about certain values or ways to attain them, e.g. to establish that he is wrong that wives are subordinated to their husband in marriage.

What many critics seem to overlook is that they cannot have it both ways. If they are persuaded that particular moral judgments of Suárez (and the tradition upon which he relies) are mistaken, then they *cannot* at the same time reject the existence of lasting moral values and standards. For holding that Suárez was mistaken about (say) the status of women in marriage is tenable if and only if the moral standard which allows the critics to make this judgment is a moral standard which *holds good for Suárez as much as for us today*! Even those who consider themselves to be moral relativists discover, upon reflecting on such instances, that they actually believe in lasting moral values and at least some lasting moral standards (the prohibition of murder is an obvious candidate). Of course, these values and standards were neglected in earlier times and are being neglected in some or all parts of the world today. This neglect is, however, not a reason to deny the values and standards themselves, but rather a reason to think of values as potentialities and to distinguish between values and our (imperfect) understanding and/or actualization of them.

Could the idea of a peaceful world order—an idea which exists independently of the work of a Suárez or Aquinas—also be such a lasting ideal and does this ideal still guide the most highly qualified publicists of international law as well as many governments and ordinary citizens today?

3. Historical background: Modern or medieval?

Characterizations become perhaps even more contentious when we turn from a description of Suárez' intellectual background to the larger historical picture. Recent accounts tend to argue that Suárez is either a modern thinker or, at the very least, a transitory figure placed at the watershed between the Late Middle Ages and (Early) Modernity. In support of this view, scholars mainly refer (i) to the Reformation, and (ii) to the discovery of the New World in 1492 leading to an increase in Spain's military and economic power as well as to great intellectual and artistic flourishing in the sixteenth century (*siglo de oro*).[17]

[16] See his discussion in *De Actibus Qui Vocantur Passiones*, in vol. 4, Opera Ominia (n. 7), esp. Disp. III, s. IV, §8 (*incontinentia*) and s. VII.

[17] In addition to the accounts in the works referred in n. 1 above, see e.g. Norbert Brieskorn, 'Francisco Suárez und sein Gesetzesbegriff im Kontext', in M. Walther, N. Brieskorn, and K. Waechter (eds.), *Transformation des Gesetzesbegriffs im Übergang zur Modern? Von Thomas von Aquinas zu Francisco Suárez* (2008), pp. 105–23.

The standard account is correct that Suárez reacted to these major events. Yet, scholars mistakenly claim that they led Suárez to develop a modern position. Instead and in line with his—in a literal sense—conservative mindset, Suárez reacted by defending a long established Catholic position—already articulated by Aquinas.[18]

None of the aforementioned events forced Catholics to revise their worldview. (i) From a Christian perspective, the discovery of the New World was less radical than its portrayal by non-Christians today makes it appear. For Christians, their religion did not exist from the dawn of time (of course, God existed prior to creation). Instead, Christianity arose at *a particular point in history* in a *Judeo-pagan* environment, i.e. in a mainly Jewish community within the Roman Empire: with the birth of Christ in Bethlehem.[19] It *slowly spread* from Jerusalem to Asia Minor and Rome and from there to other parts of Europe (Scandinavia, for instance, was Christianized between the eighth and the twelfth centuries). At least among Christian intellectuals, awareness of pagans inhabiting more or less distant lands *never faded* and trade with non-Christians continued throughout.[20] It is difficult to see, then, what dramatic change intervenes with Columbus's discovery of simply yet another series of pagan peoples. (ii) The schism of the Church into a Catholic and several Protestant parts was foreshadowed by the eleventh-century schism between the Western and the Eastern Church. As for the theological challenges posed by Protestantism, these did not require a fundamental modification of Catholic dogmas, but their restatement and defence.[21]

III. Theory

1. Suárez' theological approach to law

Although an authority in law and philosophy, Suárez was first and foremost a theologian. He approaches law, like all matters of morality, from a theological perspective because, for him, only the theologian (or Christian) is capable of a comprehensive understanding of the human condition.[22]

Suárez follows Aquinas in conceiving of the human condition as marked by a grand scheme devised by God. All creation—inanimate things, animals, and human beings—has come forth from God (*exitus*) and is called to return to him (*reditus*).[23] Unlike non-rational animals which follow their natural instinct by

[18] Suárez denied both the Pope and the Emperor universal temporal jurisdiction, see Section III.2.c) below.

[19] On the transition from the Old (Jewish) Law to the New Law see Suárez, *De Legibus*, vol. 6, *Opera Omnia*, Bk. IX and X (n. 7). For a historical account of the spread of Christianity see e.g. Jean Daniélou, *L'Eglise des Premiers Temps* (1985).

[20] Consider only Augustine's critical engagement with paganism and that of Aquinas with Judaism and Islam in his *Summa Contra Gentiles*.

[21] The issue is obviously complex and would require detailed engagement, above all, with the Council of Trent (1545–1563).

[22] Suárez, *De Legibus*, Preface (n. 8).

[23] For Suárez' reliance on the *exitus–reditus* scheme, see e.g. *De Fine Hominibus*, Preface §1 and §8, and Disp. V, s. II, §§4–5 (n. 15). For the following points see the works cited in n. 11 above.

necessity, human beings are capable of returning to God in a self-directed way because they possess reason and (free) will. For Suárez, God is not only the creator of the world, but also an ocean of perfection: perfect actualization of being, truth, and moral goodness (perfect love, perfect justice, etc).[24] The way back to this ocean of perfection requires human beings to perform good moral actions so as to gain a state of peace within themselves as well as with other human beings and God.[25] The way to such peace with oneself and others is chiefly a life of love and justice; divine laws and counsel as well as human laws guide us on this way.[26]

A perfect state of peace is attainable only among the blessed who see God in the next life (Augustine's City of God): the blessed are confronted with an object of such overwhelming goodness that they cannot but love what they see. This perfect peace at the heart of theology transcends the peace attainable in this life, whether the peace of the soul—the subject matter of ethics—or the temporal peace between citizens or nations—the subject matter of political philosophy. From this briefest of sketches of Suárez' intellectual framework we can already start to see that the idea of a peaceful order plays a central role in Christian theology.

In the Preface to *De Legibus*, Suárez deploys this multi-faceted idea of peace in order to articulate the difference between his theological approach to law and the approach of ancient (pagan) philosophers and lawyers trained in Roman law. These latter only explain

> those human laws which help to keep a commonwealth or state in justice and in peace; and, at the most, they touched somewhat upon natural law in so far as it can be made known by human reason and serves as guide for the moral rectitude of acquired virtues.[27]

Suárez recognizes the temporal ends of peace and justice which are knowable by human reason without revelation, i.e. knowable by so-called 'natural reason'. Yet, for him, the pagan philosophers' and jurists' way of treating 'of the laws . . . fails to transcend the natural end; nor does it even touch upon all its phases, but only upon such phases as are necessary to preserve the external peace and justice of the commonwealth'.[28] The theologian, by contrast, in addition to considering the peace and justice of the commonwealth, also considers what is necessary to attain an inner peace of the soul and peace with God. For Suárez, like for Aquinas, all just laws offer guidance on our way back to God, either directly (as in the case of divine worship) or indirectly by disposing us to goods connected to God (as is the case for justice).[29]

As a theologian, Suárez devotes the most detailed observations to the relationship between human beings and God rather than to the relationship between nations and temporal peace. He does, however, also make important observations on the

[24] Suárez, *De Fine Hominis*, Disp. V, s. III, §§3–4; also s. II, §7 (n. 15).

[25] Suárez, *De Charitate*, vol. 12, Opera Omnia, Disp. II s. III, §6, p. 646 (n. 7).

[26] Suárez, *De Legibus*, Preface (n. 8).

[27] Suárez, *De Legibus*, Preface (n. 8). The acquired virtues are (i) practical reasonableness (*prudentia*), (ii) temperance (reasonable use of alcohol, food, sex, and wealth), (iii) courage, and (iv) justice.

[28] Suárez, *De Legibus*, Preface (n. 8).

[29] See e.g. Suárez, *De Bonitate et Malitia Humanorum Actuum*, vol. 4, Opera Omnia, Disp. II, s. II, §14, pp. 295–6 (n. 7).

relationship between human beings themselves when he turns to state law (*jus civile*) and to the law of nations (*jus gentium*).

2. Communities as orders of practical reasoning

a) A Suárezian critique of legalistic approaches to the state

For a proper understanding of Suárez' approach to the law of nations, it is (again) useful to contrast his approach to that of today's international lawyers. The latter have the tendency of limiting their attention to three main actors in the 'inter-national' order: states, international organizations, and individuals. States are, moreover, still commonly defined by reference to the 1933 Montevideo Convention on the Rights and Duties of States:

> The state as a person of international law should possess the following qualifications: (a) a permanent population; (b) a defined territory; (c) government; and (d) capacity to enter into relations with the other states.

Suárez would have rejected the idea that one can define the state in purely legal terms and without an account of its purpose. He recognizes that the existence of states or political communities can only be adequately understood from the perspective of political philosophy offering an account of their formation.[30] For him, unlike for most of today's lawyers, neither the existence of states nor that of any other community should be taken for granted. Following Aristotle's observation that 'man is a social animal',[31] he gives an account of how families decided to unite as political communities or states and how these form a universal community of states. For Suárez, each such community represents a distinct *order of practical reason*: its members direct their actions to the realization of the particular community's distinct end or ends.

b) The political community as an order of practical reason

For Suárez, we understand the formation of communities by adopting the *internal, practical perspective of their founders*: it is from their perspective that we can identify the end they chose to pursue in common. Like the forming of a family, the founding of a state depends on human choice and human actions directed at a certain good or end. States are not naturally given.[32] As Suárez notes:

> there is a further necessity among human beings for a political community, consisting at least of a city state (*civitas*), and formed by a coalition of a number of families . . . if the

[30] The terms 'state' and 'political community' are used interchangeably as referring to communities of citizens. The state, thus understood, is distinguished from its government and other public authorities.

[31] Suárez, *De Legibus*, vol. 5, Opera Omnia, Bk. III, Ch. I, §3 (n. 7) (referring to Aristotle's *Politics*, Bk. I, Ch. V); see also §§4–5.

[32] Suárez, *De Legibus*, Bk. III, Ch. I, §11 (n. 7) (natural law has not in and of itself, and without the intervention of human will, created political subjection); and with regard to state law, Bk. III, Preface, §2.

individual families were divided one from another, *peace* could scarcely be preserved among men, *nor could wrongs (iniuriae) be duly averted or avenged.*[33]

Natural practical reason indicated to the founders that only a community larger than the family and under the rule of a government with coercive force is strong enough to secure *peace* vis-à-vis *other communities*, i.e. freedom from invasion, and *a peaceful and just order within its boundaries.*[34] In referring to wrongs (*iniuriae*) Suárez is thinking of crimes as well as acts of injustice like a breach of contract: a political community consists of members who do not commit such acts against each other (they recognize each other as citizens). If the members nevertheless commit an injustice, it is either corrected spontaneously or through law courts. Elsewhere Suárez adds that the political community, in addition to peace and justice, should also seek to secure sufficient material goods for people to survive and to lead a convenient life and to enforce the probity of morals necessary for peace and justice.[35] The Aristotelian–Thomists call this compound end the '(political) common good' or 'the common good of the political community' (*bonum commune*).[36]

Suárez also offers a definition of the political community. It must consist of (i) a multitude, (ii) bound together by some agreement or alliance (*foedus*), (iii) existing under a head, and (iv) with a certain end.[37] When he refers to an agreement or alliance, Suárez does not think of a written constitution, but of the alliance between the isolated families. It is a 'special volition or common consent' to gather 'together into one political body through one bond of fellowship and for the purpose of aiding one another in the attainment of (*in ordine ad*) {one} political end'.[38] For Suárez, the family and the state, although distinct orders of practical reasonableness also form part of two larger communities each of which has its own end distinct from the other communities.

c) *The church and the state–church relationship*

It is tempting to assume that Suárez' conception of the Church is irrelevant for his approach to international law. Yet, this is a mistaken assumption: for him, Jesus had come to replace the Jewish synagogue, which was open only to Jews, with a universal Church, a community open to all human beings.[39] For Suárez, the Church

[33] Suárez, *De Legibus*, Bk. III, Ch. I, §3 (emphasis added) (n. 8).

[34] Suárez, *De Legibus*, Bk. III, Ch. I, esp. §§2–12 (n. 8).

[35] Suárez, *De Legibus*, vol. 5, Opera Omnia, Bk. III, Ch. XII, §7 (n. 7); and *De Fide*, Disp. XVIII, s. III, esp. §7 (n. 8).

[36] Often Suárez omits the qualification 'political' because it is clear from the context which concept of common good he envisages, see e.g. *De Legibus*, Bk. III, Ch. II §4 (n. 8).

[37] Suárez, *De Legibus*, Bk. I, Ch. VI, 19 (n. 8).

[38] Suárez, *De Legibus*, Bk. III, Ch. II, §4 (n. 7), curly brackets, i.e. '{}', indicate passage where I have corrected the English translation. *Nota bene*: In tyrannical states, state law and practice are directed at the good of the ruler or the ruling elite, e.g. their desire for (immoral) ends such as power or wealth, see Suárez, *De Legibus*, Bk. I, Ch. I, §6; Ch. VII, §11; Ch. IX, §4 (n. 8).

[39] Suárez, *De Legibus*, Bk. I, Ch. VI, §18 (n. 7); vol. 5, *Opera Omnia*, Bk. IV (n. 7); and Suárez, *Defensio Fidei Catholicae et Apostolicae contra Errores Anglicanae Sectae*, trans. George Moore and Peter Simpson, <http://www.aristotelophile.com/Books/Translations/Suarez%20Defense%203.pdf>, Bk. III, Ch. VI, §8.

is thus a universal community (he uses the term 'Church'—Latin *ecclesia*—to refer to the visible community of the baptized, not to its institutions and officials). The laws of the Church apply across state-borders to all its members worldwide. Given this universal community whose officials have global jurisdiction, one may wonder why Suárez should continue to see any need for states.

In answering this question, it is again important to remember that the Christian Church was established in a Judeo-pagan environment. The Bible reports that Jesus taught that a good Christian renders unto Caesar what is Caesar's and unto God what is God's.[40] For the early Christians and for *one strand* of Christian theologians (not for all, see below) this was an exhortation to respect the *sovereign power* of the state *within its own, temporal sphere* (*in suo ordine*).

As emerges clearly from Suárez' work, one can only determine how far the sovereign independence of Christian states extend vis-à-vis the Church by identifying the end of the political community—i.e. temporal peace and justice—as well as the end(s) of the Church. For Suárez the Church has two ends which are reflected in Canon law:

> The one consists in the establishment in the whole ecclesiastical state of a due political order, the preservation in that state of peace and justice, and the regulation by right reason of all that relates to the *forum externum* of the Church. The other end consists in the right and prudent ordering of all things relating to divine worship, the salvation of souls and the purity of faith and moral conduct.[41]

The passage reveals two points about the Church–state relationship: the Church has (i) exclusive competence over the 'purity of faith and moral conduct' in the *forum internum*, and (ii) seemingly shared competence concerning 'a state of peace and justice' in the *forum externum*. Such shared competence would, of course, jeopardize the independence of the state in its own sphere. The Church's jurisdiction concerning peace and justice applies, however, chiefly to the clergy or 'ecclesiastical state'. In addition, it is a jurisdiction which allows the Church to impose, for the sake of peace and justice within *its distinct* community, stricter rules on its members *qua Christians* than those found in the political community. Canon law, for instance, prohibited the charging of interests—so-called usury—while state law tolerated usury (of course still without morally approving of interests).

Suárez followed a strand of Catholic theologians in inferring from the separate ends of Church and state that the Church only holds *indirect power* over the state, it has no direct jurisdiction in temporal affairs over citizens qua citizens.[42] State

[40] Suárez, *Defensio Fidei*, Bk. III, Ch. IX, esp. §9 (n. 39).

[41] Suárez, *De Legibus*, Preface (n. 8); see also vol. 5, *Opera Omnia*, Bk. IV, Ch. VIII, §4 (n. 7).

[42] Suárez, *De Legibus*, vol. 5, *Opera Omnia*, Bk. III, Ch. VI (n. 7); *Defensio Fidei*, Bk. III, Ch. 5, esp. §8 (referring to Major, Cajetan, Victoria, Soto, Bellarmin, Covarruvias, Navarrus, Bertrandi, and several Popes) and Ch. XXIII (n. 39). There is abundant literature on the indirect power of the Church over the state, see e.g. Heinrich Rommen, *Die Staatslehre des Franz Suárez S.J.* (1926), pp. 235–69; Reinhold Schwarz, *Die eigenberechtigte Gewalt der Kirche* (1974), esp. pp. 39–53 and pp. 72–89; a (too) critical account is given by Harro Höpfl, *Jesuit Political Thought: The Society of Jesus and the State, c. 1540–1630* (2004), Ch. 14.

authorities thus enjoy relative sovereignty in the temporal order directed towards earthly peace and justice; the Church can intervene only if rulers jeopardize their own spiritual good or that of their citizens.

It is common among historically interested international lawyers to assume that *the* authentic Catholic position was to affirm that the Pope had full jurisdiction over states, Christian and non-Christian alike. Proponents of this view like to refer to the Papal Bulls by which the Pope seemed to divide the newly discovered lands between Spain and Portugal. This 'Papal donation' suggests that states were insufficiently sovereign for a true international law to develop as long as the one *respublica Christiana* was in place.

Some Popes and canonists affirmed this position. Yet, Suárez expressly denies that the Church has temporal power over states: when Popes divide territories of unbelievers among temporal princes, they do so

> not in order that the former may take possession of these regions according to their own will, for that would be tyranny, . . . but in order that they may make provision for the sending of preachers . . . and may protect such preachers.[43]

The Pope's intervention is thus directed exclusively at the salvation of people's soul, not at a temporal end. Regarding the issue of preaching in foreign lands, we should note in passing that Suárez staunchly opposed direct coercion for the purpose of conversion.[44] For him, 'God has reserved for His own judgement . . . the sin of unbelief', 'because otherwise the human race could not be governed with peace and justice'.[45]

Suárez even expressly affirmed the *sovereign independence* of states *within* the one *respublica Christiana* (which for Suárez extends before and after the Reformation): the state's relative sovereignty in the temporal sphere gave rise to 'inter-national' relationships between *independent* states—he expressly names Spain, France, and England—even though they were 'kingdoms of the Church'.[46] This is even more true for non-Christian states which are not 'kingdoms of the Church'. We shall now turn to Suárez' account of the great community of nations formed by all states.

d) *The great community of nations*

Following Aristotle, Suárez emphasized that too large a community cannot be reasonably governed. According to him, it would 'hardly be possible, and much less would it be expedient' to set up a single (temporal) government over mankind (i.e. a world-state).[47] For Suárez, 'it is not necessary to the preservation or welfare of

[43] Suárez, *De Fide*, Disp. XVIII, s. 1, §7 (n. 8).
[44] Suárez, *De Fide*, Disp. XVIII, s. I, §9 and s. III, esp. §§5–7 (n. 8). On indirect conversion see Suárez, *De Fide*, Disp. XVIII, s. I, §§8–11.
[45] Suárez, *De Fide*, Disp. XVIII, s. III, §12 (n. 8).
[46] Suárez, *Defensio Fidei*, Bk. III, Ch. V, §7 (n. 39).
[47] Suárez, *De Legibus*, Bk. III, Ch. II, §5 (n. 8). The qualification 'hardly' is perhaps intended to make room for the universal government of the Church.

nature, that all men should thus congregate in a single political community'.[48] The community of states lacks a head or legislator and an agreement (*foedus*) of the kind one associates with a state.[49] Suárez *rejected* the view of Bartolus and some other jurists that the Emperor has supreme temporal power over states, even over states belonging to the Roman Empire.[50]

Although the human race does not form a state, the separate political communities are, according to Suárez, united as a quasi-moral and political community with a distinctive end: a common good of a temporal and political nature. It is worth quoting his explanation in full, since his understanding of an international legal order depends on these points:

> [H]uman race, into howsoever many different peoples and kingdoms it may be divided, always preserves a certain unity, not only as a species, but also a {quasi} political and moral unity, {as is indicated by} the natural precept of mutual love and {compassion}; a precept which applies to all, even to strangers of every nation. Although a given {perfect} state (*civitas*), commonwealth (*respublica*), or kingdom (*regnum*) may constitute a perfect community in itself, consisting of its own members, nevertheless, each one of these [perfect communities] is also, in a certain sense, and viewed in relation to the human race (*ad genus humanum*), a member of that universal society, for these states when standing alone are never so self-sufficient that they do not require some mutual assistance, association, and intercourse, at times for their own greater welfare and advantage, but at other times because also of some moral necessity or need.[51]

Suárez presents the distinctive common good of the universal society of nations as consisting of two components: a necessary component—consisting, as he clarifies elsewhere, of peace and justice—and a component which is concerned with the greater welfare and advantage (*ad melius esse majoremque utilitatem*).[52] This greater welfare encompasses, for instance, a higher standard of living achieved through cross-border commerce. He even gave as an example of *jus gentium* the 'freedom to contract commercial agreements with persons not actively hostile'.[53] The common good of nations is thus a complex good. Peace and justice are architectonic ends: the community of states ought to secure these ends whatever further ends it pursues. Thus an increase in the freedom of trade must not jeopardize peace and justice, a point relevant for instance in case of arms trades with hostile nations.

For Suárez, the peaceful order of the great society of states is, however, only a temporal good, subordinate to salvation. It is not the goal of the community of

[48] Suárez, *De Legibus*, Bk. III, Ch. II, §5 (n. 8).

[49] Suárez, *De Legibus*, Bk. II, Ch. XX, §1 and Bk. III, Ch. II, §6 *in fine* (n. 8).

[50] Suárez, *Defensio Fidei*, Bk. III, Ch. 5, §§6–7 (n. 39).

[51] Suárez, *De Legibus*, Bk. II, Ch. XIX, §9 (see also §10) (n. 8) curly brackets, i.e. '{}', indicate passage where I have corrected the English translation. Suárez goes on to add that his observations are based on actual usage.

[52] Suárez returns to the idea of this two-fold common good and clarifies that the necessary part consists of peace and justice at *De Legibus*, Bk. III, Ch. II, §6 (n. 8).

[53] Suárez, *De Legibus*, Bk. II, Ch. XIX, §7 (n. 8).

states to directly foster our salvation other than by securing the subordinate end of a just peace between states. State authorities have only jurisdiction in the *forum externum*: they are entitled to punish subjects who violate *temporal peace and justice* through their *external* acts; state authorities have no coercive jurisdiction to punish merely internal acts, nor to punish sins against virtues other than justice (justice is understood here in a narrow sense, mainly acts against life, bodily integrity, and property).[54] These limits on state jurisdiction apply both in the domestic order and in the international order.[55] It is the universal (Catholic) Church which has, as we saw, exclusive jurisdiction over the purity of people's mind (inner peace) and the salvation of their souls in its *forum internum* (i.e. the forum of the confessional).[56] Having clarified Suárez' teachings on the community of states and its distinct, temporal end, we can now finally turn to his treatment of the law of nations (*jus gentium*).

3. The law of nations as a legal order of natural and positive laws

It is tempting to approach Suárez' concept of the law governing the relationship between nations anachronistically by discussing only his teachings on the law between *nations* and only insofar as *positive* law is concerned, i.e. law laid down by nations. Yet, Suárez did not focus on legal precepts applicable to states as juridical entities (see Section III.3.a) below), nor did he limit his discussion to positive law (see Section III.3.b) below). After clarifying these issues, we will consider his concept of the law of nations (see Section III.3.c) below).

a) *Primary focus on individuals*

To the limited extent that Suárez discussed particular legal precepts, e.g. those governing just war, he focused on rules which apply to individual human beings, both to ordinary persons and to rulers. He wrote from the perspective of a theologian: his primary concern is the salvation of souls; yet states—or mystical persons (*persona mystica*) as he calls them—do not have a soul. Similarly, Suárez ascribed rights to human beings; here again, his focus is on the rights of persons (not of states) and the individual's duty to respect other persons' rights.[57]

At one point, he did, however, expressly establish the analogous applicability of a legal rule applicable between individuals to whole states (*respublicae*).[58] The case concerns blasphemy. For Suárez, blasphemy, although a sin against natural reason, does not involve an act of injustice against human beings (i.e. harming others). Injustice is only

[54] This distinction is, for instance, relevant to determine the causes of just war, see Suárez, *De Bello*, s. IV, §8 (n. 8).

[55] Suárez held that only the injured state is entitled to punish crimes in the 'inter-national' order, see *De Bello*, s. IV, §5 (n. 8).

[56] See Suárez, *De Censuris*, vol. 23, Opera Omnia, Disp. I, s. 2, §2 (n. 7).

[57] For a useful discussion see Doyle, 'Suárez on Human Rights' (n. 9).

[58] Suárez, *De Fide*, Disp. XVIII, s. IV. §3 (n. 8).

involved in blasphemy if, for instance, heathens sacrifice innocent people to their gods. State law grants impunity to an individual or ruler who commits blasphemy without harming others. According to Suárez, this impunity is also granted to states: states committing simple blasphemy (without human sacrifice) benefit from impunity from punitive war. Although we may assume that for Suárez such analogies hold in a great variety of cases, his treatment differs from that of today's international lawyers by tending to treat primarily of the rights and duties of individuals and only secondarily of states.

b) A legal order consisting of natural and positive law

It would be equally anachronistic to move straight to a consideration of Suárez' account of the *positive* law of nations. For Suárez, positive *jus gentium* is only one part of the law governing the relationship between nations. In addition to positive *jus gentium*, these relationships, e.g. war, are subject to rules belonging to natural law, (positive) divine law and, in the dealings between Christians, to canon law. The natural law prohibition of murder, for instance, is applicable in war between states: it prohibits the unjust party from killing its opponents. This natural law prohibition is not only confirmed by positive *jus gentium*, but also by positive divine law (the Ten Commandments) and canon law, all equally applicable between (Christian) nations. Given the interplay of these different types of law, it would be mistaken to present Suárez' treatment of the law of nations as if it was limited to positive law of nations. This is all the more true, since a number of rules of positive law *merely confirm or declare* rules of natural law, as in the case of the prohibition of murder declared by e.g. a statute of criminal law (*lex declarativa*), but holding independently from the statute.[59]

Still, Suárez devoted a separate chapter to the concept of *jus gentium* in the sense of *positive* law applicable *between* nations (*inter gentes*), for instance (unwritten) customary rules concerning the reception and immunity of ambassadors or norms governing the treatment of prisoners of war. In the chapter, Suárez explains that the positive law of nations, where it does not simply declare rules of natural law, *adds* something to the limited or minimal regime of natural law: here positive law has a *constitutive* force (so-called *lex constitutiva*). His point can be illustrated using the *positive law* institution of ambassadors as an example. The example also serves to clarify the relationship between natural law and positive law.

For Suárez, temporal peace and justice are subordinate, yet necessary (i.e. indispensable) ends of a moral life leading to God or eternal peace. We are called to preserve these goods at the very least by not thwarting them (e.g. by abstaining from unjust war). Yet, peace and justice among nations could be preserved either

[59] On the distinction between declarative and constitutive positive law, see Suárez, *De Legibus*, Bk. II, Ch. XVI, §5 and Ch. XIX, §3 (n. 8); vol. 5, *Opera Omnia*, Bk. III, Ch. XXI, §10 and vol. 6, *Opera Omnia*, Bk. IX, Ch. IV, §§18–19 (n. 7). The Ten Commandments are *lex declarativa*, they declare precepts of natural law, see Bk. II, Preface and Ch. VII, §§6–7; Ch. X, §1 (n. 8); and vol. 6, *Opera Omnia*, Bk. IX, Ch. IV, §18 (n. 7).

without the institution of ambassadors at the courts of other nations (e.g. simply by abstaining from unjust war) or through other means (e.g. by means of ad hoc envoys). This institution is therefore *not strictly necessary* for the common good of nations: nations have a *choice* between different means.[60]

If permanent ambassadors were the *one and only* means, nations would have no choice. In this case, natural reason would recognize the institution as a *strictly necessary* means (like taking a boat to cross the sea) and *dictate* its adoption: it would be prescribed by natural law (*nota bene*: natural law consists of the dictates of natural reason).[61] As pointed out above, the regime of natural law rules is limited or minimal: it only consists of a small set of precepts. This is the case because it is rare that human beings are left with one, and only one, means to attain their moral ends.

Although not the only means, the institution of ambassadors is such a *highly useful* means for 'inter-national' peace and justice that the usefulness was recognized by 'all or nearly all nations'.[62] The choice by which the institution was introduced has constitutive force. For Suárez, the introduction of such unwritten rules of positive *jus gentium* does not require all nations to consent at one and the same time; customary rules are gradually introduced.[63]

c) Suarez' concept of the law of nations and its connection to the common good

In Section III.3 we have so far seen that Suárez conceives the law of nations as applicable primarily to individuals and only secondarily to states and as consisting of rules of natural law and of human and divine positive law. But what allows him to group these rules under the single concept of the law of nations, i.e. what makes them a distinct legal order? This question brings us back to the idea of the common good of mankind. The central role of this idea emerges from the way Suárez distinguishes *jus gentium* in the sense of the law between nations from *jus gentium* in the old, Roman law sense. As an illustration of the latter, Suárez refers to the prohibition of marrying a person of another religion, a prohibition found in many states in his time. This prohibition is part of *jus gentium* in the Roman law sense, because it is similar to laws in other countries, yet it does not serve 'the general intercourse and fellowship of the human race, but rather the {particular good} of the {community} within which the prohibition is found'.[64] From this passage, we can see how Suárez distinguishes between domestic legal orders and the 'inter-national' legal order: the former serves the good of a particular political community or state, the latter serves the common good of the human race. What remains to be clarified is whether

[60] Suárez, *De Legibus*, Bk. II, Ch. XIX, §7 (n. 8); on positive law (*jus gentium*) as based on free will (*liberum arbitrium*) or will (*voluntas / ab arbitrium hominum*) see Bk. II, Ch. XIX, §3 and §5; and Ch. XX, §2.

[61] Suárez, *De Legibus*, Bk. II, Ch. XIX, §2 (n. 8); for the boat example see Aquinas, *Summa Theologiae*, Ia q. 19 a. 3; Ia q. 82 a. 1; IIIa q. 1 a. 2 c.; q. 65 a. 4 c. (n. 10).

[62] Suárez, *De Legibus*, Bk. II, Ch. XIX, §6 (n. 8).

[63] Suárez, *De Legibus*, Bk. II, Ch. XX, §1 (n. 8).

[64] Suárez, *De Legibus*, Bk. II, Ch. XIX, §10 (n. 8).

Suárez considers that the rules belonging to this legal order form a legal system and can be systematically treated by jurists.

4. Systematic legal scholarship on the law of nations

Asking whether, for Suárez, the law of nations forms a legal system confronts the interpreter with an immediate difficulty: Suárez did not write the kind of treatise that most of us today regard as the paradigm of systematic legal scholarship, a treatise like Hugo Grotius' *De Jure Belli ac Pacis*.[65] In this (systematic)[66] treatise, Grotius presents the fundamentals of public law, of private law, i.e. property law, contract law, and tort law, of certain rules of the law of nations, and of criminal law, following a clearly perceptible order.[67]

The fundamental, albeit not exclusive,[68] aim of *De Jure Belli ac Pacis* is that of the jurists whom Suárez describes in the Preface to *De Legibus* (see Section III.1 above): he sets out the law which orders nations to the temporal peace and justice of the human race (*forum externum*). In his lectures on war (*De Bello*), Suárez, by contrast, approaches war as a theologian writing for the *forum internum*. He treats war from the perspective of the theological virtue of love that directs us to the common good of the next life. Yet, although Suárez did not write a systematic treatise of the law of nations for the *forum externum*, his Aristotelian–Thomist understanding of communities as distinct orders of practical reason and his teleological concept of law are the very key that Grotius used to construct the system underlying *De Jure Belli ac Pacis*.

The greatest model of all systematic doctrinal treatises was, perhaps, a theological treatise: Aquinas' *Summa Theologiae*. In its preface, Aquinas expressly points out that *the plan of his treatise reflects the order of the world*.[69] Thus, Part I of the *Summa Theologiae* treats of God and the flowing of creation from God (*existus*); Part II treats of the way back to God (*reditus*) through human action, virtue, law, and grace. Part III presents Jesus' exemplary way back to God. This same *exitus-reditus* scheme underpins Suárez' systematic presentation of theology.[70]

We may assume that, for Suárez, jurists should seek to reflect the order of the temporal world in their treatises on the law of nations. This is compatible with the theological outlook, since Aristotelian–Thomists consider the community of nations as a distinct *locus* of practical reasoning. The distinct end of this community—temporal

[65] Hugo Grotius, *De Jure Belli ac Pacis*, trans. Francis W. Kelsey (1925).

[66] Like Suárez, Grotius nowhere uses the word 'system' and its cognates; he instead speaks of 'imposing the form of an art' (*forma artis*) on law, see *De Jure Belli ac Pacis*, Prol. §30 (n. 65).

[67] Even just a brief look at the table of contents will confirm this, see esp. Grotius, *De Jure Belli ac Pacis*, Bk. I, Chs. III–V, and Bk. II, Chs. II–XXI (n. 65); for the treatise's overall plan see Prol. §§33–5.

[68] See the many references to love (*caritas*) and the law of love (*lex dilectionis*) throughout the treatise, e.g. *De Jure Belli ac Pacis*, Bk. II, Ch. I (n. 65), and the requirements to attain heaven in Bk. III, Ch. X, §iii; and the discussion in my 'The Eudaemonist Ethics of Hugo Grotius' (n. 12).

[69] Aquinas, *Summa Theologiae*, Preface (n. 10), where he affirms that a treatise on moral theology ought to be structured 'according to the order of the subject matter' rather than 'according as the plan of the book might require'.

[70] See n. 11 above.

peace and justice—is in harmony with, albeit subordinate to, the otherworldly peace. Accordingly, jurists should divide their systematic treatment of the law of nations into two parts: an outline of the rules governing the peaceful order among nations characterized by the respect of other nation's rights, followed by the rules on just war which govern the way back to peace, in case unjust war has disrupted peace.

What remains to be clarified is whether the large number of norms prescribing very diverse actions and omissions contributing to peace and justice among nations form a single legal system. The still popular voluntaristic approach to international law has difficulty justifying this view; for why should international law form a (coherent) system if a norm qualifies as a norm of international law solely because it has been established by the (at least potentially) *arbitrary* will of states?

Aristotelian–Thomists, by contrast, have no difficulty explaining the existence of legal systems. This can be seen from Aquinas' explanations concerning the diversity of precepts of the Ten Commandments. As he notes, many actions and omissions 'may happen to be necessary or expedient to an end; and, accordingly, precepts may be given about various things as being ordained to one end.'[71] Similarly, Suárez justifies the attribution of diverse rules to natural law by noting that they 'proceed, by a certain necessity, from nature, and from God as the Author of nature, and all tend *to the same end*, which is undoubtedly the due preservation and natural perfection of felicity of human nature' (emphasis added).[72]

Law, although consisting of different branches, forms a single system, because the conduct prescribed by the different branches contributes to the one political common good. The ideal of a peaceful order in the practical sphere is thus reflected in the system of legal norms in the practico-theoretical sphere. This systematic order extends beyond the precepts of natural law to positive *jus gentium*, despite the fact that positive *jus gentium* is based on the *choice* of all or nearly all nations. This is the case, because (or *to the extent that*) the choices do not rely on arbitrary will (this is *nota bene* the point which proponents of the voluntaristic approach to international law as well as many textbook writers refuse to address). Rather, the rules of positive law of nations *determine* a specific way of preserving the common good of nations by selecting (choice) one reasonable way and prescribing it for all. The actions chosen and prescribed by positive *jus gentium*, like the actions prescribed by natural law, contribute to the same end: a peaceful and just 'international' order. This directedness towards the same practical end makes them part of one legal system.

IV. The Reception of Suárez' Aristotelian–Thomist Theory

The international lawyer interested in the history of the discipline asks for the reception of Suárez' work in treatises on the law of nations. It is useful, however,

[71] Aquinas, *Summa Theologiae*, I-II q. 99 a. 1 c. (n. 10).

[72] Suárez, *De Legibus*, Bk. II, Ch. VII, §7 (to be read in conjunction with §5) (n. 8); see also Ch. VIII.

to remember that the narrow focus on the law of nations, whilst compatible with Suárez' theology,[73] is the focus adopted by lawyers, not by theologians. There is a history of the reception of Suárez' thought in Catholic theology and a very different history of its reception in international legal thought.

It makes little sense to examine Suárez' influence on the discipline of the law of nations solely by reference to his own work. First, he makes only scant references to substantive norms of the law of nations apart from treating war (see esp. Section II.1 above). Second, Suárez understood himself to be part of a broad theological movement, Aristotelian–Thomism. We should therefore ask for this movement's influence on international legal thought.

Members of this movement, including Domingo de Soto, Louis Molina, and Suárez' pupil Leonard Lessius dealt with substantive law in treatises entitled *De Justitia et Jure*. As theologians, they wrote their treatises for the *forum internum*. It was these treatises—more than Suárez' work—which served Hugo Grotius as a guide for his *De Jure Belli ac Pacis*: from them (as well as from e.g. Gentili's *De Jure Belli*) he took many of the substantive rules for his book on the law of nations. Yet, unlike the theologians, Grotius wrote his treatise mainly with a view to temporal peace and the *forum externum*.[74]

Whilst Grotius openly acknowledged his debt to the Catholic theologians, some later Protestant natural law scholars—above all Samuel Pufendorf and Christian Thomasius—hailed him as a great innovator who rejected Aristotelian–Thomism.[75] In the nineteenth century, confessional bias led Protestant historians to stylize Grotius as the 'father of international law'. This image was questioned only in the wake of the broad revival of Thomism, so-called neo-Thomism, in the late nineteenth century.[76] For the past one hundred years, historians have sought to determine the extent of Grotius' debt to the Spanish Thomists.[77]

In the same period, we can also witness renewed interest in Suárez' thought and Spanish Aristotelian–Thomism more generally.[78] One prominent international lawyer who highlighted the relevance of Suárez' views for the present time was the Austrian Alfred Verdross (1890–1980).[79] Verdross expressly defended the lasting validity of the common good of the large society of states. More recently, John Finnis (born 1940) has drawn on Suárez (of whom he is generally very critical) as

[73] The idea of communities as distinct orders of practical reasonableness with their distinct ends allows for such specialization.

[74] See my 'The Eudaemonist Ethics of Hugo Grotius' (n. 12), esp. the references cited at n. 40.

[75] See my 'The Eudaemonist Ethics of Hugo Grotius' (n. 12).

[76] See esp. Josef Kohler, 'Die spanischen Naturrechtslehrer des 16. und 17. Jahrhunderts', *Archiv für Rechts- und Wirtschaftsphilosophie* 10(3) (1917), 235.

[77] For an overview with references to the works of Hans Thieme, Ernst Reibstein, Robert Feenstra, Alfred Dufour, and many others see Wim Decock, *Theologians and Contract Law: The Moral Transformation of the Ius Commune* (2013), pp. 643–6.

[78] See Rommen, *Die Staatslehre des Franz Suárez* (n. 42).

[79] See Alfred Verdross and Bruno Simma, *Universelles Völkerrecht: Theorie und Praxis* (3rd edn, 1984), pp. 8–13, esp. p. 12; Verdross, 'Der klassische Begriff des "*bonum commune*" und seine Entfaltung zum "*bonum commune humanitatis*"', *Österreichische Zeitschrift für öffentliches Recht und Völkerrecht* 28(1) (1977), 143–62, 157–8.

well as on Aquinas in a remarkable essay on just war.[80] In philosophy, Suárez has found an eminent defender in the Oxford Professor Terence Irwin.[81] Most recently, Markus Kremer translated a selection of Suárez' writings relevant to the law of war.[82] Kremer's introduction to the translation (as well as his doctoral thesis listed in the Bibliography below) marks a clear turn to interpretations of Suárez which pay attention to his theological outlook.

V. Conclusion

A contribution on Suárez' work which takes his outlook seriously cannot end with a historical account of his work's reception. Typically, the question of a work's reception is a question asked by historians. But why should we accept that Suárez' work is the proper subject matter of the history of international legal thought? This seems natural, of course, if we accept the still popular understanding that international law is exclusively grounded in the will of states. Lacking state authority, legal treatises written by private scholars such as Suárez' treatises then appear naturally as irrelevant for contemporary international law and hence as the proper subject matter for legal historians.

International lawyers seem also barred from consideration of Suárez' work, because the modern doctrine of sources qualifies the writings of all publicists, even of more recent publicists than Suárez, only as subsidiary source of international law. Surprisingly, however, this is exactly the view taken by Suárez himself, and the tradition in which he stands. For him too, treatises written by scholars possess no special authority. From his point of view, the problem with the modern doctrine of sources does not consist in relegating the publicists to a subsidiary role, but its failure to acknowledge the central role of the values which lie *beyond or behind* the primary sources as well as behind the subsidiary sources: the ideal of a peaceful and just order among states. For Suárez, these values are as much sources of international law as are international treaties or customary law. They are even its 'meta-sources', yet they are not mentioned in the ICJ Statute and perhaps for this reason textbooks do not accord them the place they deserve. As we saw, Suárez would readily admit that there is need for a mechanism—such as treaties or customs—to *authoritatively* determine which one of a number of reasonable ways of preserving a just and peaceful order should be binding for all states (see Section III.3.b above). For him, this authoritative determination is effected by the law of nations. The law of nations, if it is directed towards a peaceful and just order, is based on will and reason, not on state will alone.[83]

[80] John Finnis, 'War and Peace in the Natural Law Tradition', in *Collected Essays*, vol. 3 (1996, reprint 2011).

[81] Terence Irwin, *The Development of Ethics: From Suárez to Rousseau*, vol. 2 (2008).

[82] Francisco Suárez, *Über den Frieden – über den Krieg*, Markus Kremer ed. (2013).

[83] I would like to thank the editors for their helpful comments on an earlier draft.

Selected Bibliography

Finnis, John, 'War and Peace in the Natural Law Tradition', in John Finnis (ed.), *Human Rights and Common Good: Collected Essays*, vol. 3 (Oxford: Oxford University Press, 2011), pp. 183–208.

Irwin, Terence, *The Development of Ethics: From Suárez to Rousseau*, vol. 2 (Oxford: Oxford University Press, 2008).

Kremer, Markus, *Den Frieden verantworten: Politische Ethik bei Francisco Suárez (1548–1617)* (Stuttgart: Kohlhammer, 2008).

Rommen, Heinrich, *Die Staatslehre des Franz Suárez S.J.* (Mönchengladbach: Volksverein Verlag, 1926).

Verdross, Alfred, 'Der klassische Begriff des "*bonum commune*" und seine Entfaltung zum "*bonum commune humanitatis*"', *Österreichische Zeitschrift für öffentliches Recht und Völkerrecht* 28(1) (1977), 143.

4

Jean Bodin on International Law

Merio Scattola†

I. The Problem of Sovereignty, or: Is Jean Bodin a Classic Author in International Law?

Undoubtedly Jean Bodin (1530–1596) is a classic writer in the history of political and legal thought, whose name is closely linked with his masterpiece, *Six livres de la république*[1] (*Six Books of the Commonwealth*), and to the doctrine of sovereignty that he explained in the famous eighth chapter of the first book. Therefore we may not understand Bodin as a classic in international law, and actually his name and his work do not appear among the twenty-two books of the series 'Classics of International Law', edited by James Brown Scott (1866–1943) and published between 1911 and 1950 by the Carnegie Institution of Washington, a series that fostered, in the early twentieth century, the idea that a small number of outstanding writers, living mainly in the sixteenth and seventeenth centuries, are responsible for the foundation of the international law.[2] Among his contemporaries, the names of Pierino Belli (1502–1575), Baltasar Ayala (1548–1584) and Alberico Gentili (1552–1608) have been preferred as a choice for the publication, since they

[1] Published in French in 1576; Latin edition 1586.

[2] The following books were all published in the series 'Classics of the International Law': 1. Richard Zouche, *Iuris et iudicii fecialis, sive, Iuris inter gentes* (1650); 2. Balthazar Ayala, *De jure et officiis bellicis et disciplina militari libri III* (1582); 3. Hugo Grotius, *De jure belli ac pacis libri tres* (1646); 4. E. de Vattel, *Le droit des gens* (1758); 5. Samuel Rachel, *De jure naturae et gentium dissertationes* (1676); 6. Johann Wolfgang Textor, *Synopsis juris gentium* (1680); 7. Franciscus de Vitoria, *De Indis et de iure belli relectiones* (1696); 8. Giovanni da Legnano, *De bello, de repraesaliis et de duello* (1477); 9. Alberico Gentili, *Hispanicae advocationis libri duo* (1661); 10. Samuel von Pufendorf, *De officio hominis et civis juxta legem naturalem libri duo* (1682); 11. Cornelius van Bynkershoek, *De dominio maris* (1744); 12. Alberico Gentili, *De legationibus libri tres* (1594); 13. Christian von Wolff, *Jus gentium methodo scientifica pertractatum* (1764); 14. Cornelius van Bynkershoek, *Quaestionum iuris publici liber duo* (1737); 15. Samuel von Pufendorf, *Elementorum jurisprudentiae universalis libri duo* (1672); 16. Alberico Gentili, *De iure belli libri tres* (1612); 17. Samuel von Pufendorf, *De iure naturae et gentium libri octo* (1688); 18. Pierino Belli, *De re militari et bello tractatus* (1563); 19. Henry Wheaton, *Elements of international Law* (1836); 20. Francisco Suárez, *Selections from three works: De legibus, ac Deo legislatore* (1612); *Defensio fidei catholicae, et apostolicae adversus anglicanae sectae errores* (1613); *De triplice virtute theologica, fide, spe, et charitate* (1621); 21. Cornelius van Bynkershoek, *De foro legatorum liber singularis* (1721); 22. Hugo Grotius, *De iure praedae commentarius* (1604).

explicitly addressed, in their works, topics of the relationships among nations like warfare and diplomacy.

Both modern scholarship and the ancient legal or political literature share this opinion. Critical assessments of Bodin's contribution to topics related to international law are quite rare,[3] and the comprehensive introductions to his work dedicate their explanations mainly to issues of the interior life in a commonwealth (sovereignty, the form of constitutions, the best constitution, climate and constitutions, harmonic justice), but they do not pay attention to the doctrines related to the relationships among commonwealths.[4] The impression that Bodin is to be regarded as a 'classic in the doctrine of sovereignty' becomes even stronger when we consider the immediate reception of his doctrines in the late sixteenth and in the early seventeenth century. This process began quite early, and already the first discussions on Bodin's work concentrated on a small number of theories. For instance, the first Latin translation was issued in Germany as early as 1581, five years before the Latin translation provided by Jean Bodin himself in 1586. This partial version, composed by the German Catholic Johann Schröder, contained only the second book, *De la république*, and presented it as a treatise on the different forms of constitutions, with particular attention to the changes of constitutions and to political revolutions.[5] In this sense, it already identified, at this early stage, a main topic in the history of the reception of Jean Bodin's *œuvre*. His *Six livres de la république* were not composed like a close deductive system, departing from a single principle as was the custom in the late seventeenth century, but rather they departed from a collection of doctrines that are gathered together in a series of commonplaces. Among the interesting and sometimes original doctrines of this books are: sovereignty, the different forms of constitutions (a question that was linked with the legal and historical judgment on the Holy Roman Empire),[6] the best constitution, the transformations of the constitution and the historical revolutions, the climate, and the political order. The polemical debates of the early seventeenth century concentrated on the regal prerogatives (what the monarch might and might not do) and, among all doctrines of the *Six livres de république*, paid the most attention to the question of sovereignty. This was the case in France, during the religious wars that provided the backdrop to the composition of this work. In the Italian territories, the same question arose by dint of the papal interdict launched against the Republic of Venice in 1606; in England, the oath of allegiance and, in the Empire, the formation of opposed

[3] Guillaume Cardascia, 'Machiavel et Jean Bodin', *Bibliothèque d'Humanisme et Renaissance*, 3 (1943), 129–67; Virgilio Ilari, *L'interpretazione storica del diritto di guerra romano fra tradizione romanistica e giusnaturalismo* (1981), p. 51; Margherita Isnardi Parente, 'Introduzione', in Margherita Isnardi Parente (ed.), *Jean Bodin, I sei libri dello stato: Volume primo*, (1964), pp. 11–100, at pp. 76–7; Diego Quaglioni, *I limiti della sovranità. Il pensiero di Jean Bodin nella cultura politica e giuridica dell'età moderna* (1992), pp. 107–39.

[4] Simone Goyard-Fabre, *Jean Bodin et le droit de la république* (1989). Cf. Artemio Enzo Baldini, ed. *Jean Bodin a 400 anni dalla morte: Bilancio storiografico e prospettive di ricerca* (1997), p. 390.

[5] Jean Bodin, *Iohannis Bodini Galli, De speciebus rerumpublicarum liber ob eruditionem et historiarum multiplicitatem lectu non indignus, interprete Iohanne Schrodero. Subiectus iudicio amplissimorum Magdeburgensis archidioecesis aulae consiliariorum* (1581), fo. A1-N8.

[6] Cf. Jean Bodin, *Methodus, ad facilem historiarum cognitionem* (1566).

religious alliances were supported by similar debates about the competence of the highest power in a commonwealth. Clearly, the main problem was whether legal autonomy should be allowed within a republic or a kingdom, whereas the Catholic church laid claim to a particular form of autonomy that granted the pope a right of intervention against the king if the latter degenerated into a tyrant and threatened the existence of the 'true' religion. This doctrine of the indirect power of the pope in secular affairs configured the specific form of a Catholic right of resistance, and therefore the discussion on sovereignty was always connected with the permissibility of resistance. Incidentally, this question also touched on an international topic because from different sides it was maintained that a prince could intervene in a war if foreign subjects were menaced by their legitimate sovereign who had degenerated into a tyrant. This situation configured what we would now call an international right of humanitarian intervention.[7] However, religious reasons could also be understood as sufficient, thus presenting a basis for a right to religious intervention.

The doctrine of sovereignty of Jean Bodin was exactly in the middle of these discussions, and in the early seventeenth century two different interpretations or alternatives in political thought were formulated about the whole question of political and supreme power. Some authors, guided by Iustus Lipsius (1547–1606), maintained that the supreme power of a king derives from its personal virtues, which sometimes has supernatural elements and corresponds to a ray of divine light. This line, which can refer back to Eusebius of Caesarea (263–339),[8] conceives political power, *imperium*, as *maiestas*. The second line, on the contrary, considers *imperium* as *summa potestas*, that is, as a right, a set of rights, or a legal construct.[9] The most famous promoter of this interpretation was Jean Bodin, who therefore appeared positively in numerous books and dissertations on majesty and

[7] Merio Scattola, 'Das Ganze und die Teile. Menschheit und Völker in der naturrechtlichen Kriegslehre von Francisco de Vitoria', in Norbert Brieskorn and Gideon Stiening (eds.), *Francisco de Vitorias 'De Indiia' in interdisziplinärer Perspektive. Interdisciplinary Views on Francisco de Vitoria's 'De Indiis'*, (2011), pp. 97–120; Francisco de Vitoria, 'De Indis / Über die Indianer', in Ulrich Horst, Heinz-Gerhard Justenhoven, and Joachim Stüben (eds.), *Francisco de Vitoria, Vorlesungen (Relectiones). Völkerrecht – Politik – Kirche* (1995/97), vol. II, pp. 370–541, at pp. 478–80. Jean Bodin, *Les six livres de la république* (1583), liv. II, ch. 5; Stephanus Iunius Brutus, *Vindiciae contra tyrannos, sive de principis in populum populique in principem legitima potestate* (1600), pp. 170–87; Guilelmus Rossaeus, *De iusta reipublicae Christianae in reges impios et haereticos authoritate, iustissimaque Catholicorum ad Henricum Navarraeum et quemcumque haereticum a regno Galliae repellendum confoederatione* (1592), pp. 576–659; Iohannes Althusius, *Politica methodice digesta atque exemplis sacris et profanis illustrata* (3rd edn, 1614), p. 784. Vgl. Adhémar Esmein, 'La théorie de l'intervention internationale chez quelques publicistes français due XVIe siècle', *Nouvelle revue historique de droit français et étranger*, 24 (1900), 549–74, at 564–9; Merio Scattola, 'Diritto medievale e scienza politica moderna nella dottrina della sovranità di Jean Bodin' *Ius commune*, 26 (1999), 165–209, at 202; Mario Turchetti, *Tyrannie et tyrannicide de l'Antiquité à nos jours* (2001), pp. 441–2.

[8] Eusebius Caesariensis, 'De laudibus Constantini oratio in eius tricennalibus habita', in Jacques-Paul Migne (ed.), *Patrologiae cursus completus. Series Graeca* (1857), to. 20, coll. 1315–1440; Eusebius Caesariensis, *On the Theophania or Divine Manifestation of Our Lord and Saviour Jesus Christ*, trans. Samuel Lee (1843).

[9] Merio Scattola, 'Die Frage nach der politischen Ordnung: *Imperium, maiestas, summa potestas* in der politischen Lehre des frühen siebzehnten Jahrhunderts', in Martin Peters and Peter Schröder (eds.), *Souveränitätskonzeptionen. Beiträge zur Analyse politischer Ordnungsvorstellungen im 17. bis zum 20. Jahrhundert* (2000), pp. 13–39.

sovereignty published in the early seventeenth century. We can remember here the explicit contributions given by Henning Arnisaeus (*c*. 1575–1636), Jakob Bornitz (*c*. 1560–1625), and Christoph Besold (1577–1638).[10]

But the doctrine of sovereignty was at the same time strongly refused and opposed as it happened with Fabio Albergati and Antonio Possevino, who elaborated the idea of a kinship, a participation in a similar 'unorthodoxy', between Jean Bodin and Niccolò Machiavelli, an interpretation that was accepted in the *historia literaria* until the eighteenth century, of course closely linked to the name of Thomas Hobbes.[11] Even in the late eighteenth century, a Catholic philosopher like Salvatore Maria Roselli (*c*. 1710–1784) still wrote that all disorder in moral and political questions had come from the three evil-doers Machiavelli, Bodin, and Hobbes.[12]

Nevertheless, Bodin dedicates two chapters in his masterpiece to a presentation of the relationships among independent commonwealths. However, these observations of his seem to provide only a very loose link to his theory of sovereignty. They can be seen as two unrelated parts of the same complex of commonplaces, but still they can even throw a very interesting light on the more familiar question of sovereignty. If we take these chapters seriously into account, we can formulate the following theses:

1. The theory of sovereignty applies only to the interior life of the commonwealth, that is, to rule the relationships between the supreme power and its subjects. It is an interior concept.
2. The relationships between independent supreme powers are not ruled by the idea of sovereignty, which has no meaning and no application in this context *inter gentes*. It does not even affect this situation, and therefore independent powers cannot be understood as sovereign from one another, nor as completely independent. In their interactions, dealings, wars, and communications, they actually follow the rules of an external law.
3. We can divide the political life of a commonwealth into two spheres: the internal dominion has a top-down pattern and is regulated by the idea of absolute sovereignty, whereas the external sphere has a bottom-up pattern and obeys the rule of law.

[10] Henning Arnisaeus, *De iure maiestatis libri tres* (1610); Henning Arnisaeus, *De autoritate principum in populum semper inviolabili seu quod nulla ex causa subditis fas sit contra legitimum principem arma movere* (1612); Jakob Bornitz, *Torgensis iurisconsulti et consiliarii Caesarei et. c. tractatus duo. I. De maiestate politica et summo imperio eiusque functionibus. II. De praemiis in republica decernendis, deque eorum generibus, differentiis et mutationibus* (1610); Christoph Besold, 'De politica maiestate in genere. Resp. Daniel a Wensin', in *Collegii politici classis prima, reipublicae naturam et constitutionem XII. disputationibus absolvens*, edited by Christoph Besold (1614), disp. 2, p. 30; Alberico Gentili, *Regales disputationes tres: id est, De potestate regis absoluta, De unione regnorum Britanniae, De vi civium in regem semper iniusta* (1605).

[11] Daniel Georg Morhof, *Polyhistor, in tres tomos* (1708), lib. II, par. 4, p. 12.

[12] Salvatore M. Roselli, *Summa philosophica ad mentem Angelici doctoris sancti Thomae Aquinais. Pars quarta. Ethicam complectens. Tom. VI* (1788), quaest. 7, art. 1, pp. 316–30, qui par. 541, pp. 327–30.

4. However, we can finally also apply the external pattern to the internal domain and find that the sovereignty itself is not as absolute as it seems; rather, it admits in the internal life of a commonwealth the presence of an eternal order of law which is superior to the sovereign.

II. Relationships among Commonwealths in the *Six Livres de la République*

Jean Bodin introduces explicitly what we may call 'international law topics' in the fifth book of his *République*, particularly in the fifth and in the sixth chapter, presenting in the former the questions related to warfare, and treating and reconstructing the ancient *jus feciale* in the latter. Actually, although Bodin points out the existence of a clear link between both chapters,[13] the former begins rather casually and treats the question whether the building of castles and fortresses can improve or damage the virtue of the citizens in a commonwealth. It is evidently a question that echoes a main Machiavellian concern and that Bodin also explains by introducing Machiavellian arguments and suggestions, such as the idea that a popular state should be at best maintained in a condition of perpetual conflict with the surrounding enemies.[14] Following the thread of Machiavelli's arguments, Bodin touches on the main points in a doctrine of war, albeit without any systematic arrangement. In the treatment of this question, Bodin is clearly guided by the concern for identifying the rules of prudent conduct in all different situations. Given this fortuity, it cannot be said that both chapters together constitute a clearly defined part of legal knowledge. They do not make up a separate discipline or a branch of political and legal knowledge, a forerunner of the modern international law, but rather they touch on two important issues in the right and prudent behaviour of a sovereign.

Bodin answers the question of the fifth chapter in a way that is very significant for his method. In actual fact, he makes a subtle and articulated distinction because different commonwealths have diverging natures and constitutions and therefore react to the same problem in very different ways.

> For, if you would like to say something generally valid, you must necessarily be mistaken because different polities must be governed by different institutions and laws.[15]

However, it must be said in general that every war must be just and waged only for defending a country from an aggression or for avenging an accepted offence. Still, although some constitutions like in the Venetian Republic preferred to avoid

[13] Jean Bodin, *De republica libri sex, Latine ab autore redditi multo quam antea locupletiores* (1586), lib. V, cap. 6, p. 578 C.

[14] Bodin, *De republica libri sex*, lib. V, cap. 5, p. 566 (n 13). See further the contribution by Roth-Isigkeit in this volume.

[15] Bodin, *De republica libri sex*, lib. V, cap. 5, p. 557 (n. 13): 'Nam si de toto genere dictum velint, in maximis erroribus versari necesse est, cum dissidentes inter se rerumpublicarum status discrepantibus institutis ac legibus moderari oporteat.' English translation by the editors.

conflicts as much as possible and to settle their quarrels with the enemies in a peaceful way and through compromise, other democratic states like Switzerland maintain its citizens in a permanent readiness for combat.[16] A second main principle is that war must be necessary (*necessarium*) because it implies great destruction and great peril for the whole commonwealth, and consequently it must be waged only if there is no other way and the commonwealth is obliged to choose a path of violence, when the citizens come *ad extrema vitae pericula*.[17] In this case also, however, the sovereign must accurately weigh up the gain in case of victory against the loss in case of defeat, opting for war only when the gain is greater than the loss.[18] Thirdly, the war must be fought respecting all precepts of virtue, both with regard to the reasons of beginning a war and the way of conducting it. Desire of conquest or longing for richness and other forms of personal interest can never clearly constitute sufficient reasons for a just war, and in fighting the enemy, the highest measure of temperance must be observed.[19]

According to these three main principles, Bodin's explanations on warfare remain in the mainstream of traditional just war doctrines. Nevertheless, they formulate a particular point of view because they combine two different and apparently opposite observations, which we could easily identify with the Scholastics, on the one hand, and with Machiavelli, on the other. On the one hand, it is actually evident that a war must always be just and therefore can be waged only for the conservation of peace and for the vindication of offences (traditional doctrine, Vitoria); but on the other hand, it is also clear that a commonwealth defends itself in the best way by instilling terror in its enemies, which can be done by maintaining its citizens continuously under arms (Machiavelli). Justice and virtue seem here to contradict one another. Only the ancient Romans succeeded in overcoming this problem, because they fought only just wars with the highest religious respect for all rules; and by waging war, they could constantly improve the virtue of their citizens.[20]

The sixth chapter in the fifth book is dedicated to a systematic reconstruction of the ancient *jus feciale*, which Bodin understands as a law that regulates the relationships between foreign nations. The ancient 'law of the nations' actually reached much further than modern 'international law' and indicated all kinds of legal situations that could occur between two citizens of different nations, who therefore used different civil laws in their countries. Contracts, marriage, and slavery belonged to this part of the Roman law, and public matters, like war or boundaries, occupied only a small part of it, whereas its main interest lay in questions of the private sphere.[21] The *jus feciale* was, on the contrary, a religious institution that ruled exclusively over the

[16] Bodin, *De republica libri sex*, lib. V, cap. 5, p. 558 D (Respublica Venetorum) and p. 566 C (Helvetii) (n. 13).

[17] Bodin, *De republica libri sex*, lib. V, cap. 5, p. 560 A (n. 13).

[18] Bodin, *De republica libri sex*, lib. V, cap. 5, p. 570 C-D (n. 13).

[19] Bodin, *De republica libri sex*, lib. V, cap. 5, p. 560 A and p. 571 B (n. 13).

[20] Bodin, *De republica libri sex*, lib. V, cap. 5, p. 563 D-564 A (n. 13).

[21] *Digesta*, lib. I, tit. 1, leg. 5 (Hermogenianus): 'Ex hoc iure gentium introducta bella, discretae gentes, regna condita, dominia distincta, agris termini positi, aedificia collocata, commercium, emptiones venditiones, locationes conductiones, obligationes institutae: exceptis quibusdam quae iure civili introductae sunt.'

ceremonies of war and peace and was therefore understood by Bodin as that part of the law which could offer a kind of 'public law of nations'. Bodin defines it firstly through its issues and secondly through its principle. The topics of this *jus feciale* are the treaties of peace with the enemies, the treaties of alliance or federation, the treaties of union when a new country or new citizens are accepted in a commonwealth or when a prior unity got lost in a civil war and the enemy parties rebuild the original society.[22] All these relationships depend on a single first principle, on faith or loyalty (*fides*), so that we could observe that all relationships inside a commonwealth are ruled by *maiestas* or sovereignty, but all relationships outside a commonwealth refer to *fides*. The former requires the presence of political subordination, while the latter operates whenever no subordination is possible or when it has got lost. The fundamental insistence on the principle of faith necessarily produced a violent polemic against Niccolò Machiavelli, who is not quoted directly in the text, but is indirectly referred to in the subject index as the defender of a perverse kind of politics applied by Pope Alexander VI and by his son, Cesare Borgia.

> They say, that Cesar Borgia, sonne to pope Alexander the sixt, was like unto this monster [Caracalla], whome Machiavel doth produce for the paragon of princes: he had learned of his father to poyson such as he invited to a banquet: it cannot be said, which did exceed other in treachery. Alexander the father never did that which he said, and Cesar his sonne never spake that which he did: and both of them did religiously hold, that faith was to be given to all men [fidem omnibus dari oportere], but to be kept with no man. Cesar gave his faith and sware great oathes for the assurance of the peace which he had made with the princes that were in league against him: and having drawn them together upon his faith, hee murthered them cruelly whereas his father laughing, said, that he had shewed them a Spanish tricke. But it was an extreame folly for the princes to put their lives into the hands of the most disloyall and perfidious man living, and knowne for such a one: and even at such a time as he was but subiect to the pope [alienae maiestatis subdito], and had no power to give his faith to them [nec hostibus dare fidem] he put to death: so as the pope might have excused them as his subiects and vassals [pontifex maximus, penes quem erat imperii maiestas], without any note of treacherie. But none of them knew the *jus feciale* or any other decent thing.[23]

The given word must always be respected, and Bodin applies this rule to all different situations that appear in the *jus feciale*. We can choose one of the extreme cases in order to exemplify all other ordinary cases. In particular, Bodin accuses

[22] Bodin, *De republica libri sex*, lib. V, cap. 6, p. 578 B-C (n. 13).

[23] Bodin, *De republica libri sex*, lib. V, cap. 6, p. 602 B and Index, voc. Fides (n. 13): 'Huic pesti [= Caracallae] quamsimillimum fuisse ferunt Borgiam Alexandri VI pontificis Romani filium, qui a patre, quos ad convivium invitaret, veneno necare didicerat. Uter utrum perfidia superaret, vix dici potest: alterum enim ferunt numquam dicere, quae facturus esset, alterum numquam efficere, quae dixisset, ac utrumque id unum pro summa religione persuasum habuisse, fidem omnibus dari oportere, servandam nemini. Cum enim hostium duces ad pacis actionem deinde blanditiarum illecebris ac iureiurando Alexandri filium ad se pertraxisset, crudelissime necari iussit, cui flagitio pater irridens: "O factum bene!" inquit. Sed non minori temeritate homini perfidiosissimo quam imprudentia seipsos alienae maiestatis subdito committendos putabant, qui nec hostibus dare fidem nec sine pontificis maximi, penes quem erat imperii maiestas, consensu pacisci utiliter poterant. Neuter tamen ius feciale aut boni quidquam didicerat.' English text: Bodin, *The Six Bookes of a Commonwealth*, trans. Richard Knolles (1606); last sentence translated by the editors.

some Roman lawyers of the past, amongst whom are Bartolo da Sassoferrato, Baldo degli Ubaldi, and the canonist Francesco Zabarella, of having perverted the correct interpretation of Roman law, since they admitted that a peace treaty signed after a defeat implies a constraint for the losing party. In such a treaty, there is also a kind of violence exerted by the winner on the loser, but a contract agreed to under violence or the threat of violence is not valid. At the end of their argument, the aforementioned jurists concluded that a prince forced under these conditions to sign a treaty can honestly break his word and be disloyal and treacherous.[24] But if we admit this interpretation, no treaty will resist firmly and all peace treaties will be broken with the argument that they were agreed under the threat of violence. In this sense, no war can ever be brought to an end other than with the complete destruction of one of the warring parties. But the meaning of a peace treaty is precisely to put an end to a war when one of the parties has prevailed and could use its force or its victory to set forth the violence and possibly destroy the loser. The latter accepts the peace conditions under the premise that otherwise his situation would be much worse. Even in this case, where there is a clear asymmetry between the parties in a treaty, faith must be conserved rigorously.[25] And this principle applies to all cases and situations of a correctly understood *jus feciale*, that is, the most important relationships amongst a free and independent commonwealth. Faith is *The Trew Law of Free Monarchies*,[26] and in the field of faith a king or a sovereign commonwealth cannot decide and judge in his own case, but they must follow a rule that is above them.

We should therefore conclude that princes and kings and sovereigns in general may freely create, change, and use the positive laws of their countries, where they do not acknowledge any superior power above themselves. But when they go outside the boundaries of their kingdoms, they are subject to a superior form of law that does not depend on their will. This superior form of law must be before their will and is part of the natural law. In this domain, the arguments of the sovereignty have no force at all, and therefore we can observe that a sphere of the legal world, namely the sphere that includes the war and the relationships among commonwealths, is not subject to sovereignty and is ruled by natural law.

III. A Method for a Missing Public Law of Nations

Bodin is to some extent conscious that he is going down a new path with his doctrine of *jus feciale* because the jurisprudence of his time needed integration and

[24] Alessandro Tartagni, *Consilia*, lib. IV, cons. 48 [cf. III, 98]; lib. V, cons. 17 [= 16]; Francesco degli Accolti detto l'Aretino, *Consilia*, 14; Filippo Decio, *Consilia et responsa*, 219; Baldo degli Ubaldi, *Consilia*, III, 364 and 26; I, 40; Domenico da San Gimignano, *Consilia*, 124; Francesco Zabarella, *Consilia*, 137, Bartolo da Sassoferrato, *In Iam Digesti veteri partem*, in leg. Conventionum, De pactis [Digesta, lib. II, tit. 15, leg. 5].

[25] Bodin, *De republica libri sex*, lib. V, cap. 6, p. 594 C (n. 13).

[26] James I King of England, 'The Trew Law of Free Monarchies. Or the Reciprock and Mutual Duetie betwixt a Free King, and his Natural Subjects, 1598 and 1603', in Charles Howard McIlwain (ed.), *The Political Works of James I* (1918), pp. 53–70.

improvement about a topic that had been completely neglected, both in the legal and in the political learning of the past, although it was well known in the Roman world.

This treatie depends of the former, the which ought not to be omitted, seeing that neither lawyer nor politician hath ever handled it: and yet there is nothing in all affaires of state that doth more trouble Princes and Commonweales, then to assure the treaties which they make one with an other, be it betwixt friends or enemies, with those that be newters, or with subiects.[27]

Although ancient Roman jurisprudence knew a large number of institutions in the law of nations dealing with the private sphere, it did not develop a similar doctrine for the public sphere, which remained vacant and defective, somehow longing for fulfilment. The whole *Corpus juris civilis* was understood as a collection of private law, while public law was identified with the ceremonies, the institutions, and the magistrates of the city of Rome.[28] This was one reason that prevented Roman jurisprudence from the foundation of both a universal public law and of a universal international law; and, as we can read in the last quotation, Bodin was aware of this deficiency and of the duty that consequently fell upon the jurisprudence of his time.

In this sense, we can observe that this chapter underwent a particular evolution between the French first edition of 1576 and the Latin translation of 1586. In the first French editions of 1576 and 1577, it took the place of the eighth chapter in the first book, i.e. the place of the famous chapter on sovereignty in the later editions, and was entitled: 'The keeping of treaties and alliances between princes'. Since the third French edition in 1578, it was moved to its final position at the end of the fifth book, and in the Latin translation of 1586 it received a new title, which pointed out the presence of a particular variety of law: 'On the *ius feciale*, on alliances and on the way of making and enforcing treaties of peace between nations', and it was consistently enlarged with a schematic explanation of the most relevant notions in the *jus feciale*. In this way, the same chapter was organized in a straight line of argumentation and became much more systematic than before; it now figured as perhaps the most systematic chapter in the whole work, so systematic in fact that it actually looked like an independent treatise that could also be published and read on its own. In 1583, the diplomat and lawyer Barnabé Brisson (1531–1591) published his *De formulis et sollemnibus populi Romani verbis libri octo*,[29] in which he tried to give a

[27] Bodin, *De republica libri sex*, lib. V, cap. 6, p. 578 B (n. 13): 'Iura fecialia, quae superioribus sunt consequentia, nec ab iureconsultis nec ab iis, quotquot der republica scripserunt, pertractata fuisse videmus, cum tamen nulla re principes ac populi gravius periclitentur quam in pace cum hostibus sancienda aut in foederibus feriendis aut in coeunda societate seu cum peregrinis seu cum civibus, secessione quadam aut civili bello ab unione mutua distractis, agatur.' English text: Bodin, The Six Bookes of a Commonweale, trans. Richard Knolles (1606).

[28] *Digesta*, lib. I, tit. 1, leg. 1, par. 1 (Ulpianus): 'Huius studii duae sunt positiones, publicum et privatum. publicum ius est quod ad statum rei romanae spectat, privatum quod ad singulorum utilitatem: sunt enim quaedam publice utilia, quaedam privatim. publicum ius in sacris, in sacerdotibus, in magistratibus constitit. privatum ius tripertitum est: collectum etenim est ex naturalibus praeceptis aut gentium aut civilibus.'

[29] Cf. Ernst Holthöfer, 'Barnabé Brisson', in Michael Stolleis (ed.), *Juristen: Ein biographisches Lexikon. Von der Antike bis zum 20. Jahrhundert* (2001), p. 102.

complete description of the ancient Roman customs in the exchanges with other nations. Using these new materials also, Bodin continued, in this chapter, a common path in the construction of a public law of nations that still did not exist at the time, and his merit was soon acknowledged by Alberico Gentili and Hugo Grotius (1583–1641), who both gave a definitive form to this branch of human knowledge.[30]

For the solution to this problem, the foundation of a public law of nations, Bodin refers first of all to the legal tradition and to the arguments of the lawyers, who commented on the *Corpus juris civilis*, which is particularly evident in the chapter on the law of war. It has been observed that he prefers, for his definition of the just war, the straight civil law materials and omits, especially in the French version, the authorities that referred to the canon law tradition.[31] He therefore follows a traditional doctrine of the just war, but pursues more legal sources than theological authorities, which was rather mainstream in the discussion of this topic in the sixteenth century. He quotes Cicero on the necessity of respecting the given word even under the worst conditions, but he ignores the fourfold distinctions of the different kinds of war given by Isidore of Seville (560?–636), which was commonplace in theological discussions.[32]

This preference of Bodin's can be assumed as late evidence for the hypothesis of Michel Villey (1914–1988), who argues that in the Middle Ages and early modern times two separate traditions in natural law were active and influential for the understanding of war: a legal tradition linked to the study of the Roman law and a theological line influenced by the Stoic philosophy mediated by Cicero. This hypothesis can perhaps still be useful if we consider those lines of transmission not as substantial 'traditions', as Villey wanted them to be understood, but rather as 'communities of discourse' that used the same language and referred to the same authorities in order to treat common problems.[33]

[30] Ilari, *L'interpretazione storica del diritto di guerra romano* (n. 3); Diego Quaglioni, 'Note', in Margherita Isnardi Parente and Diego Quaglioni (eds.), *Jean Bodin, I sei libri dello stato: Volume terzo* (1988), p. 212.

[31] Isnardi Parente, 'Introduzione', in *Bodin, I sei libri dello stato*, pp. 76–7 (n. 3).

[32] Cicero, *De officiis* (44 BC), lib. I, cap. 13, par. 41: 'Ac de bellicis quidem officiis satis dictum est. Meminerimus autem etiam adversus infimos iustitiam esse servandam. Est autem infima condicio et fortuna servorum, quibus non male praecipiunt, qui ita iubent uti, ut mercennariis, operam exigendam, iusta praebenda. Cum autem duobus modis, id est aut vi aut fraude, fiat iniuria, fraus quasi vulpeculae, vis leonis videtur; utrumque homine alienissimum, sed fraus odio digna maiore. Totius autem iniustitiae nulla capitalior quam eorum, qui tum, cum maxime fallunt, id agunt, ut viri boni esse videantur. De iustitia satis dictum.' Isidorus Hispalensis, 'Etymologiarum libri XX', in Jacques-Paul Migne (ed.), *Patrologiae cursus completus. Series Latina* (1850), to. 82, lib. XVIII, cap. 1, par. 2, col. 639: '2. Quatuor autem sunt genera bellorum, id est, iustum, iniustum, civile, et plusquam civile. Iustum bellum est, quod ex praedicto geritur de rebus repetitis, aut propulsandorum hostium causa. Iniustum bellum est, quod de furore, non de legitima ratione initur. De quo in Republica dicit Cicero: *Illa iniusta bella sunt, quae sunt sine causa suscepta.*'

[33] Merio Scattola, *Krieg des Wissens – Wissen des Krieges. Konflikt, Erfahrung und System der literarischen Gattungen am Beginn der Frühen Neuzeit* (2006); Merio Scattola, 'Konflikt und Erfahrung. Über den Kriegsgedanken im Horizont frühneuzeitlichen Wissens', in Heinz-Gerhard Justenhoven and Joachim Stüben (eds.), *Kann Krieg erlaubt sein? Eine Quellensammlung zur politischen Ethik der Spanischen Spätscholastik* (2006), pp. 11–53; Merio Scattola, 'Zu einer europäischen Wissenschaftsgeschichte der Politik', in Christina Antenhofer, Lisa Regazzoni, and Astrid von Schlachta (eds.), *Werkstatt Politische Kommunikation. Netzwerke, Orte und Sprachen des Politischen* (2010), pp. 23–54.

Faced with the problem of rebuilding or reconstructing an already existing ancient public law of nations, however, the whole legal tradition or community of discourse did not offer sufficient materials. Bodin was clearly aware of this deficiency, since we no longer possess any collection of rules that the ancient Romans applied in their international relationships, and such a collection had actually never existed, but we now only have quite a large series of examples that show us all different forms of exchange between nations in antiquity. All these samples have been gathered together in the ancient histories, above all in the history *Ab Urbe condita* of Livy (59 BC–AD 17), and what we can now do is to compare all the different examples and extract from them all implicit general rules that the ancient Romans applied and that constitute the ancient public law of nations. We should therefore conclude that a general doctrine or a general description of a public law of nations can be reached only on the basis of history: not theology, not jurisprudence, but history.

In ancient *foedera*, nothing was inscribed except the names of the *fetials* of both peoples; in *sponsiones*, the names of the military commanders or the envoys were inserted, as a Roman consul [= Spurius Postumius Albinus], having made peace with the Samnites without orders from the Roman people, discussed in a public assembly. Based on his speech [Livius, lib. IX, cap. 8] and on historic accounts we can draw a distinction between *foedus* and *sponsio* on the one hand and between both of them and *pactio* on the other, even if this is generally confused by those inexperienced with the matter.[34]

This is exactly what Jean Bodin did in his two chapters on 'international' topics, above all in the sixth chapter on treaties, since he gathered together a large number of historical examples, from Livy, Polybius, Plutarch, and other ancient historians, and developed his doctrine mainly with their help.

On such a historical foundation of the public law of nations we can formulate two different observations dealing with the development of this discourse or form of knowledge in the early seventeenth century. Firstly, what Bodin did in this part of his work was highly congenial not only to his own method, but also to the way of arguing in legal and political matters, a way that was characteristic for the French kingdom in the late sixteenth and early seventeenth century. We notice that in early modern times political debates were clearly articulated within a number of detached communities that used a common language, were made of similar social components, developed exclusive literary genres for their communication and recognized one another as members of the same overarching community mostly by the way of quoting. In France, the political discussions were led (especially during the religious wars) by writers with a legal education who were inclined towards a historical explanation or foundation of the jurisprudence of their time. Most

[34] Bodin, *De republica libri sex*, lib. V, cap. 6, p. 578 D (n. 13): 'In foederibus antiquis praeter nomina fecialium utriusque populi nulla inscripta erant; in sponsionibus nomina ducum legatorumve inserebantur, ut consul Romanus [= Spurius Postumius Albinus], qui cum Samnitibus pacem iniussu populi Romani fecerat, in concione disseruit, ex cuius oratione [Livius, lib. IX, cap. 8] et ex historicorum fontibus discrimen foederis a sponsione et utriusque a pactione hausimus et expressimus, tametsi haec ab imperitis confunduntur'; English translation by the editors.

of them were also trained in legal matters and had a legal profession: as judges, attorneys, counsellors, or even as presidents of a court or parliament. The names of François Hotman (1524–1590), Étienne Pasquier (1529–1615), Jean Bodin, Barnabé Brisson, and Charles Loyseau (1566–1627) spring to mind. All of these figures used legal arguments in their works, referring preferably to Roman law sources that they interpreted in a historical way with the method of the *mos Gallicus* or humanistic jurisprudence. They also used the works of the great contemporary French historians like Philippe de Commines (1447–1511) or Jacques-August de Thou (1553–1617), who was a lawyer and magistrate. The legal treatise is the literary genre preferred in this French community of discourse.

Secondly, we can also observe that what Bodin did in his two chapters—and this was so familiar to his cultural environment—became, after him, exactly the program for a new and somehow independent branch of legal knowledge, that is, what we can call a 'public law of nations' built on the materials of ancient traditions. Through his strong inclination towards the *mos Italicus*, Alberico Gentili gave a broad historical foundation to his doctrines about warfare and diplomacy, and the historical examples of the ancient Romans were for him, too, the starting point of his explanations.[35] This programme was then developed in all its details by Hugo Grotius, who was also considered, in the first history of *jus naturae et gentium*, the founder of the discipline. He worked with an even more consistent method with historical and literary sources, and therefore this line of international law, which we call the 'public law of nations' and which had in him its first and most representative writer, had a humanistic and historical origin.

IV. Conclusions for the Doctrine of Sovereignty

The result of our considerations on the chapters that Jean Bodin dedicated to topics of 'international law' in his *Six livres de la république* can be summarized as follows:

1. As regards the quantity and perhaps also the quality of his arguments on the law of nations, Jean Bodin cannot be considered a 'classic' in international law.
2. Nevertheless, he offers important issues for discussion because he explicitly tried to develop, albeit briefly, a new branch of legal knowledge that had not existed before his time. This discipline had to comprise and to explain all rules that regulated the 'public' intercourse among commonwealths or 'nations'. In this sense, and in the language of the sixteenth century, Jean Bodin worked on the foundation of a 'public law of nations', a project that he shared with other authors of his time, chiefly with the theologians in Salamanca.
3. Given the fact that Roman jurisprudence did not contain a systematic and authoritative description of this topic, all rules, institutes, and customs of this 'public law of nations' had to be obtained and extracted from a careful study

[35] See, for further elaboration, the contribution by Wagner in this volume.

of examples and models preserved in ancient history and elaborated in the customs of 'at least the more civilized nations'.[36] This new branch of human knowledge was developed by Hugo Grotius mainly on the basis of historical and literary sources and therefore had a humanistic quality at its origin.

4. Jean Bodin and the authors who followed him conceived the sphere of the relationships among commonwealths with the traditional conceptual means of the *justum bellum* and of the *fides*, and this whole domain of legal and political experience was set under the principle of faith and loyalty. This implied that these relationships were ruled by a higher form of law, that is, by natural law, to which all sovereigns must be subjected. In this sense, kings and aristocratic or democratic councils did not recognize any superior instance when they were in their own territory, but when they went outside their boundaries and entered into an exchange with other commonwealths they had to acknowledge that there was a law superior to them, which they had to obey.

This result in the exterior is not without consequences for the interior of a commonwealth, since we can apply the same observation to the relationships within the commonwealth, and with this model or pattern we can ask whether a sovereign, that is, a king or a council, is really superior to all institutions and laws in his country. In other words, we must ask whether the sovereign is really absolute in his or her country. Looking at the interior situation, do all laws really depend on the will of the sovereign, or is there any law that is independent and superior to the sovereign? If this is the case, then the sovereign must obey it and would not be absolute in his power.

This is the case with the sovereignty of Jean Bodin because, as the famous eighth chapter of the first book explains, there are some situations that limit the power of a king. It is true that a king can freely decide on the laws in his country, and that he is in this sense sovereign, but at the same time there are some limits (*bornes*) that he cannot exceed. Firstly, he may not violate the commandments of natural law; secondly, he must respect the treaties he has entered into with other kings, since these are regulated by the natural law that is valid on the outside; thirdly, he must remain loyal to all constitutional contracts he has agreed upon with his subjects, because both parties of such a compact are free and equal and the king, as long as he is not

[36] Hugo Grotius, *De iure belli ac pacis libri tres* (1625), lib. I, cap. 1, par. 12: 'The existence of the Law of Nature is proved by two kinds of argument, a priori, and a posteriori, the former a more abstruse, and the latter a more popular method of proof. We are said to reason a priori, when we show the agreement or disagreement of any thing with a reasonable and social nature; but a posteriori, when without absolute proof, but only upon probability, any thing is inferred to accord with the law of nature, because it is received as such among all, or at least the more civilized nations. For a general effect can only arise from a general cause. Now scarce any other cause can be assigned for so general an opinion, but the common sense, as it is called, of mankind. There is a sentence of Hesiod that has been much praised, that opinions which have prevailed amongst many nations, must have some foundation. Heraclitus, establishing common reason as the best criterion of truth, says, those things are certain which generally appear so. Among other authorities, we may quote Aristotle, who says it is a strong proof in our favour, when all appear to agree with what we say, and Cicero maintains that the consent of all nations in any case is to be admitted for the law of nature.'

yet acknowledged as supreme magistrate, is not yet sovereign; fourthly, he cannot infringe a treaty or a compact that he has agreed on with his subjects before he was made king, because at that time he was not yet sovereign.[37] We would be correct in saying that a king is perfectly sovereign over positive law, which depends totally on his will, but he is not sovereign over natural law and divine law, which are still valid in his country and rule over some domains in the life of the subjects.

All these cases tell us that the sovereignty proposed by Jean Bodin is less absolute than we would imagine at first sight. We have gone an indirect way because we came to the interior of a commonwealth after observing its exterior; we came to sovereignty after considering faith and natural law. But in so doing we can discover through international law a side of public law that would otherwise remain hidden: the fact that sovereignty cannot be so absolute.

Selected Bibliography

Baldini, Artemio Enzo (ed.), *Jean Bodin: a 400 anni dalla morte. Bilancio storiografico e prospettive di ricerca* (Florence: Olschki, 1997).

Cardascia, Guillaume, 'Machiavel et Jean Bodin', *Bibliothèque d'Humanisme et Renaissance* 3 (1943), 129–67.

Goyard-Fabre, Simone, *Jean Bodin et le droit de la république* (Paris: PUF, 1989).

Ilari, Virgilio, *L'interpretazione storica del diritto di guerra romano fra tradizione romanistica e giusnaturalismo* (Milan: Giuffre, 1981).

Isnardi Parente, Margherita, 'Introduzione', in Margherita Isnardi Parente (ed.), Jean Bodin, *I sei libri dello stato: Volume primo* (Turin: U.T.E.T., 1964).

Quaglioni, Diego, *I limiti della sovranità. Il pensiero di Jean Bodin nella cultura politica e giuridica dell'età moderna* (Padova: Cedam, 1992).

Scattola, Merio, 'Diritto medievale e scienza politica moderna nella dottrina della sovranità di Jean Bodin', *Ius commune* 26 (1999), 165–209.

[37] Merio Scattola, 'Diritto medievale e scienza politica moderna nella dottrina della sovranità di Jean Bodin', *Ius commune* 26 (1999), 165–209; Merio Scattola, 'Ordine della giustizia e dottrina della sovranità in Jean Bodin', in Giuseppe Duso (ed.), *Il potere: Per la storia della filosofia politica moderna* (1999), pp. 61–75.

5

Alberico Gentili

Sovereignty, Natural Law, and the System of Roman Civil Law

Andreas Wagner

I. Introduction

The theory of international law offered by Alberico Gentili (1552–1608) is marked by a delicate, if not confusing, combination of the two principles of equal and unrestrained sovereignty of states, on the one hand, and of an international legal integration grounded on natural law, on the other. He achieves this by separating the presumed fact of universal natural and international legal obligation from the authority to interpret and enforce it, of which there is no universal agent (in the secular realm). Then, each sovereign (head of) state is the supreme interpreter of her own natural obligations. However, Gentili complements this principled argument with an emphasis on the historical convergence of many such interpretations, which makes for a more integrated international order than one would expect. The contingency of the factual convergence, both in terms of its substance and in terms of eventual incoherencies and inconsistencies, is offset by the system of the Roman *jus civile* that, according to Gentili, mirrors or incorporates the convergence and, at the same time, possesses a rationality that has been established by a long tradition of reflexive jurisprudence.

After a brief biographical sketch including an introduction to Gentili's most important texts on matters of international law (II), I will present his theory of international order and how it is articulated as a system (III). Besides its merits, I will also mention what I consider to be a major shortcoming of Gentili's theory, i.e. its deficit of effectively equal chances of participation in the interpretation and development of international law. I will then consider the various phases of the reception of Gentili's theory and relate these to its distinctive traits and to the agenda the respective recipients were pursuing (IV). The discussion of Gentili's role in the present debate will bring both the report on the reception and the chapter as a whole to a conclusion, explaining how the reception relates to and seems to affirm the criticism voiced in the systematic exposition (V).

II. Biographical Sketch

The eldest of seven children, Alberico Gentili was born in the Italian town of San Ginesio. He received a humanist education and, at the age of fifteen, was sent to the famous university of Perugia to study Roman civil law. He obtained his doctorate in 1572 and started to work as a judge, and soon after as an advocate for his native city. In 1579, Alberico had to flee the Inquisition because of the family's Protestant leanings, together with his father, Matteo, and his youngest brother, Scipio. After a short period of having moved from place to place, Scipio settled in Tübingen and later went to Altdorf, while Alberico and (soon after) his father continued to England.[1]

Gentili was able to gain the protection of Robert Dudley, Earl of Leicester, who at the time was also Chancellor of Oxford University. In 1581, the university acknowledged Gentili's doctoral degree, enabling him to teach Roman civil law. Besides the special problem of the marginal relevance of Roman law in England at the time, the main issue in discussions of Roman law was the dispute between the traditional *mos italicus* and the recent, humanist *mos gallicus*: Inspired by renaissance philological discussions, legal scholars of the 'modern' or 'French' mode—such as François Hotman, Jacques Cujas, Hugues Doneau, and others—would criticize the historically distorted and misleading pictures of ancient Roman law that traditional jurisprudence had established, using methods of textual criticism and focusing on the original wording and meaning. By contrast, scholars of the 'Italian' mode emphasized the gain in flexibility, in applicability to current problems as well as in consistency and coherence that the later (non-ancient) interpreters such as Baldus, Bartolus, or Accursius had brought to the law, perhaps to the negligible detriment of historical accuracy. From his early days at the Bartolist university of Perugia, Gentili was approaching matters according to the *mos italicus*.[2] However, the dispute is quite complex and especially in Gentili's case, the reception of the *mos gallicus* writings and ideas was much more sustained than a mere rebuke would have been.[3] In any case, it was important to Gentili to read Roman law texts

[1] For a more complete biographical account, Gesina van der Molen's, *Alberico Gentili and the Development of International Law: His Life Work and Times* (1937) (2nd rev edn, 1968) is still the most comprehensive work available in English. See also Angela de Benedictis, 'Gentili, Alberico', in *Dizionario biografico degli Italiani*, vol. 53 (1999), pp. 245–51; and Pepe Ragoni (ed.), *Alberico Gentili vita e opere* (2000).

[2] Among Gentili's earlier works unrelated to international law, *De Juris Interpretibus Dialogi Sex* (1582) should be mentioned. In this and other commentaries on Roman law, Gentili was defending Bartolus, Accursius, and others against both early and later writers of the *mos gallicus*: Budé, Alciati, Zasius, Cujas, and also, to an extent, against Hugues Doneau and François Hotman. Doneau was also one of Scipio Gentili's teachers during the latter's stay in Leiden; moreover, he helped him get established in Altdorf. Scipio also finished the edition of Doneau's *Commentarii de Iure Civili* (1604) after the author had died in 1591. François Hotman was the father of Jean Hotman, who was slightly less famous than his father; the son was a colleague of Gentili in Oxford, with whom the latter agreed on many points.

[3] Cf. Giovanni Minucci, 'Per una rilettura del metodo gentiliano', in Ferdinando Treggiari (ed.), *Alberico Gentili: La tradizione giuridica perugiana e la fondazione del diritto internazionale* (2010), pp. 29–56; G. Minucci, *Alberico Gentili tra* mos italicus *e* mos gallicus: *L'inedito commentario* Ad legem

from the perspective of current problems and, with this motivation, to study how they had come to be interpreted and applied to analogous problems over the course of time by jurisprudential discourse. The systematic rationality that the scholarly discourse and reception of Roman law had established was to become very important for Gentili, as we will see below.

In 1584, Gentili was asked by the court for his opinion regarding the appropriate verdict for Bernardino de Mendoza, the Spanish ambassador to England, who had been found involved in a conspiracy to kill Queen Elizabeth I. Gentili argued that he should be expelled rather than executed, and this was also the solution finally adopted by the court.[4] The following year, Gentili had further developed his theory of diplomatic immunity and published his first major work on subjects of international law: *De legationibus libri tres*.[5] While referring directly to Mendoza's case, it had obvious implications for the ongoing trial against Mary Stuart as well. At the age of thirty five, Gentili was named Regius Professor of Roman Law in 1587, and in 1588/89 he delivered three lectures on the law of war, initially published as *De iure belli commentationes tres* and nine years later, in a considerably expanded form, as *De iure belli libri tres* (1598).[6] While Gentili was consistently critical of the Humanists' tendencies to replace questions of law and justice with philological ones, he showed considerable humanist erudition and versatile rhetorical capabilities, e.g. in a work *On the Wars of the Romans*, which he published one year later.[7] Gentili had more or less close friendships with Giordano Bruno, with his fellow Oxonian Jean Hotman, and with his mentors and literary patrons Robert Dudley, Earl of Leicester, and the latter's nephew, the poet Philip Sidney. Among the more recent theological and juridical authors Gentili cited, there were members of the Iberian scholastics, like Vitoria, Soto, and Covarrubias as well as the Protestants Melanchton, Beza, Andreae, and others; however, there are also Italian and English authors, such as Nicolò de' Tudeschi (Panormitanus) and Thomas More. Among Humanist authors, Gentili mentions, among others, Erasmus, George Buchanan, Paulus Manutius, and Julius Caesar Scaliger.

In 1600, Gentili was admitted to the bar, joined the company of advocates at Gray's Inn and started working as advocate and legal counsellor in London. Near the end of his career, he was practising more than he was teaching: he spent most of his time at the Admiralty Court, where 'international' cases were adjudicated and where he, despite having been very critical of Spain and the Spanish foreign policy in earlier publications, had been appointed as an advocate for Spain. (Although

Julian de adulteriis (2002); Italo Birocchi, 'Il *De iure belli* e 'l'invenzione' del diritto internazionale', in Luigi Lacchè (ed.), *'Ius gentium ius communicationis ius belli' Alberico Gentili e gli orizzonti della modernità* (2009), pp. 101–38; and Guido Astuti, *Mos italicus e Mos gallicus nei Dialoghi 'De iuris interpretibus' di Alberico Gentili* (1937).

[4] As a second opinion, Gentili's fellow Oxonian Jean Hotman was approached as well, and he came to the same result.

[5] Cf. Alberico Gentili, *De Legationibus Libri Tres* (1924).

[6] Cf. Alberico Gentili, *De Iure Belli Commentationes Tres* (1589) and A. Gentili, *De Iure Belli Libri Tres* (1933).

[7] Cf. Alberico Gentili, *The Wars of the Romans* (2010).

Spain and England had reached peace in 1604,[8] the war between Spain and the United Provinces continued, and the court often heard cases of maritime law dealing with controversies that arose in England or in English waters between Spaniards and Dutch privateers.) While absent from teaching, Gentili's writing activities continued. For example, in 1605, he published his *Regales Disputationes Tres*, wherein he defined the rights of the king and rejected the right of the subjects to rebellion.[9] Finally, Gentili's last work, his *Hispanicae advocationis libri duo*, must be mentioned, in which he provided a summary of this practical work, mostly a collection of cases he had been involved in and of the arguments presented therein. It was left unpublished when Alberico Gentili died in London in 1608, but his brother Scipio published it posthumously in 1613.[10]

In the next part, I will present Gentili's general methodology and the main traits of his interpretation of international law. First, I will discuss in some detail his theory of sovereignty. This establishes the nature of the agents and the chief problem of international law, since it implies the impossibility of executive or interpretative institutions above the competing states. Second, I will turn to how Gentili's uptake of Stoic cosmopolitan morality establishes a natural law applicable to all states and constituting a universal legal order. Third, I will describe how Roman civil law establishes the rationality, i.e. the knowability, coherence, and consistency of that order, and also for its necessary flexibility, that is to say, how Roman law constitutes the international legal order as a *system* of law. Finally, the quasi-private law character of Gentili's Roman law (which allows it to cater for the principles of equal sovereignty of all states) leads me to critically discuss the lack of equal access of all affected parties to the processes of legal reasoning.

III. System and Order: Gentili's Synthesis of Sovereignty and Legal Integration

It is quite clear that Gentili was most interested in laws or rules regulating the relations between sovereign states. Bodin's theory of sovereignty had been around for a while already, and it proved to be immensely influential for Gentili. It meant that international law could only be based on either the actual consent of the parties or on natural law. It also meant that natural law could not be armed with authoritative institutions and coercive force above the level of the sovereign state. On the one hand, Gentili developed an approach to international relations that respected and even emphasized the sovereign equality of states, and, at the same time, held peace to be in fact attainable through the *voluntary adoption* of legal procedures such as arbitration and the regulations of what would today be called humanitarian

[8] According to van der Molen (n. 1), p. 58, Gentili was probably even involved in the drafting of the peace treaty.

[9] Cf. Alberico Gentili, *Regales Disputationes Tres* (1605). On the notion of sovereignty and especially on its implications for international law, see below, Section III.1.

[10] Cf. Alberico Gentili, *Hispanicae Advocationis Libri Duo* (1921).

law, i.e. the law of war.[11] On the other hand, treaties, arbitration, and explicitly consented agreements clearly represented only a very limited part of international law, so Gentili had to find a conceptual place for, and some substantial content of, *natural law*. And while this might be more obvious in questions concerning voluntary law, Gentili insisted that questions involving natural law should also be dealt with by legal scholars. One of the most famous aspects of his approach was his opposition to theologians. In fact, Gentili's famous exhortation for the theologians to remain silent in the domain of other disciplines[12] points to methodological as well as political issues of the time: With it, Gentili did not refer so much to earlier theologians who had dealt with international law. Rather, he referred to the Puritan faction that had, at the time, become very influential in the University of Oxford and among the advisors to the Crown, and whose aim was to morally purify the legal and political order by relying on and proceeding from the Holy Scriptures.[13] Against this, Gentili insisted that there had to be *juridical sources* and *juridical reasoning* constituting international legal rules and institutions.[14] The Roman civil law that Gentili was teaching comprised a corpus of norms and abstract principles, and of principles for their interpretation, which constituted a coherent and consistent system of a distinctly legal character.[15] But *prima facie*, it was also clear that it was a municipal law, linked to a very different context and to a very specific culture of reception and interpretation—according to both the *mos italicus* and the *mos gallicus* approaches—and was neither meant to, nor even could, provide the needed international laws or rules.[16] So Gentili first had to establish a new juridical argument about the possible sources of such rules, in terms of the grounds of their validity, but also in the more technical sense of where to look in order to discover those rules. His approach implied the use of ample examples of both ancient and contemporary history. Here Gentili's humanist education and erudition shines through; he used even more examples from historiographic or even literary sources than from legal texts in a narrow sense.[17] Using arguments such as overlapping

[11] One should, however, not miss the fact that the third book of Gentili's *De iure belli libri tres* is concerned with the *jus post bellum*, i.e. with the principles and rules that must be followed in order for a post-victory peace to be a lasting one.

[12] 'Silete theologi in munere alieno' (*De iure belli*, lib. I, ch. 12, ed. James Brown Scott (1933), vol. 2, p. 57.

[13] Cf. G. van der Molen (n. 1), pp. 210–19 and 245–68. Cf. also Christopher N. Warren, *Literature and the Law of Nations, 1580-1680* (2015), p. 231.

[14] This could be the reason why throughout his entire career Gentili has no problems quoting authors of the Spanish Scholastics like Francisco de Vitoria and Domingo de Soto affirmingly, who seem to agree with him on that point to a considerable extent. Besides theological authorities in the narrow sense, these authors included the legal tradition among their preferred authorities and they pushed a good part of moral theological discourse into the direction of a somewhat juridical reasoning, focused on considerations of rights and legitimacy. Cf. Andreas Wagner, 'Francisco de Vitoria', in Rafael Domingo and Javier Martínez-Torrón (eds.), *Great Christian Jurists in Spanish History* (forthcoming 2017); Andreas Wagner and Anselm Spindler, 'The School of Salamanca', in Marco Sgarbi (ed.), *Encyclopedia of Renaissance Philosophy* (forthcoming 2017); and the various essays in Kirstin Bunge et al. (eds.), *Kontroversen um das Recht. Contending for Law* (2013).

[15] For more on the conception of a system and its applicability to Roman law, see below, Section III.3.

[16] And neither could the English common law, nor canon law, of course.

[17] On the relation between literature and early modern international law cf. Warren (n. 13), on Gentili see esp. ch. 2 and Christopher N. Warren, 'Gentili, the Poets, and the Laws of War', in Benedict

customs, the test of time, and an analogy between sovereigns and private citizens, he finally identified Roman civil law to be as good an expression of natural law as one can hope to find, and he set out to explain and adapt its rules and concepts for the cases and issues he was interested in:

Moreover, the law which is written in those books of Justinian is not merely that of the state, but also that of the nations and of nature; and with this last it is all so in accord, that if the empire were destroyed, the law itself, although long buried, would yet rise again and diffuse itself among all the nations of mankind. This law therefore holds for sovereigns also, although it was established by Justinian for private individuals.[18]

1. Doctrine of sovereignty

Gentili's theory of war very clearly shows how much he subscribed to a Bodinian notion of *sovereignty* as the supreme, indivisible, and absolute power of the ruler over the citizens. For him, this fundamental concept also implies the impossibility of any exterior legal authority superior to the sovereign—except, of course, for God and natural law.[19]

Kingsbury and Benjamin Straumann (eds.), *The Roman Foundations of the Law of Nations: Alberico Gentili and the Justice of Empire* (2010), pp. 146–62; Merio Scattola, *Krieg des Wissens, Wissen des Krieges: Konflikt, Erfahrung und System der literarischen Gattungen am Beginn der Frühen Neuzeit* (2006).

[18] Gentili, *De iure belli libri tres*, lib. I, ch. III, ed. Brown Scott (n. 3), p. 17. Also note how Justinian and the *Corpus juris* keep reappearing throughout Gentili's presentation of the sources of his arguments in *De iure belli*, ibid., pp. 8–11: In a first approach based on custom, Gentili explains how, through the vast reach of the Roman Empire and through its even more extensive commerce, 'knowledge could be gained of all peoples, thus the law of nations could be defined' and 'our jurists then have been able to compile this law from absolutely all nations' (p. 9). In a second approach based on natural reason, Gentili mentions intuitive self-evidence, supported by examples, the examples and utterances of great authorities, arguments and reasoning, the Holy Scripture and 'not a few things from the civil law of Justinian which it will be possible to adapt to our uses [and that most properly so, for] the laws which were laid down by the philosophers and approved by the judgement of every age undoubtedly possess natural reason' (p. 11). Cf. Benjamin Straumann / Benedict Kingsbury, 'Introduction', in Benedict Kingsbury and Benjamin Straumann (eds.), *The Roman Foundations of the Law of Nations: Alberico Gentili and the Justice of Empire* (2010), pp. xviii–xxii; Benjamin Straumann, 'The *Corpus iuris* as a Source of Law Between Sovereigns in Alberico Gentili's Thought', in Benedict Kingsbury and Benjamin Straumann (eds.), *The Roman Foundations of the Law of Nations: Alberico Gentili and the Justice of Empire* (2010), pp. 101–23; or Jeremy Waldron, 'Ius gentium. A Defence of Gentili's Equation of the Law of Nations and the Law of Nature', ibid., pp. 283–96. According to van der Molen (n. 1), Gentili assumed rather a clear *separation* of international and Roman civil law, but the analytic and formal separation of the two systems of law does not negate their analogy, on the basis of which it is possible to infer rules and principles of international law.

[19] Cf. Peter Schröder, 'Vitoria, Gentili, Bodin: Sovereignty and the Law of Nations', in Benedict Kingsbury and Benjamin Straumann (eds.), *The Roman Foundations of the Law of Nations* (2010), pp. 163–86; Christian Zendri, 'Alberico Gentili e il *De iure belli*. Metodo e fonti', *Laboratoire italien* 10 (2010), pp. 45–63; Diego Quaglioni, 'The Italian "Readers" out of Italy - Alberico Gentili (1552-1608)', in Howell A. Lloyd (ed.), *The Reception of Bodin* (2013), pp. 371–86. See also the contribution of Merio Scattola to the present volume. For the roots of the discourse on sovereignty in Roman legal discourse, see Kenneth Pennington, *The Prince and the Law, 1200-1600: Sovereignty and Rights in the Western Legal Tradition* (1993).

In contrast to Gentili's elaborate discussions of natural law,[20] the concept of sovereignty is more of a basic axiom of his theory of international law: it is not so much justified in a meta-juridical explanation, but rather presupposed by his legal arguments. It is only in a late text, *Regales Disputationes Tres* (1605), that he explicitly and extensively addresses the internal constitution of sovereign rule, its limits, and the rights of the subjects. And while one can find in *De iure belli* dispersed arguments to the effect that ruler and subjects are mutually bound by a social compact, and that the subjects—when they manage to find a legitimate representation in some noblemen—have a certain right of deposing a tyrannical ruler, in this later text, Gentili leans quite unequivocally to an absolutist conception of sovereign rule. He starts the first of these disputations, quite fittingly entitled *De potestate Regis absoluta*, with the Ulpianian 'What pleases the prince has the force of law, for by a regal law the people has transferred to him and conferred upon him all its power and authority'.[21] And going through classical authors, civil law, Aristotle, and Bodin, he identifies the English Royal Prerogative Powers with a '*potestas extraordinaria, legibus absoluta*'.[22]

On the one hand, this conception of sovereignty allows for a ruler to be an agent in legal relations and interactions; she is not only representing her commonwealth, but is related to it and to all her subjects in a way that explicitly provides her with the competences to commit the whole of it and all of them to legal obligations, to claim and to possess titles in the name of all of it and all of them.[23] On the other hand, and at the same time, this also puts limits on international law: with the strong concept of sovereignty comes the impossibility of any human institution that would be superior to the sovereign. There cannot be any (human) legislator above the sovereign, no legal proceedings to which she would be obliged to submit and no interpreter of the sovereign's obligations, duties and entitlements other than the sovereign herself. Thus, in the end, the term 'legal obligation' might boil down to the principle of sovereign equality.[24]

[20] On the often rather metaphorical nature of his arguments, and on the moral character of international legal obligation according to Gentili, cf. Andreas Wagner, 'Francisco de Vitoria and Alberico Gentili on the Legal Character of the Global Commonwealth', *Oxford Journal of Legal Studies* 31(3) (2011), 565–82.

[21] 'Quod principi placuit, legis habet vigorem: utpote cum lege regia, quae de eius imperio lata est, populus ei et in eum omne suum imperium et potestatem conferat.' (D. 1.4.1 pr., quoted in *Regales Disputationes Tres* [n. 9], p. 5).

[22] *Regales Disputationes Tres* (n. 9), p. 10. This doctrine is an expression of the general legitimatory outlook that leads Diego Panizza to describe Gentili as *giurista ideologo*, cf. Diego Panizza, *Alberico Gentili, giurista ideologo nell'Inghilterra Elisabettiana* (1981). On Gentili's doctrine of sovereignty cf. also van der Molen (n. 1), pp. 219–40, who writes 'just as Bodin in France, he was the theoretical founder of absolutism in England' (p. 239). Cf. also Alain Wijffels, 'Assolutismo politico e diritto di resistenza: la disputatio gentiliana "De vi civium in Regem semper iniusta"', in *Alberico Gentili: l'uso della forza nel diritto internazionale* (2006), pp. 433–57; and Diego Quaglioni (n. 19).

[23] Relating this to literary taxonomies, Warren associates this with the trope of *epic distance*, implying both distance and detachment, on the one hand, and representation, on the other. Cf. Warren (n. 13).

[24] With regard to Gentili's conception of war, Diego Panizza makes this very point in 'Political Theory and Jurisprudence in Gentili's *De iure belli*. The Great Debate Between 'theological' and 'humanist' perspectives from Vitoria to Grotius', *IILJ Working Paper* 15 (2005), 53.

As an aside, it also means that *only* sovereigns, or those who can legitimately claim some form of authorization or sponsorship from a sovereign, are agents in international legal relations and interactions. This sponsorship is unspectacular insofar as it is a default assumption. Nevertheless, it is explicitly denied to rebels, pirates, brigands, and runaway slaves who have disrupted precisely the ties to their sovereign. They have 'withdrawn from the agreement and broken the treaty of the human race', thereby making them 'common enemies of all mankind' to which international law (and the law of war, in particular) no longer applies.[25]

Hence, war, for example, cannot be defined as the enforcement of law on a perpetrator, since the latter has just as much authority to define the rights and obligations in play, the compliances and infringements as anyone else. War is a legally regulated mechanism necessary to produce a decision in cases of conflict where legal judgment cannot be rendered:

> [T]here cannot be judicial processes between supreme sovereigns (*summos Principes*) or free peoples unless they themselves consent, since they acknowledge no judge or superior. . . . Therefore it was inevitable that the decision between sovereigns should be made by arms. 'War', says Demosthenes, 'is made against those who cannot be controlled by the laws, but judicial decisions are rendered in the case of private citizens.'[26]

However, at this very point, having just articulated the definition of sovereignty and the inevitability of war, Gentili continues to point out that he is 'speaking here only of a real and actual necessity',[27] and not merely a theoretical one: the Roman institution of appeal, and its international counterpart, the institution of arbitration, provide mechanisms that quite often enabled the settlement of conflicts without either defining the parties as subjects to a superior authority or resorting to the violence of war. Again, multiple historical examples allow him to argue:

> that those who avoid this kind of contest by arbitration and resort at once to the other, that is, to force, may understand that they are setting their faces against justice, humanity, and good precedent, and that they are rushing to arms of their own free will, because they are unwilling to submit to any one's verdict.[28]

Hence the inference from the unavailability of a superior authority to the legitimacy of war is not cogent, and it is a duty of morality and of natural law to seek compromise and arbitration. War is a last resort—the justice of which depends on it being in fact necessary. And the uncertain expectations of compliance to international commitments are not sufficient to create such factual necessity, for if the

[25] With these concepts of *unjust enemy* and *hostis humani generis*, Gentili places certain individuals and communities outside of the legal realm altogether. Commentators have pointed out that this plays a role in colonial policies no less than in dealing with pirates and brigands in the strict sense. Cf. the contributions of Noel Malcolm, Alexis Blane/Benedict Kingsbury, Anthony Pagden, and Randall Lesaffer to Benedict Kingsbury and Benjamin Straumann (eds.), *The Roman Foundations of the Law of Nations: Alberico Gentili and the Justice of Empire* (2010).

[26] Gentili, *De iure belli libri tres*, lib. I, ch. III (ed. Brown Scott [n. 6], p. 16). See also ch. XIV (pp. 61–3).

[27] Gentili, *De iure belli libri tres*, lib. I, ch. III (ed. Brown Scott [n. 6], p. 16).

[28] Gentili, *De iure belli libri tres*, lib. I, ch. III (ed. Brown Scott [n. 6], p. 16).

norms and agreements are fair, i.e. if they truly provide for the common advantage based on equal respect for all parties, they result in compliance and a secure and lasting peace.[29]

A couple of consequences can be extrapolated to follow from this set-up: the legal character of the international order and of international law is neither constituted by, nor even necessarily related to, their reliable enforcement. On the one hand, there are reasons and historical precedent for trusting an international order based on fair agreements and equal respect to establish a secure and lasting peace and promote the advantages of each individual state—even when the rights and obligations of each state in principle are up for more or less unrestricted interpretation of that state. On the other hand, there is a law prescribing the compliant behaviour of the individual sovereigns and which lies outside of their discretion, even though it is not enforced. The whole constellation of equally sovereign states deliberately coming to fair agreements and submitting to arbitration procedures is framed by the order of international law. The obligatory character of this order is then explained in terms of natural law, and there is a certain propensity of Gentili to use moral terms and metaphors. For Gentili, putting the norms of the international order beyond the scope of subjective reasoning means assuming that it has been generated and legitimized outside of, independently of, and prior to any political association and deliberation. Second, it explains the private character of the subjects of such law and of their resolutions. And third, it suggests that in the search for effective and substantial norms, history and historical systems of norms seem to respond better to the private authority of those subjects than philosophical constructions of their presumed resolutions.

2. Stoic morality

Gentili is deeply influenced by Stoic moral philosophy, which makes for a second characteristic trait of his theory: the values of peace, liberty, unity, civility, and humanity are central to Gentili's outlook. Translated to the legal realm, they are concentrated in the different aspects of the guiding principle of *justice* and constitute a normative framework of *natural law*. The Stoic roots of Gentili's principle of justice are above all apparent in its universalist dimension: for Gentili, justice can only be rightly understood against the horizon of a universal community, a *respublica magna*, which connects all mankind and which abstracts from social, cultural, and even religious particularities.[30] However, this conception is also Stoic insofar as

[29] In this passage (at p. 15), Gentili explicitly discusses the problem of the uncertain compliance of parties to treaties and refers the reader to the third book of his treatise, where he discusses measures that parties should take to ensure lasting peace. The most important common denominator is justice and equal respect: cf. Gentili, *De iure belli libri tres*, lib. III, ch. XIII (ed. Brown Scott [n. 6]), pp. 353–5.

[30] This relationship of justice to a form of community is similar in Machiavelli's oeuvre. Machiavelli, however, understands this only with respect to a particular community while Gentili refers to the universal frame. See the contribution by Roth-Isigkeit in this volume.

it abstracts even from political institutions—it is not the law of any political community or of concrete institutions that would legislate or enforce it.

On the one hand, then, the orientation of natural law towards justice and the orientation of international relations towards those values are often spelled out in *moral* terms and in appeals to moral values (such as *amor, benevolentia, caritas*);[31] in this sense, the universal principle of justice constitutes moral rights for, and places moral obligations on, the sovereigns in their relation to one another. On the other hand, the universal community and its normative order conceives and addresses its subjects directly, in their humanity, without the mediation of common institutions, which makes it akin to a *private* law order. In this sense, sovereigns stand in relation to each other just as private citizens stand in relation to each other within the state.

Moreover, both the abstract notion of transcultural humanity as an order and the origin of that order in plain human nature itself make the recognition and formulation of substantial norms implementing those universal principles a particularly difficult epistemological problem. For Gentili, these norms are not easily available to the sober reasoning of individuals:

> Such laws are not written, but inborn; we have not learned, received, and read them, but we have wrested, drawn, and forced them out of nature herself. We have not received them through instruction, but have acquired them at birth; we have gained them, not by training, but by instinct.[32]

Thus, in spite of occasional recourses to 'philosophers and other wise men' whose habit it is 'to speak according to the promptings of nature',[33] in the end Gentili opts to look for such norms in processes and insights that transcend individual reasoning—it is the examples, historical precedent as well as historically tested and proven norms that offer an articulation of natural law.

In the end, Gentili identifies this natural law with international law: he heaps up examples of 'international' issues, of state conduct towards other states, as they have been reported in ancient literature and notable from contemporary history; and connecting these issues with their appraisal by historians and legal scholars with their public evaluation and their historical reception, he shows how they transcend particular polities and conjunctures and how they exhibit universal rules. Vice versa, if it is by historical examples of customs and treaties that one identifies natural law, one can immediately recognize its international dimension. In effect, the beginning of the passage just quoted above indicates that the 'inborn laws' that have been 'forced out of nature herself' are precisely international law: 'But there is another more elegant definition of the law of nations . . . that there are everywhere certain unwritten laws, not enacted by men . . . but given to them by God'.[34]

[31] See also the contribution by Schaffner in this volume.
[32] Gentili, *De iure belli libri tres*, lib. I, ch. I (ed. Brown Scott [n. 6], p. 10).
[33] Gentili, *De iure belli libri tres*, lib. I, ch. I (ed. Brown Scott [n. 6], p. 11).
[34] Gentili, *De iure belli libri tres*, lib. I, ch. I (ed. Brown Scott [n. 6], p. 9f). For Gentili's identification of natural and international law, cf. e.g. Waldron (n. 18).

3. Roman civil law as substance and as system

In this approach of seeking historical norms of 'international' practice and of its critical reception by historical and contemporary authors, Gentili finds Roman law to be *the prime* example of such law: It had been designed to be applicable throughout the Roman empire and hence is suitable to a diverse set of social contexts. (Gentili points out that the laws that the Roman jurists have established have been found in commercial, diplomatic, and belligerent interaction with 'absolutely all nations' known at the time.[35]) Also with respect to the temporal dimension, the sheer duration of its operative validity, i.e. being in effect, means that it has been tested and historically proven to provide a mechanism for social integration effective in the most diverse circumstances. And while it provides very concrete norms, which lend themselves to easy application to factual situations, it has been proven flexible enough to be adjusted to new requirements. All of this signifies a certain emancipation of Roman law from its genesis in the legislative will of concrete human beings and substantiates its articulation to human nature's universal normative reason. Thus, Gentili writes:

> [T]hat which has successively seemed acceptable to all men should be regarded as representing the intention and purpose of the entire world (*totius orbis decretum fuisse existimetur*).[36]

Moreover, to a large extent, the Roman law of the *Corpus juris civilis* is a private law, regulating the relations and interactions between free and equal citizens. Its republican heritage guarantees the fundamental respect for—in fact it implies the utmost relevance of—the equal liberty of its subjects. Thus, the legal subjects and acts that it regulates are highly analogous to the context of international relations, and Roman law is perfectly suitable to conceptualize the status and interactions between sovereigns.[37] In this perspective, and in terms of both its structure and its substance, Roman law is quasi identical to natural law and, therefore, identical to international law.

Thus, Gentili's 'natural-historical' approach allows him to reconstruct many substantial norms of the international order through an investigation of Roman law. But it does not solve the task of establishing a *system* of international law: while history may expose some rules, it does not, in and of itself, render them as a coherent and comprehensive set of rules, the relations between which follow rational rules themselves. In logic and philosophy of science, a *formal system* consists of a language (alphabet, words, and grammar), basic axioms and rules of inference.[38] It is remarkable that the Roman law of Gentili's time—with its definitions of categories (e.g. in Gaius's *Institutions*, I, 8-12), its norms (e.g. on usucaption *Inst* II, 42–44) as well as its principles of argumentation and interpretation (e.g. in *Digest*

[35] Gentili, *De iure belli libri tres*, lib. I, ch. III (ed. Brown Scott [n. 3], p. 9).

[36] Gentili, *De iure belli libri tres*, lib. I, ch. I (ed. Brown Scott [n. 3], p. 8).

[37] Cf. Straumann (n. 18).

[38] Cf. e.g. Haskell B. Curry, *Outlines of a Formalist Philosophy of Mathematics* (1951), chapter IV. For an application of a related, albeit more differentiated, concept of 'system' to the history of ideas, cf. Scattola (n. 17).

D. 50.17)—corresponded, to an extent, to such a system. In fact, in some respects it represented an even more 'rational' type of system, where glossators and post-glossators had invested great effort to establish that the whole system was consistent (non-contradictory) and complete (i.e. that all the problems and solutions one may encounter are susceptible to be expressed and treated in the system).

However, there is a tension between a narrowly logical constructivist perspective and Gentili's historicist approach. Our assessment in terms of systematic construction is then not meant to suggest that Gentili sought to derive or develop a comprehensive system of natural law in a logical or 'geometrical' fashion from a few axioms or a single grounding principle. Such an approach would in effect seem even contrary to his insistence on historical reason and on empirically founded knowledge. Also, his texts are concerned with special areas of international law, such as the law of war or of diplomatic immunities, rather than with constructing a complete account of international law and its analytical structure. Thus, some basic principles, concepts, and ambitions of the construction and partitioning of the ancient 'system'—like Gaius's orderly treatment of persons, things, and actions,[39]—do not feature in analogous ways in Gentili's arguments. And yet, in terms of legal practice, it would without doubt be immensely advantageous if the rules of international law, which could be found by historical investigation and by interpretation of historical phenomena, were exhaustive — and if they would not, at some point, turn out to be contradictory. It is in this sense that the second decisive trait of the Roman legal tradition, its systematic character, weighs in. It is precisely the Bartolist tradition of post-glossators and commentators, so dear to Gentili, who have sought to harmonize the different sets of norms in the *Corpus juris civilis*, to elaborate its systematic rationality and to articulate it with other contemporary sources of law in order to re-establish it as a living, flexible and applicable law.[40]

In terms of this volume, the *international order* then is the set of legal subjects—sovereign heads of states—the relations of whom are governed by a historically grown complex of rules. The substance of these rules is defined topically, but two forceful formal principles can be discerned: sovereign equality and cosmopolitan morality. The topical and historical character of that order makes a systematic knowledge of it impossible, at least insofar as that would mean a priori knowledge in the form of sentences that would be methodologically deduced from simple fundamental principles. On the other hand, in spite of its topical character, it is possible to reasonably acknowledge the coherence and consistency of this order, since it corresponds to a corpus of normative knowledge the rationality of which has been long discussed and historically tested: Roman law is a *systematization* of the international order in the slightly different sense of a transparent and reliable cognitive representation of it.

[39] Cf. *Institutions* I, 3.

[40] Cf. Jan Schröder, *Recht als Wissenschaft. Geschichte der juristischen Methodenlehre in der Neuzeit (1500-1933)* (2nd edn, 2012), pp. 25–96; Alain Wijffels, 'Early-Modern Scholarship on International Law', in Alexander Orakhelashvili (ed.), *Research Handbook on the Theory and History of International Law* (2011), pp. 23–60.

Roman law carefully balances respect for sovereign autonomy and cosmopolitan morality, and Gentili invests considerable effort to demonstrate how it is expedient for, and malleable by, sovereign commonwealths, and how, at the same time, it puts a moral force in effect. In and of itself, it is not applicable to the relations and processes between sovereign rulers; however, taken as an articulation of natural law, it makes for a law to which even sovereign rulers are subject. And it brings along its self-knowledge, its flexible structure and its respect for the ultimate relevance of the individual person. In other words, international law is operating analogous to private law, yet without overarching legislative or executive authority, thereby allowing extensive freedom to its subjects: the sovereigns.[41]

4. A brief critical comment

On the one hand, Gentili clearly puts great emphasis on the fact that natural law and international law bind sovereign rulers, and that it can hence coordinate their relations towards an ideal of peace and justice. On the other hand, the sweeping role of sovereignty, the private law character of international law leaves considerable discretion to the sovereigns in interpreting their respective claims and obligations. Finally, the close relationship between Roman law and a particular tradition of interpretation and scholarship together make for a tendency of *reification* of natural law. Its universalism and dynamic character are conceptualized only *ex post*, not as characteristics of its procedures that could find an analogous expression in current institutions and diplomatic practices open to all concerned agents as well. As Gentili's own text, *De armis Romanis*, shows, the factual asymmetries of power and the injustices resulting from them, are not easily made a subject of legal discussions if every sovereign is free to move in her own interpretative universe, and especially so if history has worked towards a quasi-monopoly of legal interpretation coinciding with the wielders of international power.[42]

Structurally, what Gentili's private/international/natural law paradigm may be missing most urgently is a forum to prevent the law from only ever working to the benefit of the powerful, a forum for all parties concerned to participate in effectively on equal standing, and to agree on *common interpretations* of the law and its purposes, and hence also on *common interests and values*.

In the final section, I will turn to various phases of the reception of Gentili's theory of international law and not only explain how different stakes and interests could be articulated to shifts in emphasis, but also what one can discern as recurring traits of the various references to Gentili. This will take me to the final, conclusive

[41] Cf. Waldron (n.18).

[42] On the fact that identifying a particular domain of scholarly authority, of professional expertise with and for an otherwise purportedly universal normative system, in turn, implies asymmetrical relations of power, cf. Anthony Pagden, 'Gentili, Vitoria, and the Fabrication of a "Natural Law of Nations"', in Benedict Kingsbury and Benjamin Straumann (eds.), *The Roman Foundations of the Law of Nations: Alberico Gentili and the Justice of Empire* (2010), pp. 340–61.

section where, in a more tentative appraisal, current debates will be linked to the historical reception as well as to the previously mentioned point of criticism.

IV. Reception

1. (Near) contemporaries

While Gentili may have been involved in disputes with Puritan scholars in Oxford, the more prominent contemporary authors of a Catholic theory of international law hardly took notice of him. The theologian Suárez does not cite him in his *De legibus*, which appeared shortly after *De iure belli*, and the Spanish jurist Juan de Solórzano Pereira cites Gentili only once in his compendium of the law concerning colonial policy (though he cites the brother, Scipio, twice on marriage law).

In the domain of international law, more specifically, and outside of Ibero-Scholastic discourse, however, the reception is clearly visible. In particular, Grotius' *De Jure Belli ac Pacis* contains a dozen references to Gentili's *De Jure Belli, De Legationibus*, and the *Hispanica Advocatio*; Grotius acknowledges his debt to Gentili in the Prolegomena to this work, even though, at the same time, he sharply criticizes the topical approach described above (§ 38).[43] But also later authors of the Anglo-Dutch debates, such as John Selden, Richard Zouche, Samuel Rachel, and Cornelis van Bijnkershoek, referred to Gentili as one of several important authors, for example, in the debate on the freedom of the seas, concerning diplomatic immunities and, of course, in arguments about the law of war. In subsequent discussions, and in a variety of fields, Gentili is regularly quoted, although he does not appear to occupy a particularly prominent role.[44]

2. International arbitration (late nineteenth century)

As Martti Koskenniemi has argued,[45] in the 1870s there had been a decisive development in international law: at the time, a group of lawyers established the domain of modern international law as a special field of law and jurisprudence, and it fought to establish a liberal international law as a compulsory framework for international politics. One key moment in this period was the establishment of international arbitration as a means of conflict resolution before recourse to war and military

[43] Cf. early studies such as Carl von Kaltenborn, *Die Vorläufer des Hugo Grotius auf dem Gebiete des* ius naturae et gentium (1847), but above all the thorough and balanced study by Peter Haggenmacher, 'Grotius and Gentili: A Reassessment of Thomas E. Holland's Inaugural Lecture', in Hedley Bull, Benedict Kingsbury, and Adam Roberts (eds.), *Hugo Grotius and International Relations* (1992), pp. 133–76. Haggenmacher also reports on a couple of letters Grotius wrote confirming Gentili's influence as well.

[44] He is mentioned, in some cases frequently, in works of Samuel Pufendorf, Johann Gottlieb Heineccius, Adam Friedrich Glafey, Christian Thomasius, and others.

[45] Cf. Martti Koskenniemi, *The Gentle Civilizer of Nations: The Rise and Fall of International Law 1870-1960* (2002).

measures could be taken. The success of early arbitration procedures led to ambitious projects of codification and ratification of international law in treaties such as the first Geneva Convention in 1864, or the Hague Convention in 1899.

In this struggle by peace societies and liberal international lawyers to establish arbitration and large treaties, Gentili was seen to have played an exceptional role in the genesis of international law: his theory provided the adequate measure between sovereignty and international legal coordination. Consequently, the identity of natural and international law as well as the reliance on the substance of Roman law in Gentili's thought were downplayed, and emphasis was put on the possibilities of integrating a strong conception of sovereignty with compulsory legal procedures and on giving a systematic account of international legal rules. In this way, Gentili appeared as a founder of a positivist and liberal tradition in international law.

Moreover, Gentili's rebuke of theological interference in legal matters—*Silete theologi in munere alieno*—was much emphasized in the wake of Italian post-Risorgimento and made him a very influential, even iconic, figure in some contexts.[46]

The central text establishing Gentili as one of the figureheads of international law at the time was certainly Thomas Erskine Holland's Inaugural Lecture in Oxford of 1874. This was shortly thereafter followed by a new Latin edition of Gentili's *De iure belli* prepared by Holland and an Italian translation of that same work by Antonio Fiorini, both in 1877.[47]

3. Breakdown of the League of Nations and the question of non-discrimination (early twentieth century)

After the First World War, the League of Nations built upon what the Hague conventions had already established. On the other hand, problems that had beset the League from the outset were exacerbated and, in many crises during the 1930s, the League could not (or did not) do much to prevent or contain these events. Given the sobering development regarding the League of Nations and the fickle commitment of its members, questions concerning arbitration as well as the integration of national sovereignty and interests with compulsory international legal procedures were constantly on the table. Since Gentili's texts responded to this

[46] On this phase of reception in general, on Holland's role in the 'discovery' of the previously 'forgotten' author and on the Italian *Gentili-mania* and its relation to the development of international law, see Luigi Nuzzo, 'Alberico Gentili "internazionalista" tra storia e storiografia', in Luigi Lacchè (ed.), *'Ius gentium ius communications ius belli': Alberico Gentili e gli orizzonti della modernità* (2009), pp. 73–99; and Luigi Lacchè, '"Celebrato come una gloria nazionale": Pietro Sbarbaro e il "Risorgimento" di Alberico Gentili', in Pepe Ragoni (ed.), *Alberico Gentili: Atti dei Convegni nel quarto centenario della morte*, vol. II (2010), pp. 189–295.

[47] Cf. Thomas Erskine Holland, 'Alberico Gentili', reprinted in Thomas Erskine Holland, *Studies in International Law: Reprint of the Edition Oxford 1898* (1979), pp. 1–39; Antonio Fiorini, *Del diritto di guerra di Alberigo Gentile* (1877); for a recent bibliography, see Diego Quaglione, 'Introduzione', in Alberico Gentili, *Il diritto di guerra* (2008), pp. IX–XXXIII.

problem, they formed part of the academic and publicist initiatives that sought to strengthen international law. It was an American initiative, the *Carnegie Endowment for International Peace,* established in 1910 by the industrialist Andrew Carnegie, which was one of the most powerful social and cultural forces advocating for the adoption of strong mechanisms of international law (and for the United States to join the League of Nations). Among other activities, the Carnegie Endowment funded a series of *Classics of International Law*, coordinated by James Brown Scott, which featured original and translated versions of the works of classical authors such as Grotius, Vitoria, and Gentili: Beginning in the 1920s, Gentili's *Hispanicae Advociationis* (1921), his *De legibus* (1924) and, once more, his *De iure belli* (1933) appeared in this series.[48] In this vein, Gentili was presented as one of the champions of an effective, institutionalized order of international law.

While the *Classics* series was a larger attempt to represent the general pedigree of international legal theory and doctrine, its diversity, and the theoretical precision of solutions that had historically been developed, there were also more focused approaches: in 1937, the Dutch jurist Gesina van der Molen presented her dissertation on the biography of Alberico Gentili. Beyond the general ambitions presented above, she underlined the close connection between Gentili's jurisprudential views, his publication activities, and his religious conviction. She identified both a tendency in Gentili to maintain the superior position and importance of God for natural and international law, and, at the same time, an insistence on a framework of public religious toleration.

After the end of the Second World War, the Nuremberg trials of 1945–1946 and the establishment of the United Nations in 1945, the stakes of reading Gentili seemed to have changed fundamentally: Carl Schmitt's favourite quote from Gentili was the famous 'Silete theologi'. For Schmitt, who famously placed the responsibility for deciding on the state of emergency on the coming into effect of the legal system as a whole and in the hands of the sovereign,[49] this meant the conceptual repudiation of any normative authority above the state, be it theological, moral, or legal. The bottom line of Gentili's theory, Schmitt argued in his *Nomos of the Earth* from 1950, was Gentili's non-discriminatory conception of war, fitting his (Schmitt's) idea of sovereignty as the point from which it is possible to define legality and ethical principles of law in the first place.[50] Thus, Gentili was used rather to argue *against* an internationally institutionalized legal framework that would curtail the freedoms of individual sovereign states.

4. Historiographic work (late twentieth century)

While, to some extent, Holland's lecture from 1874 was already based on thorough historical research and provided a number of historical details, van der

[48] Cf. Christopher Rossi, *Broken Chain of Being: James Brown Scott and the Origins of Modern International Law* (1998).

[49] Carl Schmitt, *Politische Theologie. Vier Kapitel zur Lehre von der Souveränität* (8th edn, 2004), p. 13.

[50] Carl Schmitt, *Der Nomos der Erde im Völkerrecht des* Jus Publicum Europaeum (1950), p. 92.

Molen's biography from 1937 was, for a long time, the only work that had an openly critical–historical approach. It aimed to critically reconstruct Gentili as a historical figure and his texts, so that attempts of appropriating him for contemporaneous legal–political projects could be assessed critically, and van der Molen's normative and contemporaneous orientations show only very faintly between the lines. This primarily historiographic approach gained much traction in the later 20th century, beginning with Diego Panizza's important monograph, *Alberico Gentili, Giurista Ideologo nell'Inghilterra Elisabettiana*, from 1981.[51] Panizza was also the driving force and long-time scientific director of the *Centro Internazionale Studi Gentiliani* in San Ginesio, which was founded in the same year. It has since become the academic centre of research and international debate about Gentili, hosting among others a series of biannual conferences, the *Convegni Giornate Gentiliane*, inaugurated in 1983. With the pressure regarding the seminal importance of Alberico Gentili for Western international law removed, many works now investigate different aspects of Gentili's life, his historical context, and his doctrine in great detail and with considerable investigative effort.[52]

V. The Present Role of Gentili's Non-Public Global Law, its Advantages and Drawbacks

By focusing on the examples of two present authors who seem to be inspired by Gentili, this last section will conclude the discussion of the reception of Gentili, and at the same time pick up and assess the advantages and drawbacks of Gentili's approach. Even though historical sobriety has led to a sort of detachment between historical research on the one hand and debates of systematic issues in current international law on the other, one strand of relating these two has recently become vaguely perceptible again: without making their inspiration explicit, some current developments feature authors who, on the one hand, publish on Gentili and on his role in the history of international law, and who, on the other hand and on other occasions, contribute to discussions about a global legal order alternative to both the constitutionalization of international law and more 'realist' models of states making merely instrumental use of international law. Since the relation between both discussions is never made explicit, an attempt to reconstruct it is necessarily somewhat speculative—even more so as it concerns present and ongoing discussions. Nonetheless, I will risk two such attempts, if only to elucidate repercussions of those traits of Gentili's theory that have been criticized

[51] Diego Panizza, *Alberico Gentili, giurista ideologo nell'Inghilterra Elisabettiana* (n. 22).

[52] Panizza's work makes the point that Gentili was the first author to establish an ideological mode of theorizing, i.e. writing in order to methodologically legitimize (and thereby also to set limits to) political rule. The present author, however, considers Panizza to be of great importance primarily due to his sustained historiographic effort and the organizational work that he has accomplished rather than for that particular thesis.

above.[53] The first example concerns a 'Gentilian' understanding of the everyday workings of international law, the second one a more exceptional constellation.

1. Global administrative law struggling with political ambivalence

Taking the organization of international law according to the paradigm of private law and the simultaneous endowment of this 'private' international law with the normative force of natural law frees it from the need to be legislated and justified in an institutionalized public procedure. If this is the gist of Gentili's approach, the analysis of 'bottom-up' private ordering might be seen as the starting point for the discovery of more general rules of international law and Gentili as an inspiring author for attempts to theorize such general rules, their applicability, and their binding force. If one is not bewildered by such a combination of historical and contemporary systematic interests in the first place, one will find it interesting to learn that Benedict Kingsbury, one of the organizers of the project behind a couple of recent initiatives around Gentili,[54] is also strongly involved in attempts to formulate and normatively develop the theory of global administrative law (GAL):[55] against 'laissez-faire' private ordering and *lex mercatoria*, on the one hand, and against unifying and monolithic tendencies of global constitutionalization, on the other, the GAL approach is set to identify many diverse arenas of global and transnational governance and examine (or promote) the application of common procedural principles known from domestic administrative law in these arenas. The ideas of transparency, accountability, and participation feature prominently among such principles and provide some foothold for attempts at justification of transnational governance regimes. Yet, the approach renounces strong overarching institutions and authorities corresponding (arguably) to pre-globalization normative political and legal theories that legitimize institution by their derivation from one such fundamental jurisgenerative institution, i.e. from the constitution. From early on, Kingsbury has connected the normative force of said principles to the publicness of law, but explained that publicness as an *inter*-public relation without taking recourse to the assumption of a unified global public.[56] That is, the normative

[53] Cf. above, Section III.4.

[54] Cf. articles such as Benedict Kingsbury, 'Confronting Difference: The Puzzling Durability of Gentili's Combination of Pragmatic Pluralism and Normative Judgment', *American Journal of International Law* 92(4) (1998), 713–23; id., 'Gentili, Grotius, and the Extra-European World', in Harry N. Schreiber (ed.), *The Law of the Sea: The Common Heritage and Emerging Challenges* (2000), pp. 39–60; edited volumes such as in Benedict Kingsbury (ed.), *Alberico Gentili e Il Mondo Extraeuropeo: Atti Del Convegno, Settima Giornata Gentiliana* (2001); Benedict Kingsbury and Benjamin Straumann (eds.), *The Roman Foundations of the Law of Nations. Alberico Gentili and the Justice of Empire* (2010); and Benedict Kingsbury and Benjamin Straumann (eds.), trans David Lupher *Alberico Gentili, The Wars of The Romans: A Critical Edition and Translation of* De Armis Romanis (2011); and institutional projects like the Gentili fellowship at the IILJ at NYU Law School.

[55] Cf. e.g. Benedict Kingsbury, Nico Krisch, and Richard B. Stewart, 'The Emergence of Global Administrative Law', *Law and Contemporary Problems* 68(15) (2005), 15–61.

[56] Benedict Kingsbury, 'International Law as Inter-Public Law', *Nomos* 49 (2009), 167–204; id., 'The Concept of 'Law' in Global Administrative Law', *European Journal of International Law* 20(1) (2009), 23–57.

weight is distributed between the respective domestic constitution of parties to such regimes, on the one hand, and procedural rules for the interaction between those parties, on the other. Quite similar to Gentili's conception then, the different agents of inter-, trans-, and supranational governance as well as their (quasi-)legal products are in principle not subject to a higher authority or institution. At the same time, agents and regimes are restrained (on a theoretical level and in a non-enforceable way) by procedural rules that introduce presumably universal principles and establish at least thin standards of legitimacy of regimes and their outcomes. Moreover, the tradition of jurisprudential discourse on domestic administrative law brings additional assumptions of systematic rationality to the table, as the quasi-system of Roman law did in the case of Gentili's natural/international law.

Do the points of criticism that have been raised above with regard to Gentili resurface in the debates around GAL? One of them was that the cultural particularity of Roman law insofar as it is an institutional scholarly discourse and a forensic practice belies its universal scope and its purported provision of equal access and equal consideration for all parties. In terms of speaker positions, this has resulted in an uneven factual distribution of discursive resources (and finally in unequal treatment of equal persons and cases). In terms of the plasticity of Roman law, it meant a reification that impeded the alleged flexibility and the dynamic adjustment to new constellations to a considerable extent. As both Carol Harlow and Ming-Sung Kuo have argued, in many discourses on GAL, the political and particular character of the movement was not acknowledged or glossed over, and the GAL approach turned out more substantial than it was ready to admit.[57] Then there was an inverse problem, Gentili's renunciation of an international institutional venue for public deliberation about the law: while Gentili held that there was an international legal binding force for the sovereigns, he did not want to provide for a mechanism to establish common interpretations of that law. In that sense, while the universal community of mankind was a moral category, there was no room for it to appear as a legal subject with its own public authority and to confront sovereigns and their particular justifications and interpretations with community interests and values. Authors such as Neil Walker have argued that, analogously, the publicness constraint emphasized in the GAL approach needs to be developed into a more substantial normative concept in order for the procedural principle to do the rationalizing and legitimizing work it is supposed to do.[58] One of the salient points is the requirement of publicness as a criterion for the 'second-order' level

[57] Carol Harlow, 'Global Administrative Law: The Quest for Principles and Values', *European Journal of International Law* 17/1 (2006), 187–214; Ming-Sung Kuo, 'Inter-Public Legality or Post-Public Legitimacy? Global Governance and the Curious Case of Global Administrative Law as a New Paradigm of Law', *International Journal of Constitutional Law* 10/4 (2012), 1050–75.

[58] Neil Walker, 'On the Necessarily Public Character of Law', in Claudio Michelon, Haris Psarras, Gregor Clunie, and Christopher McCorkindale (eds.), *The Public in Law* (2012), pp. 7–33; for a similar point about the accountability principle, cf. Danielle Hanna Rached, 'Doomed Aspiration of Pure Instrumentality: Global Administrative Law and Accountability', *Global Constitutionalism* 3/3 (2014), 338–72.

of international regimes, i.e. the public constitution of an authority from which first-order (GAL) norms and institutions can be derived. Interestingly, in a recent article, Kingsbury and other authors have acknowledged the substantial normative commitments of their approach.[59] They have conceded a political ambivalence of their strong focus on a purely instrumental understanding of GAL, but pointed out the inevitability of political struggles over the development of the concept and the practice of GAL and the emancipatory potential of such struggles. In the same article, they have brought forward a contribution to such far-reaching debates, drawing parallels between GAL and conceptions of deliberative democracy where one would elucidate the other and suggest ways to unfold latent normative potentials.

2. Sovereign interpretive authority and self-judgment struggling with *jus cogens* norms

The awkward situation that the attribution of the ultimate interpretive authority of international law to the sovereigns might lead to an erosion of international law can be illustrated also by a quite different constellation.[60] In 1997, John Yoo, at the time Professor of Law at UC Berkeley, wrote a 25-page introduction to an edition of Gentili's *De Legationibus.*[61] And Gentili also appeared regularly in more recent works of his on the law of war, discussing, among others, 'asymmetrical', undeclared, partisan wars and different categories of involved or uninvolved persons.[62] In another text, Yoo explained how the 2003 invasion of Iraq has been covered by international law's right to anticipatory self-defence.[63] While this general idea of anticipatory self-defence might equally be referred to Gentili,[64] in this text Yoo did not resort to Gentili. He argued for reduced standards required in the justification of such warfare due to contemporary factors such as terrorism and weapons of mass destruction, but on the other hand he based one important strand of his argument for pre-emptive warfare on a definition of imminence of a threat from 1837, thereby blinding out more recent legal developments such as the Kellogg-Briand pact's renunciation of war as an instrument of national policy and the whole development of the 1870s mentioned above. In fact, the development of international law in the twentieth century exhibits clear attempts to limit the principle of self-judgment implied by theories of sovereignty like that of Gentili. Issues

[59] Benedict Kingsbury, Megan Donaldson, and Rodrigo Vallejo, 'Global Administrative Law and Deliberative Democracy', forthcoming in Anne Orford and Florian Hoffmann, *The Oxford Handbook of International Legal Theory* (2016), available as preprint at <http://ssrn.com/abstract=2575435> (accessed 26 January 2016).

[60] The example is discussed in Christopher N. Warren, *Literature and the Law of Nations, 1580-1680* (n. 13), pp. 229–33.

[61] Alberico Gentili, *De Legationibus libri tres* (1997).

[62] Cf. John Yoo, *Point of Attack: Preventive War, International Law, and Global Welfare* (2014), p. 63; cf. also John Yoo and Robert J. Delahunty, 'Making War', *Cornell Law Review* 93/1 (2007), 143–5.

[63] John Yoo, 'International Law and the War in Iraq', *American Journal of International Law* 97(3) (2003), 563–76, esp. sect. III.

[64] Cf. Gentili, *De iure belli libri tres,* lib. I, ch. 14 (ed. Brown Scott [n. 6], pp. 61ff.).

of self-defence and of imminent threat are the most pointed way of putting the question and even with regard to these, the subjective element is not the ultimate criterion—the international legality that it is capable of establishing is 'provisional', or 'temporary', and subject to later revision by a third-party arbiter.[65] As Oscar Schachter put it: 'For it is incontrovertible that if a state or an individual claiming a right has the exclusive authority to decide on the lawfulness of its exercise, the law has reached a vanishing point.'[66] Yoo for his part expresses no such concern.

In an even more prominent and controversial case, Yoo mentioned Gentili as an important witness in legal, rather than scholarly, arguments: Acting as head of the Office of Legal Counsel of the United States Department of Justice, Yoo in 2003 issued a memorandum arguing that

> the application of these [generally applicable, limiting] statutes to the conduct of interrogations of unlawful combatants would deprive the sovereign of a recognized prerogative. Historically, nations have been free to treat unlawful combatants as they wish . . .[67]

Gentili is then quoted explicitly on the issue as one of the witnesses for this opinion: 'malefactors do not enjoy the privileges of a law to which they are foes'.[68] This complete lack of legal standing of the 'malefactors', the authority of the sovereign as interpreter of her own international legal obligations and other factors allow Yoo to argue for the admissibility of cruel and degrading interrogation techniques, at the bottom line sidestepping what was and is considered a peremptory norm of international law, i.e. the prohibition of torture.[69] The little role of peremptory norms in international legal practice and the lack of progress in identification of *jus cogens* norms have been argued to have as one of their causes precisely an insufficient legitimacy and public authority of international adjudicative institutions.[70] As far as Gentili is concerned, and besides the problem of self-judgment implied by Gentili's theory of sovereignty, the crucial importance of sovereignty plays out also in his idea of pirates being without the protection of international law. As the example illustrates, this puts Gentili's theory clearly at odds with universal individual rights, however indispensable these may seem to us. There is a clear connection between Gentili's insistence on the public constitution of sovereigns within the particular context of their respective state, and the putting outside of the reach of any law of certain persons. And there is again a clear connection between these

[65] Cf. David Kaye, 'Adjudicating Self-Defense: Discretion, Perception, and the Resort to Force in International Law', *Columbia Journal of Transnational Law* 44 (2005–2006), 159f.

[66] Oscar Schachter, 'Self-Judging Self-Defence', *Case Western Reserve Journal of International Law* 19 (1987), 123.

[67] Cf. John Yoo, 'Memorandum for William J. Haynes II, General Counsel of the Department of Defense' from 14 March 14 2003 (online at <http://www.aclu.org/files/pdfs/safefree/yoo_army_torture_memo.pdf>, accessed 23 November 2015), p. 15.

[68] Ibid., n. 14. Cf. Gentili, *De iure belli libri tres*, lib. I, ch. 4 (ed. Brown Scott [n. 6], p. 22).

[69] Cf. David Kretzmer, 'Torture, Prohibition of', in *Max Planck Encyclopedia of Public International Law*, MPEPIL 880 (accessed 12 February 2016).

[70] Cf. Matthew Saul, 'Identifying *Jus Cogens* Norms: The Interaction of Scholars and International Judges', *Asian Journal of International Law* 5 (2015), 26–54.

two aspects of his conception: the assignment of ultimate authority to interpret international law without an international authority available to intervene to the sovereigns, and the factual, opportunist use of such arguments for particular interests and expediency that ignore or reverse inconvenient developments of international law. This is present both in Gentili's texts and in some arguments advanced in today's debates.

3. Conclusion

Given the present relevance of patterns of arguments used by Gentili, and given the present, perhaps inescapable, asymmetries in power between sovereigns, it is appropriate then to repeat an earlier critical assessment: Gentili does not seem to provide conceptual resources to establish—as a necessary component of international law's procedures, or at least as an aim—a forum to prevent the law from only ever working to the benefit of the powerful. For Gentili, there is a strong incentive, and even a moral imperative, to resort to arbitration and to aim for peace, even for the powerful sovereigns. But there is no conceptual, let alone institutional, room for public (in the sense of universal) deliberation of all parties on equal standing so that the affected parties—rather than some authority with either a particularistic pedigree or with more universal, but shaky legitimacy—could agree on *common interpretations* of the law. A core issue one might have with Gentili's theory is related to the fact that, obviously and inevitably, one of the central tenets of normative legal theory, '*nemo iudex in causa sua*' is connected to the presence of public institutions of international law (in a strong sense of publicness).

More generally, to end on a more positive note, the fact that Gentili's original arguments (and their shortcomings) seem to converge on the same serious issues and points of contention as today's debates suggests that his theory is located right at the centre of core problems of international law.

Selected Bibliography

Haggenmacher, Peter, 'Grotius and Gentili: A Reassessment of Thomas E. Holland's Inaugural Lecture', in Hedley Bull, Benedict Kingsbury, and Adam Roberts (eds.), *Hugo Grotius and International Relations* (Oxford: Oxford University Press, 1992), pp. 133–76.

Holland, Thomas Erskine, 'Alberico Gentili', reprinted in idem, *Studies in International Law: Reprint of the Edition Oxford 1898* (Aalen: Scientia, 1979), pp. 1–39.

Kingsbury, Benedict, 'Confronting Difference: The Puzzling Durability of Gentili's Combination of Pragmatic Pluralism and Normative Judgment', *American Journal of International Law* 92 (1998), 713–23.

Kingsbury, Benedict and Straumann, Benjamin (eds.), *The Roman Foundations of the Law of Nations: Alberico Gentili and the Justice of Empire* (Oxford: Oxford University Press, 2010).

Panizza, Diego, *Alberico Gentili, giurista ideologo nell'Inghilterra Elisabettiana* (Padova: La Garangola, 1981).

Panizza, Diego, 'Political Theory and Jurisprudence in Gentili's *De Iure Belli*: The Great Debate Between "Theological" and "Humanist" Perspectives from Vitoria to Grotius', *IILJ Working Paper* 15 (2005).
van der Molen, Gesina, *Alberico Gentili and the Development of International Law: His Life Work and Times* (Amsterdam: Paris, 1937, 2nd rev edn Leyden: Sijthoff, 1968).
Wagner, Andreas, 'Francisco de Vitoria and Alberico Gentili on the Legal Character of the Global Commonwealth', *Oxford Journal of Legal Studies* 31(3) (2011), 565–82.

6

Althusius

Back to the Future

Thomas O. Hueglin

The contribution of Johannes Althusius (1563–1638) to system and order in international law lies in his early-modern construction of a federal theory of politics not yet based on the distinction of national and international law and thus of heuristic value for a post-modern system of transnational order. The main objective of this theory, the *Politica Methodice Digesta*,[1] is the stable organization and preservation of political plurality. To this end, it emphasizes negotiated agreement over majoritarian decision-making, and power sharing based on considerations of subsidiarity over exclusive power assignment to separate levels of governance. It thus can help conceptualizing a post-Westphalian international political order in which individual rights would be complemented by the collective or group rights of a plurality of smaller and larger communities.

While the *Politica* was primarily occasioned by the struggle of religious minorities against rising state absolutism in the aftermath of the Reformation, it was also meant to provide a systematic justification for the autonomy of smaller communities in a composite commonwealth modelled after the Holy Roman Empire. Still writing in a pre-Westphalian world of overlapping plural rule, Althusius combined the Aristotelian foundation of politics with principles of Roman law as well as drawing on Reformed theology and theories of resistance against tyranny that had sprung from it. The result is a theory of con-federal federalism carried throughout by a spirit of shared or co-sovereignty. It is entirely constructed bottom-up: each level in a multilevel commonwealth is governed by a council of delegates from what he calls consociations at the next lower level. The emphasis is on mutual cooperation and consensus rather than power separation and majority rule. The main normative guideline for the allocation of power is subsidiarity. Widely read at the time,

[1] Johannes Althusius, *Politica Methodice Digesta Atque Exemplis Sacris Et Profanis Illustrata* (1614); this is the usually cited 3rd edn, which has also been reprinted in facsimile (1981). A slightly abridged English translation is Frederick S. Carney ed. and trans. Johannes Althusius, *Politica*, together with the forewords (*Praefatio*) to the 1st (1603) and 3rd (1613) edns ([1964] 1995). Citations in this chapter largely follow Carney but will deviate when the original Latin text suggests a slightly different own translation.

Althusius was harshly condemned during the age of absolutism and largely forgotten in a modern world of sovereign nation-states. Moreover, the rise of the modern federal state with its strict separation of powers and the assumption of indivisible centralized sovereignty also kept him at the margins as a theorist of federalism. His place among the classics of political thought, however, is no longer in dispute, and his relevance has been acknowledged particularly in the context of the European Union as a novel form of con-federal federalism. Herein also lies his significance for international law in a post-Westphalian global order.

I. Early-Modern Context: Territorial Absolutism and Political Calvinism

The life of Althusius falls into a most dramatic and traumatic period of transition. The Reformation had brought to an end the last vestiges of medieval Christian universalism. The plurality of overlapping rule under the formula of *rex imperator in regno suo*[2] was giving way to the rise of a European territorial state system with exclusive sovereignty claims. Under the Augsburg Religious Peace of 1555, those claims included the determination of an official state religion according to the individual ruler's preference and own denomination. Religious dissenters and minorities had to fear suppression or outright persecution.

Althusius was born into a peasant family in Diedenshausen in the County of Wittgenstein-Berleburg.[3] During his years of education, which would take him to Marburg, Cologne, Basle, and Geneva, he received support from Count Ludwig the Elder of Sayn-Wittgenstein, the ruler of Wittgenstein Berleburg and a prominent figure among Germany's Reformed princes. After his promotion as doctor of both civil and ecclesiastical law 1586 in Basle, he received, still in the same year, a call to the Hohe Schule Herborn, a Calvinist academy founded by Count Johann the Elder of Nassau-Dillenburg, another prominent Reformed prince and brother of William of Orange. There, with some interruptions, he taught law and politics until 1604. In that year, after having published the first edition of his *Politica*, he accepted appointment as city syndic[4] in Emden, a Reformed German seaport in the vicinity of the Netherlands. Until his death in 1638, Althusius guided the city through turbulent times, remained active as a scholar,[5] and served as church elder. The most traumatic events during Althusius' long life as a Reformed

[2] A king possesses as much power over his particular realm as does the emperor over the whole.

[3] Biographical information on Althusius is available mostly in German. A synopsis is provided in Thomas O. Hueglin, *Early Modern Concepts for a Late Modern World: Althusius on Community and Federalism* (1999), pp. 29–41; while the older literature assumed that Althusius was born in 1557, it now seems more likely that his year of birth was 1563.

[4] As syndic, Althusius was the city's chief executive officer and as such accountable to the city council.

[5] Apart from subsequent revised and enlarged editions of the *Politica*, Althusius also published a major work on jurisprudence: Johannes Althusius, *Dicaelogicae Libri Tres* (1617); a 2nd edn (1649) was still revised by Althusius but published after his death.

Christian were the St. Bartholomew's Day massacres of 1572, the Dutch Revolt against Catholic Spain culminating in the 1581 Act of Abjuration and subsequent assassination of Wilhelm of Orange in 1584, and the Thirty Years' War (1618–1648), which began as a religious war between Catholicism and Protestantism and ended with territorial consolidation among territorial rulers.

The St. Bartholomew's Day massacres were the most distressing event by far. Some 10,000 Huguenots may have been savagely cut to pieces by Catholic mobs after the murder of their leaders had been ordered by the Catholic French monarch Charles IX and his queen mother Catherine de' Medici. The most prominent victim was the Admiral of France, Gaspard II de Coligny, whom Catherine suspected of persuading the indecisive Charles to adopt the Reformed faith as well as harbouring plans to draw France into a war with Catholic Spain by intervening in the Dutch Revolt.[6] This first organized killing of fellow Christians in the name of reason of state propelled into publicist overdrive a new kind of political Calvinism no longer content with securing minority rights under the umbrella of unquestioned monarchical rule. A series of Reformed pamphlets printed and disseminated all over Europe by the so-called Monarchomachs not only justified resistance and even tyrannicide but moreover argued that legitimate governance required popular consent, and that even foreign intervention was warranted against oppression in neighbouring countries.[7] Survivors of the massacres fled into emigration. An impressionable young Althusius may have met some of them in Geneva.

The revolt of the Reformed Dutch provinces against religious and political oppression by Catholic Spain was the prelude to the final unravelling of the old Christian Europe in the Thirty Years' War. In 1581, when the Reformed Dutch provinces repudiated allegiance to King Philip II of Spain, they did not opt for outright independence—as yet unthinkable in a world generally thought to be governed by kings and princes. Instead, their intention was to submit to the lawful governance of another sovereign, and only when they could not find a taker, they resorted to republican self-governance. Althusius would later suggest exactly the same in his own theory of lawful resistance against tyranny: When 'the head of a province does not protect his subjects in time of need, or refuses to support them, they can submit themselves to another'.[8] Ten years after Althusius' death, the Westphalian Peace Treaties at Münster and Osnabrück recognized the independence of the Dutch Republic and brought on its way a new world of sovereign territorial states.

Althusius already was in Emden when he wrote the preface to the second edition of the *Politica* in which he reflected on his time at the Herborn academy. His ambition had been to establish politics as a discipline in its own right, and as

[6] A recent account of this traumatic event is Barbara D. Diefendorf, *The Saint Bartholomew's Day Massacre: A Brief History with Documents* (2008).

[7] See Robert M. Kingdon, 'Calvinism and Resistance Theory', in J.H. Burns (ed.), *The Cambridge History of Political Thought 1450-1700* (2004), pp. 193–218.

[8] *Politica*, chapter VIII, paragraph 92 (n. 1) (*Quod si talis provinciae praeses tempore necessitatis suos subditos non protegit, vel auxilia illis ferre recusat, tum illi se alii submittere possunt*).

distinguished from both jurisprudence and theology. For him political science was a crucible in which answers to the two most intricate questions of the epoch had to be melded, the proper sources and ownership of the rights of sovereignty, and the organization of a pious and just life as demanded by the moral prescriptions of the Decalogue. He would not take anything away from jurists or theologians, he assured his sceptical colleagues, because 'where the political scientist ceases, there the jurist begins', just as he takes from the Decalogue only what is 'proper to political science insofar as it breathes a vital spirit into symbiotic life'.[9]

It was in Emden where theoretical ambition then turned into practical politics.[10] Situated at the north-western corner of the Empire adjacent to the Netherlands, Emden was at the time one of the wealthiest seaports in all of Europe, a hub of the North Sea trade that had been displaced from Dutch ports during the turmoil of the Revolt. The city was Calvinist and known as the 'Geneva of the north'. It had given refuge to a large number of Dutch emigrants. The Calvinist city, however, also was located in the Imperial province of East Frisia, which in turn was under the rule of Lutheran counts. The ambition of these counts was to transform their backward provincial fiefdom into a modernized absolutist state along the lines already accomplished or in progress elsewhere. To this end, they demanded that the city adopt the Lutheran faith as was their right under the August Religious Peace agreement, and they required unlimited powers of taxation over the province's richest burghers.

The city denied both the religious and financial impositions. Already before Althusius arrived, decisive action had been taken in the so-called revolution of 1595: the count's governing city magistrate was forcefully removed and replaced by a city council; the post of city syndic was created for strategic guidance and executive leadership; and a military garrison was established under a Dutch commander. The city obtained guarantees of religious freedom as well as autonomous rights of taxation. With Althusius at the helm of business, the city would repeatedly avail itself of the garrison's soldiers to press for further concessions. Once, in 1618, the ruling count even found himself under arrest in his own city residence. By 1627, Althusius had succeeded in re-writing the city's formal oath of allegiance to the count, from a one-sided declaration of loyalty, to a two-sided contract with mutual obligations: practical politics inspired by theoretical ambition indeed.

II. Conceptual Foundations: Federal Theology and the Question of Sovereignty

'On the morrow of Saint Bartholomew, Europe awoke to a new epoch in the history of its political doctrines.' Thus wrote Harold Laski in the foreword to a

[9] *Politica, Praefatio* 1613 (n. 1) (*Propriam vero politicae vindico, quatenus spiritum vitae symbioticae inspirat... quod politicus ibi desinat, ubi incipit jurisconsultus*).
[10] See again Hueglin, *Early Modern Concepts*, pp. 29–41 (n. 3).

modern English edition of one of the most famous and influential pamphlets the Monarchomachs had written, the anonymously published *Vindiciae contra Tyrannos* of 1579.[11] At stake was nothing less than the question of sovereignty, of who should hold ultimate power and authority in an increasingly divided Christian world. It was a question that had been left open in the pre-Reformation world of *rex imperator in regno suo*. Emperors, kings, and princes all happily relied on the Roman law principle according to which they were above the law, *legibus solutus*, but in practice this meant only that as far as their actual authority reached, and in line with however vague appeals to divine or natural law, they could change their own laws, or those of their predecessors. Divine or natural law was grounded in the moral teachings of the universal church. The Reformation had already led to religious wars among countries and princes. What Saint Bartholomew changed was the spectre of civil war within countries. And there were two diametrically opposed answers to the question of how to regain peace and stability.

In 1576, Jean Bodin gave one answer with his epochal definition of sovereignty as 'absolute and perpetual power'.[12] Moreover, he declared that the 'prerogatives of sovereignty are indivisible'.[13] He did so because he feared that anarchy would result from the Huguenots' assertions of a right of resistance against a king whom he unquestioningly assumed to be the sovereign.[14] Welcomed by Europe's territorial princes, Bodin's definition gave a whole new meaning to the formula of *princeps legibus solutus*: it eliminated whatever had been thought of as the autonomous rights of smaller communities within a larger realm. For religious minorities such as the Huguenots in France this meant that survival was at stake. Three years after Bodin, therefore, the *Vindiciae* gave a very different answer by postulating a deliberately polemical counter-formula: the people are released from all obligations, *populus... omni obligatione solutus*, when kings violate their rights.[15]

The question about the origin of these rights forms the political core of the *Vindiciae's* argument, and of what was taught as 'federal theology' at Herborn and other Calvinist academies in Europe. It is the argument of a double covenant between God and the people of Israel mainly taken from Deuteronomy in the Old Testament. The argument in brief is this: by entering into a first covenant, God, king, and people pledge to each other mutual allegiance and loyalty. God will lead the people to the promised land in return for their promise to piously uphold his laws. A second and similar covenant, however is established between the king and

[11] Harold J. Laski, 'Historical Introduction', in *A Defence of Liberty Against Tyrants*, anonymously published under the pseudonym of Junius Brutus in 1579 (1924), pp. 1–60.

[12] Cited from the 1606 English edition and translation by Richard Knolles: Jean Bodin, *The Six Books of a Commonwealth*, ed. and trans. Richard Knolles (1606), I.8; available online at <https://archive.org/details/sixbookesofcommo00bodi>.

[13] Bodin, *The Six Books*, II. 1 (n. 12).

[14] Julian H. Franklin, 'Introduction', in Julian H. Franklin (ed. and trans.), Jean Bodin, *On Sovereignty* (2005), pp. xxii–xxiii.

[15] Hubert Languet, Johann Baptist Fickler, and Philippe de Mornay, *Vindiciae Contra Tyrannos* (1622), Quaestio III; available online at <http://babel.hathitrust.org/cgi/pt?id=osu.32435017667882;view=1up;seq=7>.

the people: because both people and king are directly responsible for upholding the first covenant with God, they both must also hold each other to account for violations of God's law. Herein lies the seed for all Reformed resistance theories. In addition, the Calvinists pointed out that the kings had entered or joined the original covenant between people and God only at a later time. From this they deduced that in the second covenant the king 'promised absolutely, and the people conditionally'.[16] The people, in other words, only had to obey the king's laws only so long they were just laws. Herein in turn lies the seed for the Calvinists' claims of the people's superiority over their rulers.

The victory of royal absolutism over claims of popular sovereignty during the two centuries that followed had as much to do with the elegant simplicity of Bodin's formula as with the fact that these claims came from religious minorities. The Calvinist Monarchomachs also had no clear answer as to how their claims might be transformed into political practice. They 'postulated a government by consent of the governed and a right to rebel against tyranny'.[17] How could consent be obtained, however, when there was no unified people to be asked in the first place? This is the question that Althusius asked when he was confronted, at Herborn, with the incompatibility between, on the one hand, the teachings of federal theology, and, on the other hand, what he already saw as 'common opinion,' the 'rights of sovereignty and their sources... belonging to the prince and supreme magistrate'.[18] Against 'Bodin's clamors',[19] Althusius insisted in the 1603 foreword to the first edition of the *Politica*, that the rights of sovereignty instead belong 'to the commonwealth and people'.[20] In the foreword to the second edition of 1610, already at Emden, he elaborated with much more precision: the owner and beneficiary of the rights of sovereignty is 'none other than the total people consociated in one symbiotic body from a plurality of smaller consociations'.[21]

The logic leading Althusius to this early-modern postulation of the people's collective ownership of sovereignty was not just dictated by strategic considerations of stability and survival. Such considerations had led the Monarchomachs to the postulation of a covenanted relationship between king and people in which the people's loyal obedience was conditional upon the king observing certain limits of governance. In this way the people could be considered superior to their rulers, but this superiority did not include any original grant of power.[22] The people was only *legibus solutus* and could resist the king when he violated his obligations under

[16] Languet, Fickler, and de Mornay, *Vindicae contre Tyrannos*, Quaestio III (n. 15) (*promittebat rex pure, populus sub conditione*).

[17] Reinhard Bendix, *Kings or People* (1980), p. 325.

[18] *Praefatio* 1603 (n. 1) (*communi calculo... majestatis capita & jura... principi & summi magistratui propria adsignari*).

[19] *Praefatio* 1603 (n. 1) (*Bodini clamores*).

[20] *Praefatio* 1603 (n. 1) (*Reipublicae & populo*).

[21] *Praefatio* 1614 (n. 1); the 1610 foreword was also retained for all subsequent editions (*nullum alium, quam populum universum, in corpus unum symbioticum ex pluribus minoribus consociationibus consociatum*).

[22] See J.W. Gough, *The Social Contract* (1967), p.14.

the covenant. Althusius arrived at his far more radical postulation of the people's sovereignty by converting the idea of a covenanted relationship between people and ruler into a constitutional system of legitimate governance. In doing so, he not only turned from federal theology to natural law, but moreover transformed the medieval assumption of plural rule into a systematic order of divided and shared rule by turning the *rex imperator in regno suo* formula on its head.[23]

According to 'natural law', Althusius declared, 'all men are equal and not subject to anyone's jurisdiction except by their own consent and voluntary act'. This is so because 'in the beginning of the human race, there were neither empires . . . nor rulers of them'. Both were 'constituted only later, out of necessity, by the people itself'.[24] It is therefore the ruler or supreme magistrate who does not possess an original grant of power. Instead, he is constituted by a 'reciprocal contract' in which his obligations as the 'mandatory' precede those of the 'universal consociation' as the 'mandator'.[25] This is a far cry indeed from the traditional assumption of plural rule under the *rex imperator* formula, under which the emperor's sovereign powers over the 'whole' of the empire had in principle been considered as constrained only by the exercise of de facto similar powers by kings and princes in their respective realms. Althusius turned the logic of this formula upside down by limiting the powers of the emperor or supreme magistrate, not as a consequence of the de facto powers exercised by the other members of the empire or commonwealth, but by means of a clear mandate received from these members: 'The supreme magistrate receives only as much right as is explicitly conceded to him by the consociated bodies or members of the realm.'[26]

Althusius effectively turned the Calvinist double covenant in to a triple covenant: a first one between people, ruler, and God meant to establish the parameters of a just and pious life; a second one securing mutual accountability between people and ruler, reformulated as a contract of mandated executive government; and a third one as the necessary precondition for the second, a social contract establishing the people as an organized body.[27] It is this social contract that gives both expression to the sovereignty of the people as such an organized body, and circumscribes the limits of the ruler's executive power. As was the case in the Holy Roman Empire, Althusius thought of the election of a supreme magistrate as the default option.[28] Regarding this election, then, he expounded, the 'highest concern must be given to

[23] See Hueglin, *Early Modern Concepts*, pp.169–93 (n. 3).

[24] *Politica* XVIII. 18 (n. 1) (*jure naturali omnes homines sunt equales & nullius jurisdictioni subjecti, nisi ex suo consensu & facto voluntario. . .Nec enim in principio generis humani fuerunt imperia. . ., neque horum rectores, quae tamen postea necessitate postulante an ipsomet populo sunt constituta*).

[25] *Politica* XIX. 6–7 (n. 1) (*In contractu autem hoc reciproco inter magistratum summum mandatarium. . .& consociationem universalem mandantem, praecedit obligatio magistratus. . .*).

[26] *Politica* XIX. 6–7 (n. 1) (*Tantum autem juris habet hic summus magistratus, quantum illi a corporibus consociatis, seu membris regni, est expresse concessum*).

[27] It is this third covenant that renders unconvincing the view of some according to which *Politica* must be seen primarily as the construction of a religious state; for a more balanced recent assessment see Bettina Koch, 'Johannes Althusius: Between Secular Federalism and the Religious State', in Ann Ward and Lee Ward (eds.), *The Ashgate Research Companion to Federalism* (2009), pp. 75–90.

[28] *Politica* XVIII (n. 1); election by so-called ephors analogous to electoral princes in the Empire.

the fundamental law of the realm, which is nothing other than those pacts by which many cities and provinces come together and agree to establish and defend one and the same commonwealth'.[29]

Obviously, the Althusian social contract that precedes and is distinct from the government contract that follows is not a social contract among individuals, as Thomas Hobbes would propose, half a century later, collapsing social and government contract into one. It is a contract among a plurality of smaller and larger communities. It is also not a fictitious contract. Despite all Bodinian 'clamors', Althusius still saw the Empire and all other realms like it as a composite commonwealth in which nobody possessed exclusive and indivisible authority, and major governance decisions depended on agreement and compromise. Sovereignty in such a commonwealth was co-sovereignty shared by its members. In fact, the Althusian insistence on the organized body of the people as the collective owner of ultimate authority points to a procedural understanding of sovereignty: it only exists when the deliberative process of negotiation and compromise works. How that process works is the subject matter of Althusius' theory of federalism proper.

III. A Theory of Federalism: Council Governance, Subsidiarity, and Consent

It is not a theory of federalism in the conventional modern sense. That would be a theory almost exclusively based on the constitutional model of the American centralized federal state. It was first brought on its way by the authors of the *Federalist Papers* defending and justifying the American constitutional draft of 1789.[30] The core of that defence was a rejection of confederalism with its reliance on intergovernmental agreement instead of direct agency of a strong federal government in the name of efficiency and stability. The model rests on the combination of three institutional and procedural mechanisms: a constitutional division of powers between two levels of government; dual representation of population and constituent member units in two elected legislative chambers at the national level; and compound majoritarianism as the default mode of decision-making whereby legislative acts have to be passed by both chambers.

The dominance of the American model has obscured the existence of a European procedural model of federalism that followed the tradition of the Holy Roman Empire and has found its most recent reconfiguration in the European Union.[31] Instead of dividing powers, it relies on power sharing under the principle of

[29] *Politica* XIX. 49 (n. 1) (*In electione vero summi magistratus, summa cura legis fundamentalis regni, habenda est. . . . Est autem haec fundamentalis lex, nihil aliud, quam pacta quaedam, sub quibus plures civitates & provinciae coierunt & consenserunt in unam eandemque Rempubl. habendam & defendam*).

[30] Alexander Hamilton, John Jay, and James Madison, *The Federalist* ([1787–1788] 2001).

[31] Thomas O. Hueglin, 'Comparing Federalisms: Variations or Distinct Models?', in Arthur Benz and Jörg Broschek (eds.), *Federal Dynamics: Continuity, Change, and the Varieties of Federalism* (2013), pp. 27–47.

subsidiarity; instead of an elected second legislative chamber, there is a council of ex officio delegates of the member unit governments; and decision making remains characterized by a search for intergovernmental agreement 'in the shadow' of formal majority rule.[32] Subsidiarity, council governance, and a consent requirement for questions of vital interest to individual members were hallmarks of legitimate Imperial governance before the dawn of modern parliamentary governance. For Althusius, these are the systematic building blocs for what amounts to a procedural theory of federalism.

That theory quite deliberately begins with Aristotle. Bodin had dismissed Aristotle because his definition of sovereign power as absolute and indivisible could be reconciled neither with the Aristotelian doctrine of a mixed regime or constitution,[33] nor with the philosopher's definition of a good citizen as someone who actively participates in politics.[34] In the opening chapter of the *Politica*, Althusius conversely affirms that, in explicit reference to Aristotle, 'man is a social animal by nature',[35] and that, therefore, 'the subject matter of politics are precepts for the communication of those goods, services and rights that we bring together as common advantages of social life'.[36] Contrary to Bodin's rights-based definition of politics, in other words, Althusius emphasizes politics as a communicative process. Politics is not defined by the question of who has the right to govern and who does not. Instead, Althusius defines it as 'symbiosis', the 'art of consociation', *ars consociandi*, whereby those who live together as 'symbiotes', *symbiotici*, 'pledge themselves each to the other, by explicit or tacit agreement, to mutual communication of whatever is useful and necessary for the harmonious exercise of social life'.[37]

The definition of politics as mutual communication echoes Aristotle's anti-Platonic dictum that the virtue of the citizen was the ability 'to rule and to be ruled'.[38] Althusius departs from the philosopher, however, by applying the precepts of citizenship not just to the members of a single small community or *polis* as Greek political thought did in general, but to a larger and composite commonwealth in which the smaller units are the constituent members of the larger ones. This was a radical proposition occasioned by the threat to autonomy and survival that smaller civic and religious communities such as Emden suffered from territorial state building. It was radical because it went squarely both against the dualistic juxtaposition of emperor and territorial princes under the old *rex imperator* formula in the Empire, and against the monism of the new doctrine of sovereignty. Under the old formula, the role of the emperor and the political status of territorial estates had been left conspicuously ambiguous. Under the new doctrine, the emperor could

[32] Eva Krick, *Verhandlungen im Konsensverfahren: Varianten kollektiver Entscheidung in Expertengremien* (2013), p. 280.

[33] Bodin, *The Six Books*, I.10 (n. 12).

[34] Bodin, *The Six Books*, I.6 (n. 12).

[35] *Politica* I. 32 (n. 1) (*homo natura ipsa sociale animal est*).

[36] *Politica* I. 31 (n. 1) (*subjectum politicae sunt praecepta de communicatione quarundam rerum, operarum & juris, quae ad... commune commodum vitae socialis conferimus*).

[37] *Politica* I: 2 (n. 1) (*inter se invicem ad communicationem mutuam eorum, qua pacto expresso, vel tacito, quae ad vitae socialis usum & consortium sunt utilia & necessaria, se obligant*).

[38] Aristotle, *The Politics* (1981), 1277a25.

only be seen either as the absolute ruler over the whole of the Empire, which he clearly was not, or as a mere figure-head presiding over an aristocracy of sovereign princes, which was Bodin's view.[39]

For Althusius, the emperor or supreme magistrate is the administrator of a universal consociation constituted from a plurality of particular such consociations. The modalities of governance in this multilevel commonwealth form the core of a theory of federalism that is neither 'confederal' nor 'federal' in the modern sense of this distinction. The universal consociation does have direct agency and significant powers of its own, yet these powers remain tied to approval by its constituent members in significant ways. Similarly, approval will be based on majority decisions in principle but remain tied to a consent requirement in significant ways yet again. Althusius avails himself of the Empire as the most obvious example in practice but in methodologically systematic intention, he will formulate general principles transcending that template.

The systematic intention is most clearly visible in the way Althusius describes the construction of the multilevel commonwealth. Leaving aside the early chapters on family and kinship, which Althusius insists are part of politics because the same rules of mutuality apply as elsewhere, subsequent chapters of the *Politica* explain how guilds and colleges come together forming cities and rural towns; how many such minor and particular consociations then form provinces as larger particular consociations, and how many cities and provinces finally agree to form the universal consociation or commonwealth. In principle, each consociation at each level is governed by a council composed of delegates from its constituent members, i.e. the consociations at the next lower level. What is systematic, here, is the level of inclusiveness by constructing membership in the commonwealth from the bottom up instead of relying on tradition or privilege bestowed from the top down. All cities are included, for instance, and not just Imperial cities. Likewise, as was the case in East Frisia but otherwise uncommon throughout Europe, 'peasants and shepherds' are included in the representative composition of provincial estates.[40]

In principle also, these councils are headed by an elected magistrate or prefect. In practice, Althusius knew full well that the ruling princes in the provinces of the Empire received their mandate not fromounciliar election but from Imperial privilege, a fact which he downplayed by insisting that in 'grave matters' such as war and peace, taxation and other matters of general legislation, these princely provincial 'prefect(s) can do nothing without the consent of the assembled provincial orders',[41] just as the 'opinion of the combined estates and orders prevails over the presiding officer or supreme magistrate' at the universal councils of the realm.[42] What is systematic in this instance is that all executive governance is dependent

[39] Bodin, *The Six Books*, II. 6 (n. 12).

[40] *Politica* VIII. 47 (n. 1) (*agricolae & pastores*).

[41] *Politica* VIII. 50 (n. 1) (*In negotiis arduis. . .prefectus hicce sine consensu & conventu ordinum provinciae, nihil aget*).

[42] *Politica* XXXIII. 20 (n. 1) (*sententia igitur universorum statuum & ordinum praevalet praesidis seu summi magistratus sententiae*).

on counciliar approval regardless of whether the legitimation of office holders is derived from election or hereditary privilege.

That kings and princes depended on the approval of estates and orders within their respective realms was nothing new. Althusius in fact employs the old medieval formula derived from Roman law according to which 'what touches all should be approved by all'.[43] In its medieval understanding, however, this consent requirement gave expression to a duality of authority. King and estates embodied different spheres of authority. The king needed approval when his actions 'touched' rights and liberties of the estates. If he only exercised his own authority, no approval was needed.[44] Althusius transformed this consent requirement in two significant ways.

First, as already discussed above, the collective body of the people is the sole owner of the rights of sovereignty, and the supreme magistrate is only given a mandate for executive governance. The old duality of authority is overcome by the separation of social and government contract. Moreover, the estates and other orders such as cities no longer embody authority of their own, they represent, at each level of consociation, the collective will of the people organized into those smaller and particular consociations by whom they are constituted. The councils of cities and rural areas represent the collective will of guilds and colleges including those of peasants and shepherds, provincial assemblies represent the collective will of cities and rural areas, and the universal council of the commonwealth in turn represents the collective will of cities and provinces. This is of course not equivalent to direct representation of individual citizens in the modern sense. What Althusius constructs instead is an indirect and ascending chain of counciliar governance in which citizens are collectively represented according to local, regional. and universal spheres of common interest.

Second, Althusius transformed the medieval consent requirement into a differentiated mode of decision making that also went beyond early-modern practice at the Imperial assemblies or Reichstage, which he described in detail in a passage of the *Politica* omitted from the abridged English translation.[45] After outlining the general rules of convocation, composition, and voting rights, Althusius turns to the procedures of decision making.[46] There are three parties to the process: the Electoral Princes and the Imperial Princes as the major 'colleges', and the Imperial Cities, which do not possess full voting rights but play a role of mediator in case the two other colleges disagree. These three colleges first deliberate separately, and then come together in search of a common position or resolution. The Electoral Princes deliberate first and then pass their resolution on two the Imperial Princes. The Imperial Cities will only be drawn into the process in case of disagreement

[43] Althusius refers to this formula twice, verbatim in his discussion of decision making in guilds and colleges, *Politica* IV. 20 (n. 1) (*quod omnes tangit, ab omnibus. . .approbari debet*), and modified in a reference to the representative purpose of universal councils, *Politica* XVII. 60, where he says that what touches all, should also and in fairness be acted upon by all (*quod omnis tangit, ab omnibus etiam peragi aequum est*).

[44] See Harvey C. Mansfield, Jr., 'Modern and Medieval Representation', in J. Roland Pennock and John W. Chapman (eds.), *Representation* (1968), pp. 78–9.

[45] *Politica* XXXIII. 46–110 (n. 1).

[46] *Politica* XXXIII. 70–7 (n. 1).

of the other two colleges. In that case, they can either side with one of the differing opinions or offer their own. Decisions at the Imperial Assemblies of the Holy Roman Empire could be made by majority rule. However, a final resolution could only be adopted when the disagreement of one of the major colleges is just one of being 'indifferent but not of outright opposition'.[47]

As this last formulation suggests, the entire process is meant to encourage deliberation in order to achieve consensus and avoid open conflict. Althusius in fact describes this process as one of 'dual consent' formation,[48] first in the colleges' separate deliberations, and then in the final decision-making process among them. Yet he also notes that binding decisions can be made 'either by unanimous consent of all colleges, or by the larger part'.[49] What seems to be a contradiction, here, finds explanation in another passage where Althusius characterizes the process of decision making within the colleges as one driven by 'consultation, which endures until all are of the same opinion or the minority bows to the majority'.[50] As in the final round of deliberation among all three colleges, this will obviously only happen, and make majority decisions acceptable, when there is no 'outright opposition'.

Thus far, Althusius has provided a description of the Imperial decision-making process of which it has been said that it is remarkably clear and comprehensive.[51] Clearly, that process was driven by a search of agreement 'in the shadow' of majority rule.[52] Clearly also, the Empire was his prime example with which he meant to illustrate (*exemplis illustrata)* what he intended to set out methodologically as general principle (*methodice digesta*). But Althusius would not be Althusius had he not thought about differentiating between consent requirement and majority rule in more systematic fashion. This he did in his discussion of decision making at provincial assemblies. He added the chapter on provincial administration only in later editions after the move to Emden where his task was not only not only to protect Calvinist Emden from the absolutist aspirations of the Lutheran provincial ruler but also defend the interests of its wealthy burghers against the other and impoverished provincial estates. Consent or majority rule was a vital question for the city in that latter context. Majority decisions, Althusius therefore declares categorically, shall apply only to matters 'that concern all orders in the same way but not to matters only concerning individual orders separately'.[53] The question of consent becomes the key question for the entire process of decision making in a multilevel commonwealth. For Althusius, the consent requirement is meant to protect each consociation in its particular rights of self-determination. Only when there is agreement that a matter is of common concern to all can decisions be made by majority

[47] *Politica* XXXIII. 76 (n. 1) (*indifferens, non apertè contraria*).
[48] *Politica* XXXIII. 70 (n. 1) (*consensus... duplex*).
[49] *Politica* XXXIII. 19 (n. 1) (*ex consensu unanimi omnium collegiorum, vel majoris partis*).
[50] *Politica* XXXIII. 71 (n. 1) (*consultatione... donec vel omnes collegae inter se consentiant, vel major pars, quibus numero pauciores cedunt*).
[51] F. H. Schubert, *Die deutschen Reichstage in der frühen Neuzeit* (1966), pp. 417–18.
[52] Hueglin, 'Comparing Federalisms', pp. 27–47 (n. 31).
[53] *Politica* VIII. 70 (n. 1) (*quae simul universos ordines concernunt, non quae seorsim singulos*).

rule. If that is the case, individual members of the commonwealth can be overruled by the universal decision-making process of the higher order. It is then the higher order of government that is autonomized.

These considerations are of particular and obvious relevance for any international or global order intent on pushing the non-majoritarian boundaries of international law towards majoritarian rules of supranationality. At its core, the question comes down to the problem of how to come to a common understanding about what is of such universal interest that majority decisions become acceptable. A possible answer lies in the principle of subsidiarity, which avoids the rigid distinction between particular and universal rights typical for modern federalism. Instead of asking the classical federal question of who has the power to do what, subsidiarity considerations aim at providing an answer to the question of who should have the authority to do how much of what.[54]

In modern federal states, the distinction between particular and universal rights is determined by a constitutional division of powers. Althusius did not provide such a division of powers. Instead he provided what can be appreciated as an early-modern pre-formulation of the principle of subsidiarity according to which decisions should be taken at the lowest possible level of authority and governance. As such, subsidiarity was an implicit part of the Protestant move against church hierarchy. At the 1571 General Synod of the Dutch Reformed Churches, held in exile in Emden, it had been resolved that 'provincial or general assemblies must not deliberate on matters already decided at a lower level', and that 'they shall concern themselves only with such matters as pertaining to all churches generally'.[55] Just as implicitly, Althusius echoes this resolution by limiting majority rule in principle to matters 'that concern all orders in the same way but not to matters only concerning individual orders separately'.[56] The very purpose of his multilevel commonwealth construction was to ensure that the 'mutual communication of whatever is useful and necessary for the harmonious exercise of social life'[57] could take place at each level 'according to the nature of each consociation'.[58] The consent requirement protects the particular nature of each consociation. Considerations of subsidiarity facilitate agreement on the extent to which autonomous self-regulation of any given specific matter is essential in order to protect the particular nature of each member in a larger union, and on the extent to which regulation can be assigned to a realm of common generality. Majority rule at the level of such generality then allows moving beyond mere confederalism and towards the establishment of common purpose in a multilevel federal polity.

[54] Thomas O. Hueglin and Alan Fenna, *Comparative Federalism: A Systematic Inquiry* (2015), p. 160.

[55] J.F. Gerhard Goeters (ed.), *Die Akten der Synode der Niederländischen Kirchen zu Emden vom 4. – 13. Oktober 1571* (1971), pp. 79–83.

[56] *Politica* VIII. 70 (n. 1) (*quae simul universos ordines concernunt, non quae seorsim singulos*).

[57] *Politica* I. 2 (for the original text, see n. 37).

[58] *Politica* I. 7 (n. 1) (*qualibet consociatione pro natura ejusdem*).

IV. Reception: Refuted, Condemned, Forgotten, Misread

With five editions during the first half of the seventeenth century, the *Politica* must be considered a bestseller in its time, and surely so at least in Reformed circles. The second edition of 1610 was published in the Netherlands at a time when some of the English Puritans stayed there in exile before their departure to the New World as Pilgrim Fathers. There is no evidence that a copy of the book sailed along on the Mayflower but it is at least noteworthy that one of the first political documents of the New World, the Articles of Confederation of the United Colonies of New England, 1643, in its opening paragraph speaks of 'a present Consociation amongst ourselves, for mutual help and strength' because 'we can not according to our desire with convenience communicate in one government and jurisdiction'.[59]

According to Otto von Gierke's extensive investigation of primary sources, three subsequent phases can be identified in the reception of Althusius' political theory. Initially, he had his supporters and opponents, with the postulation of the people's unalienable rights of sovereignty the main bone of contention. Academic refutation turned to outright condemnation with the consolidation of the age of absolutism after the conclusion of the Westphalian Peace Treaties. Althusius came to be accused of being the worst of the Monarchomachs, his theory a 'pestilential error turning the world into turmoil,' his book in general 'poison for the youth' and 'worthy of being thrown into the flames'.[60] Finally, however, he was simply forgotten once political theory had turned to Locke's advocacy of individual liberalism as the foundation of representative government, and Rousseau's idea of a general will among individual citizens freed from all associational impositions as the foundation of democracy. The modern understanding of popular sovereignty emerging from these theories no longer had use for a seemingly outmoded conceptualization of the people as a community of communities.

It was in the context of his research on guilds and fellowships that Otto von Gierke 'rediscovered' Althusius towards the end of the nineteenth century. The great professor of fellowship law not only declared that the most outstanding characteristic of the *Politica* was its 'spirit of federalism throughout',[61] but moreover suggested that because of 'remarkable similarities' it was 'highly probable' that Rousseau had read it and drawn from it.[62] It is remarkable indeed that there is this sentence in the *Politica* according to which what the people decide by common consent cannot be changed 'unless something else pleases the common will'.[63] And Rousseau did refer to Althusius explicitly once, albeit in an aside, as someone who

[59] The Articles of Confederation of the United Colonies of New England are available online at <http://avalon.law.yale.edu/17th_century/art1613.asp>.

[60] Otto von Gierke, *Johannes Althusius und die Entwicklung der naturrechtlichen Staatstheorien* ([1880] 1958), pp. 4–8.

[61] von Gierke, *Johannes Althusius*, p. 226 (n. 60).

[62] von Gierke, *Johannes Althusius*, p. 9 (n. 60). See further the contribution by Heller in this volume.

[63] *Politica*, IX. 18 (n. 1) (*nisi communi voluntate aliud placeat*).

like himself had made enemies for the boldness of his thoughts.[64] To stylize the largely unknown Althusius into a German precursor of the great French Rousseau at a time of mounting nationalism, however, probably was not a prudent move if the goal was to rescue the author of the *Politica* from obscurity. Yet in the context of Gierke's careful and contextually erudite analysis of Althusius' political theory, the comparison has considerable merit: while the *Contrat Social* in its disdain for '*associations partielles*'[65] logically points to the construction of a Jacobin state, the *Politica* in its structured approach to organized social life retains the tradition and promise of a federal polity.

After Gierke, Althusius no longer could be ignored so easily. Yet he mostly remained relegated to scholarly footnotes pointing out his importance without exactly explicating why. A few exceptions notwithstanding, which will be discussed in the next and last section, the author of the *Politica* rarely has been taken seriously in his own right, and nowhere less so than by that kind of critical social science for which federalism smacks of the old feudalism that the French Revolution had sought to overcome. To Franz Borkenau, for instance, writing his famous book about the ideological transition from the feudal to the bourgeois world view in French exile and with the rising tide of German fascism before his eyes, Althusius' defense of particular autonomies could only mean support for the 'democratic Caesarism of the House of Orange'.[66] At the time Borkenau obviously had little or no knowledge of Althusius' life and political contexts and therefore simply speculated that 'an absolutist provincial administration would hardly have allowed a professor, whom it employed', . . . to write anything that was opposed to its interests.[67]

Curiously, however, the *Cambridge History of Political Thought* more than half a century later essentially still reiterates the same misinformed verdict, this time on the basis of a rather selective reading of the text as 'distinctly oligarchic' and 'doubtless to the satisfaction of the Dutch'.[68] The verdict is based on a passage where Althusius is quoted as saying that 'the individual people of the realm by themselves are the subjects and servants of their administrators'. This is only half of what Althusius is saying, however. The full passage reads that with regard to their ownership and delegation of the supreme right of realm, the members of the realm are masters of their administrators who in turn are their servants; only with regard to administration itself, outside or below the constitutional plane, as mandated and approved by the people, the individual inhabitants of the realm are in turn the subjects and servants of their ministers.[69]

[64] Jean-Jacques Rousseau, *Lettres ecrites de la Montagne* [1764], Sixieme Lettre, available online at <http://www.inlibroveritas.net/oeuvres/3146/lettres-ecrites-de-la-montagne>.

[65] Jean-Jacques Rousseau, *Du Contrat Social* (1993), II. 3.

[66] Franz Borkenau, *Der Uebergang vom feudalen zum buergerlichen Weltbild* (1934), p. 131.

[67] Borkenau, *Der Uebergang*, pp. 123f. (n. 66).

[68] Howell A. Lloyd, 'Constitutionalism,' in J.H. Burns (ed.), *The Cambridge History of Political Thought 1450-1700* (1991), p. 292.

[69] *Politica* XVIII. 14–15 (n. 1) (*Ratione consitutionis & juris supremi atque proprietatis, universi subditi et regni membra sunt domini horum rectorum & ministrorum. . .rectores hi, sunt istorum famuli & ministri. Extra constitutionem hanc & ratione administrationis demandatae, & a populo acceptatae, ipsi regnicolae singuli, per se, sunt subditi & famuli suorum administratorum & rectorum*).

What stands in the way of an adequate interpretation and appreciation of Althusian political thought are, first of all, 800 pages of early-modern Latin written in a dichotomizing style of logic following the Ramist method fashionable at the time and also employed, if less pedantically, by Bodin.[70] The overall sense of this thought does not reveal itself easily and also cannot be captured by snippets of text taken out of context. While this obviously holds true for other authors and even those firmly belonging to the classical canon of political thought, an adequate understanding of Althusius is further hampered by the fact that his insistence on the maintenance of a plurally structured political order based on collective loyalties and negotiated agreements does not easily fit into a classical canon that has been constructed retroactively from the perspective of modern state and society. Even the early Habermas, not yet swayed by his own theory of communicative action, only had a few and dismissive comments on Althusius. In his account of the early-modern transformation of that old plural order into a modern bourgeois world unfolding under the regulatory and protective umbrella of centralized bureaucratic state absolutism, he celebrated Hobbes as the rational beginning of 'social philosophy as science'. In Althusius, he only saw a trickster presenting as political system what he thought did not go beyond the 'schematization of accidental relationships'.[71] With the outcome of the epochal transformation, centralization and bureaucratization, no longer in doubt, it is easy to dismiss the Althusian political system as accidental or irrelevant. What Habermas failed to recognize, however, is that this political system very much transcended the accidental relationships of the time and offered an alternative vision and path into the future that at the time still was every step as rational as the Hobbesian one. But history is written by victors and rational social science is its handmaiden.

V. Relevance in Ascendance?

Gierke's assessment of Althusius' *Politica* as imbued by a spirit of federalism was entirely valid. The federalism Gierke had in mind, however, was not that of the American federal state but that of the Bismarck federation, which had followed in the footsteps of the Holy Roman Empire by retaining 'long-standing norms of diplomatic *Verhandlung* (negotiation)'.[72] To be sure, the Bismarck constitution had taken from the American precedent a bicameral legislature with a parliamentary lower chamber and a regional upper chamber. And in this upper chamber, the Bundesrat, still composed of hereditary princes representing their territories, decisions now could also be taken by weighted majority rule. But as in the Holy Roman Empire before, and in the European Union thereafter, majority decisions, even

[70] Kenneth D. McRae, 'Ramist Tendencies in the Thought of Jean Bodin', *Journal of the History of Ideas* XVI (1955), 306–23.

[71] Jürgen Habermas, *Theorie und Praxis* (1972), pp. 67–9.

[72] Daniel Ziblatt, *Structuring the State: The Formation of Italy and Germany and the Puzzle of Federalism* (2006), p. 139.

though easily orchestrated by Prussian hegemonic might, were generally avoided. Negotiations in the shadow of majority rule typically went on until agreement was reached.[73] Althusius did not schematize accidental relationships: indeed he elevated the characteristics of those traditional European relationships to the timeless and systematic level of a procedural theory of federalism.

As transmitted through Gierke's book, Althusius influenced the associational thought of British state pluralists from John Neville Figgis to Harold Laski,[74] and he became a major inspiration for a young and impressionable Carl Joachim Friedrich who published a—slightly abridged—new edition of the *Politica* for the first time in 300 years. Friedrich went on to become one of his epoch's most influential political scientists, and he was at hand as an adviser at the end of the Second World War when the new West German republic drafted its first fully democratic federal constitution under Allied supervision. Friedrich credited Althusius with having formulated the first-ever 'full-bodied concept of federalism'. More importantly, he probably took from the *Politica* the understanding that 'federalism is a process rather than a static pattern'.[75] This procedural understanding not just of federalism but of all political order became so paramount for him that when his influential *Man and his Government* was translated into German, he had it titled as: *Politics as a Process of Community Building*.[76]

Friedrich's 1932 edition of the *Politica* spawned some renewed interest in Althusius but the problem of accessibility remained until 1964 when Frederick S. Carney published his—likewise abridged—English translation of the Latin text.[77] Notwithstanding a few excerpts here and there, this was the first translation of the *Politica* into a modern language. Carney's thoughtful and generally perceptive introduction further helped to introduce Althusius to a wider readership. Among the new 'Althusiasts' was the doyen of American federalism studies at the time, Daniel J. Elazar, who was particularly attracted by Althusius' reference to the biblical covenant as the foundation of structured human sociability and politics.[78] Elazar never ceased to sing Althusius' praise as the 'real father of modern federalism'.[79] The praise, however, continued to fall on mostly deaf ears in a scholarly community of federalism specialists who almost invariably associate modern federalism with the American model of a rights-based constitutional federal state rather than with the European tradition of procedural federalism.[80]

So what *is* the relevance of Althusius for international law and political order? His place among the classics of political thought is no longer in question. Yet

[73] Gerhard Lehmbruch, *Parteienwettbewerb im Bundesstaat* (2000), pp. 63–4.
[74] See Paul Q. Hirst (ed.), *The Pluralist Theory of the State* (1993).
[75] Carl J. Friedrich, *Trends of Federalism in Theory and Practice* (1968), p. 12.
[76] Carl J. Friedrich, *Politik als Prozess der Gemeinschaftsbildung* (1970).
[77] Cf. (n. 1) reference.
[78] Daniel J. Elazar, 'Althusius' Grand Design for a Federal Commonwealth', in *Politica*, xxxv–vii (n. 1).
[79] Daniel J. Elazar, 'Federalism', in D.L. Sills (ed.), *International Encyclopedia of the Social Sciences* (1968), p. 363.
[80] See Hueglin, 'Comparing Federalisms' (n. 31).

notwithstanding the sustained work by members of an international society in his name,[81] Althusius has remained at the margins of scholarly interest in federalism, and federalism has hardly played a role in the search for a global order of peace and stability. It is not difficult to see why. Althusian federalism squares poorly with the idea and practice of the modern centralized federal state, and that modern centralized federal state hardly offers a promising model for what is for the most part still considered to be a Westphalian global order of sovereign nation-states. It is therefore not coincidental that Althusius' name has cropped up in contexts pointing to the emergence of a post-Westphalian world:

In Canada, at a time when national sovereignty came under siege by Quebec separatism and aggressive forces of regional power assertion more generally, the political scientist and Bodin expert Kenneth McRae, in his final address as the president of the Canadian Political Science Association, asked his colleagues the provocative question: 'Have we, under the 400-year-old spell of national sovereignty, unwisely neglected other sectors of Western thought. . .Should we devise an alternative curriculum in political thought that would stress Althusius over Bodin. . . Gierke over Hegel. . . ?'[82] And in a speech to one of the largest gatherings of scholars and practitioners of federalism ever assembled, the vice-president of the European constitutional convention and former Italian prime minister, Giuliano Amato, conjured up the name of Althusius no less than four times as evidence that the—ultimately ill-fated—constitutional project would remain faithful to the European tradition of federalism. 'Organizations inspired by the thinking of [Althusius]', he assured his audience, 'deny exclusivity as a matter of principle. No one in a pluralistic system is the exclusive holder of public authority.'[83]

An international political order without the assignment of exclusive authority is very much what Hedley Bull some forty years ago anticipated—and ultimately rejected for a post-Westphalian age: an anarchical neo-medieval world of overlapping plural powers.[84] Writing against the rising tide of exclusive state sovereignty at the end of the Pre-Westphalian age, Althusius wanted to preserve that medieval plurality, by transforming its anarchical tendencies into a stable form of organized con-federal federalism. This federalism would have two main characteristics distinct from the two-tiered modern federal state model. First, it would be a multilevel federal system with the same rules of representation and decision-making at all levels of governance. Second, subsidiarity considerations would guide the process of power sharing in its application of majority rule or unanimous agreement. In this way, the autonomy of smaller communities could be preserved without ignoring the rising importance of larger communities, of states, or even of a universal commonwealth.

[81] International Althusius Society, see <http://www.althusius.de/althusiuse.htm>.

[82] Kenneth D. McRae, 'The Plural Society and the Western Political Tradition', *Canadian Journal of Political Science* XII(4) (1979), 685–6.

[83] Giuliano Amato, 'Plenary Speech', in Raoul Blindenbacher and Arnold Koller (eds.), *Federalism in a Changing World: Learning From Each Other* (2002), p. 579.

[84] Hedley Bull, *The Anarchical Society: A Study of Order in World Politics* ([1977] 2012).

Selected Bibliography

Carney, Frederick S., 'Translator's Introduction', in Frederick S. Carney (ed.), *Johannes Althusius, Politica* (Indianapolis: Liberty Fund, [1964] 1995), pp. ix–xxxiii.

Elazar, Daniel J., 'Althusius and Federalism as Grand Design', in Giuseppe Duso, Werner Krawietz, and Dieter Wyduckel (eds.), *Konsens und Konsoziation in der politischen Theorie der fruehen Neuzeit,* Beiheft 16 *of Rechtstheorie* (Berlin: Duncker & Humblot, 1997), pp. 209–18.

Friedrich, Carl J., 'Introduction', in Carl J. Friedrich (ed.), *Politica Methodice Digesta of Johannes Althusius* (Harvard: Harvard University Press, 1932), pp. xv–xcix.

Hueglin, Thomas O., *Early Modern Concepts for a Late Modern World: Althusius on Community and Federalism* (Waterloo: Wilfrid Laurier University Press, 1999).

Koch, Bettina, 'Johannes Althusius: Between Secular Federalism and the Religious State', in Ann Ward and Lee Ward (eds.), *The Ashgate Research Companion to Federalism*, (Aldershot: Ashgate, 2009), pp. 75–90.

Wyduckel, Dieter, 'Einleitung', in Johannes Althusius, *Politik* (Berlin: Duncker & Humblot, 2003), pp. vii–lxvii.

7

Hugo Grotius: On the Conquest of Utopia by Systematic Reasoning

Stefan Kadelbach

I. Introduction

In the introduction to this book, we subscribed to a moderate anachronism, meant as a term to mark an intermediate position between a contextual perspective on the one hand, and mere interpretive abstraction on the other.[1] Methodically contestable as it is, the position is the more difficult to hold with respect to Hugo Grotius, given the enormous number of original texts, revisions, new editions, translations, commentaries, interpretations, lines of reception, expositions of 'Grotian' traditions and their refutation, as well as discourse on the way everyone reads Grotius, and on those who read those who have read Grotius. A strictly historical stance probably leads to a selective grouping of what is to constitute context; the other extreme is obviously open for inappropriate retrospective projections.[2] A similar dilemma occurs with respect to the problem as to how to approach the texts. The attempt at a fresh look would be both naïve and impossible, given the vast amount of literature, but merely to historicize some four hundred years of exegesis would be bound (to borrow from an exhortation by *Ernst Gombrich*) to miss a museum's paintings while checking the catalogue.[3] The present contribution does not try to detach the reconstruction of the basic elements of Grotian thinking from existing interpretations (below, Section II). However, since some of what is called 'Grotian' is not much more than a standard taxonomy of the history of ideas, the ensuing sections will deal with adaptations of Grotius' philosophy in natural law thinking (Section III) and internationalist reception (Section IV), respectively, in order to assess how much of Grotianism came about in later epochs.

As for Grotius himself, to stick to pictures, catalogues abound and all of them begin with a description of a portrait, the tale of his life.[4] Due to his connections

[1] On the two approaches, see Quentin Skinner, 'Meaning and Understanding in the History of Ideas', *Hist & Theory* 8 (1969), 3–53.

[2] Cf. Martti Koskenniemi, 'Vitoria and Us', *Rechtsgeschichte* 22 (2015), 1–20.

[3] Ernst Gombrich, *The Story of Art* (16th edn, 1995), p. 37.

[4] For a recent biography, see Henk Nellen, *Hugo Grotius: A Lifelong Struggle for Peace in Church and State, 1583-1645* (2015).

with varying political elites, Grotian philosophy of law depends perhaps more than others on the political and economic environment of birthplace, family, and education. The biography has it all: efforts to emancipate the Netherlands from Spanish rule and the search for support abroad; rising wealth and expansionism overseas, paradoxically unaffected by civil war and inner disintegration; and an endless fight without rules, with mixed alliances across religious adherence before and during the Thirty Years' War.[5]

The Grotius story tells us of a gifted offspring of the Delft political elite who went through a humanist *studium generale* at the university of Leiden as a child. At the age of fifteen, he was a political adviser to the chairman of the States of Holland, Land's Advocate Johan Oldenbarnevelt, and a member of his delegation to the French court to remind Henry IV, Catholic at the time, of an old promise of alliance ('*voici le miracle d'Hollande*'). Subsequently, at the age of sixteen, he began to practise as a solicitor, with time to write poetry and with temporary remuneration as an official historiographer. Ambitions towards a political career took shape with positions as a fiscal advocate in the province of Holland (1607) and as a legal adviser of the city of Rotterdam (1613). However, as a member of the patrician faction he also shared its misfortune. In the inner-confessional struggle with orthodox Calvinists, Oldenbarnevelt and Grotius adhered to the Arminian (or remonstrant) party, which opted for confessional tolerance, decentral rule, and a course of compromise vis-à-vis Spain. In a coup of the opponent camp, Prince Maurits, the *stadhouder* and commander-in-chief of five of the seven provinces, sided with the more popular counter-remonstrant party. In 1618, Oldenbarnevelt was sentenced to death, Grotius was condemned to lifetime imprisonment, and his goods were seized. His wife arranged an escape with a daring plot, so that Grotius could emigrate to Paris, where he lived from 1621 to 1631. He subsequently worked as a (poorly talented) diplomat in Swedish services from 1635 to 1645, an attempt to return home having failed. After a passage from Sweden ended in a shipwreck, the philosopher of the freedom of the seas died of exhaustion in Rostock in 1645, at the age of sixty two.

Contemporary commentators stressed Grotius' merits in history, theology, and private law.[6] The significance of Grotius' work on these fields for the better-known treatises is only slowly being rediscovered. A historic booklet about the origins of the States of Holland (1610), a legal pamphlet intended to prove the sovereignty of the Dutch provinces by its descent from Antiquity, already contains the idea of rights and of public authority as their guardian.[7] Grotius' theological notions are of interest for his concept of natural law. Ideas of Christian unification unfold, for

[5] Jan de Vries and Ad van der Woude, *The First Modern Economy: Success, Failure, and Perseverance of the Dutch Economy, 1500-1815* (1997); Jonathan Israel, *The Dutch Republic: Its Rise, Greatness, and Fall, 1477-1806* (1995), pp. 233–505.

[6] Cf. Hasso Hofmann, 'Hugo Grotius', in Michael Stolleis (ed.), *Staatsdenker in der frühen Neuzeit* (1994), pp. 52–77, at p. 53.

[7] *Liber de antiquitate reipublicae Batavicae*, ed. and trans. Jan Waszink et al. (2000), chs. I and VI; for the 'Batavian myth', see Gustaaf van Nifterik, 'Hugo Grotius, Privileges, Fundamental Laws and Rights', *Grotiana* 32 (2011), 1–19, at 4–7.

instance, in *Meletius* (1611), where Grotius displays a preference for consent over dogma and condenses theology into a more abstract form of inter-confessional morality.[8] Seeking for proven agreement thus is a general philosophical disposition to favour established common ground over purity of thought, which is also characteristic of the legal writings. The combination of natural law with systematic legal studies appears, apart from the treatises on the law of nations, in Grotius' introduction to Dutch law, which sets out different categories of rights, many of which are found in *De jure belli ac pacis*.[9] All of this, a historical method of proof, reductionist ethics, and civil-law structuring of the subject-matter, are typical patterns of Grotius' writings on the law of nations.

II. Texts, Intentions, Method

Grotius' theory on the law of nations spreads over several of his more than 100 books and treatises, many of which are unpublished.[10] However, it essentially unfolds in two works, both of which have their own history of reception, *De jure praedae* (hereafter JP in this chapter) and *De jure belli ac pacis* (hereafter JBP in this chapter).

1. *De jure praedae* and *Mare liberum*

The famous manifesto of the freedom of the seas, *Mare liberum*, was originally part of a counsel's opinion, its predecessor *De jure praedae*, written in Grotius' years as a private lawyer.[11] On 25 February 1603, Admiral van Heemskerck, a cousin of Grotius',[12] had seized the Portuguese vessel Santa Caterina in the Straits of Singapore on its return from Japan and Macao.[13] Heemskerck and

[8] *Meletius sive de iis quae inter Christianos conveniunt epistola*, ed. and trans. Guillaume Posthumus Meyjes (1988); cf. Henk Nellen, 'Disputando Inclarescet Veritas: Grotius as a Publicist in France (1621-1645)', in Henk Nellen and Edwin Rabbie (eds.), *Hugo Grotius Theologian* (1994), pp. 121–44.

[9] *Inleidinge tot de Hollandsche rechts-geleertheyd*, written in captivity and published 1631; see Robert Feenstra, 'Grotius et le droit privé européen', *RdC* 182 (1983), 453–69; Franz Wieacker, *Privatrechtsgeschichte der Neuzeit* (1967), pp. 287–301.

[10] Of interest for the genesis of Grotius' concept of law is a chapter from *Parallelon rerum publicarum*, on thought and morals in Antiquity and the Netherlands, probably written in 1602; Wolfgang Fikentscher (ed.), *De fide et perfidia* (1979), pp. 89–145; Hans Blom, 'The Meaning of Trust: Fides Between Self-Interest and Appetitus Societatis', in Pierre-Marie Dupuy and Vincent Chetail (eds.), *The Roots of International Law* (2014), pp. 39–58.

[11] *De iure praedae commentarius*, written in 1604 and 1605, was rediscovered as a whole only in 1864. Grotius had entitled it, alluding to Vitoria, as *De rerum Indicorum*. The name it has today stems from the ed. H.G. Hamaker (1868); citations here are to ed. and trans. Gwladys L. Williams and Walter H. Zeydel (1950), by chapter and page; cf. also recent ed. by Martine Julia van Ittersum (2006).

[12] Richard Tuck, *The Rights of War and Peace* (1999), p. 79, with reference.

[13] Robert Fruin, *An Unpublished Work of Hugo Grotius's*, trans. F. Hopman (1925), pp. 8–40; Peter Borschberg, 'Hugo Grotius' Theory of Trans-Oceanic Trade Regulation: Revisiting *Mare Liberum* (1609)', *Itinerario* 29, 3 (2005), 31–53; Martine Julia van Ittersum, *Profit and Principle: Hugo Grotius, Natural Rights Theories and the Rise of Dutch Power in the East Indies, 1595-1615* (2006), pp. 1–52.

the Portuguese competed for trade with the Sultan of Johor, who had decided to enter into direct commercial relations with the Dutch. The capture of the ship answered a blockade inflicted by the Portuguese on the Sultan to enforce older claims. After the Amsterdam Admiralty Court had ruled that Heemskerck's action was within his powers and the unusually valuable prize could be retained, the United East India Company (Verenigte Oostindische Compagnie, VOC), the successor of the regional company for which Heemskerck had sailed, entrusted Grotius with the mandate to pronounce a statement on the lawfulness under the law of nations.[14]

The structure along the lines of which the argument runs anticipates much of JBP. The initial chapters offer an exposition of rules and laws of just war (*dogmatica*) in scholastic style, a language a Portuguese counterpart would understand. But different from scholastic opinion, the virtue of 'justice', in the sense of not being unjust, here not only meant to avoid harm to others; it is an obligation to guard one's own interest (JP I, pp. 2–3). After a narrative of the conflict with Spain and of Portuguese conduct in the East Indies (*historica*), the remaining sections vindicate the prize (chs. XI to XV). In chapter XII on the right of private companies (like VOC) to wage war, Grotius on its face follows an argument Vitoria had developed in *De Indis*, where he had derived a right of peoples to visit and to entertain commerce with others (JP XII, p. 218). As a corollary, no title over the high seas could lie, as it had been derived by Portugal and Spain from the papal award of 1493, for the pope did not hold secular authority (JP XII, p. 223). Since subjective rights were conferred upon man by God (JP II, p. 9), liberty was characteristic of human beings in the state of nature and self-preservation, a natural means to secure existence.[15] The faculty to pursue self-interest is a consequence of man's natural power over himself. In the given context, it encompassed the right to send ships and to engage in trade with other nations, the more so since all society benefited from it. Interference by others, as by Portugal in this case, was an act of piracy and could be responded to accordingly. Usually, punishment of the wrongdoer was with the ruler, but since there was no property in the high seas (JP XII, p. 231), there was no public authority with which punishment could interfere.[16] Justification of punitive private wars was something new in the history of just-war treatises. However, having declared the oceans a good common to all, Grotius had made sure that the enforcement of trading interests also served the entire community of mankind.[17]

The crucial chapter XII appeared separately under the title *Mare liberum* on request by the VOC, which hoped that it would help to guard their stakes in the

[14] It is suggested that VOC was established with the capital gained from proceeds of the prize; see Tuck, *Rights*, p. 79 (n. 12).

[15] Grotius was influenced here (as in many ways) by Fernando Vázquez de Menchaca ('the pride of Spain', JP XII, p. 249), adviser to Philipp II. See Kurt Seelmann, *Die Lehre des Fernando Vazquez de Menchaca vom Dominium* (1979), pp. 106–31; Peter Borschberg, *Commentarius in Theses XI* (1994), pp. 73–101; Annabel Brett, *Liberty, Right and Nature: Individual Rights in Later Scholastic Thought* (1997), pp. 165–204.

[16] In addition to the right to reparation for injury, assistance to the Malayan allies justified war (JP XIII, pp. 314–6).

[17] Annabel Brett, *Changes of State* (2011), p. 105.

course of truce negotiations with Spain.[18] Since the justification of privateering aimed at the heart of colonial trade, it was set to prompt reactions in Spain and England.[19] During the two colonial conferences in 1613 and 1615, Grotius had to realize that his English counterparts turned the argument against him in that they claimed freedom of commerce with the East Indies and rejected Dutch insistence on older rights. Now, for Grotius, the *pacta sunt servanda* principle was the ground to defend the Dutch position, which included contractual rights acquired from local rulers, and the principle could, along the lines of JP, be defended by force. The response by John Selden, later published under the title *Mare clausum* as a quasi-official statement of the English king,[20] sets out a different idea of the acquisition of property in the state of nature. Grotius had held that land and sea were initially owned by no one (*res nullius*, JP XII, p. 227); whereas land could be divided and taken in possession as *dominium*, the seas remained free of title and jurisdiction (JP XII, p. 231) and could be used by everyone for travel and trade. Grotius' right of communication has therefore been interpreted as a return to the 'lost world' of the state of nature.[21] Selden, by contrast, described land and sea as being in an English-type common property (*res communis*) from the beginning, so that it required a convention to own them—by the force of which England ruled all neighbouring waves including the Atlantic.

JP and *Mare liberum* already contain most of what comes up again in much greater detail in JBP, and can be read, as it has been done, in diametrically opposite ways. The traditional line used to consider JP as a defence of the freedom of the seas against imperial claims of Spanish hegemony.[22] A different reading takes it as the justification of a rigid protection of commercial interest and imperial expansionism,[23] some even of bellicism and a generally hostile stance against non-European peoples.[24] The latter point may be an overstatement, since Grotius had stressed prominently the importance to protect allies irrespectively of faith (JP XII, p. 315). But indeed, the notion that native people could sell away their rights, the concept of shared sovereignty as well as the strictly binding force of promises and the right to enforce them in war suited commercial and colonial interests. That the shift in emphasis changed over time from the freedom of trade and navigation to the *pacta sunt servanda* principle does not make it look any better. The fact that Grotius

[18] *Mare liberum – Sive de iure quod Batavis competit ad Indicana commercia dissertatio*, recently published as Robert Feenstra (ed.), *Hugo Grotius Mare liberum* 1609–2009 (2009), based on the first anonymous publication of 1609; the second edn 1618 appeared under Grotius' name.

[19] Mónica Brito Vieira, '*Mare Liberum* vs. *Mare Clausum*: Grotius, Freitas, and Selden's Debate on Dominion over the Seas', *J Hist Id* 64 (2003), 361–77.

[20] The first version was written in 1616–1617; published as *Mare Clausum, Seu De Dominio Maris* (1635), trans. Marchamont Nedham (1652); see Tuck, *Rights*, pp. 116–20 (n. 12).

[21] Brett, *Changes*, p. 199 (n. 17).

[22] For a contemporary view, see Benjamin Schmidt, *Innocence Abroad: The Dutch Imagination and the New World, 1570-1670* (2001), pp. 181–2.

[23] Edward Keene, *Beyond the Anarchical Society: Grotius, Colonialism and Order in World Politics* (2002), pp. 50–9; van Ittersum, *Profit and Principle*, pp. 108–13, 167–86 (n. 13); Erik Thomson, 'The Dutch Miracle Modified', *Grotiana* 30 (2009), 107–30.

[24] Tuck, *Rights*, pp. 78–108 (n. 12).

distanced himself later (JBP II 3, 8) does not in itself have to mean a change of mind. Grotius in the 1620s still hoped to return to his home country, the commercial power of which had consolidated in the meantime. Freedom is good for newcomers, whereas established powers seek cartel and monopoly.[25] Thus, JP offers material to deconstruct Grotian idealism and to render it a myth.

2. *De jure belli ac pacis*

Even though JP has attracted considerably more attention in recent years, JBP is the main opus on which Grotius' reputation rests as one of the central figures in the history of natural law, international law, and international relations. Much in it is indebted to JP, and the question arises how far it can be perceived as being independent from its reasonably partisan predecessor.[26] For Grotius, the situation had changed dramatically since JP was written. JBP is not the product of an admired mind in proximity to power, but of one of captivity, exile, and limited financial resources. Former affiliations were not cut off, but loose at best. The dedication is to Louis XIII, who once had backed up Grotius' faction in the inner-Dutch conflict and then had supported him by paying a modest, albeit irregular, pension during Grotius' years in Paris. Thus, JBP is the product of a subsidized scholar who addresses the European world of states.

Its difficult reading has been a challenge ever since.[27] The structure roughly follows the *dogmatica* of JP, but as a whole changes from a rather predetermined exposition for specific purposes to the style of systematic private law science. After a general explanation of the concept of law (a.), it deals with all sorts of reasons to resort to war (b.). Book III is devoted to conduct of warfare (c.).

a) The concept of law

The Prolegomena start by lamenting that, as opposed to civil law, no one had dealt with the law among states[28] 'in a systematic and comprehensive manner' (Pr. 1: *universim ac certo ordine*),[29] although nothing less than the 'welfare' of mankind

[25] Cf. van Ittersum, *Profit and Principle*, pp. 371–412 (n. 13); Andrea Weindl, 'Grotius' *Mare Liberum* in the Political Practice of Early-Modern Europe', *Grotiana* 30 (2009), 131–51, at 142f.; Martti Koskenniemi, 'International Law and the Emergence of Mercantile Capitalism: Grotius to Smith', in *Roots of International Law*, pp. 3–37, at p. 22 (n. 10).

[26] For continuity and changes in just war doctrine, see Peter Haggenmacher, *Grotius et la doctrine de la guerre juste* (1983), pp. 588–91; in political theory Richard Tuck, *Philosophy and Government 1572-1651* (1993), pp. 196–201.

[27] The most common English edition of JBP comprises some 900 pages with about a million words, *De Jure Belli ac Pacis Libri Tres* (1646), trans. Francis W. Kelsey (1925). Citations here are from this edition (former editions were published in 1625, 1631, 1632, and 1642). There have been 117 editions in twelve languages until today, with twelve in French and thirteen in English alone; see Hofmann, *Grotius*, pp. 60–1 (n. 6). The recent English edition, with an introduction by Richard Tuck (2005), is a reprint of the 1738 translation by Barbeyrac.

[28] The term 'state' is used here in the sense of a political and legal entity distinct from its people and with an authority to act on its behalf, i.e. a commonwealth in Grotian terminology (*societas civilis* or *civitas*).

[29] This verdict included Vitoria, see Pr. 37.

so demanded. By setting out such a system, Grotius writes, he wanted to contribute to the 'philosophy of law' (*jurisprudentia*, Pr. 30). As a definition, the law of nations (*jus gentium*) is distinguished from *jus civile* (municipal law). This term 'strictly speaking' (JBP II 8, 1.2) is reserved to the law between nations, so that it does not have the dual meaning of *jus gentium* contended by Vitoria and mentioned by Suarez, who also used it for a common law that is valid for all human beings.[30]

The first step is to prove that such law exists at all. Grotius illustrates the opinion that states among themselves were in an anarchical state of nature without rules with a citation taken from Thucydides, which represents the position that history advocated for the law of the fittest. Whether this addressed contemporary philosophical scepticism or referred back to a remark by Richelieu to Grotius is hard to verify.[31] Grotius replies along the lines of a stoicist refutation of utility as the governing principle: man had not only an interest in self-preservation, but also an impelling desire for society (*appetitus societatis*), what stoics called *oikeiosis* (Pr. 6), and for social order (*societatis custodia*), 'peaceful and organized according to his [. . .] intelligence, with those who are of his own kind' (Pr. 8). The sociable nature of man is the source of law, and to its sphere belong the abstaining from the goods of others, the obligation to fulfil promises, reparation for loss, and punishment of those who violate the law. These principles constitute most of the essence of the law of nature. Hobbes' political philosophy can be read as a commentary of this.[32]

The question where natural law comes from is addressed in a well-known passage which states that the law of nature would be binding 'even if we should concede [. . .] that there is no God' (*etiamsi daremus [. . .] non esse Deum*) (Pr. 11). Not even God can change it (I 1, 10.5).[33] Rationalist schools read the phrase as an expression of distance to law based on the will of God and hence as the emancipation of natural law from theology.[34] The context of the passage, however, does not warrant unequivocal conclusions.[35] It seems more plausible that Grotius refers to an old debate in which the impious hypothesis was used as an argument against Ockham's voluntarism.[36] Accordingly, what is right directly relates to God's will, whereas

[30] Cf. Brett, *Changes*, pp. 13–14 (n. 17). For Suarez (in this context LDL II 19, 8) see below n. 80.

[31] The relation to contemporary scepticism forms part of the argument made by Richard Tuck, 'Grotius, Carneades and Hobbes', *Grotiana* 4 (1983), 43–62; but see Petter Korkman, 'Barbeyrac on Scepticism and on Grotian Modernity', *Grotiana* 20/21 (1999/2000), 77–106; on Grotius and Richelieu, see Cornelis G. Roelofsen, 'Grotius and the State Practice of his Day', *Grotiana* 18 (1997), 97–120, at 116–19.

[32] See III. below.

[33] Why JBP was placed on the index, as JP had been before, is not entirely clear; J. St. Leger, *The 'Etiamsi Daremus' of Hugo Grotius* (1962), p. 22, reports an opinion that JBP II 29, 50 was one reason, where it is held that wars against those who err in faith are not justified for that reason alone.

[34] Cf. A.P. d'Entrèves, *Natural Law: An Introduction to Legal Philosophy* (1970), pp. 50–5; Charles Edwards, *The Miracle of Holland* (1981), pp. 9–25.

[35] The background could have been the inner-Calvinist controversy, see St. Leger, *Etiamsi Daremus*, pp. 141–2 (n. 33); Tadashi Tanaka, 'Grotius' Method: With Special Reference to Prolegomena', Yasuaki Onuma (ed.), *A Normative Approach to War* (1993), pp. 11–31, at pp. 27–9.

[36] It is found in Gregory of Rimini, cited (but rejected) by Suárez and used by Vázquez de Menchaca, see St. Leger, *Etiamsi Daremus*, pp. 96–147 (n. 33); Edwards, *Miracle*, pp. 48–69 (n. 34); Leonard Besselink, 'The Impious Hypothesis Revisited', *Grotiana* 9 (1988), 3–63; Knud Haakonssen, *Natural Law and Moral Philosophy: From Grotius to Scottish Enlightenment* (1996), p. 29.

intellectualism builds on human reason as a component of man's natural ability to recognize what is just. Grotius would then have taken a third way in deriving natural law from both sources. Since God's inexistence is not a possible assumption to make (Pr. 11), both 'the free will of God' (Pr. 12) *and* human sociability and reason, which equally flow from divine will (Pr. 7 and 8), constitute natural law. This position would also be in keeping with protestant ethics. Accordingly, the true will of God is inaccessible as long as it is not revealed, but indications of it can be found by reason; law can be both secular and in harmony with belief.[37] Thus, even though the secularization thesis proves difficult to hold, Grotius still marks a change in paradigm.[38] The passage is also a clarification of the reasoning for the law of nature in comparison to JP, which had begun with a statement of divine will and common consent as the sources of natural law (rules I and II, JP II, pp. 8 and 12), without, however, relating them to each other.[39]

Natural human sociability brings about common accord (Pr. 17). Within the commonwealth, public authority builds on a contract (II 14)[40] by which people choose to whom they entrust power (II 5, 17) and thus their political system.[41] If not subject to another human will, such authority is supreme (*imperium, summum imperium*, or *summa potestas civilis*).[42] By the same act, such contracts establish states (*civitates*) as 'complete associations' (*consociationes*, I 1, 14.1; II 5, 17), which are bodies external to the peoples themselves (*corpora artificialia*, II 9, 3.1) and capable of entering into legal relations.[43] Man's natural consciousness of the need to conclude contracts also applies to society beyond boundaries (Pr. 17), the realm of *jus gentium*. JBP restates the notion, already developed in JP, that subjects of *jus gentium* are states, rulers, and private persons alike. They form the society of mankind (*magna civitas universitatis*, Pr. 17, or *societas humana*). From the fusion of natural sociability with a contract as a legal source it follows that *jus gentium* consists of both natural law and human volitional law (I 1, 14.1). As far as it is volitional law alone, it has a purely external effect (*in foro externo*) if it does not coincide with genuine justice (Pr. 41).

[37] Cf. Sergio Dellavalle, *Dalla comunità particolare all'ordine universale* (2011), vol I, pp. 162–6; John Haskell, 'Hugo Grotius in the Contemporary Memory of International Law', *Emory IL Rev* 25 (2011), 269–98, at 277–9.

[38] Franco Todescan, *Le radici teologiche del giusnaturalismo laico* (1983), pp. 99–111.

[39] The departure from JP in that point is overstated by Giovanni Ambrosetti, *I presupposti telogici e speculativi delle concezioni giuridiche di Grozio* (1955), pp. 93–127; see Haggenmacher, *Guerre juste*, pp. 496–504 (n. 26).

[40] D.F. Schelten, 'Grotius' Doctrine of the Social Contract', *Neth IL Rev* 30 (1983), 43–60; Michael P. Zuckert, *Natural Rights and the New Republicanism* (1994), pp. 123–6; Annabel Brett, 'Natural Right and Civil Community: The Civil Philosophy of Hugo Grotius', *Hist J* 45 (2002), 31–51; Frank Grunert, 'Der Vertrag als rechtliches Medium sozialer Gestaltung: Zum Kontraktualismus bei Hugo Grotius', in Norbert Konegen and Peter Nitschke (eds.), *Staat bei Hugo Grotius* (2005), pp. 125–37.

[41] That this is not the only way to constitute authority, but also that conquest is a possible basis (JBP I 3, 8.6), shows that Grotius' interest is in the mere fact of sovereignty, not the character of rule; for an exposition in a former work of Grotius', see Borschberg, *Commentarius* (n. 15).

[42] The three terms are used synonymously, cf. I 3, 6, and 7.

[43] Tadashi Tanaka, 'State and Power', in *Normative Approach*, pp. 122–46 (n. 35).

The question arises as to how the different layers of law relate to each other. Grotius is not explicit in that respect. The answer depends on the secularization dispute reflected in the impious hypothesis conundrum (Pr. 11). If we follow the secularization thesis, natural law is the highest;[44] if not, divine volitional law is superior (cf. I 1, 10.1). At any rate, the latter is binding only for those to whom it is revealed, be they Jews or Christians, unless it has become 'adequately known' to all men (I 1, 15); it rarely lends itself to enforcement. Natural law then is the next source in rank. It is complete law in that it is both internally and externally binding, and it is universal since its existence would not depend on God. However, it is confined to some basic principles, hence less concrete and leaves space for change, so that it is supplemented by human volitional law. Human volitional law can be of an equally universal character, since pacts may be concluded between all nations (I 1, 14.1). More often, however, consent is implicit. The last layers are the norms of morality, for which different terms are employed (II 1, 11: *caritas*; III 13, 4.3: *regulae humanitatis* etc.); the overarching concept is *interna justitia*, which also empowers man to recognize natural law. It is, however, broader than law and distinguished from it. From the defence of law against utility it followed that all natural law coincides with morals (Pr. 5-27). But since human law is not necessarily congruent with it, morality serves a supplementary function where natural law is permissive. Both are distinct in their consequences. Although promise and legal obligations do not depend on sanctions (Pr. 20), only law may be enforced by coercive means (Pr. 25; II 22, 16).

In book I, Grotius proceeds to prepare his system of subjective rights by further elaborating on the notion of law. He discerns three different concepts of *jus*, which are set out in three steps. The first is justice, 'what is just' in the sense that it is not 'in conflict with the nature of society of beings endowed with reason' (I 1, 3.1). The second meaning is a moral quality innate to all humans. By virtue of this quality, man has rights to have and to do 'what is just'. This law is present in two variants: perfect rights, which Grotius calls *facultas*, and imperfect rights, called *aptitudo*. The distinction is based on the Aristotelian twin concept of attributive (according to Grotius: expletive) and distributive (allocative) justice, but Grotius gives a new meaning to it. Only the former type is hard law and enforceable (I 1, 5). It comprises powers (*potestas*), as over oneself (*libertas*) and over others, ownership (*dominium*), and contractual rights (*creditum*). *Aptitudo*, by contrast, is a matter of mercy and charity, lastly administered by the state or the Church, so that there is no enforceable claim to it (I 1, 7). This transformation of *facultas* into right in a legal sense is one of the core concepts of JBP.[45] The third meaning of *jus* equates *jus* with *lex*, which denotes anything that is binding law in a community (I 1, 9), be it natural or volitional, which includes *jus gentium*.

[44] Tadashi Tanaka, 'Grotius' Concept of Law', in *Normative Approach*, pp. 32–56, at pp. 51–4 (n. 35).
[45] Cf. Brett, *Changes*, p. 105 (n. 17).

The consequences of the relationship between natural law and human volitional law are difficult to spot and have been a constant source of critique. In that respect, the famous treatment of slavery (I 1, 5; I 3, 8.1) is an example, which according to Grotius can be subject to contract and permission (III 7, 1). It does not help much to demand that volitional law be 'just';[46] the question is what the consequences are if it is not. Natural law, as far as it does not command behaviour, is dispositive in the sense that it leaves room for permissible conduct. Volitional law is there to indicate consent and to clarify what the law is. If such law commands or allows what natural law permits, the former prevails. The reverse case that volitional law contradicts natural law is less clearly stated. There are various categories of exceptions, to which permission of cruelties in the course of war belong (see c. below). A related conflict between natural law and volitional law is behind the problem of resistance which natural law does not permit. If a people can decide to subject itself even to slavery, this holds the more true for transfer of government to an absolute ruler (JBP I 3, 8), and all these contracts are, as a rule, binding (I 4),[47] unless under extreme conditions of necessity (I 4, 7.2-4; II 14, 12.2).[48] Only humanitarian intervention can promise relief, when the intervener guards the rights of the oppressed on behalf of human society (II 25, 8.2 and 3; III 20, 40). The solution to the problem of resistance then is caution in constitution-making, as can be seen in many states (cf. I 3, 8.14): if the authority can be as a whole transferred to the ruler, this must also be true of parts of it, so that the right to resistance may be retained in the contract (I 4, 14). Obviously, the prohibition of rebellion under natural law does not prevent derogating from it by consent.

b) System of rights and just war

The second book is on just war. It deals systematically with subjective rights (law in the second meaning of *jus*), as far as they are binding law (*jus* in its third meaning), so that they can be enforced.[49] Their violation is unjust (*jus* in the first meaning), so that it justifies defence, seeking recovery, and punishment, each of which is a just cause (II 1, 2). War is the transformation of a legal affair: where peaceful means of

[46] Benedict Kingsbury and Benjamin Straumann, 'State of Nature versus Commercial Sociability as the Basis of International Law', in Samantha Besson and John Tasioulas (eds.), *The Philosophy of International Law* (2010), pp. 33–51, at pp. 42–3.

[47] Thus, Grotius combines constitutional rule *and* the option for absolutism; see Deborah Baumgold, *Contract Theory in Historical Context* (2010), pp. 35–6, 78. It is not surprising that Rousseau found Grotius' theory was favourable to tyrants, but not to individuals; see *Du contrat social* (1762), ed. Bernard Gagnebin et al. (1964), liv. I 2, pp. 352–3. Suárez' *De Legibus*, which justified tyrannicide under certain circumstances, had been burnt publicly in Paris, the place of Grotius' exile; see St. Leger, *Etiamsi Daremus*, pp. 106–8 (n. 33). After all, whereas Grotius had left the choice of the political system to the contracting people, Hobbes will later explain that the only option *is* absolutism, Baumgold, *Contract Theory*, pp. 90–1 (n. 47).

[48] JBP I 14, 12.2 mentions that 'there can be laws that are plainly foolish and ridiculous'. The passage is related to resistance; but see Peter Pavel Remec, *The Position of the Individual in International Law according to Grotius and Vattel* (1960), pp. 79–80, 89, 96–7.

[49] For Haggenmacher, *Guerre juste*, pp. 549–52, 615 (n. 26), the genuine achievement of JBP is its system of *justitia belli*.

law end, war begins. The natural right of self-defence within the commonwealth is transferred to the state (II 4, 2.1), so that it has the authority (*jurisdictio*, II 1, 1) to wage public war. But beyond borders, as already developed in JP, private war can be just as permissible (II 1, 3).

Most violations refer to private rights of individuals (*potestates*), such as *dominium* (rights vis-à-vis persons or to property) and obligations (*creditum*). Rights of the governing power (*imperium*) form but a category of rights flowing from *potestas* over persons and, by derivation, over property (*dominium*). Thus, territorial sovereignty (II 9) is a function of rule which can be acquired overseas by contract with local authorities or by just war, and its violation may constitute in itself a reason for enforcement.[50] The right to migrate and settle is an extension of the rights to navigation and trade equally defended already in JP. A special case is war for the sake of others; Grotius' humanitarian intervention, as mentioned, can assume the strange character of an act on behalf of a people that has no right to resist.[51]

The subjective character of law, on the one hand, and its relation to state authority, on the other, gives rise to the question where this concept stands in the development of individual or human rights. Given the emphasis on man's natural equipment with rights ('[b]y nature a man's life is his own, not indeed to destroy, but to safeguard', II 17, 2.1) and their concrete shape ('body, limbs, reputation, honour'), one might see this derivation of rights from human faculty as an important step in that direction.[52] However, it is not more than that. Methodologically, the rights system is an adaptation of Roman civil law to the laws of nations; how far its substance can be traced back to medieval theology is subject to a controversy between legal historians and historians of political thought.[53] But from a modern public-law perspective on the function of these rights, it is notable that the individual has a role in this system foremost in creating authority. Freedom as such, be it of human beings or of entire peoples, is present in the state of nature, but it can be lost by waiver or conquest, as the treatment of slavery and resistance has shown. Human persons are seen as members of a community, but not as isolated individuals who confront a powerful state.[54]

[50] Unsurprisingly, the construction has been received as to affirm the old design for colonization; cf. Tuck, *Rights*, pp. 104–8 (n. 12); Koskenniemi, *Emergence*, p. 17 (n. 25).

[51] Cf. Yasuaki Onuma, 'War', in *Normative Approach*, pp. 57–121, at pp. 107–11 (n. 35).

[52] Cf. Hans Blom, 'The Great Privilege (1477) as "Code of Dutch Freedom" ', in Barbara Dölemeyer and Heinz Mohnhaupt (eds.), *Das Privileg im europäischen Vergleich* (1997), vol. I, pp. 233–47; Peter Haggenmacher, 'Droits subjectifs et système juridique chez Grotius', in Luc Foisneau (ed.), *Politique, droit et théologie chez Bodin, Grotius et Hobbes* (1997), pp. 73–130, at p. 130; van Nifterik, *Grotius*, pp. 15–16 (n. 7); but see Christoph Stumpf, *The Grotian Theology of International Law* (2006), pp. 58–63, who holds that the system was not on rights, but on obligations. This would be in line with prior natural law conceptions of justice as virtue and duty, see Leo Strauss, *Natural Right and History* (1953), pp. 146–8.

[53] See Laurens Winkel, 'Problems of Legal Systematization from *De iure praedae* to *De iure belli ac pacis*', *Grotiana* 26–8 (2005–2007), 61–78, at 76–7.

[54] Knud Haakonssen, 'Hugo Grotius and the History of Political Thought', *Pol Thr* 13 (1985), 239–65; Brian Tierney, *The Idea of Natural Rights* (1997), pp. 333–6.

The place of rights is in the doctrine of war, for they are the standard against which use of force is justified. This opens up another problem. If there are as many reasons for war as there are rights, why bother outlawing war in the first place? Obviously, there is a second part to it. As explained in book I, Grotius conceives war as a legal relationship, a certain state in the course of a dispute. For that purpose, he combines the just war tradition with a notion of form and status as Gentili understood it,[55] and like in the just-war theories before, further requirements must be met, i.e. authority, proportionality, and right intention. Private war is linked to authority in that it depends on the non-availability of public power. As to proportionality, war should only be the last resort; in case of doubt, negotiation, conferences (II 23, 7) and, famously, arbitration (II 23, 8) are recommended. The requirement of just intention aims at concealing impermissible interest behind allegedly just causes. In the end, war can only be justified in rare cases (II 24, 8). The weakness of this concept is that proportionality is not a compelling standard, and intentions are hard to verify. One might conclude that *raison d'état* has become domesticated by law,[56] but at the price of a plethora of just reasons to wage war.

c) Laws of war

Book III deals with 'what is permissible in war' (III 1, 1). The concept of 'permission' (*quod liceat*, III 1, 1) is decisive. Natural law coincides with moral precepts, but just as there is immoral behaviour that goes unpunished by men (like lying, for example), natural law also leaves room for permitting inhuman conduct in war. In that space, law of a merely outward effect (Pr. 41), i.e. volitional *jus gentium*, can develop. Thus, book III consults consecutively natural law, the law of nations, and commandments of Christian duty.[57] Since not all that is done in the course of conflict is punishable under natural law, the rules of conflict are, for the most part, merely limited by morality. The cruelty of these laws has often been deplored.[58] They allow wanton killings of anyone on the enemy's territory, including women and children, the right to refuse surrender, destruction, pillage, torturing of prisoners, and enslavement (III 4, 6 to 18).

This lack of legal restraint is said to pay tribute to what was known from the wars at the age; but it also looks as if Grotius fell back to his habit of relying on antique sources against his own intentions.[59] One may also question whether this description is in line with the stoic assumption of the sociable nature of man. Obviously, the international society has serious shortcomings, and the strategy to overcome

[55] Onuma, 'War', in *Normative Approach*, p. 62 (war as a 'lawsuit') (n. 35).

[56] Cf. Istvan Hont, *Jealousy of Trade* (2005), p. 15; Kingsbury and Straumann, *State of Nature*, p. 35 (n. 46).

[57] Hans Wehberg, Die Unterscheidung von Natur- und Völkerrecht in der Lehre von Hugo Grotius, in *Mensch und Staat in Recht und Geschichte* (1954), pp. 227–32.

[58] Karma Nabulsi, *Traditions of War: Occupation, Resistance and the Law* (1999), pp. 155–8.

[59] As opposed to practice, law was not necessarily as cruel; see Kenneth Ögren, 'Humanitarian Law in the Articles of War decreed 1621 by King Gustavus II Adolphus of Sweden', *IRRC* 36 (1996), 438–42.

them is to offer certain advantages, such as enslavement and property seized in war, for abstaining from even more destructive conduct.[60] However, atrocities, if not punishable, were nevertheless immoral (III 4, 3); a sorry comfort as it is, the argument is a critique of what was conceived then as voluntary law.[61] There were only two ways out of these savage customs to the forces of reason, the virtue of moderation (*temperantia*), and change of *jus gentium*.[62] An accurate restatement of contemporary law was not intended. Later Vattel was to elevate such principles to the normativity of law. Grotius' project was to frame a realist picture of the laws of war in a plea for moral progress.

3. Intention and method

a) Intention

Given the large proportion devoted to war, it is at times observed that relatively little attention appears to be paid to peace itself.[63] However, peace is mentioned at the beginning as the stated intention (Pr 28).[64] It is the central perspective from which everything is supposed to make sense, the Alpha and Omega of the whole exercise.[65] It serves as the justification behind problematic or contradictory parts of JBP like the binding force of contracts and treaties under all circumstances, the refusal of a right of resistance, the according of benefits of war also to the unjust party, and it is the regulative idea behind the principles of conduct in war. Peace prevails over freedom and justice.[66]

The question is what kind of peace this means. The second book depicts peace as the absence of war, which appears against the background of contemporary bellicism as a plausible end in itself. However, there is a further normative dimension to it. If the purpose of war is re-establishing or securing peace (I 1, 1) by restoration

[60] Daniel Schwartz, 'Grotius on the Moral Standing of the Society of Nations', *J Hist IL* 14 (2012), 123–46.

[61] G. I. A. D. Draper, 'Grotius' Place in the Development of Legal Ideas About War', in Hedley Bull et al. (eds.), *Hugo Grotius and International Relations* (1992), pp. 177–208, at p. 207; Tadashi Tanaka, 'Temperamenta', in *Normative Approach*, pp. 276–307, at pp. 302–3 (n. 35); Steven Forde, 'Hugo Grotius on Ethics and War', *Am Pol Sc Rev* 92 (1998), 639–48.

[62] See Remec, *Individual*, pp. 107–18 (n. 48).

[63] Hofmann, *Grotius*, p. 65 '*[v]om Frieden ist gar nicht die Rede*' (n. 6).

[64] 'Throughout the Christian world I observed a lack of restraint in relation to war, such as even barbarous races should be ashamed of; I observed that men rush to arms for slight causes, or no cause at all, and that when arms have once been taken up there is no longer any respect for law, divine or human; it is as if, in accordance with a general decree, frenzy had openly been let loose for the committing of all crimes.'

[65] The bracket of peace also determines the structure of JBP, cf. I 1, 1 (*controversiae* as the first word of book I) and, in the end, III 23, 16 (prayer for peace); see also Haggenmacher, *Guerre juste*, pp. 565–7 (n. 26).

[66] An objection to this view is that the treatment of valid law of the time undermined this declared purpose; see Bert Röling, 'Are Grotius' Ideas Obsolete in an Expanded World?' and Georg Schwarzenberger, 'The Grotius Factor in International Law and Relations', both in *Hugo Grotius and International Relations*, pp. 281–300 and 301–12, respectively (n. 61).

of rights, the underlying idea is a concept of order. A peaceful and organized society was described as the natural condition of man at the beginning (Pr. 6). If this is the description of a perfect peace, the Grotian order has features of a backward utopia, which would in a way comply with the line of reasoning already found in JP. True, while JP was concerned with explaining why the pursuit of self-interest is just, JBP was about the failure of justice in the pursuit of self-interest.[67] However, both coincide in the general structuring of the argument towards an underlying notion of a state of nature to be recovered, undivided commons of the seas in the first case, order by peace in the second.

b) Method

This intention behind JBP has certainly contributed to decisions on difficult choices in its course. However, it does not, for the most part, guide visibly the process of developing the content of specific rules. The question how the components of the system were filled with substance is one of method. Grotius discerns a deductive and an inductive element, both of which are in the end similar to each other. Natural law and volitional law are dealt with separately. Natural law, including the first principles of nature (*prima naturae*), the 'first duty' to take care of oneself (I 2, 1.1), can be ascertained by virtue of human reason, since a sense of what complies with it and what does not is part of the human condition (Pr. 9, 23, 39). Proof can be found in the testimony of those who have expressed themselves on the matter with sufficient authority. The inductive method, by contrast, seeks evidence for practice. For 'when many at different times, and in different places, affirm the same thing as certain, that ought to be referred to a universal cause' (Pr. 40). Both methods serve as proof for the existence of a common consent that is present in the law of nations (Pr. 40, I 1, 14.2). The natural ('which is truly and in all respects law') and volitional law of nations ('which produces merely a kind of outward effect') can only be distinguished 'by the character of the matter'. Thus, both the deductive and inductive methods start with practical reasoning and rely on the same material in finding evidence. The Grotian method is an abstraction from customs of the time (Pr. 58),[68] and its result is an abstract notion of law rather than codification.[69]

Canvassing just how much influence which source really had in JBP has become a science of its own. Grotius mentions Aristotle in particular, who 'holds the foremost place' (Pr. 42), Greek and Roman history, poets and orators,[70] the Bible, and

[67] Brett, *Changes*, pp. 70–1 (n. 17).

[68] When Pr. 58 refers to method as 'mathematics', Grotius means verification in this sense and not what Cartesian rationalism denotes as *mos geometricus*; previously, he had denoted the method to set out axioms (rules and laws) before proving them as mathematical (JP I, p. 7).

[69] To what extent Grotian thought had an impact on practice is a different question; see Edgar Müller, 'Hugo Grotius und der Dreißigjährige Krieg', *Tijdschrift voor Rechtsgeschiedenis* 77 (2009), 499–538.

[70] Benjamin Straumann, *Roman Law in the State of Nature: The Classical Foundations of Hugo Grotius' Natural Law* (2015).

Roman law.[71] It is obvious that Grotius drew from stoicism, be it immediately or as taken up by humanism and scholasticism alike.[72] *Oikeiosis* and the demand for justice even in relations external to the state are stoic (JBP Pr 5-18), as is the merger of natural justice and imperial claims in just-war theory (cf. Pr 53).[73] The Humanist spirit coined the immediate environment of the Leiden school, but its precise impact on JBP is hard to detect.[74] Some aspects show traces of Erasmus' (qualified) pacifism, which may be seen in an expressed principal aversion to war (Pr. 28), but Grotius rejects his general admonishment not to use arms against Christians (Pr. 29).[75] From Gentili, a humanist, but by no means a pacifist, JBP profited largely, particularly so in the part on the conduct in war, even though it rarely expresses outright approval.[76] Traditional interpretation credits the strongest influence to scholastic heritage like the Aristotelian social character of man,[77] the distinction between natural and conventional justice, the subdivision into attributive and distributive justice, and further distinctions of this kind; furthermore, we should mention the hierarchy between divine, natural, and human law, the dual origin of *jus gentium* in natural and human law, as well as the extraction of subjective rights from moral capacities.[78] Grotius' *communis societatis generis humani* is not only a stoic concept; it also parallels Vitoria's *totus orbis*, as does the embedding of *jus communicationis* in the just-war theory.[79] A special case is Grotius' relationship with Suárez, whose *De Legibus ac Deo Legislatore* (LDL) had been published twelve years before JBP.[80] Whereas frequent reference is made to Vitoria, Soto, Vázquez de Menchaca, Covarruvias, Molina, and Ayala,[81] Suárez is cited only rarely and in passing.[82] The

[71] Pr. 40, 42, 47, 48, 52, 58. For a concordance of citations, see David Bederman, 'Reception of the Classical Tradition in International Law: Grotius' De Jure Belli ac Pacis', *Emory IL Rev* 10 (1996), 1–49, at 41–9.

[72] On the stoic influence, see contributions in Hans Blom and Laurens Winkel (ed.), *Grotiana* 21 (2001–02).

[73] Christopher Brooke, 'Grotius, Stoicism and "Oikeiosis"', *Grotiana* 29 (2008), 25–50.

[74] On Grotius in Leiden, see Fiorella de Michelis, *Le origini storiche e culturali del pensiero di Ugo Grozio* (1967), pp. 62–81. On different opinions about the influence of Justus Lipsius, see Straumann, *Roman Law*, p. 45 (n. 70) and Christopher Ford, 'Preaching Propriety to Princes: Grotius, Lipsius, and Neo-Stoic International Law', *Case W Res JIL* 28 (1996), 313–66, at 341–66.

[75] On the stand vis-à-vis Erasmus, see Matthijs de Blois, 'Blessed [Are] the Peacemakers . . . : Grotius on the Just War and Christian Pacifism', *Grotiana* 32 (2011), 20–39, at 27–31.

[76] Peter Haggenmacher, 'Grotius and Gentili', in *Grotius and International Relations*, pp. 133–76 (n. 61).

[77] But see Tuck, *Rights*, p. 89 (n. 12): Sociability only in a European sense and thus a restriction of the Aristotelian human notion.

[78] Koskenniemi, *Emergence*, pp. 10–17 (n. 25).

[79] This ancestry is rejected by Tuck, *Rights*, p. 108 (n. 12), who sees older just-war doctrines perverted by Grotius' advocacy of intervention for commercial and expansionist purposes.

[80] Citations are from Francisco Suárez, *De Legibus ac Deo Legislatore* (1612), in James Brown Scott (ed.), *Selections of Three Works* (1944).

[81] For an overview, see Borschberg, *Commentarius*, pp. 47–101 (n. 15). Counts of citations are found in Antonio Truyol Serra, 'Grotius dans ses rapports avec les classiques espagnols du droit des gens', *RdC* 182 (1983), 431–51, at 451.

[82] Defendants of the Spanish origins theory blame Grotius for quoting Suárez only four times in subordinate contexts and for concealing his indebtedness to him in *De jure praedae* (1604) by inserting a summary taken from LDL (1612) at a later point in time; on this episode, see Edwards, *Miracle*, pp. 148–55 (n. 34).

modest record of quoting has caused some frowning, and resemblances with Suárez' notions are at the core of debates about Grotius' originality. Central elements are the universal human society united by solidarity (actually love and mercy, LDL II 19, 9), the reception of the rationalist/voluntarist debate as to the origin of natural law, the openness of natural law to change and permission, and the adaptation of *dominium* to the notion of free commerce as a component of a system of law, to name just some of those which have been dealt with here.[83] If a short formula is sought, the Grotian mindset can be described as a fusion of the scholastic form of structuring and the humanist style of argument.

This admittedly cursory account at least shows that JBP had drawn from so many sources that Grotius' reputation as a syncretist, compilator, and synthesizer of pre-existent thought is understandable. To do justice to this style, however, it is worth pondering that recourse to sources in JBP is not in the first place a matter of pure doctrine and scholarly authority, but rather of proving what Grotius considered as the reality of the relations between states.

4. Some characteristic features

Given the ambitious intentions of JBP, the array of sources cited and the different currents they represent, the degree of its originality was debated in various ways. Instead of taking up this debate, five features will be distilled here which seem to be characteristic for Grotius' international legal thought.

The first is an attitude that accounts for both the originality dispute and inconsistencies in the technique of reasoning, but which has also contributed to Grotius' success in the later tradition of political thought. There is a proverbial inclination in JBP towards a middle approach between the extremes. It shows in the treatment of the impious hypothesis, in the ambivalence of social contract, in the position between pacifism and reason of state, and in the precarious balancing between a realist view at the usages of war and idealist pleas for the better.

The second feature is Grotius' contract theory. The fusion of Aristotelian sociability with the sanctity of contracts, which carries the commonwealth and international society alike, did not yet yield a social contract proper nor a *société des nations* of any sort. The Grotian concept of law still represents natural law as one monistic legal order. Rights and contract are the keys to a concept of law in which individuals and states are subjects. In that form, it is a precursor of later contractualism.

A third characteristic is the claim to a universal reach of *jus gentium*. The reconstruction of the dual origin of natural law and its emergence from old controversies has shown that natural law has a place in Grotian theology. The reductionist method of verifying norms in law and in ethics alike does not necessarily prove natural law to be secular. One will note from today's perspective that this plan was pursued by inappropriate means, since the Humanist–Protestant background is always present, and the material used was inevitably European. But the purpose was

[83] Cf. Edwards, *Miracle*, pp. 86–105 (n. 34); Koskenniemi, *Emergence*, p. 17 (n. 25).

inter-confessional with the objective to explain its binding force also vis-à-vis (and for) non-Christian nations.

Fourthly, the structuring of the problem of a just war against the background of subjective rights is probably the first description of the law of nations to revolve around the subjects of law.[84] Adam Smith referred to Grotius as 'the first who attempted to give the world any thing like a system of those principles which ought to run through, and be the foundation of the laws of all nations'.[85] Liberal as it appears, this 'system' can be interpreted as the set-up of the state as a protector of economic interest.[86]

The last characteristic to be mentioned here is of a methodological kind and concerns the sources of international law. Their most important function is to prove the existence of law between states as a social fact. The method to identify sources is unique. Apart from the most basic rules of natural law, which are recognized a priori, reflection by reason alone does not carry very far when it comes to verifying binding law. Grotius relies to a substantial extent on an a posteriori ascertaining of principles and rules.[87] As long as there are not yet collections of practice as they are promulgated in later epochs, human knowledge from the books must suffice to verify custom. Municipal (Roman) law has a supplementary role in it. Thus, it becomes visible what later will be classified as custom and general principles.

III. Grotius and Ensuing Natural Law Philosophy

The measuring of Grotius' influence on further history of political thought and international law theory largely depends on the willingness to interpret later reference as contributions to a tradition. Whereas more recent research has taken an increasing interest in Grotius' relation to Hobbes, traditional historiography points at an authoritarian and a liberal pedigree.

It has been noted that Hobbes' philosophy can be read as a conversation with Grotius.[88] Therefore, some consider Grotius as proto-Hobbesian, given his ultimate basing of natural law on the need for self-preservation and the irritating concept of contractual absolutism.[89] Internationalists may recall findings concerning

[84] One can object that this is not true international law, since most rules entitle private persons, and it is not complete, so that it is not a 'system'; see Peter Haggenmacher, 'Hugo Grotius', in Bardo Fassbender and Anne Peters (eds.), *The Oxford Handbook of the History of International Law* (2012), pp. 1098–1101.

[85] Adam Smith, *The Theory of Moral Sentiments*, Knud Haakonssen (ed). (2002), p. 404.

[86] Koskenniemi, *Emergence* (n. 25).

[87] Cf. Jules Basdevant, 'Hugo Grotius', in Antoine Pillet (ed.), *Les fondateurs du droit international* (1904, repr. 2014), pp. 119–206, at p. 177; Roberto Ago, 'Le droit international dans la conception de Grotius', *RdC* 182 (1983), 375–98, at 391–2.

[88] Baumgold, *Contract Theory*, pp. 30–41, 57–9, 81–4 (n. 47).

[89] Tuck, *Grotius* (n. 31); Tuck, *Rights*, pp. 13 and 135 (n. 12); Haakonssen, Natural Law, pp. 31–5 (n. 36). This reading goes back to Rousseau, 'Emile, ou de l'éducation', in *Œuvres complètes* 8 (1831), liv. V, p. 236 ('La vérité est que leurs principes sont exactement semblables, ils ne diffèrent que par les

the laws of war.[90] Intriguing as this version of the secularization theory is, it carries the point too far.[91] Obviously, Hobbes and Grotius start from different assumptions as to the nature of man: for Grotius, human beings are social with the effect that law precedes the state, whereas Hobbes' ploy was to take away the moral ontology of man which Grotius had inherited from scholasticism. And whereas Hobbes constructed state, authority, and command, Grotius' very point was to preserve order without such authority and to tame anarchy with the prerequisites of a law alone.

Reading Grotius as an authoritarian means ascribing to him what has its traits in Pufendorf. The contention that Grotius secularized natural law goes back to him and to Barbeyrac, the translator of both Grotius and Pufendorf. The latter, Pufendorf, depicted JBP as a new start in the philosophy of natural law, and Barbeyrac found that Grotius was the first who had attempted 'to give a system' to the science of natural law,[92] the interest behind this reading being in a law that did not depend on the authority of (Catholic) theology.[93] Pufendorf himself had not expressed himself explicitly in that sense, but could have done so.[94] However, as has often been noted, Pufendorf's Hobbesian departures from Grotius' thinking are significant.[95] He construes rule and authority as the means to keep human self-interest in check. Law rests on command, not on consent. Law beyond the state is exclusively public law, and the law of nations is merely an external law of the state.

The liberal tradition[96] begins with Grotius' influence on Locke's notion of natural law, which becomes apparent in the concepts of *dominium* and rights.[97] For Locke, natural law is always in harmony with universal divine law, so that there is no need to distinguish one from the other, the result being both a reinforcement of theology and a 'secularizing effect'.[98] A genuine conversion of Grotian patterns

expressions. Ils diffèrent aussi par la méthode. Hobbes s'appuie sur des sophismes, et Grotius sur des poëtes; tout le reste leur est commun').

[90] Cf. Hersch Lauterpacht, 'The Grotian Tradition in International Law', *BYIL* 23 (1946), 1–53, at 13–14.

[91] Robert Shaver, 'Grotius on Scepticism and Self-Interest', *Arch Gesch Phil* 78 (1996), 27–47, at 30–9; Zuckert, *Natural Rights*, pp. 137–8 (n. 40); Perez Zagorin, 'Hobbes Without Grotius', *Hist Pol Thgt* 21 (2000), 16–40; Blom, *Trust*, pp. 51–8 (n. 10).

[92] Cf. Barbeyrac's preface to the 1729 edition of Pufendorf's *De jure naturae et gentium*, sec. 29, quoted by St. Leger, *Etiamsi Daremus*, p. 39 (n. 33).

[93] Frank Grunert, 'The Reception of Hugo Grotius' *De Jure Belli Ac Pacis* in the Early German Enlightenment', in T.J. Hochstrasser and P. Schröder (eds.), *Early Modern Law Theories* (2003), pp. 89–105, at pp. 96–7.

[94] For Pufendorf's treatment of the impious hypothesis, see *De jure naturae et gentium Libri Octo* (1688), ed. and trans. C.H. and W.A. Oldfather (1934) lib. I 2, mn 20 (p. 30).

[95] Cf. Renée Jeffery, *Hugo Grotius in International Thought* (2006), pp. 57–61.

[96] A reading against the background of Rawlsian liberalism is offered by Stumpf, *Grotian Theology*, p. 9 and *passim* (n. 51).

[97] Cf. James Tully, *An Approach to Political Philosophy: Locke in Contexts* (1993), pp. 101–17. On Locke's justification of slavery and its Grotian roots, see James Farr, 'Locke, Natural Law, and New World Slavery', *Pol Thr* 36 (2008), 495–522.

[98] Gabriella Silvestrini, 'With Grotius against Grotius: Jephta's 'Appeal to Heaven' in John Locke's Two Treatises of Government', in *Roots of International Law*, pp. 59–94, at 93 (n. 10). For an

concerns the merger of the right to opposition and just-war theory. While Grotius, as we have seen, rejected self-defence against unjust rule in unequivocal terms, Locke imports the reasons for a just war into the internal realm and considers resistance justified if there is a just cause.[99]

As for international law, the 'Grotian' notion refers to a liberal universalism that does not from the beginning stress individual rights, but instead emphasizes international society. It starts from Leibniz, who learned from Grotius via Pufendorf and reconstructed the fusion of morality and law, which Pufendorf had dissolved. Leibniz also went back to the idea of sovereignty as a fact rather than as an expression of legitimate rule.[100] The Grotian concept of securing peace on common ground reappeared in the *civitas dei* of Leibniz. From there, it was but one further step to Wolff.[101] Wolff saw in Grotius' notion of society the predecessor of his *civitas maxima*, which nature itself had established, but constructed voluntary law as being directly determined by it; man-made customary law was to be distinguished from them both. In this modified way, Wolff reinstated the dual origin of *jus gentium*.[102]

As early twentieth-century reception has it, Vattel was the gravedigger of the Grotian vision.[103] Accordingly, despite distinguishing necessary law from voluntary law, Vattel considered agreement as the sole source of law and decomposed international society into a loose assemblage of sovereign states. The political theories of the enlightenment brought the process of the secularization of law to an end. Since man-made law had become the only enforceable source of obligation between nations, the Grotian record of mandatory rules began slowly to be replaced.

Recent scholarship, however, which has begun to focus on the Grotian theory of the state, stresses the theory of rights rather than the theory of international society. Accordingly, the line to be drawn from him to Locke, Hume, and Smith deserves more attention. The Grotian system, then, is not only one of international law or society, but also one of rights, a position closer to the eighteenth century than some philosophers of the Enlightenment would wish to make it appear.[104]

expansionist understanding Tuck, *Rights*, pp. 171–81 (n. 12); Locke's rejection of conquest as a title (*Two Treatises of Government*, ed. Peter Laslett (1970) II, ch xvi, §§ 180–4) is then put in relation to Spanish claims.

99 Silvestrini, *With Grotius*, pp. 60–1, 70–83 (n. 98).

100 Jeffery, *Grotius*, p. 63 (n. 95).

101 See the contribution by Kleinlein in this volume.

102 On Grotius and Wolff, see Ernst Reibstein, 'Deutsche Grotius-Kommentatoren bis zu Christian Wolff', *ZaöRV* 15 (1953/54), 76–102.

103 Hamilton Vreeland, *Hugo Grotius, The Father of the Modern Science of International Law* (*1917*), pp. 171–2; Cornelius van Vollenhoven, *The Three Stages in the Evolution of the Law of Nations* (*1919*); Cornelius van Vollenhoven, 'Grotius and the Study of Law', *AJIL* 19 (1925), 1–11.

104 If it was not for the authoritarian gist of it, see Koskenniemi, *Emergence*, pp. 33–7 (n. 25): Grotius continued a tradition of scholasticism to emancipate subjective rights from objective legal order and to connect them with the interest of the state. But this is a controversial reading; see above (n. 91); cf. also James Tully, Editor's Introduction, in *Samuel Pufendorf, On the Duty of Man and Citizen* (1991), pp. xviii–xxi; Hont, *Jealousy of Trade*, pp. 164–84 (n. 55).

IV. The 'Grotian Tradition'

1. 'Grotian moments' and the 'Grotian quest'

Reminiscences to Grotius are used to prove the rooting of a rule in tradition, to witness the originality and prophetic qualities of a classic, and to indicate a need for progress. Apart from the freedom of the seas,[105] the other aspects belonging to the catalogue of allegedly Grotian institutions are human rights and humanitarian intervention,[106] humanitarian law,[107] the law of treaties and their interpretation,[108] the law of state responsibility,[109] and the peaceful settlement of disputes including arbitration.[110] Anachronistic as these references may seem, they illustrate that the name of Grotius is used synonymously for a comprehensive system of international law for the components of which he is considered an authority of intuitive persuasiveness.

On a more abstract level, the associations that allusions to Grotius were supposed to provoke were morality, idealism, and progress.[111] In this vein, one way to speak of Grotius is to deploy an argument for a shift in paradigm, from insufficient order to a structuring by new rules or new forms of political organization.[112] It is by this token that a former Secretary-General of the United Nations saw a 'Grotian moment' in the prospect of new mulitilateralism after the Cold War.[113] Such invocations stand in the tradition of the 'Grotian Quest', which draws inspiration from Grotius' idealist potential and seeks to preserve Grotian heritage in further course,[114] as it was the case with the two Hague peace conferences, the foundation of the League of Nations, the establishment of the United Nations, and the Nuremberg and Tokyo Trials.[115]

This use of Grotian philosophy is erratic, but in line with various cycles of reception which circled around the initial question of JPB, the impact of legal norms

[105] W.E. Butler, 'Grotius and the Law of the Sea', in *Hugo Grotius and International Relations*, pp. 209–20 (n. 61).

[106] Ove Bring, 'Hugo Grotius and the Roots of Human Rights Law', in Jonas Grimheden et al. (eds.), *Human Rights Law from Dissemination to Application* (2006), pp. 131–47, at pp. 140–1.

[107] For a dark interpretation of a 'Grotian tradition of War', see Nabulsi, *Traditions of War*, pp. 158–76 (n. 58).

[108] Makoto Kimura, 'Treaties and Good Faith with Enemies', in *Normative Approach*, pp. 308–32, at pp. 314–15 (n. 35).

[109] Lauterpacht, *Grotian Tradition*, p. 48 (n. 90).

[110] van Vollenhoven, *Grotius*, p. 5 (n .103).

[111] See Christopher Weeramantry, 'Opening Tribute to Hugo Grotius', *Am U IL Rev* 14 (1999), 1516–20.

[112] For an attempt to build a theory of customary law on this concept, cf. Michael Scharf, *Customary Law in Times of Change: Recognizing Grotian Moments* (2013).

[113] Boutros Boutros-Ghali, 'A Grotian Moment', *Fordh ILJ* 18 (1995), 1609–16.

[114] Edwards, *Miracle*, pp. 157–81 (n. 34).

[115] The District Court of Jerusalem invoked Grotius to derive a right to punish from international law; see *Attorney-General v Adolf Eichmann*, 36 ILR 5 (1961), paras. 14, 32, 38; Hannah Arendt, *Eichmann in Jerusalem* (German edn, 1964), p. 56.

founded in morality on international relations. Whereas the debate about who was the true founder of international law still continued after the Second World War, focusing on Grotius' employment as a secularizer, reference to Grotius as the 'father of international law' assumed a new accent. The 'Grotian tradition' now marked a defined position in the 'grand debate' between realism and idealism in the wake of the establishment of international relations as an academic discipline (2. below), to which International Relations theory reacted (3.). This discourse declined with the end of the Cold War. Recent reception deconstructs Grotian thought as a precursor to colonialism, authoritarianism, and capitalism (4.).

2. International law

That the fatherhood diagnosis began to become disputed only in the second half of the nineteenth century seems to affirm a verdict by Hegel that Grotius was not read anymore.[116] This was probably not even accurate at the time. Grotius was quite popular in the early American republic and was cited with approval or even recommended as essential reading by Jefferson, Hamilton, and Franklin.[117] What apparently appealed to American readers was the notion of divided sovereignty, the idea of civilized conduct in international relations, which was a desire for the young state to demonstrate, and a perception of Christian morals in international law.[118] In continental legal thought, most particularly in Germany, Grotius had also always been present. Thus, his re-discovery in the wake of the humanitarian movement in the second half of the nineteenth century is less of a surprise than it might appear. When Grotius was chosen as the symbol figure of the Hague Peace Conference in 1899,[119] the decisive reason was the recommendation to resort to peaceful means of settlement before resorting to war (JBP II 23, 8).[120] At the time when the revival of Spanish scholastics began,[121] such attributions had been quite common.[122] However, the dispute about them appears to resemble a new version of the secularization debate.[123] After the First World War, it

[116] Georg Wilhelm Friedrich Hegel, 'Vorlesungen über die Geschichte der Philosophie', in Hermann Glockner (ed.), *Sämtliche Werke* (1959), vol. 19, p. 440.

[117] Jeffery, *Grotius*, pp. 77–84 (n. 95), with reference.

[118] Cf. Mark Weston Janis, 'American Versions of the International Law of Christendom: Kent, Wheaton and the Grotian Tradition', *Neth IL Rev* 39 (1992), 37–61.

[119] Because of Grotius, the Holy See was not invited, since JBP still figured on the index, though it was removed soon after; see Hofmann, *Grotius*, p. 54 (n. 6).

[120] Cf. van Ittersum, *Profit*, p. xxxii (n. 13).

[121] Ernest Nys, *Le droit de la guerre et les précurseurs de Grotius* (*1882*).

[122] Edward Keene, 'The Reception of Grotius in International Relations Theory', *Grotiana* 20/21 (1999/2000), 135–58, at 144–5. Keene points to a reference by Georg Friedrich von Martens, *Summary of the Law of Nations* (1795), p. 8 ('father of this science'), and a tradition in counter-revolutionary international law theory at the time to define order in legalistic terms; see also Carl von Kaltenborn, *Die Vorläufer des Hugo Grotius* (1848), pp. 231–46.

[123] For the Spanish origins thesis, see James Brown Scott, *The Spanish Origin of International Law* (1932), pp. ixf., 3f.; Alfred Verdross, *Abendländische Rechtsphilosophie* (2nd edn, 1963), pp. 112–13; Truyol Serra, *Grotius* (n. 81); Randall Lesaffer, 'The Grotian Tradition Revisited: Change and Continuity in the History of International Law', *BYIL* 73 (2002), 103–39.

was under these auspices that confessing Grotians competed with post-Vitorian law-of-nature theorists about the authorship for the design of an organized world community.[124]

After the Second World War, the debate continued,[125] but soon assumed a new direction that drew on the Grotian self-perception as a middle-way approach. By the 1920s, it had become a habit to describe Grotius as an intermediate position between natural law and positivism.[126] In this line, it was a reaction both to Carr's version of political realism and Kelsen's pure theory of law that Hersch Lauterpacht presented his exposé of the stoic defence of law and his own definition of what represented the Grotian tradition.[127] Accordingly, 'Grotian' is a synonym for reliance on international law as a system and its foundation in morality. Lauterpacht specifies this position in eleven principles:[128] (1) The subjection of international relations to the rule of law rather than to the interest in self-preservation; (2) the acceptance of the law of nature as an independent source of international law, so that law is not only the product of the express will of states, but also represents general principles of law; (3) the affirmation of the social nature and rational constitution of man as the basis of law, in contrast to Machiavelli and Hobbes; (4) the essential identity of states and individuals as to their moral and legal obligations; (5) consequently, the rejection of 'reason of the state' as a manifestation of double standards; (6) the distinction between just and unjust wars, since all war has to be justified; (7) a doctrine of qualified neutrality, since there can be no full neutrality against a state that wages an unlawful war; (8) the binding character of promises as a cornerstone of law; (9) fundamental rights and freedoms of the individual, at least a general attitude of humanity; (10) the idea of peace and the obligation to seek negotiation and arbitration; and (11) a general idealism and belief in progress.

Thus, the 'Grotian' position is no longer one on the originality of a natural law concept or a specific idea of a system. With Lauterpacht, Grotianism has become part of a dispute of the faculties. For the time being, it was in IR theory where Grotian thought lingered on.

3. International Relations

Lauterpacht's taxonomy was taken up by the so-called English school in the 1950s, in particular by Martin Wight and, more schematically, by Hedley Bull. Wight distinguished between revolutionarism, rationalism (to which he counted 'Grotians'),

[124] van Vollenhoven, *Three Stages* (n. 103); cf. P. H. Kooijmans, 'How to Handle the Grotian Heritage: Grotius and Van Vollenhoven', *Neth IL Rev* 30 (1983), 81–92.

[125] Edward Dumbauld, 'Hugo Grotius: The Father of International Law', *J Publ L* 1 (1952), 117–37; Walter Schiffer, *The Legal Community of Mankind* (1954), pp. 38, 46.

[126] Lassa Oppenheim, *International Law* (3rd edn, 1920), p. 107.

[127] Lauterpacht, *Grotian Tradition* (n. 90); Arthur Nussbaum, *A Concise History of the Law of Nations* (1954), pp. 105–14; Lassa Oppenheim and Hersch Lauterpacht, *International Law*, vol. I (8th edn, 1955), p. 98.

[128] Lauterpacht, *Grotian Tradition*, pp. 19–51 (n. 90).

and realism,[129] which provided the design for the well-known standard account ascribed to Hedley Bull, who placed Grotius between Hobbes' realism and Kantian idealism.[130] Accordingly, Grotius left old natural-law thinking behind and conceived a new notion of international society in the sense of an interdependent community of states.

Bull posits his own picture of international society in contrast to Grotius' 'solidarist' view, from which, however, some of the elements identified as Grotian are retained.[131] System, then, was not a whole of legal and moral interrelations between persons and states, but a neutral descriptive term. Accordingly, a system exists when two or more states are in contact with each other and mutually influence their behaviour. Order is a 'pattern of activity that sustained the elementary or primary goals of the society of states'.[132] Whereas only order can provide for justice, the existence of the system of states does not depend on it. Since justice is an inherently subjective concept, system and order are in tension with each other. Hence Bull's (though in the end mitigated) critique of 'solidarism' and affirmations of unity of the international order in its wake rather pointed at the question whether this was an adequate description of the international landscape of his own day. Bull conceived international society as a loosely structured system of states characterized by minimum consent and an indulgence of pluralism. His picture of Grotius' philosophy served as a foil against which he sought an accurate description of the modern system of states and with which he confronts a view of an ideal order.

4. History of political thought

Historiography of political theory dismisses such juxtapositions as anachronistic and recommends reading Grotius in his contemporary context. Accordingly, all efforts to interpret history of thought coherently already mean constructing a theory of its own. It is on this track that more attention is paid to other Grotian texts and the sources from which they profited in order to reconstruct better the underlying assumptions of the principal tenets, contents, and methods of JBP.[133] This approach does not necessarily coincide, but is at times in harmony with a methodologically realistic posture that stresses political power and economic interest as forces that cannot be phased out when we deal with Grotian theory.[134] As a consequence,

[129] Martin Wight, *International Theory: The Three Traditions*, eds. Gabriele Wight and Brian Porter (1991), p. 14; M. Wight, 'Grotius', in Gabriele Wight and Brian Porter (eds.), *Four Seminal Thinkers in International Theory: Machiavelli, Grotius, Kant, and Mazzini* (2004), pp. 29–61.

[130] The fact that Bull's taxonomy is not trivially schematic is stressed by Benedict Kingsbury, 'A Grotian Tradition of Theory and Practice?' *Quinnipiag LR* 17 (1997), 3–33. For a reconstruction, see also Keene, *Reception*, pp. 135–58 (n. 122); Jeffery, *Grotius*, pp. 124–38 (n. 95).

[131] Hedley Bull, 'The Grotian Conception of International Society', in Herbert Butterfield and Martin Wight (eds.), *Diplomatic Investigations* (1966), pp. 51–73.

[132] Cf. Hedley Bull, *The Anarchical Society: A Study of World Order in Politics* (1995), pp. 8–21, 75–89 (quotation p. 8).

[133] An example for such an approach is also Haggenmacher, *Guerre juste*, cf. pp. 549–52 (n. 26).

[134] Koskenniemi, *Emergence* (n. 25).

many recent studies are devoted to JP, which directs the interpretation towards an understanding in the context of an expansive pursuit of trade interests.[135] Against this background Grotius figures as an illustration of the dilemma between apology and utopia underlying all reasoning on international law.[136] Lauterpacht's 'Grotian tradition' is thus an old-fashioned 'Victorian' way of giving Grotius an unhistorical and overly harmonious sense.[137]

Clearly, the warnings of creating a theory of their own making can also be directed against historical and critical approaches.[138] However, the merit of the constant appeal to take the intellectual context and the risk of falling to partisanship more seriously is twofold. Firstly, it helps to accept that JBP is not a non-contradictory whole that only has to be understood correctly by appropriate exegetic means or, worse, by *ex post* reconstruction in an imagined relation to later thought. Thus, it suggests that Grotius' own claim to set out a 'system' does not have to be taken too seriously, and to examine what it means for later 'systems' is more a constructive than an analytical exercise. As a consequence, it is presumably inappropriate to speak of a 'Grotian tradition' at all. The second point is related, in that readers are encouraged to face the darker sides of Grotius more openly. It is difficult to tell how much political opportunism and partisanship was in Grotius' mind when he wrote JBP. As to religion, however, the impact is probably deeper than the secularization narrative has it. Consulting theological texts opens a different view at the universal reach of Grotian normativity, which is not only qualified by the claim that Christianity disposes of the more profound reservoir for achieving higher standards of morality and law, but is also underlain by irritating views on other religions which do not lend themselves for a 'liberal' reading.[139] In this context, the hope that Christian states would enter a league against the enemies of Christianity (JBP II 15, 12) is not in clear harmony with the irenic tune otherwise called for in JBP.

V. Conclusion: System and Order in Grotius

What follows from this look at Grotius' philosophy? Shall we conclude that Grotius must be left to the historians? Contestable as it is, the look at Grotian connotations to system and order shows at least the desire to see a normative sense in the

[135] Despite passages where Grotius rejects the unwillingness to adopt the Christian faith (JBP III 20, 48–9) and the desire for conquest (JBP II 22, 3) as just causes for war (JBP II 20, 48–9). For reference, see above, Section II.1; cf. also contributions in Hans Blom (ed.), *Property, Piracy and Punishment: Hugo Grotius on War and Booty in De iure praedae* (2009).

[136] Martti Koskenniemi, *From Apology to Utopia* (1989). On 'apologetic' and 'utopian' readings of DJ, see Eric Wilson, *The Savage Republic: De Indis of Hugo Grotius, Republicanism, and Dutch Hegemony within the Early Modern World System (c. 1600-1619)* (2008), pp. 235–50, 479–80.

[137] On Lauterpacht's picture of Grotianism, see Martti Koskenniemi, *The Gentle Civilizer of Nations* (2002), pp. 408–11.

[138] Georg Cavallar, 'Vitoria, Grotius, Pufendorf, Wolff and Vattel: Accomplices of European Colonialism and Exploitation or True Cosmopolitans?', *J Hist IL* 10 (2008), 181–209.

[139] See the quotes from *The Truth of the Christian Religion* (1627) in Haskell, *Grotius*, pp. 286–8 (n. 37) on Judaism and Islam.

interrelations between states. It has taken us to a vast array of conceptions that are found in former designs, adapted by Grotius and analysed and projected with varying focus by later reception and research. Uses of the Grotian idea of a system related it to different contexts: a system of reasons for war, a system of international law as a network of rights and duties independent of state will, a system of states and its resemblances to Grotian 'international society', and a system of rights as one of an economy protected by an expansive state.

The stated ambition expressed in JBP was to achieve the order of peace by a system of laws on war. System and order in that sense form the brackets of JBP. Intention, method, and sources let it appear as a backward utopia, both conservative and faithful in progress. The claim to unfold a system that is analogous to civil law expresses the plan to translate the language of morals into the language of law. Whether this claim holds in terms of consistency and scientific standards might be an issue when it comes to the question of the function of a system for the unity of law,[140] but seems to have been less relevant to JBP than later systems architects would be willing to accept. Rather, the 'mathematic' method to analyse the laws of the time serves the purpose of keeping different grades of normativity apart and thus of developing a (moderate) critical potential when law is confronted with demands of morality. System and order are thus characterized by a relationship of tension. If the lesson of Grotian studies is that there is no point in forcing the effort to make a simple message of JBP, but to recognize that there are partisanship, syncretism, inconsistencies, and shortcomings, a conciliatory resume could be just that, and also to use 'realist' analysis as a tool to explore the prospect for innovation.

Selected Bibliography

Brett, Annabel, *Changes of State: Nature and the Limits of the City in Early Modern Natural Law* (Princeton and Oxford: Princeton University Press, 2011).

Edwards, Charles S., *Hugo Grotius – The Miracle of Holland. A Study in Political and Legal Thought* (Chicago: Nelson-Hall, 1981).

Haggenmacher, Peter, *Grotius et la doctrine de la guerre juste* (Paris: Presses Universitaires de France, 1983).

van Ittersum, Martine Julia, Profit and Principle: *Hugo Grotius, Natural Rights Theories and the Rise of Dutch Power in the East Indies (1595-1615)* (Leiden: Brill, 2006).

Keene, Edward, *Beyond the Anarchical Society: Grotius, Colonialism and Order in World Politics* (Cambridge: Cambridge University Press, 2002).

Koskenniemi, Martti, 'International Law and the Emergence of Mercantile Capitalism: Grotius to Smith', in Dupuy, Pierre-Marie and Chetail, Vincent (eds.), *The Roots of International Law – Liber Amicorum Peter Haggenmacher* (Leiden/Boston: Martinus Nijhoff Publishers, 2014), pp. 3–37.

[140] Lauterpacht, *Grotian Tradition*, p. 17 (n. 90); Cornelius Murphy, 'The Grotian Vision of World Order', *AJIL* 76 (1982), 477–98, at 482; for a contemporary critique, see Grunert, *Reception*, pp. 92–4 (n. 93).

Lauterpacht, Hersch, 'The Grotian Tradition in International Law', *British Year Book of International Law* 23 (1946), 1–53.
Nellen, Henk, *Hugo Grotius: A Lifelong Struggle for Peace in Church and State, 1583-1645* (Leiden/Boston: Brill, 2015).
Onuma, Yasuaki (ed.), *A Normative Approach to War: Peace, War, and Justice in Hugo Grotius* (Oxford: Clarendon Press, 1993).
Straumann, Benjamin, *Roman Law in the State of Nature: The Classical Foundations of Hugo Grotius' Natural Law* (Cambridge: Cambridge University Press, 2015).
Tuck, Richard, *The Right of War and Peace: Political Thought and International Order from Grotius to Kant* (Oxford: Oxford University Press, 1999).

8

Orders in Disorder

The Question of an International State of Nature in Hobbes and Rousseau

Jonas Heller

In the political philosophy of Hobbes and Rousseau, law and order are necessarily linked concepts: *Order* denotes a political association which is founded and upheld by law; *law* (in the sense of positive law) is established by a political order which guarantees its legitimation and its enforceability. The focal point of their reflections is order, not law: Hobbes and Rousseau ask how a good political order is possible, and they are interested in law insofar as it is a means of such an order. If we want to know about law, we have to start with order.

The order Hobbes and Rousseau are primarily concerned with is not international. They both focus on the national order of the state and on the law enacted and enforced by it. A state, however, is never alone. It is surrounded by other orders and this means that, according to the perspective of Hobbes and Rousseau, it is surrounded by enemies. If the international sphere is a sphere of hostility, the question arises as to how an order can exist in such an environment: is international law and order necessary, and is it even possible? The focal point here is, again, order and not law. Hobbes and Rousseau, however, do not describe the international sphere as order but as a state of nature between sovereigns. Thus, the question about international law arises in the context of their conception of a state of nature. In the first section, (Section I) I deal with the characteristics of this international state of nature. Its specifity consists in the fact that it is neither an order nor entirely beyond order but a mixed (and hence disorderly) condition between order and disorder. Thus, the relation of order and disorder plays a major role in this chapter. I examine this relation at the point when a national order passes into disorder (Section II) and when pre-political disorder changes into national orders—which is the beginning of the international sphere (Section III). Between the orders constituting this sphere there is, as indicated, a condition of war. This condition is evaluated very differently by Hobbes and Rousseau. Whereas in Hobbes' view there is no need for international law and order, Rousseau considers an international legal framework necessary for the establishment of any good order on a national level (Section IV.). This is why Rousseau, in contrast to Hobbes, extensively reflects about the possibilities of bringing law and order into the international sphere. He is concerned with the case of Europe at that time which constituted a 'system' of violence in his eyes. The order which should replace this violent system takes shape as a (European) confederation. Such a confederation is, according to Rousseau, necessary but utopian: he considers it impossible that sovereign states could approve of an international legal framework which would restrain their competences (Section V). Rousseau, however, states that a weak form of international law already exists in his time. The reason why Rousseau observes international law where Hobbes does not, is not that they lived in different centuries but rather that they have different concepts of (international) law. I deal with these concepts (Section VI) before sketching the different lines of reception Hobbes and Rousseau have met (Section VII). The political philosophy of Hobbes and Rousseau is a philosophy about peace; for peace is the desired consequence of a good order which can only be established and perpetuated by means of law. In their opinion, such an order can never be international. As I argue in conclusion (Section VIII), this is the reason why international law and order are not full-fledged topics of their political thinking. Inevitable disorder remains marginal within a philosophy engaged with the possibilities of peace.

I. The Question of an International Disorder in Hobbes and Rousseau

When we reflect about the international sphere in Hobbes and Rousseau, we reflect about the state of nature. For it is a state of nature in which the relations of sovereign states take place.[1] In the political philosophy of both Hobbes and Rousseau, there are three different situations denominated by this term. Firstly, the state of nature is the situation before a sovereign state is founded. Secondly, the state of nature is the situation which results from the dissolution of a sovereign state. And thirdly, the state of nature is the international situation, the situation between sovereigns. What is the characteristic which allows us to describe these three situations by the same term? First of all, it is not true that they are all 'natural'. This is eminently evident with regard to the international sphere: an international situation is no natural condition as it presupposes states, and states are not naturally given but politically founded. States establish a political sphere which is, as such, beyond nature.[2] This

[1] Cf. Thomas Hobbes, *Leviathan*, ed. Richard Tuck (1991), p. 90; Jean-Jacques Rousseau, 'Discourse on the Origin and the Foundations of Inequality among Men', in Victor Gourevitch (ed.), *The Discourses and Other Early Political Writings* (1997), p. 174.

[2] It is this difference between nature and politics that Hobbes makes in the first five sentences of the introduction to his *Leviathan*. 'Nature' is here defined as the art of God whereby he has made (besides the rest of the world) 'the most excellent worke of Nature, *Man*'. The 'State' is built by imitating this work of nature, and it is nothing else than 'an Artificiall Man'. Cf. Hobbes, *Leviathan*, p. 9 (n. 1). The state (politics) is not nature because it imitates it. As an imitation it is not natural, but artificial. It is exactly the imitation (of nature) which distinguishes politics from nature.

political sphere is defined by the borders of the states. In Hobbes and Rousseau, the sphere of politics is only within states—it does not extend between them. Thus, the international sphere is beyond politics. And it is for this reason that it is a state of nature. In Hobbes and Rousseau, 'nature' first and foremost means nothing else than 'not within politics'.

Whereas a condition of politics is a condition of order, the state of nature is a condition of disorder. To reflect about the state of nature means to reflect about disorder. If we want to know about the international sphere, we have to ask what kind of disorder it is and in what respect it differs from the other two situations of a state of nature. First of all, we have to make clear how the notion of disorder is used by Hobbes and Rousseau. The specific meaning of disorder helps to understand why the state of nature (as a state of disorder) is radically distinct from the political sphere. The notion of disorder is not used to describe a (defective) aspect, part, or condition of a political situation but rather marks the point when a situation is not yet political or not any more. 'Disorder' means that a situation *as a whole* is or becomes unpolitical; and this is because the term 'disorder' denominates nothing else than a discord which is not reconcilable with the existence of a political unity, in other words: with order.[3] The relation between order and disorder is one of exclusion. Between them, there is no liminal zone: Either you are within order or you are within disorder. 'Order' and 'disorder' are radically distinct concepts used to describe radically distinct situations of human coexistence.

The fact of an international sphere disrupts this distinction. The international sphere is not totally beyond order. It is a disorder formed from orders (states). The question about the international sphere is the question about this particular relation between order and disorder. It is the question how two situations which by definition exclude each other can form a situation which is neither political nor completely beyond politics.

This question is not only a problem of concepts but, as Rousseau points out, a problem of lifeworld as well. It is the problem of living at the same time in order and in disorder. The disruption in the distinction of the two concepts is experienced by all the individuals subjected to a state. Rousseau says:

> The first thing I notice, in considering the condition of the human species, is an open contradiction in its constitution which causes it to vacillate incessantly. As individual men we live in a civil state subject to laws; as people we each enjoy a natural liberty: this makes our position fundamentally worse than if these distinctions were unknown. For living simultaneously in the social order [*l'ordre social* in the French text, J.H.] and in the state of nature we are subjected to the inconveniences of both, without finding security in either.[4]

[3] It is in this sense that Hobbes uses the notion 'discord' when talking about the 'Intestine Discord' which is a reason for the mortality of sovereignty. Cf. Hobbes, *Leviathan*, p. 153 (n. 1). Since sovereignty is the artificial soul which gives life to the whole body politic, cf. Hobbes, *Leviathan*, p. 9 (n. 1), 'discord' (as the end of sovereignty) is the death of this body or the time before its generation. In the same sense—as irreconcilable conflict—but in regard to conflicts between states, Rousseau uses the French term 'discorde' in his writing *The State of War*. Cf. Jean-Jacques Rousseau, 'L'état de guerre', in Charles E. Vaughan (ed.), *The Political Writings of Jean Jacques Rousseau*, vol. I (1962), pp. 293–307, at p. 296.

[4] Jean-Jacques Rousseau, 'The State of War', in Stanley Hoffmann and David P. Fidler (eds.), *Rousseau on International Relations* (1991), pp. 33–47, at p. 44.

According to Rousseau, the contradiction of the international situation is a contradiction between what individuals strive for and what they get. By founding a state, they strive for security, and what they get is the insecurity of a mixed condition between order and disorder which is worse than the disorder they left. As I will show, Hobbes evaluates the consequences for the individuals differently, but the fact of a mixed condition is the same. The contradiction Rousseau mentions can be put in another form: the international disorder contains more than itself because it *is* the relation between itself (as disorder/state of nature) and the social orders from which it is made. If we deal with the question of international disorder we thus have to deal with the question of national order as well. If we detach the international question from the domestic one, we at the same time lose track of the philosophical approach of Rousseau and Hobbes. We have to consider what Stanley Hoffmann pointed out in regard to Hobbes, Rousseau, and Kant: 'Any sharp separation between their conceptions of human nature, of the state and of the international milieu, destroys the unity of their philosophy.'[5] As national orders are the presupposition for an international situation, I want to start with them and deal with them in the same respect which is relevant for the international situation: I will focus on the relation between order and disorder, between state and state of nature—not the international state of nature but the state of nature which is entirely beyond politics. Given the fact that on a domestic level order and disorder are in a relation of mutual exclusion, they only get 'in touch' during the shift from one to the other—from disorder to order, or from disorder to order. Hobbes and Rousseau are interested in the formation of orders. Thus, their focus is on the transition from disorder to order, from the state of nature to the political society. As the question of this chapter concerns disorder, I will focus primarily on the other transition, the transition from order to disorder. It occurs when states fail.

II. The Beginning of Disorder

In Hobbes and Rousseau, order is established all at once. The moment when politics begins, when the state is founded and the state of nature is left, is a juridical moment, a moment of contract.[6] Whereas it is obvious that the contractual foundation of the state takes place in a single moment (not a real moment but a juridical one), it is not as evident that the rise of disorder, the end of the state, occurs equally abruptly. It is also possible—and at a first glance it may seem even more plausible—to think of the decline of the state as a long process which leads from order to disorder and which opens up a liminal zone between them. But if we look from the perspective of Hobbes and Rousseau at the causes of disorder, we get a clear idea

[5] Stanley Hoffmann, 'Rousseau on War and Peace', *The American Political Science Review* 57, 2 (1963), 317–33, at 317. Equally argues Jean-François Thibault, 'Les relations internationales et la crise de la pensée politique moderne selon Jean-Jacques Rousseau', *Études internationales* 37, 2 (2006), 205–22, at 208.

[6] Cf. Hobbes, *Leviathan*, 16 (n. 1), and Jean-Jacques Rousseau, 'The Social Contract', in Victor Gourevitch (ed.), *The Social Contract and Other Later Political Writings* (1997), I, 6–8.

why according to them the failing of orders happens all at once, in a determinable moment, and does not take place in a slow process. We first have to localize this moment in the theories of Hobbes and Rousseau.

When Hobbes deals with the collapse of the commonwealth in his *Leviathan*, he distinguishes dissolution by external violence from dissolution by 'intestine disorder'. He is interested in the latter because only the internal disorder can be prevented by means of a rational formation of order (and can thus be subject of a theory of such an order).[7] Regarding the occurrence of internal disorder, 'the fault is not in men, as they are the *Matter*; but as they are the *Makers*, and orderers' of the commonwealth.[8] What does it mean to see the fault in men as *makers* and *orderers*? It means to assume that men are capable to solve the problem of men as *matter* by the formation of a good order.[9] And this means to connect disorder with the beginning of the state: internal disorder refers to the (failed) institution of order. Consequently, Hobbes reckons 'in the first place, those that arise from an Imperfect Institution, and resemble the diseases of a naturall body, which proceed from a Defectuous Procreation'[10] among the infirmities of a commonwealth. If an order fails and this failing is primarily rooted in the very moment of its formation, then a real order has never been formed. If the orderers have failed in forming an order, they actually were not orderers.

Similarly, in his *Second Discourse* Rousseau explicates the inconstancy of the first political condition (*état Politique*) by referring to its wrongful institution. He argues that it 'always remained imperfect because it was almost a product of chance and because, having begun badly, time revealed its flaws and suggested remedies but could never repair the vices of the Constitution'.[11] Rousseau takes account of external causes of disorder as well; but like Hobbes he considers a 'healthy and strong constitution' the 'first thing to strive for', not only in order to prevent internal causes of disorder but also in order to prevent the conquest by other states.[12] He thus focuses on the 'conditions for the institution of a people',[13] conditions which have to be given in the moment when the state is founded.[14] What if they are not given? As order begins with a strong constitution, it is, again, as if order in

[7] Hobbes, *Leviathan*, 29, p. 221 (n. 1). External causes receive attention only insofar as they can be influenced by internal factors. Cf. Hobbes, *Leviathan*, p. 118 (n. 1) where Hobbes discusses the danger of attacks, i.e. external violence, and suggests an internal solution. He does so by stressing the importance of adjusting the number of members of the own politcal society 'by comparison with the Enemy we feare'.

[8] Hobbes, *Leviathan*, 29, p. 221 (n. 1).

[9] Regarding Hobbes' confidence in this human capability cf. Leo Strauss, *Natural Right and History* (1976), p. 194.

[10] Hobbes, *Leviathan*, 29, pp. 221f (n. 1).

[11] Rousseau, *Discourse*, II, p. 175 (n. 1). Rousseau likewise argues in the *Social Contract* that it is within men's capacity 'to prolong the State's life as far as possible by giving it the best constitution it can have'. Cf. Rousseau, *Social Contract*, III, 11, p. 109 (n. 6).

[12] Cf. Rousseau, *Social Contract*, II, 9, p. 75 (n. 6).

[13] Rousseau, *Social Contract*, II, 10, p. 77 (n. 6).

[14] Rousseau's French terms *contrat* and *constitution* are both related to the foundation of the state, but they are not synonyms. *Contrat* refers to the unification of all individual forces which together found the political society. The term *constitution* refers to the specific political form given to this society.

the narrower sense had never begun. It is exactly this scenario of a not-beginning order which Rousseau describes in the second part of his *Second Discourse*: order cannot begin because it is the opposite of what he considers as an ideal in his *Social Contract*. Firstly, the political association as he describes it lacks legitimation as it does not guarantee a free coexistence but establishes servitude.[15] Secondly, the constitution is not 'healthy and strong' (*saine et forte*) but extremely 'weak' (*foible*), as there is an initial lack of conventions and a lack of authority to enforce them.[16] And finally, after the appointment of magistrates, their ambition and vanity impedes the wealth of the people which is a declared purpose of the state.[17] In this scenario, a wrongful contract and a deficient constitution do not so much *lead* into disorder; but rather the contract and the constitution are ever lacking force to establish what can actually be considered as order: there is no decline from order into disorder and no liminal zone between them because order has never begun.

In the *Social Contract*, however, Rousseau describes a different scenario: there is an initially well-working order (i.e. an order in the narrower sense) which changes into disorder. According to Rousseau's conception, a well-working order is composed of the following elements: there are the members of the people who on the one hand enact laws as participants in the sovereign authority and who on the other hand obey these laws as its subjects;[18] and there are magistrates who govern, that is who are charged with the execution of these laws.[19] Order is upheld as long as the sovereign authority, the subjects, and the magistrates fulfil their tasks. As soon as the sovereign, the magistrate or the subjects transcend their given competences, order stops and disorder follows: 'If the Sovereign wants to govern, or the magistrate to give laws, or the subjects refuse to obey, disorder replaces rule, force and will no longer act in concert, and the dissolved State thus falls into despotism or anarchy.'[20] In this scenario it is not appropriate either to talk of a decline in the sense of a process leading from order to disorder. Disorder is not what destroys the rule from the inside. It is not what causes the order to stop, it is what comes after it: disorder *succeeds* the rule—*le désordre succède à la règle*. When the state falls into despotism or anarchy, it is already dissolved (*dissous*). The fact of disorder means that there is no state any more. Disorder is not a messed order, it is not just misorder (as such it would still be within order), but it is rather the condition when order has gone.

These passages in the texts of Hobbes and Rousseau can give a clearer notion of the characteristics of a state of nature and its theoretical function. *Firstly*, the conception of a state of nature as a state of disorder makes clear that the coexistence of men does not necessarily have a political form. In *On Revolution,* Hannah Arendt

Cf. also the remarks of Heinrich Meier in Jean-Jacques Rousseau, *Discours sur l'inégalité*, ed. Heinrich Meier (6th edn, 2008), n. 271, pp. 224f.

[15] Cf. Rousseau, *Discourse*, II, p. 173 (n. 1).

[16] Cf. Rousseau, *Discourse*, II, pp. 175f (n. 1).

[17] Cf. Rousseau, *Discourse*, II, pp. 181f (n. 1).

[18] Cf. Rousseau, *Social Contract*, I, 6, p. 51 (n. 6).

[19] cf. Rousseau, *Social Contract*, III, 1, p. 83 (n. 6).

[20] Rousseau, *Social Contract*, III, 1, p. 83 (n. 6). Further descriptions of the end of the political entity as the beginning of 'disorder'. Cf. Rousseau, *Social Contract*, III, 6, p. 97 and III, 10, p. 108 (n. 6).

argues that exactly this insight is the reason why 'the assumption of a prepolitical state, called "state of nature"' has not lost actuality: 'Its relevance even today lies in the recognition that a political realm does not automatically come into being wherever men live together, and that there exist events which, though they may occur in a strictly historical context, are not really political and perhaps not even connected with politics.'[21] Arendt stresses that the idea of a state of nature not only implies the fact of non-political events but of events which 'perhaps' do not even have a connection with politics. Referring to Hobbes and Rousseau, I have described the existence of such events beyond politics as 'disorder'. *Secondly*, the passages quoted above show that in Hobbes and Rousseau such events are not only disconnected from politics, but moreover they imply the absence of a political sphere. Political and non-political events cannot take place simultaneously because they belong to different phases. When one phase begins, it is because the other has ended.[22] Arendt explicitly mentions this radical separation of beginning and ending as well: '[T]he hypothesis of a state of nature implies the existence of a beginning that is separated from everything following it as though by an unbridgeable chasm.'[23]

The unbridgeable chasm, the border between politics and state of nature is, according to Arendt, defined as occurrence of violence. In her German translation which she published two years later (1965), Arendt writes that violence is only able to protect the borders of the political realm; wherever violence invades politics itself, politics has come to an end.[24] Arendt also points out what has often been noticed before and after her—and with good reason: that it is not by a coincidence that the conception of a state of nature was developed in the seventeenth century, a period characterized by the violence of civil wars. What informed the reflection about the state of nature was the threatening occurrence of a backfall from order to disorder which the above quotations describe.

However, as mentioned before, it is not this backfall that Hobbes and Rousseau were primarily interested in. And it is thus not the state of nature 'as backfall' which they primarily focused on. They were both interested in the escape of disorder by formation of orders. In this case, the state of nature is not a backfall, but an (imagined) condition before politics. Whereas the state of nature as a backfall from order shows the failing of the state (or, more precisely, that the state has failed), this pre-political state of nature is the reason for any foundation of a state. As such, the pre-political state of nature is of the greatest importance in the theories of Hobbes and Rousseau. I will deal with the change from the pre-political state of nature to

[21] Hannah Arendt, *On Revolution* (1963), p. 10.

[22] It is this separateness which Adorno and Horkheimer critically address in their *Dialectic of Enlightenment*: 'Men have always had to choose between their subjection to nature or the subjection of nature to the Self.' There was no third option between the domination of nature and the domination of men—with the result that domination is omnipresent. Cf. Theodor W. Adorno and Max Horkheimer, *Dialectic of Enlightenment* (1999), p. 32.

[23] Arendt, *On Revolution*, p. 10 (n. 21).

[24] 'Die Gewalt kann nie mehr, als die Grenzen des politischen Bereichs schützen. Wo die Gewalt in die Politik selbst eindringt, ist es um die Politik geschehen.' Hannah Arendt, *Über die Revolution* (4th edn, 2014), p. 20.

the sovereign state because the egress from this state of nature is the beginning of another state of nature, the one within the international sphere: the foundation of the sovereign state is in the same logical moment the ending and the beginning of the state of nature, and it is a question of perspective—domestic or international—how it is perceived.

III. The Social Contract as Foundation of an International State of Nature

In their political writings, Hobbes and Rousseau have a principal question in common. This question is twofold: why is the state necessary and what can make it legitimate? The state is necessary because the state of nature, a condition of coexistence beyond sovereign power, is unbearable.[25] In such a condition, there is no security because there is 'too much' freedom: everyone's life is threatened by everyone's unlimited freedom. The necessity of the state is the necessity to limit this original freedom. It is at this point where the question of legitimation arises. Whereas the state is necessary because the state of nature has to be left and freedom has to be limited, the question of legitimation is about *how* freedom is limited. Consequently, the (imagined) moment *when* freedom is limited takes centre stage. This moment is the entering of the political society by the formation of the state. According to both Hobbes and Rousseau, this moment—in order to be legitimate—requires a juridical form: a contract in which all future members of the political society participate. The twofold question about the necessity and the legitimacy of the state is unfolded by bringing two theoretic figures in a strong alliance: state of nature and social contract.

There are, however, important differences between Hobbes and Rousseau concerning the question of how the problems which necessitate the contract evolve and how the contract is supposed to solve them. Hobbes presupposes a stable human being which does not change either within the state of nature or within the political society. It is characterized by the core faculties of physical force, experience, reason, and passion.[26] Because of the competition about honour and about goods which cannot be shared, the coexistence of human beings is conflictual. Hobbes furthermore presupposes a natural 'willingness to hurt each other'.[27] Since he postulates that the abilities of human beings are substantially equal, especially the ability to kill each other, nobody can consider himself safe from harm while being in the state of nature. The ubiquitary danger of a violent death makes self-preservation impossible.[28] The political society does not eliminate this danger by changing human

[25] Cf. Thomas Hobbes, *On the Citizen*, ed. and trans. Richard Tuck and Michael Silverthorne (1998), I, 13, and 15; Rousseau, *Social Contract*, I, 6 (n. 6).

[26] Cf. Hobbes, *On the Citizen*, I, 1, p. 21 (n. 25).

[27] Hobbes, *On the Citizen*, I, 3, pp. 25f (n. 25).

[28] Cf. Hobbes, *On the Citizen*, I, 13, p. 30 and 15, p. 31 (n. 25); Hobbes, *Leviathan*, 13, p. 89 (n. 1).

nature;[29] it only establishes a 'power able to over-awe them all'.[30] The sovereign state guarantees security at the cost of the natural freedom.

Rousseau agrees that the purpose of entering the sphere of politics by the foundation of the state is to guarantee self-preservation. He also agrees that men do not naturally aspire to a life within society. But he objects that men are naturally peaceful and characterized not by a willingness to harm but by pity.[31] Unlike Hobbes who imagines the state of nature as an unvarying state, Rousseau conceives it as changing for the worse. The drive to compare oneself with others emerges only in society which evolves—caused by many coincidences—already *within* the state of nature. In Rousseau's account of the state of nature in his *Second Discourse*, the state of war (*état de guerre*[32]) *results* from the '[n]ascent Society',[33] and it is this conflictual society which necessitates the foundation of a political body by contract. The state of nature is not essentially unbearable but reaches a point when self-preservation becomes impossible.[34] Rousseau is not only a 'historical' thinker regarding the development within the state of nature. In his *Social Contract*, he claims that 'the transition from the state of nature to the civil state produces a most remarkable change in man by substituting justice for instinct in his conduct, and endowing his actions with the morality they previously lacked'; the moment of contract transforms 'a stupid and bounded animal' into 'an intelligent being and a man'.[35] However, the most important distinction from Hobbes' conception of the social contract consists in the fact that according to Rousseau men not only lose their natural unlimited freedom but gain a 'civil freedom' instead.[36] In contrast to Hobbes, Rousseau's aim is not only to develop a theory of a state which legitimately guarantees security but of a state in which security is guaranteed while its citizens who are part of the sovereign power remain as free as before (exactly because they are part of the sovereign power).[37] This difference has essential consequences regarding the form of social contract in Rousseau and Hobbes. Hobbes' contract has the form of authorization. Everyone agrees with everyone else to give up their right of governing themselves and to make themselves the authors of all acts of a person or an assembly in order that this person or assembly undertakes all measures which appear appropriate to maintain peace and to guarantee the common defense: 'And he that carryeth this Person, is called *Soveraigne*, and said to have *Soveraigne Power*; and every one besides, his *Subject*.'[38] Whereas the subjects are

[29] Cf. Hobbes, *On the Citizen*, I, 2, p. 25 (n. 25); Hobbes, *Leviathan*, 13, p. 89 (n. 1).

[30] Hobbes, *Leviathan*, 13, p. 88 (n. 1).

[31] Rousseau formulates his objection directly against Hobbes: 'By reasoning on the basis of the principles he establishes, this Author [Hobbes, J.H.] should have said that, since the state of Nature is the state in which the care for our own preservation is least prejudicial to the self-preservation of others, it follows that this state was the most conducive to Peace and the best suited to Mankind.' Rousseau, *Discourse*, I, p. 151 (n. 1); cf. Rousseau, *State of War*, pp. 33f and 45–7 (n. 4).

[32] Rousseau, *Discours sur l'inégalité*, II, p. 212 (n. 14).

[33] Rousseau, *Discourse*, II, p. 172 (n. 1).

[34] Cf. Rousseau, *Discourse*, II, pp. 171–3 (n. 1) and also Rousseau, *Social Contract*, I, 6, p. 49 (n. 6).

[35] Rousseau, *Social Contract*, I, 8, p. 53 (n. 6).

[36] Cf. Rousseau, *Social Contract*, I, 8, pp. 53f (n. 6).

[37] Cf. Rousseau, *Social Contract*, I, 6, and 7 (n. 6).

[38] Cf. Hobbes, *Leviathan*, 17, pp. 120f (n. 1).

excluded from sovereignty, this is not the case in Rousseau's account in his *Social Contract*. The form of contract in Rousseau is not authorization but alienation (*aliénation totale*): the clauses of the contract 'all come down to just one, namely the total alienation of each associate with all of his rights to the whole community'.[39] The public person formed by the union of all associates is called 'Republic' or 'body politic'. The individuals are both citizens (insofar as they are 'participants in the sovereign authority') and subjects (insofar as they are 'subjected to the laws of the State').[40] In contrast to Hobbes, the political entities 'subjects' and 'sovereign' do not include different individuals or groups. The fact that all associates of the body politic are part of the sovereign and involved in the sovereign competence of legislation creates the civil freedom of the individuals as citizens.[41] This including character of the conception of sovereignty in Rousseau does not diminish its absoluteness. Like Hobbes, Rousseau argues that the sovereign is bound to no law because he cannot obligate himself.[42]

Even if the figure of contract differs in many ways, the fact of the contract and its reasons open up a shared perspective. In this social contract theory perspective, the contract draws an impervious line between a non- or pre-political sphere which is before the contract and a political sphere which is after the contract. If a backfall into the state of nature occurs, it is not a backfall into an original state of nature. A civil war is not a 'natural' condition at all.

In the social contract theory perspective, the non- or pre-political sphere is of no interest in its own right: it is as if what is before the contract had never existed.[43] And indeed both Hobbes and Rousseau suggest that there was in fact no such time as an original state of nature. They do not locate it somewhere in history, they do not claim that it really happened.[44] The state of nature is a fiction which makes the idea of a radical beginning of politics possible—thus a beginning which is empty, not occupied by already existing social unjustice which could penetrate the political form of the state.

Rousseau explicitly underscores the importance of an unburdened beginning when he deals with the question of legislation: 'What makes the work of legislation difficult is not so much what has to be established as what has to be destroyed; and what makes success so rare is the impossibility of finding the simplicity of nature linked with the needs of society. [...] This is one reason why one sees few

[39] Rousseau, *Social Contract*, I, 6, p. 50 (n. 6).

[40] Cf. Rousseau, *Social Contract*, I, 6, pp. 50f (n. 6).

[41] However, not every inhabitant ranks as a citizen. Rousseau quotes the example of the republic of Geneva where there are five different orders of men whereof only two form the republic as the association of citizens. Cf. Rousseau, *Social Contract*, I, 6, p. 51 (n. 6).

[42] Hobbes, *On the Citizen*, VI, 14 (n. 25); cf. Rousseau, *Social Contract*, I, 7, pp. 51f (n. 6); Robert Derathé has pointed out that in Rousseau's time the idea of absolute power meant the absence of any *constitutional* restraints but not of any restraints at all; the exercise of sovereignty should still be limited by the law of nature and the public good. The obvious question, then, is how operative such limitations are. Cf. Robert Derathé, *Jean-Jacques Rousseau et la science politique de son temps* (1950), pp. 339f.

[43] There is no 'before the contract' because, as Hans Blumenberg points out, the contract has always already been entered. Cf. Hans Blumenberg, *Die Legitimität der Neuzeit* (1996), p. 108.

[44] Hobbes, *Leviathan*, 13, p. 90 (n. 1); Rousseau, *Discourse*, I, Preface, p. 125 (n. 1).

well-constituted States.'[45] Rousseau points to the following problem: men have lost the simplicity of nature which consists in a pre-social peaceful life; they have moved towards a conflictual society which makes the state necessary. In order to be built on a proper fundament, the state requires men in the 'simplicity of nature'—the very simplicity of nature which has made the state necessary because it has been lost. The institution of the state was possible when it was not needed (because men lived peacefully) and became impossible when it was needed (because men lost their peaceful nature).[46] The decisive aspect of this aporetic situation is that the disorder which makes the state necessary is *socially produced.* When Hobbes mentions that the 'Americans' of his century and other peoples of the past were living the life of a state of nature, he also assumes that they are not isolated individuals but members of a community. He speaks of them as peoples [*gentes* in the original Latin version of *On the Citizen*] and thereby acknowledges that they do not live the life of isolated individuals.[47] But this is not more than an implication, and it is the project of Rousseau to explicitly elaborate, against Hobbes as well, the social genesis of disorder (as a result of inequality) in his *Second Discourse*. In this work, Rousseau puts his assumption in an even more radical form: the disorder which makes a political sphere necessary is neither caused by nature nor produced within a pre-political society. Rather, this disorder is itself a product of the political sphere: the laws of this sphere are not just the remedy against disorder but its cause:

It has to be granted from the first that the more violent the passions, the more necessary are Laws to contain them: but quite aside from the fact that the disorders and the crimes they daily cause among us sufficiently prove the inadequacy of the Laws in this respect, it would still be worth inquiring whether these disorders did not arise together with the Laws themselves; for then, even if they could repress them, it is surely the very least to expect of them that they put a stop to an evil that would not exist without them.[48]

Rousseau here suggests that disorder is *never* natural or prepolitical. Disorder is a result and not a presupposition of the political sphere. If the state of nature as disorder is never natural, it only exists as a backfall from order and as the international sphere. Whereas the former is the end of the political state,[49] the latter

[45] Rousseau, *Social Contract*, II, 10, p. 78 (n. 6). The same argument can be found in the *Second Discourse* where Rousseau praises Lycurgus who set 'aside all the old materials [. . .] in order afterwards to erect a good Building' in Sparta. Rousseau, *Discourse*, II, p. 175 (n. 1).

[46] In a similar way, Rousseau refers to the paradoxical situation of the foundation of a political society when he claims in the *Second Discourse* that 'the same vices that make social institutions necessary make their abuse inevitable'. Rousseau, *Discourse*, II, p. 182 (n. 1).

[47] Cf. Hobbes, *On the Citizen*, I, 13, p. 30 (n. 25); Hobbes, *Leviathan*, 13, p. 89 (n. 1).

[48] Rousseau, *Discourse*, I, p. 155 (n. 1). As it becomes clear in the second part of the *Second Discourse*, Rousseau's argument against the law is that the law established with the political society primarily serves the juridification of property which reinforces the evolving inequality. As all forms of inequality can be reduced to riches (cf. Rousseau, *Discourse*, II, pp. 183f (n. 1)) and as inequality is the reason of the collapse of the political society, the law is an essential contributory cause of the backfall into disorder. Cf. Rousseau, *Discourse*, II, pp. 166f, 169, 171–3 (n. 1).

[49] Hobbes and Rousseau both stress that any state will inevitably dissolve some day as nothing which is humanly produced can last forever. Cf. Hobbes, *Leviathan*, 17, p. 120 and 29, p. 221 (n. 1); Rousseau, *Social Contract*, III, 11, p. 109 (n. 6).

is an everyday phenomenon. It begins in the very moment when states appear. According to Rousseau, the formation of one political order is sufficient to provoke an international sphere:

As soon as the first society is formed, the formation of all the others necessarily follows. One has either to join it or to unite to resist it; to imitate it or let oneself be swallowed up by it. Thus the whole face of the earth is changed; everywhere nature has disappeared; everywhere human artifice takes its place.[50]

The international sphere is a side effect of the foundation of the state. It is a state of war which goes along with the normality of the political sphere.

IV. The International State of Nature as a Condition of War

Both Hobbes and Rousseau call the state of nature a 'time of Warre'[51] and an 'état de guerre', respectively.[52] There are three important characteristics in their concept of war. Firstly, war is always bad.[53] Secondly, war has some extension in time; it is not the single event of a battle but a period. Thirdly, war in the proper sense is not an affair between individuals.

Hobbes distinguishes the 'actuall fighting' from 'the known disposition thereto'.[54] War is this disposition, it is the 'tract of time'[55] in which the outbreak of actual fighting is not utterly out of the question. This has never been the case between individuals, but it is the permanent situation between sovereigns:

But though there had never been any time, wherein particular men were in a condition of warre one against another; yet in all times, Kings, and Persons of Soveraigne authority, because of their Independency, are in continuall jealousies, and in the state and posture of Gladiators; having their weapons pointing, and their eyes fixed on one another; that is, their Forts, Garrisons, and Guns upon the Frontiers of their Kingdomes; and continuall Spyes upon their neighbours, which is a posture of War. But because they uphold thereby, the Industry of their Subjects; there does not follow from it, that misery, which accompanies the Liberty of particular men.[56]

[50] Rousseau, *State of War*, p. 36 (n. 4). Cf. also Rousseau, *Discourse*, II, pp. 173f (n. 1): 'It is easy to see how the establishment of a single Society made the establishment of all the others indispensable, and how, in order to stand up to united forces, it became necessary to unite in turn.'

[51] Hobbes, *Leviathan*, 13, p. 89 (n. 1).

[52] Cf. Hobbes, *Leviathan*, 13, p. 89 (n. 1) and Rousseau, *Discours sur l'inégalité*, II, p. 212 (n. 14).

[53] Simone Goyard-Fabre points out that Hobbes rejects a non-pessimistic idea of war: he neither continues the tradition of 'just war' (Augustine, Thomas Aquinas) nor the tradition of war as art (Machiavelli). Both Hobbes and Rousseau consider war not as a mission or a skill but just as a fact which has to be averted if possible. Cf. Simone Goyard-Fabre, *Le droit et la loi dans la philosophie de Thomas Hobbes* (1975), pp. 62–5.

[54] Hobbes, *Leviathan*, 13, pp. 88f (n. 1).

[55] Hobbes, *Leviathan*, 13, p. 88 (n. 1).

[56] Hobbes, *Leviathan*, 13, p. 90 (n. 1). Cf. as well Hobbes, *On the Citizen*, XIII, 7, p. 145 (n. 25): 'For the state of commonwealths towards each other is a *natural* state, i.e. a state of hostility. Even when the fighting between them stops, it should not be called Peace, but an intermission during which each watches the motion and aspect of its enemy [. . .]'.

War is possible because of the independency of the sovereigns. They have not given up their natural right and thus remain in the state of nature: not only towards other sovereigns but towards their subjects as well. But this is not enough to explain why there has never been 'a condition of warre one against another'. What is lacking between individuals is everything that is 'continuall'—and due to this lack, there is no 'condition' between them and thus no war. This correlation becomes more explicit in Rousseau. He argues that the (early) state of nature is no state of war not only because men are timid, peaceful and endowed with pity but also because there are no continuous relationships between private individuals.[57] This is the reason why there is no 'true war between individuals' but only between 'public persons', i.e. sovereigns.[58] Thus, Rousseau defines war as follows: 'I call then war between power and power[59] the effect of a constant, overt, mutual disposition to destroy the enemy state, or at least to weaken it by all the means one can. When this disposition is transformed into action it is war properly called; in so far as it remains untransformed it is only the state of war.'[60] What is properly called 'war' presupposes a constant disposition—a state of war. In Hobbes and Rousseau, this leads to the conclusion that the state of nature as a state of war has its only actual appearance in the international sphere.

Hobbes and Rousseau agree in their distinction between a hypothetical state of nature between individuals and a real state of nature in the international realm, but they fundamentally disagree in their appraisal of the international condition of war. In Hobbes' view, the international state of war does not cause major problems. Admittedly, the formation of states causes the problem of an international state of war but it is at the same time the principal part of minimizing its threats. The purpose of the state is not only to guarantee 'Peace at home' but also to enable mutual assistance against the 'enemies abroad'.[61] To save the citizens from both 'foreign and civil war' is the sovereign task.[62] Apart from this, Hobbes claims that the

[57] Cf. Rousseau, *State of War*, p. 35 (n. 4): 'War is a permanent state which presupposes constant relations; and these relations are a rare occurrence between men, for between individuals there is a continual flux which constantly changes relationships and interests. Thus a matter of dispute rises and disappears almost at the same moment; a quarrel begins and ends within a day; and one can have fights and murders, but never, or very rarely, long enmities and wars.'

[58] Rousseau, *State of War*, p. 41 (n. 4).

[59] In the *Social Contract* which appeared six years later (1762) Rousseau uses the term 'power' [*puissance*] in order to describe the body politic 'when comparing it to similar bodies'. Rousseau, *Social Contract*, I, 6, p. 51 (n. 6). 'Power' is the term for bodies politic in the international perspective, whereas 'sovereign' denominates these bodies when perceived in their internal activity.

[60] Rousseau, *State of War*, p. 40 (n. 4).

[61] Cf. Hobbes, *Leviathan*, 17, pp. 120f (n. 1).

[62] Hobbes, *On the Citizen*, XIII, 6, p. 144 (n. 25). Robinson Grover stresses that the crucial difference between individuals in a state of nature and nations in a state of nature 'is the shielding effect of national institutions which interpose themselves between the international anarchy of sovereign nations and the solitary citizen'. Robinson A. Grover, 'Hobbes and the Concept of International Law', in Timo Airaksinen and Martin A. Bertman (eds.), *Hobbes: War Among Nations* (1989), pp. 79–90, at p. 88. Grover turns this argument against Hobbes' conception of absolute sovereignty: if the states can interpose themselves between the international anarchy and the individuals, why should it not be possible to mitigate the individual state of nature by interposing other institutions between the individuals, for example the law, the church, or the family (instead of a national absolute sovereign)? In other words: if an absolute (super-national) sovereign is not needed to protect the individuals in

condition of war between sovereigns is less miserable than a state of nature between individuals, as the industry of the subjects of a state is not infringed but upheld in the international condition.

In his *Second Discourse* and his treatises about peace and war, Rousseau develops a dialectical perspective which is less conciliatory than the one of Hobbes. In contrast to Hobbes, Rousseau points to the paradoxical situation caused by the formation of the state. The unification of private individuals constitutes a new kind of individuals 'for with regard to foreigners it [the body politic, J. H.] becomes a simple being, an individual'[63]. The unification causes a new division—and this division between public or national individuals produces a dimension of violence hitherto unknown on earth: the 'first discernible effects of the division of Mankind into different Societies' were wars between nations, battles, murders, and reprisals 'that make Nature tremble'. The trembling of nature shows how far from nature such a state of nature is, and how far it is from Rousseau's hypothesis of an original state of nature between individual men. This is because in the rising international sphere 'more murders were committed in a single day's fighting, and more horrors at the capture of a single town, than had been committed in the state of Nature for centuries together over the entire face of the earth'.[64] The foundation of states here only causes the problem of war without providing a means to prevent its outbreak. This is also the radical conclusion Rousseau draws against Hobbes in his essay about *The State of War:* 'Far from the state of war being natural to man, war springs from peace, or at least from the precautions that men have taken to ensure a lasting peace.'[65] The precautions consist in building political associations—but 'in joining a particular group of men, we have really declared ourselves the enemies of the whole race'.[66] The deadly irony lies not only in the fact that the prevention of eventual private 'wars' produces actual wars between nations but that these wars between nations are by far more disastrous than the wars one sought to prevent.

The difference between Hobbes and Rousseau is as drastic as it can be. Whereas Hobbes consequently looks at the formation of the political society from the perspective of unification and peace, Rousseau—at least in the *Second Discourse, The State of War*, and *The Abstract of Saint-Pierre's Project for Perpetual Peace*—looks at it

an international state of nature, why is an absolute (national) sovereign needed to protect them in an individual state of nature? Cf. Grover, 'Hobbes', in *Hobbes: War Among Nations*, p. 89 (n. 62).

[63] Cf. Rousseau, *Social Contract*, I, 7, p. 52 (n. 6). Georg Cavallar considers Rousseau's account of the state of nature between these public individuals as a 'structural interpretation' of Hobbes' hypothesis of a state of nature between private individuals. Cf. Georg Cavallar, 'Jean-Jacques Rousseau', in Bardo Fassbender and Anne Peters (eds.), *The Oxford Handbook of the History of International Law* (2012), pp. 1114–17, at p. 1115. Indeed the similarity between Rousseau's depiction of the destructive aspiration for power of the sovereigns and Hobbes' depiction of the will of private individuals is noticeable.

[64] Rousseau, *Discourse*, II, p. 174 (n. 1).

[65] Rousseau, *State of War*, p. 45 (n. 4). In the *Abstract of Saint-Pierre's Project for Perpetual Peace*, Rousseau also blames the precautions against war as the cause of war. Jean-Jacques Rousseau, 'Abstract and Judgement of Saint-Pierre's Project for Perpetual Peace', in Stanley Hoffmann and David P. Fidler (eds.), *Rousseau on International Relations* (1991), pp. 53–100, at p. 54.

[66] Rousseau, *Abstract and Judgement*, p. 54 (n. 65).

from the perspective of division and war.[67] According to Rousseau, the formation of political societies does not give an answer to the question of war. It rather makes this question relevant.[68] This could explain why Rousseau, in contrast to Hobbes, dealt extensively with the question of bringing order into the international sphere. He did so in his *Abstract and Judgement of Saint-Pierre's Project for Perpetual Peace.* I now want to outline the reasons why in Rousseau's perspective such an international order is preferable but impossible and which conclusions he draws from this insight.

V. Rousseau and the Question of Perpetual Peace

In his *Abstract of Saint-Pierre's Project for Perpetual Peace*, Rousseau only deals with the international situation within Europe. The question of perpetual peace is a European question. The vision of peace has its borders at the borders of Europe. The relation between Europe and the rest of the world remains in a state of nature. According to the *Abstract*, the European situation of war is more disastrous than anywhere else—not because there is unbridled disorder but because there is some order in disorder. A balance [*équilibre*] of forces stabilizes the European condition of war and makes it impossible to arrive at a decision which brings violence to an end: 'The present balance of Europe is just firm enough to remain in perpetual oscillation without losing itself altogether; and, if our troubles cannot increase, still less can we put an end to them, seeing that any sweeping revolution is henceforth an impossibility.'[69] In the French original text, Rousseau uses the term 'système de l'Europe' which has a certain 'degré de solidité'.[70] The European states do not build an order as order implies a situation of non-violent coexistence.[71] But neither are they in mere disorder: although they are in a state of war, European sovereigns are juridically, ethically, and religiously connected. These ties make it possible to talk of a *système*: 'C'est ainsi que toutes les Puissances de l'Europe forment entre elles une sorte de système qui les unit par une même religion, par un même droit des gens, par les moeurs, par les lettres, par le commerce, et par une sorte d'équilibre qui est l'effet nécessaire de tout cela [...].'[72] The social bond which constitutes this system

[67] Regarding this difference between Hobbes and Rousseau cf. also Thibault, 'Les relations internationales', in *Études internationales*, pp. 217–20 (n. 5).

[68] The question of foreign affairs is explicitly excluded from the reflections in the *Social Contract*. Cf. Rousseau, *Social Contract*, IV, 9, p. 152 (n. 6).

[69] Rousseau, *Abstract and Judgement*, pp. 61f (n. 65).

[70] Rousseau, 'Extrait de la Paix perpétuelle', in *The Political Writings of Jean Jacques Rousseau*, pp. 364–87, at p. 370 (n. 3).

[71] It is in this sense of non-violent, i.e. peaceful coexistence Rousseau uses the term 'order' in the first sentence of the first book of his *Social Contract* when he speaks of the 'civil order' [*l'ordre civil*]. Cf. Rousseau, *Social Contract*, Introduction, p. 41 (n. 6).

[72] Rousseau, 'Extrait de la Paix perpétuelle', in *The Political Writings of Jean Jacques Rousseau*, p. 366 (n. 3). 'Thus the powers of Europe constitute a kind of a whole [in the French original: 'système', J.H.], united by identity of religion, of moral standard, of international law; by letters, by commerce, and finally by a species of balance which is the inevitable result of all these ties [...].'; Rousseau, *Abstract and Judgement*, pp. 55f (n. 65).

remains imperfect but it is still tighter than the general knots of humanity, i.e. the knots existing in a state of nature. Imperfect bonds, however, are worse than no bonds at all—a 'system' is worse than mere disorder.[73]

Whereas living in any state is bad because it combines the inconveniences of the state of nature and of society, living in a European state is worse because the European state of nature has a societal structure. The imperfection of this *société*[74] causes a miserable situation. But it is exactly the existence of such imperfect social bonds which could facilitate a European society in the form of a *Confédération* which he calls *République européenne*.[75] Only in this form of a real confederation (*Confédération réelle*) would the European society be a true body politic (*un vrai Corps politique*).[76]

The condition of a true body politic is a legal framework. First of all, the European sovereigns would have to be willing to sign a treaty which declares their 'perpetual and irrevocable alliance'.[77] At the heart of the confederation would be a *tribunal judiciaire*[78] which should establish the laws and regulations obliging all sovereign members. Armed with a coercive power, the confederation would be able to enforce its laws.[79] According to Rousseau, it is this enforceability which is essential for law to be law. In order to be legitimate, the law has to be enacted by an assembly of the sovereign states which will be bound to this law. The question of an international body politic—which is, according to Rousseau, the only possibility of an international order—and the question of legitimate law are intertwined: a body politic needs enforceable law, and enforceable law needs the approval of the members of the political body. Rousseau argues that the common tribunal does not affect the rights of sovereignty; sovereigns do not become less absolute, but instead their crown will rather be assured.[80]

According to Rousseau, firstly there is no doubt that the confederation, once established, would achieve its purpose to guarantee a lasting peace within Europe. This peace would be peace in the strict sense (and not just a temporary truce which is still a condition of war)[81] as the eventuality of war would be out of the question: 'Let no one threaten us with a sudden invasion. It is perfectly obvious that Europe has no invader to fear, and that the "first comer" will never come. The day of those barbarian irruptions, which seemed to fall from the clouds, is gone forever.'[82] Secondly, there is no doubt that the established confederation would be in the

[73] Cf. Rousseau, *Abstract and Judgement*, p. 67 (n. 65).

[74] Rousseau, 'Extrait de la Paix perpétuelle', in *The Political Writings of Jean Jacques Rousseau*, p. 374 (n. 70).

[75] Cf. Rousseau, 'Extrait de la Paix perpétuelle', in *The Political Writings of Jean Jacques Rousseau*, pp. 375f (n. 70).

[76] Cf. Rousseau, *Abstract and Judgement*, p. 67 (n. 65).

[77] Cf. Rousseau, *Abstract and Judgement*, p. 69 (n. 65).

[78] Rousseau, 'Extrait de la Paix perpétuelle', in *The Political Writings of Jean Jacques Rousseau*, p. 374 (n. 70).

[79] Cf. Rousseau, *Abstract and Judgement*, p. 68 (n. 65).

[80] Cf. Rousseau, *Abstract and Judgement*, pp. 80f (n. 65).

[81] Cf. Rousseau, *Abstract and Judgement*, p. 60 (n. 65).

[82] Rousseau, *Abstract and Judgement*, p. 84 (n. 65).

interest of all sovereign states.[83] At the end of his *Abstract*, Rousseau radicalizes this second claim. He argues that an international peace is not only in the interest of the states but that beyond such peace there is a total impossibility to establish a good government.[84] Rousseau, however, adds for consideration that there is one right that sovereign states have to waive when entering the confederation: it is their right to take measures against one of the members, i.e. their right to decide on war.[85]

In Rousseau's perspective, this deprivation is the reason why a perpetual peace within Europe is not achievable. This is his argument in his *Judgement of Saint-Pierre's Project for Perpetual Peace*. The kings and those who serve them only aim at two objects: 'to extend their rule beyond their frontiers and to make it more absolute within them'.[86] Rousseau assumes that sovereign states are governed by individuals who follow more their private than the public interest.[87] And he makes clear that the princes governing the states are not aware about what is best for them. Deluded by appearances, they do not realize that their own interest (being rich and powerful) is pursued by acting in the public interest.[88] Instead of entering a federation, they continue to conduct war. This is the reason why the project of perpetual peace in Europe is desirable but will not be carried out without violent means: 'No federation could ever be established except by a revolution. That being so, which of us would dare to say whether the league of Europe is a thing more to be desired or feared? It would perhaps do more harm in a moment than it would guard against for ages.'[89]

In contrast to the Abbé de Saint-Pierre, Rousseau is not a proponent of an international (European) order. International order would require an obliging legal framework. As Rousseau considered such a framework as beyond reach, he could only think of international order and peace as a wishful dream.[90] But still, he admits that there is *some kind* of international law. In a last step, I want to clarify why such an international law is possible in Rousseau's theory and why it is impossible in Hobbes' approach.

VI. Can International Law Be Possible?

If we now deal with the question of international law, it is no longer a question about international order (in the strict sense of order as implied by Hobbes and

[83] Cf. Rousseau, *Abstract and Judgement*, pp. 71–82 (n. 65).
[84] Cf. Rousseau, *Abstract and Judgement*, p. 86 (n. 65).
[85] Rousseau, *Abstract and Judgement*, pp. 69f and 76 (n. 65).
[86] Rousseau, *Abstract and Judgement*, p. 90 (n. 65).
[87] Cf. Rousseau, *Abstract and Judgement*, p. 97 (n. 65).
[88] Cf. Rousseau, *Abstract and Judgement*, pp. 92f and as well p. 82 (n. 65).
[89] Rousseau, *Abstract and Judgement*, p. 100 (n. 65).
[90] Olaf Asbach plausibly argues that there is also a structural reason why Rousseau does not advocate an international order: it would necessarily curtail the autarky and independence of the political entities, and it is exactly the autarky and independence of small republics which is in the center of his political philosophy. Cf. Olaf Asbach, 'Staatsrecht und Völkerrecht bei Jean-Jacques Rousseau. Zur Frage der völkerrechtlichen Vollendung des *Contrat social*', in Reinhard Brandt and Karlfried Herb (eds.), *Vom Gesellschaftsvertrag oder Prinzipien des Staatsrechts* (2nd edn, 2012), pp. 243–71.

Rousseau). Rousseau's probably most dismissive reference to international law can be found in *The State of War*: 'As for what is commonly called international law, because its laws lack any sanction, they are unquestionably mere illusions.'[91]

Because it lacks sanctions, the law of nations is not assured. In the case of conflict, it is not this law which is enforced but the 'law' of the stronger.[92] This is the principal deficiency of the existing international situation. Rousseau puts it first in the summary at the end of his *Abstract*: 'Nul droit assuré que celui du plus fort.'[93] No assured law except that of the stronger. Rousseau points out in the *Social Contract* that the law of the stronger actually is no law.[94] Pure enforceability (the fact of sanction) does not create law. Law always needs legitimation and the criterion of legitimation, according to Rousseau, is the same in the international sphere as in the domestic one: those obliged by the law have to approve it, in other words, they have to participate in the legislation process. Regarding the international law of his time, Rousseau not only criticizes a lack of enforceability but also a lack of legitimation. He does so when considering the public law of Europe (*le Droit public de l'Europe*): it has not been established or authorized in concert ('n'étant point établi ou autorisé de concert').[95] This is the second deficiency. The third deficiency is that the law of nations is not based on general principles and that it varies ceaselessly in the course of time and from place to place. It is therefore riddled with contradictions which, again, are only solved by the force and in favour of the stronger.[96] Due to these deficiencies, the law of nations which takes shape as a public law of Europe lacks legal character. This is why Rousseau states that the laws of what is called 'law of nations' (*Droit des gens*) are only illusions. And still it is this common law of nations which, lacking systematicity in itself, contributes to the cohesion of Europe as an (imperfect) *système*.[97] Together with religion, morals, and commerce it establishes interstate relations which are beyond a political federation. Rousseau describes the efficacy of these relations as less apparent but not less real.[98] The formation of the law of nations takes place silently and it only consists in 'a few tacit conventions'.[99] We can conceive the term 'tacit' as 'not explicitly approved within a legislation process'. As such, the law of nations is not part of the political sphere—and consequently not part of Rousseau's political philosophy in the narrower sense.

[91] Rousseau, *State of War*, p. 44 (n. 4); Rousseau, 'L'état de guerre', in *The Political Writings of Jean Jacques Rousseau*, p. 304 (n. 3): 'Quant à ce qu'on appelle communément le droit des gens, il est certain que, faute de sanction, ses lois ne sont que des chimères plus faibles encore que la loi de nature.'

[92] The term that Rousseau uses for the law of nations is *Droit/droit des gens* (cf. n. 91 and Rousseau, *Discourse*, II, p. 174 (n. 1)). This *droit des gens* is powerless against the *droit du plus fort*, the law/right of the stronger.

[93] Rousseau, 'Extrait de la Paix perpétuelle', in *The Political Writings of Jean Jacques Rousseau*, p. 385 (n. 70).

[94] Cf. Rousseau, *Social Contract*, I, 3, p. 44 (n. 6).

[95] Cf. Rousseau, 'Extrait de la Paix perpétuelle', in *The Political Writings of Jean Jacques Rousseau*, p. 369 (n. 70); for the English translation cf. Rousseau, *Abstract and Judgement*, p. 60 (n. 65).

[96] Cf. Rousseau, *Abstract and Judgement*, p. 60 (n. 65).

[97] Cf. Rousseau, *Abstract and Judgement*, pp. 55f (n. 65).

[98] Cf. Rousseau, *Abstract and Judgement*, p. 55 (n. 65).

[99] Rousseau, *Discourse*, II, p. 174 (n. 1).

In Hobbes, there is no such weak form of international law. In his account, the international sphere (which is beyond all kind of system and cohesion) is an empty space from a legal point of view. This is due to the strict concept of law that Hobbes establishes when dealing with 'civil laws' or 'laws of the commonwealth': '*Civil laws* (to define them) are nothing other than commands about the citizens' future actions from the one who is endowed with *sovereign authority* [*summa potestas*].'[100] Sovereignty is the presupposition for law; as only sovereigns can enact laws, there is no law beyond sovereignty.[101] This is the reason why there is only (domestic) civil law and no international law. As long as there is no overarching sovereign in the international sphere, that is to say as long as there is a plurality of sovereign states, there is no possibility of international law. In contrast to Rousseau, the idea of international law and the idea of sovereign states exclude each other in a Hobbesian conception of law. The relations between sovereigns are only characterized by an unrestrained natural right. Without any restraint of this right (which can only be achieved by the enactment of laws) 'there cannot possibly be any Peace'.[102] But when Hobbes claims that the law 'which is commonly called the *Law of Nations*' is 'the same thing' as the law of nature, he does not claim that sovereigns are exempt of all duties.[103] The law of nature demands to seek peace. This applies to individuals and to 'Soveraign Princes, and Soveraign Assemblies' alike—even though there is no other 'Court of Naturall Justice', but the conscience and the legal character of such a court is doubtful.[104]

Whereas in the final analysis Hobbes and Rousseau agree that there is no effectual international law, they disagree about the value of an eventual international

[100] Hobbes, *On the Citizen*, VI, 9, p. 79 (n. 25). Cf. as well Hobbes, *Leviathan*, 26, pp. 183 and 200 (n. 1). M. M. Goldsmith classifies Hobbes not only as 'a command theorist' but also as a 'legal positivist'. Hobbes fulfils two conditions of legal positivism: on the one hand, the validity of law is not attached to general principles of morality, justice, or rationality; on the other hand, laws and authorities are organized hierarchically and integrated in a system which is closed by a supreme authority. Cf. M.M. Goldsmith, 'Hobbes on Law', in Tom Sorell (ed.), *The Cambridge Companion to Hobbes* (1996), pp. 274–304, at p. 275 and p. 278.

[101] This is also the basis of Hedley Bull's assumption of an international anarchy: according to Hobbes, what is called the law of nations is not law in the proper sense (not positive law) but just the law of nature (prudential rules of self-preservation). Insofar as there is no central authority, the international sphere remains anarchic—which is, Bull argues, not only true for Hobbes' time but for the time of Bull's own article as well. On the other hand, Bull points out that Hobbes' account neglects all the legal and non-legal relations and cooperations between states which already existed in Hobbes' time and which are extended today. Cf. Hedley Bull, 'Hobbes and the International Anarchy', *Social Research* 48, 4 (1981), 717–38, at 723 and 736f.

[102] Hobbes, *Leviathan*, 26, p. 185 (n. 1).

[103] Noel Malcolm insists that Hobbes considers international law to be law *precisely because* he identifies it with the law of nature: as distinct from civil law, international law qualifies as law not by being positive law but by being 'directly derived from (or identical with) natural law'. It is for this reason that Malcolm refuses to align Hobbes with the tradition of legal positivism. Cf. Noel Malcolm, *Aspects of Hobbes* (2004), pp. 439f. For a critique of Malcolm's argument cf. Benedict Kingsbury and Benjamin Straumann, 'State of Nature versus Commercial Sociability as the Basis of International Law: Reflections on the Roman Foundations and Current Interpretations of the International Political and Legal Thought of Grotius, Hobbes and Pufendorf', in Samantha Besson and John Tasioulas (eds.), *The Philosophy of International Law* (2010), pp. 33–51, at pp. 44f.

[104] Hobbes, *Leviathan*, 30, p. 244 (n. 1).

order and a forceful international law. As I will show in the next step, the agreement and the disagreement of Hobbes and Rousseau are reflected in their reception: concerning their descriptive account, they have mainly been received as representatives of the same direction; concerning their normative claims, they have been sorted in different traditions.

VII. Remarks about the History of Reception

Considering the history of the reception of Hobbes and Rousseau, we can distinguish between two questions: how have Hobbes and Rousseau been classified regarding their appraisal of international law? How have they influenced important normative positions regarding the question of international law?

Concerning the question of classification, both Hobbes and Rousseau have predominantly been considered as precursors of 'realism' because they both characterize the international sphere as a condition of war.[105] In other words, they have been considered 'realists' because they did not advocate a legal framework which makes international cooperation possible.[106] The objections against this 'realist' interpretation (regarding Hobbes) are based on an understanding of natural law as a law 'in its own right', a law which is binding despite the lack of enforceability[107] and (regarding Rousseau) on the emphasis that Rousseau developed elements and fragments of an ideal theory of supranational organization which he, however, never elaborated in a book.[108] Even though both Hobbes and Rousseau have mainly been classified as precursors of 'realism', their influence on later positions has been very different. I only want to mention two positions—one drawing on Hobbes and one on Rousseau—in order to illustrate the different directions of reception.

Hobbes' conception of war as a disposition to fight together with the Hobbesian relation of protection and obedience are the core of Carl Schmitt's *The Concept of the Political.*[109] This book (published in 1932) is prominent in the debate until today. Schmitt argues that 'the real possibility of war' is the condition of the existence of states. If there is no disposition to fight, there is no longer any friend and enemy

[105] Regarding Hobbes cf. the list of authors classifying Hobbes as 'realist' in Malcolm, *Aspects of Hobbes*, pp. 432–5 (n. 103); regarding Rousseau cf. Cavallar, 'Jean-Jacques Rousseau', in *The Oxford Handbook of the History of International Law*, p. 1116 (n. 63).

[106] Simone Goyard-Fabre has called this the 'silence' of Rousseau and Hobbes. Cf. Simone Goyard-Fabre, 'Les Silences de Hobbes et de Rousseau devant le droit international', *Archives de philosophie du droit* 32 (1987), 59–69, and Simone Goyard-Fabre, 'La guerre et le droit international dans la philosophie de Rousseau', *Études Jean-Jacques Rousseau* 7 (1995), 45–78.

[107] This is, as mentioned, also the prominent argument in Malcolm, *Aspects of Hobbes*, pp. 439f (n. 103).

[108] Francis Cheneval calls this Rousseau's 'unfinished' or 'unwritten' doctrine. Cf. Francis Cheneval, *Philosophie in weltbürgerlicher Bedeutung. Über die Entstehung und die philosophischen Grundlagen des supranationalen und kosmopolitischen Denkens der Moderne* (2002), pp. 365 and 390. Rousseau outlines the structure of such a book about the relations between political societies in *Emile or On Education*, trans. by Allan Bloom (1979), pp. 466f.

[109] Cf. Carl Schmitt, *The Concept of the Political*, trans. by George Schwab (2007), p. 52.

grouping, which means, according to Schmitt, that there is no state any more. A global organization of states which could preclude the possibility of war is tantamount to the nonexistence of states. The realization of a league of nations is thus, according to Schmitt, the end of the political sphere.[110]

This question of a league of nations is the most important starting point of one of the most prominent receptions of Rousseau. In the seventh proposition of his *Idea for a Universal History from a Cosmopolitan Perspective*, Kant remarks that 'Rousseau's preference of the state of savages was not all that far off the mark, that is, if one leaves out this last stage, which our species has yet to surmount.'[111] What Kant calls 'this last stage' is the federation of states (*Staatenverbindung*). Kant tackles exactly the problem which Rousseau had in mind: 'The problem of establishing a perfect civil constitution is dependent upon the problem of a law-governed *external relation between states* and cannot be solved without having first solved the latter.'[112] Rousseau noticed this problem and made it explicit but yet focused on a strong national constitution as the first thing to strive for. In *Toward Perpetual Peace*, Kant stresses the importance of an 'internal legal constitution'[113] as well. For without a juridical condition (i.e. without states), there is no public law and thus no possibility for a federation which, like in Rousseau, can only exist in an international legal framework.[114] The only aim of such a federation is to guarantee peace since any other purpose would restrain the freedom of its members.[115] The crucial difference between Rousseau and Kant is not that Kant considers such an ideal federation as attainable whereas Rousseau does not, but that Kant focuses on the federation and on perpetual peace as a condition which cannot be fully achieved in a single moment of contract but which has to be pursued 'in the form of an endlessly progressing approximation'.[116] It is not surprising that regarding the normative question of how an international legal order should look like, the reference to Rousseau and Kant has been much more frequent than the reference to Hobbes—even though Kant's position in *Toward Perpetual Peace* shares many of Hobbes' premises.[117]

[110] Cf. Schmitt, *Concept*, p. 55 (n. 109).

[111] Immanuel Kant, 'Idea for a Universal History from a Cosmopolitan Perspective', in Pauline Kleingeld (ed.) and David L. Colclasure (trans.), *Toward Perpetual Peace and Other Writings on Politics, Peace, and History* (2006), pp. 3–16, at p. 12. Cf. as well in this volume the contribution by Vischer.

[112] Kant, *Idea for a Universal History*, p. 9 (n. 111).

[113] Cf. Kant, 'Toward Perpetual Peace: A Philosophical Sketch', in *Toward Perpetual Peace*, pp. 67–109, at p. 80 (n. 111).

[114] Kant, *Toward Perpetual Peace*, p. 107 (n. 113).

[115] Cf. Kant, *Toward Perpetual Peace*, pp. 107f (n. 113). Regarding Kant's reception of Rousseau's idea of a necessary nexus of freedom on the one hand and legal condition on the other cf. Ernst Cassirer, *Das Problem Jean Jacques Rousseau* (1970), pp. 18f.

[116] Cf. Kant, *Toward Perpetual Peace*, p. 109 (n. 113). It is because of his ideal of a federation and his idea of an endless approximation that Kant has been classified as 'anti-realist'. Cf. Pauline Kleingeld, 'Immanuel Kant', in *The Oxford Handbook of the History of International Law*, pp. 1122–6, at p. 1124 (n. 63).

[117] Two important premises are a) the crucial difference between war as a single event of a battle and war as a lasting condition, and b) the relation of protection and obedience within the state. Cf. Kant, *Toward Perpetual Peace*, pp. 79 and 105f (n. 113).

VIII. Conclusion: National Orders in International Disorder

Peace in the sense of a condition in which the eventuality of war is excluded is not possible within the international sphere, neither in the theory of Hobbes nor in the theory of Rousseau. In both Hobbes and Rousseau, the condition of peace presupposes a political order established and maintained by means of law. 'Order', 'peace', and 'law' are necessarily linked concepts. Whereas these concepts are pivotal in Hobbes' and Rousseau's philosophy of the state, there is no reference point for these concepts in their understanding of the international sphere. In their perspective, the international sphere cannot be peacefully handled and it is for this reason that it does not play a major role in their political philosophy. In his *Judgement*, Rousseau criticizes Saint-Pierre for having chosen the wrong means: international peace cannot be 'set up by a book'.[118] The peaceful federation could only be founded 'by the violent means from which humanity must needs shrink'.[119] The political philosophy of Hobbes and Rousseau is about the necessity and legitimation of the foundation of a national political order. According to Rousseau, the foundation of an international political order cannot have a legitimate form; according to Hobbes, the foundation of an international political order is not necessary. Thus, such an order is for Hobbes as well as for Rousseau—for different reasons but in equal measure—out of the question. As a result, the international sphere remains in a state of disorder. To deal with this disorder is not an international task but the task of national orders. The task of political philosophy, as Hobbes and Rousseau understand it, is to elaborate the preconditions and fundaments of an order which is able to accomplish this task: as there is no international politics, international peace is a national responsibility.

Selected Bibliography

Goyard-Fabre, Simone, 'La guerre et le droit international dans la philosophie de Rousseau', *Études Jean-Jacques Rousseau* 7 (1995), 45–78.

Grover, Robinson A., 'Hobbes and the Concept of International Law', in Timo Airaksinen and Martin A. Bertman (eds.), *Hobbes: War Among Nations* (Aldershot and Brookfield: Gower, 1989), pp. 79–90.

Hobbes, Thomas, *On the Citizen*, ed. and trans. Richard Tuck and Michael Silverthorne (Cambridge: Cambridge University Press, 1998).

[118] This conviction (and not modesty) may be the reason why Rousseau explicitly refused to choose a title for his *Abstract* and *Judgement* which would have connected his person directly with the project of a perpetual peace within Europe: 'A l'égard du titre, je ne puis consentir qu'il soit changé contre un autre qui m'approprieroit davantage un Projet qui ne m'appartient point.' Jean-Jacques Rousseau, *Friedensschriften*, trans. and ed. Michael Köhler (2009), p. 8. The full title of the *Abstract* is: 'Extrait du projet de paix perpétuelle de Monsieur l'Abbé de Saint-Pierre. Par J.J. Rousseau, Citoyen de Genève'. Cf. Rousseau, *Friedensschriften*, p. 2 (n. 118).

[119] Rousseau, *Abstract and Judgement*, p. 100 (n. 65).

Kant, Immanuel, 'Toward Perpetual Peace: A Philosophical Sketch', in Pauline Kleingeld (ed.) and David L. Colclasure (trans.), *Toward Perpetual Peace and Other Writings on Politics, Peace, and History* (New Haven/London: Yale University Press, 2006), pp. 67–109.

Malcolm, Noel, *Aspects of Hobbes* (Oxford: Oxford University Press, 2004).

Rousseau, Jean-Jacques, *Extrait de la Paix Perpétuelle*, in Charles E. Vaughan (ed.), *The Political Writings of Jean Jacques Rousseau, Volume I* (Oxford: Basil Blackwell, 1962), pp. 364–87.

Strauss, Leo, *Natural Right and History* (Chicago/London: The University of Chicago Press, 1976).

9

The International Legal Argument in Spinoza

*Tilmann Altwicker**

I. Introduction

Living in Amsterdam in the seventeenth century—'arguably one of the most cosmopolitan and transnational environments on the globe at the time'[1]—it is not surprising that Spinoza wrote about international relations and international law. It is worthwhile reconstructing his international legal argument as he does not develop a remote ideal of an international order, but instead aims to provide an explanation of why states are compelled to cooperate internationally.

There are only few references to Spinoza in the current theory of international relations and international law.[2] To many, Spinoza's contribution to the field seems merely a reflection of the 'Westphalian law' that needs to be sharply distinguished from an international legal order based on common ethical values.[3] Under 'Westphalian law', international law was unconcerned with universal values as causes for action (war, peace, agreements etc.).[4] During Spinoza's lifetime

* This contribution is based on my earlier study on 'Spinozas Theorie der internationalen Beziehungen', in Wolfgang Bartuschat, Stephan Kirste, and Manfred Walther (eds.), *Spinoza, Politischer Traktat: Ein Kommentar* (2014), pp. 67–77. I am grateful to Alexandra Hansen and Nuscha Wieczorek for excellent research assistance.

[1] Cesare Casarino, 'Marx before Spinoza: Notes toward an Investigation', in Dimitris Vardoulakis (ed.), *Spinoza Now* (2011), pp. 179, 191.

[2] Other than in the beginning of the twentieth century, Spinoza's theory of international law rarely receives attention today: Hersch Lauterpacht, 'Spinoza and International Law', *The British Yearbook of International Law* 8 (1927), 89–107; Adolf Menzel, 'Spinoza und das Völkerrecht', *Zeitschrift für Völkerrecht* 2 (1908), 17–30; Alfred Verdross, 'Das Völkerrecht im Systeme von Spinoza', *Zeitschrift für öffentliches Recht* (1928), 100–5. For recent studies see Francis Cheneval, 'Spinozas Philosophie der internationalen Beziehungen', in Marcel Senn and Manfred Walther (eds.), *Ethik, Recht und Politik bei Spinoza* (2001), pp. 195–208; Manfred Walther, 'Natural Law, Civil Law, and International Law in Spinoza', *Cardozo Law Review* 25 (2003), 657–65; Altwicker, Tilmann, 'Spinozas Theorie der internationalen Beziehungen', in Wolfgang Bartuschat, Stephan Kirste, and Manfred Walther (eds.), *Spinoza, Politischer Traktat: Ein Kommentar* (2014).

[3] For example, Oscar Schachter writes that 'Spinoza, the great rationalist, urged states to give their highest priority to increasing their power', 'The Role of Power in International Law', *Proceedings of the Annual Meeting* (American Society of International Law) 93 (1999), 200.

[4] See Martti Koskenniemi, *From Apology to Utopia: The Structure of International Legal Argument* (2005), p. 94 (stating that in the Peace of Westphalia it was recognized that 'even the possible existence of universal values was not a sufficient *casus belli*').

and until the late nineteenth century, 'international law' was equated with the *jus publicum Europaeum*, the European public law governing the relations between Christian sovereigns that allowed the particular national interest to function as a legitimate reason to go to war.[5] When the *Tractatus Politicus* (Political Treatise, referred to hereafter in this chapter as TP)[6] was first published (posthumously) in 1677, the 'Peace of Westphalia' barely dated back some thirty years. It was the peace treaty of Munster and Osnabruck in 1648 that confirmed the sovereignty of the European powers for the first time. 'Sovereignty' became the central concept of the Westphalian era, reflecting the new self-perception of European powers. The modern concept of sovereignty that evolved in the fifteenth and sixteenth centuries referred to the supreme command *(summa potestas)* that rested with the sovereign rulers (and later became an attribute of the state).[7] 'Westphalian law', thus, stands for the idea of a conception of international law based on sovereign political units and the rejection of the far older conception of a universal society *(societas humana)*.[8]

At a first glance, Spinoza's treatment of international relations in Book III of the TP appears indeed to provide merely a realist account of the world of diplomacy in his day. A realist interpretation could be easily squared with Spinoza's intention voiced at the beginning of the TP not to suggest 'anything that is novel or unheard of, but only to demonstrate by sure and conclusive reasoning such things as are in closest agreement with practice'.[9] Accordingly, many commentators (Gustav Adolf Walz, Arthur Nussbaum, and, more recently, Cornelius Murphy) have considered Spinoza—along with Thomas Hobbes—to be a classical 'denier' of international law.[10]

Others have underscored that Spinoza's denial of binding international law is inconsistent with his political philosophy. It is claimed that had he been consistent with his own basic assumptions, he should have accepted the legal bindingness of at least some international treaties. For example, Charles Edwyn Vaughan claims that Spinoza did not sufficiently distinguish between non-binding treaties such as peace treaties dictated by the victorious party or pacts of aggression on the one hand, and binding defensive pacts or trade agreements on

[5] Koskenniemi, *From Apology to Utopia*, p. 94 (n. 4).

[6] Baruch Spinoza, *Political Treatise*, trans. Samuel Shirley (2000).

[7] On the concept of sovereignty see the seminal study by Helmut Quartisch, *Entstehung und Entwicklung des Begriffs in Frankreich und Deutschland vom 13. Jh. bis 1806* (1986).

[8] Gerry Simpson, 'International Law in Diplomatic History', in James Crawford and Martti Koskenniemi (eds.), *The Cambridge Companion to International Law* (2012), pp. 25, 31.

[9] TP 1/4, p. 35.

[10] Arthur Nussbaum, *A Concise History of the Law of Nations* (1947), pp. 18–26; Cornelius F. Murphy, 'The Grotian Vision of World Order', *AJIL* 76 (1982), 477, 484; G.A. Walz, *Wesen des Völkerrechts und Kritik der Völkerrechtsleugner* (1930), pp. 18–26 ('Yes, one can say that the radical denial of international law in the Western legal philosophical literature after the epoch-making work of Grotius, proclaiming the legal nature of international law, occurs for the first time with full clarity in Baruch Spinoza.') On Grotius see the contribution by Kadelbach, on Hobbes see the contribution by Heller (in this volume).

the other hand.[11] For Vaughan, the latter are binding as they pursue just aims.[12] Similarly, Hersch Lauterpacht argues that, given the *raisons d'être* Spinoza developed for the state, he should have also claimed that international defensive pacts are binding.[13] In a context of *prima facie* hostile neighbouring states, defensive pacts guarantee the conditions of individual self-preservation. Then, on the basis of his political theory, Spinoza should have assumed their legal bindingness. According to Lauterpacht, the absence of any notion of binding international law in Spinoza's theory reflects the reality of international relations in the seventeenth century.

In contrast, other commentators (Alfred Verdross, Adolf Menzel, and more recently, Francis Cheneval and Manfred Walther) claim that Spinoza indeed recognized the bindingness of international law.[14] Their conclusion is that Spinoza's account of international relations must be understood as a precursor to a consensus-based society of states bound by international law. For example, early on Adolf Menzel argued that 'from the remarks in paragraphs 15 and 16 of the *Political Treatise* emerges a new point of view which seems suitable to modify the previous statements [on the non-bindingness of international treaties, T.A.]. It opens up the possibility, at least prospectively, to form a community of states, which sets a barrier to the arbitrariness and the egoism of individual states'.[15]

In this chapter, it is argued that Spinoza is far from being a 'denier' of international law. Instead, it is shown that Spinoza offers a nuanced argument for why states are compelled to cooperate with one another in the form of international law. The argument is developed as follows: Section II outlines Spinoza's realist starting point which can be called the 'international state of nature'. Section III reconstructs—drawing on his ethical and ontological theory outlined in the *Ethica Ordine Geometrico Demonstrata* (Ethics, E)[16] and in the *Tractatus Theologico-Politicus* (Theological-Political Treatise, referred to hereafter in this chapter as TTP)[17] —Spinoza's international legal argument, i.e. the conditions that must be fulfilled for international law to exist. Section IV condenses and generalizes Spinoza's international legal argument in the form of three analytical concepts (normativity of international law, being a state *sui juris* and the concept of international cooperation). Section V concludes by outlining Spinoza's lasting contribution to the theory of international relations and law.

[11] Charles Edwyn Vaughan, *Studies in the History of Political Philosophy Before and After Rousseau*, vol. 1, ed. A.G. Little (1939), pp. 80–4.

[12] It should be critically noted here that Vaughan's reliance on the justness of some treaties can hardly be squared with Spinoza's doctrine of the absence of normativity and morality in the international state of nature.

[13] Lauterpacht, 'Spinoza and International Law', pp. 89, 97 (n. 2).

[14] Verdross, 'Das Völkerrecht im Systeme von Spinoza', p. 104 (n. 2); Walther, 'Natural Law, Civil Law, and International Law in Spinoza', pp. 657, 664 (n. 2).

[15] Adolf Menzel, *Beiträge zur Geschichte der Staatslehre* (1929), p. 414.

[16] Baruch Spinoza, *The Essential Spinoza: Ethics and Related Writings*, ed. Michael L Morgan, trans. Samuel Shirley (2006).

[17] Baruch Spinoza, *Theological-Political Treatise*, ed. Jonathan Israel (2012).

II. The Absence of Normativity in the International State of Nature

Spinoza's account of international relations starts out from what can be called a 'realist' position: Spinoza assumes a natural antagonism between states, which he describes as an 'international state of nature'. In this regard, Spinoza's conceptualization of international relations is influenced by Hobbes.[18] The international state of nature according to Spinoza's account, rests on two premises: First, at various points in the TP, Spinoza relies on an analogy between the individual and the state (individual/state-analogy).[19] Following this analogy, Spinoza reasons that states, too, must be considered in a state of nature. Spinoza uses the individual/state-analogy as a tool for the analysis of conditions of agency.[20] Accordingly, and important for his argument, Spinoza claims that states have a 'will' and can act on 'passions'. Second, the socialization of individuals comes to an end with the creation of the nation-state. There can be no world society or integration of all societies in one, superior world state. Thus, Spinoza treats international law, similarly as Hegel later, as 'external state law'.[21] Contrary to individuals, states have the potential to provide for their self-preservation (security).[22] Given this difference, there is no natural need for further association of individuals beyond the socialization at the state-level.

Based on these premises, Spinoza outlines three characteristics of the international state of nature: the absence of substantive international values, the non-bindingness of international treaties, and the character of international relations as a (latent) 'state of war'. First, unlike the Spanish scholastics (e.g. Francisco Vitoria or Francisco Suárez) and in contrast to Hugo Grotius,[23] Spinoza does not base his theory of international relations on any notion of substantive universal values or a

[18] See Thomas Hobbes, *Leviathan*, ed. Edwin Curley (1994), ch. XXX, p. 233 ('Concerning the offices of one sovereign to another, which are comprehended in that law which is commonly called the law of nations, I need not say anything in this place, because the law of nations and the law of nature is the same thing. . . . And the same law that dictateth to men that have no civil government, what they ought to do, and what to avoid in regard of one another, dictateth the same to commonwealths, that is, to the consciences of sovereign princes and sovereign assemblies, there being no court of natural justice but in the conscience only, where not man, but God reigneth, whose laws (such of them as oblige all mankind) in respect of God, as he is the author of nature, are *natural*, and in respect of the same God, as he is King of kings, are *laws*' [emphasis in the original]).

[19] 'For since . . . the sovereign's right is nothing other than the right of Nature itself, it follows that two states are in the same relation to one another *as* are two men in a state of Nature . . .' (TP 3/11, p. 54 [emphasis by the author]). 'Now in a civil order the citizens as a body are to be considered *as* a man in a state of Nature' (TP 7/22, p. 87 [emphasis by the author]).

[20] Spinoza is mindful of the difference in *potentia* between individuals and states, as TP 3/11, p. 54 shows.

[21] G.W.F. Hegel, *Elements of the Philosophy of Right*, ed. Allen W. Wood, trans. H.B. Nisbet (trans.) (2003), paras. 330–40.

[22] TP 3/11, p. 54. Later, it will be shown that this potential is conditioned upon the existence of a particular power structure (see IV.).

[23] On universal values as justification for internationalism see Nigel Dower, *World Ethics: The New Agenda* (2nd edn, 2007), p. 60.

universal society *(societas humana)*. Rather, Spinoza emphasizes what we would call 'particularism' in international relations.[24] States are considered as isolated entities for which their own 'security' or 'welfare' *(salus)* is the 'highest law'.[25]

Second, Spinoza claims that treaties between states concluded in the international state of nature, are non-binding.[26] It is important to distinguish between the existence of 'rules for action under natural law' and their binding nature.[27] The reason is that Spinoza does not give a teleological account, but a naturalist account of international relations and international law. Accordingly, it can be useful for a state in the state of nature to conclude 'treaties' (rather bargains) with other states (while the question of their bindingness follows other, naturalist principles, see Section III.). Spinoza mentions two such 'treaties': non-aggression pacts concluded due to a 'fear of loss' and trade agreements made in 'hope of gain'.[28] Though it is rational (in the sense of advantageous) for a state to enter into such international agreements, they are non-binding on Spinoza's account. According to a central passage in his theory of international relations, 'if the fear or the hope is lost to either of the two commonwealths, that commonwealth is left in control of its own right, and the tie by which the two commonwealths were bound together automatically disintegrates'.[29] International agreements in the state of nature, thus, are stable only as long as it is in the mutual interest to keep them. If the international agreement ceases to be in the interest of one of the parties, the agreement as such collapses (without any remedy for the other parties). Once a government discovers that an international treaty is harmful to the interests of the state, it must break the agreement. For otherwise, the government would violate its pledge of allegiance to its own subjects.[30] The 'rules for action under natural law', thus, have the status of rules of prudence rather than (legal) obligation. As such, they do not amount to binding international law. To the contrary, as Spinoza's mockery makes clear: 'If, then, a commonwealth complains that it has been deceived, it certainly cannot blame the bad faith of its ally but only its own folly in entrusting its security to another who is in control of his own right and for whom the safety of his own state is the supreme law'.[31]

Third, Spinoza leaves no doubt that the international state of nature is a state of (latent) war. Two commonwealths are enemies 'by nature', as Spinoza writes, relying again on the analogy between states and individuals: The natural antagonism among individuals, following from their conflicting 'passions' *(affectus)*, creates a state of (latent) war.[32] Spinoza writes, there are 'certainly some things to fear for a commonwealth', just like for individuals in the state of nature.[33] Hence, from the

[24] See David Boucher, *The Limits of Ethics in International Relations: Natural Law, Natural Rights, and Human Rights in Transition* (2009). For a general philosophical analysis of the dichotomy 'universalism/particularism' see Ernesto Laclau, *Emancipation(s)* (1996), ch. 2.

[25] TP 3/14, p. 55. [26] TP 3/14, p. 55.

[27] See Cheneval, 'Spinozas Philosophie der internationalen Beziehungen', pp. 195, 201 (n. 2).

[28] TP 3/14, p. 55. [29] TP 3/14, p. 55. [30] TTP 16/16, p. 203.

[31] TP 3/14, p. 55.

[32] See TP 2/14, p. 43 ('In so far as men are assailed by anger, envy, or any emotion [*affectus*, better translated as 'passion', T. A.] deriving from hatred, they are drawn apart and are contrary to one another . . .').

[33] TP 3/9, p. 52.

individual/state-analogy it follows that the international state of nature must also be considered a state of war.[34] As shall be argued in the next section (III.), this realist position taken by Spinoza is only the backdrop against which his international legal argument is developed.

III. Reconstruction of the International Legal Argument

Spinoza's international legal argument, i.e. the conditions under which international law exists, is contained in a dense and demanding passage in the TP. The text is difficult to understand because it draws on concepts and arguments outlined earlier in the TP and some contained in his major work, *Ethics*. Spinoza's international legal argument can be outlined in six steps (followed by short remarks):

(1) There is a fundamental 'disproportionality' (Manfred Walther) between the individual's judgment of what is good for him or her (the desired good or status) on the one hand, and the individual's 'power' *(potentia)* to achieve that good on the other.[35]

In the TTP, Spinoza argued that individuals are 'carried away by sensual desire and by their passions (which have no regard for the future and for other things)'.[36] Spinoza's doctrine of the passions is crucial for an understanding of his political philosophy because passions function both as a catalyst for the need to establish institutionalized social life and as a limit to the design of political institutions. Essentially, Spinoza believes that passions are an unchangeable constant in human actions that cannot be eliminated. Consequently, his political philosophy is about channelling the passions into social benefits *by institutional means* (e.g. through laws backed by threats).[37] It is the transformative aspect of institutions that makes Spinoza's political philosophy highly relevant for today's discussions of the functioning and the limits of institutions. Furthermore, it is important to see that in the aggregate, insofar as judgments on the good by the individuals are irreconcilable, these individuals will be 'adversaries'.[38] The individuals' power of action is thus limited—most importantly, in the political context, by the other individuals' power.

[34] See TP 3/12, p. 54, missing in the Hackett edition: 'Haec autem clarius intelligi possunt, si consideremus, quod duae civitates natura hostes sunt: homines enim ... in statu naturali hostes sunt; qui igitur jus naturae extra civitatem retinent, hostes manent' [translation by the author: This can be understood more clearly if one considers that two commonwealths are enemies by nature: because men ... are enemies in the state of nature; those who retain the law of nature outside the commonwealth remain enemies].

[35] Manfred Walther, 'Elementary Features of Spinoza's Political Philosophy (4P37S2)', in Michael Hampe, Ursula Renz, and Robert Schnepf (eds.), *Spinoza's Ethics: A Collective Commentary* (2011), pp. 211, 220.

[36] TTP 5/8, p. 73.

[37] Walther, 'Elementary Features of Spinoza's Political Philosophy (4P37S2)', pp. 211, 215 (n. 32).

[38] TP 2/14, p. 43.

It should be noted that Spinoza's international legal argument makes use of his dual conception of power: *potentia* and *potestas*. 'Power' as *potentia* refers to the individual's ability to cause factual change (causal power). 'Power' as *potestas* is used by Spinoza in social and political contexts to denote authority or coercive power.[39] Whereas *potentia* is inalienable, *potestas* may be transferred (most importantly, the individual transfers his or her *potestas* to the state).[40] Thus, Manfred Walther translates *potentia* as 'power of action' and *potestas* as 'power of direction'.[41]

(2) The 'power of action' *(potentia)* increases when individuals join together and combine their individual power in the form of the 'power of the multitude' *(potentia multitudinis)*.[42]

In Spinoza's naturalistic political philosophy, the increase of power through cooperation can be understood as an 'addition of forces' in a Newtonian sense. Spinoza gives reasons that drive individuals to conspire: the primary reasons are common fear or the will to avenge a common injury.[43] In the TTP, Spinoza adduces further reasons of utility for the association of individuals, all relating to the idea of division of labour.[44] It is, however, important to emphasize again that Spinoza does not give a teleological, but a naturalistic account of the formation of associations. Thus, given the fundamental, indisposable condition of 'disproportionality' between individual judgment and individual power outlined above, cooperation among individuals is self-evident and—as Manfred Walther argues—'alternativeless'.[45]

(3) The association of individuals is called a 'state' *(civitas)* when it has the power *(potestas)* to prescribe and enforce 'laws', i.e. common rules of behaviour sanctioned by threats.[46]

It is important to note that for Spinoza normativity of any kind (law or morality), i.e. being bound to perform or to abstain from an action, requires institutionalized social life. Only in the context of institutionalized social life is the individual compelled—by the 'power of the multitude' *(potentia multitudinis)* —to perform an act or to abstain from performing it.[47] Again, underlying this reasoning is evidently a physical conception of power: The multitude with its superior power

[39] Justin Steinberg, 'Spinoza on Being *sui iuris* and the Republican Conception of Liberty', *History of European Ideas* 34 (2008), 239.

[40] Justin Steinberg, 'Spinoza's Political Philosophy', in *The Stanford Encyclopedia of Philosophy*, Edward N. Zalta (ed.) (Winter 2013 edn), accessed 15 September 2015, <http://plato.stanford.edu/archives/win2013/entries/spinoza-political/>, ch. 3.6.

[41] Walther, 'Elementary Features of Spinoza's Political Philosophy (4P37S2)', pp. 211, 220 (n. 32). See also Oliver Lembcke, 'Spinozas Theorie der Souveränität', in Wolfgang Bartuschat, Stephan Kirste, and Manfred Walther (eds.), *Naturalismus und Demokratie: Spinozas 'Politischer Traktat' im Kontext seines Systems* (2014), pp. 45, 47–51.

[42] TP 2/13, p. 43.

[43] TP 3/9, p. 52; *Ethics* 4P37S2, p. 122. Here, and in the following, 'P' denotes proposition, 'S' denotes scholium.

[44] TTP 5/7, p. 72.

[45] Walther, 'Elementary Features of Spinoza's Political Philosophy (4P37S2)', pp. 211, 220 (n. 32).

[46] *Ethics* 4P37S2, p. 122.

[47] TP 2/16, p. 44.

overcomes any resistance of particularity (e.g. the individual). Of course, it needs to be asked how the *multitudo* is composed in the first place. Spinoza does not give much guidance here. For him, it is its function as a normativity-generating entity that characterizes the *multitudo*, not e.g. common history, geographical unity, or language. This openness of the *multitudo*-concept has proven useful to thinkers such as Michael Hardt and Antonio Negri who in their seminal work *Multitude* explicitly rely on Spinoza, arguing that there is an emerging transnational multitude of the exploited.[48]

(4) Given the individual/state-analogy, the supreme right of the state reaches as far as the power of action *(potentia)* it possesses,[49] and it is diminished to that extent that it causes fear in other individuals who, in turn, associate and establish other, foreign states.[50]

Spinoza's international legal argument is based on two assumptions of fact: first, that there exists a plurality of states (each of which has the supreme right in that state), and, second, that there exist things each state has to fear.[51] The assumptions are related because it is the fear of domination by others that drives people to associate in a plurality of states.

The 'vanishing point' of Spinoza's theory of international relations is the stability of the institutionalized social life of individuals in the form of associations, the primary example of which is the state. The stability of the state can be threatened both from the inside and from the outside: It is threatened *from the inside* if the governed subjects are given cause to join in conspiracy against it, i.e. if the rules are such that it makes no sense for some individuals to remain part of the state.[52] The stability of a state can also be threatened *from the outside* in the case of domination by other states, i.e. if a state fears the power of action *(potentia)* of another state, or is prevented by that state from carrying out its intent, or where it depends on the other state's help for its own preservation or prosperity.[53]

(5) If two or more states associate, their power of action *(potentia)* increases and together they have more 'rights' than each of them in isolation.[54] The greater the number of states that join the association of states, the less each individual state must be feared.[55]

Given that institutionalized social life (within a state) is under threat from the outside, there must be a form of association available that reaches beyond the single state. This is the association of states. It should be noted that Spinoza does not speak about a transnational association relating to individuals. In the TTP and in

[48] Michael Hardt and Antonio Negri, *Multitude: War and Democracy in the Age of Empire* (2004), p. 190.

[49] TP 3/2, p. 48. [50] TP 3/9, p. 52. [51] TP 3/9, p. 52.

[52] In an interesting passage, Spinoza discusses what cannot be part of (domestic) law-making. The supreme right of the state *(summum potestas)* is limited: '[A]ll such things as no one can be induced to do by reward or threats do not fall within the rights of the commonwealth.'

[53] TP 3/12, p. 54. [54] TP 3/12, p. 54. [55] TP 3/16, p. 56.

the TP, Spinoza speaks of 'allies' *(confoederati)* and of an 'association' or 'league' of states *(foedus)*.[56] As already stated, Spinoza does not advocate the socialization of individuals beyond the state—a 'world state', a *societas humana* in the way the Spanish Scholastics had contemplated, is ruled out in Spinoza's theory of international relations and international law. In the TTP, Spinoza explicitly mentions that 'allies' retain their respective governments.[57] In other words, statehood is a constant in international relations for Spinoza.

Each individual member (state) of the association of states has that much less 'right' *(jus)* the more it is exceeded in power by the others collectively. By the individual/state-analogy, the individual member (state) of the association of states has only the 'right' that the association grants.[58] In all other actions, the individual member (state) is compelled by the 'common will' of the association of states *(communis foederatorum voluntas)*.[59] Spinoza does not mention any international institutions or organs (as Kant famously does later).[60] Nevertheless, there must be some forum in which the 'common will' of the allies may be formed and expressed. One is tempted to draw from Spinoza's treatment of (domestic) democracy and his belief in group rationality: Spinoza famously states that 'there is less reason in a democratic state to fear absurd proceedings. For it is almost impossible that the majority of a large assembly would agree on the same irrational decision'.[61] In other words, deliberation among a great number of people or—in the case of the association of states—state governments is a way to 'avoid the follies of appetite and as much as possible to bring men within the limits of reason, so that they may dwell in peace and harmony'.[62]

(6) Since being compelled to act in accordance with an association's common rules of behaviour means following a 'law', the existence of binding international law is possible.[63]

In general, Spinoza speaks of 'law' in a weak normative sense (and refers to it) as 'guidance' or 'rule for living'.[64] The weak normative meaning of law is due to his naturalistic account of political philosophy.[65] Instead of a normative theory, Spinoza provides a psycho-sociological theory of international law and international relations. He outlines the psychological ('passions'-related) and sociological

[56] TTP 16/16, p. 203; TP 3/13, p. 55. On the 'association of states' *(foedus)* see TP 3/14, p. 55. See also the contrast between 'allies' and 'cities' as components of a single state, TP 9/4, p. 121.

[57] TTP 16/16, p. 203. [58] Cf. TP 2/16, p. 44. [59] TP 3/16, p. 56.

[60] Kant mentions the 'permanent congress of States', see Immanuel Kant, *The Metaphysics of Morals*, ed. and trans. Mary Gregor (2003), pp. 119–20 (para. 61).

[61] TTP 16/9, pp. 200–1. That on many questions groups produce a more accurate answer than individuals has recently been confirmed by Cass R. Sunstein and Reid Hastie, *Wiser: Getting Beyond Groupthink to Make Groups Smarter* (2015), pp. 143–56.

[62] TTP 15/9, p. 201.

[63] TTP 4/3, p. 59 ('[L]aw . . . is nothing other than a rule for living which men prescribe to themselves or to others for a purpose . . .').

[64] TTP 4/3, p. 59.

[65] For a more nuanced view on normativity in his international legal argument, see Section IV below.

(power-related) conditions under which international law is really 'law', i.e. the conditions under which the overriding 'passion' by the states is to comply with the 'common will' of the association of states.[66] Thus, Spinoza describes the effect of laws as guiding the conduct of all individuals 'as if by one mind' *(omnes una veluti mente ducuntur)*.[67] Therefore, since a situation can be imagined in which the conduct of allies (in the association of states) is guided 'as if by one mind', binding international law has the potential to exist.

IV. Three Analytical Concepts in Spinoza's International Legal Argument

Spinoza's international legal argument gives a particular meaning to three concepts which are of general analytical value when studying the theory of international law and international relations: normativity of international law, being a state *sui juris* and the concept of international cooperation.

(1) Applying the notion of 'normativity', i.e. the idea of being bound to perform or to abstain from an action, to a naturalistic account of international law such as Spinoza's poses evident difficulties. It is common to distinguish—with Joseph Raz—two conceptions of normativity: 'justified' and 'social' normativity.[68] In the present context of international law, 'justified normativity' refers to the legitimacy of international legal norms measured by some external standard (justice etc.) and their acceptance as binding by the subjects acting in the international realm. 'Social normativity' means the relevance of the international legal norms in guiding the actual behaviour of states.

It is not an easy task to square Spinoza's naturalistic account with this common understanding of normativity. Spinoza does not employ the concept of 'normativity' explicitly. However, in the context of international relations, he uses (weakly) normative expressions reminding of the idea of 'social normativity': Spinoza argues that 'each [member state of the association of states] is the more *bound* to observe

[66] Similarly, Manfred Walther, 'Spinozas Beitrag zu den Bedingungen eines internationalen Rechts im Politischen Traktat', in Tilmann Altwicker, Francis Cheneval, and Oliver Diggelmann (eds.), *Völkerrechtsphilosophie der Frühaufklärung* (2015), pp. 49, 57 (arguing that the enduring relevance of Spinoza's theory of international law lies both in his diagnosis of the problems of international law as well as the realization-conditions for an international law).

[67] TP 2/16 [translation by the author].

[68] Joseph Raz, *The Authority of Law* (2nd edn, 2011), p. 134 ('Two conceptions of the normativity of law are current. I will call them justified and social normativity. According to the one view legal standards of behaviour are norms only if and in so far as they are justified. They may be justified by some objective and universally valid reasons. They may be intuitively perceived as binding or they may be accepted as justified by personal commitment. On the other view standards of behaviour can be considered as norms regardless of their merit. They are social norms in so far as they are socially upheld as binding standards and in so far as the society involved exerts pressure on people to whom the standards apply to conform to them.').

the conditions of peace; that is . . . [the member state] *must the more adapt* itself *[sese accomodare tenetur]* to the common will of the allies' [my emphasis] the greater the number of states that join the association of states.[69] What Spinoza has in mind, as stated above, may be characterized as a psycho-sociological interpretation of normativity. Normativity in Spinoza's theory of international relations refers, first of all, to the determination of an action by an overriding passion (e.g. the fear of being sanctioned for non-compliance by the association of states) or intellectual insight (e.g. in the utility of contributing individually to the security and stability of the association of states).[70]

The conception of 'justified normativity' poses greater problems: for a naturalistic account of international relations and law, there are no transcendent or a priori standards for the 'law'. To Spinoza, thus, there can be no juxtaposition of an ideal, natural law order of things versus the non-ideal, factual order of things.[71] Nevertheless, Spinoza does not propose a simple 'social fact'-based legal positivism either. Even though there is no transcendent or a priori-standard for the 'justness' of international legal norms, there is an immanent, contextual standard which is the 'utility' of an action under the prevailing power structure: Spinoza writes in the TTP that an agreement among allies (members of the association of states) 'will be valid as long as its foundation, the source of the danger or advantage, persists. No one makes an agreement, and no one is obligated to honour a pact, except in the hope of some good or apprehension of some adverse consequence'.[72] The utility-standard of international legal norms emerges even clearer from the following passage: 'This treaty of alliance remains effective for as long as the motive for making the treaty—fear of loss or hope of gain—remains operative.'[73] It is crucial to note that the determination of what is 'useful' does not only take into account the subjective judgment of the state's government on what is momentarily good or harmful for their state, but it necessarily reflects the prevailing power structure. The reason is that the 'passions' attributed to states (or—rather—their governments), namely fear of loss and hope of gain, remain *unaltered* within the context of the association of states. The only difference is that the association of states has the 'power of direction' *(potestas)* to compel the individual state member to acting in conformity with the 'common will'. In consequence, the 'common will' of association must 'legislate' wisely as it will otherwise give rise to adverse 'passions' that may lead to insurrection by a group of member states and may ultimately lead to the destruction of the association of states.

[69] TP 3/16, p. 56.

[70] See, mutatis mutandis, Walther, 'Elementary Features of Spinoza's Political Philosophy (4P37S2)', pp. 211, 216 n. 11 (n. 32).

[71] Steinberg, 'Spinoza's Political Philosophy', ch. 2 (n. 37). On normativity in Spinoza's legal and political philosophy, see Michael A. Rosenthal, 'Politics and Ethics Spinoza: The Problem of Normativity', in Matthew J. Kisner and Andrew Youpa (eds.), *Essays on Spinoza's Ethical Theory* (2014), p. 85.

[72] TTP 16/16, p. 203. See also TP 2/12. See Steinberg, 'Spinoza's Political Philosophy', ch. 2.2 (n. 37).

[73] TP 3/14, p. 55.

(2) Another difficult, yet essential analytical concept in Spinoza's political philosophy is that of being (a person or a State) *sui juris*.[74] The concept derives from the Roman law classification of citizens into persons *alieni juris* and persons *sui juris*.[75] The persons lacking the capacity of being *sui juris* are slaves but the term is also used in relation to children (until the death of the *paterfamilias*) and women who are not the head of the household.[76] *Sui juris* is thus a concept used in legal contexts, denoting the capacity to act in a legal manner.[77] Several influential juristic accounts in the 16th and 17th century (e.g. by Hugo Grotius) employed the concept of *sui juris*.[78] In the TP, Spinoza introduces the *sui juris*-concept with regard to the individual person, giving it primarily the meaning of 'independence' or 'self-ownership'.[79] Essentially, being *sui juris* implies the power of retribution of harm done to oneself and the power to avert all attempts of domination by others.[80] The concept of *sui juris* is then applied to the state. Spinoza writes that a state 'is in control of its own right *[sui juris]* to the extent that it can take steps to safeguard itself from being subjugated' by another state.[81] This idea of independence from another's will or self-governance of citizens would count Spinoza into a pre-republican line of thought.

However, as Justin Steinberg has forcefully argued, Spinoza attaches a second idea to the concept of *sui juris* which diverges from its meaning in republicanism thought: while the first understanding of *sui juris* stresses self-governance in contrast to being *sub potestate* of another person, the other meaning of *sui juris* emphasizes wise or rational governance.[82] On rational governance, Spinoza writes in the TTP, 'no one can doubt how much more beneficial it is for men to live according to laws and the certain dictates of reason, which as I have said aim at nothing but men's true interests'.[83] It is this idea of *sui juris* as 'rational governance' that can also be found in the TP when Spinoza makes the (in)famous claim that the state—to remain *sui juris*—must 'preserve the causes that foster fear and respect',[84] or when Spinoza denounces absolute rule by a monarch.[85] In both cases, 'rational

[74] On the *sui juris*-concept see Steinberg, 'Spinoza on Being *sui iuris* and the Republican Conception of Liberty', p. 239 (n. 36); Gunnar Hindrichs, 'Spinozas Begründung der praktischen Vernunft', in Wolfgang Bartuschat, Stephan Kirste, and Manfred Walther (eds.), *Naturalismus und Demokratie. Spinozas 'Politischer Traktat' im Kontext seines Systems* (2014), pp. 21, 40–3.

[75] Paul du Plessis, *Borkowski's Textbook on Roman Law* (4th edn, 2010), p. 102; Quentin Skinner, 'States and the Freedom of Citizens', in Quentin Skinner (ed.), *States and Citizens: History, Theory, Prospects* (2003), pp. 11, 13.

[76] Du Plessis, *Borkowski's Textbook on Roman Law*, p. 110 (n. 72); Steinberg, 'Spinoza on Being *sui iuris* and the Republican Conception of Liberty', pp. 239, 242 (n. 36).

[77] See also the antonym, '*alieni iuris esse*', Adolf Berger, *Encyclopedic Dictionary of Roman Law* (2008), p. 360.

[78] Steinberg, 'Spinoza on Being *sui iuris* and the Republican Conception of Liberty', pp. 239, 243 (n. 36).

[79] See TP 2/9, pp. 41–2. [80] TP 2/9, pp. 41–2. [81] TP 3/12, p. 54.

[82] Steinberg, 'Spinoza on Being *sui iuris* and the Republican Conception of Liberty', pp. 239, 246–9 (n. 36).

[83] TTP 16/5, p. 197. [84] TP 4/4, p. 59. [85] TP 6/8, p. 66.

governance' is endangered because the government itself gives rise to adverse passions (or omits to arrange for 'loyal' passions) in the individuals subject to their rule. This may ultimately lead to upheaval and the overthrow of the government, i.e. threaten the stability of institutionalized social life.

The second interpretation of *sui juris* as rational governance best explains the idea of what it means to be *sui juris* in an association with other states: Just as any individual loses his or her capacity to be *sui juris* in the (first) sense of independence or self-governance once he or she is under the civil rule of the state, the state itself loses its independence when joining the association of states.[86] However, what is gained from joining the respective associations is (additional) *potentia*, the 'power of action'.[87] Once one distinguishes the two conceptions of *sui juris*, it becomes clear that, by joining the association of states, a state loses its independence and submits to the *potestas* of the association. Nevertheless, it is *sui juris* as it gains in *potentia*, and it is therefore ruled rationally.

(3) A third analytical concept is that of 'international cooperation'. Spinoza himself does not use the term 'international cooperation' explicitly, but the idea is very much present in both the TTP and the TP. In the TTP, Spinoza argues that States conclude a 'mutual agreement not to harm one another, and to give assistance to each other when the need arises'.[88] Similarly, in the TP, he says that allies 'afford each other mutual help'.[89] Spinoza also reveals the areas or goals of international cooperation. He writes that the motive *(causa)* for joining the association of states is 'fear of loss' and 'hope of gain'.[90] The first motive, 'loss' *(damnum)*, relates to concerns of security. Military alliances are formed to reduce the risk of war for all members. The other motive, 'gain' *(lucrum)*, relates to economic affairs. While the security-aspect of international cooperation often appears more urgent to Spinoza, he nevertheless clearly identifies making profit by international trade as a motive for international cooperation. Spinoza must have been impressed by the volume of international trade done in Amsterdam in the 17th century.[91]

Again, in a naturalistic account of international relations it is not teleological reasons that bring states together. Thus, it would be improper to claim with Spinoza that international law is created for the purpose of facilitation of cross-border 'trade' or 'security'. Spinoza's international legal argument is much more sophisticated: states are *compelled* to engage in international cooperation to remain *sui juris*. States must enter into a relationship with other states that enables each to be *sui juris* in the sense of being under rational governance (see above).

[86] See TP 3/5, p. 50 (in relation to the individual); TP 3/16, p. 56 (in relation to the state).
[87] See TP 3/12, p. 54. [88] TTP 16/16, p. 203. [89] TP 3/12, p. 54.
[90] TP 3/14, p. 55.
[91] On the importance of Amsterdam to international trade see David Ormrod, *The Rise of Commercial Empires: England and the Netherlands in the Age of Mercantilism, 1650–1770* (2005), pp. 13, 207–8 (emphasizing the importance of the large-scale grain imports in the agricultural sector).

Adapting a formulation by the political scientist Robert Axelrod, the fundamental question that Spinoza seeks to answer with his conception of international cooperation can be put as follows: under what conditions will cooperation in the form of law emerge in a world of egoistic states without central authority?[92] Spinoza's answer—one that is full of insight into the psychology of international relations—is this: as long as there is 'fear of loss or hope of gain' by one state in relation to others.[93] Spinoza, therefore, neither simply describes international relations 'as they are', nor 'as they should be', but rather depicts international relations 'as they have the potential to be' given what law 'is' and given the psycho-sociological conditions of human action. Spinoza's great sense for the reality of international relations cannot be stressed enough: the idea to choose political isolation, the belief to be able to stand apart when other states establish alliances or engage in other forms of international cooperation would have been considered short-sighted, even irrational by Spinoza.

V. Conclusion: Spinoza's Contribution to the Ordering of International Relations

What is Spinoza's lasting contribution to the theory of international relations and international law? Three suggestions shall be made here: the exposition of a 'non-ideal theory' of international relations, international relations as part of a theory on the institutionalization of individual freedom, and the idea of precedence of rational international governance over independent governance.

First, Spinoza offers—in the best sense of the term—a 'non-ideal theory' of international relations and international law. Other than John Rawls, who introduced the distinction between an 'ideal' and a 'non-ideal' theory of international relations in his *Law of Peoples*, Spinoza does not make this distinction.[94] Instead, Spinoza outlines a unique theory which is both relying on a philosophical system (the principles 'proven' in his major work *Ethics*) *and* providing a practical theory which can have universal application in the interaction of states (regardless of how the state or a society is structured internally).[95] As was shown above, Spinoza's idea of the international interaction of states builds upon principles he developed in the *Ethics*, like the doctrine of the passions and of power *(potentia)*. However, the state of ordered international relations cannot be deduced from 'teachings of reason'.[96] It must take into account the realities of social interaction and, above all, the constitution of man. In other words, Spinoza does not 'derive' his theory of international relations and international law from ontological principles

[92] Robert Axelrod, *The Evolution of Cooperation* (1984), p. 3.
[93] TP 3/14, p. 55.
[94] John Rawls, *The Law of Peoples* (2002), pp. 89–120.
[95] See TP 1/1, p. 33.
[96] TP I/7, p. 36.

contained in the *Ethics*.[97] Instead, he purports to develop a theory of practice which is—though not deduced from ontological principles—nevertheless in conformity with them.[98] Accordingly, he does not assume perfectly rational actors in the international sphere. Rather, Spinoza's theory of international relations operates on the premise that states remain egoistic, utility-maximizing, and antagonistic associations of individuals driven by passions and not necessarily by reason.[99] This 'thin' assumption regarding the constitution of states turns Spinoza's account of international relations into a forceful international argument.

Second, though the individual does not appear in the short paragraphs dealing with international relations in the TTP and the TP (for the simple reason that there is no socialization of individuals in a super-state, as explained above), Spinoza's theory of international relations connects to individual freedom. In fact, individual freedom is the common theme running through both the *Ethics* and the TP. In the *Ethics*, Spinoza showed the way to individual freedom, in the TP he expounds the political institutions required to put individual freedom into practice.[100] As the foreword to the TP states, his intention is to show 'how a community . . . should be organised if it is not to degenerate into a Tyranny, and if the Peace and Freedom of its citizens is to remain inviolate'.[101] Spinoza's treatment of international law must also been seen in this light of institutionalizing individual freedom. In other words, the path towards a realization of individual freedom only comes to a conclusion when international relations among states are ordered by international law. Only under a stable power structure—safeguarded by the common will of the association of states—is lasting freedom of individuals within their respective states possible. Thus, Spinoza, in both his works on political philosophy views stable international relations ultimately as a condition of individual freedom (within a state).

Most powerful is, third, the idea of precedence of 'rational international governance' over 'domestic self-governance' regarding two fields of policy: 'security' and 'trade'. Spinoza's theory does not require the internationalization of all fields of policy. Neither does he suggest that statehood must be abolished. To the contrary, the existence of states remains a condition of individual freedom in Spinoza's political philosophy. Only with regard to two transnational goods, 'security' and 'trade', does his theory envisage the submission of the individual state under the 'common will' of the allies or association of states. Regarding these two policy fields, a compelling

[97] Accordingly, the field of politics is elaborated separately from the *Ethics*, Wolfgang Bartuschat, 'Spinozas Ontologie und Erkenntnistheorie als Hintergrund seiner politischen Philosophie', in Wolfgang Bartuschat, Stephan Kirste, and Manfred Walther (eds.), *Naturalismus und Demokratie: Spinozas 'Politischer Traktat' im Kontext seines Systems* (2014), p. 2.

[98] TP 2/1, p. 37. See Stephan Kirste and Manfred Walther, 'Politische Philosophie als Theorie der Praxis', in Wolfgang Bartuschat, Stephan Kirste, and Manfred Walther (eds.), *Naturalismus und Demokratie. Spinozas 'Politischer Traktat' im Kontext seines Systems* (2014), p. 13.

[99] TP 1/7, p. 36. [100] Steinberg, 'Spinoza's Political Philosophy', ch. 4 (n. 37).

[101] TP Foreword, p. 33.

force drives states towards international cooperation. Here, international governance has a rationality-benefit over domestic self-governance.

Selected Bibliography

Altwicker, Tilmann, 'Spinozas Theorie der internationalen Beziehungen', in Wolfgang Bartuschat, Stephan Kirste, and Manfred Walther (eds.), *Spinoza, Politischer Traktat: Ein Kommentar* (Heidelberg: Mohr Siebeck, 2014).

Cheneval, Francis, 'Spinozas Philosophie der internationalen Beziehungen', in Marcel Senn and Manfred Walther (eds.), *Ethik, Recht und Politik bei Spinoza* (Zurich: Schulthess, 2001).

Lauterpacht, Hersch, 'Spinoza and International Law', *The British Yearbook of International Law* 8 (1927), 89.

Santos Campos, André (ed.), *Spinoza and Law* (Abingdon, UK and New York, USA: Routledge, 2015).

Walther, Manfred, 'Natural Law, Civil Law, and International Law in Spinoza', *Cardozo Law Review* 25 (2003), 657.

Walther, Manfred, 'Spinozas Beitrag zu den Bedingungen eines internationalen Rechts im Politischen Traktat', in Tilmann Altwicker, Francis Cheneval, and Oliver Diggelmann (eds.), *Völkerrechtsphilosophie der Frühaufklärung* (Heidelberg: Mohr Siebeck, 2015).

10

States, as Ethico-Political Subjects of International Law

The Relationship between Theory and Practice in the International Politics of Samuel Pufendorf

Vanda Fiorillo

I. International Law as a Moral Politics: The Correlation between the Fulfilment of the 'Offices of Humanity' and the Exercise of the Natural Rights of States

'The specific character' of Pufendorf's theory of the international order 'is recognisable in embryonic form in the very foundations of his moral philosophy', but also has 'factors (. . .) not solely related to phylosophical elements pertaining to natural law'.[1] From such a standpoint, this chapter aims to focus on the dialectical relationship between the various principles upon which the theory of international law as developed by Samuel Pufendorf is founded and supported. In fact, this theory is substantiated as much by principles of natural law, arising from the complex edifice of the duties of peace, as by strictly political criteria among which there are also, and not least, international treaties.

In order to reconstruct the dialectic between these two sets of principles, it should be said that the international scenario to which Pufendorf refers no longer coincided with that outlined by the Christian Commonwealth. This is because he had, as it were, 'completely atomised', in conceptual terms, 'the universal juridical community of the Middle Ages', conceived 'as a *corpus mysticum politicum*',[2] breaking it down into a 'constellation' of sovereign states, which he

[1] Cf. Maurizio Bazzoli, 'La concezione pufendorfiana della politica internazionale', in Vanda Fiorillo (ed.), *Samuel Pufendorf, filosofo del diritto e della politica*, International Conference Proceedings, Milan, 11–12 November 1994 (1996), pp. 46–7 (*here and below, works cited which are not in English have been translated by the author, unless otherwise stated*).

[2] Cf. Hermann Klenner, 'Bileams Pferd auf die Kanzeln! Zur Naturrechts- und Völkerrechtslehre des Samuel Pufendorf', in Bodo Geyer and Helmut Goerlich (eds.), *Samuel Pufendorf und seine Wirkungen bis auf die heutige Zeit* (1996), p. 200.

interpreted as *moral entities*[3] and more specifically, as *compound moral persons.*[4] Thus, Pufendorf's conception of international law bears witness to the crumbling of the compact unity of the mediaeval *corpus christianorum* and the emergence, twenty years on from the Peace of Westphalia, of territorial states as new actors in international politics. Indeed, it is widely known that the seventeenth century saw the 'reinforcing (. . .) of national states, organising law according to the needs of their statehood. The idea of an Empire looming over them gradually disappeare[d]'.[5]

Within this framework, sovereign states, like all other moral persons, are conceived by Pufendorf 'in the Manner of Substances'.[6] As with *natural entities*, that perform their physical movements within a space, states carry out their actions and cause their moral and legal effects within the moral entity 'state of nature'.[7] Consequently, the relations between sovereign entities—like those that once united the ancient household heads or 'patriarchs' at the dawn of human history—exemplify, for Pufendorf, a *tempered* or *'qualified'* state of nature towards others.[8] He qualifies this state as *real*, not *fictitious*,[9] and more precisely as the state of nature that really exists.[10] And as, in the earliest days of anthropological history, the ancient household heads lived in a state of anarchy, so in Pufendorf's day, the different peoples were not subject, in his view, to the power of any common master, nor were they linked by a relationship of

[3] On the fundamental division, drawn by Pufendorf between natural entities and moral entities, cf. all of chapter I of book I, pp. 3–22, of his most important work on natural law, *De Jure Naturae et Gentium*, libri octo, cited here and below in the Lausannae et Genevae, 1744 edition, unless otherwise stated (Samuel Pufendorf, *De Jure Naturae et Gentium, libri octo* [1744]). As is well known, moral entities are, in turn, grouped into four categories by Pufendorf as follows: moral persons, state, moral qualities, and moral quantities. On the quadripartite division of the moral entities and their internal subdivisions, see in particular paragraphs V–XXII of chapter I of book I of *De Jure*, on pp. 6–21, cited here.

[4] As is well known, for Pufendorf, the compound moral persons are formed when a number of men come together in such a way that what they do and want is judged, by virtue of the moral bond between them, as but one action and one sole will. On this, cf. Pufendorf, *De Jure*, bk. I, ch. I, para. XIII, p. 14 (n. 3).

[5] Horst Denzer, *Moralphilosophie und Naturrecht bei Samuel Pufendorf. Eine geistes- und wissenschaftsgeschichtliche Untersuchung zur Geburt des Naturrechts aus der Praktischen Philosophie* (1972), p. 218.

[6] Cf. Pufendorf, *De Jure*, bk. I, ch. I, para. VI, p. 7 (n. 3); here cited from Samuel Pufendorf, *Of the Law of Nature and Nations*, 8 bks., trans. Basil Kennet, with notes of Jean Barbeyrac (1729), bk. I, ch. I, para. VI, p. 4.

[7] In Pufendorf's practical philosophy, the moral entity 'state', including the state of nature, presents itself as an *ens suppositivum*, i.e. as a system of reference, without which persons could not have moral existence. Thus, it may be said to correspond ultimately to the sphere of the carrying out of life in society. On the moral entity 'state', see Samuel Pufendorf, *Elementorum Jurisprudentiae Universalis*, libri duo (1669), bk. I, def. III, para. 1, p. 9.

[8] In Pufendorf's vision, in fact, the natural state towards other men is 'real only in a limited way and in part, in the case where sections of humankind live in communities, which, in turn, find themselves mutually in the *status naturalis*': Hans Welzel, *Die Naturrechtslehre Samuel Pufendorfs: Ein Beitrag zur Ideengeschichte des 17. und 18. Jahrhundert* (1958), p. 29. On the *temperatus et velut partialis* state of nature towards others cf. Pufendorf, *De Jure*, bk. II, ch. II, para. IV, pp. 159–61 (n. 3).

[9] Cf. Samuel Pufendorf, *De Officio Hominis et Civis secundum Legem Naturalem*, libri duo, cum Adnotationibus Everardi Otti (1711), bk. II, ch. I, para. VI, pp. 397–8.

[10] Cf. Pufendorf, *De Officio*, p. 398 (n. 9).

command and subordination. In short, peoples lived in a state of international anarchy.[11]

Despite the parallels that Pufendorf repeatedly drew between the natural state existing at his time between sovereign states and what had once mutually bound the household heads, he does not fail, however, to highlight a significant difference between these two natural societies, even though they are united by the absence of a higher-level political power, able to give lasting protection to their members. According to Pufendorf, in fact, natural men—precisely because of their limited strength,[12] i.e. their constitutive 'weakness'[13]—would not have found it particularly pleasant or helpful not to recognize some supreme power over them, to whom they could entrust the task of ensuring their preservation. Conversely, states and their rulers may boast that they live in a state of supreme natural liberty,[14] i.e. of natural freedom par excellence, precisely because they are self-sufficient and strong enough to be able to enjoy their liberty[15] in safety. This freedom should be understood here as the faculty of states to decide for themselves, using their own judgment, on the questions that concern their preservation and security.[16] However, despite the acknowledged superiority of the state over the 'weak' natural man in achieving its own self-preservation without risk, Pufendorf admits that no sovereign entity is sufficiently rich or strong as to have no need of friendship or the aid of others nor not to fear harm from an enemy coalition.[17]

Despite the not insignificant difference between the natural state of men and that of states in the successful pursuit of the goal of security, Pufendorf—critically qualifying Hobbesian *war of all against all* as the life and condition of beasts[18]—characterizes both these conditions as states of *universal* peace, prescribed solely by the obligation of the law of nature.[19] In fact, as occurs in the natural state of men, it would prove superfluous in the creation of peace in international society to reinforce it by means of pacts or alliances, which add nothing to the natural obligation. This is because, as happens with a single individual, also a sovereign entity

[11] Cf. Samuel Pufendorf, *De Statu Hominum Naturali*, in Samuel Pufendorf, *Dissertationes Academicae Selectiores* (1675), para. 7, p. 600. On this point see also Pufendorf, *Elementorum*, bk. I, def. XIII, para. XXIV, p. 282 (n. 7); Pufendorf, *De Jure*, bk. I, ch. I, para. VII, p. 9 (n. 3).

[12] Cf. Pufendorf, *De Jure*, bk. II, ch. II, para. IV, p. 160 (n. 3).

[13] On the anthropological characteristic of 'weakness' (*imbecillitas*), meaning the original incapacity of man to acquire arts, crafts, and techniques to satisfy his own needs, and thus his inability to fully develop his humanity without the aid of his fellow humans cf., for example Pufendorf, *De Jure*, bk. II, ch. II, para. II, pp. 151–4 (n. 3); Pufendorf, *De Statu Hominum Naturali*, para. 5, pp. 592–7 (n. 11).

[14] Cf. Pufendorf, *De Jure*, bk. II, ch. II, para. IV, p. 160 (n. 3). On the difference between the state of nature of men and the state of nature of states, cf., in the context of the literature on the subject, Ernst Reibstein, *Völkerrecht: Eine Geschichte seiner Ideen in Lehre und Praxis. I. Von der Antike bis zur Aufklärung* (1957), p. 490; Ernst Reibstein, 'Pufendorfs Völkerrechtslehre', *Österreichische Zeitschrift für Öffentliches Recht*, vol. VII (1956), p. 48.

[15] See further Pufendorf, *De Jure*, bk. II, ch. II, para. IV, p. 160 (n. 3).

[16] Cf. Pufendorf, *De Jure*, bk. VII, ch. V, para. XX, p. 207 (n. 3). See also Samuel Pufendorf, *De Systematibus Civitatum*, in Pufendorf, *Dissertationes Academicae Selectiores*, para. 18, pp. 314–15 (n. 11).

[17] Cf. Pufendorf, *De Jure*, bk. II, ch. III, para. X, p. 192 (n. 3).

[18] Cf. Pufendorf, *De Jure*, bk. I, ch. I, para. VII, p. 8 (n. 3).

[19] Cf. Pufendorf, *Elementorum*, bk. I, def. III, para. 5, pp. 15–16 (n. 7).

is violated with equal injustice and wrongfulness whether a pact has been entered into or otherwise. Therefore, universal peace can be said to be realized for mankind organized into political societies only through the mutual respect of those duties of natural law that consist mainly in refraining from causing unjust harm to others and in settling possible disputes between states by resorting to a mutual accord or an arbitral award.[20]

More specifically, Pufendorf applies his usual tripartite division of the duties towards other men[21] to the coexistence of states. Such duties are deduced from the first law of nature, which prescribes to human beings a pacific sociality[22] and at the same time universal peace to states.

Peace comes about, first of all, through the mutual fulfilment of the duty of reciprocal non-aggression (*neminem laedere*)—which should be seen as the fundamental obligation for coexistence, whether international or interpersonal—and secondly, through the mutual satisfaction of the two natural obligations of equality and humanity towards other peoples. Taken as a whole, such duties considered in relation to others come, in particular, under what Pufendorf calls the *absolute* law of nature. This coincides with the set of the natural precepts, that oblige members of mankind at all times and in which ever condition they find themselves in, setting aside any institution, deed, or covenant entered into or introduced by man.[23] In essence, in Pufendorf's vision, such precepts of the absolute law of nature—from which duties between states originate—exemplify those metahistorical moral principles, valid for all men and for all states in both diachronic and synchronic terms. On this basis, Pufendorf equates international law, to its fullest legal extent, precisely to the range of the absolute natural obligations towards others.[24] In his definition of international law, he especially takes up Hobbes's thesis that the law of nations is merely another name for natural law, when, with no change to its content, it is applied to states, which have essentially the same properties as individuals.[25]

Bearing in mind the conceptual definition of international law as the set of the absolute natural duties towards others, it is appropriate at this point to mention some special characteristics assumed by two of the three above-mentioned kinds of obligations[26] (equality and the duties of humanity), when these refer to states and not to individuals.

[20] Cf. Pufendorf, *Elementorum*, bk. I, def. III, para. 5, pp. 15–16 (n. 7).

[21] On Pufendorf's tripartite division of the duties towards other men into those of non-aggression (*neminem laedere*), equality and the obligations of humanity or charity, cf. Pufendorf, *De Jure*, bk. III, ch. I–III, pp. 297–356 (n. 3); Pufendorf, *De Officio*, bk. I, ch. VI–IX, pp. 163–238 (n. 9).

[22] On sociality, as the fundamental proposition of Pufendorf's law of nature, cf. Pufendorf, *De Jure*, bk. II, ch. III, para. XV, pp. 202–5 (n. 3).

[23] Cf. Pufendorf, *De Jure*, bk. II, ch. III, para. XXIV, p. 224 (n. 3).

[24] On the same interpretative lines, cf. Erik Wolf, *Grosse Rechtsdenker der deutschen Geistesgeschichte* (1951), esp. pp. 348–50 (n. 1), who identifies the 'true locus of validity' of Pufendorf's absolute natural law in the 'reciprocal relationship between legislative powers'. Thus, the above-mentioned law 'would merge with *ius gentium*, with international law (insofar as it does not derive from a positive law agreement)'.

[25] Cf. Thomas Hobbes, *Elementa Philosophica de Cive* (1649), ch. XIV, para. IV, p. 240.

[26] On Pufendorf's tripartite division of the duties towards others, see n. 21 above.

Starting with the duty of equality, it may be seen how it is interpreted in the international scenario as the *equal liberty* of states, regardless of their size, strength, or wealth.[27] It is evident that in the inter-state context, freedom may be enjoyed 'in equal measure as much by the sovereign, with absolute power, as that who is limited in the exercise of [such power]'.[28] And if one considers that liberty of the political entities is understood by Pufendorf as the faculty that all states may exercise to establish, on condition that they are reciprocal, the ways and means most appropriate for their conservation,[29] then the duty of their *equal freedom* coincides with the mutual moral commitment of sovereigns to allow the application of the *same power and right to preservation* of all the other political societies. Moreover, in sovereign entities such a power and such a right to self-preservation seem very similar to Pufendorf's particular understanding of natural equality among men, consisting in their equal right and power to preserve themselves.[30] With regard to *how* it can be put into practice, it should be emphasized here that the duty of equality between states—like the other two kinds of natural obligations towards others[31]—is converted into practice through the criterion of *reciprocity*. In fact, this represents 'the basis of equality',[32] constituting the formal structure, which, in the practical sphere, regulates the equal treatment of another state. In this regard, it may be said that it is precisely the violation, or the not always perfect application in the practice of the criterion of reciprocity that gives rise to the most pressing theoretical and practical issues in international law, including that of Pufendorf. Moreover, the moral principle of equality between states, despite the disparity in their degree of power—repeatedly sustained theoretically in his works on natural law—is then also included by Severinus de Monzambano-Pufendorf among the concrete measures which he suggests for 'curing' the constitutional 'disease' of the German Empire of his time. So much so that in order to preserve the internal

[27] Cf. Pufendorf, *De Jure*, bk. VIII, ch. IV, para. XVIII, p. 395 (n. 3). On this matter, despite sustaining that in internationalistic theory 'no man has ever, neither before nor since, assumed such a narrow and unilaterally naturalistic view as Pufendorf', Arthur Nussbaum identifies, nevertheless, the 'most important (. . .) contribution [of this thinker] to the history of international law' precisely 'in his thesis of the natural equality of states': cf. Arthur Nussbaum, *Geschichte des Völkerrechts in gedrängter Darstellung* (1960), pp. 165–6.

[28] Wilfried Schaumann, *Die Gleichheit der Staaten: Ein Beitrag zu den Grundprinzipien des Völkerrechts* (1957), p. 45. On this point, cf. Pufendorf, *De Jure*, bk. VIII, ch. IV, para. XIX, p. 396 (n. 3).

[29] See n. 16, above.

[30] On the meaning of equality as the equal power and right of natural men to preserve themselves, cf. Pufendorf, *De Statu Hominum Naturali*, para. 13, pp. 611–12 (n. 11). On the various meanings of equality recurring in the works on natural law or theology of Pufendorf, see Vanda Fiorillo, 'L'altro, "ut aeque homo": eguaglianza e "dignitas individui" nell'antropologia politica di Samuel Pufendorf', in Vanda Fiorillo, Friedrich Vollhardt (eds.), *Il Diritto Naturale della Socialità: Tradizioni Antiche ed Antropologia Moderna nel XVII Secolo*, International Conference Proceedings, Naples, 24–25 October 2003 (2004), pp. 105–38; partially republished in German with the title: 'Der Andere "ut aeque homo": Gleichheit und Menschenwürde in der politischen Anthropologie Samuel Pufendorfs', *Archiv für Rechts- und Sozialphilosophie*, Vol. 99, 1 (2013), 11–28.

[31] Still referring here—as stated above—to the duty that no man be hurt and the offices of humanity.

[32] Cf. Gerhard Sprenger, 'Die Bedeutung der Lehre von der imbecillitas bei Samuel Pufendorf. Einige anthropologische Anmerkungen', in *Pufendorf, filosofo del diritto*, p. 263 (n. 1).

concord between the sovereign entities participating in the disharmonious political body of the Empire—which suffered from the dual 'disease' of a badly organized monarchy and a disorderly confederation of states[33]—Pufendorf deems it necessary that states unequal in power may, nevertheless, enjoy equal freedom and security.[34]

Turning now to examine briefly the third kind of absolute duties towards others, the offices of humanity, also known as offices of peace, it should be noted that Pufendorf slightly adapted them to the nature of states. These, in fact, in their capacity as subjects of international law, seek to attain above all mutual security. And it is for this reason that—in accordance with this purpose—such duties, of a (logically) *positive* character, if applied to states rather than individuals, are properly restricted in their range of action, ending up not encompassing 'any of the social prescriptions of the natural law that look beyond considerations of security'.[35]

Finally, of all the obligations towards others, for Pufendorf, abiding by one's word and fulfilling promises and agreements has a special value in ensuring peaceful international coexistence, as this obligation is one of the most sacred imperatives in natural law.[36] So much so that if this duty were not respected, much of the benefit that states may derive from their mutual exchange of services and goods would be lost. But most importantly, failing to keep his word, no sovereign would be able to rely in any way on the help of others in pursuing his goals.[37] In Pufendorf's view, the evident importance of the duty of keeping faith in international society finds its theoretical justification in the fact that 'promises can already have binding force in the state of nature'.[38] This is because every sovereign, i.e. he who recognizes no superior above him, is surely the only one who can be regarded, in the strict sense, as a natural man, in accordance with the logical-rational construction of the state of nature as a condition of anarchy. However, he—while not recognizing any earthly power above himself—should constantly be 'determined in his actions by the voice of (. . .) conscience to keep to moral rules'.[39] In fact, the reason for the inner binding force, on conscience, of the sovereign's promise—as, indeed, the

[33] Cf. Severinus de Monzambano (pseudonym of Samuel Pufendorf), *De Statu Imperii Germanici*, liber unus (1668), ch. VII, para. 8, p. 130. Among the other measures recommended by Pufendorf to remedy the constitutional irregularity of the German Empire, mention should be made here only of his original proposal to establish a permanent council, which would represent the confederate states, carrying out the task of attending to the current affairs of the confederation itself. This council, in fact, and in conjunction with certain and carefully produced laws, would have had—in Pufendorf's design—the overarching aim of limiting and mitigating the power of any supreme head of the *Reich*, so that he would be prevented from aspiring to a despotic dominion over it. On Pufendorf's proposal for a permanent council of the states that were associated within the German Empire, see Monzambano, *De Statu Imperii Germanici*, ch. VIII, para. 4, p. 141.

[34] Cf. Monzambano, *De Statu Imperii Germanici*, ch. VIII, para. 4, p. 141 (n. 33).

[35] Cf. Leonard Krieger, *The Politics of Discretion: Pufendorf and the Acceptance of Natural Law* (1965), p. 169.

[36] Cf. Pufendorf, *De Jure*, bk. III, ch. IV, para. II, p. 358 (n. 3).

[37] On the duty of keeping faith in Pufendorf, see also Pufendorf, *De Officio*, bk. I, ch. IX, para. III, pp. 207–8 (n. 9).

[38] Cf. Gerald Hartung, Vertragstheorie und Konstruktion der Souveränität bei Samuel Pufendorf, in Dieter Hüning (ed.), *Naturrecht und Staat bei Samuel Pufendorf* (2009), p. 47.

[39] Cf. Hartung, Vertragstheorie, p. 47 (n. 38).

obligatory value of any other peace duty valid in all relations between states—stems from the specific theologico-voluntaristic basis that the concept of duty takes on in Pufendorf's moral philosophy: it is, in short, 'the divine legislator that obliges men to shape their behaviour in a manner consistent with moral norms'.[40] Indeed, in investigating the origin of those obligations, which from some points of view can be distinguished from civil obligations, that derive from other men's power,[41] Pufendorf states that God as creator of mankind must also be considered as the author of the obligation in man and of the law of nature.[42]

The theologico-voluntaristic basis of duties, including international ones, is also part of a general and broader but equally voluntaristic definition of the concept of law, from which 'obligation' arises in the first place. In fact, law, in its capacity as *decree of a sovereign*,[43] always implies a 'distance between the superior [himself] and the one who receives the order' through which the law itself, 'as such, acquires binding force'.[44] However, as there is no political power above the sovereign entities, Pufendorf denies the existence of a voluntary or positive international law, with true legal force, binding peoples, as this would emerge from a legislator superior to them.[45] On this important point of his international law theory, the German philosopher departs, however, from Grotius's thesis, whereby 'the *jus gentium voluntarium* requires the consensus, if not of all nations, then at least of the greatest number of them'.[46] Thus, Pufendorf shows that his criticism of Grotius's voluntary or positive international law rests 'essentially on the rejection of the idea of the 'universal consensus of nations' as well as on the idea of 'the consensus of the more civilised peoples'.[47] Indeed, Pufendorf holds that it is not possible to 'establish international law on the Grotian *consensus gentium*, because the law that governs the free life of states cannot be the law of nations as a changing positive law, but

[40] Gerald Hartung, *Die Naturrechtsdebatte: Geschichte der Obligatio vom 17. bis 20. Jahrhundert* (1999), p. 36. On Pufendorf's theory of duties and their classification, see further Albrecht Randelzhofer, *Die Pflichtenlehre bei Samuel von Pufendorf* (1983); Hans-Ludwig Schreiber, *Der Begriff der Rechtspflicht: Quellenstudien zu seiner Geschichte* (1966), on Pufendorf pp. 9–12. On this topic, see furthermore Vanda Fiorillo, *Tra egoismo e socialità: Il giusnaturalismo di Samuel Pufendorf* (1992), pp. 169–212.

[41] Samuel Pufendorf, *Appendix* to *Epistola ad Adamum Scherzerum, super censura quapiam in librum suum inique lata*, in Pufendorf, *Eris Scandica, qua adversus libros de iure naturali et gentium obiecta diluuntur* (1743), in the appendix to his *De Jure Naturae et Gentium*, p. 77 (n. 3).

[42] Pufendorf, *Appendix* to *Epistola*, p. 78 (n. 41).

[43] Cf. Pufendorf, *De Jure*, bk. I, ch. VI, para. IV, p. 89 (n. 3).

[44] See Hartung, *Die Naturrechtsdebatte*, p. 35 (n. 40).

[45] Cf. Pufendorf, *De Jure*, bk. II, ch. III, para. XXIII, p. 220 (n. 3). On the theoretical reasons for Pufendorf's denial of a voluntary or positive international law, see Thomas Behme, *Samuel von Pufendorf: Naturrecht und Staat: Eine Analyse und Interpretation seiner Theorie, ihrer Grundlagen und Probleme* (1995), p. 167, n. 312; and Schaumann, *Die Gleichheit der Staaten*, p. 43 (n. 28). On this matter, Ziegler recognizes, on the other hand, in the 'rejection' by Pufendorf of 'a positive international law (...) a weakness—albeit immanent in the system—of his work': Karl-Heinz Ziegler, *Völkerrechtsgeschichte* (1994), p. 197.

[46] Cf. Simone Goyard-Fabre, *Pufendorf et le droit naturel* (1994), p. 222.

[47] Cf. Bazzoli, 'La concezione pufendorfiana', pp. 47–8, n. 35 (n. 1). On Pufendorf's critique of *consensus gentium* see Pufendorf, *De Jure*, bk. II, ch. III, paras. VII–IX, pp. 184–90 (n. 3). On Pufendorf's confutation of Grotius's position on the consensus of the peoples as a valid principle of legitimation of international law, cf., in the literature on the subject, Massimo Panebianco, *Ugo Grozio e la tradizione storica del diritto internazionale* (1974), esp. pp. 108–9. On this critique of Grotius by Pufendorf, see Fiorillo, *Tra egoismo e socialità*, pp. 155–64 (n. 40).

only the law of nature, which is "not subject to change"'.[48] Starting from these assumptions, Pufendorf believes that what is inappropriately called voluntary or positive international law would in effect derive from the correspondence between the civil laws common to a plurality of nations. Thus, it would not constitute a particular kind of law, as the shared characteristics of the rules of civil law, recurring in a number of legislations, do not depend on some sort of mutual convention or obligation among these nations, but simply on the particular will of their individual legislators.[49]

In the light of the rejection of a positive law of nations and the claim that international law and natural law are identical, it is precisely the fundamentally ethical nature of the obligations making up international law that allows Pufendorf to consider peace as the *ordinary proper state of man*, i.e. the condition closest to human nature and—like the first law of nature that prescribes sociality to men—particularly suited to the ultimate goal of safety of mankind.[50] As we have seen, peace is the result of the reciprocal moral fulfilment, and thus the spontaneous satisfaction of international duties, especially not to harm other states, to mutually fulfil the common offices of humanity and to carry out spontaneously what has been agreed upon through pacts.[51] For this reason, the nature of peace can only be grasped by man as a rational being with his peculiar God-given disposition to act ethically, which makes him apt to conform to that law of nature from which obligations spring in the first place. Thus, peace originates from a principle whereby man prevails over beasts, which tend to survive by brute force, as their will is not reined in by any kind of inner moral bond.[52] Indeed, it is in the nature of peace to do something spontaneously for others, and to refrain from harming them as the result of some obligation in one, and the correlative right in another. These are all things, says Pufendorf, that cannot be understood except through the use of reason. In his words: 'Man alone understands the Nature and Constitution of *Peace*. For it is he only, that can voluntarily undertake or forbear the Performance of any Action, which may bring Good or Harm upon another Person, *upon a Consideration of certain Obligations on one Side, and certain Rights on another*.'[53]

[48] Bazzoli, 'La concezione pufendorfiana', p. 48 (n. 1). On Grotius's distinction between natural law and the law of nations cf., e.g. Ugo Grozio, *De Jure belli ac pacis*, libri tres, cum annotatis Auctoris, nec non J.F. Gronovii Notis, & J. Barbeyracii Animadversionibus; Commentariis Henr. L. B. De Cocceii, insertis quoque Observationibus Samuelis L. B. De Cocceii (1758), Tomus I, Prolegomena, para. 40, p. 21.

[49] Cf. Pufendorf, *Elementorum*, bk. I, def. XIII, para. 24, p. 283 (n. 7).

[50] Cf. Pufendorf, *De Jure*, bk. VIII, ch. VI, para. II, pp. 431–2 (n. 3).

[51] Cf. Pufendorf, *De Jure*, bk. VIII, ch. VI, para. II, pp. 431–2 (n. 3).

[52] Cf. Pufendorf, *De Jure*, bk. II, ch. I, para. IV, p. 144 (n. 3). On the man–beast relationship in Pufendorf's moral theory, see Vanda Fiorillo, '"Non canis, sed homo": dignità umana ed onore nel giusnaturalismo di Samuel Pufendorf', *Il Pensiero Politico*, XL, 2 (May–August 2012) pp. 177–80; republished in German in Vanda Fiorillo, Michael Kahlo (eds.), *Wege zur Menschenwürde. Ein deutsch-italienischer Dialog in memoriam Mario A. Cattaneo, International Conference Proceedings, Trier, 20–24 February 2012* (2015), pp. 111–30.

[53] Pufendorf, *De Jure*, bk. VIII, ch. VI, para. II, p. 432 (*my italics*) (n. 3); here cited from Pufendorf, *Of the Law of Nature and Nations*, bk. VIII, ch. VI, para. II, p. 833 (n. 6).

As may be seen from the correlation clearly described above between the duties and rights existing among states, Pufendorf considers the relationship between states as a *moral relationship*, built on the necessary mutual relation between an obligation of one international subject and a right of another. To fully understand the ethical nature of this interdependence between a duty and a (subjective) right in the international context, it is necessary first of all to underline that Pufendorf applies this correlation indifferently to the relationship between *simple moral persons*—which comprise natural men—and between *compound moral persons*, which include states.[54] On this basis, it may be said that in Pufendorf's conception of international law, the correlation between right and duty determines, in the first instance, the specific nature of the relationship between states. To understand what this correlation is, it is necessary to reflect a little on the particular idea he has of these two concepts. In the works of Pufendorf on natural law, both these notions are included in his quadripartition of the moral entities,[55] and are specifically identified with two different kinds of moral qualities: a duty with a passive operating moral quality[56] and a (subjective) right with an active operating moral quality. More specifically, the latter, a right, may refer to '*active Qualities*, as by virtue of it any thing may be requir'd of others'.[57] In the language of Pufendorf, in fact, a right is 'a power, *potestas*, in a person, enabling this person to act with moral effect. The effect is that an obligation is laid on somebody else', where obligation is conceived as 'an inner bond on the will'.[58] It is clear that a right is here included in the broader category of power, which enables the person who holds the latter to act '*lawfully and with a moral Effect*'.[59] And this moral efficacy consists in eliciting from the counterpart an 'obligation (. . .) to perform some certain Business, which he requires, or to admit some Action of his as valid, or not to stop and hinder it'.[60] In other words, a right, as a moral faculty, 'places fellow humans, as partners in a contractual exchange, in an obligatory relationship'.[61] Thus—also in Pufendorf's internationalistic vision—the holder of a right establishes, as such, a moral relationship with the other party, which is bound to fulfil the correlative (moral) obligation of non-resistance to the right itself.

On the basis of these premises, the mutual and spontaneous (being moral) fulfilment of the peace duties in relations between sovereigns is—at this level of

[54] The distinction between simple and compound moral persons, as well as their inner subdivisions is set out by Pufendorf in *De Jure*, bk. I, ch. I, paras. XII–XIII, pp. 12–14 (n. 3).

[55] On Pufendorf's classification of the moral entities, see n. 3, above.

[56] The definition of duty as a passive moral quality is given in Pufendorf, *De Jure*, bk. I, ch. I, para. XXI, p. 21 (n. 3).

[57] Cf. Pufendorf, *De Jure*, bk. I, ch. I, para. XX, p. 20 (n. 3); here cited from Pufendorf, *Of the Law of Nature and Nations*, bk. I, ch. I, para. XX, p. 12 (n. 6).

[58] Cf. Karl Olivecrona, *The Concept of a Right according to Grotius and Pufendorf* in Peter Noll, Günter Stratenwerth (eds.), *Rechtsfindung: Beiträge zur juristischen Methodenlehre: Festschrift für Oscar Adolf Germann zum 80 Geburtstag*, (1969), p. 178.

[59] Cf. Pufendorf, *De Jure*, bk. I, ch. I, para. XIX, p. 19 (n. 3); here cited from Pufendorf, *Of the Law of Nature and Nations*, bk. I, ch. I, para. XIX, p. 11 (n. 6).

[60] Cf. Pufendorf, *De Jure*, bk. I, ch. I, para. XIX, p. 19 (n. 3); here cited from Pufendorf, *Of the Law of Nature and Nations*, bk. I, ch. I, para. XIX, p. 11 (n. 6).

[61] Cf. Hartung, *Die Naturrechtsdebatte*, p. 34 (n. 40).

Pufendorf's theory—the main condition, allowing, in the first instance, the exercise of the natural rights of states, and especially their freedom, as the right to self-preservation and security. In short, for Pufendorf, the moral applicability of the absolute natural duties towards others, attributable to states, allows the undisturbed exercise of the natural rights of sovereign entities, and therefore the potential *physiological* development of non-conflictual international relations.

It may thus be supposed that, at this stage of Pufendorf's theorization on international law based on the coincidence of the law of nations and natural law, states in their capacity as *compound moral persons* are conceived, in the first instance, as *ethical subjects of international law*. They appear, namely, as the main actors on a possible world stage in a kind of barely outlined *moral politics*, i.e. in the same theoretical politics that, in the climate of the mature German Enlightenment, would be referred to as *politische Weisheit, political wisdom*. At the close of the eighteenth century, in fact, it was no coincidence that this form of politics would be closely identified with the law of nature, built up as a theory of natural duties;[62] a theory, that, in our case, would set out the specific obligations to be performed within the international community.

II. A Pragmatic Politics: International Treaties as Politico-Diplomatic Instruments Converting the Peace Duties into Inter-State Practice

In international relations, however, it is also, and above all, the necessity to resort to inter-state coercion, i.e. war,[63] which shows that the law of nations, as absolute law of nature, despite being valid for mankind over the centuries, is not always effective or applicable. In fact, although natural law is adapted, by virtue of divine wisdom, to human nature, so that its observance is always connected to the personal benefit of individuals,[64] nevertheless the true reason for it lies not so much in 'the useful', as in the nature of men. Therefore, taking up the stoic idea of the universal relationship between human beings, Pufendorf sees, for example, the reason

62 Essential reading on the concept of *politische Weisheit*, as the specifically theoretical level of the Enlightenment conception of politics in Germany is the work of Diethild Maria Meyring, *Politische Weltweisheit: Studien zur deutschen politischen Philosophie des 18 Jahrhunderts*, phil. diss. (1965), esp. ch. I, pp. 16–60. For a further examination of this concept, cf. n. 70, below.

63 On the concept of war in Pufendorf, refer to Pufendorf, *De Jure*, bk. VIII, ch. VI, pp. 431–54 (n. 3). In Pufendorf's thought, war appears as a *status subsidiarius*, which takes over when the criterion of reciprocity has been violated in the fulfilment of the duties of peace. This is because the violation of this criterion is—as we have seen—the violation of the natural rights of peoples. Thus, the state of war is the last resort to which one is driven when it is impossible to protect one's safety and one's own rights without using force. War is, therefore, a state of mutual and excessive coercion, which necessarily occurs because of the irrationality of men, similar in this respect to animals, which are not, in themselves, likely to be moderated in their behaviour by any moral bond. On this point, see Pufendorf, *Elementorum*, bk. I, def. III, para. 6, pp. 17–18 (n. 7) and Pufendorf, *De Jure*, bk. VIII, ch. VI, para. II, p. 432 (n. 3).

64 See Pufendorf, *De Jure*, bk. II, ch. III, para. X, p. 191 (n. 3).

why a man should not do harm to another not so much in utility itself (even if this is actually extremely useful), but because the other is also a man, i.e. a creature similar in nature, whom it is wrong to harm.[65] Thus, although respect for natural law is also accompanied by a utility that is of benefit to all mortals, while, on the other hand, violation generally causes a remorse of conscience[66] and hence unhappiness in individuals, this law turns out to be, due to the irrationality of man, not sufficiently suited to bringing about tranquillity and security of mankind.[67]

For this reason, precisely because of the wickedness of man, who is not always inclined to act on the basis of the sole law of humanity, the law of nations, as natural law, requires states to draw up contracts in order to strengthen through promises and pacts their mutual transactions.[68] So much so that without pacts it would not be possible to maintain sociality and peace among men.[69] It might thus be supposed that it is the law of nature itself—as a 'political wisdom' or a theoretical politics in embryo—that seeks the aid, in a subordinate role, of prudence or pragmatic politics.[70] To this would be assigned, in this case, the specific task of finding the most useful and appropriate means to realize the natural duties of peace in international practice. In this sense, prudence would appear to form the applicative part or the way of realizing in the practical sphere the law of nations, as a moral politics, constituted by the offices of humanity. Also in Pufendorf's view, however, political prudence seems only to play a subordinate role to international law, as a 'political wisdom', insofar as it appears to have a merely instrumental function in promoting the moral dynamics of the latter. Consequently, what has been rightly observed on Pufendorf's state doctrine may be extended to his theory of international law.

[65] Cf. Pufendorf, *De Jure*, bk. II, ch. III, para. XVIII, p. 208 (n. 3).
[66] Cf. Pufendorf, *De Jure*, bk. III, ch. IV, para. VI, p. 363 (n. 3).
[67] See Pufendorf, *De Jure*, bk. VII, ch. I, para. XI, pp. 124–5 (n. 3).
[68] Cf. Pufendorf, *De Jure*, bk. III, ch. IV, para. I, p. 357 (n. 3).
[69] See Pufendorf, *De Jure*, bk. III, ch. IV, para. I, p. 358 (n. 3).
[70] With the dialectical connection between moral politics and political prudence, which seem to underly Pufendorf's very conception of international law, he would appear, then, to prepare the terrain for the debate in the following century, made famous in 1793 by Kant in his *On the Old Saw*—which would attempt to answer one of the most important theoretical questions which animated critical public discussion in Germany: that of establishing the proper relationship between theory and practice. In particular, this public debate gave expression to yet another attempt to define the nature of politics, leading to a definition, also from the disciplinary point of view, of the relationship between 'political wisdom' (*politische Weisheit*), as theoretical politics, and prudence (*Klugheit*), which corresponds conversely to pragmatic politics. Within this framework, the formal structure of eighteenth-century German political philosophy, known at the time as *Philosophia practica, Philosophia moralis*, or else *practische Weltweisheit*, was divided, in particular, into the two disciplines of 1) natural law, as a theory of socio-political duties, and 2) the doctrine of prudence (*Klugheitslehre*), which was identified, on the other hand, with politics *stricto sensu*. The first, natural law, formed the specifically theoretical part of the *Weltweisheit*, while the second, prudence, provided instructions on *how* to fulfil in the practical sphere, and in the most advantageous way, the socio-political duties suggested by the law of nature. On the formal division of eighteenth-century German political philosophy, refer, once again, to the apposite observations of Meyring, *Politische Weltweisheit*, pp. 17ff. (n. 62). For an analysis of the dialectic between political wisdom and prudence applied to two German Enlightenment theories of different ideological standpoints, one liberal (that of Ernst Ferdinand Klein), and the other radical-democratic, (that of Johann Adam Bergk), see Vanda Fiorillo, *Autolimitazione razionale e desiderio. Il* dovere *nei progetti di riorganizzazione politica dell'illuminismo tedesco* (2000), passim.

In fact, according to Pufendorf, as the science of natural law, 'as a practical discipline, also needs prudence alongside normative science (. . .), in order to be able to determine action in concrete situations', which represent 'facts that cannot be constructed *more geometrico*', equally, 'also in the doctrine of state, the discipline of political prudence is an indispensable means of application of the natural-law construction of state to practice, i.e. of conversion of the natural law definition of the purpose of the state [itself] into concrete provisions to act (. . .) related to the condition and situation of individual political communities'.[71] More specifically, political wisdom and prudence—whose criteria would seem to be inherent in the very international law of Pufendorf—also appear to imply two distinct criteria for assessing inter-state relations. While prudence seems to proceed according to the *useful-useless* binomial, wisdom or moral politics would evaluate what exists starting from the *just-unjust* concept pair.

Based on these assumptions, it is precisely the insufficient applicability of the law of nature that gives rise to the necessity, at international level, to open up the field of pragmatic politics. This finds its parallel (in terms of relations between individuals) in the necessity to found a state with positive laws, assisted by coercion. More specifically, the not always perfect effectiveness of the duties of peace in relations between sovereigns involves a shift from universally valid utility—which, based on reason and recommended by the norms of international law, coincides with what is of lasting benefit to humanity[72]—towards a delicate and difficult compromise between the peculiar utilities of individual states. In fact, such a compromise is reached precisely by means of those political principles that complement Pufendorf's theory of international law, working together in a subordinate role with its natural law canons. And this is how 'in Pufendorf the two extremes of natural-law rationalism and political opportunism come into contact'.[73]

Among the political principles which contribute to defining Pufendorf's doctrine of the law of nations, there are undoubtedly also international treaties, which flank war as the main instrument of empirical politics. It is no coincidence that Pufendorf considers them to be 'legal transactions of the political and diplomatic kind, belonging as such not to jurisprudence but to history'.[74] In fact, according to Pufendorf, the special conventions between two or more states, such as alliances or peace treaties, do not come under the law of nations, despite their being carried out in fulfilment of the duty to religiously abide by the given word. Not only do many

[71] Behme, *Naturrecht und Staat*, p. 168 (n. 45).

[72] Cf. Pufendorf, *De Jure*, bk. II, ch. III, para. X, pp. 191–2 (n. 3).

[73] Cf. Reibstein, *Völkerrecht*, p. 493 (n. 14).

[74] Reibstein, 'Pufendorfs Völkerrechtlehre', p. 63 (n. 14). Concerning in particular Pufendorf's discussion of the law of embassies, it should be recalled that in his opinion, the inviolability of ambassadors is sanctioned by natural law itself, as such figures contribute, for him, to re-establishing, conserving, or making peace more solid through alliances or treaties. This, however, is on condition that ambassadors do not behave like spies, plotting hostile acts against the host sovereign. Yet, precisely because they are protected by the law of nature itself, delegates are not, however, subject to the jurisdiction or the punitive power of the host state. Other kinds of privilege, that may or may not be granted to them depend, on the other hand, solely on the customs of the ruler who offers them hospitality. On the law of embassies, according to Pufendorf, see Pufendorf, *De Jure*, bk. II, ch. III, para. XXIII, p. 223 (n. 3).

such treaties have obligatory force only for a limited time, but they are also similar to those private contracts between citizens which are not included under civil law, but are rather part of history and custom or practices that may or may not be followed, depending on the will of the contracting parties.[75]

In this regard, it is important to note the analogy that exists in the relationship between international law and treaties in the field of external relations, and between natural law and positive law systems, concerning relations within individual political societies. In both cases, the law of nature forms 'the basis of validity'[76] of treaties between states on the one hand, and positive legal orders on the other. This is because 'whether from the systematic point of view, or regarding their validity', natural laws can boast 'pre-eminence over positive laws' and over international treaties themselves, precisely 'by virtue of their claim to universal validity, and their more general scope'.[77] This scope does not in fact coincide with the specific public safety of the individual state, but the safety of mankind. 'Therefore, since the general is logically superordinate to the particular', in Pufendorf's vision, natural law—precisely because it is equipped with universal validity—is superior to both international conventions and positive laws, neither of which pursue, on the other hand, 'the good of mankind', but rather 'a particular interest (. . .) of certain groups'.[78]

Consequently, both international treaties and the positive legal orders of states limit themselves, in turn, to specifying natural law in its more indeterminate precepts, integrating it within the field of what is permitted, authorized, or indifferent.[79] In fact, defining the relationship between the law of nature and nations and those particular treaties of friendship or alliance between peoples which he called *foedera* or confederations of states, Pufendorf states that international alliance agreements[80] can concern things to which one was already bound by virtue of the

[75] Cf. Pufendorf, *De Jure*, bk. II, ch. III, para. XXIII, p. 223 (n. 3).

[76] Cf. Denzer, *Moralphilosophie und Naturrecht*, p. 224 (n. 5), who here refers, however, only to the relationship between the internal legal order and natural law. In the same interpretative direction cf., furthermore, Goyard-Fabre, *Pufendorf et le droit naturel*, p. 234 (n. 46), where she rightly points out that, for Pufendorf, '*natural law* (. . .) constitutes (. . .) the founding principle of all juridical normativeness'. On the relationship between natural law and positive law, according to Pufendorf, see e.g. Pufendorf, *De Jure*, bk. II, ch. III, paras. XI and XXIV, pp. 194–5 and 224–5 (n. 3); Pufendorf, *De Jure*, bk. VIII, ch. I, para. I, pp. 285–7 (n. 3).

[77] See Wolfgang Röd, *Geometrischer Geist und Naturrecht: Methodengeschichtliche Untersuchungen zur Staatsphilosophie im 17. und 18 Jahrhundert* (1970), p. 93.

[78] Cf. Röd, *Geometrischer Geist*, p. 93 (n. 77).

[79] Making, also in this case, exclusive reference to relationships within civil states, Denzer underlines how in Pufendorf, the object of positive law is 'things, that are not regulated by natural law, [i.e.] that [are] left by the law of nature to the field of permission, "the authorized" and "the indifferent" ': Denzer, *Moralphilosophie und Naturrecht*, p. 222 (n. 5).

[80] It is precisely in the theory of international treaties that Ernst Reibstein sees the clear emergence of the 'positivistic attitude' of Pufendorf, who, for the critic, applies to this subject 'simply the points of view on the basis of which the Spanish jurists had defined the relationship between *jus naturae* and *jus civile*'. More specifically, 'the model not mentioned by Pufendorf' would seem to have been Fernando 'Vasquez, who in this way meant to assert the natural law criterion of every positive law': Reibstein, 'Pufendorfs Völkerrechtslehre', pp. 68–9, n. 94 (n. 14). On this theoretical point, see Fernando Vázquez de Menchaca, *Controversiarum Illustrium, aliarumque usu frequentium*, libri tres (1572), libri primi, ch. XXIX, para. 21, p. 82. On the distinction between *jus gentium primaevum*

law of nature, or add to this more specific duties, or else make some hitherto more indeterminate natural law prescriptions certain.[81]

Before examining the link between international law and alliance pacts or confederations in greater detail, it is, however, necessary to briefly refer first to the characteristics of the latter. In this regard, it should first be pointed out that in Pufendorf's political theory, confederations of states represent a specific variant of the innovative concept of the composite state or 'state-system' (*systema civitatum*), which the author in turn distinguishes, on the basis of the unity or the division of sovereign power, from the simple forms of the state itself.[82]

In this distinction between simple and composite states, he identifies the 'state-system' with several political entities, mutually connected so as to form one body, though each of these entities retains its sovereignty.[83] In turn, the 'state-system' is subdivided, in Pufendorf's opinion, into associations of states under one sovereign[84] and into confederations of states. The latter forms, in particular, permanent associations, based on a federal pact between two or more sovereign states.[85] In this way, Pufendorf introduces 'a new category' into his political theory, that of 'state-system'.[86] This would prove to be 'a very effective conceptual and terminological instrument for the analysis and representation of the international political order'.[87] For Pufendorf, in fact, the inter-state order does not depend 'so much [on] static bilateral equilibria, as especially [on] balanced relations between allied groups of powers, or between groups and single states'.[88]

Starting from this premise, in chapter IX of book VIII of *De Jure*, Pufendorf begins with an analysis of the so-called 'treaties of friendship', specifying the relationship of the latter with the law of nations, as natural law. According to his reconstruction, in this kind of alliance it is simply agreed upon to mutually exercise the

and *jus gentium secundarium* according to Vázquez, refer to Reibstein, 'Pufendorfs Völkerrechtslehre', pp. 58–9 (n. 14); and Franco Todescan, *Lex, Natura, Beatitudo: Il problema della legge nella Scolastica spagnola del sec. XVI* (2014), esp. pp. 221–2.

[81] Pufendorf, *De Jure*, bk. VIII, ch. IX, para. I, p. 467 (n. 3).

[82] On the fundamental distinction between simple states and compound states or 'state-systems', cf. Samuel Pufendorf, *De Republica irregulari*, in Pufendorf, *Dissertationes Academicae Selectiores*, para. 6, pp. 393–5 (n. 11). On this distinction, as well as on the general typology of the constitutional forms in Pufendorf, cf., in the literature on the subject, Bazzoli, 'La concezione pufendorfiana', in particular pp. 38–40, 57–9 (n. 1); Alfred Dufour, 'Féderalisme et Raison d'État dans la pensée politique pufendorfienne', in *Pufendorf, filosofo del diritto*, esp. pp. 115–25 (n. 1); Krieger, *The Politics of Discretion*, esp. pp. 153–64 (n. 35); Welzel, *Die Naturrechtslehre Samuel Pufendorfs*, pp. 74–9 (n. 8); Simone Zurbuchen, 'Samuel Pufendorfs Theorie der Staatsformen und ihre Bedeutung für die Theorie der modernen Republik', in *Naturrecht und Staatstheorie*, pp. 138–60 (n. 38).

[83] See Pufendorf, *De Systematibus Civitatum*, para. 2, p. 266 (n. 16).

[84] In Pufendorf's view, such associations of states ruled over by a single king, are, in turn, formed either by virtue of marriage among ruling dynasties or of transmission of entitlement to sovereignty by inheritance, this giving rise to *personal unions*, or also on the basis of a contractual agreement between sovereigns, which brings about *real unions*. On the distinction between personal unions and real unions, cf. Pufendorf, *De Jure*, bk. VII, ch. V, paras. XVII–XVIII, pp. 202–6 (n. 3).

[85] Cf. Pufendorf, *De Jure*, bk. VII, ch. V, para. XVIII, pp. 204–6 (n. 3).

[86] Cf. Bazzoli, 'La concezione pufendorfiana', p. 38 (n. 1).

[87] See Bazzoli, 'La concezione pufendorfiana', p. 38 (n. 1).

[88] Cf. Bazzoli, 'La concezione pufendorfiana', p. 57 (n. 1).

obligation of non-aggression (*alterum non laedere*) and the duties of humanity.[89] Therefore, the 'treaties of friendship' do not establish anything other than what rulers are bound to do according to the principles of natural law. Agreements of this kind thus add nothing to the law of nature, making them unnecessary for civilized peoples who are accustomed to respecting the law of humanity (*lex humanitatis*).[90] Conversely, the sometimes vague content of the natural duties of international law is elaborated on and specified by those leagues that Pufendorf differentiates between as equal and unequal.[91] In general, such leagues—whether equal or unequal—aim, in the practical sphere, to specify the more indeterminate precepts of natural law precisely through the pursuit of the fundamental goal of 'creating a situation of dynamic balance of power, which concept (if not the term itself) is recurrent in the political writings of Pufendorf'.[92] With this common purpose, the first, or equal, type of league is the *foedera,* that are based on the perfect equality of both parties.[93] In contrast, the second, or unequal, type of alliance, 'occur[s] because there are considerable differences between the powers',[94] and the alliance is therefore based on a *foedus inaequale* establishing a disparity between performance and consideration, making one of the allies inferior to the other.[95]

As we have seen so far, also from the characteristics of such alliances—which specify the more indeterminate offices of humanity that substantiate Pufendorf's international law—it is possible to see the general role played by international conventions, which are treated by Pufendorf like private contracts between citizens having a customary rather than positive nature.[96] In fact, the agreements between states, like the aforementioned private contracts between citizens, have in international society the specific function of 'turning the universal duties of humanity towards our fellows into coercible rights'.[97] In other words, in Pufendorf's view, a contract, including international ones, 'serves' as an instrument of political prudence, 'the fulfilment of the duties'[98] of humanity, prescribed by the law of nations, as a moral politics. For this reason, such international agreements turn out not to be 'means of free disposal, but instruments for organising duties relating to the aid'[99] of other states. Therefore, if treaties between states are essentially means of prudently

[89] Cf. Pufendorf, *De Jure*, bk. VIII, ch. IX, para. II, p. 467 (n. 3).

[90] Cf. Pufendorf, *De Jure*, bk. VIII, ch. IX, para. II, p. 467 (n. 3).

[91] Cf. Pufendorf, *De Jure*, bk. VIII, ch. IX, para. III, p. 468 (n. 3).

[92] Cf. Bazzoli, 'La concezione pufendorfiana', p. 56 (n. 1). On the notion of balance between the European powers in Samuel Pufendorf, cf. Hans Fenske, under 'Gleichgewicht, Balance', in Otto Brunner, Werner Conze, and Reinhart Koselleck (eds.), *Geschichtliche Grundbegriffe: Historisches Lexikon zur politisch-sozialen Sprache in Deutschland* (1975); on Pufendorf see pp. 969–70.

[93] On alliances between equals, cf. Pufendorf, *De Jure*, bk. VIII, ch. IX, para. III, pp. 468–9 (n. 3).

[94] See once again Bazzoli, 'La concezione pufendorfiana', p. 56 (n. 1).

[95] On unequal alliances, cf. Pufendorf, *De Jure*, bk. VIII, ch. IX, para. IV, pp. 469–71 (n. 3). Pufendorf returns to the distinction between equal and unequal *foedera* also in his *De Republica irregulari*, para. 12, pp. 406–9 (n. 82).

[96] Cf. n. 75, above.

[97] Cf. Klaus Luig, 'Pufendorfs Lehre von der Wirksamkeit des Staates und das Privatrecht', in *Pufendorf und seine Wirkungen*, p. 95 (n. 2).

[98] See Luig, 'Pufendorfs Lehre', p. 96 (n. 97).

[99] Cf. Luig, 'Pufendorfs Lehre', p. 95 (n. 97).

putting into practice the moral duties of the law of nations, then there is no space in Pufendorf's internationalistic theory for a 'selfish contractual freedom'.[100] In this regard, it is true that international conventions are manifestations of the equal freedom of states in practice, i.e. their equal faculty to judge and decide on matters concerning their own self-preservation and security. Nevertheless, given the (subordinate) relationship of prudence to moral politics—which also appears implicit in Pufendorf's internationalistic conception—'the administration of mutual security by a state is the only way in which self-interested natural liberties can be necessarily related to other-oriented natural obligations'.[101] This shows after all that the content of such international conventions—precisely because they are directed towards the practical realization of the duties of peace—is 'in absolute terms, more what is [*morally*] *due*, than what is *wanted*'.[102] For this reason, even in exchanges between states 'there cannot be (. . .) total contractual freedom oriented solely to the will of the single individual'.[103] On such a basis, in Pufendorf's view, the field of free negotiation between states, for example, regarding alliances or trade—far from being a space of unbridled competitive selfishness—integrates 'a model of cooperation'[104] between peoples inspired by the moral criteria suggested by the law of nations as natural law.

III. Conclusion

In summary, Pufendorf creates a model of international *ethico-political* order which, being based on a concept of international law as a set of duties of peace, shows a balance rooted, in the first instance, in the moral dynamics of these duties. These dynamics mean that relations are set up between states, which—far from corresponding, as in the case of Hobbes, to a mere collision of opposing forces—are ethical in nature, because they are founded on the correlation between the (moral) fulfilment of the obligations of peace and the undisturbed exercise of the natural rights of states, and, above all, their free faculty of self-preservation and security. However, given the not always sufficient applicability of the law of humanity on the ethical plane alone, Pufendorf recognizes—this time inspired for his part by political realism—the necessity for the duties of peace to be *opportunely* converted into the practice of international relations with the help of merely instrumental political criteria which, as such, must be constantly animated by the supreme moral aspiration to realize peace among peoples.

[100] Cf. Luig, 'Pufendorfs Lehre', p. 95 (n. 97).

[101] Krieger, *The Politics of Discretion*, p. 169 (n. 35). However, in denying the connection in Pufendorf between theory and practice in inter-state relationships, this critic concludes his argument recognizing 'no logical or legal relationship between the interests of state and the universal obligations of natural law in the international field'. This is precisely because of the absence in this field of a political power above sovereign entities: cf. Krieger, *The Politics of Discretion*, p. 169 (n. 35).

[102] Cf. Luig, 'Pufendorfs Lehre', p. 97 (*my italics*) (n. 97).

[103] Cf. Luig, 'Pufendorfs Lehre', p. 96 (n. 97).

[104] Cf. Luig, 'Pufendorfs Lehre', p. 96 (n. 97).

It is possible, on these grounds, to state conclusively that it is precisely the dialectical relationship that Pufendorf establishes between international law, as a moral politics, and the interests of states as an expression of pragmatic politics, that constitutes the thin 'red line' that keeps the disparate elements, be they moral or political, united and in which he roots his concept of international law. Consequently, only by taking into account the dual, but interdependent conceptual level on which Pufendorf's discussion of international relations unfolds, is it possible to recognize the inherent organic nature of his conception of the law of nations, based on both natural law and political principles, which, if they are considered unrelated, cannot but appear highly contradictory. With his model of cooperation between peoples, constantly underpinned by the latent but tenacious dialectic between the moral and pragmatic planes of politics, Pufendorf effectively creates 'a major general vision (. . .) of international order, which is [certainly] not lacking in organic conceptual unity'.[105]

Selected Bibliography

Bazzoli, Maurizio, 'La concezione pufendorfiana della politica internazionale', in Vanda Fiorillo (ed.), *Samuel Pufendorf, filosofo del diritto e della politica, International Conference Proceedings, Milan, 11–12 November 1994* (Naples: La Città del Sole, 1996), pp. 29–72.

Bazzoli, Maurizio, *Il piccolo stato nell'età moderna. Studi su un concetto della politica internazionale tra XVI e XVIII secolo* (Milan: Jaca Book, 1990).

Klenner, Hermann, 'Bileams Pferd auf die Kanzeln! Zur Naturrechts- und Völkerrechtslehre des Samuel Pufendorf', in Bodo Geyer, Helmut Goerlich (eds.), *Samuel Pufendorf und seine Wirkungen bis auf die heutige Zeit* (Baden-Baden: Nomos, 1996), pp. 195–208.

Reibstein, Ernst, 'Pufendorfs Völkerrechtslehre', *Österreichische Zeitschrift für Öffentliches Recht*, vol. VII (1956), pp. 43–72.

Reibstein, Ernst, *Völkerrecht: Eine Geschichte seiner Ideen in Lehre und Praxis. I. Von der Antike bis zur Aufklärung* (Munich: Karl Alber, 1957), on Pufendorf pp. 488–95.

Stolleis, Michael, 'Textor und Pufendorf über die Ratio Status Imperii im Jahre 1667', in M. Stolleis (ed.), *Staat und Staatsräson in der frühen Neuzeit. Studien zur Geschichte des öffentlichen Rechts* (Frankfurt am Main: Suhrkamp, 1990), pp. 106–33.

[105] Cf. Maurizio Bazzoli, *Il piccolo stato nell'età moderna. Studi su un concetto della politica internazionale tra XVI e XVIII secolo* (1990), p. 65.

11

Christian Wolff

System as an Episode?

Thomas Kleinlein

Christian Wolff is known as an encyclopaedic 'systematizer of all areas of knowledge',[1] and his contribution to international legal thought has also received praise, specifically for having brought international law into a system. Dietrich Heinrich Ludwig von Ompteda wrote in 1785: 'Grotius raised natural international law to the dignity of a science, Wolff was the first to give it a complete order and bring it into a system.'[2] Still, international lawyers today mostly know Wolff best as Vattel's precursor, a scholar chronologically somewhere between Grotius and Vattel, from whom Vattel distanced himself because he did not know what to make of his systematic method and his unrealistic claim of a supreme state termed '*civitas maxima*'. What Wolff considered to be his original contribution to the study of international law—his systematic method—therefore got lost early on in the further history of international legal thought. Therefore, despite the fact that Wolff was a very renowned scholar in his time, his systematic method apparently remained an episode in international legal thought. The aim of this chapter is to explain the reasons for this peculiar development: it sets out by presenting a short overview of the life and work of Wolff as a universal systematizer and champion of academic freedom (I) before turning to the significance of methodological considerations in the development of international legal thought from Grotius via Wolff to Vattel (II). The next section analyses in detail Wolff's systematic method and its implications for his writings on *jus gentium* (III). The final section presents three transitions in international legal thought that are already discernible, but not explicit, in Wolff's writings. Arguably, this ambiguity contributes to explaining Wolff's later reception (IV).

[1] Knud Haakonssen, 'Christian Wolff (1679-1754)', in Bardo Fassbender and Anne Peters (eds.), *The Oxford Handbook of the History of International Law*, pp. 1106–9, at p. 1106.

[2] Dietrich Heinrich Ludwig von Ompteda, *Litteratur des gesammten sowohl natürlichen als positiven Völkerrechts nebst vorangeschickter Abhandlung von dem Umfange des gesammten sowohl natürlichen als positiven Völkerrechts, und Ankündigung eines zu bearbeitenden vollständigen Systems desselben* (Regensburg, 1785), p. 328 (my own translation).

I. A Universal Systematizer and Champion of Academic Freedom

The eighteenth-century polymath Wolff was born in Breslau, Silesia, which was at the time a Protestant part of the Habsburg monarchy, on 24 January 1679.[3] From 1699 on, he studied at the University of Jena, first divinity, then focusing on mathematics and natural sciences. After he had finished his studies in Leipzig, Wolff was invited to be a staff member of the leading German scholarly journal, the *Acta Eruditorum Lipsiensium*. Strongly supported by Gottfried Wilhelm Leibniz, Wolff became a professor of mathematics at the University of Halle in 1706. He succeeded both as a lecturer, later also covering the field of philosophy and finally physics—which implied an additional nomination as professor of physics—and as a scholar. He was elected as Fellow of the Royal Society in London, became a member of the Berlin, St. Petersburg, and Paris Academies and later a Prussian *Hofrat* (court councillor).

The career of this prolific and celebrated teacher and scholar was interrupted abruptly. In 1723, Wolff was dismissed from his position by the Prussian King Frederick William I (known as the 'soldier king'), who also ordered that Wolff had to leave the city of Halle and all other Prussian lands within 48 hours or suffer punishment by the rope. Wolff was forced to flee because he had given a lecture in which he expressed his admiration for Chinese philosophy, the *Oratio de Sinarum philosophia practica*.[4] For Wolff, Chinese philosophy demonstrated that there was a transcultural natural morality available to any reasonable human being without the help of divine revelation. This obviously provoked his pietist colleagues in Halle, who were reportedly jealous of his success anyway, and who charged him with heresy. Fortunately, Wolff did not have to worry about his future. He merely had to travel to Marburg in Hesse. There, he accepted a professorship that had been offered to him earlier. Far from damaging his career, the affair contributed to Wolff's international reputation as a 'martyr of science',[5] and his renown spread throughout Europe. Even twentieth-century observers stress Wolff's paramount importance

[3] On Wolff's biography, see Johann Christoph Gottsched, *Historische Lobschrift des weiland hoch= und wohlgebohrnen Herrn Herrn Christians, des H.R.R. Freyherrn von Wolf, Erb=Lehn= und Gerichtsherrn auf Klein=Dölzig, Sr. Königl. Maj. in Preussen geheimen Raths, der Universität zu Halle Kanzlers und Seniors, wie auch des Natur= und Völkerrechts und der Mathematik daselbst, Der kaiserl. Akademie zu Petersburg Prof. honor. der königl. Akad. der Wissenschaften zu London, Paris, Berlin und der zu Bologna, Mitglied. Nebst des hochseligen Freyherrn Kupferbilde* (1755); Wolfgang Drechsler, 'Christian Wolff (1679-1754): A Biographical Essay', *E.J.L. & E.* 4(2/3) (1997), 111–28, at 111; Otfried Nippold, 'Introduction (1917)', in Joseph H. Drake (ed.), *Christian Wolff, Jus Gentium Methodo Scientifica Pertractatum (1764)* vol. 13; and James Brown Scott, *The Classics of International Law* (1934), pp. ix–lii, at xi–xxiv.

[4] Christian Wolff, *Oratio de Sinarum philosophia practica: Rede über die praktische Philosophie der Chinesen*, ed. Michael Albrecht (1985). English translation: Anonymous, *The Real Happiness of a People Under a Philosophical King Demonstrated: Not only from the Nature of Things, but from the undoubted Experience of the Chinese under their first Founder Fohi, and his Illustrious Succcessors, Hoam Ti, and Xin Num* (1750). See Mark Larrimore, 'Orientalism and Antivoluntarism in the History of Ethics: On Christian Wolff's *Oratio de Sinarum philosophia practica*', *J Religious Ethics* 28(2) (2000), 189–219.

[5] Arthur Nussbaum, *A Concise History of the Law of Nations* (Rev Edn, 1954), p. 151.

for the independence of scholarship. In his introduction to the *Classics* edition of Wolff's *Jus gentium methodo scientifica pertractatum*, Otfried Nippold praised him as a 'champion of academic freedom and unhampered search after truth'.[6] Obviously, the incident also made Wolff an appealing role model for twentieth-century international lawyers and their project of an international law that would overcome raw power politics. Remarkably, in the first paragraph of his *Jus gentium*, Wolff equates law and the science of law in his definition of the law of nations: 'By the Law of Nations we understand the science of that law which nations or peoples use in their relations with each other and of the obligations corresponding thereto.' For present-day readers, this only highlights Wolff's self-consciousness.[7]

Wolff received flattering invitations from Saxony, Sweden, and even Russia. In 1740, Frederick II ('The Great', the 'philosopher king'), in one of his first actions as a monarch, extended to Wolff a very generous invitation. Wolff returned to Halle where he became a professor of public law and of mathematics, Prussian *Geheimer Rat* (privy councillor), and vice chancellor of the university. He remained in Halle until he died as a wealthy man in 1754. In 1745, Wolff was ennobled and became a *Reichsfreiherr* (Imperial Baron of the Holy Roman Empire). Commentators stress the rather exceptional fact that Wolff—the champion of academic freedom—received this honour exclusively on the basis of his scholarly work.[8] Others take a more critical stance, pointing to Wolff's lack of familiarity with affairs of state or with the practice of law.[9] In any case, at the end of his career, Wolff's popularity as a teacher was in decline, as apparently even a Royal commission in 1748 noted. Hegel is often quoted for his seemingly malicious remark that Wolff 'had survived his acclaim, and in the end, his auditorium was completely empty'.[10]

II. Grotius, Wolff, Vattel, and the Riddle of Scientific Method

Wolff's writing began to focus completely on practical philosophy and on natural and international law only after his return to Halle.[11] Accordingly, his contributions to the study of international law appear, at first, to be contained in late works. The

[6] Nippold, 'Introduction (1917)' (n. 3), p. xvi.

[7] As another twentieth-century writer remarked, it also points to the significance of scholarship, especially in international law, where a real lawmaking procedure is absent: see Walter Schiffer, *The Legal Community of Mankind: A Critical Analysis of the Modern Concept of World Organization* (1954), p. 73. Nicholas Greenwood Onuf, '*Civitas maxima*: Wolff, Vattel and the Fate of Republicanism', *Am. J. Int'l L.* 88(2) (1994), 280–303, at 284, criticized that the identification of law with the science of that law was 'muddled'.

[8] Drechsler, 'Christian Wolff' (n. 3), pp. 117–18.

[9] Nussbaum, *A Concise History of the Law of Nations* (n. 5), p. 151.

[10] Georg Wilhlem Friedrich Hegel, *Vorlesungen über die Geschichte der Philosophie, als Vorschule zur Encyklopaedie, mit einigen Anführungen und Anmerkungen zur Erlaeuterung, Verteidigung oder Berichtigung, für den akademischen Gebrauch*, ed. Gerardus Johannes Petrus Josephus Bolland (1908), p. 940 (my own translation).

[11] Ernst Reibstein, 'Deutsche Grotius-Kommentatoren bis zu Christian Wolff', *ZaöRV* 15 (1953–1954), 76–102, at 81. Also, see Masaharu Yanagihara, *Borufu-no-kokusaihoriron (Christian Wolff's Theory of International Law)* (1998) (in Japanese).

relevant works *Jus gentium methodo scientifica pertractatum*[12] and the *Institutiones juris naturae et gentium*,[13] in German: *Grundsätze des Natur- und Völckerrechts*,[14] were only published in 1750 and 1754, respectively. However, the earlier multi-volume treatise *Jus naturae, methodo scientifica pertractatum* (1740–1748)[15] must not be overlooked. Actually, the volume on *Jus gentium* brought Wolff's *Jus naturae* to a conclusion, and the whole work represents a *jus naturae et gentium*,[16] the *Institutiones* offering a brief take of the whole subject. Furthermore, Wolff had edited Grotius's *De jure belli ac pacis* as early as 1734.[17] Apparently, he had long considered himself a methodologically superior successor of Grotius. In the introduction to his Grotius edition, Wolff writes that Grotius abided by a way of teaching that was common 'before we had thought about a thorough method of scholarly presentation'. Wolff regarded it as his discovery that Grotius started from fundamental ideas that could 'easily be brought into a system'. According to Wolff's own account, the substantive overlap of Grotius's teachings and Wolff's philosophy was considerable. It was the method and not the substance that made the difference.[18]

This insistence on a systematic method was received in a dubious manner. In international law scholarship, Wolff is taken as an authority for *jus cogens*[19] or for the doctrine of fundamental rights of states,[20] and we can also find a theory of customary international law as tacit agreements in his treatise.[21] What Wolff considered to be his main achievement beyond Grotius, his systematic method, by contrast, obviously did not achieve a sustainable impact. Generally, scholars across the disciplines tend to have strong views on Wolff's writings:[22] the philosopher Ernst

[12] Christian Wolff, *Jus Gentium Methodo Scientifica Pertractatum (1764)*, ed. Joseph H. Drake (1934); Christian Wolff, *Jus Gentium, methodo scientifica pertractatum, in quo jus gentium naturale ab eo, quod voluntarii, pactitii et consuetudinarii est, accurate distinguitur (1749)*, ed. Marcel Thomann (1972).

[13] Christian Wolff, *Institutiones juris naturae et gentium: in quibus ex ipsa hominis natura continuo nexu omnes obligationes et jura omnia deducuntur* (1754); Christian Wolff, *Institutiones juris naturae et gentium*, ed. Marcel Thomann (1969).

[14] Christian Wolff, *Grundsätze des Natur- und Völckerrechts*, ed. Marcel Thomann (1980).

[15] Christian Wolff, *Jus Naturae, methodo scientifica pertractatum (1740–1748)*, ed. Marcel Thomann, 8 vols (1968–1972).

[16] Nippold, 'Introduction (1917)' (n. 3), at xxvi.

[17] Christian Wolff (ed.), *Hugo Grotius, De jure belli ac pacis: Editio nova cum annotatis et praefatione Chr. Wolfii* (1734); see Reibstein, 'Deutsche Grotius-Kommentatoren bis zu Christian Wolff' (n. 11).

[18] Wolff (ed.), *Hugo Grotius, De jure belli ac pacis* (n. 17), Introduction, excerpts reprinted in Reibstein, 'Deutsche Grotius-Kommentatoren bis zu Christian Wolff' (n. 11), p. 77 (the translations are my own).

[19] Marcel Thomann, 'Introduction', ed. Marcel Thomann, in *Christian Wolff Gesammelte Werke, Abteilung III, vol. 25* (1972), pp. V–LI; critically Stefan Kadelbach, 'The Function and Identification of Jus Cogens Norms', *NYIL* 46 (2015), 147–72, at 150: invention of nineteenth-century Pandectism.

[20] Nussbaum, *A Concise History of the Law of Nations* (n. 5) p. 152; Miloš Vec, 'Grundrechte der Staaten: Die Tradierung des Natur- und Völkerrechts der Aufklärung', *RG* 18 (2011), 66–94, 70, *passim*; Helmut Philipp Aust, 'Fundamental Rights of States: Constitutional Law in Disguise?', *CJICL* 5 (2016), 521–46, at 525–6.

[21] Wolff, *Jus Gentium Methodo Scientifica Pertractatum* (1764) (n. 12), § 24.

[22] Critically, Reibstein, 'Deutsche Grotius-Kommentatoren bis zu Christian Wolff' (n. 11): 'superlatives and summary judgments'. For a collection of some statements of philosophers, see Francis Cheneval, *Philosophie in weltbürgerlicher Bedeutung: Über die Entstehung und die philosophischen*

Bloch severely criticized his philosophy as an apology of the mercantilist welfare and police state,[23] while Ernst Cassirer praised him as a father of human rights.[24] Henry Wheaton, in his *History of the Law of Nations*, regarded Wolff's works as an 'injudicious attempt to apply the phraseology and forms of mathematics to moral sciences which do not admit of this strict method of reasoning'.[25] The legal scholar Josef Kohler accused Wolff of a 'philistine intellectual impoverishment' that buried Grotian natural law,[26] and Arthur Nussbaum, in his *Concise History of the Law of Nations*, admonished that Wolff's 'pseudo-mathematical' syllogistic way of reasoning lead him to 'frequent pretentious trivialities and tautologies'.[27]

In the international law scholarship, Wolff's reception is largely influenced by how his 'translator' Vattel presented his writings, and this presentation is rather enigmatic on the face of it. As said before, Wolff distinguishes himself from Grotius by explicitly underlining the significance of his system and his method. The significance of method is already highlighted by the subtitle 'methodo scientifica pertractatum' ('treated according to a scientific method'). In the preface of his *Jus gentium*, Wolff states: 'And in that we part company with Grotius, to whose time system was an unknown name, an abuse which still exists in our time . . .'.[28] A generation later, Vattel—in a move comparable to Wolff's insistence on the continuity in substance between Grotius and himself—admits to drawing heavily on Wolff's authority and 'borrowing' from him. In turn, Vattel criticizes Wolff's systematic method:

> The treatise of the philosopher of Hall[e] on the law of nations is dependent on all those of the same author on philosophy and the law of nature. In order to read and understand it, it is necessary to have previously studied sixteen or seventeen quarto volumes which precede it. Besides, it is written in the manner and even in the formal method of geometrical works. [. . .] The method followed by Monsieur Wolf has had the effect of rendering his work dry, and in many respects incomplete. The different subjects are scattered through it in a manner that is extremely fatiguing to the attention. . . .[29]

Accordingly, what Wolff claims to be his major achievement compared to Grotius's earlier work—his systematic method—is turned against him by Vattel as his

Grundlagen des supranationalen und kosmopolitischen Denkens der Moderne, vol. 4, Schwabe philosophica (2002), 134.

[23] See Ernst Bloch, *Natural Law and Human Dignity*, Dennis J. Schmidt, Studies in Contemporary German Social Thought (1986); Bloch, *Natural Law and Human Dignity* (n. 23), at pp. 50–1.

[24] See Ernst Cassirer, *Freiheit und Form: Studien zur deutschen Geistesgeschichte* (3rd edn, 1961), pp. 314–15.

[25] Henry Wheaton, *History of the Law of Nations in Europe and America: From the Earliest Times to the Treaty of Washington, 1842* (1845), p. 177.

[26] Josef Kohler, 'Die spanischen Naturrechtslehrer des 16. und 17. Jahrhunderts', *ARSP* 10(3) (1917), 235–63, 236 (my own translation).

[27] Arthur Nussbaum, *A Concise History of the Law of Nations* (1947), p. 153. Like Wheaton before him, Nussbaum considered Wolff's method, at least as applied to the social sciences, 'a delusion' because social sciences required a different method from mathematics.

[28] Wolff, *Jus Gentium Methodo Scientifica Pertractatum (1764)* (n. 12), p. 8.

[29] Emer de Vattel, *The Law of Nations, Or, Principles of the Law of Nature, of Nations and Sovereigns, with Three Early Essays on the Origin and Nature of Natural Law and on Luxury*, ed. Béla Kapossy and Richard Whatmore (2008), p. 12.

severest flaw. On the one hand, both Wolff and Vattel treat method as an issue of presentation. On the other hand, Vattel is unsatisfied with Wolff's *civitas maxima* and acknowledges only a society of nations.[30] Vattel does not make this explicit, but this transposition seems to be closely related to the change in method. The meaning of method therefore seems to reach beyond issues of presentation, or style.

The fact that Vattel praised Wolff as a scholarly authority and still distanced himself from Wolff is well known. In light of how Wolff distinguished himself from Grotius, however, this move is rather puzzling: how could Vattel claim closely to follow Wolff and change, of all things, the very method that took centre stage for Wolff? Was Wolff's system just an episode in the history of international legal thought and, if so, why?

One reason for the twists in Wolff's reception arguably are due to the fact that his *jus gentium*—published right in the middle of the eighteenth century—needs to be situated in the middle of three major shifts in international legal thought that are already visible in his work, but not fleshed out clearly because Wolff—in a somehow indecisive attitude and a self-perception of timelessness—does not break with the past and includes the new ideas seemingly seamlessly. This is why we can see both continuity and change when we compare Grotius and Wolff and Wolff and Vattel, respectively. Arguably, the three major shifts are (1) the autonomization of international law from the old *jus gentium et naturae*, (2) an interrelated transition from natural law to positivism, and (3) a shift from law to political economy. We will approach these shifts in two steps. A short presentation of Wolff's method and its major implications for his approach to international law (III.) will be followed by a contextualization of all three shifts and an analysis of how they rendered Wolff's writings ambiguous in the eyes of later readers (IV.).

III. The Systematizer's Scientific Method and International Law

1. The logical or mathematical method and Wolff's system of science

In the dedicatory letter at the beginning of his *Jus gentium*, Wolff claimed to 'communicate a knowledge' of the law of nations by the same scientific method which he had used in all of the law of nature and in other departments of philosophy.[31] Wolff saw human knowledge in a continuous progress and believed that there was an intelligible order and interconnectedness between the many different subjects of human inquiry.[32] His claim of ultimate authority that Wolff attaches to his

[30] Ibid., p. 14; on the limited consequences of this difference, see Peter Haggenmacher, 'Le modèle de Vattel et la discipline du droit international', in Vincent Chetail and Peter Haggenmacher (eds.), *Vattel's International Law in a XXIst Century Perspective*, vol. 9, Graduate Institute of International and Development Studies (2011), pp. 3–48, at pp. 38–46.

[31] Wolff, *Jus Gentium Methodo Scientifica Pertractatum (1764)* (n. 12), p. 3.

[32] Matt Hettche, 'Christian Wolff', in Edward N. Zalta (ed.), *Stanford Encyclopedia of Philosophy (Winter 2014 Edition)*, <http://plato.stanford.edu/archives/win2014/entries/wolff-christian/>.

universally applicable method would not allow him to focus on any field of knowledge in isolation. Wolff's integration of the scholarly disciplines by deductions from highest principles 'more geometrico' with the aim of consistency establishes a complex meshwork of syllogisms.[33] Following in Leibniz's footsteps, the rationalist polymath Wolff claims that the mathematical method as a universal method can be consistently applied across all areas of knowledge.[34]

Due to its overarching character, method determines the architecture of Wolff's philosophical system.[35] The basis of Wolff's universal science[36] is the 'metaphysica generalis', which he identifies with ontology.[37] The highest principles in ontology are the principle of sufficient reason and the principle of non-contradiction.[38] Ontology is followed by the 'metaphysica specialis'. The system further spreads out to physics and finally practical philosophy. Practical philosophy is made up of general practical philosophy and natural law as theoretical disciplines (consisting of the parts of *jus naturale ethicum*,[39] *oeconomicum*,[40] and *politicum* (*jus publicum universale*).[41] The practical counterparts of these parts of the natural law are practical ethics,[42] economics,[43] and politics.[44] Remarkably, the classical social studies—ethics, economics, and politics—are transferred to legal concepts in this structure.[45] In practical philosophy and natural law, Wolff's method aims at founding social norms in seemingly objective and therefore neutral grounds. The background of this kind of a secular natural law in general is provided by the experience of the religious war. Wolff pushes this idea of scientific objectivism to its limits, thereby also

[33] Klaus-Gert Lutterbeck, *Staat und Gesellschaft bei Christian Thomasius und Christian Wolff: Eine historische Untersuchung in systematischer Absicht* (2002) pp. 144–5.

[34] Ibid., pp. 146–8. [35] Ibid., p. 149.

[36] For an outline of Wolff's system of science, see Christian Wolff, *Discursus praeliminaris de philosophia in genere, Einleitende Abhandlung über die Philosophie im Allgemeinen, historisch-kritische Ausgabe (1728)*, eds. Günter Gawlick and Lothar Kreimendahl (1996), Caput III: De partibus Philosophiae, §§ 55–114; Christian Wolff, *Philosophia rationalis sive logica, pars II sive practica*, ed. Jean École (1983), § 829 (here distinguishing himself from the scholastic method). On the structure of Wolff's philosophy, see also Jean École, 'Introduction de l'éditeur', in Jean École (ed.), *Philosophia rationalis sive logica, pars I sive theoretica* vol. 1.2, Christian Wolff, Gesammelte Werke. II. Abteilung, Lateinische Schriften (1983), V–LXXXVII, XIV–XXXIV, in particular the chart on pp. XXVIII–XX.

[37] Wolff, *Discursus praeliminaris de philosophia in genere, Einleitende Abhandlung über die Philosophie im Allgemeinen, historisch-kritische Ausgabe (1728)* (n. 36), § 73. By making ontology the basis of his universal science, Wolff follows Leibniz's example. See Lutterbeck, *Staat und Gesellschaft bei Christian Thomasius und Christian Wolff* (n. 33), pp. 146–8.

[38] Christian Wolff, *Philosophia prima sive Ontologia*, ed. Jean École (1977) §§ 27, 56; Lutterbeck, *Staat und Gesellschaft bei Christian Thomasius und Christian Wolff* (n. 33) 151.

[39] Wolff, *Jus Naturae, methodo scientifica pertractatum (1740–1748)* (n. 15), vol I.

[40] Ibid., vol VII. [41] Ibid., vol VIII.

[42] Christian Wolff, *Philosophia moralis sive ethica, methodo scientifica pertractata (5 vols, 1750–1753)*, eds. Jean École et al., 5 vols (1970–1973).

[43] *Oeconomica, methodo scientifica pertractata, pars prima, in qua agitur de societatibus minoribus conjugali, paterna et herili; pars reliqua, continuata et absoluta a Michaele Christophoro Hanovio*, 2 vols, reprint of the first edition, Halle 1754 and 1755, 1972 (partly authored by Wolff's disciple Hanov).

[44] Michael Christoph Hanov and Christian Wolff, *Philosophia civilis sive politica: exhibens principia cum generalia politicae publicae tum simplicibus civitatem formus propria*, vol. 47, Christian Wolff, Gesammelte Werke. III. Abteilung, Materialien und Dokumente, ed. Jean École, Hans Werner Arndt, J.E. Hofmann, and R. Thies (1998) (I–IV, partly authored by Wolff's disciple Hanov).

[45] Lutterbeck, *Staat und Gesellschaft bei Christian Thomasius und Christian Wolff* (n. 33), p. 183.

demonstrating his ambitious understanding of the role of the scholar or, as some would claim, of *himself* as a scholar.[46] Nevertheless, he does not break radically with the so-called *Schulphilosophie* or scholasticism. Rather, he tries to update classical thought and aims at a scientification of teleology.[47]

In Wolff's thought, logic as a general theory of knowledge provides the rules for reaching reliable conclusions in any scientific discipline, and it is also a path to a synthetic knowledge of the legal system.[48] Logic serves to ascertain a priori objective knowledge, the transcendental 'essence' of objects, or philosophical truth.[49] Objects in their 'existence' vary in an unpredictable manner, whilst in their 'essence' they are always the same, necessary and identical with themselves.[50] Since it is impossible that something can arise out of nothing (*ex nihilo nihil fit*),[51] everything that exists in time and space (*existentia*) must have its basis in something else (*essentia*) from which one can comprehend why it exists: a sufficient ground (*ratio sufficiens*, Leibniz) to its existence. Wolff calls this the principle of sufficient reason.[52] Based on the so-called principle of contradiction, Wolff claims that that which constitutes the reason cannot at the same time be based on something else, for what necessarily exists in this way requires no further ground for why it exists in this way.[53] That which is in itself the reason for everything else is the 'being'. It becomes perceivable to reason only through its manifestations. In a movement from possibility to reality, the manifestation is determined temporally and spatially—it is individualized and attaches accidental and coincidental attributes to necessary ones.

In parallel with Aristotle's distinction between knowledge of the cause of the fact and knowledge of fact,[54] Wolff distinguishes philosophical and historical knowledge: philosophical or scientific knowledge relates to *essentia*. Philosophy must strive to attain 'absolute certainty'; in other words, it must be a science that proves its assertions by deriving conclusions 'from certain and unshakable principles by valid

[46] For a critique of Wolff's monologist and restricted understanding of scholarship, see Frank Grunert, 'Absolutism(s): Necessary Ambivalences in the Political Theory of Christian Wolff', *Tijds Rgeschied* 73(1) (2005), 141–52, at 145–7.

[47] Max Wundt, *Die deutsche Schulphilosophie im Zeitalter der Aufklärung*, vol. 32, Heidelberger Abhandlungen zur Philosophie und ihrer Geschichte (1945), pp. 151–2.

[48] Claes Peterson, 'What Has Logic Got to Do with It? On the Use of Logic in Christian Wolff's Theory of Natural Law', *Sc.St.L.* 48 (2005), 310–20, at 310.

[49] For a comprehensive study on Wolff's method, see Juan Ignacio Gómez Tutor, *Die wissenschaftliche Methode bei Christian Wolff*, vol. 90, Christian Wolff, Gesammelte Werke. III. Abteilung, Materialien und Dokumente, ed. Jean École, Hans Werner Arndt, J.E. Hofmann, and R. Thies (2004). For this method applied to law, see Herbert Stupp, 'Mos geometricus oder Prudentia als Denkform der Jurisprudenz: Eine Untersuchung an Hand der methodologischen Lehren des Christian Wolff und des Thomas von Aquin' (1970), pp. 4–79.

[50] Christian Wolff, *Vernünfftige Gedancken von Gott, der Welt und der Seele des Menschen, auch allen Dingen überhaupt (Deutsche Metaphysik)*, ed. Charles A. Corr (1983), § 576. English translation (excerpts): Christian Wolff, 'Rational Thoughts on God, the World and the Soul of Human Beings, Also All Things in General (1720)', in Eric Watkins (ed.), *Kant's Critique of Pure Reason. Background Source Materials* (2009), pp. 7–53.

[51] Christian Wolff, *Vernünftige Gedanken von dem gesellschaftlichen Leben der Menschen und insonderheit dem gemeinen Wesen: 'Deutsche Politik'*, ed. Hasso Hofmann (2004), § 28.

[52] Ibid., § 30. [53] Ibid., § 32.

[54] Aristotle, *Posterior Analytics*, Edmund Spenser Bouchier ed. (1901) Book I, ch. XIII.

inference'.[55] Here, Wolff, like many philosophers of the modern period, believed that the method of mathematics could be used.[56] It rested on the conviction that it was possible, with the help of logic, to cross over the realm of experience and reach an a priori reason. So far, Wolff offers a specific formulation of the positions that Kant would later criticize as 'pure reason'.[57]

However, different from other rationalists,[58] Wolff insists that there are no a priori truths, i.e. truths discovered by reason alone, independent of experience. Philosophical demonstration is not sufficient because a priori reasons lack content and must be filled in with the help of historical knowledge or induction. This can be understood as an accommodation of the claims raised by the so-called empiricists, like Locke or Newton, who were the contemporary adversaries of the rationalists. Actually, Wolff wrote at a time when the intellectual climate was rather hostile towards the authority of reason.[59] He undertook to find correct definitions in which the logical attributes concur with the ontological, reason and experience being the two paths for cognizing the truth. They correspond to philosophical and historical knowledge; the former is grounded in the understanding, the latter in the senses[60] and refers to *existentia*. In a syllogistic way, there are two movements in knowledge: a movement from experience to reason—which is inductive, ascendant, or analytical—, and a movement from reason to experience—which is deductive, descendant, or synthetic. The former is the way to demonstrate positive law, while the latter is applied to demonstrate natural law propositions that stem from necessary reasons. Wolff therefore provides for a 'marriage of reason and experience',[61] and his rationalism is thereby qualified.[62]

Systematization plays a special role in Wolff's reasoning. Systematization in the realm of objects is defined with the help of logic and provides for a path to scientific knowledge.[63] A system is a combination of truths, a concept that appears relatively late in Wolff's works. It is closely related to his method because a combination of propositions in a system constitutes a demonstration. The combination of truths forms a 'systema doctrinarum'. In his essay 'De differentia intellectus systematici &

[55] Wolff, *Discursus praeliminaris de philosophia in genere, Einleitende Abhandlung über die Philosophie im Allgemeinen, historisch-kritische Ausgabe (1728)* (n. 36), § 33.

[56] Ibid., §139, Wolff states: 'The philosophical method follows the same rules as the method of mathematics' ('Methodi philosophicae eaedem sunt regulae, quae methodi mathematicae').

[57] See Eric Watkins, 'Introduction', in Eric Watkins (ed.), *Kant's Critique of Pure Reason: Background Source Materials* (2009), pp. 1–4, at p.2.

[58] See Tim J. Hochstrasser, *Natural Law Theories in the Early Enlightenment*, vol. 58, Ideas in Context (2000), 161, who claims that Wolff—even in the course of a lengthy correspondence—failed to engage fully with the metaphysics of Leibnizian ontology.

[59] Hettche, 'Christian Wolff' (n. 32).

[60] Wolff, *Vernünftige Gedanken von dem gesellschaftlichen Leben der Menschen und insonderheit dem gemeinen Wesen: 'Deutsche Politik'* (n. 51), § 372.

[61] Lewis White Beck, 'From Leibniz to Kant', in Robert C. Solomon and Kathleen Marie Higgins (eds.), *The Age of German Idealism*. vol. 6, Routledge History of Philosophy (1993), pp. 5–39, at p. 10.

[62] Jean École, 'En quels sens peut-on dire que Wolff est rationaliste?', *Studia Leibnitiana* 11(1) (1979), 45–61.

[63] Peterson, 'What Has Logic Got to Do with It? On the Use of Logic in Christian Wolff's Theory of Natural Law' (n. 48), p. 312.

non systematici', which is contained in the first volume of his 'Horae subsecivae Marburgenses',[64] Wolff refers to four distinct advantages of demonstration qua system: First, a combination of propositions makes their truth more evident than isolated propositions. Second, if one makes sure that the premises of the system are not erroneous, a system allows a safe development of scholarship. Third, the system avoids contradictions, and fourth, it makes errors easily detectable.[65]

Wolff's understanding of his method somehow disqualifies his image as a champion of academic freedom. His defence of the *libertas philosophandi* only refers to those who engage in philosophy 'according to philosophical method', and not to freedom of thought in general. Wolff also has a narrow understanding of what defines philosophy and which methods are philosophical. Actually, the true philosophical method is his own. Philosophical criticism does not take place in a public discourse, but is somehow monologist and restricted to a certain method.[66]

2. Meaning and function of the *civitas maxima*

While the principle of sufficient reason and the principle of non-contradiction explained so far determine the form of Wolff's practical philosophy, the principle of perfection determines its content. In Wolff's practical philosophy, 'perfection' is a central concept.[67] Wolff derives the notion of perfection from the notions of order ('Ordnung') and truth ('Wahrheit').[68] Wolff's legal philosophy as part of his practical philosophy is built on two lines of argument: on the one hand, he develops a contractual model of rationalism, using the concepts of fiction, of the fictitious moral person and the fictitious presumed consent, contract, and quasi-contract. On the other hand, he refers to ontological assumptions and natural teleology.[69] Supposedly, Wolff is the last systematic thinker to give this teleological vision unqualified support.[70]

Optimal perfection will only be reached if all acts of all men and associations are optimally coordinated in an organized world association. The pursuit of self-perfection implies association. Natural law therefore comprises the imperative to form associations.[71] Ultimately, nature herself has established a society among

[64] Christian Wolff, *Horae subsecivae Marburgenses, anni MDCCXXIX, quibus philosophia ad publicam privatamque utilitatem aptatur*, ed. Jean École (1983), pp. 107–54.

[65] On the relation between Wolff's 'methodus scientifica' and system, see Gómez Tutor, *Die wissenschaftliche Methode bei Christian Wolff* (n. 49), pp. 271–7.

[66] Grunert, 'Absolutism(s): Necessary Ambivalences in the Political Theory of Christian Wolff' (46), pp. 145–6, 150.

[67] See Frank Grunert, 'Vollkommenheit als (politische) Norm: Zur politischen Philosophie von Christian Wolff, 1679–1754', in Bernd Heidenreich and Gerhard Göhler (eds.), *Politische Theorien des 17. und 18. Jahrhunderts. Staat und Politik in Deutschland* (2011), pp. 164–84.

[68] Wolff, *Vernünfftige Gedancken von Gott, der Welt und der Seele des Menschen, auch allen Dingen überhaupt (Deutsche Metaphysik)* (n. 50), §§ 132, 142, 145; cf. Lutterbeck, *Staat und Gesellschaft bei Christian Thomasius und Christian Wolff* (n. 33), p. 173.

[69] See, generally, Christian Schröer, *Naturbegriff und Moralbegründung: Die Grundlegung der Ethik bei Christian Wolff und deren Kritik durch Immanuel Kant*, vol. 3, Münchener philosophische Studien (1988).

[70] Onuf, '*Civitas maxima:* Wolff, Vattel and the Fate of Republicanism' (n. 7), p. 283.

[71] Wolff, *Jus Naturae, methodo scientifica pertractatum (1740-1748)* (n. 15), vol VII, § 138.

mankind and binds them to preserve it. This *societas magna* represents the association of humanity.[72] Wolff assumes that, after humanity was divided into nations, the society that so far had existed between individuals continued to exist between nations.[73] Individual states are equated with 'individual free persons living in a state of nature'.[74] Optimal self-perfection cannot be accomplished within the state, but necessitates the universal *civitas*.[75] States would be established contrary to the law of nature if their particular societies did away with the *societas magna*. Accordingly, states have the natural-law duty to preserve and perfect themselves by associating in the *civitas maxima*.[76] In contrast to the *societas magna*, the *civitas maxima* is constituted of states as moral persons, an association of associations,[77] not a homogenous world state.[78] The purpose of the *civitas maxima* is to 'give mutual assistance in perfecting itself and its condition', the 'promotion of the common good by its combined powers'.[79]

With the *civitas maxima* as an association of associations, Wolff shares an Aristotelian view of the steps of human association.[80] By way of modernizing Aristotelian metaphysics, Wolff also refers to Leibniz. His *civitas maxima* builds on Leibniz's *civitas dei*.[81] As indicated by the epithet 'maxima',[82] the *civitas maxima* is the most inclusive of all human communities.[83] However, even the *civitas maxima* is not the endpoint of perfection of individuals, which is unachievable. For Wolff, the common goal of humanity is identical with the goals of any individual, but cannot be realized by the individual on its own; rather, it presupposes the optimal cooperation in a world system.[84] Since Wolff's natural law does not lay down any goals external to the pursuit of self-perfection, it has been called a 'Hobbesian instrument of the "self"'.[85] According to this 'individualist' origin, Wolff's *civitas maxima* has an ethical and communitarian purpose, but is a decentralized legal community.

[72] Ibid., vol VII, § 142.

[73] Wolff, *Jus Gentium Methodo Scientifica Pertractatum (1764)* (n. 12), § 7, commentary.

[74] Ibid., § 16.

[75] Hanov and Wolff, *Philosophia civilis sive politica* (n. 44), pars 1, exhibens principia cum generalia politicae publicae tum simplicibus civitatum formis propria, § 73.

[76] Wolff, *Jus Gentium Methodo Scientifica Pertractatum (1764)* (n. 12), §§ 8, 9.

[77] Ibid., § 10; see Onuf, '*Civitas maxima:* Wolff, Vattel and the Fate of Republicanism' (n. 7), p. 295; Francis Cheneval, 'Der präsumtiv vernünftige Konsens der Menschen und Völker – Christian Wolffs Theorie der civitas maxima', *ARSP* 85(4) (1999), 563–80, at 565.

[78] But see Otfried Höffe, 'Für und wider die Weltrepublik', *IZPh* 2 (1997), 218–33, 224.

[79] Wolff, *Jus Gentium Methodo Scientifica Pertractatum (1764)* (n. 12), § 8.

[80] Hanns-Martin Bachmann, *Die naturrechtliche Staatslehre Christian Wolffs*, vol. 27, Schriften zur Verfassungsgeschichte (1977), p. 120.

[81] Cheneval, *Philosophie in weltbürgerlicher Bedeutung* (n. 22), p. 132.

[82] Wolff, *Jus Gentium Methodo Scientifica Pertractatum (1764)* (n. 12), § 10, commentary; cf. Onuf, '*Civitas maxima:* Wolff, Vattel and the Fate of Republicanism' (n. 7), pp. 292–6.

[83] For a dissertation on Wolff's *civitas maxima*, see Kurt Prigge, 'Christian Wolffs Lehre von der civitas maxima gentium' (1953).

[84] Cheneval, 'Der präsumtiv vernünftige Konsens der Menschen und Völker – Christian Wolffs Theorie der civitas maxima' (n. 77), p. 571.

[85] Martti Koskenniemi, *From Apology to Utopia: The Structure of International Legal Argument* (1989), p. 86.

Therefore, despite their conceptual differences, the discrepancy between Wolff's and Vattel's teachings may not be as great as one might imagine.[86] For Wolff, there is a reciprocal relationship between the whole and its parts: inasmuch as nations are understood to have combined in the *civitas maxima*, the individual nations are understood to have bound themselves to the whole because they wish to promote the common good, but the whole to the individuals, because it wishes to provide for the especial good of the individuals.[87] Sovereignty in the *civitas maxima* is divisible: 'Some sovereignty over individual nations belongs also to nations as a whole.'[88]

The *civitas maxima* is a fiction,[89] based on a fictitious treaty, a 'quasi-agreement' between states ('as if by agreement'):[90]

> [S]ince nations, which know the advantages arising therefrom, by a natural impulse are carried into this association, which binds the human race or all nations one to the other, since moreover it is assumed that others will unite in it, if they know their own interests; what can be said except that nations also have combined into society as if by agreement? So all nations are understood to have come together into a state, whose separate nations are separate members or individual states.[91]

Wolff founds any form of association on a contract or quasi-contract, which he understands to be of merely hypothetical character, based on conditions of rational reciprocity and normativity.[92] He compares the states' situation in the *civitas maxima* to tutelage, where it is presumed that the pupil agrees. Comparably, nations are presumed to agree to this association, even if—through lack of insight—they fail to see how great an advantage it is to be a member of the *civitas maxima*:

> [I]n establishing this quasi-agreement we have assumed nothing which is at variance with reason, or which may not be allowed in other quasi-agreements. For that nations are carried into that association by a certain natural impulse is apparent from their acts [. . .]. Therefore do not persuade yourself that there is any nation that is not known to unite to form the state, into which nature herself commands all to combine. But just as in tutelage it is rightly presumed that the pupil agrees, in so far as he ought to agree, nay, more, as he would be likely to agree, if he knew his own interest; so none the less nations which through lack of insight fail to see how great an advantage it is to be a member of that supreme state, are presumed to agree to this association. And since it is understood in a civil state that the tutor is compelled to act, if he should be unwilling to consent of his own accord, but that even when the agreement is extorted by a superior force that does not prevent the tutelage from resting upon a quasi-agreement; why, then, is it not allowable to attribute the same force to the natural obligation by which nations are compelled to enter into an alliance as

[86] Alexander Orakhelashvili, 'The Origins of Consensual Positivism: Pufendorf, Wolff and Vattel', edited by Alexander Orakhelashvili, in *Research Handbook on the Theory and History of International Law*. Research Handbooks in International Law (2011), pp. 93–110, pp. 97–8.

[87] Wolff, *Jus Gentium Methodo Scientifica Pertractatum (1764)* (n. 12), § 12.

[88] Ibid, § 15.

[89] Ibid., § 21.

[90] Ibid., § 9. See Wolfgang Dzialas, 'Christian Wolffs Völkerrechtstheorie: Herkunft und Wirkung' (1956) 31: association 'more geometrico'.

[91] Wolff, *Jus Gentium Methodo Scientifica Pertractatum (1764)* (n. 12), § 9.

[92] Cheneval, 'Der präsumtiv vernünftige Konsens der Menschen und Völker – Christian Wolffs Theorie der civitas maxima' (n. 77), p. 569.

is attributed to the civil obligation, that it is understood to force consent even as from one unwilling?[93]

One can well imagine that this comparison with tutelage makes sovereign rulers uneasy. They would be ready to benefit from scholarly knowledge but not in need of an academic guardian. Yet, the notions of the quasi-contract and the presumed consent, initially only heuristic devices and regulative ideas, also introduce an element of paternalism into contract theory.[94]

Fictions are important for philosophical knowledge, as explained above, philosophy being the science of the possible, insofar as it can be that.[95] Fictions are defined as that which we presume to be possible despite the fact that reality goes against it.[96] They can be understood as the exclusive product of human reason and are only based on the principle of non-contradiction.[97] Wolff was well aware of the fact that there was no such thing as a real world state; nor did he suggest establishing one.[98] Therefore, the critique that the *civitas maxima* does not capture the reality of international relations[99] is somehow misleading. The *civitas maxima* is also, quite counterfactually, a 'kind of democratic form of government' ('quidam popularis') because nations are free and equal to each other.[100] Neither under natural law nor under the law of nations does power give one nation a special privilege over another.[101]

3. Categories of norms

The *civitas maxima* is considered to be the 'most original trait of Wolff's system of international law'.[102] It is also this trait of his system that goes to the core of the differences between Wolff and Grotius and the meaning of the *civitas maxima*. In the *Prolegomena* to his *Jus gentium*, Wolff claims that the concept of a *civitas maxima* was not unknown to Grotius, 'nor was he ignorant of the fact that the law of nations

[93] Wolff, *Jus Gentium Methodo Scientifica Pertractatum (1764)* (n. 12), § 9, commentary.

[94] Cheneval, 'Der präsumtiv vernünftige Konsens der Menschen und Völker – Christian Wolffs Theorie der civitas maxima' (n. 77), p. 570.

[95] Werner Schneiders, 'Deus est philosophus absolute summus: Über Christian Wolffs Philosophie und Philosophieverständnis', in Werner Schneiders (ed.), *Christian Wolff 1679–1754: Interpretationen zu seiner Philosophie und deren Wirkung*, Mit einer Bibliographie der Wolff-Literatur. vol. 4, Studien zum achtzehnten Jahrhundert, Deutsche Gesellschaft für die Erforschung des 18. Jahrhunderts (1983), pp. 9–30.

[96] Ontologia, I, ii, 3, § 140 (my own translation).

[97] Cheneval, 'Der präsumtiv vernünftige Konsens der Menschen und Völker – Christian Wolffs Theorie der civitas maxima' (n. 77), p. 567.

[98] Schiffer, *The Legal Community of Mankind* (n. 7), pp. 73–4.

[99] Prigge, 'Christian Wolffs Lehre von der civitas maxima gentium' (n. 83), *passim*; Schiffer, *The Legal Community of Mankind* (n. 7), pp. 78 and 319 (endnote 141).

[100] Wolff, *Jus Gentium Methodo Scientifica Pertractatum (1764)* (n. 12), § 19.

[101] Ibid., § 18.

[102] Louis Olive, 'Wolff', in Antoine Pillet and Denis Alland (eds.), *Les fondateurs du droit international* (2014), pp. 447–79, p. 459.

was based on it, but nevertheless he did not derive from it the law of nations which is called voluntary, as he could and ought to have done'.[103] In Wolff's system, the *jus gentium voluntarium* is directly related to the *civitas maxima*; it is deduced from the notion and purpose of the *civitas maxima*—'which nature herself established' so that nations are bound to agree to that law—on the basis of the equality of (civilized) states.[104] Vattel, in turn, will derive the *jus gentium voluntarium* essentially from 'the natural liberty of nations'.[105]

The *civitas maxima* has the right to promulgate 'laws with respect to those things which concern it' and 'prescribe the means by which its good is maintained'. For Wolff, it is 'evident enough of what sort those laws ought to be that nations ought to agree to' and consequently may be presumed to have agreed to.[106] The actual practice is, however, less promising:

> Nevertheless, since in a democratic state it is necessary that individuals assemble in a definite place and declare their will as to what ought to be done, since moreover all the nations scattered throughout the whole world cannot assemble together, as is self-evident, that must be taken to be the will of all nations which they are bound to agree upon, if following the leadership of nature they use right reason. Hence it is plain, because it has to be admitted, that what has been approved by the more civilized nations is the law of nations.[107]

It is actually approval by 'the more civilized nations' that matters. As other writers before him, Wolff distinguishes between 'barbarous nations' and 'cultured and civilized nations'.[108] Not surprisingly, Wolff is therefore also mentioned in the context of the 'colonial origins' of international law.[109] Wolff even refers to a fictitious ruler of the *civitas maxima*, who promulgates the *jus gentium voluntarium*:

> [H]e can be considered the ruler of the supreme state who, following the leadership of nature, defines by the right use of reason what nations ought to consider as law among themselves, although it does not conform in all respects to the natural law of nations, nor altogether differ from it.[110]

The *jus gentium voluntarium* is 'considered to have been laid down by this fictitious ruler and so to have proceeded from the will of nations'. Wolff points out that the voluntary law of nations is therefore 'equivalent to the civil law' and 'derived in the same manner from the necessary law of nations, as [...] the civil law must

[103] Wolff, *Jus Gentium Methodo Scientifica Pertractatum (1764)* (n. 12), § 10.

[104] Ibid., § 20, commentary; § 26. On natural law equality: Wolff, *Jus Naturae, methodo scientifica pertractatum (1740–1748)* (n. 15), vol VIII, §§ 50–3.

[105] Vattel, *The Law of Nations, Or, Principles of the Law of Nature, of Nations and Sovereigns, with Three Early Essays on the Origin and Nature of Natural Law and on Luxury* (n. 29), p. 16.

[106] Wolff, *Jus Gentium Methodo Scientifica Pertractatum (1764)* (n. 12), § 11, commentary.

[107] Ibid., § 20. [108] Ibid., §§ 52, 53.

[109] Brett Bowden, 'The Colonial Origins of International Law. European Expansion and the Classical Standard of Civilization', *J Hist Int Law* 7(1) (2005), 1–24, at 14–15. See, however, for a defence of Wolff, Georg Cavallar, 'Vitoria, Grotius, Pufendorf, Wolff and Vattel: Accomplices of European Colonialism and Exploitation or True Cosmopolitans?', *J Hist Int Law* 10(2) (2008), 181–209, at 200–4: Wolff's as 'The First Culturally Sensitive International Legal Theory'.

[110] Wolff, *Jus Gentium Methodo Scientifica Pertractatum (1764)* (n. 12), § 21.

be derived from the natural law [...]'.[111] This distinguishes Wolff from the 'sorry comforters' Vattel, Grotius, and Pufendorf: they do not apply the theory of civil law to public international law, but continue to work on the theory of just war under the conditions of the absence of an international ruler under the rule of law.[112]

The *jus gentium voluntarium* also reflects the two movements of knowledge. It is deeply rooted in Wolff's scientific method and combines reason and experience by taking into account that 'the condition of men is such that in a state one cannot completely satisfy in all details the rigour of the law of nature'. For this reason, Wolff sees a need of positive laws, 'which do not differ altogether from the law of nature, nor observe it in all details'. On the other hand, since the common welfare itself of nations demands the immutable natural law, nations are none the less bound by nature to an observance of natural law.[113] A post-modern observer described the *jus gentium voluntarium* as a 'strategy of reconciliation', 'a reconciliation between a given natural law and a law which emerges from international reality'.[114] This is obviously an appropriate way to put it. However, the roots of this reconciliatory strategy go much deeper and lie in the combination of philosophical and historical knowledge.

The contents of the *jus gentium naturale vel necessarium* are limited. They include the duty of states to associate with the *civitas maxima*, the moral equality of states and of their rights and obligations[115] and a right of the *civitas maxima* to coerce the individual states.[116] The central natural law obligation is to overcome the state of nature: *exeundum est e statu naturali*.[117] Natural law, or a 'necessary law of nations', binds nations in conscience.[118]

Altogether, Wolff distinguishes four categories of norms: the two categories already referred to—the natural or necessary law of nations (*jus gentium naturale vel necessarium*) and the voluntary law of nations (*jus gentium voluntarium*)—and, beyond these two categories of 'universal' international law, international treaty or stipulative law (*jus gentium pacititium*, § 23) and customary international law (*jus gentium consuetudinarium*, § 24). The positive law of nations (*jus gentium positivum*) is the generic term for the voluntary, the stipulative, and the customary law of nations.[119] However, Wolff is not very interested in the two categories of the 'particular' law of nations, stipulative and customary law.[120] The stipulative

[111] Ibid., § 22.

[112] Cheneval, 'Der präsumtiv vernünftige Konsens der Menschen und Völker – Christian Wolffs Theorie der civitas maxima' (n. 77), p. 564.

[113] Wolff, *Jus Gentium Methodo Scientifica Pertractatum (1764)* (n. 12), Preface, pp. 5–6.

[114] Koskenniemi, *From Apology to Utopia* (n. 85), pp. 86–7.

[115] Wolff, *Jus Gentium Methodo Scientifica Pertractatum (1764)* (n. 12), § 16–17.

[116] Ibid., § 13. See also Wolff, *Institutiones juris naturae et gentium* (n. 13), § 1089, where Wolff refers to the equality, liberty, and integrity as contents of the *jus gentium naturale*.

[117] Wolff, *Jus Naturae, methodo scientifica pertractatum (1740–1748)* (n. 15), vol 8, § 138; cf. Onuf, '*Civitas maxima:* Wolff, Vattel and the Fate of Republicanism' (n. 7), p. 283.

[118] Wolff, *Jus Gentium Methodo Scientifica Pertractatum (1764)* (n. 12), § 4.

[119] Ibid., § 25.

[120] Very critically, Nussbaum, *A Concise History of the Law of Nations* (n. 5), p. 154, 'practically ignored by Wolff'. Nussbaum particularly refers to the law of ambassadors where Wolff's treatment contradicts the state of the law. Wolff is obviously aware of this discrepancy, but not interested in

law of nations derives its validity from natural law, which commands that agreements should be observed (*pacta sunt servanda*). Wolff divides stipulations into treaties (which are reciprocally entered into forever or for a considerable time) and compacts (which contain temporary promises or those not to be repeated).[121] Customary international law is presented as a tacit agreement, accordingly also binding under natural law. Distancing himself from Grotius, Wolff insists that customary international law be distinguished from the common law of nations, i.e. natural law or voluntary law. The voluntary law of nations (*jus gentium voluntarium*) is not determined from acts of nations and is 'not left to their caprice as to whether they should prefer to agree or not'.[122] States, in their actual practice, can err. This may influence their tacit agreements, but it leaves both the natural and the voluntary law unaffected.[123] Different from Grotius, Wolff is interested neither in legal sources nor in juristic literature. His references are mostly to his own works, in particular his *Jus Naturae*.[124] He also cites legal philosophers such as Cicero or Grotius, albeit very rarely.[125]

Most of the space is dedicated to the *jus gentium voluntarium*. The treatise *Jus gentium methodo scientifica pertractatum* comprises 1068 paragraphs and covers a broad area of subjects such as ownership by nations, the law of treaties and other agreements, the method of settling controversies between nations, the law of war and the rules of warfare, peace, and peace treaties, and the law of embassies. The longest chapters refer to the law of treaties and other agreements (ch. IV), the law of war (ch. VI) and the rules of warfare (ch. VII).[126]

IV. Three Transitions and Wolff's *Jus Gentium Voluntarium*

We have seen thus far that the particular way in which Wolff understands the *jus gentium voluntarium* is closely related to this systematic method and the combination of philosophical and historical knowledge. Wolff's method also explains why the *civitas maxima* and the *jus gentium voluntarium* take centre stage, while the *jus gentium pacititium* and the *jus gentium consuetudinarium* are more or less neglected. We will now move on to analyse in what way it not only represents a reconciliation between reason and experience, but subconsciously also marks three transitions in

bringing his treatment of the law of nations, necessary or volitional, in line with what Nussbaum would later call 'the actual law'.

[121] Wolff, *Jus Gentium Methodo Scientifica Pertractatum (1764)* (n. 12), § 369.

[122] Ibid., § 20, commentary; § 26. [123] Ibid., 7.

[124] Wolff, *Jus Naturae, methodo scientifica pertractatum (1740–1748)* (n. 15).

[125] Nussbaum, *A Concise History of the Law of Nations* (n. 5), pp. 151–2.

[126] *Prolegomena*: §§ 1–26; Ch. I: *Of the Duties of Nations to Themselves*: §§ 27–155; Ch. II: *Of the Duties of Nations toward Each Other*: §§ 156–273; Ch. III: *Of Ownership by Nations*: §§ 274–367; Ch. IV: *Of Treaties and other Agreements, and Of Promises*: §§ 368–560; Ch. V: *Of the Method of Settling Controversies of Nations*: §§ 562–606; Ch. VI: *Of the Law of War of Nations*: §§ 607–776; Ch. VII: *Of the Law of Nations in War*: §§ 777–958; Ch. VIII: *Of Peace and the Treaty of Peace*: §§ 959–1040; Ch. IX: *Of the Law of Embassies*: §§ 1041–68.

international law scholarship. First, we can observe a process of an autonomization of international law (1); second, a shift from natural law to positivism (2); and third, a shifting focus from law to political economy (3). In a paradoxical manner, Wolff's specific approach to the study of international law and his scientific method contributed to these transitions in international legal thought and, at the same time, hid them behind ambiguity.

1. The autonomization of international law

First, we can locate Wolff in the middle of the autonomization of international law as a distinct field of law, as 'a law peculiar to nations'.[127] In this regard, Wolff plays an important role in the emergence of classic international law and can be seen as a true precursor to Vattel. *Jus gentium* as understood by Wolff does not apply to individuals but to nations as moral persons. Obviously for the first time, the abstract personality of the 'state' (and not the ruler) becomes really the exclusive subject of a distinct category of norms, rights, and duties.[128] Essentially, the *jus gentium* becomes an independent category of its own as positive law between states. Different from the *jus gentium* as known before and in Grotius, it is no longer a law between human beings. Johannes Althusius, in his *Politica methodice digesta*,[129] had already clearly expressed the idea of the *populus* as a fictional corporate person, of which the ruling individual or group is merely the highest agent.[130] Grotius was less clear in this regard. He spoke of the *civitas* as the general subject of sovereignty, and of the ruling individual or group as its particular subject.[131] Hobbes and Pufendorf referred to institutions and representatives as fictitious persons.[132] Pufendorf, in 1672,[133] described the state as 'a composite moral person whose will, compounded of the concord of many, is deemed the will of all'.[134] Compared to these authors, Wolff can be regarded as an innovator in this respect.

Several scholars have highlighted this contribution of Wolff's to the autonomization of *jus gentium* as the law between states as legal persons. While Emmanuelle Jouannet approaches Wolff with the primary aim of understanding Vattelian thought and classical international law, Nicholas Onuf points to a complex change from a 'republican' law of nature and nations to a 'liberal' distinction between the

[127] Wolff, *Jus Gentium Methodo Scientifica Pertractatum (1764)* (n. 12), p. 5.

[128] Percy Ellwood Corbett, *Law and Society in the Relations of States* (1951), p. 54; Emmanuelle Jouannet, *Emer de Vattel et l'émergence doctrinale du droit international classique*, vol. 50, Publication de la Revue Générale du Droit International Public (1998), pp. 394–5.

[129] Johannes Althusius, *Politica methodice digesta (1614)*, ed. Carl Joachim Friedrich (1932) Chap. ix, secs. 14–19.

[130] See Corbett, *Law and Society in the Relations of States* (n. 128), p. 54; Onuf, '*Civitas maxima:* Wolff, Vattel and the Fate of Republicanism' (n. 7), p. 295.

[131] Hugo Grotius, *De Jure Belli ac Pacis Libri Tres, in quibus Jus Naturae & Gentium, item Juris Publici praecipua explicantur* (1925) Bk. I, ch. iii, sec. 7.

[132] Thomas Hobbes, *Leviathan (1651)* (1929), ch. 16; Samuel Pufendorf, *De jure naturae et gentium libri octo (1688)*, Charles Henry Oldfather and William Abbott Oldfather, vol. 17, The Classics of International Law, ed. James Brown Scott (1934) Bk. VII, ch. ii, sec. 13.

[133] Ibid.

[134] Corbett, *Law and Society in the Relations of States* (n. 128), p. 54.

domestic and international legal spheres. According to Onuf's account, this change took place still under the 'aegis of republicanism', but resulted in 'liberalism and the impersonal state'.[135] As we have already seen, in Wolff's *civitas maxima*, an association of associations or, in Onuf's parlance, a 'republica composita',[136] there is no direct link between the *civitas maxima* and the individual. Scholars have also pointed out that this 'autonomization' or, in that sense, 'liberalization' of international law is not necessarily a story of progress. One can also regard it as a kind of decay,[137] and many of the scholars who take a critical stance towards Wolff obviously have one major point of criticism exactly here.[138]

Be that as it may, Wolff was farther away from Grotius than he admitted or was even aware of. Contrary to his own self-perception, Wolff was heavily influenced by how Grotius's writings had been received in the 115 years that had passed since the publication of Grotius's *De Iure Belli Ac Pacis* when Wolff started writing his *Jus Gentium.*[139] His writing 'set the seal' on an ongoing autonomization of international law,[140] and yet he did not fully accomplish it. Apart from Wolff's explicit announcement, on the first page of the *Preface*, that *jus gentium* would be treated 'separately as a law peculiar to nations',[141] the distinctness of the *jus gentium* as a separate category of law and its particular significance is already signalled by the fact that the work on *jus gentium* is published separately from the eight volumes on *jus naturae*. However, in the *Institutiones*, Wolff deals with the treatise on *jus gentium* as a ninth volume of his *Jus naturae*.[142] Beyond a certain indecisiveness which we can witness here, there is a certain ambiguity or even irony in the very fact that just a polymath and systematizer of all knowledge like Wolff played an important role in the autonomization of international law as a distinct area of law and ultimately as an academic discipline. Therefore, it was left to Vattel to take a further step forward in the autonomization of international law by cutting the methodological ties that linked Wolff's *jus gentium voluntarium* to the rest of his philosophy.

2. From natural law to positivism

A second, interrelated transition discernible in Wolff's work is a movement from natural law to positivism.[143] This seems similarly paradoxical at first, given the scant attention that Wolff dedicates to stipulative and customary international law. Also,

[135] Onuf, '*Civitas maxima*: Wolff, Vattel and the Fate of Republicanism' (n. 7), p. 281.

[136] Ibid., p. 296.

[137] Reibstein, 'Deutsche Grotius-Kommentatoren bis zu Christian Wolff' (n. 11), p. 100; Jouannet, *Emer de Vattel et l'émergence doctrinale du droit international classique* (n. 128), 398.

[138] See e.g. Kohler, 'Die spanischen Naturrechtslehrer des 16. und 17. Jahrhunderts' (n. 26).

[139] Reibstein, 'Deutsche Grotius-Kommentatoren bis zu Christian Wolff' (n. 11), p. 81.

[140] Ibid., p. 97.

[141] Wolff, *Jus Gentium Methodo Scientifica Pertractatum (1764)* (n. 12), p. 5.

[142] See Jouannet, *Emer de Vattel et l'émergence doctrinale du droit international classique* (n. 128), p. 396.

[143] Cheneval, 'Der präsumtiv vernünftige Konsens der Menschen und Völker – Christian Wolffs Theorie der civitas maxima' (n. 77), p. 564: a major contribution to the positivist turn in international legal thought.

the subtitle of Wolff's *Jus gentium* ('in quo jus gentium naturale ab eo, quod voluntarii, pactitii et consuetudinarii est, accurate distinguitur')[144] emphasizes that it is an exposition of natural law that is 'accurately' distinguished from voluntary law, stipulative, and customary law as forms of positive law. As we have seen, the natural law foundation of the treatise guarantees its scientific character.[145]

Indeed, it might be misleading to regard Wolff as an originator of consensual positivism.[146] The idea becomes clearer if we think of the Kelsenian variant of positivism. Kelsen, in his 1920 work on *The Problem of Sovereignty*, indeed embraced Wolff's concepts of the *civitas maxima* and *jus gentium voluntarium*. Both fit neatly with Kelsen's pure theory of law. As understood by Kelsen, Wolff's stipulative and customary international law derive their validity from volitional international law (*jus gentium voluntarium*), which in turn is positive law in the sense that it is derived from a presupposed hypothetical basic norm of international law. For Kelsen, Wolff's decisive move is that he restricts the contents of natural law to the idea of a legal community based on the freedom and equality of states as moral persons and the imperative to overcome the state of nature. Accordingly, the natural law basis of international law—as a juridical hypothesis—has the limited function of allowing for the positive making of international law between coordinate subjects. Furthermore, the concept of a moral person allows an emphasis of the identity of state and world state.[147] Drake's translation of *civitas maxima* with 'supreme state',[148] which has been much criticized,[149] would not have been a problem for Kelsen.[150] The decisive point—in which Wolff also distinguishes himself from Pufendorf—is that Wolff identifies the natural law basis for the binding force of positive law. Unlike in Pufendorf's understanding, natural and positive law are not mutually inimical, but the natural law provides for the very basis from which the validity of positive law is derived.[151] Beyond this, it can also be assumed that the critical function of method in Wolff's work was very appealing for the founder of a pure theory of law.

Wolff's theory still rested on the idea that there existed a universal law of nature and reason in which all legal rules had their ultimate common basis,

[144] English translation: 'in which the natural law of nations is carefully distinguished from that which is voluntary, stipulative, and customary'.

[145] See Walter Jaeschke, 'Vom Völkerrecht zum Völkerrecht. Ein Beitrag zum Verhältnis von Philosophie und Rechtsgeschichte', *DZPhil* 56(2) (2008), 277, 284.

[146] Schiffer, *The Legal Community of Mankind* (n. 7), p. 79: 'Wolff's volitional law of nations had not been really positive law because its general rules did not have their origin in human will but were derived from the presumed consent of the members of the international community'. But see Orakhelashvili, 'The Origins of Consensual Positivism: Pufendorf, Wolff and Vattel' (n. 86).

[147] Hans Kelsen, *Das Problem der Souveränität und die Theorie des Völkerrechts: Beitrag zu einer reinen Rechtslehre* (1920), pp. 241–4, 249–55.

[148] Wolff, *Jus Gentium Methodo Scientifica Pertractatum (1764)* (n. 12), p. 3, *passim*.

[149] See Onuf, '*Civitas maxima:* Wolff, Vattel and the Fate of Republicanism' (n. 7), pp. 287–92.

[150] Kelsen, *Das Problem der Souveränität und die Theorie des Völkerrechts* (n. 147), p. 249.

[151] Orakhelashvili, 'The Origins of Consensual Positivism: Pufendorf, Wolff and Vattel' (n. 86), p. 100.

Der Hausknecht der Deutschen Gesandtschaft in Brüssel wurde beauftragt, einen dort herumlungernden Asiaten von der Wahnvorstellung, er sei ein Preuße, zu heilen.

Plate 1. Albert Einstein's departure from Germany.
This cartoon from the *Deutsche Tageszeitung* of 1 April 1933 says, 'The manservant at the German Embassy in Brussels was charged with curing a loitering Asian of the crazy idea that he was a Prussian'. Einstein had left Berlin for the United States in December 1932, just before the Nazis came to power. However several months later, he returned briefly to Europe, renting a house in Belgium. From there, he gave up the German citizenship he had acquired in 1914 and soon left Europe for good. The publication date of the cartoon was not accidental. It marked the official Nazi boycott of Jewish shops and businesses, the beginning of a campaign of systematic persecution. (Bildarchiv Preussischer Kulturbesitz, courtesy Réunion des musées nationaux, agence photographique, Paris)

Plate 2. *Reichstag* fire, 1933.
In February 1933, the *Reichstag*, the German Parliament building in Berlin, went up in flames. Nobody knows for sure who was responsible, but it gave the newly elected Nazis the chance to blame the disaster on others. Hitler pushed through 'emergency' legislation to enable political decisions to be taken without parliamentary approval. One of the first of these acts was the 'Restoration of the Civil Service', which purged German universities of Jewish professors and teachers. (Photo Imperial War Museum, London)

Plate 3. Nobel Prize for Physics, 1933.
In 1933, the Nobel Prize for Physics, 1933 was awarded to Erwin Schrödinger, Werner Heisenberg, and Paul Dirac for their development of quantum mechanics (Heisenberg's award being held over from 1932). None of them was Jewish. This photograph, taken at Stockholm railway station, shows (*right to left*) Schrödinger, aged 46, Heisenberg, 32, and Dirac, 31, with Dirac's mother, Schrödinger's wife Anny, and Heisenberg's mother. Schrödinger's flamboyant attire contrasts with the others' sedateness. Such was his lifestyle: Anny Schrödinger had by that time ceased to play a conventional matrimonial role in his life. Schrödinger had recently left Germany in protest against Nazi policy in general, and their treatment of the Jews in particular. In spite of his Nobel Prize, Heisenberg's career in Germany became blocked, the Nazis stigmatizing him as a 'White Jew' because of his unconventional science. (Photo Max-Planck Institute, courtesy AIP Emilio Segrè Visual Archives)

Plate 4. *Kristallnacht* 1938.
Berlin's Fasanenstrasse synagogue, built in 1912 and a symbol of the emancipation of German Jewry, lay in ruins after *Kristallnacht*, the night of broken glass, in November 1938. This pogrom marked the escalation of the Nazi persecution of the Jews: what had been discrimination now became outright attack. After seeing what the Nazis were prepared to do, refugee scientists became convinced that they had to get to the Atomic Bomb first. (Photo Imperial War Museum, London)

Plate 5. Lise Meitner.
As a woman scientist in the early twentieth century, and as a Jewess, Lise Meitner had to struggle continually against prejudice. Early photographs such as this show an attractive woman, fashionably dressed and self-possessed. Later ones show her seated alongside grim Nobel laureates, the only woman in a room full of famous men, and demurely, often dowdily, dressed. As an Austrian she was able to retain a research post in Berlin until 1938, when the annexation of her country by Nazi Germany made her subject to the Nazi race laws. Soon after she fled to Sweden, her former colleagues in Berlin discovered new nuclear effects. During Christmas 1938, she and her nephew Otto Frisch saw the significance of these discoveries. Called by Frisch 'nuclear fission', a new genie was let loose. (Photo AIP Emilio Segrè Visual Archives)

Plate 6. Otto Frisch and Rudolf Peierls.
Otto Frisch (*left*) and Rudolf Peierls, both from highly assimilated Jewish families, left Nazi Germany in the 1930s for posts at British universities. At the University of Birmingham in 1940, they realized that uranium-235 could provide a fission bomb small enough to be carried by air, capable of producing an explosion equivalent to that of several thousand tonnes of dynamite. Their 'Frisch–Peierls memorandum' was a landmark in the development of nuclear weapons. Both scientists went on to join the Atomic Bomb development team at Los Alamos. (Photo Corbis Images)

Plate 7. Leo Szilard.
Born in Budapest in 1898, Leo Szilard was the human catalyst who made the Atomic Bomb possible, managing always to be in the right place at the right time. He contrived to leave Germany one day before the first official anti-Semitic legislation became law. Convinced that Nazi Germany would make its own Atomic Bomb, Szilard pushed for the Americans to start a crash programme to beat them to it. Part of his political master-plan was to write a letter to President F. D. Roosevelt, above Einstein's signature to give it weight. (Photo Digital Photo Archive, Department of Energy (DOE), courtesy AIP. Emilio Segrè Visual Archives)

Plate 8. John von Neumann, Richard Feynman, and Stanislaw Ulam.
A lot of brain power in a single photograph. (*Right to left*) John von Neumann, Richard Feynman, and Stanislaw Ulam, during a sightseeing trip in New Mexico in the mid-1940s. All three came from Jewish families. Ulam, born in Lviv, and von Neumann, born in Budapest, both managed to leave Europe in the 1930s before they were forced to do so. Among many other accomplishments, they played vital roles in the development of nuclear weapons at Los Alamos. Feynman, who also worked at Los Alamos, went on to share the 1965 Nobel Physics Prize. His grandparents had emigrated to the USA from Minsk in 1895. (Photo AIP Emilio Segrè Visual Archives, Ulam Collection)

Plate 9. The first Atomic Bomb explosion.
At 05:30 on 16 July 1945, in New Mexico's desolate Jornada del Muerto desert, a blinding flash lit up the surrounding hills, and rumbling thunder never seemed to stop. For hundreds of miles around, unsuspecting witnesses thought the Sun rose twice that day. The first dawn had been an Atomic Bomb explosion, the end result of an effort initially sparked by Jewish scientists who had been forced to leave Nazi Germany. (Photo Los Alamos National Laboratory)

Plate 10. Victor Weisskopf.
The influential quantum physicist Victor Weisskopf (1908–2002), from a highly cultured Jewish family in Vienna, knew more culture than Judaism. He is seen here teaching in Germany in the early 1930s. In 1937, before his Austrian nationality would make him an automatic victim of Nazi race laws, he emigrated to the United States, where he was later invited to join the Atomic Bomb development team at Los Alamos. In 1961 he became Director General of CERN, the new European Organization for Nuclear Research in Geneva, Switzerland. His return to Europe was itself symbolic, and his accomplishments as CERN's head ensured that specialists from a wide variety of backgrounds and cultures could work together harmoniously in teams whose combined strength became bigger than the sum of their individual parts. CERN is now the world centre for subnuclear research. (Photo CERN, Pauli Archives)

Plate 11. Edward Teller.
Dr Strangelove? Edward Teller, born Teller Ede in 1908 into a Jewish family in Budapest, lost his university post at Göttingen as a result of the 1933 Nazi Civil Service Laws. Moving to the USA, he was invited to join the Atomic Bomb development work at Los Alamos, but was disappointed not to be nominated as head of its Theory Division. He distanced himself from the wartime fission bombs, focusing instead on the more remote possibility of thermonuclear fusion. In 1950, he returned to Los Alamos to play a key role in the development of such a bomb. Again miffed when not nominated to head the programme, he left Los Alamos, but went on to help guide the Strategic Defense Initiative—'Star Wars'—in the 1980s. (Photo AIP Emilio Segrè Visual Archives, Wheeler Collection)

Plate 12. Eugene Wigner.

Eugene Wigner, born Wigner Jeno in 1902 into a Jewish Family in Budapest, came to Princeton at the same time as John von Neumann (*see Plate 8*). The world's first nuclear engineer, Wigner guided the design, construction, and operation of the huge nuclear reactors which manufactured plutonium for the first fission bombs. In 1963 he shared the Nobel Prize for Physics for work he had done before he left Europe. (Photo Argonne National Laboratory, courtesy AIP Emilio Segrè Visual Archives)

Plate 13. Jack Steinberger.
Jack Steinberger, born into a religious Jewish family in Bad Kissingen, Germany, in 1921, left the country in 1934 to continue his schooling in the United States. After becoming a leading figure in post-war subnuclear physics, he moved back to Europe in the 1960s. Science's swing westward across the Atlantic, symbolized by Einstein's departure for the USA in 1932, was beginning to bounce back. In 1988 Steinberger shared the Nobel Prize for Physics. (Photo Columbia University Nevis Cyclotron Laboratory, courtesy American Institute of Physics Emilio Segrè Visual Archives)

a law of mankind uniting all members of the human race and constituting a general standard of justice. Furthermore, as we have seen, Wolff does not pay much attention to stipulative and customary law. Later positivists expressly reject these natural-law concepts and pay much closer attention to treaties and international custom.[152] Therefore, a transition from natural law to positivism is discernible in Wolff's writings, but at the same time its close connection to Wolff's system and method provides a barrier for the development of 'classic' international law.

3. From law to political economy

There is a further movement in Wolff's writings hidden behind the natural law language and his perception as a 'great expositor [. . .] of natural law'.[153] Wolff contributes to a new understanding of the art of government informed by the emergence of a political economy and based on three interrelated organizing ideas: mercantilism, the police state, and the European balance. This is a development carved out by Matt Craven, who refers to Foucault.[154] From this point of view, Wolff's discussion of the 'Duties of the Nation to Itself' in Chapter I of his treatise on *Jus gentium*, otherwise 'almost occult',[155] suddenly makes sense. Matters of statecraft thereby find their place in the volume on *jus gentium*. For example, several paragraphs are devoted to the power and wealth of nations. § 70 states that nations ought to strive for power; § 72, however, condemns the waging of an unjust war to increase power.[156] It is not without reason that Wolff's textbooks became axiomatic in justifications of enlightened despotism[157] and that Frederick II was Wolff's benefactor.[158]

[152] Schiffer, *The Legal Community of Mankind* (n. 7) pp. 80–1. For an early example of a more practically oriented treatise that focuses more on the collection of the contents of international law than on its foundation, see Johann Jakob Moser, *Grundsätze des jetzt üblichen europäischen Völker-Rechts in Fridenszeiten, auch anderer unter denen Europäischen Souverainen und Nationen zu solcher Zeit fürkommender willkührlicher Handlungen, zum Gebrauch seiner Staats- und Cantzley-Academie entworffen* (1750).

[153] Onuf, '*Civitas maxima:* Wolff, Vattel and the Fate of Republicanism' (n. 7), p. 282.

[154] Matthew Craven, 'On Foucault and Wolff *or* from Law to Political Economy', *LJIL* 25(3) (2012), 627–45, at 627, referring to Michel Foucault, *Security, Territory, Population: Lectures at the Collège de France, 1977-78*, Michel Senellart, François Ewald, and Alessandro Fontana (eds.) (2007). For a broader analysis, see Martti Koskenniemi, 'International Law and *raison d'état*: Rethinking the Prehistory of International Law', in Benedict Kingsbury and Benjamin Straumann (eds.), *The Roman Foundations of the Law of Nations. Alberico Gentili and the Justice of Empire* (2010), pp. 297–339.

[155] Jouannet, *Emer de Vattel et l'émergence doctrinale du droit international classique* (n. 128), pp. 399–400.

[156] Onuf, '*Civitas maxima:* Wolff, Vattel and the Fate of Republicanism' (n. 7), pp. 291–2.

[157] Hochstrasser, *Natural Law Theories in the Early Enlightenment* (n. 58), p. 36.

[158] Nippold, 'Introduction (1917)' (n. 3), pp. xxi–ii; Paul Sonnino, 'Introduction', in Paul Sonnino (ed.), *Frederick, The Refutation of Machiavelli's* Prince *or Anti-Machiavell* (1981), pp. 1–22.

As we have seen in the general discussion of his scientific system and method, Wolff transferred practical ethics, economics, and politics to legal concepts.[159] The duties of the nation to itself correspond to its obligations, aimed at self-preservation and self-perfection. Apart from these obligations that nations have toward themselves, there are also obligations that nations owe to other nations and that are aimed at assisting the other nations' preservation and perfection. The corresponding right of the other nations is a so-called imperfect right only. Imperfect rights can be made perfect by treaty, otherwise a nation must assist another nation only to the extent that this is possible without sacrificing its own self-perfection, and this evaluation is subject to the respective nation's own evaluation.[160] The most prominent example of this kind of imperfect rights is probably the right to commercial relations, which becomes only perfect through a commercial treaty.[161] On the one hand, this system of rights and obligations gives rise to the claim, referred to above, that Wolff establishes a 'Hobbesian instrument of the "self"';[162] on the other hand, in the words of Arthur Nussbaum, these 'gratuitous and nugatory' imperfect rights, served Wolff 'to represent the relations among nations conveniently in legal terms—to fill the world arbitrarily with international "rights"'.[163]

This focus on political economy, on the one hand, and the derivation of the *jus gentium voluntarium* from the *civitas maxima*, on the other, creates an inherent tension between legitimation and critique of political absolutism.[164] In line with the goals of the Enlightenment, Wolff's concept of philosophy has genuine potential for political criticism. By introducing the concept of the *civitas maxima*, Wolff was one of the first thinkers who addressed the cosmopolitan implications of contract theory.[165] Again and again, Wolff stressed this critical dimension of his thinking, especially in his *Deutsche Politik* of 1721. He does not want to be a 'storyteller' who only narrates what is customary,[166] but rather he speaks as a 'philosopher of that which has to happen when reason is put into practice'.[167] This claim, however, is somehow compromised. Ultimately, even natural law can be subordinated to the final purpose of the state, to public welfare, and security, in order to prevent greater

159 See text accompanying nn. 42–4.

160 Wolff, *Jus Gentium Methodo Scientifica Pertractatum (1764)* (n. 12), §§ 156–9.

161 Ibid., §§ 73–4.

162 See n. 85.

163 Nussbaum, *A Concise History of the Law of Nations* (n. 5), p. 152.

164 See Lutterbeck, *Staat und Gesellschaft bei Christian Thomasius und Christian Wolff* (n. 33), p. 150.

165 Cheneval, 'Der präsumtiv vernünftige Konsens der Menschen und Völker – Christian Wolffs Theorie der civitas maxima' (n. 77) p. 575; Francis Cheneval, 'Die kosmopolitische Dimension des "Consensus Praesumtus": Von Christian Wolff zu John Rawls und darüber hinaus', in Matthias Lutz-Bachmann (ed.), *Kosmopolitanismus. Zur Geschichte und Zukunft eines umstrittenen Ideals* (2010), pp. 122–45; cf. Wolfgang Kersting, *Die politische Philosophie des Gesellschaftsvertrags* (1994) pp. 212–16.

166 Wolff, *Vernünftige Gedanken von dem gesellschaftlichen Leben der Menschen und insonderheit dem gemeinen Wesen: 'Deutsche Politik'* (n. 51), § 379.

167 Ibid., Vorrede, § 270. See Grunert, 'Absolutism(s): Necessary Ambivalences in the Political Theory of Christian Wolff' (n. 46), p. 143.

damage. Natural law itself in many cases demands the violation of natural law if this is to the benefit of the perfection of man, i.e. if it is advantageous for the entire body politic.[168]

The sovereign can change something that is permitted by natural law through positive law into a duty or a prohibition—'as the final purpose of the republic demands'.[169] He can also prevent a collision between different norms of natural law by making an exception to the rule[170] with the help of positive law. In this case, he may even accept injustice in order to avert serious detriment. Although the authorities are in principle not in a position to give orders that directly contradict natural law, Wolff considers deviations from this rule, justified in 'some cases' if the order that runs counter to natural law is advantageous to the entire body politic. The subject is then no longer obliged to obey, but the duty of obedience comes into force again if his refusal 'attracts more calamity than if he obeyed'.[171] Since man, by natural law, is obliged to perfect himself and thus has to avoid anything that could worsen his interior and exterior condition,[172] the violation of a prescription of natural law is in most cases demanded by natural law itself. Wolff also refers to a hierarchy between the norms of natural law. This move allows him to reconcile the conflict between positive law and natural law because a conflict between positive law and a norm of natural law can almost always be eliminated by recourse to a higher norm of natural law. In this way, a positive law that contradicts natural law is justified by natural law itself. With the help of a 'natural theory of civil or positive law', which he sees as a part of a general theory of natural law, Wolff explicitly wants to reconcile the conflicts between the two types of law in a 'most beautiful concord'.[173]

Taking into account this aspect, it becomes understandable how Wolff furnishes monarchs with a concept of a *Wohlfahrtsstaat* (welfare state) and provided a cameralist set of justifications for state intervention to promote, *inter alia*, economic growth as well as military and diplomatic aggrandisement. The polymath offered a comprehensive account of the legitimate outreach of the enlightened state that could be detached from all the scholastic detail of Wolffian metaphysics.[174] In making practical use of Wolff's writings and at the same time detaching the knowledge based on his method from this very method, Frederick II could benefit from Wolff's

[168] See e.g. Wolff, *Vernünftige Gedanken von dem gesellschaftlichen Leben der Menschen und insonderheit dem gemeinen Wesen: 'Deutsche Politik'* (n. 51), § 434.

[169] Wolff, *Jus Gentium Methodo Scientifica Pertractatum (1764)* (n. 12); Wolff, *Grundsätze des Natur- und Völckerrechts* (n. 14), §1071.

[170] See e.g. Wolff, *Vernünfftige Gedancken von Gott, der Welt und der Seele des Menschen, auch allen Dingen überhaupt (Deutsche Metaphysik)* (n. 50) § 165.

[171] Wolff, *Vernünftige Gedanken von dem gesellschaftlichen Leben der Menschen und insonderheit dem gemeinen Wesen: 'Deutsche Politik'* (n. 51), § 434.

[172] Wolff, *Grundsätze des Natur- und Völckerrechts* (n. 14), § 36.

[173] Ibid., Vorrede; Grunert, 'Absolutism(s): Necessary Ambivalences in the Political Theory of Christian Wolff' (n. 46), pp. 148–9.

[174] Hochstrasser, *Natural Law Theories in the Early Enlightenment* (n. 58), 36.

work in a manner resembling Vattel's 'translation' into a more 'classic' international law, at least structurally.

V. Conclusion

To conclude, we return to the riddle of why Wolff's systematic method—which he considered to be his main contribution to the study of international law—was largely ignored while Wolff himself was treated as a scholarly authority. Arguably, the key to this puzzle is not only the fact that Wolff's philosophy of international law builds on his general philosophy and 'is written in the manner and even in the formal method of geometrical works', as Vattel writes in the introduction to his *Droit des Gens*.[175] Rather, method is not only a matter of style, but deeply entangled with substance, and Wolff dealt with substantive questions in a rather ambiguous way from the point of view of the subsequent reader trained in international law. He was manoeuvring between international law as an autonomous discipline and its integration into a system of science, between natural law and positivism, and between law and political economy, thereby mirroring relevant developments of his epoch. In this way, Wolff is a figure of transition. His responsiveness to these developments of his time, however, contrasts with Wolff's own belief in the timelessness of his system. Ernst Reibstein pointed out a long time ago that Wolff obviously ignored the fact that the abstract ideas that he presented as based on axiomatic reason were actually rooted in a long history of ideas. In that sense, he is indeed the cause of the misunderstandings through which his system persisted,[176] and his system and method had to remain an episode in the history of international legal thought. Nevertheless, his writings in all their ambiguity are a rich source for the study of decisive shifts in international legal thought that took place in the middle of the eighteenth century.

Selected Bibliography

Cheneval, Francis, 'Der präsumtiv vernünftige Konsens der Menschen und Völker—Christian Wolffs Theorie der civitas maxima', *ARSP* 85(4) (1999), 563–80.

Craven, Matthew, 'On Foucault and Wolff *or* from Law to Political Economy', *LJIL* 25(3) (2012), 627–45.

Grunert, Frank, 'Absolutism(s): Necessary Ambivalences in the Political Theory of Christian Wolff', *Tijds Rgeschied* 73(1) (2005), 141–52.

[175] Vattel, *The Law of Nations, Or, Principles of the Law of Nature, of Nations and Sovereigns, with Three Early Essays on the Origin and Nature of Natural Law and on Luxury* (n. 29), p. 12.

[176] Reibstein, 'Deutsche Grotius-Kommentatoren bis zu Christian Wolff' (n. 11), p. 101.

Haakonssen, Knud, 'Christian Wolff (1679-1754)', in Bardo Fassbender and Anne Peters (eds.), *The Oxford Handbook of the History of International Law* (Oxford: Oxford University Press, 2012), pp. 1106–09.
Olive, Louis, 'Wolff', in Antoine Pillet and Denis Alland (eds.), *Les fondateurs du droit international* (Paris: Édn Panthéon-Assas, 2014), pp. 447–79.
Orakhelashvili, Alexander, 'The Origins of Consensual Positivism: Pufendorf, Wolff and Vattel', in Alexander Orakhelashvili (ed.), *Research Handbook on the Theory and History of International Law* (Cheltenham, UK; Northampton, Mass., USA: Edward Elgar, 2011), pp. 93–110.
Peterson, Claes, 'What Has Logic Got to Do with It? On the Use of Logic in Christian Wolff's Theory of Natural Law', *Sc.St.L.* 48 (2005), 310–20.
Reibstein, Ernst, 'Deutsche Grotius-Kommentatoren bis zu Christian Wolff', *ZaöRV* 15 (1953–1954), 76–102.

12

The Law of the Nations as the Civil Law of the World

On Montesquieu's Political Cosmopolitanism

Christian Volk

Today, Montesquieu's fame seems to be due mainly to his appraisal of the English constitution and his thoughts on the separation of powers. Such a focus might be related to the large shadow cast by the French Revolution.[1] However, although his thoughts on this matter are definitely significant,[2] the almost exclusive concentration of the reception on these aspects of his oeuvre has left other important things in the shade. One aspect that has received very little attention yet—both in Montesquieu scholarship and in the philosophy of international law—and which forms the subject of analysis here, is the classification of Montesquieu's thoughts on the law of nations. I will point out that Charles-Louis de Secondat, Baron de La Brède et de Montesquieu (1689–1755)[3] argues in favour of a specific kind of political cosmopolitanism. I will come to this conclusion on the basis of an interpretation of his conception of the law of nations 'as the civil law of the whole globe, in which sense every nation is a citizen'.[4] Elsewhere he also speaks of the 'civil law . . . of the whole world'.[5]

[1] See Ernst Forsthoff, 'Zur Einführung', in *Vom Geist der Gesetze (Charles de Montesquieu)*, ed. Ernst Forsthoff (1992), p. V.

[2] See inter alia Sharon R. Krause, 'The Spirit of Separate Powers in Montesquieu', *The Review of Politics* 62(2) (2000), 231–65. However, a critical account of Montesquieu's interpretation of the English constitutional tradition is given by Claus, 'Montesquieu's Mistakes and the True Meaning of Separation'.

[3] For a general overview of the life and work of Montesquieu see inter alia Robert Shackleton, *Montesquieu: A Critical Biography* (1961); Georges Benrekassa, *Montesquieu* (1968); Melvin Richter, *The Political Theory of Montesquieu* (1977).

[4] Charles de Montesquieu, *The Spirit of the Laws*, eds. Anne M.Cohler, Basia Carolyn Miller, and Harold Samuel Stone (1989), Book 26, Ch. 1.

[5] Charles de Montesquieu, *Lettres Persanes*, ed. Pierre Grimal (1961), no. 94. The English translation of the *Lettres Persanes*, published by Oxford University Press, deviates significantly in places from the French original in terms of the numbering of the letters and the content. For this reason I have reverted to the French edition, translated directly from the original French text and stated the number of the respective letter.

This kind of Montesquieuian political cosmopolitanism makes clear reference to the republican Roman thinking of Cicero[6] or the 'modern' thoughts of Grotius on the law of nations; he also develops this perspective relatively systematically and identifies it by means of a critique of the Hobbesian tradition.[7] Nevertheless, Montesquieu was not an expert on the law of nations, but did *also* think about and addresses questions of international law. Therefore, when reading Montesquieu, one might get the impression that his comments on the law of nations arise less from scientific aspirations, but instead were motivated to a much greater degree by two specific historical incidents. (This impression is reinforced by the fact that, methodologically, Montesquieu's thoughts on the law of nations run contrary to his actual approach (see Section I). These two historical incidents are, firstly, Montesquieu's shock and moral indignation about Spanish colonial behaviour in South America. His shock is expressed repeatedly in all of his works and in *The Spirit of the Laws* he calls these crimes 'one of the most dangerous wounds that the human species ever received'.[8] Secondly, and closely connected, is Montesquieu's rejection of slavery.[9]

The key problem identified by Montesquieu with a view to the law of nations is that the concepts of the public lawyers of his age did not draw the correct conclusions either from the tragedy of Spanish colonialism or from slavery. Instead, these concepts imagine a law of nations that continues to legally justify both phenomena—colonialism and slavery. His political cosmopolitanism is directed against that. Essentially, therefore, it can be said that Montesquieu conceives of a law of nations that attempts to avert both the exploitation of other communities and also slavery. At the same time, however, he is not concerned with equating the law of nations with global ethics, or with establishing morally substantial yet politically ineffective obligatory requirements. One consequence of this is that the idea of human rights virtually does not appear in his considerations. For Montesquieu, the protection of individual rights is a matter for the constitutional, civil, and criminal law of individual states and discussed in this context. To put it another way: in his thoughts on the law of nations, too, Montesquieu tries to remain a political thinker who assumes the reality of individual state interests, but who wishes to integrate these in an international legal order that represents more than the consensus between states.

The entire complexity of his international legal and political thoughts arises from this. For Montesquieu's thoughts on the law of nations are thus not only reconstructive, but also normatively constructivist and prospective in character, with a view to justifying universal legal norms. At first glance, therefore, Montesquieu breaks away to a certain extent from the specific political methodology he develops in *The Spirit of the Laws*, which always refers the laws of a country back to the

[6] But cf. Paul A. Rahe, *Montesquieu and the Logic of Liberty* (2009), pp. 219–21.

[7] For a thorough account of Montesquieu's critique of Hobbes see Michael Zuckert, 'Natural Law, Natural Rights, and Classical Liberalism', *Social Philosophy and Policy* 18(1) (2001), 227–51.

[8] Charles de Montesquieu, *Spirit of the Laws*, Book 4, Ch. 6 (n. 3).

[9] On this point see my comments in Section III.2.a.

general spirit (*esprit général*) among the people, which itself in turn results from such different aspects as geography, climate, the quality of the soil, history and the way of life, religion, trade, customs, and state constitution, and which differs from country to country.[10] Similar to the program of global ethics, which is able to formulate abstract moral obligations, Montesquieu is also concerned with justifying political relationships of responsibility. At the same time, however, he formulates these with a view to the fact that every kind of abstract law that aims to develop an effectiveness must not only be well justified, but must also refer closely to the real-world living conditions of the actors. In other words: to the general spirit of a community. That is also true of the law of nations. Against this background there are two key civilizing and cultivating mechanisms to be found in Montesquieu's work: conquest and trade.[11]

The question of conquest marks a systematic component of Montesquieu's thoughts on the law of nations and shall be discussed in detail in all of its ambivalence (see Section III.2).[12] Although Montesquieu believes that the conquering state always assumes a large amount of political guilt, which must be redeemed, at the same time Montesquieu sympathizes in a certain sense with the view that a benevolent conqueror can set in motion a process of civilization and—at least to an extent—cultural homogenization, on whose basis the claims to universal validity of international legal norms can be realized. Just as ambivalent as Montesquieu's discussion of the question of conquest is his discussion of trade. For Montesquieu, the 'natural effect of trade' is 'peace'. In his view, the reason for this is that those peoples who conduct trade with each other 'become reciprocally dependent': 'one has an interest in buying, the other has an interest in selling; and thus their union is founded on their mutual necessities'.[13] In this regard, Rosow speaks of a 'cosmopolitan vision of mutuality'.[14] On the other hand, however, Montesquieu warns against the commodification of life. In countries, he writes, which are inspired exclusively by the spirit of trade, trade is also conducted with all human actions and all moral virtues. The consequence is that even 'the most trifling things, those which humanity would demand, are there done, or there given, only for money.'[15]

[10] For elaborations on Montesquieu's method see inter alia Melvin Richter, 'Montesquieu's Theory and Practice of the Comparative Method', *History of Human Sciences* 15(2) (2002), 21–33; Karsten Fischer, 'Demokratie und Differenzierung bei Montesquieu', *Zeitschrift für Politik* 56(1) (2009), 19–34, at 20–2; Paul A. Rahe, 'Forms of Government: Structure, Principle, Object, and Aim', in David W. Carrithers, Michael A. Mosher, and Paul A. Rahe (eds.), *Montesquieu's Science of Politics: Essays on the Spirit of Laws* (2001), p. 69.

[11] See also Katya Long, 'Civilizing International Politics: Republicanism and the World Outside', *Millennium Journal of International Studies* 38(3) (2010), 773–96, at 789.

[12] See also Michael Mosher, 'Montesquieu on Conquest: Three Cartesian Heroes and Five Good Enough Empires', *Revue Montesquieu* 8 (2006), 81–110.

[13] Montesquieu, *Spirit of the Laws*, Book 20, Ch. 2 (n. 3).

[14] Stephen J. Rosow, 'Commerce, Power and Justice', *The Review of Politics* 46(3) (1984), 346–66, at 346. See also Bernard Manin, 'Montesquieu, la république et le commerce', *European Journal of Sociology* 42(3) (2001), 573–602.

[15] Montesquieu, *Spirit of the Laws*, Book 20, Ch. 2 (n. 3). Howse identified very clearly the peace-bringing effect of trade according to Montesquieu. However, I do not share Howse's view that the 'stateless merchants' anticipate for Montesquieu an order that is 'of a transnational, transpolitical kind' (Howse, 'Montesquieu on Commerce, Conquest, War, and Peace', *Brooklyn Journal of International*

In order to work out Montesquieu's view of the law of nations, I shall proceed in four large steps: first I shall present Montesquieu's specific methodology in dealing with political and legal questions. In doing so, I shall demonstrate that his methodology on the one hand appears to be incompatible with his concerns relating to the law of nations—thus throwing light on the status of his thoughts on the law of nations. At the same time, however, his methodological approach gives a specific direction to his considerations on international law. In a second step, Montesquieu's concept of law as relationship (*rapport*) is addressed and applied to the question of the nature of the law of nations. In a third step, the systematics of Montesquieu's considerations on the law of nations are developed. The confederate republic as the political-institutional form of Montesquieu's political cosmopolitanism is outlined in a fourth and last step.

I. Montesquieu's Methodology and the Status of his Thoughts on the Law of Nations

In contrast to John Locke or Immanuel Kant, Montesquieu is not interested in the question of the morally–normatively justified legitimacy of order—in other words the question by what right political power is executed. His reading of travelogues appears to have made him 'staunchly empirical'[16] and immune to a moral–philosophical claim to universality, whether based on reason or natural law. What drives Montesquieu—and places him in the direct vicinity of Machiavelli in his *Discorsi*—is the political–normative question as to what holds a political community together or, more generally: what creates a political cohesion of order; what gives it 'duration and prosperity',[17] and what leads to its collapse. Montesquieu developed a specific methodology, which at its core is anti-universalistic, precisely

Law 31(3) (2006), 694–708, at 708) which could replace an order created by and on the basis of states. Such a contention is undermined by the fact that, firstly, for Montesquieu there is practically no trade that is separate from the basic structure of the state (nature of the form of government). It is precisely Montesquieu's aim to work out the relationships between trade and the respective basic structure. Paradigmatically, he begins Book 20, Ch. 4 with the sentence: 'Trade has some relation to forms of government.' Secondly, Montesquieu still assumes that there is no trade that is separate from the state and its interests. All 'the grand enterprises of merchants are always necessarily connected with the affairs of the public' (Montesquieu, *Spirit of the Laws*, Book 20, Ch. 4 (n. 3)). Elsewhere he writes: the goal of 'commerce is the exportation and importation of merchandises, with a view to the advantage of the state: Customs are a certain right over this same exportation and importation, founded also on the advantage of the state' (Montesquieu, *Spirit of the Laws*, Book 20, Ch. 13 (n. 3)).

16 Lorenzo Zucca, 'Montesquieu, Methodological Pluralism and Comparative Constitutional Law', *European Constitutional Law Review* 5(3) (2009), 481–500, at 481.

17 Montesquieu, *Spirit of the Laws*, Book 2, Ch. 2 (n. 3). For Machiavelli see Niccolo Machiavelli, *Discourses on Livy* (2009), Book I, Ch 2. For Montesquieu's Machivellianism see Paul A. Rahe, 'Montesquieus anti-Machiavellian Machiavellianism', *History of European Ideas* 37(2) (2011), 128–36, at 128. Machiavelli and Montesquieu are genuine political thinkers. For both of them, the field of politics is an area with its own intrinsic reference to meaning and not merely a special case of moral or immoral behaviour. (On this point see also Forsthoff, 'Zur Einführung', in *Vom Geist der Gesetze (Charles de Montesquieu)*, p. XXI (n. 1).)

in order to answer this political–normative question. The problem now is that his thoughts on the law of nations, as I shall show below, break with this anti-universalism, and set out precisely with the aim of justifying universal norms.

1. Montesquieu's political methodology

Montesquieu's specific methodology for discussing political matters consolidates in the analytical *interplay between the nature and principle of government*. The *nature of government* means the essence of a political order; this is manifested in the basic structure specific to it. According to Montesquieu there are three types of such basic structures: republic, monarchy, and despotism.[18] However, the form of government not only means the form of state organization, but instead the term represents the fundamental constitution of a community. In brief: it stands for a whole way of life of political and social coexistence, which is shaped decisively by the nature of government.[19]

The *principle of government* refers to the principle that allows the government in particular and the citizens in general to act in accordance with the nature of government. It therefore concerns the—in each case specific—human passion (love, honour, or fear) that drives the actions of people and institutions in each form of government, or through which each form of government is preserved.[20] Thus the difference between nature and principle indicates in the first instance that, according to Montesquieu, every form of government or constitution is allocated to a specific manner of action (principle). This manner of action is specific because it corresponds with the nature of government upon which it depends.

To explain briefly the specific character of this doctrine of constitutional form, it should be noted that Montesquieu, in his work, differentiates somewhat

[18] The relevant section reads: 'That a republican government is that in which the body or only a part of the people is possessed of the supreme power: monarchy, that in which a single person governs by fixed and established laws: a despotic government, that in which a single person directs every thing by his own will and caprice.' Montesquieu, *Spirit of the Laws*, Book 2, Ch. 1 (n. 3).

[19] Therefore, Sebastian Huhnholz is right to argue that Montesquieu's political constitutional ideas are closer to the republican pole than to the liberal pole in so far as they do not identify the social constitution of a society with the (constitutional or state) legal disposition of their political ruling bodies. (Sebastian Huhnholz, 'Von republikanischer Mächtebalance zu liberaler Verfassungstrinität? Zur Dementierung des Montesquieuschen Mischverfassungserbes durch die Gewaltentrennungsdokrtin', in Thorsten Thiel and Christian Volk (eds.), 'Die Aktualität republikanischer Theorie' (2016), pp. 45–72, at p. 46). In this sense see also Karsten Malowitz and Veith Selk, 'Republikanischer Konstitutionalismus. Die Bewältigung der Furcht als Schlüssel zur Freiheit in Montesquieus Verfassungslehre', *Zeitschrift für Politische Theorie* 5(1) (2014), 31–50. A different perspective on Montesquieu's sorting is taken by Carrese who speaks of Montesquieu's 'moderate liberalism' (Paul O. Carrese, *The Cloaking of Power* (2003), p. 1). Such a perspective is supported by Annelien de Dijn, 'On Political Liberty. Montesquieu's Missing Manuscript', *Political Theory* 39(2) (2011), 181–204; Annelien de Dijn, *French Political Thought from Montesquieu to Tocqueville: Liberty in a Levelled Society?* (2008); Robin Douglas, 'Montesquieu and Modern Republicanism', *Political Studies* 60(3) (2012), 703–19.

[20] The driving force of the republic is political virtue; that of the monarchy is honour and that of despotism is fear. Montesquieu, *Spirit of the Laws*, Book 2, Chs. 3–9 (n. 3).

casually between a form of government in which the people as a whole (democracy) act as holders of supreme power and a form of government in which only a section of the people (aristocracy) do so. Both democracy and aristocracy are categorized under the basic structure of the republic. What makes aristocracy and democracy republican forms of government is their common principle: political virtue. If the basic structure of a political community provides that the people as a whole or a section of the people rules, then the community must be constituted in such a very specific manner that the principle—in the case of the republic: political virtue[21]—is manifested in the form of a common spirit (*esprit général*) among the whole people (democracy) or only part of the people (aristocracy) and combines the citizens, the political institutions, society, and the legal order into units.[22]

Consequently, the classification of Montesquieu's types of constitution is motivated by his discovery of the principles. These principles allow him to differentiate political communities not according to constitutional structures, organizational forms, or other institutional criteria, but instead according to the mindset that determines the actions of the citizens, the organization of the legal order, the work of the institutions and that of the governing apparatus.[23] In his preface to *The Spirit of the Laws* he makes it clear that his central analytical starting point lies here.[24]

From his empirical observations Montesquieu assumes that different actions, passions, and motives of the actors involved in social and political processes are predominant under different constitutions. Indeed, even more: the functioning of the—republican, monarchist, or despotic—community as a whole depends on the validity and social effectiveness of the respective principle. Therefore, the state and civil laws in a country must be compatible not only with the basic structure, the so-called nature of government, but also and especially with the principle of government. Otherwise, decline threatens.[25]

[21] However, by making a strict distinction between political virtue on the one hand and moral and Christian virtue on the other, Montesquieu caps the link between virtue and morality that was typical of the Aristotelian tradition and of the entire Christian Middle Ages. Montesquieu's concept of political virtue stands for the mindset of the political agents in a republic; political virtue, seen as a mindset, gains its value from its suitability for political-republican practice (see also Larrère, 'Montesquieu and the Modern Republic', in Jonathan Mallinson, David W. Carrithers, and Patrick Coleman (eds.), *Montesquieu and the Spirit of Modernity* (2003), pp. 235–49, at p. 236; Judith N. Shklar, 'Montesquieu and the new republicanism', in Gisela Bock, Quentin Skinner, and Maurizio Viroli (eds.), *Machiavelli and Republicanism* (1990), pp. 265–80, at p. 266.

[22] Michael Hereth, *Montesquieu: Eine Einführung* (2005), p. 61.

[23] Hereth, *Montesquieu. Eine Einführung*, p. 61 (n. 21).

[24] See Montesquieu, *Spirit of the Laws*, Preface (n. 3).

[25] Montesquieu, *Spirit of the Laws*, Book 8, Ch. 1 (n. 3). An exemplary extract reads: 'When once the principles of government are corrupted, the very best laws become bad, and turn against the state: but, when the principles are sound, even bad laws have the same effect as good; the force of the principle draws everything to it.' Montesquieu, *Spirit of the Laws*, Book 8, Ch. 11 (n. 3). For a thorough elaboration on Montesquieu's motif of 'decline' see Sharon R. Krause, 'The Uncertain Inevitability of Decline in Montesquieu', *Political Theory* 30(5) (2002), 702–27.

2. Methodological anti-universalism vs. universal norms of the law of nations

A key consequence of this methodical approach is that Montesquieu cannot argue in universal terms which political decisions are right or wrong, good, or bad. The normative standard changes with the basic structure: he begins his comments on the nature of government with the democratic republic. This, says Montesquieu, demands much more from the people than monarchy or despotism. In a monarchy, laws regulate life; in despotism, it is violence. The republic, in contrast, depends significantly on the aforementioned political virtue. Thus that which can be beneficial to durability and prosperity in a monarchy can, in a republic, represent a sure sign of decay. In this very sense, Montesquieu writes:

> Clear it is, also, that a monarch, who, through bad advice or indolence, ceases to enforce the execution of the laws, may easily repair the evil; he has only to follow other advice, or to shake off this indolence. But when, in a popular government, there is a suspension of the laws, (as this can proceed only from the corruption of the republic,) the state is certainly undone.[26]

One of many other examples for the fact that the normative standard differs from basic structure to basic structure is presented by Montesquieu's discussion of inheritance law. Whereas, in a monarchy, the father may be permitted to pass his inheritance on to one of his children, such a law in a democracy could prove to be very dangerous. Excessive wealth not only destroys the 'spirit of ... frugality'[27] and contradicts the principle of relative material equality, but it also leads one to succumb to luxury and abandon work. (And Montesquieu also restricts these thoughts to so-called trading republics.)

In *The Spirit of the Laws* Montesquieu differs between the natural laws, the laws of religion, the moral laws formulated by the philosophers, the state and civil laws, and the laws that regulate the relationships between the peoples. Without any doubt, it is the state and civil laws that interest him most in *The Spirit of the Laws*. However—and this is key—they interest him with a view to their suitability for a specific historical society and not with regard to their moral or universal–reasonable content. It is true that reason plays an important role for Montesquieu's venture. After all, the specific laws of a society must be identified and the relationships that exist there between people at a specific historic point in time must be understood, arising from such different aspects as geography, climate, quality of the soil, history and the way of life, religion, trade, customs, and state constitution—with the objective of drafting such state laws that suit this specific community.[28] But due to the differences between the countries and communities with regard to the aforementioned criteria, it would be, according to Montesquieu, 'a great chance if those of one nation suit another'.[29] The 'spirit of the laws' that emerges from all of the

[26] Montesquieu, *Spirit of the Laws*, Book 3, Ch. 3 (n. 3).
[27] Montesquieu, *Spirit of the Laws*, Book 5, Ch. 6 (n. 3).
[28] Montesquieu, *Spirit of the Laws*, Book 5, Ch. 1 (n. 3).
[29] Montesquieu, *Spirit of the Laws*, Book 1, Ch. 3 (n. 3).

relationships mentioned, and which Montesquieu wishes to examine, differs from country to country. 'An Englishman, a Frenchman, an Italian: three esprits.'[30] Only by observing all of the named areas (climate, morals, trade, form of government, etc.) collectively is it possible to state which laws are suitable and which are not.[31]

In his thoughts on the law of nations, Montesquieu now breaks with this methodology, including its anti-universalistic implications, and adopts nothing less than a universal perspective. Driven by the shock mentioned at the outset about the cruelty of Spanish colonialism, and motivated by the battle against slavery, he is essentially concerned with, first, (re-)constructing a law of nations that is based on the 'true Principles'[32] and secondly to think about how to address the problem that each nation obviously has its own national law and that 'our law of nations' has no validity there.[33] There is a passage that illustrates this twofold problem clearly:

> All countries have a law of nations, not excepting the Iroquois themselves, though they devour their prisoners; for they send and receive ambassadors, and understand the rights of war and peace. The mischief is, that their law of nations is not founded on true principles.[34]

It will require great effort to spell out, from Montesquieu's comments on the law of nations, these 'true principles' and to clarify the epistemological standpoint behind these principles.[35] At the same time, however, Montesquieu is aware that the law of nations is a law that must be considered both from the position of the logic and structure of interstate interaction and from the perspective of the states and the peoples themselves. Precisely this is what he means with his remark that all countries have a law of nations: the existence and the validity of norms of the law of nations always refer directly to the general spirit and the form of government of a community as well. As a result, a republic can agree to norms of the law of nations that would not be acceptable to a monarchy, and certainly not to a despotic state. In the event of a conquest, for example, according to Montesquieu, a democratic state must democratize the state and the conquered people. If it does not do so and instead merely sends civil servants there to administer the state, it not only fails to fulfil its political responsibility, but also jeopardizes its own order.[36] A monarchy, in contrast, should rather leave things as they are in the event of a conquest.[37] In Montesquieu's view, things look very bleak in despotic states. Here, the law of a nation generally has little influence, since the despot is not accustomed to resistance and contradiction. The fear is therefore that war can be conducted 'in its full natural fury'.[38]

[30] Charles de Montesquieu, *My Thoughts*, ed. and trans. Henry C. Clark (202), no. 376.
[31] See also Sharon R. Krause 'Laws, Passion and the attractions of right action in Montesquieu', *Philosophy Social Criticism* 32(2) (2006), 211–30, at 220.
[32] Montesquieu, *Spirit of the Laws*, Book 1, Ch. 3 (n. 3).
[33] Montesquieu, *Spirit of the Laws*, Book 10, Ch. 4 (n. 3).
[34] Montesquieu, *Spirit of the Laws*, Book 1, Ch. 3 (n. 3).
[35] On this point see my comment in Section II.
[36] Montesquieu, *Spirit of the Laws*, Book 10, Ch. 6 (n. 3). For a more detailed explanation see Section II.
[37] Montesquieu, *Spirit of the Laws*, Book 10, Ch. 9 (n. 3).
[38] Montesquieu, *Spirit of the Laws*, Book 5, Ch. 14 (n. 3).

Thus although Montesquieu's thoughts on the law of nations contradict his methodology, due to their universal focus and their normative–constructivist character, he becomes sensitized to the question of the conditions of validity of the norms of the law of nations due to this very methodology. At the same time, however, it is this nexus between the law and the general spirit, between norms, culture, and forms of government, which motivates him to seek for civilizing and cultivating mechanisms (trade and conquest).

II. What Is Law? Montesquieu's Basic Legal–Philosophical Assumptions about the Essence of Law and its Consequences for the Law of Nations

One of the central debates related to the law of nations that was conducted on the threshold from the seventeenth to the eighteenth century was 'whether or not there was, alongside the *ius naturae*, also an independent *ius gentium positivum*.'[39] Following Hobbes, large parts of the scientific community disputed the existence of an independent *jus gentium positivum*. The relationship between the states, such was the widespread assumption, was regulated solely by means of the *jus naturae*. Yet law enters the world by being imposed by a responsible and higher authority. However, since there is no such authority for dealings between sovereign states, the states live in a state of nature in which, per definition, there is no law in the strictest sense of the word. Therefore not even custom can be considered as law as long as it does not have the consent of the sovereign.

In contrast to this, Montesquieu, who has long been neglected in the philosophy of international law, approaches the discussion on law in general and the law of nations in particular in a very different manner. He neither shares the premise of the state of nature—irrespective of whether this is applied to the domestic or to global level—neither does he see the essence of the law in the command. One could say that Montesquieu 'de-sovereignizes' the discourse on law and the discourse on power.[40] This shows to what extent the question of whether the *jus gentium positivum* exists arises from a 'sovereign-centred political theorizing'[41] in the first place. In other words: the question itself is the consequence of a very specific epistemology.

Montesquieu does not agree with this epistemology. To certain extent, he has to be considered as a materialistic thinker who always discusses the ideas, wishes, and hopes of the people with recourse to their political–social living conditions.

[39] Heinhard Steiger, 'Völkerrecht', in Otto Brunner, Werner Conze, and Reinhardt Koselleck (eds.), *Geschichtliche Grundbegriffe* (2004), p. 116.

[40] Hereth, *Montesquieu: Eine Einführung*, p. 45 (n. 21). One consequence of his methodology is that the duration and prosperity of a community precisely does not depend on the assertiveness of a central sovereign instance, the sovereign. The power of a community feeds upon the successful interplay between the nature of government, the principle of government, the general spirit (formed by climate, geography, religion, customs, etc.), and the laws passed.

[41] Jonathan Havercroft, *Captives of Sovereignty* (2011), p. 5.

Althusser e.g. speaks of Montesquieu's 'mechanistic materialism'.[42] Like Marx (and also Hegel), society in general and the political community in particular is therefore also not an artificial work of the people that, moreover, has come into being by social contract. For Montesquieu, the people have always been people in society, and these societies, peoples, nations, or states have always stood in relationship to each other.[43]

It is true that Montesquieu formulates thoughts on a human state of nature and on natural laws. However, on the one hand, all of his comments on such a state are made in the subjunctive and demonstrate by these means the distance maintained by Montesquieu to the theoretical conception of a natural state as the starting point of all contractual–theoretical considerations. For Montesquieu, there are also no rights that could be separated from these natural laws—in Montesquieu this refers to peace, the impulse to search for food, sexual lust between the sexes, and the urge to live in society—in order to then transfer them to a higher authority in the course of a contract.[44] On the other hand, these considerations on the natural laws serve to underpin the fact of the natural relationship-forming nature of human life: peace, for example, is not something that is dictated by reason, God, or nature, but instead a general human yearning which, according to Montesquieu, *is likely to* result from a feeling of weakness, fear, and inferiority. What Montesquieu makes clear right at the beginning of the first book of *The Spirit of the Laws* is that laws are best conceived as relationships (*rapport*): 'Laws in the broadest sense of the word are relationships that emerge necessarily from the nature of things.'[45]

With his understanding of laws, he distances himself both from the Greek tradition of nomos, which conceives of laws as a fence or enclosure, and from Hobbes, who defines law as command.[46] Though Montesquieu talks about a 'Creator and Preserver' of the universe and writes of the 'state of nature' and the laws of nature, these laws describe, in his view, merely the references between the creator and creation or between humans in their natural state.[47] Following Hannah Arendt's reading of Montesquieu on this point, what the laws reveal are the 'rules or règles which determine the government of the world and without which a world would not exist at all'.[48]

These explications on Montesquieu's understanding of law as relation are of key significance in order to properly classify his thoughts on the legal character of the law of nations. One essential reason for this is that, according to Montesquieu, the question of the origin of these international relationships is just as 'ridiculous' as

[42] Louis Althusser, *Politics and History: Montesquieu, Rousseau, Marx* (2007), p. 44.

[43] Montesquieu, *Lettres Persanes*, no. 94 (n. 4).

[44] Montesquieu, *Spirit of the Laws*, Book 1, Ch. 2 (n. 3). Georges Benrekassa, *Montesquieu: La liberté et l'histoire* (1987), p. 101. See also Hereth, *Montesquieu: Eine Einführung*, p. 49 (n. 21). But cf. Michael Zuckert, 'Natural Rights and Modern Constitutionalism', *Northwestern Journal of International Human Rights* 2(1) (2004).

[45] Montesquieu, *Spirit of the Laws*, Book 1, Ch. 1 (n. 3).

[46] Thomas Hobbes, *Leviathan*, ed. J.C.A. Gaskin (2009), Ch. 26.

[47] Montesquieu, *Spirit of the Laws*, Book 1, Ch. 2 (n. 3).

[48] Hannah Arendt, *On Revolution* (1963), p. 189.

that of the origin of societies. Just as all people are already 'born connected to one another'[49], one can assume that relationships have also always existed between the different peoples, nations, or states that constitutes that which Montesquieu calls the 'world'.[50] Of course, Montesquieu is concerned with defining the status and the legal and political quality of these interstate relationships—also from a normative perspective. But he rejects the assumption that states, nations, or peoples live or have ever lived in a state of nature, i.e. in an anarchic condition without relationships and thus without laws.[51] In parody of Hobbes, he argues that precisely the *possibility* of a state of war between peoples leads to the creation of public law.[52]

Considered as inhabitants of so great a planet, which necessarily contains a variety of nations, they *have* laws relative to their mutual intercourse, which is what we call the law of nations (emphasis added).[53]

All things in this world—humans, states, people—stand in relationship to one another. Accordingly, 'the world' is not created in a political or legal sense only by means of the foreign policy activities of the state. Montesquieu's epistemological anti-Descartianism is transferred to his political thinking. One could say, that we have with Montesquieu a threefold break with sovereignty: (1) from an epistemological perspective, the relationship forming nature of the world replaces Descartes' *cogito ergo sum*; (2) society gets its stability and permanence not from the omnipotence of the sovereign, but rather from the fact that the laws passed are related to the principle of government and the general spirit of the society; (3) in a political and legal sense, the world already exists before the will of a state to design its foreign policy relationships and is based on the fact that different peoples inhabit the Earth and demonstrate reciprocal bonds to one another.

Speaking in theoretical conceptual terms, it is important to be aware of the fact that the starting point of Montesquieu's thoughts is the aforementioned relationship forming nature of the world and the things in the world. Therefore, in a very similar manner to the Roman tradition of the *jus gentium*, the people *do not make* the laws, but instead they 'have' laws that regulate their relationships with each other, as it reads in the quotation above. These laws include in equal measure contracts, customs, principles, and a legal conviction, which results from discussion between the leading thinkers of a particular age.

While the law of nations is *in use* among the individual nations, and regulates the relationship between peoples, the validity of this law is, according to Montesquieu,

[49] Montesquieu, *Lettres Persanes*, no. 94 (n. 4).

[50] Montesquieu, *My Thoughts*, no. 1814 (n. 29).

[51] Therefore, Katya Long is mistaken when she argues that Montesquieu invented the 'idea of a federation as a solution to the anarchy of international politics' (Long, *Civilizing International Politics*, p. 774 (n. 10)). The point in Montesquieu's international political, and legal thought is that there is no anarchy in international politics. He starts, in epistemological terms, from the assumption of the relationship forming nature of the world.

[52] Montesquieu, *Lettres Persanes*, no. 95 (n. 4). See Montesquieu, *Spirit of the Laws*, Book 1, Ch. 2 (n. 3). The possibility of a state of war, which can arise both between peoples and within a society, emerges when people live in a society and lose the feeling of weakness.

[53] Montesquieu, *Spirit of the Laws*, Book 1, Ch. 3 (n. 3).

independent of whether or not it is confirmed by the sovereign legislating power of the individual states. Or to put it less strongly: according to Montesquieu, interstate contracts are only *one* source of the law of nations. In Montesquieu's view, with regard to the use of the law of nations, individual states can assume incorrect legal principles—with the consequence that their actions become illegitimate from the perspective of a law of nations. In the *Persian Letters*, for example, Montesquieu writes that an alliance between two states must be 'just . . .' in order to truly obligate both states. An alliance formed between two nations for the purpose of suppressing a third nation '. . . is not legitimate, and can be violated without crime.'[54]

The validity of such a law of nations cannot be custom, contract, or sovereign command alone; for Montesquieu, the law of nations is always also subject to a political reason which, in its reasoning, is oriented towards the conditions of the possibility that a world of peoples is preserved. In the *Persian Letters* he even speaks of the law of nations as the 'law of reason'.[55] Montesquieu formulates the directive of such an understanding of the law of nations in *Mes pensées*:

> If I knew something useful to my Country and harmful to Europe, or else useful to Europe and harmful to the mankind [*genre humain*], I would regard it as a crime.[56]

Certainly, a law of nations understood in this manner must continue to regulate the relationships between states as well, but in contrast to a state-centred view of the law of nations, it is conceived from two sides: first from the perspective of an order of the world that is a reality due to the relationships between the peoples. In other words, an international world order represented by the term mankind. At the same time, however, Montesquieu also includes in his considerations the interest of the individual state or states in their separateness, as will become even clearer in his thoughts on the right to war, self-preservation, and conquest.[57] For without states there is no world. According to Montesquieu, states and the world are co-original. However, these interests of the individual states are not absolutized as in the Hobbesian tradition and declared as the epistemological crux of the matter—with the consequence that the existence of a law of nations is essentially negated by Hobbes. Montesquieu's law of the nations is inspired by a 'cosmopolitan imagining'.[58]

In contrast to Hobbes, with Montesquieu one can speak of a post-sovereign law of nations, in which the dogma of sovereignty is qualified insofar as that legitimate state behaviour must always be able to justify itself with reference to the nature of the interstate order. Not only did the Spanish, and many other European nations, breach the legitimate law of nations with their colonialism, but also the Iroquois,

[54] The original French sentence is: 'Mais, pour que l'alliance nous lie, il faut qu'elle soit juste: ainsi une alliance faite entre deux nations pour en opprimer une troisième n'est pas légitime, et on peut la violer sans crime' (Montesquieu, *Lettres Persanes*, no. 95 (n. 4)).

[55] Montesquieu, *Lettres Persanes*, no. 95 (n. 4).

[56] Montesquieu, *My Thoughts*, no. 741 (n. 29).

[57] See Section III.2.

[58] Genevieve Lloyd, 'Imaging Difference: Cosmopolitanism in Montesquieu's *Persian Letters*', *Constellations* 19(3) (2012), 480–93, at 482.

who 'devour their prisoners', applied a law of nations that 'is not founded on true principles'.[59] What is incorrect about these principles is that they negate the conditions of the possibility of a world of peoples and they endanger peace. According to Montesquieu, whoever invokes 'humanity' or 'the world' does not want to cheat; 'the world' or 'humanity' is a central reference of reason in the endeavour to justify universal norms of the law of nations. In the following I will show how this view of the law of nations is revealed in a systematic manner.

III. Montesquieu and the System of his Thoughts on the Law of Nations

1. War and self-preservation in Montesquieu's thoughts on the law of nations

When we set out to examine the systematics of Montesquieu's thoughts on the law of nations, our attention is grabbed primarily by the (occasional) comments in Book 1 and his remarks in Book 10 of *The Spirit of the Laws*. In Book 1, Chapter 3, Montesquieu names the two principles of the law of nations from which all other laws can and must be derived and on which the law of nations is 'naturally founded'. The first is the principle 'that different nations ought in time of peace to do one another all the good they can, and in time of war as little injury as possible. . .'.[60] Secondly, Montesquieu states that the objective of war is to win. The objective of the victory must be to conquer; and the objective of the conquest, however, is preservation.[61] In Book 10, Montesquieu once again takes up these thoughts on the principles of the law of nations. His starting point here is the assumption that the law of nations is there to regulate the 'offensive force' between states.[62]

At first glance, his remarks appear to be more or less conventional. Conventional in the sense that the law of nations is conceived apparently as a purely interstate law—Montesquieu speaks of the *loi politique* of the peoples in their mutual relationships—and its very purpose is to regulate all those things which, due to their nature, can be regulated either by force or by contract (whereby contract is the postponement of force).[63] In other words: at first glance, Montesquieu also considers the law of nations to exist in order to define more precisely the *jus ad bellum*[64] and the question of the just war.[65]

[59] Montesquieu, *Spirit of the Laws*, Book 1, Ch. 3 (n. 3).
[60] Montesquieu, *Spirit of the Laws*, Book 1, Ch. 3 (n. 3).
[61] It is interesting here that Montesquieu states in *Mes pensées* that the objective of war is peace—and that therefore such measures may not be taken that make peace impossible (see Montesquieu, *My Thoughts*, no. 1814 (n. 29)). A thought that later can be found in Kant's Perpetual Peace (Immanuel Kant, *Zum ewigen Frieden*: p. 7, ed. Rudolf Malter (1984)).
[62] Montesquieu, *Spirit of the Laws*, Book 10 (n. 3).
[63] See Montesquieu, *My Thoughts*, no. 741 (n. 29).
[64] Montesquieu, *Spirit of the Laws*, Book 10, Ch. 2 (n. 3).
[65] See Montesquieu, *Lettres Persanes*, no. 95 (n. 4).

Accordingly, Montesquieu begins with a double analogy: first he compares states with people and in this manner ascribes to the state—once again quite conventionally—the status of subject. Second, he draws a comparison between the individual right to natural defence and the right of the state to self-preservation: just as humans have the right to kill in self-defence, so also do states have the right to conduct war for the sake of their self-preservation.[66] Every person has the right to kill in the case of natural defence, because his life belongs to him just as that of his attacker belongs to him. Analogously, Montesquieu argues that the state may conduct war for the sake of its self-preservation, because its self-preservation is equally as justifiable as the preservation of any other state.

What becomes clear here is that Montesquieu distances himself in his considerations from Locke's natural law tradition, or better: modernizes it. For Locke, the right to life is based on the circumstance that man is considered to be the property of God and therefore may not be used by another as a means to an end.[67] (This is the origin of the natural law concept of human dignity.) For Montesquieu, however, each person's individual life is his own. But more important is that he also distances himself from a state-centred positivism that comes from Hobbes. Hobbes justifies the right to self-preservation with reference to a nature that is so 'arranged that all desire good for themselves. Insofar as it is within their capacities, it is necessary to desire life, health, and further, insofar as it can be done, security of future time'.[68] With Montesquieu, in contrast, the right to self-preservation is not simply given, but rather its value is once again questioned—and the answer is: the self-preservation of Country A is equally as just as that of Country B. And precisely for this reason, Country A may defend itself. But just in relation to what? Montesquieu does not address that question at this point, but in the style of modernized concept of natural law, his answer will be: just against the background of a 'world...' for which it is '... as necessary ... that nations preserve themselves as it is necessary to each nation that its citizens not be destroyed'.[69]

So already at the level of the justification of a right to state self-preservation we can see that Montesquieu does not follow the powerful Hobbesian tradition. Instead he justifies the right to self-preservation with reference to the preservation of a higher, natural totality, which he calls world. Thus on the one hand he joins the ranks (naturally with some limitations) of the Roman *jus gentium* tradition, such as that found in Cicero, Livy, or Gaius, for which the 'law of nations' is the law of humanity—*jus commune omnium hominium*.[70] On the other hand, he follows the thinking of Vitoria, Suarez, and above all Grotius on the 'modern law of nations' as a natural and un-intentional or non-constituted community of states.[71] With reference to the general direction of this volume and as outlined in the introduction,

[66] Montesquieu, *Spirit of the Laws*, Book 10, Ch. 2 (n. 3).
[67] John Locke, *Second Treatise of Government*, ed. C.B. Macpherson (1980), Ch. II, § 6, § 7: 9.
[68] Thomas Hobbes, *Man and Citizen*, ed. Bernard Gert (1991), p. 48.
[69] Montesquieu, *My Thoughts*, no. 1814 (n. 29).
[70] See Steiger, 'Völkerrecht', p. 102 (n. 38).
[71] See Steiger, 'Völkerrecht', p. 111 (n. 38).

Montesquieu's considerations on this issue can be conceived in terms of system and order.

As already stated, Montesquieu does not go any deeper into this matter and also does not clarify the references. Instead he restricts the sustainability of his analogy: while people have the right to natural defence, this right does not include the necessity to attack. Rather, people must turn to the courts, and may become violent only in an instance of present danger. States, on the other hand, have the right to a pre-emptive strike for the purpose of their self-preservation.

'But, with states, the right of natural defence carries along with it sometimes the necessity of attacking; as, for instance, when one nation sees that a continuance of peace will enable another to destroy her, and that to attack that nation instantly is the only way to prevent her own destruction.'[72]

As well as the fact that Montesquieu concludes from this that smaller societies more frequently have the right to conduct wars than larger ones, the perspective adopted by Montesquieu here in order to justify an international legal norm is interesting: here, Montesquieu (apparently) seems to conceive the law of the nation from the self-preserving logic of the state. The state is obliged to address the matter with the neighbouring country and to take the necessary measures. If a state feels that its self-preservation is threatened, it may attack. At first glance, therefore, Montesquieu appears to follow the same line as Thomas Hobbes. According to Hobbes, it is not a system of obligating norms of natural law that regulates interstate relationships, but rather rational utilitarian considerations. These dictate 'that every man ought to endeavour peace, as far as he has hope of obtaining it; and when he cannot obtain it, that he may seek, and use, all helps, and advantages of war'.[73]

At the same time, however, Montesquieu again departs from the state-centred view of the law of nations in the very next sentence, adopts a more general perspective, and limits the room for possible arbitrariness. For the point of his considerations is that one can speak of a 'legitimate right' to war *only* in the narrow context of self-preservation.[74] To underline this view, Montesquieu becomes drastic and argues that if this is not observed, then 'everything is lost' and when one 'proceeds on arbitrary principles of glory, convenience, and utility, torrents of blood must overspread the earth.'[75] Here, too, it is difficult to ignore the anti-Hobbesian impulse of his thinking.

2. The right of conquest—a discussion with the thinking of his time on the state and the law of nations

Although a quick study of Montesquieu, possibly limited only to *The Spirit of the Laws*, might give the impression that he understands the law of nations in the traditional sense as an interstate law, as the *loi politique* of states, it already becomes clear

[72] Montesquieu, *Spirit of the Laws*, Book 10, Ch. 3 (n. 3).
[73] Hobbes, *Leviathan*, Book 1, Ch. 14 (n. 45).
[74] Montesquieu, *Spirit of the Laws*, Book 10, Ch. 3 (n. 3).
[75] Montesquieu, *Spirit of the Laws*, Book 10, Ch. 3 (n. 3).

at this point, however, that he is concerned with fundamentally restricting the room for individual state arbitrariness. This impulse is very evident especially in Book 10, Chapter 3 'Of the Right of Conquest'. For one thing, in this chapter he works out a fundamental critique of contemporary thoughts on the state and the law of nations that were prevalent during his age, which were ignited by the question of conquest (a). It should be borne in mind that among some authors (in particular Abbé de Saint-Pierre),[76] a critique of the European state system had become established to an ever-increasing degree from the eighteenth century, which was consolidated in the topos of war and conquest. The accusation was that the structure of the absolutist state was the actual cause of war, because it was unable to restrict the monarchs' desire for enlargement.[77] Montesquieu's thoughts on the law of nations are also rooted in this context, understood as an area that is obliged to regulate the question of war and conquest. On the other hand, however, Montesquieu formulates a 'right of conquest' in this chapter. The paradox of this right of conquest is that it legitimizes the violent subjection of another nation—Ramgotra interprets it as a plea for a 'moderate colonial empire'[78]—while at the same time opening up the perspective of a completely different kind of international law (b).

a) Revisiting the question of conquest

His implicit discussion with the existing positions of his time—primarily of course with a scepticism, formulated by Pufendorf, Thomasius and others in line with Hobbes, of the idea that an independent *jus gentium positivum* exists at all alongside natural law[79]—he begins by naming the four fundamental ways in which a conqueror could treat a conquered people: one possibility, that would conform with the 'law of nations that we follow today',[80] is that the conqueror continues to rule according to the existing laws, and takes over only the execution of the political and civil government. Or he could establish a new political and civil government or, thirdly, he could dissolve society and divide it among other states. The fourth and final possibility would be to exterminate all of the citizens.

If we examine the existing public law positions against this background, says Montesquieu, then it becomes clear that they grant too much room to the freedom

[76] See Wilhelm Janssen, 'Krieg', in Otto Brunner, Werner Conze, and Reinhart Koselleck (eds.), *Geschichtliche Grundbegriffe*, Band 7 (2004), p. 584.

[77] See Janssen, 'Krieg', pp. 584–5 (n. 76). However it is misleading to see Montesquieu's discussion of conquest primarily as a critique of the desire for enlargement of the eighteenth-century state, as suggested by Janssen (see Janssen, 'Krieg', p. 586 (n. 76)). Montesquieu is not exactly averse to a certain form of conquest.

[78] Manjeet Kaur Ramgotra, 'Republic and Empire in Montesquieu's Spirit of the Laws', *Millenium: Journal of International Studies* 42(3) (2014), 790–816, at p. 800.

[79] See Steiger, 'Völkerrecht', p. 116 (n. 38).

[80] Montesquieu, *Spirit of the Laws*, Book 10, Ch. 3 (n. 3). Here I deviate from the English translation and revert to the French original. The English translation does not fully express Montesquieu's meaning of 'our national law' as it is currently applied and followed. The original French sentence reads: 'La première manière est conforme au droit des gens que nous suivons aujourd'hui.' (Charles de Montesquieu, *De l'esprit de loix* (1750), Book 10, Ch. 3).

of states in the matter of a right to kill, thus opening the floodgates to arbitrariness. Their thinking is based on false principles of the law of nations. Why?

According to Montesquieu, the 'authors of our public law' grant the conquerors with the right to destroy the political community and they deduce from this that the conqueror can even exterminate or enslave the people in the conquered state if it corresponds with his utilitarian considerations.[81] For Montesquieu, however, that is 'a wrong consequence from a false principle'.[82] Following a completed conquest, the conqueror may no longer kill, 'because he has no longer the plea of natural defence and self-preservation'.[83] Since natural defence and self-preservation are the only justifications for war, the lapse of such a situation removes any legitimate right to kill. That is Montesquieu's criticism of the major premise.

His criticism of the 'wrong consequence' comes down to an attack on the public lawyers for their careless separation of people and citizens. Even if the political community may be destroyed—and as I shall show, Montesquieu did not believe this was the case—it does not mean, in Montesquieu's view, that the people that form that community may be exterminated. 'The state is the association of men, and not the men themselves; the citizen may perish, and the man remain.'[84]

The enslavement of people in the course of a conquest is also unlawful. Only if it is necessary to safeguard the conquest does one have the right to enslave people *temporarily*. However, slavery can never be the legitimate goal of a conquest; indeed, permanent slavery contradicts the principle of conquest. According to Montesquieu, it is the duty of a conqueror to lead a conquered people back out of bondage.[85] There are ways and means of doing this. In the first instance, naturally, by means of peace treaties, which he calls 'sacred'.[86] Montesquieu's most plausible example of a 'successful' conquest, however, is Alexander the Great, who, after the conquest of the Persians, strived only to unite the two peoples and to extinguish the differences between the victors and the defeated people. He achieved this, says Montesquieu, by adopting the customs of the others, and by allowing, indeed encouraging marriages.[87]

b) Between imperialism and humanity

For Montesquieu, the question of conquest is the burning lens for the debate in the law of nations. Montesquieu postulates that the conqueror must comply with a whole range of legal principles in his treatment of the conquered people: on the one hand, according to natural law, that everyone should strive for the preservation of his species. But he must also observe the law of natural reason, which he

[81] Montesquieu, *Spirit of the Laws*, Book 10, Ch. 3 (n. 3).
[82] Montesquieu, *Spirit of the Laws*, Book 10, Ch. 3 (n. 3).
[83] Montesquieu, *Spirit of the Laws*, Book 10, Ch. 3 (n. 3).
[84] Montesquieu, *Spirit of the Laws*, Book 10, Ch. 3 (n. 3).
[85] See Montesquieu, *Spirit of the Laws*, Book 10, Ch. 3 (n. 3).
[86] The original French sentence reads: 'Les traités de paix sont si sacrés parmi les hommes qu'il semble qu'ils soient la voix de la nature qui réclame ses droits' (Montesquieu, *Lettres Persanes*, no. 95 (n. 4)).
[87] See Montesquieu, *Spirit of the Laws*, Book 10, Ch. 14 (n. 3).

identifies in the so-called golden rule. Furthermore, the law that leads to the formation of political communities must also be followed, whose duration is unlimited by nature. That probably means that Montesquieu considered the existence of people to be a value in itself, because this existence manifests the presence of a specific general spirit.[88] The fourth law mentioned by Montesquieu is the law that arises from the nature of the thing.[89] Here, the nature of the thing means that the conquest represents an acquisition. In line with Locke, he sees preservation and usage as the spirit of acquisition, rather than destruction. Accordingly, the law dictates that the conquered country and its people should be preserved.

Most of Montesquieu's views on the law of nations are expressed in his thoughts on the right of conquest, and these views are condensed in the following paragraph:

> It is a conqueror's business to repair a part of the mischief he has occasioned. The right, therefore, of conquest I define thus: *a necessary, lawful, but unfortunate right*, which leaves the conqueror under a heavy obligation that must be redressed before humanity. (emphasis added)[90]

By characterizing the right of conquest as a 'necessary right', Montesquieu acknowledges the circumstance that 'the world', in a political sense, is also dependent on the interests of individual states and the accompanying reason of state, which differs from state to state. A law of nations that denies its reference to the state as the subject of the law of nations and which ignores the state's doctrine of self-preservation is inconceivable to him. In brief: the right of conquest cannot be invalidated for Montesquieu by referring to individual human rights.

Yet the right of conquest is not only necessary; it is also legitimate. What makes conquest legitimate in Montesquieu's eyes? Here we touch upon a delicate point in Montesquieu's thinking, his cultural imperialism. For according to Montesquieu, conquest is legitimate, because it can even create some advantages for the subjected peoples. First he argues that conquered states are no longer fully in control of their constitution anyway. Laws are usually flouted, with the resulting threat of both a collapse in morals and political decay. Thus a conquest could help to prevent the negative consequences of such a development. Second, conquest often leads to the removal of tyrannical leaders.[91] And, third, a conquest 'may destroy pernicious

[88] A similar argument can be found in Michael Walzer's thoughts on the 'moral standing of a state' (Michael Walzer, 'The Moral Standing of States. A Reponse to Four Critics', *Philosophy and Public Affairs* 9(3) (1980), 209–29, at 211).

[89] Montesquieu, *Spirit of the Laws*, Book 10, Ch. 3 (n. 3).

[90] Montesquieu, *Spirit of the Laws*, Book 10, Ch. 4 (n. 3). Here I deviate from the English translation and revert to the French original. The right of conquest is not 'a necessary, lawful, but unhappy, power', as it says in the English translation, but rather a necessary, lawful, but unfortunate right. Furthermore, the injuries were inflicted not only on humanity, as it says in the English translation, but instead the idea is that amends must be made in order to free oneself from the guilt one has incurred, before the eyes of humanity. The passage in the French original reads: 'C'est à un conquérant à réparer une partie des maux qu'il a faits. Je définis ainsi le droit de conquête: un droit nécessaire, légitime et malheureux, qui laisse toujours à payer une dette immense, pour s'acquitter envers la nature humaine.' (Montesquieu, *De l'esprit de loix*, Book 10, Ch. 4 (n. 79)).

[91] The idea behind this might be that a tyranny, to Montesquieu's mind, is the most violent form of government. But because it cannot rely on the support of its subjects, but rather is based on fear and violence, Montesquieu believes that it is also the weakest form of government.

prejudices, and lay, if I may presume to use the expression, the nation under a better genius'.[92] The public lawyers, according to Montesquieu, would have detected these advantages more easily 'were our law of nations exactly followed, and established in every part of the globe'.[93]

Against the background of the colonial expansion of Europe, which Montesquieu witnessed, the last point in particular must be interpreted in a value– and cultural–imperial perspective. What is interesting, however, is that this perspective is not inspired either solely by the superiority belief of the Enlightenment or by humanist convictions.[94] With Montesquieu, it is also linked to how he thinks about the law in general and the law of the nations in particular. To remind us: for Montesquieu, laws are relationships that arise necessarily from the nature of the thing. Accordingly, for Montesquieu, the law of nations is not something that can be observed in complete isolation from the specific historical disposition of the individual societies. According to Montesquieu, the law of nations is also related to the general spirit of a nation. To put it bluntly, Montesquieu formulates this thought in the sentence that each nation has its own national law; or it appears in the phrase referring to 'our [European] law of nations'—in contrast to the national law of the Chinese. At the same time, however, Montesquieu tries to justify universal norms of the law of nations—an endeavour, as shown above, that represents a methodical contradiction of the actual leanings of his legal and political thoughts.[95] For how can it be ensured that the universal norms of the law of nations that are (re-) constructed by Montesquieu can be harmonized with the general spirit of the peoples, and also with other cultural circles? One answer is: by means of conquest by an enlightened, prudent, benevolent, conqueror (as Alexander the Great allegedly was). Montesquieu sympathizes with the idea that such a conqueror could initiate a process of civilization and cultural homogenization—a process which provides the ground for the universal validity of international legal norms. Trade would be the other alternative.[96]

At the same time it is absolutely crucial not to reduce Montesquieu to this cultural imperialistic strain of his thoughts on the law of nations, which declares conquest to be legitimate for the purpose of civilizational progress. For one thing, he is very much aware that the 'civilized nations' who would come into question as

[92] Montesquieu, *Spirit of the Laws*, Book 10, Ch. 4 (n. 3).

[93] Montesquieu, *Spirit of the Laws*, Book 10, Ch. 4 (n. 3).

[94] There can be no doubt that Montesquieu was convinced by the superior cultural value of western European ways of life. The indications are very obvious in his work. Equally obvious is the fact that Montesquieu's comments about people with dark skin must be judged as clearly racist from today's perspective. When Montesquieu speaks of the human race, black people are not included, for it is 'impossible for us to suppose these creatures to be men' (Montesquieu, *Spirit of the Laws*, Book 15, Ch. 5 (n. 3)). Montesquieu's remarks about the people of South America or Asia also frequently appear in figures of speech of infantilization. However, I disagree with Ramgotra's account who argues that Montesquieu's political thinking 'constructs a republican constitution that supports the pursuit of empire abroad and allows a greater number of people to enjoy the benefits of colonial commerce and trade' (Ramgotra, 'Republic and Empire in Montesquieu's Spirit of the Laws', p. 791 (n. 77)).

[95] Howse, 'Montesquieu on Commerce, Conquest, War, and Peace', p. 6 (n. 14).

[96] On this point see Howse, 'Montesquieu on Commerce, Conquest, War, and Peace', p. 9 (n. 14).

actors in such a project, 'very often violated'[97] key norms of the law of nations, especially in their treatment of non-European peoples, and caused the 'most dangerous wounds that the human species ever received'.[98] Furthermore—and more importantly—Montesquieu also labels the right of conquest an 'unfortunate right'. A conquest always 'leaves the conqueror under a heavy obligation that must be redressed before humanity'.[99]

With the conquest, the conqueror assumes a debt of guilt. This guilt is not moral in nature, which would require the duty of atonement and whose final authority might be God. Here Montesquieu aims at a political concept of guilt, which demands liability and the 'redressing of the injury'[100] before the conquered people, with humanity as the instance. Humanity is the world court that shall judge, both from a contemporary and historical perspective, whether or not a conqueror has absolved his guilt with regard to the conquered people. The term humanity not only means an abstract, universal claim of reason to observe a minimal moral consensus justified naturally, rationally, or legally; here the term represents the idea of a specific order of human coexistence on this planet, which results from the relationships of the peoples with each other, which is accompanied by political responsibilities, and which is reflected in the obligations of the law of nations.

IV. The Confederate Republic as the Political–Institutional Form of a Montesquieuesque Law of Nations

A confederate republic (*république fédérative*) is the form of government that comes closest to representing Montesquieu's thoughts on the law of nations.[101] There are many reasons for this.

1. Cultivation of a civil law of the world by means of a specific interstate way of life

The confederate republic is the political–institutional form in which a law of nations could best be cultivated as a civil law of the world. In previous research on Montesquieu, the idea of the confederate republic was discussed primarily from the logic of the republic as a form of government. From the perspective of the republic as a form of government, the confederate republic famously imposes itself because it provides an answer to the two dangers facing a republic, namely the danger of conquest by a foreign power if the republic is too small, or internal collapse if the republic is too large. In contrast, according to Montesquieu the confederate

97 Montesquieu, *My Thoughts*, no. 1560 (n. 29).

98 Montesquieu, *Spirit of the Laws*, Book 4, Ch. 6 (n. 3).

99 Montesquieu, *Spirit of the Laws*, Book 10, Ch. 4 (n. 3).

100 Montesquieu, *Lettres Persanes*, no. 95 (n. 4). Montesquieu speaks in the French original of '*de la réparation du tort*'.

101 See also Long, 'Civilizing International Politics', p. 783 (n. 11).

republic combines the internal advantages of a republican form of government with those of a monarchy constituted by size and with an external show of strength. The fact that the confederate republic now imposes itself against the background of the thoughts on the law of nations as nothing less than the ideal form of government is due on the one hand to the fact that Montesquieu explicitly calls it a 'form of government'. The nature of the confederate republic as a form of government is

> a convention, by which several petty states agree to become members of a larger one, which they intend to establish. It is a kind of assemblage of societies that constitute a new one, capable of increasing by means of farther associations, till they arrive to such a degree of power, as to be able to provide for the security of the whole body.[102]

The confederate republic achieves the idea of a 'society of societies', in other words a kind of world society that consists of different peoples as its citizens. To put it in a nutshell: the confederate republic is the political–institutional form of a law of nations as the civil law of the world. The individual states remain preserved in the form of relatively small republics, and are armed against external dangers due to the alliance. At the same time, however, they cultivate the key conviction that one is dependent in many ways on the other peoples, and that cooperation is the only suitable behaviour.[103] Thus, according to Montesquieu, a nation in a confederate republic may no longer form an alliance without the consent of the other states; decisions on behalf of the confederate republic are made in a joint council and in accordance with gradated voting rights, depending on the size of the republic; the contributions to the confederate republic, in turn, depend on the votes in the council and the judges and civil servants should also ideally be elected by the council, in Montesquieu's view.[104] Since, for Montesquieu, the universal norms of the law of nations can be justified by means of reflection, but can be brought to life only through the relationship to the general spirit of a community, these considerations on the political–institutional form are indispensable in order to allow a civil law of the world to become reality.

2. Pacification of interstate relationships

Another reason in favour of the confederate republic as a form of government is that it contributes to the pacification of the world. According to Montesquieu, this is due firstly to the fact that war and conquest contradict the nature of the thing within a confederate republic. A confederate republic that allowed such a thing would disintegrate immediately.[105] Secondly, however—and this is a much more

[102] Montesquieu, *Spirit of the Laws*, Book 9, Ch. 1 (n. 3).

[103] In *Réflexions sur la monarchie universelle en Europe* he states that 'France and England (need) the wealth of Poland and Russia, just as one of their provinces needs the other. And the state that believes it can increase its power by subjecting its neighbour usually weakens itself as a result' (Montesquieu, *Betrachtungen über die universale Monarchie in Europa*: 235). A very similar thought can also be found in *Mes pensées* (see Montesquieu, *My Thoughts*, no. 318 (n. 29)).

[104] See Montesquieu, *Spirit of the Laws*, Book 9, Chs. 1–2 and Book 4, Ch. 3 (n. 3).

[105] Montesquieu, *Spirit of the Laws*, Book 10, Ch. 6 (n. 3).

important consideration—according to Montesquieu a confederate republic can function only with republics. Yet Montesquieu argues that republics in general, and democratic republics in particular, are especially poorly suited to conquer cities or other states—or, to put it another way: the requirements for such a conquest are such that aforementioned amends would become part of the raison d'état, which would therefore lead only to benevolent conquests by republics.[106] Otherwise, in Montesquieu's view, a republic would risk its own freedom if it did not integrate a conquered people in the democratic form of government, but instead exploited them. One reason is the hate that it would provoke with this difference—here a democratic republic; there a despotic regime. Another reason given by Montesquieu is that the civil servants who would then administer the conquered country, would have too much uncontrolled power, which would have a negative impact on the home country. Hannah Arendt would later take up this idea in the form of the boomerang theory in her analysis of imperialism, applying it to the European state at the beginning of the twentieth century.[107]

3. The law of nations as a guarantee of political freedom

As well as the cultivation of a civil law of the world as a specific interstate way of life and the pacification of interstate relationships, a confederate republic that observes Montesquieu's view of the law of nations is also one of three conditions for a nation to be able to live in freedom.

When it comes to the question of political freedom in Montesquieu's work, reference is usually made to Book 11 and Book 12 of *The Spirit of the Laws*. Here Montesquieu discusses the question of political freedom with reference to the state and constitutional law on the one hand and civil and criminal law on the other. In terms of constitutional law, Montesquieu's point is to argue that political freedom does not consist in either classical autonomy or in the assertion of will, but rather a) in the fact that one may do what the laws hold in prospect, and b) that one is not forced to do things that are forbidden by law. Civil and criminal law, on the other hand, must be designed in such a manner that the presumption of innocence is safeguarded and that no citizen is at the mercy of the arbitrariness of others. Both

[106] Montesquieu, *Spirit of the Laws*, Book 10, Ch. 8 (n. 3).

[107] In the course of her thoughts on imperialism, Arendt argues that the German and other colonial powers were not only able to carry out all kinds of cruelty on the African continent at the end of the nineteenth and beginning of the twentieth century, which they would later carry out on themselves. Moreover, the racism and brutal treatment of the people living there denied the idea of universality of the values and ideals of the Enlightenment. Additionally, it revealed the fact that a legal order can be designed in such a manner that it declares the suspension of law at discretion and according to the situation to be permissible. In brief: imperialism as counter-Enlightenment, but which does not remain restricted to the African continent, but rather which, upon the return of the employees of this imperialism and their experiences, also changed the spiritual situation in the mother countries. The core of the boomerang theory is that one cannot conduct war and infringe elementary human rights somewhere or other and yet assume that that which occurs at the other end of the world stays there. Like a boomerang, this story comes back to the mother country (see Hannah Arendt, *Origins of Totalitarianism*, p. 155 (1994)).

perspectives are significant if we want to understand Montesquieu's discourse on political freedom.

Yet they remain incomplete. The reason for this is that one assumes, if we stay with these two perspectives, that political freedom is solely a matter for individual states and between states, which exists and can be clarified only with reference to the laws that prevail in the country in question. What one overlooks is that freedom also has an international dimension. According to Montesquieu, if freedom consists in the first instance in the fact that one cannot be coerced into an action that is not prescribed by law, then one is only free in a political sense if civil laws exist, or if one lives under civil laws. Montesquieu thus concludes that nations 'who live not among themselves under civil laws, are not free; they are governed by force; they may continually force, or be forced'.[108] Thus a law of nations as a civil law of the world is also demanded from the perspective of the realization of political freedom, which ideally accompanies the confederate republic as a political–institutional form.

Selected Bibliography

Althusser, Louis, *Politics and History: Montesquieu, Rousseau, Marx* (NY: Verso, 2007).

Howse, Robert, 'Montesquieu on Commerce, Conquest, War, and Peace', *Brooklyn Journal of International Law* 31(3) (2006), 694–708.

Krause, Sharon R., 'Laws, Passion and the Attractions of Right Action in Montesquieu', *Philosophy and Social Criticism* 32(2) (2006), 211–30.

Lloyd, Genevieve, 'Imaging Difference: Cosmopolitanism in Montesquieu's *Persian Letters*', *Constellations* 19(3) (2012), 480–93.

Rahe, Paul A., *Montesquieu and the Logic of Liberty: War, Religion, Commerce, Climate, Terrain, Technology, Uneasiness of Mind, the Spirit of Political Vigilance, and the Foundations of the Modern Republic* (New Haven, NJ: Yale University Press, 2009).

Richter, Melvin, *The Political Theory of Montesquieu* (Cambridge: Cambridge University Press, 1977).

Shackleton, Robert, *Montesquieu: A Critical Biography* (Oxford: Oxford University Press, 1961).

[108] Montesquieu, *Spirit of the Laws*, Book 26, Ch. 20 (n. 3).

13

Emer de Vattel on the Society of Nations and the Political System of Europe

Simone Zurbuchen

This chapter deals with Emer de Vattel's treatise *The Law of Nations*, one of the best-known classics in the history of international law. Despite the continuous attention it received in the scholarly literature as well as in the diplomatic and juridical practice, especially in the United States, it remained highly contested ever since its first publication in 1758. The aim of this contribution in exploring Vattel's treatise is to show why the debate about its proper interpretation is unlikely to come to a conclusion soon. After reviewing the background and career of the author in Section I, I turn to his definition of the law of nations, with the aim of showing its indebtedness to the tradition of modern natural law and, at the same time, of highlighting its originality. The latter is mainly due to the significance Vattel attributed to the sovereign state as a free and independent member of the society of nations (Section II). In Section III I expose the many dualisms Vattel established in order to develop his very broad notion of the law of nations, which comprises both positive and negative duties incumbent on states, and also accounts for certain modes of conduct states need to tolerate by necessity when the end of peace cannot be reconciled with that of justice. I also aim to explain why considering Vattel as a founding father of positivism rests on a misunderstanding of his theory of the voluntary law of nations. This is further elucidated in Section IV, where I examine how Vattel put his dualisms to work in the domain of war. In this context we see how he applies the law of nations to the 'political system' of Europe, which he considers as a kind of republic instituted for the maintenance of order and liberty and founded on the scheme of the balance of power. In the last section, I briefly deal with Vattel's contested legacy.

I. Career and Main Works

Emer de Vattel was born in 1714 at Couvet, in the Principality of Neuchâtel and Valangin, which was under Prussian rule since 1707.[1] He studied philosophy and

[1] On Vattel's biography see Ed[ouard] Béguelin, 'En souvenir de Vattel', in *Recueil de Travaux* (1929), pp. 33–176. See also the editors' introduction to the edition of Vattel's main work I will refer

theology, first at the University of Basel (1728–1730) and later at the Academy of Geneva. It is most likely that he studied natural law in Geneva under the tutelage of Jean-Jacques Burlamaqui. Together with the Huguenot Jean Barbeyrac, who taught natural law at the Academy of Lausanne from 1711–1718, Burlamaqui and Vattel belong to the so-called Swiss school of natural law. Louis Bourguet, who gave private lectures on philosophy, law, and mathematics in the city of Neuchâtel, also influenced Vattel. Unlike Barbeyrac and Burlamaqui, who taught the law of nature and nations on the basis of Pufendorf's works, Bourguet was a great admirer of Leibniz' rationalism. In 1741, Vattel published his first book, a defence of the system of Leibniz against the objections of the Lausanne professor of philosophy and mathematics Jean-Pierre de Crousaz.

The dedication of the book to the Prussian King Frederick II earned Vattel an invitation from the French ambassador in Berlin to come to the court. He failed however to obtain the diplomatic position he hoped for, and the king showed no interest in coming back to his father's promise to create an Academy in Neuchâtel. Vattel moved on to Dresden in 1743, where he was promised employment by count Brühl, first minister of Elector Friedrich August II of Saxony (who as August III was also the elective king of Poland), who in the ongoing war of the Austrian Succession sided with Austria and Great Britain against Prussia. While waiting for an occupation, Vattel returned to Neuchâtel, where he wrote essays and began studying the works of Wolff. In his *Essai sur le fondement du droit naturel*, first published in 1746 and re-edited the following year in the collection *Le loisir philosophique ou pièces diverses*, he deals with the principle of obligation and defends a middle position between Leibniz' rationalism and Pufendorf's voluntarism. In this context, he takes issue with Barbeyrac's reflections on the highly critical judgment that Leibniz had made on Pufendorf's *De officio hominis et civis* (1673).

In 1747, Vattel was sent as a diplomatic envoy to Berne. This employment secured him a modest annual pension, but did not relieve him from financial hardship. He remained in Neuchâtel for much of the next ten years and began to work on the law of nations. He was in close contact with Jean Henri Samuel Formey, in whose house he had lived in Berlin in 1742–1743. At that time, Formey was pastor and professor of philosophy at the *Collège français*. In 1748, he became the perpetual secretary of the Prussian Academy. Not least because of their interest in Wolff's philosophy and its circulation in the French speaking parts of Europe, Vattel and Formey became close friends. Their correspondence lasted from 1743 to 1767.[2] While Vattel encouraged Formey to work on Wolff's law of nature (published in eight volumes, 1740–1748) and recommended 'to

to: Emer de Vattel, *The Law of Nations*, eds. Béla Kapossy and Richard Whatmore (2008). This edition is based on the 1797 English edition of the treatise, which comprises the observations Vattel later added to the first edition of his work.

[2] André Bandelier, ed., *Emer de Vattel à Jean Henri Samuel Formey: Correspondances autour du* Droit des gens (2012). See also André Bandelier, 'De Berlin à Neuchâtel: la genèse du Droit des gens d'Emer de Vattel', in Martin Fontius and Helmut Holzhey (eds.), *Schweizer im Berlin des 18. Jahrhunderts*, (1996), pp. 45–56.

keep the principles and the essential of the method of our philosopher, but to cover all that with a varnish as elegant as lucid, in a word to cloth it *à la française*',[3] he thought about doing the same with Wolff's law of nations that he began to study in 1750. He decided however to wait for Formey's publication and to continue studying Wolff's law of nature carefully. His critical observations on it were accomplished in 1753, but only published in 1762 as *Questions de droit naturel et observations sur le Traité du Droit de la Nature de M. le Baron de Wolf.* Vattel's masterpiece, *Le Droit des Gens, ou Principes de la Loi Naturelle, appliqués à la Conduite & aux Affaires des Nations & des Souverains*, was completed in 1756. Having first envisaged publishing the treatise with Elias Luzac junior in Leyden, Vattel eventually decided to have it printed in Neuchâtel in 1757, though the title page says London 1758. A pirate edition fabricated by a certain Theodor Flaack appeared at the same time. The publication of the *Law of Nations* immediately changed Vattel's personal situation. He became privy councilor in Dresden and chief adviser to the government of Saxony on foreign affairs. Besides the *Questions de droit naturel*, Vattel also published the *Mélanges de littérature, de morale et de politique* (1760)[4] during his stay in Dresden. Due to ill health, he had to return to Neuchâtel, where he died in 1767.

II. The *Law of Nations* and the Tradition of Modern Natural Law

In the 'Preface' to the *Law of Nations*, Vattel accounts for the way in which his treatise is related to Wolff's philosophy. He originally planned to simply detach the law of nations from the other parts of Wolff's system, and to get rid of the formal method of geometry, that rendered the work dry. By doing this, he wanted to ensure Wolff's *Ius gentium methodo scientifica pertractatum* (1749) a reception in the polite world. He later decided however to form a different work, which also comprised the duties of a nation towards itself which Wolff had dealt with in the chapters on universal public law in his *Ius naturae*. In line with the teaching of modern natural law, Vattel holds that, on account of its origin, the law of nations belongs to the law of nature. States or nations being considered like individual persons living together in the state of nature, all the duties and rights that nature prescribes and attributes to men in general, must also be applied to nations. Criticizing Pufendorf and his followers, Vattel insists however that the law of nations is not the same as the law of nature, since the latter needs to be duly modified in its application to states. For this reason he sides with Wolff, who considered the law of nations as a distinct science.[5]

[3] Letter to Formey, 12 April 1749, in Bandelier (ed.), *Emer de Vattel à Jean Henri Samuel Formey*, pp. 97–98, translated into English by the author (n. 2).

[4] Reprinted in 1765 as *Amusemens de littérature, de morale, et de politique.*

[5] E. de Vattel, *The Law of Nations*, pp. 7–13 (n. 1).

Despite this, Vattel acknowledges that the study of the law of nations presupposes acquaintance with the ordinary law of nature, of which human individuals are the object. This is best visible in the way he accounts for the principle of the law of nations, on which he founds the obligation of states to fulfil the duties imposed on them by nature. This is the desire of happiness, which drives human individuals as well as nations to seek their own preservation and perfection.[6] Since Vattel subscribes to the perfectionist metaphysics of Leibniz and Wolff, his doctrine of the law of nations embraces an individualist and utilitarian dimension. The obligation of human individuals and of nations to fulfil the obligations nature imposes on them against each other ultimately derives from their obligations to preserve and perfect themselves. In case of conflict between the two kinds of obligations, the latter outdo the former.[7]

By defining the law of nations as 'the science which teaches the rights subsisting between nations or states, and the obligations correspondent to these rights',[8] Vattel acknowledges the nation-state as exclusive subject of the law of nations. Its essential property is sovereignty. Drawing a clear distinction between the state or nation as 'body politic', to which sovereignty originally belongs, and the person or senate to whom sovereignty is entrusted in the social contract,[9] he defends the right of a nation to resist a tyrannical prince.[10] Sovereignty adopts an internal as well as an external dimension. While the former is essential for a nation in order to govern itself, the latter implies the liberty and independence from other sovereign nations.[11] This does however not mean that sovereignty would be absolute or unlimited. Taking states as moral persons with understanding and will, Vattel holds them to be subjected to the law of nations. Two features are intrinsically linked with the liberty and independence of nations. Firstly, the principle of non-interference in the internal affairs of states:

> It is an evident consequence of the liberty and independence of nations, that all have a right to be governed as they think proper, and that no state has the smallest right to interfere in the government of another. Of all the rights that can belong to a nation, sovereignty is, doubtless, the most scrupulously to respect, if they would not do her an injury.[12]

There is only one exception to the prohibition of intervention: if a people has a legitimate ground for resisting the prince and revolt against his tyrannical rule, any foreign power has a right to secure it, on condition however that the people asks for assistance.[13] The second feature closely linked with the liberty and independence

[6] E. de Vattel, *The Law of Nations*, Preliminaries, § 6, p. 69, note (n. 1). On the principle of obligation see also his *Essay on the Foundation of Natural Law*, transl. T.J. Hochstrasser, published as an appendix to *The Law of Nations*, pp. 747–71.

[7] See Emmanuelle Jouannet, *Emer de Vattel et l'émergence doctrinale du droit international classique* (1998), pp. 147–9.

[8] E. de Vattel, *The Law of Nations*, Preliminaries, § 3, p. 67, italics omitted (n. 1).

[9] E. de Vattel, *The Law of Nations*, book I, ch. IV, §§ 38, 40, pp. 97, 99 (n. 1).

[10] E. de Vattel, *The Law of Nations*, book I, ch. IV, § 54, pp. 110–12 (n. 1).

[11] See Stéphane Beaulac, 'Emer de Vattel and the Externalization of Sovereignty', *Journal of the History of International Law* 5 (2003), 237–92.

[12] E. de Vattel, *The Law of Nations*, book II, ch. IV, § 54, p. 289 (n. 1).

[13] E. de Vattel, *The Law of Nations*, book II, ch. IV, § 56, pp. 290–1 (n. 1).

of nations is their equality, which implies the reciprocity of their rights and obligations: 'whatever is lawful for one nation, is equally lawful for any other; and whatever is justifiable in the one, is equally so in the other'. Juxtaposing the principle of equality with the factual inequality of nations, Vattel famously states: 'A dwarf is as much a man as a giant; a small republic is no less a sovereign state than the most powerful kingdom.'[14]

Given that Vattel conceived of the law of nations as a legal system ensuring the coexistence of sovereign entities independent from each other, his treatise is held to express in mature form what we now call 'classic international law'.[15] This would explain his immediate reception in America as well as his enduring influence in the nineteenth and early twentieth centuries.[16] Equally important in this regard is another salient feature of the *Law of Nations*. In contradistinction to his predecessors, Vattel decidedly avoided any kind of vain erudition and relied on examples taken from modern history in order to illustrate his doctrine, which he otherwise claimed to base on general principles and demonstration.[17] Drawing on various materials scattered in the literature he relied on, he produced a manual of international law that gained continuous attention since it was first published in 1758.

III. The Natural and the Voluntary Law of Nations

Given that Vattel left at one side the idea of developing the law of nations as part of a deductive system, his work marks undoubtedly a turning point in the tradition of Wolffianism. It would however be problematic to identify this turn with a shift to positivism, as was often suggested.[18] This interpretation rests on a misunderstanding of the voluntary law of nations. Siding on this issue with Grotius, who distinguished the internal or natural law from the law of nations properly so called, that rested on the common consent of mankind, Vattel proposes to supplement the natural law of nations with the voluntary law. He thus conceives of the law of nations as 'double law'.[19]

While adopting the expression 'voluntary law' from Wolff, he wholeheartedly rejects the latter's proposal to derive this law from the idea of a great republic (*civitas*

[14] E. de Vattel, *The Law of Nations*, Preliminaries, §§ 18–19, p. 75 (n. 1).

[15] Peter Haggenmacher, 'L'état souverain comme sujet du droit international, de Vitoria à Vattel', *Droits* 15–16 (1992–1993), pp. 11–20.

[16] Vincent Chetail, 'Vattel et la sémantique du droit des gens: une tentative de reconstruction critique', in Vincent Chetail and Peter Haggenmacher (eds.), *Vattel's International Law in a XXIst Century Perspective* (2011), pp. 388–433, here pp. 396–402. For more details about the reception of Vattel's treatise in America see Section 5 below.

[17] See Jouannet, *Emer de Vattel*, pp. 133–40 (n. 7).

[18] This interpretation is largely indebted to Peter Pavel Remec, *The Position of the Individual in International Law* (1960), pp. 129–57. For an excellent critique of this account see Gabriella Silvestrini, 'Justice, War and Inequality: The Unjust Aggressor and the Enemy of the Human Race in Vattel's Theory of the Law of Nations', *Grotiana* 31 (2010), 44–68.

[19] E. de Vattel, *The Law of Nations*, Preface, p. 17. For the critique of Grotius, see pp. 7–8 (n. 1).

maxima).[20] In his view, this fiction is neither admissible in itself nor would it receive the 'obedient acquiescence of sovereign states'. The main reason for this is that sovereign states claim and actually possess absolute independence from each other and acknowledge no other laws than those imposed on them by nature. It is true, Vattel admits, that there does not exist any disposition in mankind voluntarily to observe the rules of the law of nature. This is why the forming of political associations was the only means for individual men of 'securing the condition of the good, and repressing the wicked'. He contends however that the civil association is equally necessary for states, as it was for individuals, *firstly*, since men having united under the same government become able to supply most of their wants and do not necessarily depend on the assistance of other political societies. *Secondly*, states conduct themselves in a different manner from individuals: measures of the public are carried on with more deliberation and circumspection, and states make arrangements and establish regulations by treaties on important occasions. The *third* argument Vattel advances against the fiction of a great republic is that independence is necessary to states in order to discharge the duties of preservation and perfection they owe to themselves and to their citizens. Only they would know how to govern themselves in the manner best suited to their circumstances.

Instead of deducing the voluntary law of nations from the fiction of a great republic, Vattel proposes to adopt 'a mode of reasoning nearly similar to that which Monsieur Wolf has pursued, with respect to individuals, in his treatise on the law of nature'. The doctrine he adopts here, and he applies to nations, states that the rules, which must be admitted in questions of external right, do not cancel the obligation which the internal right imposes on the conscience of nations. What nations may do by internal right is stated in the necessary law of nations; the voluntary law regulates the domain of external right. Whereas the necessary law corresponds to the 'immutable laws of justice', the voluntary law indicates what needs to be tolerated 'through necessity'.[21] This dualism of the necessary and the voluntary law is at the origin of much dispute about the correct interpretation of Vattel's treatise.

In order to properly assess this dualism, we now turn to the deduction of these two kinds of law. It is important to stress from the beginning that Vattel claims to deduce both of them 'from nature'. This implies that the voluntary law does not rest on the actual consent of nations. Instead, nations are bound to consent to the latter by the law of nature:

> so that we are authorized to presume their consent, without seeking for a record in the annals of the world; because, even if they had not given it, the law of nature supplies their omission, and gives it for them. In this particular, nations have not the option of giving or withholding their consent at pleasure: the refusal to give it would be an infringement of the common rights of nations.[22]

[20] Citations in this and the next paragraph are from E. de Vattel, *The Law of Nations*, Preface, pp. 14–16 (n. 1).

[21] E. de Vattel, *The Law of Nations*, Preface, p. 16 (n. 1).

[22] E. de Vattel, *The Law of Nations*, book III, ch. XII, § 192, p. 592 (n. 1).

The first step consists in the deduction of the necessary law of nations. In this context, Vattel adopts the mode of reasoning by analogy. He begins by observing that experience sufficiently proves that man is so formed by nature that he cannot supply all his wants without the intercourse and assistance of his fellow beings, whether for his preservation or for the sake of perfecting his nature and enjoying a life suitable to a rational being. From this he concludes that it was nature's intention that men should communicate with and mutually assist each other. Since the natural society among men, in fact the universal society of the human race, is 'an institution of nature herself', men are obligated to cultivate it, and to discharge its duties. Once they unite in civil societies, for the purpose of forming a separate state or nation, men remain still bound to the performance of their duties towards the rest of mankind. All the difference consists in this, that having agreed to act in common and to submit their will to the body of the society, it thenceforth belongs to that body, the state, and its rulers, to fulfil the duties towards strangers and towards other states.

That society, considered as moral person, since possessed of an understanding, volition, and strength peculiar to itself, is therefore obliged to live on the same terms with other societies or states, as individual man was obliged, before those establishments, to live with other men, that is to say, according to the laws of the natural society established among the human race, with the difference only of such exceptions as may arise from the different nature of the subjects.[23]

Since the object of the natural society between all mankind is that they should lend each other mutual assistance, the object of the great society established by nature between all nations is also the interchange of mutual assistance for their own improvement and that of their condition.

Based on this idea of a society of nations, Vattel spells out the two general laws the natural or necessary law of nations consists of. According to the first one, 'each individual nation is bound to contribute every thing in her power to the happiness and perfection of all the others', if she does not do thereby an injury to herself. The second general law says 'that each nation should be in the peaceable enjoyment of that liberty which she inherits from nature'.[24] In light of the significance Vattel attributes to the liberty and independence of nations as well as to their right to be governed as they think proper, or the right to sovereignty,[25] it is rather surprising that he deals with the duties of assistance or offices of humanity in the first place, and relegates the duties of justice, which require nations not to violate the rights of others,[26] under the heading of the second general law of nations.

The order he adopted was however deliberate. Hence, he points to the utopian character of his teaching by observing that it would be 'a subject of ridicule' to 'many of those refined conductors of nations', and 'appear very strange to cabinet politicians'. Invoking the authority of Cicero, he defends the idea of 'universal justice,

[23] E. de Vattel, *The Law of Nations*, Preliminaries, § 11, p. 73 (n. 1).
[24] E. de Vattel, *The Law of Nations*, Preliminaries, §§ 13–15, pp. 73–4 (n. 1).
[25] E. de Vattel, *The Law of Nations*, book II, ch. IV, § 54, p. 289 (n. 1).
[26] E. de Vattel, *The Law of Nations*, book II, ch. V, §§ 63–4, p. 296 (n. 1).

which consists in completely fulfilling the law of nature',[27] and shows how important it is that nations defend a neighbouring state unjustly attacked by a powerful enemy who threatens to oppress it, that they relieve the distress of a nation afflicted with famine, or that they transfer knowledge and science to a nation 'desirous of shaking off its native barbarism'.[28] He even invokes love of other nations as 'the pure source from which the offices of humanity should proceed' and reminds the politicians how important it is to cultivate the friendship of other nations.[29] In the end, he dwells in the delightful dream of a universal republic:

> How happy would mankind be, were these amiable precepts of nature [duties of humanity] every where observed! Nations would communicate to each other their products and their knowledge; a profound peace would prevail all over the earth, and enrich it with its invaluable fruits; industry, the sciences, and the arts, would be employed in promoting our happiness, no less than in relieving our wants; violent methods of deciding contests would be no more heard of: all differences would be terminated by moderation, justice, and equity; the world would have the appearance of a large republic; men would live every-where like brothers, and each individual be a citizen of the universe. That this idea should be but a delightful dream![30]

Despite this excursion into utopia, the chapter on the offices of humanity testifies no less to Vattel's pragmatism than the rest of his work. For he goes on to stress that disorderly passions, and private and mistaken interest would forever prevent the large republic to be realized. From this realistic angle he recalls that mutual assistance is not so necessary and less frequently required between nations than between individual men, and he insists that the care of its own safety requires more circumspection and reserve from a nation than from an individual man giving assistance to others. Since 'melancholy experience' would show that most nations aim to strengthen and enrich themselves at the expense of others, to domineer over them, and, if an opportunity offers, to bring them under their yoke, prudence requires caring in the first place about one's own safety instead of strengthening an enemy. Hence, no nation is obliged to give such assistance to another as may become destructive of itself.[31] Vattel's manner of dealing with the offices of humanity perfectly illustrates his manner of developing the law of nations. As commentators have observed, he very often poses a general principle and begins, on that basis, to formulate objections and to adjust its application to various concrete cases.[32] This is no doubt the reason why Ian Hunter qualified the discursive art employed in the *Law of Nations* as 'casuistical' in the historical sense 'of a discourse

[27] E. de Vattel, *The Law of Nations*, book II, ch. I, § 1, pp. 259–60 (n. 1).

[28] E. de Vattel, *The Law of Nations*, book II, ch. I, §§ 4–6, pp. 262–5 (n. 1).

[29] E. de Vattel, *The Law of Nations*, book II, ch. I §§ 11–12, p. 267 (n. 1). See Petter Korkman, 'L'amour universel du genre humain comme fondement des relations internationals chez de Vattel', in Yves Sandoz (ed.), *Réflexions sur l'impact, le rayonnement et l'actualité du 'Droit des gens' d'Emer de Vattel*, (2010), pp. 23–9.

[30] E. de Vattel, *The Law of Nations*, book II, ch. I, § 16, pp. 268–9 (n. 1).

[31] E. de Vattel, *The Law of Nations*, book II, ch. I, § 16, pp. 269–70; see also § 3, p. 262 (n. 1).

[32] Chetail even considers ambiguity as a method and as a system, Chetail, 'Vattel et la sémantique du droit des gens', pp. 423–32 (n. 16).

that mediates between conflicting principles, and that adjusts principles to cases and circumstances'.[33]

Despite the utopian rhetoric we have just considered, Vattel leaves no doubt that the second general law pertaining to the necessary law of nations takes precedence over the first one, since 'the natural society of nations cannot subsist, unless the natural rights of each be duly respected'.[34] This is further clarified on the basis of the distinction between perfect and imperfect rights and obligations. In this context, Vattel draws on the distinction between internal and external obligation: the obligation is internal, as it derives from a nation's duty; it is external, as it is considered relative to another nation. While the internal obligation is always the same and only varies in degree, the external obligation is divided into perfect and imperfect, and the rights corresponding to it in other nations are also perfect or imperfect. While holding a perfect right entitles a nation to compel those who refuse to fulfil the correspondent obligation, an imperfect right gives her only a right to ask.[35] The distinction between perfect and imperfect obligations and rights complies with the distinction between the duties of justice on the one hand, and the duties or offices of humanity on the other. While on account of their obligatory force the two kinds of duties are the same, nations are absolutely bound to live up to the former, but are at liberty do decide whether they can or cannot contribute to the welfare of another nation without neglecting the obligation to secure their own preservation and perfection.

It is crucial not to confound this distinction between internal and external obligation with the one between internal and external right we have considered earlier.[36] While the first distinction exclusively concerns the natural or necessary law of nations, the second one serves to distinguish the necessary from the voluntary law. In consequence, the latter does not spell out what nations can be constrained to do by other nations. It rather accounts for what nations need to tolerate by necessity. The liberty of nations Vattel has in mind here is the liberty of a nation 'to form her own judgment of what her conscience prescribes to her [. . .]—of what is proper and improper for her to do'.[37] This liberty of judgment matters, first, when it comes for a nation to decide whether she can perform any duty of aid (which imposes an imperfect obligation) for another nation without neglecting the duty she owes to herself. It matters, secondly, when it comes to a dispute between nations, where each of them will in fact maintain that she has justice on its side. Since in this case 'it does not belong to either of the parties interested, or to other nations, to pronounce a judgment on the contested question', nations will have to 'suffer certain things to be done, though in their own nature unjust and condemnable'.[38]

[33] Ian Hunter, 'Vattel's Law of Nations: Diplomatic Casuistry for the Protestant Nation', *Grotiana* 31 (2010), 108–40, at 125.

[34] E. de Vattel, *The Law of Nations*, Preliminaries, § 15, p. 74 (n. 1).

[35] E. de Vattel, *The Law of Nations*, Preliminaries, § 17, pp. 74–5 (n. 1).

[36] A widespread mistake in the International Relations literature.

[37] E. de Vattel, The Law of Nations, Preliminaries, § 16, p. 74 (n. 1).

[38] E. de Vattel, The Law of Nations, Preliminaries, § 21, p. 76 (n. 1).

One of the major defects of Vattel's reasoning consists in his unclear and sometimes confusing account of the voluntary law of nations. Thus he limits himself in producing a general definition of this kind of law without however developing it in a concise manner. As he indicates at the end of the 'Preliminaries', he does not treat separately the necessary and the voluntary law of nations. Instead, having established 'under each individual head of our subject, [. . .] what the necessary law prescribes', he would immediately add 'how and why the decisions of that law must be modified by the voluntary law of nations'.[39] In order to illustrate this, I will in the next section turn to the law of war.

Before doing so, we should pause a moment and resume the complex set of dualisms Vattel has established. Considering the natural or necessary law of nations, we can easily see that the Swiss author adopts a very broad notion of law, which embraces the first two sets of dualisms we have looked at above: 1) the duties of nations towards themselves, as opposed to the duties towards others, which in turn are divided into duties of humanity, duties to consider each other as equals, and duties of justice; 2) the duties of justice imposing on nations a perfect external obligation as opposed to the duties of humanity imposing an imperfect external obligation; 3) the necessary and the voluntary law of nations. Based on a misunderstanding of the voluntary law of nations, a great number of commentators tended to focus exclusively on the perfect rights of nations that are external and coercible. By reducing the 'real' Vattelian law of nations to the core of perfect obligations and rights, deemed to protect the liberty and independence of sovereign nations, they concluded that Vattel developed a highly individualist system of international law and made of him a foundational figure of positivism. Against this reductionist reading of Vattel's treatise, it is important to underline that the latter testifies to a broad understanding of law, perfectly in line with the tradition of the modern law of nature and nations. As Jouannet stresses, this broad concept of law was especially important for Vattel and his predecessors, since they developed it in reaction to Hobbes, who in fact downscaled law to the core of perfect external obligations and rights.[40]

In the section below I propose to examine how Vattel put his dualisms to work when applying his broad concept of law to the all but peaceful relations between the European states in his own day.

IV. The Dualisms at Work: The Example of the Law of War

In his philosophical essay *Perpetual Peace* Kant famously stated that Grotius, Pufendorf, and Vattel were nothing but 'sorry comforters', whose codes could not have the slightest legal force, because states, as such, are under no common external

[39] E. de Vattel, *The Law of Nations*, Preliminaries, § 27, p. 78 (n. 1).

[40] Emmanuelle Jouannet, 'Les dualismes du *Droit des gens*', in Vincent Chetail and Peter Haggenmacher (eds.), *Vattel's International Law in a XXIst Century Perspective*, pp. 133–49, at 143–5.

authority.[41] As his critique of the fiction of a *civitas maxima* shows, it was indeed unthinkable for Vattel that nations or states would ever get united and subject them to an external authority. He thus accepted that war was an inevitable fact of international politics. Counting on the increasing number of 'wise conductors of nations', who would take his teaching seriously,[42] he hoped however to contribute to the restraining of war, firstly, by marking the just bounds of the right of nations to employ force for the preservation of their rights (*jus ad bellum*), and, secondly, by moderating the exercise of that right (*jus in bello*).[43]

Vattel's ambition to contribute by his treatise to restrain war has however been put into serious doubt by scholars who argue, in line with Carl Schmitt, that the *Law of Nations* marks the end of the medieval and early modern just war theory.[44] While admitting that Vattel retained some elements of the just war doctrine, Schmitt takes this to be a 'hallow *topos*, a true platitude', since Vattel would claim that wars in due form are, in regard of their legal effects, to be considered just on both sides, without raising any further questions concerning their just cause.[45] This observation of Schmitt's leads us to have a closer look at the teaching of the voluntary law of nations in the domain of war.

While insisting that in times of war states remain obligated to observe the necessary law in their own conduct, Vattel advises them to 'allow others to avail themselves of the *voluntary* law of nations' in order to secure the happiness and advantage of the society of nations.[46] In this context, the voluntary law consists of three basic rules. According to the first, 'regular war, as to its effects, is to be accounted just on both sides'. The second rule states that independently of which of the enemies has justice on his side, 'whatever is permitted on the one in virtue of the state of war, is also permitted to the other'.[47] This means that *jus in bello* rules are binding for both parties in war. Schmitt acknowledges this by stating that this new doctrine greatly contributed to the humanization of war. According to the third rule, the voluntary law of nations does not justify the conduct of a nation taking up arms in an unjust cause, but merely entitles it 'to the benefit of the external effect of the law, and to impunity among mankind'.[48]

The first thing that needs clarification here is the notion of 'regular war' or 'war in due form'. For Vattel, to be in 'due form', a war needs to be made by the right

41 Immanuel Kant, 'Perpetual Peace. A Philosophical Sketch', in Hans Reiss (ed.), H.B. Nisbet (trans.), *Political Writings* (1991), p. 104.

42 E. de Vattel, *The Law of Nations*, Preface, pp. 18–19 (n. 1).

43 For a more detailed account of the law of war see Simone Zurbuchen, 'Vattel's *Law of Nations* and Just War Theory', *History of European Ideas* 35 (2009), 408–17.

44 See for instance Stefan Hobe, *Einführung in das Völkerrecht* (9th edn, 2008), pp. 36–44, and Wilhelm G. Grewe, *The Epochs of International Law*, trans. and rev. Michael Byers (2000).

45 Carl Schmitt, *The Nomos of the Earth in the International Law of the Jus Publicum Europaeum*, trans. G.L. Ulmen (2003), pp. 165–7. On Schmitt's interpretation of Vattel see Isaak Nakhimovsky, 'Carl Schmitt's Vattel and the "Law of Nations" between Enlightenment and Revolution', *Grotiana* 31, (2010), 141–64, at 144–6.

46 E. de Vattel, *The Law of Nations*, book III, ch. XII, § 189, p. 590 (n. 1).

47 E. de Vattel, *The Law of Nations*, book III, ch. XII, §§ 190–1, p. 591, italics omitted (n. 1).

48 E. de Vattel, *The Law of Nations*, book III, ch. XII, § 192, p. 592, italics omitted (n. 1).

authority, i.e. by a sovereign state. Moreover, the latter needs to respect certain formalities. These formalities consist in the demand of just satisfaction, and in the public declaration of war,[49] which must be known to the state against whom it is made. It also serves for the instruction and direction of its own subjects, and allows neutral states to identify the enemies.[50] However, the crucial element in the declaration of war is the announcement of the reasons for going to war, especially in the case of an offensive war. In order for a war to count as justified, the sovereign needs to have a just cause of complaint, a due satisfaction must have been denied to him, and he ought maturely to have considered whether it be for the advantage of the state to prosecute his right by the force of arms.[51]

In light of the importance Vattel attributes to the liberty of states to form their own judgment on what conscience prescribes them, some scholars contend that by declaring regular war to be just on both sides Vattel gave carte blanche to sovereigns pursuing their self-interested ends by means of force.[52] This is however not the case. While he readily admits that wars are often fought for pretexts, i.e. for reasons that are just only in appearance or that are absolutely destitute of all foundation, he insists that 'pretexts are at least a homage which unjust men pay to justice':

> He who screens himself with them shows that he still retains some sense of shame. He does not openly trample on what is most sacred in human society: he tacitly acknowledges that a flagrant injustice merits the indignation of all mankind.[53]

Besides the link Vattel establishes between the formal declaration and the just cause of war, there is yet another reason why Schmitt's interpretation of the voluntary law of nations goes astray. By contending that regular war needs to be considered just on both sides 'as to its effect', Vattel does not exclude that nations have the right to succour another nation being the victim of an unjust attack. Indeed, he considers assistance to a nation unjustly attacked as an obligation incumbent on nations on the basis of the necessary law of nations. Since this is an imperfect obligation, sovereigns are at liberty to decide whether they can live up to this obligation in any concrete case. Vattel insists however that according to the law of nations '[i]t is lawful and commendable to succour and assist, by all possible means, a nation engaged in a just war; and it is even a duty incumbent on every nation, to give such assistance, when she can give it without injury to herself'.[54] This last remark shows that according to Vattel, third party observers of a war are by no means obligated to treat the war of an unjust aggressor as if it were materially justified: quite the contrary, they are obligated to take sides with the victim in defence of its perfect rights.

[49] E. de Vattel, *The Law of Nations*, book III, ch. IV, § 66, p. 507 (n. 1).
[50] E. de Vattel, *The Law of Nations*, book III, ch. IV, § 55, p. 502 (n. 1).
[51] E. de Vattel, *The Law of Nations*, book III, ch. IV, § 51, p. 501 (n. 1).
[52] R.L. Homes, 'Can War Be Morally Justified? The Just War Theory', in Jean Bethke Elshtain (ed.), *Just War Theory* (1992), pp. 197–233; T. J. Hochstrasser, *Natural Law Theories in the Early Enlightenment* (2000), p. 181.
[53] E. de Vattel, *The Law of Nations*, book III, ch. III, § 32, pp. 486–7 (n. 1).
[54] E. de Vattel, *The Law of Nations*, book III, ch. VI, § 83, p. 513, italics omitted (n. 1).

This example illustrates nicely how Vattel relies on the dualism between the perfect and imperfect duties on one hand, and between the necessary and the voluntary law on the other.

To conclude this discussion, let us return to the meaning of the voluntary law of nations. By stating that the latter accounts for what nations need to tolerate by necessity, Vattel simply points to the fact that the ends of justice and peace cannot be reconciled in a society of free and independent nations. Having established the first rule of the voluntary law, he declares the latter to be absolutely necessary, if people wish to set any boundaries to the calamities war produces, 'and leave a door constantly open for the return to peace'.[55] Would acquisitions made by arms in regular wars not be considered just on both sides, it would be impossible to bring war to a speedy conclusion. In order to secure the society of nations, which are free and independent and therefore acknowledge no superior judge, the voluntary law 'tolerates what cannot be avoided without introducing greater evils'.[56] To illustrate the case, Vattel draws an analogy to civil law, which authorizes a debtor to refuse payment of his debts in a case of prescription. While the debtor takes advantage of this law, he nevertheless violates his duty. Just as civil law prevents the endless increase of law suits by prescription, the voluntary law prevents endless wars by considering regular warfare to be just on both sides 'as to its effect'.[57] As stated in the third rule, a sovereign who engages in an unjust war will however not be acquitted in conscience.

What we have so far established concerning the voluntary law of nations is further confirmed by the distinction Vattel establishes between 'legitimate and formal warfare' on the one hand, and 'illegitimate and informal wars' on the other. The latter are wars undertaken 'without even an apparent cause' that 'can be productive of no lawful effect, nor give any right to the author of it'. In consequence, a nation attacked by such kinds of enemies—which are also called 'enemies of the human race'—is not 'under any obligation to observe towards them the rules prescribed in formal warfare'.[58] When dealing with the formalities of regular warfare, Vattel points out that 'this is at present the constant practice among the powers of Europe'.[59] This helps to explain the severe judgment he pronounced on the Prussian invasion of Saxony, which marked the beginning of the Seven Year's War. The fact that he does not mention this incident in the *Law of Nations* is no doubt due to his personal situation. As an employee of the Elector of Saxony, who was at the same time a citizen of Neuchâtel and a subject of the Prussian king, he was indeed in a delicate position when he witnessed the invasion.[60]

[55] E. de Vattel, *The Law of Nations*, book III, ch. XII, § 190, p. 591 (n. 1).
[56] E. de Vattel, *The Law of Nations*, book III, ch. XII, § 192, p. 593 (n. 1).
[57] E. de Vattel, *The Law of Nations*, book III, ch. XII, § 192, p. 592 (n. 1).
[58] E. de Vattel, *The Law of Nations*, book III, ch. IV, § 67, pp. 507–8 (n. 1).
[59] E. de Vattel, *The Law of Nations*, book III, ch. IV, § 52, p. 501 (n. 1).
[60] See Tetsuya Toyoda, *Theory and Politics in the Law of Nations: Political Bias in International Law Discourse of Seven German Court Councilors in the Seventeenth and Eighteenth Centuries* (2011), p. 164.

In a message Vattel addressed to the governor (*avoyer*) and council of Berne on 28 February 1757,[61] he left however no doubt that he considered the invasion of Saxony to be an illegitimate and informal war. He invokes here a principle recognized all over the world, according to which a sovereign who believes to have a cause of complaint always needs to assert his claims before taking up arms. Only when just satisfaction has been denied to him or when he cannot reasonably hope to obtain it would he be allowed to go to war. Or at least would he always need to accept fair conditions that might be offered to him. Since Saxony had disarmed and was very far from threatening preparation of war, and since the Prussian king assured it of his friendship and good neighbourhood at the moment preceding the invasion, the latter was surely illegitimate. In a letter to count Brühl he sent off around the same time, Vattel pointed out that he would show in his *Law of Nations* 'that states must unite themselves to punish the one who wishes to establish such sinister customs (of war)'.[62]

Besides warfare aimed at punishing unjust aggressors, there are yet a great number of peaceful means Vattel recommends for maintaining order and liberty between sovereign and independent states. Regarding Europe in particular, he mentions the political balance or equilibrium of power. He introduces this device with the following observation:

> Europe forms a political system, an integral body, closely connected by the relations and different interests of the nations inhabiting this part of the world. It is not, as formerly, a confused heap of detached pieces, each of which thought herself very little concerned in the fate of the other, and seldom regarded things which did not immediately concern her. The continual attention of sovereigns to every occurrence, the constant residence of ministers, and the perpetual negotiations, make of modern Europe a kind of republic, of which the members – each independent, but all linked together by the ties of common interest – unite for the maintenance of order and liberty. Hence arose that famous scheme of the political balance, or the equilibrium of power; by which is understood such a disposition of things, as that no one potentate be able absolutely to predominate, and prescribe laws to the others.[63]

The crucial question arising here is how Vattel proposed to interpret the scheme of the political balance. Many contemporary scholars follow Schmitt, who claimed that by downplaying just war theory to a 'hallow *topos*', Vattel deprived the law of nations from is claim to universality and transformed it into the *Jus publicum europaeum*, the latter being maintained by the scheme of the political balance. This interpretation is problematic, since it shoves to one side the idea of a universal society of nations we have been considering in Section III of this chapter. To recall, Vattel claims that this society of free and independent nations is instituted by nature itself and held together by the mutual obligations and rights the latter imposes on the conscience of nations. Referring to his broad concept of the natural or necessary

[61] 'Lettres de Vattel à l'Avoyer et Consil de Berne (Protestation contre l'invasion de Saxe)', quoted by Béguelin, 'En souvenir de Vattel', p. 172 (n. 1), and also reprinted in Toyoda, *Theory and Politics*, pp. 170–1 (n. 60).

[62] English translation by Toyoda, *Theory and Politics*, p. 170 (n. 60).

[63] E. de Vattel, *The Law of Nations*, book III, ch. III, § 47, p. 496 (n. 1).

law of nations, Vattel also speaks of 'that system of right and justice which ought to prevail between nations and states'.[64] When he deals with the duties of humanity, i.e. the duties of nations to promote each other's welfare and perfection, he even invokes the dream of a universal republic, which would result from the general observance of these duties. Vattel leaves no doubt that this republic is utopian, since the private and mistaken interests of nations would forever prevent it to be realized. In contradistinction to this ideal universal republic, Vattel considers modern Europe from a realistic angle. Hence he qualifies Europe as a 'political system' or 'a kind of republic' by referring to the common interests, which tie the European nations together and manifest themselves in practices such as the constant residence of ministers and perpetual negotiations. He further suggests that within this political system specific measures need to be envisaged for maintaining order and liberty. In this context he introduces the scheme of the equilibrium of power.

It remains to be assessed what function Vattel attributed to the political balance within the framework of the law of nations. Was it deemed to replace the normative order imposed on nations by the law of nations as Schmitt suggested, or was it rather conceived as an additional tool for securing the observance of the law of nations? If we consider the peaceful means for maintaining the balance such as alliances or the settlement of disputes by means of arbitration, it seems to be obvious that Vattel assigned the political balance an auxiliary function. Since he does, however, not exclude that preventive warfare against an aggrandizing power might be justified under certain circumstances, we need to further examine whether he does not thereby introduce an argument conflicting with his theory of the just causes of war.

This is not easy to establish, since in this context Vattel adopts again the discursive art of judgment Hunter qualified as 'casuistical'. He first takes it to be 'a sacred principle of the law of nations' that 'an increase of power cannot, alone and of itself, give any one a right to take up arms in order to oppose it', since the end does not sanctify the means, and since war is only justifiable on grounds of avenging an injury received or of preserving oneself from an injury one is threatened with.[65] He then considers whether a nation has good grounds to think itself threatened by the increase in power of a neighboring state. To verify this, the nation in question needs to establish whether the aggrandizement of power is accompanied by the will of the state to oppress its neighbours. Arguing that power and the inclination to oppress are 'generally and frequently united', Vattel holds it admissible to take 'the first appearances' of the will to oppress 'for a sufficient indication', and concludes:

> When once a state has given proofs of injustice, rapacity, pride, ambition, or an imperious thirst of rule, she becomes an object of suspicion to her neighbours, whose duty it is to stand on their guard against her. They may come upon her at the moment when she is on the point of acquiring a formidable accession of power, - may demand securities, - and, if she hesitates to give them may prevent her designs by force of arms.[66]

[64] E. de Vattel, *The Law of Nations*, Preface, p. 7 (n. 1).
[65] E. de Vattel, *The Law of Nations*, book III, ch. III, § 43, p. 492 (n. 1).
[66] E. de Vattel, *The Law of Nations*, book III, ch. III, § 44, p. 492 (n. 1).

It certainly comes as no surprise that scholars disagree about the proper meaning of Vattel's reasoning. As I argued at more length elsewhere,[67] I am of the opinion that the most plausible reading must account of the link Vattel establishes between his general doctrine of the just causes of war and the position he defends in regard of preventive warfare aimed at maintaining the balance of power in Europe. This reading is consistent with Vattel's recommendation that states ought to seize 'the first favourable opportunity [. . .] to weaken a potentate who destroys the equilibrium' by means of force *when this can be done 'consistently with justice'*.[68]

No sophisticated argument is however needed in case of illegitimate and informal warfare. Dealing with nations that 'seem to delight in the ravages of war' and spread it on all sides, without reasons or pretexts, Vattel speaks of 'mischievous' nations, 'enemies of the human race', or of 'unjust aggressors'.[69] He leaves no doubt that the interest of human society authorizes all the other nations 'to form a confederacy in order to humble and chastise the delinquents'.[70] In his view, '[a]ll nations have a right to join in a confederacy for the purpose of punishing and even exterminating those savage nations'.[71] Vattel takes care to explain that this right does not contradict his maxim 'that it does not belong to nations to usurp the power of being judges of each other'. For the latter would only apply in cases where one can reasonably doubt whether each of the parties has justice on its side. Only if a nation, 'by the whole tenor of her conduct', proves to be animated by a mischievous disposition, the safety of the human race requires to repress it.[72]

The notion 'enemy of the human race' and the significance Vattel attributes to it in the context of international relations has recently found increasing attention among scholars.[73] So far we have seen how Vattel defines this notion in opposition to wars undertaken for just reasons or at least for pretexts, i.e. to wars formally declared. However, he also applies this notion to wars waged in an unjust way.[74] While in the first case he refers to the *jus ad bellum* criteria of the just cause, he relies in the second one on the *jus in bello* rules he extensively deals with in his treatise, for instance the discrimination between combatants and non-combatants, the prohibition of maltreating or killing prisoners of war, or the restraint of assassination

67 Zurbuchen, 'Vattel's *Law of Nations*', pp. 411–14 (n. 43).

68 E. de Vattel, *The Law of Nations*, book III, ch. III, § 49, p. 498 (emphasis added) (n. 1). Different interpretations have been proposed, among others, by Walter Rech, *Enemies of Mankind: Vattel's Theory of Collective Security* (2013), p. 148, pp. 172–3, and by Bruno Arcidiacono, 'De la balance politique et de ses rapports avec le droit des gens: Vattel, la "guerre pour l'équilibre" et le système européen', in Vincent Chetail and Peter Haggenmacher (eds.), *Vattel's International Law in a XXIst Century Perspective*, pp. 77–100.

69 E. de Vattel, *The Law of Nations*, book II, ch. V, § 70, p. 297, book III, ch. III, §§ 34–5, p. 487 (n. 1).

70 E. de Vattel, *The Law of Nations*, book II, ch. V, § 70, p. 297 (n. 1).

71 E. de Vattel, *The Law of Nations*, book III, ch. III, § 34, p. 487 (n. 1).

72 E. de Vattel, *The Law of Nations*, book II, ch. V, § 70, p. 297 (n. 1).

73 See Silvestrini, 'Justice, War and Inequality' (n. 18); Rech, *Enemies of Mankind* (n. 68); Nakhimovsky, 'Carl Schmitt's Vattel and the "Law of Nations"' (n. 45); Michel Snellart, 'La qualification de l'ennemi chez Emer de Vattel', *Astérion* 2 (2004), 31–84, <http://asterion.revues.org/82>.

74 E. de Vattel, *The Law of Nations*, book III, ch. VIII, § 155, p. 562, ch. IX, § 167–8, pp. 570–2 (n. 1).

and poisoning. He considers the violation of the laws of war to be so serious that it authorizes the enemy nation to break these laws as well. Measures such as reprisals and retributions are justified in order to restore the respect due to the laws of war.[75] As Dan Edelstein has observed, the notion *ennemi du genre humain* had a specific meaning and a common currency in French, while the English translation of Vattel's treatise does not render it uniformly. Edelstein refers in this context to the publications of Fénélon, Rousseau, and Burlamaqui. He also observes that Wolff applied the notion *totius generi humanis hostis* to those brigands who seek for war as an end in itself.[76] One certainly needs to add to this list Pufendorf, who reserved a prominent place to this notion in his *De iure naturae et gentium* as well as in the very popular manual *De officio hominis et civis*. It is most likely that Pufendorf gave currency to the expression *ennemi du genre humain* via the French translations of his works by Barbeyrac. While Pufendorf used it to designate human individuals such as pirates, brigands, or murderers, who render themselves guilty by adopting the violation of the law of nature as the aim of their profession or mode of living,[77] Vattel was the first author who showed how this notion could also be applied to states and be put to work in the international context.

It is not possible to further examine here how Vattel applies the notion 'enemy of the human race' in concrete cases.[78] The important thing to be noted is that his reasoning concerning the preservation of a system of free and independent sovereign states rests on two different sets of rules: the first one concerns 'civilized' nations ready to submit to the law of nations in times of peace and of war. This assures them the status of dignified members of the society of nations and is deemed to guarantee their liberty and independence. The second set of rules advises these 'civilized' nations to punish and subdue 'barbarian' nations ever ready to subvert the law of nations on which the society of nations is deemed to rest. In the relationship between 'civilized' nations and 'enemies of the human race' the principle of equality and hence the reciprocity of rights and obligations does no longer hold. The distinction between nations of good standing and 'outlaw' nations rendered Vattel's

[75] On these questions see Zurbuchen, 'Vattel's *Law of Nations*', pp. 414–5 (n. 43); Stephen C. Neff, 'Vattel and the Laws of War: A Tale of Three Circles', in Vincent Chetail and Peter Haggenmacher (eds.), *Vattel's International Law in a XXIst Century Perspective*, pp. 317–34; Christoph Good, *Emer de Vattel (1714-1767). Naturrechtliche Ansätze einer Menschenrechtsidee und des humanitären Völkerrechts im Zeitalter der Aufklärung* (2011).

[76] Dan Edelstein, 'War on Terror: The Law of Nations from Grotius to the French Revolution', *French Historical Studies* 31 (2008), 229–62, at 243. See also the contributions by Heller and Fiorillo, in this volume.

[77] Samuel Pufendorf, *Le Droit de la Nature et des Gens, ou Système Général des Principes les plus importans de la Morale, de la Jurisprudence et de la Politique*, trans. Jean Barbeyrac, reprint edn Basel 1732 (1987), vol. 2, book VIII, ch. IV, §§ 1–5, pp. 414–17; Samuel Pufendorf, *Des Devoirs de l'Homme et du Citoyen, tels qu'ils lui sont precrits par la Loi Naturelle*, trans. Jean Barbeyrac, reprint edn London 1741 (Caen, 1984), vol. 2, book II, ch. IV, §§ 1–6, pp. 142–5. In addition to Pufendorf, one might also think of Jean Bodin, who in his *Six Books of the Commonwealth* (book I, ch. 1) accorded a prominent place to the notion 'enemy of mankind' when he distinguished the well-ordered commonwealth from bands of thieves or pirates.

[78] See on that issue Silvestrini, 'Justice, War and Inequality' (n. 18); Rech, *Enemies of Mankind* (n. 68).

treatise ambiguous in yet another sense than the dualisms we have been looking at above. While scholars such as Schmitt and Koselleck saw in the *Law of Nations* a major contribution to the humanization of war through the successful exclusion of natural law morality from the law of nations, others (Edelstein, Bell) contend that by introducing the notion 'enemy of the human race' Vattel made of the observance of natural law the moral criterion for defining the limits of regular warfare and prepared thereby the justification of the Jacobine regime of terror, and the unleashing of total war in the period of the French Revolution.[79]

V. Vattel's Legacy

Vattel aimed above all to transform Wolff's treatise on the law of nations into a manual of international law for the use of European sovereigns, ministers, and diplomats. Considering Europe as a kind of republic united for the maintenance of order and liberty, he gave them advice on a great number of issues such as law of the territory and the sea, treaty law, the settling of disputes between nations, the law of diplomatic relations, and the law of war we have briefly been considering here.[80] His treatise however gained nowhere more influence than in North America. As Fenwick stated more than a century ago, Vattel became a lasting authority across the Atlantic.[81] Only recently scholars have more thoroughly investigated the reasons, the scope, and duration of Vattel's influence in America. As Chetail has shown in a well-documented analysis,[82] the favourable reception of his treatise by the American Founding Fathers served as a 'catalyst' first for its influence on diplomatic and judicial practice and subsequently for the development of legal doctrine. He convincingly argues that a treatise which 'resembled a code of conduct [. . .] proved to be particularly useful for a young nation',[83] since in the book on the duties of a nation towards itself Vattel also dealt with internal affairs of states and especially the importance of the constitution as the most secure basis of political authority and liberty of the citizens. The prudence and pragmatism as well as the ambiguity of his reasoning, which recently earned him the rather dismissive

[79] For the debate on the interpretation of Vattel's theory of the 'enemy of the human race' see Nakhimovsky, 'Carl Schmitt's Vattel' (n. 45).

[80] The best overview of how Vattel dealt whith what are considered today the essential branches of international law is provided in Chetail and Haggenmacher (eds.), *Vattel's International Law in a XXIst Century Perspective* (n. 16).

[81] Charles G. Fenwick, 'The Authority of Vattel', *The American Political Science Review* 7/3 (1913), 395–410.

[82] Vincent Chetail, 'Vattel and the American Dream: An Inquiry into the Reception of the *Law of Nations* in the United States', in Pierre-Marie Dupuy and Vincent Chetail (eds.), *The Roots of International Law – Les fondements du droit international* (2014), pp. 251–300. See also William Ossipow, Domink Gerber, 'La réception du droit des gens (1758) d'Emer de Vattel aux Etats-Unis: résultats d'une recherche et quelques espériences méthodologiques avec le concept d'autorité textuelle', in Yves Sandoz (ed.), *Réflexions sur l'impact, le rayonnement et l'actualité du 'Droit des Gens' d'Emer de Vattel à l'occasion du 250e anniversaire de sa parution* (2010), pp. 79–118.

[83] Chetail, 'Vattel and the American Dream', p. 255 (n. 82)

qualification 'casuistical', must have appealed to statesmen who relied more on common sense than on scholarly arguments in order to defend the position they held in a given situation. Concerning international affairs, Vattel's treatment of the independence of nations and of neutrality was particularly relevant in the American context. Statistics show that Vattel became the most frequently cited author in the diplomatic correspondences between the United States and foreign countries up to the middle of the twentieth century, and his treatise was also frequently cited by the American courts. What is more, the *Law of Nations* became a textbook in American colleges in the late eighteenth century and was subsequently frequently cited in manuals of constitutional theory. Despite its lasting influence, Vattel's work was however not met with unanimous acclaim among American legal scholars. While some criticized it for lack of philosophical precision, others dismissed it as codification of the Westphalian state system deemed to be outdated in the twentieth century.

This favourable reception in North America stands in stark contrast with the criticism he received in Europe. As Chetail points out, Vattel 'is the only scholar of international law who has triggered off entire books to condemn and contest his ideas'.[84] To my knowledge, no one has ever tried to establish a list of the manuals and histories of international law published in Great Britain, France, and Germany dealing with Vattel's treatise.[85] There is however no doubt that despite all the criticism it earned, the *Law of Nations* became firmly established as a classic of international law since the nineteenth century. The most salient feature of its reception in the literature on international law is certainly the fact that due to his insistence on the sovereignty of nations and the conception of the law of nations as a normative system of duties, obligations, and rights deemed to guarantee a society of free and independent nations, Vattel was made the 'prince of positivists'.[86]

This highly problematic account of Vattel's treatise, which rests on a misunderstanding of his theory of the voluntary law of nations, has only been rectified in the research devoted to it in the context of the renewed interest in the history of international law since the end of the Cold War.[87] Due to the growing number of historical and philosophical studies taking account of the context in which the *Law of Nations* was elaborated and commented upon at the time of the French Revolution, a much more nuanced account of Vattel's teaching has been provided.

[84] Chetail, 'Vattel and the American Dream', p. 252, note, with a list of these books (n. 82).

[85] Only little research on the influence of Vattel in countries other than these and the United States is available. In *Réflexions sur l'impact, le rayonnement et l'actualité du 'Droit des gens'* (n. 29) some papers deal with Vattel's reception in Japan, China, and Spain.

[86] This expression was coined by Georges Scelle, *Manuel de droit international Public* (1948), p. 44, and translated into English be Chetail, 'Vattel and the American Dream', p. 299 (n. 82).

[87] Much of the recent literature is aimed at re-interpreting the history of international law and legal discourse in terms of an ideology legitimizing European colonialism and imperialism. It is however doubtful whether Vattel's treatise fits into this counter-narrative. See on this issue Emmanuelle Jouannet, 'Des origines coloniales du droit international: à propos du droit des gens moderne au 18ème siècle', in Dupuy and Chetail (eds.), *The Roots of International Law*, pp. 649–71 (n. 82); Simone Zurbuchen, 'Vattel's 'Law of Nations' and the Principle of Non-Intervention', *Grotiana* 31 (2010), 69–84.

As I attempted to show in this contribution, the dualisms Vattel relied on are at the origin of the disputes about the 'true' meaning of his work. What was lately added to the dualisms so aptly exposed by Jouannet,[88] is the dichotomy between 'civilised' and 'barbarian' nations. As Daniel Bell observed, this distinction 'constituted one of the [eighteenth] century's most dangerously double-edged legacies, for if the first had to be treated with every courtesy, the second [. . .] were left to every horror'.[89] It is most likely that this legacy of Vattel will stimulate more fruitful research in the future than his alleged positivism.

Selected Bibliography

Chetail, Vincent and Haggenmacher, Peter (eds.), *Vattel's International Law in a XXIst Century Perspective – Le droit international de Vattel vu du XXIe siècle* (Leiden: Brill, 2011).

Dupuy, Pierre-Marie and Chetail, Vincent (eds.), *The Roots of International Law – Les fondements du droit international* (Leiden: Brill, 2014).

Jouannet, Emmanuelle, *Emer de Vattel et l'émergence doctrinale du droit international classique* (Paris: A. Pedone), 1998.

Grotiana 31 (2010): volume devoted to Emer de Vattel.

[88] Jouannet, 'Les dualismes du *Droit des gens*' (n. 40).

[89] Daniel Bell, *The First Total War: Napoleon's Europe and the Birth of Modern Warfare* (2007), p. 49.

14

Towards a System of Sympathetic Law

Envisioning Adam Smith's Theory of Jurisprudence

Bastian Ronge

Writing on Adam Smith's account of international law is quite challenging. Smith's philosophy of law is based on the concept of sympathy, which is related to social interactions within small-scale communities. Hence, his jurisprudence is primarily concerned with domestic law, and it requires some speculative spirit to examine the possibility of international law within his framework. In this endeavour, the search for his concept of law is confronted with considerable difficulties: Smith presumably decided to burn his manuscript shortly before his death.[1] Dealing with Smith's philosophy of internal law is, therefore, like doing a jigsaw. One has to find and combine the various pieces which can be found in his published writings as well as in reports from his lectures on jurisprudence. Hence, a speculative mindset is required not only with respect to Smithian thinking on international law, but with respect to his account of law in general. This is probably the reason why so little research has been undertaken on his philosophy of law in general[2]—despite the fact that, as Smith points out, jurisprudence is the third essential element of his overall theoretical project.

In this chapter, I take up the challenge to reconstruct Smith's theory of internal law and speculate about his idea of an international law based on sympathy. For obvious reasons, the reconstructing part takes up more room than the speculative

[1] The influence of Smith's legal thought was, therefore, restricted to the students, who listened to his lectures at the University of Glasgow. See for this question the study 'Natural Law and Moral Philosophy: From Grotius to the Scottish Enlightenment' by Knud Haakonssen. Haakonssen examines the influence of Smith's legal thought in the work of Dugald Stewart (Knud Haakonssen, *Natural Law and Moral Philosophy: From Grotius to the Scottish Enlightenment* (1996), pp. 226; who was a student of Smith and a very important figure with regard to the reception of Smith after his death).

[2] The exception from the rule is Knud Haakonssen, who published widely on this issue and is, therefore, the major point of reference in the following. Knud Haakonssen, *The Science of a Legislator: The Natural Jurisprudence of David Hume and Adam Smith* (1981); Knud Haakonssen, 'What Might Properly Be Called Natural Jurisprudence?', in Roy Campbell and Andrew Skinner (eds.), *The Origins and Nature of the Scottish Enlightenment* (1982), pp. 205–25; Haakonssen, Natural Law and Moral Philosophy (n. 1); Haakonssen, *Natural Law and Moral Philosophy* (n. 1); Knud Haakonssen, 'Hugo Grotius and the History of Political Thought', in Knud Haakonssen (ed.), *Grotius, Pufendorf and Modern Natural Law* (1999), pp. 35–61.

Towards a system of sympathetic law: Envisioning Adam Smith's theory of jurisprudence. Bastian Ronge.

part. In detail, the chapter is structured as follows: in Section I, I examine the status of Smith's theory of jurisprudence in the context of his works (1), and take a closer look at his sentimental approach to jurisprudence (2). I then give an account of Smith's theory of sympathy (Section II), since it represents the conceptual foundation for his theory of sympathetic law, which is explored in Section III. In Section IV, I provide the reader with the example of Smith's sympathetic reformulation of inheritance law in order to illustrate the general vector of his philosophy of law. Finally, in Section V, I shift the focus to the issue of international law and examine the question of how Smith's idea of sympathetic law might be applied to the level of international law and which lessons for today could be learned from Smith's intriguing philosophy of law.

I. Adam Smith's Internal Legal Philosophy

1. Overcoming the 'Adam Smith problem': Smith's unpublished book on jurisprudence

The 'Adam Smith problem' dominated the reception of Adam Smith from the nineteenth century onwards. For the German economists of the so-called historical school, the work of Adam Smith is characterized by a fundamental contradiction: while Smith's *Theory of Moral Sentiments* (1759)[3] is based on an optimistic anthropology and describes human beings as being naturally motivated by the altruistic passion of sympathy, the *Wealth of Nations* (1776) presents a pessimistic anthropology, identifying self-interest to be the main force in human behaviour. The founders of the 'Adam Smith problem' explain this contradiction with the so-called *Umschwungtheorie*. The explanation reads like this: during his stay in France (1764–1766) Adam Smith converted from a moral philosopher of the age of sensibility to the mastermind of modern economics—due to his contact with French economic physiocracy and philosophical materialism.[4] It is quite obvious that this explanation misses any sound foundation, as was pointed out by German economist *August Oncken*.[5] On the one hand, Adam Smith was already interested in economic issues before he went to France; as proven by the

[3] See, Adam Smith, *Theory of Moral Sentiments* (1759).

[4] The *Umschwungtheorie* was defended by various representatives of the historical school, see Witold von Skarzynski, *Adam Smith als Moralphilosoph und Schoepfer der Nationaloekonomie* (1878); Bruno Hildebrand, *Die Nationalökonomie der Gegenwart und Zukunft* (1848) and Karl Knies, *Die Politische Ökonomie vom Standpunkt der Geschichtlichen Methode* (1833). A far more accurate account of Smith's journey to France is provided by Reinhard Blomert, *Adam Smiths Reise nach Frankreich oder die Entstehung der Nationalökonomie* (2012). For a full account of Smith's biography see Nicholas Philipson, *Adam Smith: An Enlightened Life* (2010) and the other references in this note.

[5] He did this in the essay 'The Consistency of Adam Smith' (1897) as well as in the one year later published article, entitled 'Das Adam-Smith-Problem' (1898). See August Oncken, 'The Consistency of Adam Smith', in *The Economic Journal* 7(22) (1897), 443–50; August Oncken, 'Das Adam Smith Problem', in *Zeitschrift für Socialwissenschaft* (1898), pp. 25–33; 101–8; 276–87.

fragments on the division of labour 'written in the 1760s'[6] and the text known as 'An Early Draft of Part of The Wealth of Nations' from 1762.[7] On the other hand, he decided to publish several other editions of his 'Theory of Moral Sentiments' after he returned from France without any considerable changes with regards to the key concept of sympathy.

Even though the *Umschwungtheorie* was rejected, the existence of the so-called 'Adam Smith problem' itself was not disputed. The Adam Smith problem survived as a problem and the search for its solution kept Smith scholars busy until now.[8] Its long lasting success is quite astonishing since its two key assumptions cannot be sustained through any serious reading of the text material. Neither is the *Theory of Moral Sentiments* based on an optimistic anthropology, since our natural inclination to sympathize with other human beings is not restricted to altruistic passions, nor is the 'stupendous palace' of the *Wealth of Nations* 'erected upon the granite of self-interest'.[9] In fact, the notion of self-interest does appear only once in the whole book, namely in a footnote about the financing strategy of the Roman Catholic Church.[10] Therefore, the well-known Smith scholars David Raphael and Alexander Macfie are absolutely right when they describe the 'so-called Adam Smith problem' as a 'pseudo-problem based on ignorance and misunderstanding'.[11]

A careful reading of the *Advertisement* which Adam Smith wrote for the sixth and last edition of the *Theory of Moral Sentiments* (1790) already suffices to realize that, for Smith himself, the *Theory of Moral Sentiments* and the *Wealth of Nations* were two equivalent elements of his theoretical project and were meant to be complemented by a third element, namely a theory of jurisprudence.

In the Advertisement, Smith draws the reader's attention to the fact that he had originally planned to continue his *Theory of Moral Sentiments* with 'an account of the general principles of law and government, and of the different revolutions they have undergone in the different ages and periods of society, not only in what

[6] Adam Smith, 'Lectures on Jurisprudence. Report dated 1766' in Ronald Meek, David Daiches Raphael, and Peter Stein (eds.), Adam Smith: *Lectures on Jurisprudence* (1978), p. 561.

[7] For the problem of dating these documents see Ronald Meek and Andrew Skinner, 'The Development of Adam Smith's Ideas on the Division of Labour', in *The Economic Journal* 83(332) (1973), 1094–116.

[8] For a comprehensive overview over the history of the Adam Smith see Martin Patzen, 'Zur Diskussion des Adam Smith Problems—ein Überblick', in Peter Ulrich and Arnold Meyer-Faje (eds.), *Der andere Adam Smith: Beiträge zur Neubestimmung von Ökonomie als politischer Ökonomie* (1991), pp. 21–54.

[9] George Stigler, 'Smith's Travels on the Ship of State', in *History of Political Economy* 3(2) (1971), 265–77.

[10] 'In the church of Rome, the industry and zeal of the inferior clergy is kept more alive by the powerful motive of self-interest, than perhaps in any established protestant church. The parochial clergy derive, many of them, a very considerable part of their subsistence from the voluntary oblations of the people; a source of revenue which confession gives them many opportunities of improving.' Adam Smith, *An Inquiry into the Nature and Causes of the Wealth of Nations*, eds. Roy Campbell and Andrew Skinner (1979), pp. 789f.

[11] David D. Raphael and Alexander L. Macfie, 'Introduction', in *The Theory of Moral Sentiments*, written by Adam Smith (1976), pp. 1–52.

concerns justice, but in what concerns police, revenue, and arms' (TMS, 342). He was not able, Smith confesses, to work out this plan in full.

In the *Enquiry concerning the Nature and Causes of the Wealth of Nations*, I have partly executed this promise; at least so far as concerns police, revenue, and arms. What remains, the theory of Jurisprudence, which I have long projected, I have hitherto been hindered from executing, by the same occupations[12] which had till now prevented me from revising the present work. Though my very advanced age leaves me, I acknowledge, very little expectation of ever being able to execute this great work to my own satisfaction [. . .]. (TMS, 3)

This passage makes three things very clear: first of all it shows that Smith himself 'regards WN as continuing the sequence of thought set out in TMS'[13], i.e. that he did not see any contradiction between his two main works.[14] Secondly, the passage hints at the fact that Smith's overall project was intended to include not just two, but three elements—the *Theory of Moral Sentiments*, the *Wealth of Nations* and, last but not least, a 'theory of Jurisprudence' (TMS, 3). And thirdly, the passage reveals that the tripartite structure of his overall project is so important to Smith that he explicitly reminds the reader on his unwritten 'great work' on jurisprudence; instead of crossing out the promising passage while editing the last edition of his *Theory of Moral Sentiments*. Against this background, it becomes clear that an adequate picture of Adam Smith's philosophy has to include his projected book on natural jurisprudence. But how should one deal with a book that does not exist (anymore)?[15]

First of all, there are various reflections on law and jurisprudence within Smith's published works, namely the *Theory of Moral Sentiments* and the *Wealth of Nations*. Furthermore, there are notes taken by students of his *Lectures on Jurisprudence*,

[12] 'From 1778 onwards Smith worked as commissioner of customs, which was quite a time-consuming activity. The office of Commissioner of Customs may have been well-paid and honourable but it was no sinecure. By Smith's day, there were 800 separate acts of parliament affecting customs duties to superintend, endless adjudications to attend to, and an entire revenue service to supervise. The Board met four days a week throughout the year, breaking only for public holidays and, as Smith commented, "it was all too likely that the remaining three days would be interrupted by Board business"'. Phillipson, *An Enlightened Life*, p. 257 (n. 4).

[13] Raphael and Macfie, 'Introduction' (n. 11).

[14] 'Smith himself provides the best evidence against any ideal that there is a conflict between his two works. In the Advertisement to edition 6 of the Theory of Moral Sentiments, he refers to the final paragraph of the book, which promises another one on law and government, and says that he has 'partly executed this promise' in WN. Clearly therefore he regards WN as continuing the sequence of thought set out in TMS'; see Raphael and Macfie, 'Introduction' (n. 11). One could argue, that 'the real Adam Smith Problem' (James R. Otteson, 'The Recurring Adam Smith Problem', *History of Philosophy Quarterly* 17 (2000), 51–74) remains unsolved, since it is still not clear, how selfishness and altruism fit together. But this problem has nothing to do with Adam Smith and should, therefore, not be posed with reference to his name and work.

[15] Shortly before his death, Adam Smith requested his close friends Joseph Black and James Hutton to burn all his unfinished manuscripts with the exception of a few essays, which were posthumously published under the title 'essays on philosophical subjects' (see John Rae, *Life of Adam Smith* (1965) [1895], p. 434; Walther Eckstein, 'Einleitung des Herausgebers', in *Theorie der ethischen Gefühle*, written by Adam Smith (2004) [1925], pp. XI–LXXXIV). There are reasons to assume, that his manuscript on natural jurisprudence has been amongst the burned manuscripts as well (see Bastian Ronge, *Das Adam-Smith-Projekt: Zur Genealogie der liberalen Gouvernementalität* (2015), pp. 401–5).

which Smith gave as a Professor for Moral Philosophy at the University of Glasgow. Theses notes, published as 'Lectures on Jurisprudence' within the Glasgow Edition of the Works and Correspondence of Adam Smith, together with the shattered remarks in *Theory of Moral Sentiments* and the *Wealth of Nations* provide us with enough material to reconstruct Adam Smith's philosophy of jurisprudence. Or, to be more precise: any reconstruction of Smith's philosophy of law remains a matter of speculation, where some parts are more and some parts are less speculative.

2. Adam Smith's sentimental approach to jurisprudence: Sympathetic natural jurisprudence

According to Smith, human beings are essentially social beings. This means, amongst other things, that '[a]ll the members of human society stand in need of each others assistance' (TMS, 85). This holds true in particular for commercial societies, in which the division of labour has arrived at such a high level that every member 'stands at all times in need of the cooperation and assistance of great multitudes, while his whole life is scarce sufficient to gain the friendship of a few persons'.[16] This dependency on others would constitute an existential threat if benevolence was the only thing to count on. If the satisfaction of our needs depended entirely on the benevolence of our fellow citizen, living in a commercial society would be a foolish, incalculable risk. Fortunately, there is another, very reliable way of making our fellow citizens giving us what we need. We do not address their benevolence, but their *self-love*. We do not need to beg like a dog in order to get our meal, but rather make an offer which the other cannot reject.

> Man [. . .] works on the self-love of his fellows, by setting before them a sufficient temptation to get what he wants; the language of this disposition is, give me what I want, and you shall have what you want. It is not from benevolence, as the dogs, but from self-love that man expects any thing. The brewer and the baker serve us not from benevolence but from self-love.[17]

The irresistible power of self-love is the foundation upon which the division of labour in modern merchant societies is based. Thanks to the natural inclination to satisfy one's own desire, social cooperation can be secured and encouraged.

Smith takes the society 'among different merchants' (TMS, 86) as an example for illustrating social cohesion that is solely based on the 'sense of its utility' (TMS, 86). Within this particular social group, no one is interested in the good luck or happiness of the other. Despite this fact, they are able to cooperate with one another and uphold their 'mercenary exchange of good offices' (TMS, 86). However, Smith leaves no doubt about the fact that this form of societal association is 'less happy and agreeable' (TMS, 86) than social forms in which the 'necessary assistance is reciprocally afforded from love, from gratitude, from friendship, and esteem' (TMS, 85).[18]

[16] Smith, *Wealth of Nations*, p. 26 (n. 10).
[17] Smith, *Lectures on Jurisprudence*, p. 493 (n. 6).
[18] This remarks shows, that Smith would be critical about the process of 'marketization', since it implies the enlargement of utility based social connections and the replacement of alternative, normative better forms of social cohesion.

In other words: societies in which the social coherence is only created and maintained by mutual utility expectations are less preferable than societies in which the social band is founded on mutual recognition. Both forms of society, however, have to maintain justice—since justice is the main foundation of every society. 'Justice [. . .] is the main pillar that upholds the whole edifice. If it is removed, the great, the immense fabric of human society [. . .] must in a moment crumble into atoms.' (TMS, 86)

Even the societal connection between 'robbers and murderers' (TMS, 86) would fall apart if they suffered injustices from one another.

> The moment that injury begins, the moment that mutual resentment and animosity take place, all the bands of it are broke asunder, and the different members of which it consisted are, as it were, dissipated and scattered abroad by the violence and opposition of their discordant affections. If there is any society among robbers and murderers, they must at least, according to the trite observation, abstain from robbing and murdering one another. (TMS, 86)

But what is justice? Like his friend David Hume, Adam Smith regards justice as a negative virtue, which means that the essence of justice is omission. Acting fair and just means avoiding actions that are unfair and unjust; and whether an action is fair or unfair is quite easy to identify. We just have to know the law. Laws express the rights of man, i.e. inform us about the ways in which we harm other people's rights.

In Smith's moral philosophy, the virtue of justice attains a special status.[19] Normally, virtuous behaviour is guided by *sympathetic interaction*, so that our conduct is 'directed by a certain idea of propriety, by a certain taste for a particular tenor of conduct' (TMS, 175f.) (I will discuss this in more detail below). The virtue of justice, however, can be performed by adhering with 'the most obstinate steadfastness to the general rules' (TMS, 175) of justice. While the general rules of justice can be declared in the form of strict and unmistakable propositions, the ethical knowledge about all other virtues can be conveyed only through 'agreeable and lively pictures of manners' (TMS, 329).[20]

> The rules of justice may be compared to the rules of grammar; the rules of the other virtues, to the rules which critics lay down for the attainment of what is sublime and elegant in composition. The one, are precise, accurate, and indispensable. The other, are loose, vague, and

[19] Smith as well as Hume were fascinated by the 'special status' of justice. 'Justice was something of an enigma to both Hume and Smith. [. . .] The thing which struck them was that justice is so different from all other virtues. It seemed to be more precise and it could therefore be formulated in strict and general rules.' Haakonssen, *The Science of a Legislator*, pp. 83–7 (n. 2). For a more detailed account, see Haakonssen, *Natural Law and Moral Philosophy*, pp. 132f. (n. 1).

[20] 'By the vivacity of their descriptions they inflame our natural love of virtue, and increase our abhorrence of vice: by the justness as well as delicacy of their observations they may often help both to correct and to ascertain our natural sentiments with regard to the propriety of conduct, and suggesting many nice and delicate attentions, form us to a more exact justness of behaviour, than what, without such instruction, we should have been apt to think of.' Smith, *Theory of Moral Sentiments*, p. 329 (n. 3).

indeterminate, and present us rather with a general idea of the perfection we ought to aim at, than afford us any certain and infallible directions for acquiring it. (TMS, 175)

With this, it is possible to define the task of jurisprudence. Jurisprudence has to set the *grammar of justice*: it has to establish a system of positive laws which enables the people to behave just and fair, while the science 'properly called Ethics' has to create 'agreeable and lively pictures of manners' (TMS, 329) in order to give people an understanding of brave, prudent, and benevolent etc. behaviour.

According to Smith, the science of jurisprudence is an inductive one. Jurisprudence is not about deducing laws from abstract legal principles. On the contrary, a system of positive laws has to reflect the ways in which people *actually* judge other people's behaviour. The *moral sentiments* of real world people about real world moral behaviour is, according to Smith, the material foundation of every system of positive law. And since humankind is still in the process of moral and sentimental refinement, all hitherto established systems of positive law have fallen short of our ideal 'natural sentiments of justice' (TMS, 341).

Every system of positive law may be regarded as a more or less imperfect attempt towards a system of natural jurisprudence, or towards an enumeration of the particular rules of justice. (TMS, 340)

These legal shortcomings for the most part stem from the imperfection of mankind's emotional sensibility. As long as the sensibility of human beings is not fully developed, their moral sentiments will be rude and barbarous, and thus their corresponding moral judgment will be rude and barbarous as well.

In some countries, the rudeness and barbarism of the people hinder the natural sentiments of justice from arriving at that accuracy and precision which, in more civilized nations, they naturally attain to. Their laws are, like their manners, gross and rude and undistinguishing. (TMS, 341)

In the eighteenth century, however, being the age of sensibility, the emotional sensibility of (European) mankind has reached such a high degree of refinement that the laws *could* be in accordance with our natural sentiments of justice. The fact that they are still not has political or even institutional reasons.

Sometimes what is called the constitution of the state, that is, the interest of the government; sometimes the interest of particular orders of men who tyrannize the government, warp the positive laws of the country from what natural justice would prescribe. [. . .] In other countries the unfortunate constitution of their courts of judicature hinders any regular system of jurisprudence from ever establishing itself among them, though the improved manners of the people may be such as would admit of the most accurate. (TMS, 341)

To sum up: according to Smith, there has never existed a single system of positive law in which the 'decisions of positive law coincide exactly, in every case, with the rule which the natural sense of justice would dictate' (TMS, 341).[21]

[21] 'Systems of positive law, therefore, though they deserve the greatest authority, as the records of the sentiments of mankind in different ages and nations yet can never be regarded as accurate systems of the rules of natural justice.' Smith, *Theory of Moral Sentiments*, p. 341 (n. 3).

Against this background, the ambitious goal of Adam Smith's 'great work' on Natural Jurisprudence becomes apparent: his projected but never realized book would have been the attempt to lay down a system of positive laws in which the laws are—for the first time in history—in correspondence with mankind's natural sentiments of justice. Just like in the *Wealth of Nations*, where he tried to establish a *natural* system of economy, Smith would now have tried to create a *natural* system of jurisprudence. And just like in the *Theory of Moral Sentiments*, where he formulates the ideal of *sensitive stoicism* as the adequate realization of Stoicism in the age of sensibility, Smith would now have tried to adjust the tradition of natural law to the eighteenth-century state of emotional sensibility.[22] Before we take a closer look at this astonishing project, however, it is necessary to recall Smith's theory of sympathy, since it provides the basic foundation for his project of sympathetic natural jurisprudence.

II. Theory of Sympathy: The Conceptual Framework

Smith's overall goal in the *Theory of Moral Sentiments* is to describe and explain why human beings make the particular moral judgment they make. Why do we consider one behaviour as appropriate and the other as inappropriate? Why do we judge a behaviour as virtuous or vicious? What are the differences between judging our own behaviour and judging other people's behaviour? These are the main questions Adam Smith attempts to answer throughout the *Theory of Moral Sentiments* by developing a complex and intriguing theory of sympathy. Sympathy is, therefore, the key concept of the *Theory of Moral Sentiments*. Unfortunately, it is not very well defined. One could say, however, that the concept of sympathy plays a key role in the three following contexts: it describes (1) our natural capability to feel with other human beings; furthermore, the notion depicts (2) emotional harmony between persons who are in different emotional states; and last not but least (3), sympathy is the reason for moral approbation.

1. Sympathy refers to our natural capability of slipping into the shoes of other people and imitating their feelings. Right in the beginning of the *Theory of Moral Sentiments*, Smith states:

[22] According to Smith, Hugo Grotius is the one who came closest to such a system of natural jurisprudence. In his *Lectures on Jurisprudence*, he states: 'Grotius seems to have been the first who attempted to give the world any thing like a regular system of natural jurisprudence, and his treatise on the laws of war and peace, with all its imperfections, is perhaps at this day the most complete work on this subject.' See Smith, *Lectures on Jurisprudence*, p. 397 (n. 6); see also Smith, *Theory of Moral Sentiments*, pp. 341f. (n. 3). Haakonssen argues that Smith grants Grotius that special status because he sees him as the one who secularized natural law for the first time. See Haakonssen, *Natural Law and Moral Philosophy*, p. 136 (n. 1); Haakonssen, *Grotius*, p. 47 (n. 2). I would argue, on the other hand, that Grotius privileged position derives from the fact that Smith regards him as the first one who tried to develop an emotional account of natural law, since he introduces the figure of the equitable civil magistrate, i.e. an impartial spectator, to set up the norms of international law. However, this thesis requires further research.

How selfish soever man may be supposed, there are evidently some principles in his nature, which interest him in the fortune of others, and render their happiness necessary to him, though he derives nothing from it except the pleasure of seeing it. Of this kind is pity or compassion, the emotion which we feel for the misery of others, when we either see it, or are made to conceive it in a very lively manner. (TMS, 9)

This passage has a long history of misinterpretation. The discoverers of the so-called 'Adam Smith problem' took it to prove their claim that the *Theory of Moral Sentiments* is grounded on an altruistic anthropology and thus stands in stark contrast with the *Wealth of Nations.* This reading, however, overlooks the circumstance that Smith in this passage refers to the altruistic feelings of pity or compassion merely *as examples* for sympathetic feelings ('Of this kind'). Indeed, the range of sympathetic feelings is much broader and encompasses all kind of emotions: Fellow joy, fellow pain, fellow shame are as sympathetic as are pity or compassion. Smith is quite clear about this. Just a few sentences after the passage quoted above, he writes:

Pity and compassion are words appropriated to signify our fellow–feeling with the sorrow of others. Sympathy, though its meaning was, perhaps, originally the same, may now, however, without much impropriety, be made use of to denote our fellow–feeling with any passion whatever. (TMS, 10)

In other words: sympathy denotes our natural capability of imitating *all kinds* of original feelings our fellow men may experience. According to Smith, every human has this capability. Even the 'greatest ruffian' and the 'most hardened violator of the laws of society' (TMS, 9) are not bare of it—although their capability is limited in comparison with that of more sentimental beings, which have cultivated their sympathizing power by cultural techniques like reading sentimental novels, visiting the theatre, or writing sentimental letters.[23]

2. The notion of sympathize also refers to the emotional harmony between two persons, namely a 'spectator' (SP) and a 'person principally concerned' (PPC). Hence, sympathy—in the sense of emotional correspondence—can only occur in emotionally asymmetric situations, where one subject is emotionally affected by an external impact (the 'person principally concerned'), while the other one is in the state of emotional indifference (the 'spectator'). This emotional asymmetry poses a great challenge. In order to overcome the asymmetry and realize sympathetic harmony, both subjects have to work hard. The spectator, on the one side, has to embrace all his imaginative powers in order 'to put himself in the situation of the other, and to bring home to himself every little circumstance of distress which can possibly occur to the sufferer' (TMS, 21).

He must adopt the whole case of his companion with all its minutest incidents; and strive to render as perfect as possible, that imaginary change of situation upon which his sympathy is founded. (TMS, 21)

[23] Smith does not refer explicitly to theses cultural techniques. There is, however, indirect evidence that Smith was aware of the educational effect of these sentimental practices, see Ronge, *Adam-Smith-Projekt*, pp. 232–6 (n. 15). He stands in contrast to Jean-Jacques Rousseau, who is well known for his scepticism against the theatre as well as the emotion of pity as a moral force.

The person principally concerned, one the other side, has to reduce his 'original passions' (TMS, 16) to that 'pitch, in which the spectators are capable of going along with him' (TMS, 22). He mitigates his feelings in the same way as the spectator embraces his, namely by slipping into the shoes of his counterpart and copying the feeling the other one feels.[24]

To sum up: the spectator copies the original passion of the person principally concerned and creates sympathetic fellow feelings, which are then copied by the person principally concerned in order to reduce his original passions to the affective level which the spectator can go along with. Through this circular interaction (which is, by the way, clearly reminiscent of the natural price mechanism described in *Wealth of Nations*), sympathy can be achieved.

3. The state of sympathy (as emotional harmony) evokes a particular feeling, both in the spectator as well as in the person principally concerned, which Smith calls 'sentiment of approbation' (TMS, 46). With this, we touch upon the overall goal of Smith's *Theory of Moral Sentiments*, namely to describe and explain our practices of making moral judgments. Sympathetic harmony, according to Smith, implies moral approbation. If we—as the spectator—have the same feeling like the person principally concerned, we will consider his behaviour as *appropriate*. If there is no sympathy, on the other hand, we will deem his behaviour as exaggerated and inappropriate.

According to Smith, this 'direct sympathy' between the spectator and the person principally concerned is the first and foundational layer of our moral judgments. Every moral judgment contains an evaluation of the appropriateness or inappropriateness of the action in question; but some moral judgments require more, something like a second layer. This is the case where our moral judgment is not only about the appropriateness or inappropriateness of an action, but also about its virtuousness or vice. In this case, we enter a situation of 'indirect sympathy', which does not involve just two, but three persons: the spectator (SP), the person principally concerned (PPC), and the *person principally acting*[25] (PPA), who performs an action that is perceived by PPC as beneficial or harmful to him. It is utterly important to understand this rather complicated model of indirect sympathy because it provides the key conceptual framework for Smith's theory of jurisprudence.

Let us take an example to illustrate the case of indirect sympathy: PPA performs an action, which is perceived as harmful by PPC. Hence, PPC feels anger and

[24] 'In order to produce this concord, as nature teaches the spectators to assume the circumstances of the person principally concerned, so she teaches this last in some measure to assume those of the spectators. [. . .] As their sympathy makes them look at it, in some measure, with his eyes, so his sympathy makes him look at it, in some measure, with theirs, especially when in their presence and acting under their observation: and as the reflected passion, which he thus conceives, is much weaker than the original one, it necessarily abates the violence of what he felt before he came into their presence [. . .].' Smith, *Theory of Moral Sentiments*, p. 22 (n. 3).

[25] While Smith uses the notion 'person principally concerned' almost like a technical term, he does not provide any notion for describing the person to whom the person principally concerned reacts. I suggest to call this third party the 'person principally acting'.

resentment against PPA and wants to harm him. If the impartial spectator (directly) sympathizes with PPC, i.e. if he successfully imitates his feeling of resentment, he will evaluate PPA's behaviour as vicious. But this direct sympathy between SP and PPC can only occur if the earlier sympathetic interaction between SP and PPA has failed. The spectator has to assess PPA's behaviour as inappropriate in order to evaluate PPC's emotional reaction to PPA as appropriate. If the spectator did not disagree with PPA's behaviour, he will not agree with PPC's reaction towards it. To put it in more abstract terms: moral judgments about the virtue or vice of actions involve not just one layer (sympathetic interaction with the PPC) but a second layer as well—namely the sympathetic interaction with the PPA. The crucial point is that the second layer works like the first layer, just with another person. The situation of indirect sympathy is nothing but the addition of two situation of direct sympathy (first with the PPA, then with the PPC).

With this, we can proceed to consider the centrepiece of Smith's philosophy of law, namely his theory about the sympathetic foundation of rights.

III. The Centrepiece of Smith's Philosophy of Law: The Sympathetic Foundation of Rights

Representatives of classical natural law usually start their theoretical reflection by examining the *natural rights* which human beings have qua being human. Afterwards, they proceed to study the *acquired rights*, namely the rights which human beings obtain as a member of society. But there is also another way of dealing with rights, represented by the 'civilians'.

> The civilians begin with considering government and then treat of property and other rights. Others[26] who have written on this subject begin with the latter and then consider family and civil government. There are several advantages peculiar to each of these methods, tho' that of the civil law seems upon the whole preferable.[27]

The reason why Smith prefers the civilian method is simple: for Smith—as for the most representatives of the Scottish Enlightenment—human beings are essentially

[26] 'Others' refers to the classical representatives of natural law, as Haakonssen points out: 'The "others" to whom Smith referred were the generality of natural law thinkers in the seventeenth and eighteenth centuries, to whose method he was introduced when a student of Francis Hutchesons' at Glasgow University. These writers divided natural law into three principal parts. The first dealt with the individual in abstraction from social groups; the second dealt with the individual as a member of the family group (often called "oeconomical jurisprudence"– that is, "household jurisprudence"); and the third dealt with the individual as a member of civil society (sometimes called "political jurisprudence"). To these topics was normally added the jurisprudence of the international community, the "law of nations".' Haakonssen, *Natural Law and Moral Philosophy*, p. 130 (n. 1).

[27] Smith, *Lectures on Jurisprudence*, p. 401 (n. 6). Again Haakonssen: 'At first it is puzzling that Smith should suggest that the "civilians" put political jurisprudence, or "government", first. Plainly, no writer on the civil law, by which Smith meant *corpus iuris civilis*, began with a discussion of the principles of political governance [. . .]. What Smith must have meant—and, one may hope, explained to his students—was that the civil law always *presupposed* the existence of political society, *civitas*, as a precondition for the law of the *civitas*.' Haakonssen, *Natural Law and Moral Philosophy*, p. 130 (n. 1).

social beings who live always and already within societal forms.[28] Society is nothing that has to be invented or constituted; society is always and already there. Starting 'with the individual in abstraction from social groups,'[29] as classical natural law does, is not very plausible to Smith.

Despite these general reservations against the method of classical natural law, Smith adopts its distinction between natural and acquired rights. For Smith, however, this does not represent a distinction in terms of origin (nature vs. society), but in terms of explanatory efforts. Even natural rights, he believes—like men's right over bodily integrity and intact reputation—are 'not pre-social moral equipment but part of living socially';[30] they are socially acquired. The crucial difference between rights called natural and acquired rights consists in the fact that the former are part of every society whereas the latter emerge only by way of socio-historic progress. While the 'origin of natural rights is quite evident', socio-historically 'acquired rights such as property require more explanation'.[31] To be more concrete: in the case of natural rights, the theorist only has to describe and explain their various formulations in time; in case of acquired rights, however, he has to tackle the question why these rights came into existence in the first place. In other words: Jurisprudence has to, therefore, come up with historical, sociological, and economical explanations.[32]

Smith's use of the distinction between natural and acquired rights should not make us lose sight of the fact that, for him, all rights—no matter, whether they are called 'natural' or 'acquired'—have one and the same origin, namely the *indirect sympathy* of the spectator. This is the key idea of Smith's philosophy of law, and he uses John Locke's example of acquiring an apple to illustrate it.

How it is that a man by pulling an apple should be imagined to have a right to that apple and a power of excluding all others from it—and that an injury should be conceived to be done when such a subject is taken for the possessor. From the system I have already explain'd[33], you will remember that I told you we may conceive any injury was done one when an impartial spectator would be of opinion he was injured, would join with him in his concern and go

[28] This Aristotelian view on the social nature of man becomes most apparent in the critique of Hobbes' contract theory, which can be found in Smith (*Lectures on Jurisprudence*, pp. 316f. (n. 6)) as well as in (Hume Knud Haakonssen (ed.), Hume, *Political Essays* (1994), pp. 186–201).

[29] Haakonssen, *Natural Law and Moral Philosophy*, p. 130 (n. 1).

[30] Haakonssen, *Natural Law and Moral Philosophy*, p. 134 (n. 1).

[31] Smith, *Lectures on Jurisprudence*, p. 401 (n. 6).

[32] See also Knud Haakonssen's remark on Smith's use of the distinction: 'Smith never makes it absolutely clear what is the basis for this distinction, but the little he does say makes it possible to find an explanation [. . .]. The thing he stresses is that natural rights are quite evident in their content and need no lengthy analysis: what constitutes an injury to a man's person or reputation is immediately 'evident to reason'. But acquired rights need much more explanation. This is simply because they are—required. They depend for their very existence, or their effective recognition, on some element of governmental authority in a society, and since the latter varies enormously from one epoch to another and from one country to another, so the rights must also vary, and consequently they can only be understood against the background of these circumstantial factors', see Haakonssen, *The Science of a Legislator*, pp. 100f. (n. 2).

[33] Smith here refers to the 'system of ethics of the Theory of Moral Sentiments, which Smith had no doubt explained earlier in the course.' See Smith, *Lectures on Jurisprudence*, p. 17, n. 16 (n. 6).

along with him when he defended the subject in his possession against any violent attack, or used force to recover what had been thus wrongfully wrested out of his hands.[34]

While Locke deduces the (acquired) property right over the apple from the (natural) right over one's own body, Smith's theory of (indirect) sympathy allows him to see the entitlement of private property in a new light. The property right over the apple derives from the fellow resentment spectators would feel with the person principally concerned if someone would take away the apple from him. Let us imagine person A picks a few apples from a tree and starts eating them. Now person B comes along and takes away an apple from A. A gets angry and wants to punish B for impinging on his property right. From Smith's point of view, the question whether A's claim is justified depends on the question whether there is sympathy between A and the impartial spectator of the scene or not. Only if the spectator sympathizes with the emotional reaction (i.e. the moral judgment) of A, he will acknowledge his claim and his right of ownership with regards to the apple.[35] To put it in another way: for Smith, all legal rights are *retroactively* constituted. Only *after* the person principally acting (PPA) has done something to the person principally concerned (PPC), to which he reacts with resentment and the wish to punish PPA, and *after* the spectators have disagreed with PPA's behaviour and successfully sympathized with PPC, PPC's claim and right is recognized and established. This sympathetic recognition of PPC's resentment, the common longing for punishment of the offender, is the original source of every endorsement—no matter whether it is called natural or acquired.[36] Hence, resentment, 'commonly regarded as so odious a passion' (TMS, 76), is not at all a threat to society but—on the contrary—an important guarantee of its continued existence.

Resentment seems to have been given us by nature for defence, and for defence only. It is the safeguard of justice and the security of innocence. It prompts us to beat off the mischief which is attempted to be done to us, and to retaliate that which is already done; that the offender may be made to repent of his injustice, and that others, through fear of the like punishment, may be terrified from being guilty of the like offence. (TMS, 79)

The 'most odious, perhaps, of all the passions' (TMS, 76) secures the administration of justice before its institutionalized and official administration through judges and arbiters. Furthermore, the official and institutionalized jurisdiction has to stay

[34] Smith, *Lectures on Jurisprudence*, p. 493 (n. 6).

[35] Interestingly enough, Smith seems to discover in the context of legal philosophy what economists in the nineteenth century will call diminishing marginal utility, i.e. the fact that the value of a particular good depends on the question how much of the same good has been already consumed. The same idea can be found here: if the person principally acting takes away the only apple from the person principally concerned, the spectator will much more easily sympathize with the resentment of the person principally concerned than if he 'steals' the thousand-and-first apple.

[36] Haakonssen comments on this in the following way: 'The object of natural Jurisprudence is justice; and the rules of justice define our rights by laying down what actions constitute injuries against us. The concept of 'injury' is understood in pure spectator-terms: what the relevant, actual spectators—such as judges and juries—in a given society recognize as injury is in legal terms injury in that society at that time and is definitive of its rights and laws.' See Haakonssen, *The Science of a Legislator*, p. 100 (n. 2).

in touch with the *real practices of moral judgment*, performed by everyday spectators. The legal system has to be mirror of the moral judgments prevalent in society.[37]

With his account of the sympathetic origin of all rights, Smith provides an alternative to utility-based conceptualizations of rights; as presented e.g. by his friend David Hume. Indeed, Smith admits that sometimes 'we both punish and approve of punishment merely from a view to the general interest of society' (TMS, 90). Nonetheless, the first and original source of claiming and defending rights is 'the sympathetic resentment of the spectator' (TMS, 78).

It is to be observed that our first approbation of punishment is not founded upon the regard to public utility which is commonly taken to be the foundation of it. It is our sympathy with the resentment of the sufferer which is the real principle.[38]

In the next part, I want to draw on Smith's thought about the inheritance law, since it is the best example to illustrate the general direction of Smith's sympathetic account of justice and law.

IV. Rewriting the Systems of Positive Law: The Example of Inheritance Law

The theory of the sympathetic foundation of rights is the key idea of Smith's sentimental approach to jurisprudence and his attempt to develop a system of positive law that—for the first time in history—fulfils the demands of sympathetic natural jurisprudence. Unfortunately, we cannot say much about the way in which Adam Smith would have set up his system of sympathetic law in concrete terms. Just one thing is fairly clear: the hierarchy and order of rights would not be based on the distinction between natural and acquired rights like in classical natural law. For Smith, all rights stem from the sympathy between impartial spectators and persons principally concerned. The ranking of rights must be deduced, therefore, from this sympathetic origin—but how? Smith gives an intriguing answer: it is the affective intensity of the fellow resentment that decides about the significance of rights: the more intense the level of sympathetic resentment, the more important the affected right.[39] For example: murder is 'the most atrocious of all crimes' and 'excites the highest degree of resentment in those who are immediately connected with the slain' (TMS, 84). Hence, rights protecting life are the most essential ones.

The most sacred laws of justice, therefore, those whose violation seems to call loudest for vengeance and punishment, are the laws which guard the life and person of our

[37] 'It is the end of jurisprudence to prescribe rules for the decisions of judges and arbiters.' Smith, *Theory of Moral Sentiments*, p. 330 (n. 3).

[38] Smith, *Lectures on Jurisprudence*, p. 475 (n. 6).

[39] See the following statement made by Haakonssen: 'For obviously both classes of rights [the natural as well as the acquired ones, B.R.] have the same foundation, namely the sympathetic resentment of the impartial spectator at the injuries against which the rights are a protection. This resentment,

neighbour: the next are those which guard his property and possessions; and last of all come those which guard what are called his personal rights, or what is due to him from the promises of others. (TMS, 84)

The sympathetic paradigm of rights would without doubt be the cardinal point of Smith's rewriting of positive law, but little can be said about the way in which Smith planned to rewrite existing laws in detail. There is, however, one example which sheds some light on this question, namely the example of the inheritance law.

According to Smith's sympathetic theory of rights, we respect the last will of another person because we sympathize with him.

We naturaly [sic] find a pleasure in remembring [sic] the last words of a friend and in executing his last injunctions. The solemnity of the occasion deeply impresses the mind. Besides, we enter as it were into his dead body, and conceive what our living souls would feel if they were joined with his body, and how much we would be distressed to see our last injunctions not performed.[40]

The sympathetic interaction with the dead is, according to Smith, the original 'foundation of testamentary succession' and is responsible for the legal practice to 'extend property a little farther than a man's lifetime'.[41] This legal practice can only be introduced in societies, which have already achieved a particular level of emotional refinement.[42] Undoubtedly, eighteenth-century European societies would be able to establish such a sympathetic inheritance law. This would not only be adequate with regards to their emotional culture, but also economically beneficial, since it would bring the disastrous praxis of *perpetual entails* to an end.

Upon the whole nothing can be more absurd than perpetual entails. In them the principals of testamentary succession can by no means take place. Piety to the dead can only take place when their memory is fresh in the minds of men. A power to dispose of estates for ever is manifestly absurd. The earth and the fullness of it belongs to every generation, and the preceding one can have no right to bind it up from posterity. Such extension of property is quite unnatural.[43]

Smith's critique of perpetual entails, motivated by his sympathetic philosophy of rights, stands in full correspondence with his economic key convictions. According to Smith, agriculture is the most productive sector of the economy,

however, is proportional to the severity of the injury done, and accordingly we get rights and the corresponding rules of justice ordered into a scale of importance. The stronger the resentment of the impartial spectator, the more important are the rules of justice that arise from it [.]' Haakonssen, *The Science of a Legislator*, pp. 101 (n. 2).

[40] Smith, *Lectures on Jurisprudence*, pp. 466f. (n. 6).

[41] Smith, *Lectures on Jurisprudence*, pp. 466f. (n. 6). Smith deals with the special case of sympathizing with the dead also in his *Theory of Moral Sentiments*, pp. 12f. (n. 3).

[42] 'It is to be observed that this practice is a considerable refinement in humanity, and never was practised in a rude nation. Before the Twelve Tables no Roman had a right to make a will. Our Saxon ancestors had no right to dispose of their lands by testament, and in the history of the Old Testament we hear of no such practice.' Smith, *Lectures on Jurisprudence*, p. 467. (n. 6).

[43] Smith, *Lectures on Jurisprudence*, p. 468. (n. 6).

since here 'nature labours along with man'[44] without generating any additional costs.[45] Every improvement in husbandry is, therefore, enormously beneficial to the wealth of the nation. If the soil is withdrawn from the market, as it happens through the practice of perpetual entails, it gets improved less than it could be. In other words: the legal practice of perpetual entails harms the economic progress of the nation.[46]

The example of the inheritance law does not only reveal how Smith's sympathetic reformulation of existing positive laws would look like; it also illustrates very clearly how the three elements of Smith's overall theoretical project—the moral, the economical, and the juridical—are closely intertwined.

It is a matter of speculation, however, which other branches of law would have been the subject of Smith's sympathetic reformulation. The *Lectures on Jurisprudence* provide us only with few hints in this direction, which are not strong enough to be extrapolated here. Speculative spirit is required also to answer the question how Smith's vision of a sympathetic international law would potentially have looked like.

V. Adam Smith's International Law: Pushing the Limits of Sympathy

At first sight, the relationship between Smith's internal legal law and international law seems to be a problematic one. If all rights are grounded in sympathy, then this means a severe constraint on the possibility of their internationalization or even universalization. It appears that Smith's theory of sympathy binds his legal theory to particularity and relativity (just as it is the case with his moral philosophy).[47] That sympathetic law is only suitable for small-scale communities, where people know each other and are bound to each other by solidarity. Actually, it's true that Smith's legal as well as moral philosophy *starts* from particularity and relativity, but

[44] Smith, *Wealth of Nations*, p. 363 (n. 10).

[45] 'No equal quantity of productive labour employed in manufactures can ever occasion so great a reproduction. In them nature does nothing; man does all; and the reproduction must always be in proportion to the strength of the agents that occasion it. The capital employed in agriculture, therefore, not only puts into motion a greater quantity of productive labour than any equal capital employed in manufactures, but in proportion too to the quantity of productive labour which it employs, it adds a much greater value to the annual produce of the land and labour of the country, to the real wealth and revenue of its inhabitants.' Smith, *Wealth of Nations*, p. 364 (n. 10).

[46] 'Entails are disadvantageous to the improvement of the country [. . .]. Heirs of entailed estates have it not in their view to cultivate lands and often they are not able to do it. A man who buys land has this entirely in view and in general the new purchasers are the best cultivators.' Smith, *Lectures on Jurisprudence*, p. 469 (n. 6).

[47] Its alleged particularity or non-universality is often presented and discussed as the mayor problem of Smith's moral philosophy. See e.g. Christel Fricke and Hans P. Schütt, *Adam Smith als Moralphilosoph* (2005).

it would be a hasty reaction to jump to the conclusion that Smith is unable to think international or universal rights.

It is widely acknowledged within the Adam Smith scholarship that his theory of sympathy has a spatial dimension. There are various 'circles of sympathy',[48] starting from the closest circle, which connects the individual and his family and friends, to the middle circle which relates the individual to his neighbours or fellow citizens, to the last circle, which links the individual to half- and far-distanced strangers. The more one moves from the inner circle to the outer circle, the strength of sympathy decreases. Hence, the sympathetic interaction between friends differs quite significantly from that between strangers. In the sympathetic interaction between friends, the person principally concerned has to mitigate his emotions less than in the interaction with a stranger, since the former is better able to slip into the shoes of the person principally concerned and to evoke intense fellow feelings than the latter. The stranger does not know the person principally concerned personally and is not familiar with his private situation. For him, the situation and the person as such must appear in a stereotypical light. Hence, the stranger's readiness to sympathize with the person principally concerned is reduced to a minimum. This means, in reverse, that the interaction with the stranger is most suitable to gain maximal control over one's own passions.

> We expect less sympathy from a common acquaintance than from a friend: we cannot open to former all those little circumstances which we can unfold to the latter: we assume, therefore, more tranquillity before him, and endeavour to fix our thoughts upon those general outlines of our situation which he is willing to consider. We expect still less sympathy from an assembly of strangers, and we assume, therefore, still more tranquillity before them, and always endeavour to bring down our passion to that pitch, which the particular company we are in may be expected to go along to. (TMS, 23)

The spatial foundation of Smith's theory of sympathy has sociological or rather social-psychological implications. The closer people live together, the more familiar they are with each other and thus the more likely they will sympathize with each other. Sympathy—as harmony of emotions—will be the easiest to achieve in the closest circle of sympathy, namely between family members and friends, more difficult in the middle circle between neighbours and fellow-citizens, and most difficult between strangers.

This spatial 'bias' of Smith's theory of sympathy has immediate consequences for his philosophy of law. If all rights originate from the sympathy between the spectator and the person principally concerned *and* if sympathy between strangers is most difficult to achieve, Smith's theory of rights seems to be bound to the closest and middle circle of sympathy, i.e. to the boundaries of the nation state. Within one nation, one could argue, the sympathetic relatedness between the people is so developed that they all accept to fall under one and the

[48] Fonna Forman-Barzilai, *Adam Smith and the Circles of Sympathy: Cosmopolitanism and Moral Theory* (2010).

same sympathetic law. They do not agree upon the idea, however, that strangers should have the same rights as well. I might be able to *feel* that the thief should get one and the same punishment no matter whether he stole from a friend of mine or from a fellow citizen. But I will not be able to have the same fellow feeling of resentment if the victim is an absolute stranger to me, for whom I have only the fewest sympathetic feelings.[49]

There are two ways in which this problem of expanding sympathetic law to the international level could be tackled. On the one hand, one could argue that the sympathetic interaction with the stranger should be the standard for national law as well. In this way, it would not make a difference if the 'victim' was a close friend or a stranger. They would all fall under the same jurisdiction. This hypothetical solution, however, apparently does not match up with Smith's overall intention. For Smith, the system of positive law should reflect the moral judgment that people actually have. In eighteenth-century refined European societies, people encounter each other not like strangers, but like sentimental beings.[50] It would therefore be highly inappropriate to establish a legal system which stands in contrast to the refined moral sentiments of the people by treating all people like strangers. Hence, Smith would not come up with this solution to solve the problem of internationalizing sympathetic law. Probably, he would use another strategy, which would be more in line with his overall intention: he would attempt to stimulate the cultural process of sympathetic refinement. Smith's vision seems to be that sympathetic refinement enters a stage where the boundaries of the national state become irrelevant. In the first instance, Smith limits this project of *sympathetic convergence* to the European nations, which is already a tough challenge, since among the European

[49] The Chinese seem to represent for Smith the 'radical other', to whom we have almost no sympathetic access. In a famous passage in his *Theory of Moral Sentiments* he states: 'Let us suppose that the great empire of China, with all its myriads of inhabitants, was suddenly swallowed up by an earthquake, and let us consider how a man of humanity in Europe, who had no sort of connection with that part of the world, would be affected upon receiving intelligence of this dreadful calamity. He would, I imagine, first of all, express very strongly his sorrow for the misfortune of that unhappy people, he would make many melancholy reflections upon the precariousness of human life, and the vanity of all the labours of man, which could thus be annihilated in a moment. [. . .] And when all this fine philosophy was over, when all these humane sentiments had been once fairly expressed, he would pursue his business or his pleasure, take his repose or his diversion, with the same ease and tranquillity, as if no such accident had happened. [. . .] If he was to lose his little finger tomorrow, he would not sleep tonight; but, provided he never saw them, he will snore with the most profound security over the ruin of a hundred millions of his brethren, and the destruction of that immense multitude seems plainly an object less interesting to him, than this paltry misfortune of his own.' Smith, *Theory of Moral Sentiments*, pp. 136f. (n. 3). China plays an important role in the cultural imagination of eighteenth-century Europe, see for example David Porter, *The Chinese Taste in Eighteenth-Century England* (2010).

[50] While in earlier societies even friends treat each other as if they were strangers, in the refined (European) societies of the eighteenth century even strangers meet as if they were friends: 'We can venture to express more emotion in the presence of a friend than in that of a stranger, because we expect more indulgence from the one than the other. And in the same manner the rules of decorum among civilized nations, admit of a more animated behaviour, than is approved of among barbarians. The first converse together with the openness of friends; the second with the reserve of strangers.' Smith, *Theory of Moral Sentiments*, p. 207 (n. 3).

nations the language of emotions differs significantly: the French and Italians are much more sentimental and sympathetic than the English, which are—according to Smith—still on the very bottom of sentimentality.[51] There is no reason, however, why this project of sympathetic convergence should end at the borders of Europe. As long as the sympathetic relationships between peoples reaches the 'middle circle' of sympathy—which means: as long as strangers recognize each other as fellow citizenships, sympathetic law can be established. Internationalizing or even universalizing sympathetic law is a target, therefore, that can be attained only by working on our emotional sensibility and creating a language of emotion that crosses social, cultural, and national boundaries. Without doubt, this idea is, in Smith, a deeply Eurocentric one, since he views eighteenth-century European societies as being ahead in the cultural process of emotional refinement. Despite this problematic historical aspect, Smith's intriguing vision of an emotionally grounded legal system could provide us with helpful insights for thinking international and universal rights today, or so I would like to argue.

First of all, Smith helps us to realize that legal force is not rooted in political sovereignty alone, as Thomas Hobbes suggested with his famous statement *Auctoritas, non veritas facit legem*. The force of law equally depends on the factual moral judgments of the *demos*. People's everyday 'legal practice' is crucial with regards to the effective enforcement of laws. A legal system which is in correspondence with the moral judgments of the people is better and more powerful then a legal system which departs from the moral intuitions of the people. Smith shows us quite clearly that the original and last foundation of law and order is the practice of making moral judgments—our emotional reactions to injustice and suffering we observe. The real substance of law is our moral sensibility and affectivity; a substance, which turns out to be highly contingent, since it is shaped by various socio-historical, cultural, and subjective conditions that change over time.

The second lesson we could learn from Smith is that the question of internationalization or even universalization of rights is not a matter of careful reasoning and convincing argumentation; it is a matter of 'Sentimental Education'. Internationalizing or universalizing sympathetic rights depends on our ability to push the limits of sympathy and to establish a common language of emotions which allows us to treat even strangers as if they were fellow citizens. The international order of sympathetic law will not be founded on reasons and arguments, but created by and maintained through sympathetic interactions.

[51] Cf. 'The emotion and vivacity with which the French and the Italians, the two most polished nations upon the continent, express themselves on occasions that are at all interesting, surprise at first those strangers who happen to be travelling among them, and who, having been educated among a people of duller sensibility, cannot enter into this passionate behaviour, of which they have never seen any example in their own country. A young French nobleman will weep in the presence of the whole court upon being refused a regiment. An Italian, says the abbot Dû Bos, expresses more emotion on being condemned in a fine of twenty shillings, than an Englishman on receiving the sentence of death.' Smith, *Theory of Moral Sentiments*, p. 207 (n. 3).

Selected Bibliography

Forman-Barzilai, Fonna, *Adam Smith and the Circles of Sympathy: Cosmopolitanism and Moral Theory* (Cambridge: Cambridge University Press, 2010).

Haakonssen, Knud, *The Science of a Legislator: The Natural Jurisprudence of David Hume and Adam Smith* (Cambridge: Cambridge University Press, 1981).

Haakonssen, Knud, 'What Might Properly Be Called Natural Jurisprudence?', in Roy Campbell and Andrew Skinner (eds.), *The Origins and Nature of the Scottish Enlightenment* (Edinburgh: John Donald Publishers, 1982), pp. 205–25.

Haakonssen, Knud, *Natural Law and Moral Philosophy: From Grotius to the Scottish Enlightenment* (Cambridge: Cambridge University Press, 1996).

Phillipson, Nicholas, *Adam Smith: An Enlightened Life* (New Haven; London: Yale University Press, 2010).

Ronge, Bastian, *Das Adam-Smith-Projekt: Zur Genealogie der liberalen Gouvernementalität* (Wiesbaden: Springer VS, 2015).

15

Systematicity to Excess

Kant's Conception of the International Legal Order

Benedict Vischer

For whatever might be the highest degree of perfection at which humanity must stop, and however great a gulf must remain between the idea and its execution, no one can or should try to determine this, just because it is freedom that can go beyond every proposed boundary.[1]

I. Introduction

In 1784, a journal reported: 'A favourite idea of Mr. Prof. Kant is that the final end of humankind is the attainment of the most perfect political constitution.'[2] Kant reacted with a seminal essay, confirming and expounding his conviction that the 'the achievement of a civil society universally administering right' constitutes '[t]he greatest problem for the human species', as well as 'the most difficult and the latest to be solved'.[3] In the future he envisions, humankind lives in a cosmopolitan legal order forming one great system. Indeed, Kant was a fervent advocate of a well-ordered international legal system. Neither the doubt nor the derision of his contemporaries could shake his defence of the duty and feasibility of a cosmopolitan order.

The efforts for the cosmopolitan idea did not constitute a political engagement isolated from Kant's philosophical work.[4] Nor was its philosophical examination

[1] Immanuel Kant, *Critique of Pure Reason*, trans. Paul Guyer and Allen W. Wood (2009), p. 397.

[2] Gothaische gelehrte Zeitungen auf das Jahr 1784, Zweytes halbes Jahr (1784), p. 95. English translation (modified here) in Günter Zöller and Robert B. Louden (eds.), Immanuel Kant, *Anthropology, History, and Education* (2007), p. 500.

[3] Immanuel Kant, 'Idea for a Universal History with a Cosmopolitan Aim', trans. Allen W. Wood, in Günter Zöller and Robert B. Louden (eds.), *Anthropology, History, and Education* (2007), pp. 112–13.

[4] For an illuminating exposition of the deep reflection of Kant's political ideas in the structures of his whole philosophy cf. Hans Saner, *Kant's Political Thought: Its Origins and Development*, trans. E.B. Ashton (1973).

merely the hobbyhorse of an aging man with decreasing mental capacities, as has been suggested.[5] On the contrary, the topic of the international legal order pervades the oeuvre from early on. Especially in shorter texts, legal development beyond the state keeps figuring as a leading subject; among them some of the author's most popular text, such as *Idea For a Universal History With a Cosmopolitan Aim* and *Toward Eternal Peace*. Yet also in Kant's larger main works, international law is of remarkable importance. Not only is the global legal order systematically detailed in the doctrine of right of the *Metaphysics of Morals*. The idea of the international legal order is also discussed in the *Critique of Judgment*, and even the *Critique of Pure Reason* reflects in passing on the perfect political constitution.[6]

No doubt then, Kant is a paragon of systematic thought on international law. He endorsed a conception of law as a cosmopolitan system, and he explicated this conception as an essential part of his whole philosophical system. Following his 'Copernican turn' from the quest of external laws to the rules of the rational subject,[7] the legal system was no more envisioned as merely given by god or nature, but as a human achievement. This led Kant to a systematicity of law that went far beyond what seemed probable considering the existing relations among human beings on a global scale. His optimism made him a principal philosophical source when law began to conquer the international domain in the twentieth century. The institutional developments substantiated the bold visions to a surprising extent. At the same time, essential aspects still await actualization. Kant's vision continues to bear its utopian appeal.

Despite this concurrence of systematic perfectionism and predictive realism, Kant's system of international law remains at essential points irritatingly vague, sometimes even contradictory. The legitimating basis vacillates between natural law and positivism, a priori reason and popular will, morality and public decision. The institutional proposals hesitate between a truly cosmopolitan world state and a looser federation. These ubiquitous ambiguities shaped the intensive reception. On the one hand, it broadened the scope of authors that could find their champion in Kant by picking and choosing the statements they preferred. On the other hand, readings tried to come to terms with the intriguing ambiguities. Examining the wavering between a world state or a world federation, interpreters have suggested that Kant got caught in a false opposition,[8] claimed that he defended a middle way,[9] or argued that he changed his view.[10] Other studies have discerned structural

[5] Hannah Arendt, *Lectures on Kant's Political Philosophy* (1982), p. 9; cf. also Arthur Schopenhauer, *The World as Will and Representation*, Vol. 1., trans. Judith Norman et al. (2010), p. 362; Friedrich Paulsen, *Immanuel Kant: His Life and Doctrine*, trans. J.E. Creighton and Albert Lefevre (1902), p. 343.

[6] The introductory quote is taken from this passage.

[7] Kant, *Critique of Pure Reason*, p. 110 (n. 1).

[8] Jürgen Habermas, 'Does the Constitutionalization of International Law Still Have a Chance', in *The Divided West* (2006), pp. 115–93.

[9] Pauline Kleingeld, 'Approaching Perpetual Peace: Kant's Defence of a League of States and His Ideal of a World Federation', *European Journal of Philosophy* 12 (2004), 304–25.

[10] Pauline Kleingeld, *Kant and Cosmopolitanism: The Philosophical Ideal of World Citizenship* (2012), pp. 40–71.

reasons behind the ambiguities, observing in Kant's philosophy elements that drive beyond any definite legal order.[11]

Indeed, as I will argue, far from revealing an inconsistency or incompleteness of the conception, the pervading tensions constitute a crucial dimension of Kant's international legal system. Kant did not intend to provide the conclusive plan for legislation that many readers seek. By contrast, following the fundamental insights of his philosophy, his sketch of the cosmopolitan system shows that the emancipatory project of law is an infinite endeavour we can never conclude. In its ultimate openness, the idea of the system points to the ongoing excess of any determined system. An integral element of Kant's philosophical system, the system of law reflects the human condition of conscious finitude; it is shaped by our situation as worldly beings who act within a historical horizon. The full actualization of law lies not in a fixed state, but in a continuous process of self-transcendence.

To comprehend Kant's system of law means primarily to grasp this constitutive openness. I will accompany Kant's systematic course beyond the system in three steps: a first chapter briefly sketches the systematicity of Kant's conception of law. Against this background, I will, secondly, consider more closely the status of the legal system. Kant exposes this status by developing the system as an idea, binding it consistently up with history, and tracking hermeneutically the implications of its practical character. In a third step, I will turn to concrete facets of the systematic openness. Law's internal impulse to push beyond its order shapes the reality of law as a whole as well as its actualization on the international level. These concrete traits of the system exploding dynamic continue to inspire central innovative perspectives in international legal thought, and outline a concept of law through and through committed to the actualization of freedom.

II. The Systematicity of International Law

Kant conceives international law decidedly as systematic. The systematicity of international law is asserted in three, interrelated respects. First, international law as such is outlined systematically. Second, law as a whole is understood as a system, international law being an essential part thereof. Third, the legal system is located at a crucial place in the philosophical system.

International law is not outlined as a collection of contracts or rights, but as 'a *cosmopolitan* whole, i.e. a system of all states'.[12] It is constructed as an encompassing

[11] Karl Jaspers, 'Kant's "Perpetual Peace"', in *Philosophy and the World: Selected Writings and Essays*, trans. E.B. Ashton (1963), pp. 88–124; Emil Angehrn, 'Kant und die gegenwärtige Geschichtsphilosophie', in Dietmar H. Heidemann and Kristina Engelhard (eds.), *Warum Kant heute?* (2004), pp. 328–51; Georg Cavallar, *Kant and the Theory and Practice of International Right* (1999); Elisabeth Ellis, *Provisional Politics: Kantian Arguments in Policy Context* (2008). Cf. also the further references in the sections below.

[12] Immanuel Kant, *Critique of the Power of Judgment*, trans. Paul Guyer and Eric Matthews (2000), p. 300.

order of two interrelated sets of publicly determined common and universal rules that establish mutual obligations among all peoples of the world. The law of peoples ('Völkerrecht') regulates the rights among states, cosmopolitan law ('Weltbürgerrecht') contains the rights of individuals beyond the state. Thus, international law is in Kant's conception strictly speaking transnational: it is not limited to interstate relations, but also recognizes and even centres on individuals as legal subjects. Both parts of the international system are based on the principle of right and directed towards the aim of an eternal peace, not only between states, but also among individuals.[13] In conjunction they establish a perfectly ordered international legal condition ensuring individuals and states universal rights.

The two components of international law form together with state law the 'system of laws' which Kant terms 'public law'.[14] This concept encompasses in Kant all law in a civil condition (including rules of private relations), whereas private law refers to law under pre-political conditions. Law is public, if it is dependent upon 'general promulgation'[15] and thus subjected to a 'uniting will'.[16] International law builds two of the three integral parts of the public legal order, and the three realms are conceived as radically interdependent: 'if the principle of outer freedom limited by law is lacking in any one of these three possible forms of legal condition, the framework of all others is unavoidably undermined and must finally collapse'.[17] The exposition of the three parts confirms this claim. They build mutually on each other and intersect in different ways.[18]

A system is defined in the *Critique of Pure Reason* as 'the unity of the manifold cognitions under one idea'.[19] In accordance with this, Kant conceives all law as based on one single idea, the universal principle of right: 'Any action is right if it can coexist with everyone's freedom in accordance with a universal law, or if on its maxim the freedom of choice of each can coexist with everyone's freedom in accordance with a universal law.'[20] The relation of the principle to the moral law is disputed in the Kant literature.[21] However, in any case, the former somehow transposes the categorical imperative to the sphere of external action: while the categorical imperative requires the universalizability of the voluntary maxim, the principle of right merely demands that the action—irrespectively of the agents' motive—conforms to a universal law. 'That I make it my maxim to act rightly is a

[13] Cf. on the ethical dimension of Kant's peace ideal Howard Williams, *Kant's Political Philosophy* (1983), pp. 260–8.

[14] Immanuel Kant, 'The Metaphysics of Morals', in Mary J. Gregor (ed. and trans.), *Practical Philosophy* (1996), p. 455 (translation modified, emphasis omitted).

[15] Ibid. [16] Ibid. [17] Ibid. (translation modified).

[18] Cf. Seyla Benhabib, *Another Cosmopolitanism* (2006), pp. 148–9; seminal on the nexus between liberal state law and international peace Michael W. Doyle, 'Kant, Liberal Legacies, and Foreign Affairs', *Philosophy & Public Affairs* 12, (1983), 205–35.

[19] Kant, *Critique of Pure Reason*, p. 691 (n. 1).

[20] Kant, 'The Metaphysics of Morals', in *Practical Philosophy*, p. 387 (n. 14).

[21] Cf. Marcus Willaschek, 'Why the Doctrine of Right Does Not Belong in the Metaphysics of Morals: On Some Basic Distinctions in Kant's Moral Philosophy', *Jahrbuch für Recht und Ethik* 5 (1998), 205–27; Arthur Ripstein, *Force and Freedom: Kant's Legal and Political Philosophy* (2009), pp. 355–88.

demand that ethics makes on me.'[22] From the defining universality follows systematicity: every right is bound up with corresponding rights of others, and different rights must be compatible with each other.[23]

Hence, the claim of right is located independently of the existence of a political community directly in practical reason. Yet it demands the institution of such a community. Without publicly determined laws binding everyone mutually, no one's rights are secured from encroachments. Lacking insurance of reciprocity, one cannot be expected to respect the others' rights. Moreover, a coordinated concretization requires common rules. The principle can therefore only be actualized through a cosmopolitan public order. Only a unified will can establish law's essential systematicity.[24]

In addition to its inner systematicity, Kant's account of law is also embedded and centrally located in his philosophical system. Kant's system is fundamentally organized by the distinction between theoretical and practical reason. While theoretical knowledge is dependent on a sensually given, practical duty is solely based on reason. Developed systematically as the first part of the *Metaphysics of Morals*, the conception of law is in some respect clearly located in the practical part of the system. Yet, while Kant relates morality to the maxim of the will, he determines the concept of right by reference to external action. Shifting from the individual will to a common will, law is comprehended as a medium organizing the actions in the world independently of the actor's individual motives—guiding even a 'nation of devils'[25]—and backed up with coercion. Law provides a means to bridge freedom and nature, mind and world, eternity and time. Thus, it assumes a role of mediation between theory and practice. That is why the cosmopolitan order is also prominently discussed outside the strictly practical philosophy, not least in the *Critique of Judgment*. As with other writings, the third Critique associates the cosmopolitan order in the part on teleological judgment with the final end of human existence, envisioning it as the venue of morality's full actualization that reconciles the latter with the empirical world. The cosmopolitan vision harmonizes the different parts of the philosophical system in the notion of a 'morally grounded system of [states]'.[26] In addition to that, Hannah Arendt famously exposed the political significance of the first part of the book on aesthetic judgment: Kant's explication reveals the logic of public judgment through which the cosmopolitan history of the legal order proceeds.[27]

This mediating function in the philosophical system gives Kant's legal thought a fairly unusual shape within his philosophy. Basic dichotomies are moderated, reason is embedded in sociality and history, and the theoretical argumentation is

[22] Kant, 'The Metaphysics of Morals', in *Practical Philosophy*, p. 388 (n. 14).
[23] Cf. Jeremy Waldron, 'Kant's Legal Positivism', *Harvard Law Review* 109, (1996), 1557.
[24] Cf. Waldron, 'Kant's Legal Positivism', *Harvard Law Review* 109, (1996) (n. 23).
[25] Immanuel Kant, 'Toward Perpetual Peace', in Mary J. Gregor (ed. and trans.), *Practical Philosophy* (1996), p. 335.
[26] Kant, *Critique of the Power of Judgment*, p. 300 (n. 12).
[27] Arendt, *Lectures on Kant's Political Philosophy* (n. 5).

bound up with pragmatic considerations in a politically engaged discourse. These anomalies constitute a great challenge for Kant scholarship and might explain the conspicuous neglect of the conception of the legal order, especially its public actualization, in many interpretations of Kant. Yet, the distinguished role and shape of the legal reflections also promise essential insights putting the whole philosophical system in a new light. Indeed, from Kant's immediate successors in German Idealism until today, these intriguing thoughts have been central to diverse seminal receptions of the Enlightener.

III. The Status of the Cosmopolitan System

1. The system as an idea

Kant's concept of the legal system assumes a peculiar status between presence and absence. On the one hand, it is developed in detail from reason as an a priori—thus always already binding—claim. On the other hand, it points to a not yet existing state to come. Reason postulates a law that differs from the prevailing legal reality. This tension between Kant's account and the *lex lata* does not simply reflect a progressive stance vis-à-vis the existing political situation. The distance from the given condition is also a structural feature of Kant's notion of the system. The mediation of freedom and nature by law is nothing we could ever conclusively achieve, but an 'idea' we infinitely have to approach.[28] Be it the perfect civil state,[29] the eternal peace,[30] the cosmopolitan constitution,[31] or the 'condition of public right' as a whole[32]—in all cases Kant insists on the system's distinct status as an aim of infinite approximation. Already the titles of Kant's political writings indicate this dynamical logic: the equivocal title of the peace treatise means 'on', but also 'for' and 'toward' eternal peace ('Zum ewigen Frieden'). The title of the essay on universal history points to the cosmopolitan as an 'intention', 'purpose', or 'aim', using a word that also reverberates with 'view' ('Absicht'). This structure is also displayed by the characteristic ambiguity and vagueness of the central components of the legal vision.

The peculiar unattainability of the idea reflects human finitude. Our limited abilities lead us always to fall short of the highest ideal: 'out of such crooked wood as the human being is made, nothing entirely straight can be fabricated'.[33] Yet the implications of human finitude exceed mere flaws in applying the commands

[28] See e.g. Kant, 'Idea for a Universal History with a Cosmopolitan Aim', in *Anthropology, History, and Education*, p. 113 (n. 3); Kant, 'The Metaphysics of Morals', in *Practical Philosophy*, p. 487 (n. 14); Kant, *Critique of Pure Reason*, p. 397 (n. 1).

[29] Kant, 'Idea for a Universal History with a Cosmopolitan Aim', in *Anthropology, History, and Education*, p. 113 (n. 3).

[30] Kant, 'Toward Perpetual Peace', in *Practical Philosophy*, p. 331 (n. 25); Kant, 'The Metaphysics of Morals', in *Practical Philosophy*, p. 492 (n. 14).

[31] Kant, 'Toward Perpetual Peace', in *Practical Philosophy*, p. 329 (n. 25).

[32] Kant, 'Toward Perpetual Peace', in *Practical Philosophy*, p. 351 (n. 25).

[33] Kant, 'Idea for a Universal History with a Cosmopolitan Aim', in *Anthropology, History, and Education*, p. 113 (n. 3).

of reason. As the hazy depiction of the system signals, our finite reason cannot even fully anticipate the content of the system. In qualifying the legal system as an idea to be approached infinitely Kant uses a concept thoroughly elaborated in his philosophy, particularly in the second part of the *Critique of Pure Reason*. The succinct definition of ideas in the *Lectures on Anthropology* reads: '*Ideas* are concepts of reason, to which no object given in experience can be adequate [. . .], concepts of a perfection that we can always approach but never completely attain.'[34] As Kant expounds, in our experience, we relate and order under the categories of the understanding a sensual given. Every possible object of experience is therefore necessarily dependent on a given content and related to another object. By contrast, the idea conceives an absolute, thus conclusive and unconditioned.[35] Such concepts provide an essential aim to guide, motivate, and sustain the course of knowledge and action. They are not least crucial to mediate the realms of theory and practice.[36] But they cannot be wholly determined, and the approximation never comes to an end. The attempt to grasp them as objects of experience leads to a contradiction. They are generally only of 'regulative' use: as a guidance for reason. Only practically are ideas also 'constitutive, i.e. practically determining'.[37] Their specific power lies precisely in their reaching beyond the realm of experience.

Accordingly, the system of law is a state we can neither set up nor even think conclusively. Indeed, the notion of its full and infinite moral perfection conflicts with the very concept of law differentiated from morality through the involvement of finite natural motives: if law matched its idea completely, it would not be law anymore.[38] Vagueness and ambiguity are necessary qualities of the system's portrait. Given that law essentially mediates morality with the empirical world, the account can only provide an 'approximation to [the system]'.[39] To be sure, the claim of systematicity calls for actualization here and now. It is implied in the a priori concept of right. Reason demands that we seek immediately for a global system of equal rights which ensures the defining universality of right. Wherever the distinct authority of law is claimed, the idea of the system is involved and requires attention. At the same time, however, in pointing to an unforeseeable, literally utopian state, and surpassing every concretization, the idea requires us to continuously reconsider and transcend established systems. It incites at once the constitution and the excess of concrete orders.

The insurmountable distance of the system from every present state is essential for the idea's liberating power. However, the radical remoteness makes the claim of this very potency at the same time precarious. If we can only approach the idea, but never attain its full content, if the thought of its full reality even leads to a

[34] Immanuel Kant, 'Anthropology from a Pragmatic Point of View', trans. Robert B. Louden, in Günter Zöller and Robert B. Louden (eds.), *Anthropology, History, and Education* (2007), pp. 306–7.

[35] Cf. Kant, *Critique of Pure Reason*, pp. 399–405 (n. 1).

[36] Cf. Kant, *Critique of Pure Reason*, p. 403 (n. 1).

[37] Kant, *Critique of the Power of Judgment*, p. 322 (emphasis omitted) (n. 12).

[38] Indeed, the idea exceeds even moral action. Moral practice also involves an external situation on which the moral law is applied.

[39] Kant, 'The Metaphysics of Morals', in *Practical Philosophy*, p. 365 (n. 14).

contradiction, then the idea also seems to be unable to guide. Lacking a definite, consistent content, it cannot provide a reliable benchmark for approximation, let alone assume normative force for that criterion. The effort of approximation seems to be a meaningless endeavour, as there is nothing that could be reliably recognized as progress.

Hegel criticized the logic of Kant's idea for this reason famously as '*bad* [. . .] infinity': Every step from the finite towards the infinite leads again to an equally finite, because the infinite is considered to be unattainable.[40] Conceived thus, Hegel pointed out, the supposed infinite is itself merely finite, because it is opposed to and thus limited by the finite.[41] The 'true infinity', instead, involves the finite.[42] It is the relation of the very process itself in which the finite moves to the other, the transcendent, finding therein its truth, the 'being with itself in its other' in Hegel's famous formula.[43] Progress is only possible, if the infinite is present in the very process and can therefore guide the latter.

The argument is compelling. An inconceivable idea cannot determine our thought and practice. However, in its central consideration, Hegel's critique articulates rather than disproves the underlying logic of Kant's conception. The truth of the idea does not lie in an ever remote future, but in the relentless dynamic it initiates here and now. Kant illustrates this with a mathematical example: 'if "the human species" signifies the *whole* of a series of generations going (indeterminably) into the infinite (as this meaning is entirely customary), and it is assumed that this series ceaselessly approximates the line of its destiny running alongside it, then it is not to utter a contradiction to say that in all its parts it is asymptotic to this line and yet on the whole that it will coincide with it, in other words, that no member of all the generations of humankind, but only the species will fully reach its destiny'.[44] The idea is present in the incessant motion, not a state brought about at any point of time. The insistence on the unattainability grasps the way we experience the ongoing vitality of the dynamic we are involved in. This persistent unrest of order–constitution and order–transcendence—present *and* coming at once—is the actuality of law. The insurmountable distance of the idea animates law's steadily present tendency to reveal and empower new claims. In their idea, legal orders bear the impetus of emancipatory transformation. The logic of presence and distance is also displayed in the title of the essay on peace. The current English translations conceal the fact that Kant does not merely term the peace here as perpetual, but as 'eternal' ('ewig'). The idea remains infinitely out of reach because it exceeds time. It

[40] Georg Wilhelm Friedrich Hegel, *Encyclopedia of the Philosophical Sciences in Basic Outline,* Part 1: Science of Logic, ed. and trans. Klaus Brinkmann and Daniel O. Dahlstrom (2010), p. 149.

[41] Hegel, *Encyclopedia,* Part 1, p. 150 (n. 40).

[42] Hegel, *Encyclopedia,* Part 1, p. 149 (n. 40).

[43] Hegel, *Encyclopedia,* Part 1, p. 149 (n. 40); cf. for a more extensive account of true and bad infinity Georg Wilhelm Friedrich Hegel, *The Science of Logic*, ed. and trans. George Di Giovanni (2010), pp. 108–25.

[44] Immanuel Kant, 'Review of J.G. Herder's "Ideas for the Philosophy of the History of Humanity" Parts 1 and 2', trans. Allen W. Wood, in Günter Zöller and Robert B. Louden (eds.), *Anthropology, History, and Education* (2007), p. 142.

makes every single moment explode, pointing it beyond itself. Precisely because it is not simply the knowledge of a future state in time, it is also opening up the possibility and demanding the endeavour for instant redemption.[45]

In careful readings of Kant's political writings, Jürgen Habermas and Axel Honneth each exposed the 'system-exploding' implications of these works.[46] They traced 'unofficial' stories behind the primary narrative leading beyond Kant's official philosophy.[47] Indeed, these explosive thoughts are even more than hidden deviations. The dialectics of system-formation and system-burst pointing beyond the anticipations of the philosopher and any other human perspective is a central point in Kant's system of law and of philosophy in general. Mere slivers of the infinite in our finite reason, ideas do not overturn our finitude. Yet they enable us to become aware of our finitude, of the limitedness and fallibility of our knowledge, and to act consciously on this condition.[48] This self-consciousness changes our condition fundamentally. It opens up a horizon of action that allows and pushes us to surpass the boundaries of constituted legal systems over and over in a never concluded and ever incalculable endeavour of emancipation.

2. Historicity of law: temporality, sociality, directedness

The unpredictable, transcending element at the core of law gives the latter a historical shape. The emancipatory consciousness of the idea is essentially a consciousness of the future. Kant's writings highlight this nexus between law and history clearly. Most of the texts dealing with the cosmopolitan legal system also address the subject of history. Even in the *Metaphysics of Morals* the conception of the legal system is embedded in a historical narrative. The doctrine of right concludes with expounding the global peace order as the end of an ongoing process of approximation.[49]

The notion of history Kant describes has three essential implications: the temporal structure of law, the social formation of legal normativity, and an evolutionary tendency beyond the intention of the interacting subjects. In the first place, the historicity of law reflects our temporal consciousness. As a normative medium determining what ought to be as different from what merely is, law is already in its most elementary logic characterized by the awareness of temporal change. Legal rules prescribe future behaviour. But the idea of the legal system Kant reconstructs goes further. It projects a future where not only the arrangement of social interactions,

45 Cf. Immanuel Kant, 'Religion within the Boundaries of Mere Reason', trans. George di Giovanni, in Allen W. Wood and George di Giovanni (eds.), *Religion and Rational Theology* (1996), p. 163.

46 Jürgen Habermas, *The Structural Transformation of the Public Sphere: An Inquiry into a Category of Bourgeois Society*, trans. Thomas Burger (1989), p. 116; Axel Honneth, 'The Irreducibility of Progress: Kant's Account of the Relationship between Morality and History', in *Pathologies of Reason: On the Legacy of Critical Theory*, trans. James Ingram and others (2009), *passim* (translated here with 'system-bursting'; the German term both authors use is 'systemsprengend').

47 Habermas, *The Structural Transformation of the Public Sphere*, p. 115 (n. 46); Honneth, 'The Irreducibility of Progress', in *Pathologies of Reason*, pp. 12, 17 (n. 46).

48 Cf. Jaspers, 'Kant's "Perpetual Peace"', in *Philosophy and the World*, pp. 117–20 (n. 11).

49 Kant, 'The Metaphysics of Morals', in *Practical Philosophy*, pp. 490–2 (n. 14).

but also the human beings themselves alter fundamentally. Essentially formed by our relation to future, legal institutions bear the idea not to be bound by timeless natural conditions underlying them. Law entertains a dialectical relationship with its conditions. It is always shaped by its historical context, but it conversely moulds the structures of the world and in particular the disposition of subjects. In this dynamic, new realities emerge. The perspective into the future points even beyond any change we can anticipate. It is bound up with the awareness of the limits of our current perspective. The modality of future consciousness is essentially openness. This is why this perspective bears the chance of imminent change. The dimension of the future liberates the emancipatory potential of law. While the expectation that everything will stay the same or even worsen threatens the readiness to endeavour moral progress, the possibility of a fundamentally other to come enables us to actualize law as a medium of morally directed transformation. This prospect is therefore an essential complement of the system the concept of right calls for.

History, however, presumes more than mere temporal change. It also involves a meaningful linkage of temporal occurrences. History as a collective singular even suggests such a connection of humankind, if not—as we increasingly realize in our days—the universe as a whole. Kant's reflections on history indeed refer to the idea of a 'universal history'.[50] Law's historicity relates to the evolution of the human species embedded in nature. For one thing, the factual development of the legal order is not at the disposition of any single individual, but depends on the entire society. Yet more importantly, the rational foundation of law is also socially formed. Since the system of rules actualizing the concept of right is not timelessly given, it has its basis in the 'united will of the people'.[51] Corresponding with Rousseau's concept of the general will, Kant does not identify this common will with the factual will of all.[52] The uniting will is rather the rational comprehension of the common aim a society reaches at a certain point of history. This will is universal in a stronger sense than factual consent, because it is justified with reasons accessible to everyone. However, this distinction from the preferences a community might approve does not locate the authorizing standpoint beyond society. Human reason has no other place than the concrete beings embodying this capacity. It is an ability of these very beings to distance themselves from their immediate perspectives. Society is not merely the aggregate of beings possessing this faculty, but the realm where reason is formed and developed: 'how much and how correctly would we *think* if we did not think as it were in community with others to whom we *communicate* our thoughts, and who communicate theirs with us!'.[53] It is the encounter with others that enables us

[50] Kant, 'Idea for a Universal History with a Cosmopolitan Aim', in *Anthropology, History, and Education* (n. 3).

[51] Kant, 'The Metaphysics of Morals', in *Practical Philosophy*, p. 457 (n. 14).

[52] Cf. Immanuel Kant, 'On the Common Saying: That May Be Correct in Theory, but It Is of No Use in Practice', in Mary J. Gregor (ed. and trans.), *Practical Philosophy* (1996), p. 297; Jean-Jacques Rousseau, 'Of the Social Contract', in Victor Gourevitch (ed. and trans.), *The Social Contract and Other Later Political Writings* (1997), p. 60.

[53] Immanuel Kant, 'What Does It Mean to Orient Oneself in Thinking?', trans. Allen W. Wood, in Allen W. Wood and George di Giovanni (eds.), *Religion and Rational Theology* (1996), p. 16.

to become aware of other perspectives, recognize the particularity of our own, and grasp in a process of continuous reconsideration a universal stance. This stance constitutes the guideline for the legal system. Pioneering a central thought of modern philosophy, Kant establishes in the exposition of law's public historicity the social fabric of reason.

Still, reason's locus in society neither ensures that the claim of reason prevails in social interactions, nor precludes a straying of collective reasoning. The members of the society do not necessarily intend the standpoint of reason to be determining, and social interactions unleash a dynamic exceeding the calculations of the involved subjects. Kant suggests institutional means to direct this dynamics beneficially. In particular, he recognizes and promotes publicity as a frame to channel the political development toward the ultimate aim of reason. However, even optimal institutional conditions can only further, but not fully control the aspired outcome. What is more, these conditions are themselves dependent on their social formation. Given humanity's flaws, finitude, and freedom, the actuality of a meaningful universal history keeps an ultimate unavailability. The continuing course toward the highest aim requires therefore a tendency beyond human feasibility.

A great deal of Kant's considerations on history concerns this dimension beyond the intentions of the subjects. In colourful examinations of human's 'unsociable sociability'[54] he suggests a directedness of nature that makes even deplorable behaviour serve a benevolent purpose in the social interplay. Kant could rely on prominent sources to make this claim: he draws on biblical passages, interpreting their narrative in the vein of the long-standing *felix culpa* tradition.[55] He refers to Rousseau's analysis of the transitional vices of cultivation.[56] Mandevilles's and Smith's contentions on the beneficial dynamics of self-interest provided further endorsements in the contemporary debate.[57] Following these suggestions and supporting them with further remarks, Kant reconstructs an overarching trend bringing the incalculable societal processes in the coherence of a history and putting law on track towards cosmopolitan perfection.

3. Hermeneutics of practice

Given its distinctive unavailability, the notion of the historical development towards the coming cosmopolitan system has a peculiar theoretical shape. It not only exceeds experience. Kant even underlines that it runs against what experience

[54] Kant, 'Idea for a Universal History with a Cosmopolitan Aim', in *Anthropology, History, and Education*, p. 111 (emphasis omitted) (n. 3).

[55] Immanuel Kant, 'Conjectural Beginning of Human History', trans. Allen W. Wood, in Günter Zöller and Robert B. Louden (eds.), *Anthropology, History, and Education* (2007), pp. 160–75.

[56] Kant, 'Conjectural Beginning of Human History', in *Anthropology, History, and Education*, p. 93 (n. 55); cf. also Kant, 'Idea for a Universal History with a Cosmopolitan Aim', in *Anthropology, History, and Education*, p. 116 (n. 3); on Rousseau's respective theory cf. Frederick Neuhouser, *Rousseau's Theodicy of Self-Love: Evil, Rationality, and the Drive for Recognition* (2010).

[57] Bernard Mandeville, *The Fable of the Bees: Or Private Vices, Public Benefits* (1988); Adam Smith, *An Inquiry into the Nature of the Wealth of Nations* (1979), pp. 25–30.

suggests.[58] 'One cannot resist feeling a certain indignation when one sees [human beings'] doings and refrainings on the great stage of the world and finds that [. . .] everything in the large is woven together out of folly, childish vanity, often also out of childish malice and the rage to destruction'.[59] Observing the course of things is more likely to evoke despair than confidence regarding the future.[60] Countering this impression, Kant considers hermeneutically what conception of the historical evolution as a whole proper human self-understanding implies.[61] He argues that, even though we cannot certainly know that the development of the world will lead to the morally required order, we have to comprehend it accordingly in order to engage with the world appropriately both in theoretical and practical terms. The *Critique of Judgment* explicates the necessity to perceive the world as a teleological system that brings about cosmopolitan perfection when inquiring experience theoretically.[62] The moral and political writings stress the even more significant role of such an underlying worldview for practice. Nature's purposiveness guiding to the unfolding of human's capabilities ensures its compatibility with morality. Trust in this harmony of our duty with the world is crucial for keeping committed to the moral imperatives.[63] The assumption of progress toward the cosmopolitan is thus implied in our self-understanding as rationally cognizing and acting subjects. It is intimated by the impression of propriety of the world for our comprehension and the experience of obligation by the moral law in our dealing with the world. Given its fundamental role for fidelity to the moral law, endorsing this conception is even normatively urged. Against this background, Kant's examination of the historical development does not attempt to prove the actuality of this cosmopolitan tendency, but only to show its possibility in order to confirm what reason suggests and commands.[64]

In one of his last writings, the *Conflict of Faculties*, Kant affirms his confidence in the course of history with another intriguing argument. The 'universal yet disinterested sympathy' of outside spectators for the French revolution 'which reveals itself *publicly*' is invoked as a 'historical sign' displaying 'a tendency and faculty in human nature for improvement' underpinning the course of history.[65] It therefore manifests, Kant argues, a continuous progress in the legal organization of

[58] Kant, 'Religion within the Boundaries of Mere Reason', in *Religion and Rational Theology*, p. 153 (n. 45): 'Experience refuses to allow us any hope in this direction.'

[59] Kant, 'Idea for a Universal History with a Cosmopolitan Aim', in *Anthropology, History, and Education*, p. 109 (n. 3).

[60] Kant, 'Conjectural Beginning of Human History', in *Anthropology, History, and Education*, p. 173 (n. 55).

[61] Cf. Honneth, 'The Irreducibility of Progress', in *Pathologies of Reason* (n. 46); Angehrn, 'Kant und die gegenwärtige Geschichtsphilosophie', in *Warum Kant heute?* (n. 11).

[62] Kant, *Critique of the Power of Judgment*, pp. 279–301 (n. 12).

[63] Kant, 'Idea for a Universal History with a Cosmopolitan Aim', in *Anthropology, History, and Education*, p. 110 (n. 3); Kant, 'Conjectural Beginning of Human History', in *Anthropology, History, and Education*, p. 173 (n. 55).

[64] Kant, 'On the Common Saying', in *Practical Philosophy*, p. 306 (n. 52); cf. also Kant, 'The Metaphysics of Morals', in *Practical Philosophy*, pp. 490–1 (n. 14).

[65] Immanuel Kant, 'The Conflict of the Faculties', trans. Allen W. Wood, in Allen W. Wood and George di Giovanni (eds.), *Religion and Rational Theology* (1996), pp. 301–2, 304.

humanity. The stunning experience of the French Revolution, driven by the claim of universal freedom, provided beyond theoretical reasoning in most palpable real developments of the time a powerful endorsement for Kant's bold optimism. Still, the far-reaching conclusions Kant draws from this are surprising. Deducing from empirical facts the direction and outcome of history seems at odds with the most foundational theses of the critical philosopher. However, the weight he attributes to the historical sign relies again on hermeneutical reasons: the sign assumes its full significance through its impact on our self-understanding. Kant's prophecy—as he frames his assertions ironically—is based on the fact that the forecasted progress is 'an occurrence that [man] himself could produce'.[66] The revolution and its reception indicate a disposition conducive to the free actualization of moral aspirations. This experience is predictive, because it encourages and informs our free endeavour to redeem the promise. It gains its significance from the prospect that 'such a phenomenon in human history *will not forget itself*'.[67] It is this lasting influence on our self-understanding that accounts for the power of the historical sign.

This line of thought brings the self-implying structure of the idea to light: the confidence in the historical tendency towards the ultimate aim liberates our free efforts in the aspired direction, and these efforts vindicate the confidence.[68] This dialectic is bound up with the curious fusion of anticipation and openness. The configuration reflects the simultaneous dependence on freedom and nature of the legal endeavour pointing ultimately to their mediation. Yet this delicate nature in no way defies the salience of the idea for an adequate account of law. Kant stresses that the conclusion he draws from the historical sign is 'not just a well-meaning and practically commendable proposition, but [...] a proposition valid also for the most rigorous theory'.[69] This obviously does not mean that the claim meets the criteria of theoretical knowledge as determined in the first Critique. By contrast, in other writings—many of them also written in the post-revolutionary period—Kant often maintains that the supposition of the historical tendency is practically justified, while exceeding theoretical knowledge.[70] The notion of the historical sign provides nothing that would change this character of the claim. Rather, the insistence on the perfect theoretical validity points out that this form of hermeneutical insight in our necessary self-understanding as engaged subjects is by no means less scientifically sound than other sorts of knowledge.

[66] Kant, 'The Conflict of the Faculties', in *Religion and Rational Theology*, p. 300 (n. 65).

[67] Kant, 'The Conflict of the Faculties', in *Religion and Rational Theology*, p. 304 (translation modified) (n. 65).

[68] Cf. Habermas, *The Structural Transformation of the Public Sphere*, pp. 115–16 (n. 46); Angehrn, 'Kant und die gegenwärtige Geschichtsphilosophie', in *Warum Kant heute?*, p. 346 (n. 11) (noting that this self-implying logic pertains to philosophy of history in general).

[69] Kant, 'The Conflict of the Faculties', in *Religion and Rational Theology*, p. 304 (translation modified) (n. 65).

[70] Kant, 'Toward Perpetual Peace', in *Practical Philosophy*, p. 332 (n. 25); Kant, 'On the Common Saying', in *Practical Philosophy*, p. 306 (n. 52); Kant, 'The Metaphysics of Morals', in *Practical Philosophy*, p. 490 (n. 14).

The chapter on the historical sign is dedicated to the conflict of the philosophical with the juridical faculty. It defends the localization of law in a horizon of historical progress against the technicist conception Kant observed in legal scholarship. Ignoring or even denying the possibility of actual transformation the jurists construct law as a mere tool to organize timeless natural dispositions according to the preferences of the authority. Such a perspective misses the most distinctive feature of law. It cannot grasp the emancipatory power that underlies its normative appeal. In this picture, law can at best serve the efficiency of benevolent administration, but it cannot liberate us from our given conditions and enable true self-determination. A rigorous theory of law that reconstructs its subject accurately is only possible, where the underlying self-understanding of this social practice is taken into account.[71]

The concern about the juridical perspective is a central motive in Kant's political works, which dwell on the deficiencies and vices of this competing view. He condemns the lawyers' appearance as 'political moralist[s]' who subject all moral considerations to the prevailing goals of the state.[72] He deplores the role of the leading figures of international law, 'Hugo Grotius, Pufendorf, Vattel, and the like', as 'only sorry comforters' whose works serve to justify every belligerent attack without ever motivating the abstention of violence.[73] What makes the juridical standpoint so problematic is that it is self-fulfilling: if the possibility of progress is not considered, then law is indeed bound by the existing preconditions whose prudent arrangement is all it can offer.[74] As our self-understanding shapes the way we act, law as a form of action cannot be described innocently. Our conception of law determines what it is. Ironically, the philosopher asks the lawyers to give due regard for the practical nature of law. The jurists examine law like an external phenomenon, and fail to take into account the complex relation between knowledge and action. Thus, their description neither bothers with the role of our underlying mindset in general, nor with the influence of their own perspective on the subject matter in particular. What results is the distorting picture and reality of a law lacking its highest virtues. Kant's conception attempts to overcome this consequential flaw. To do so, he carefully delineates the intricate structure of the cosmopolitan aim. Moreover, he embraces the involvement of theory in practice through the decidedly engaged form of his political writings. Kant imaginatively mobilizes his rhetorical talent, intervenes into contemporary debates, and addresses a greater public with short, accessible writings to engender the emancipatory mindset. The truth of theories on human things always also depends on the consequences of the theory. Still, the cosmopolitan idea

[71] Cf. Martti Koskenniemi, 'Constitutionalism as Mindset: Reflections on Kantian Themes about International Law and Globalization', *Theoretical Inquiries in Law* 8 (2007), 9–36.

[72] Kant, 'Toward Perpetual Peace', in *Practical Philosophy*, pp. 338–47 (n. 25).

[73] Kant, 'Toward Perpetual Peace', in *Practical Philosophy*, p. 326 (n. 25).

[74] Kant, 'Toward Perpetual Peace', in *Practical Philosophy*, p. 341 (n. 25); Kant, 'The Conflict of the Faculties', in *Religion and Rational Theology*, pp. 297–8 (n. 65); cf. also Immanuel Kant, 'An Answer to the Question: What Is Enlightenment?', in *Practical Philosophy*, trans. Mary J. Gregor (1996), p. 17.

ultimately remains a bet. Enlightenment can only promote its final outcome. The rest is freedom and history.

IV. Traits of Openness

The systematic openness pervades Kant's portrayal of the legal order. It shapes the apprehension of the legal system as a whole, as well as the outline of international law. As the legal relations beyond the state mark the ultimate margins of the global order, the system's openness is on this level particularly conspicuous. In what follows, I will highlight four particularly significant traits of this openness in both the legal system and its international dimension in particular.

The four elements share a basic structural logic. Kant's argumentation constantly vacillates between opposing ideals. As a result, the position appears hesitant and inconsistent. Yet in fact, this ambiguity exposes the insufficiency of each ideal and envisages a dynamic where both visions haunt each other interminably, paving the way of emancipation. In most concrete terms, Kant's engaged literature on the right of mankind reiterates the logic famously explicated in the chapter on the antinomies of pure reason of the first Critique.[75] This can be observed in the considerations on the relation of law and morality, the principle of publicity, the organization of the international community, and the notion of cosmopolitan law.

1. Openness of the legal system

a) Law and morality

As noted above, Kant derives law from the moral principle and includes it in the system of morals. Yet, his model of the legal order is also famous for its radical moral abstinence, the contention that the required republican order is even feasible for a 'nation of devils'.[76] As law only concerns the external actions, legal universality can also be achieved where people follow egoistic maxims. They only have to be organized in a way that neutralizes the selfish motives by turning them against each other. Kant's sharp distinction of the concept of right from moral motives led scholars to claim that the legal philosophy actually does not belong to the moral part of the system.[77] Kant judged differently, not only in the *Metaphysics of Morals*: only a few pages after defending the concept of a 'nation of devils', the peace essay turns to the

[75] Kant, *Critique of Pure Reason*, pp. 459–550 (n. 1).

[76] Kant, 'Toward Perpetual Peace', in *Practical Philosophy*, p. 335 (n. 25).

[77] Willaschek, 'Why the Doctrine of Right Does Not Belong in the Metaphysics of Morals', (n. 21). The independence of the concept of right from morality is also advocated by Thomas Pogge, 'Is Kant's Rechtslehre a "Comprehensive Liberalism"?', in Mark Timmons (ed.), *Kant's Metaphysics of Morals: Interpetative Essays* (2002). Cf. also the critique of the 'independence thesis' as argued by Julius Ebbinghaus, Klaus Reich, and Georg Geismann in Wolfgang Kersting, *Wohlgeordnete Freiheit: Immanuel Kants Rechts- und Staatsphilosophie* (1993), pp. 136–42.

critique of the political moralist, passionately dismissing a model that restricts law to the savvy organization of hopelessly evil people. Elsewhere, he notes the indispensability of prior cultural perfection for a lasting peace.[78] Another writing stresses the necessity of a 'prepared good will', and projects the process of being '*moralized*' as the end of the cosmopolitan order; 'everything good that is not grafted onto a morally good disposition, is nothing but mere semblance and glittering misery', he insists.[79] A further piece, however, points out that the progress can only concern 'legality', not 'morality with regard to intention'.[80]

Law cannot decree moral perfection. Kant's account indicates two reasons why this aim exceeds the scope of law. For one thing, the imposition to follow legal precepts not out of self-interest, but for their own sake would suspend the free will that morality implies and therefore would miss its objective. This is why law is by definition limited to external action. For another, even with regard to external action, law's content does not necessarily coincide with what we recognize as rationally required. Corresponding with the basic idea of Kant's critical project, he does not assert any predetermined laws in the structures of the world, but reinterprets natural law as a criterion of reason whose concretization will always be contested.[81] This procedural turn of natural law that embeds legal meaning in societal history has been fundamental for modern legal thought. It is further pursued by Hegel and underpins most important theories of the twentieth century such as the approaches of Rawls, Habermas, and Waldron.[82] Positive public rules are necessary because our views differ.[83] Law must also be distinguished from morality to respect this plurality[84] and admit of ongoing critique through independent reflection.[85]

Yet, law cannot be reduced to the arbitrary administration of selfish drives either. A legal order strictly confined to incentive and constraint would be significantly limited in its stability, efficacy, and justice.[86] Moreover, the purpose of

[78] Kant, 'Conjectural Beginning of Human History', in *Anthropology, History, and Education*, pp. 173–4 (n. 55).

[79] Kant, 'Idea for a Universal History with a Cosmopolitan Aim', in *Anthropology, History, and Education*, pp. 114 and 116 (translation modified) (n. 3).

[80] Kant, 'The Conflict of the Faculties', in *Religion and Rational Theology*, p. 307 (emphasis omitted) (n. 65).

[81] Cf. Wolfgang Kersting, 'Politics, Freedom, and Order: Kant's Political Philosophy', in Paul Guyer (ed.), *The Cambridge Companion to Kant* (1992), p. 344.

[82] G.W.F. Hegel, 'Elements of the Philosophy of Right', ed. Allen W. Wood, trans. H.B. Nisbet (2011) The subtitle 'Natural Law and Political Science in Outline' highlights the claim to redeem the idea of natural law; John Rawls, *The Law of Peoples* (1999); Jürgen Habermas, *Between Facts and Norms: Contributions to a Discourse Theory of Law and Democracy*, trans. William Rehg (2011); Jeremy Waldron, *Law and Disagreement* (1999), p. 3.

[83] Cf. Waldron, 'Kant's Legal Positivism' (n. 23); cf. also Samantha Besson, *The Morality of Conflict: Reasonable Disagreement and the Law* (2005), esp. the discussion of Kant in ch. 5.

[84] Cf. Armin von Bogdandy, 'Europäische und nationale Identität: Integration durch Verfassungsrecht?' in *Veröffentlichungen der Vereinigung der Deutschen Staatsrechtslehrer* (2003), 156–93, p. 160 and pp. 178–80.

[85] Cf. Ingeborg Maus, *Zur Aufklärung der Demokratietheorie: rechts- und demokratietheoretische Überlegungen im Anschluss an Kant* (1992), pp. 308–36.

[86] Cf. Angehrn, 'Kant und die gegenwärtige Geschichtsphilosophie', in *Warum Kant heute?*, p. 335 (n. 11).

self-determination that defines law and accounts for its normativity can be fully achieved only in moral agency. While regulation must permit the determination by self-interest, it must not suppose this to be an unalterable necessity. Otherwise, legal regulation reinforces the presumed condition and eradicates the space for moral development.[87] Law could not provide a medium to commonly overcome the constraints of self-interest. As regards disagreement on the content of legal rules, the distinction from individual judgment does not negate the foundation of law in moral reason. This rational claim bears law's normative authority and constitutes an equally essential condition for critique as the differentiation between individual morality and public law. The moral idea of right offers the reference point to assess and challenge rules even if they are legally authoritative.

Strict abstention from, as well as full identification with, moral command ultimately prevent law's critical link to morality. To serve the actualization of moral reason, law must be related to the idea of moral community, while being kept distinct from this vanishing point. Law offers a medium to establish the worldly conditions to commit to moral duty. It adapts the realm of nature to the moral demands of freedom. Paradoxically, law serves moral progress by also being apt for devils. This secures a social order that accommodates moral actions independently of the motives of other subjects, and respects the freedom of individual will determination. At the same time, it leaves room for the awareness of the disputability and fallibility of legal determinations and for the exercise of critical reflection. The moral development furthered by this setting, in turn, strengthens the legal reality, allows to reduce coercion, and invaluably informs the public struggle to improve the legal order.

Kant's ambiguity expresses that it is the division of law and morality through which they unfold their interdependence. Critically engaging with each other, they entertain the historical process of self-determination. Law provides the conditions to reconcile moral duty with nature and society; moral reflection advances the legal framework. The progress of law merely increases legality, yet this is also the fundament of realizing morality.[88] At no point does the fruitful tension between the two spheres of normativity come to rest. Only through ongoing interaction can freedom and justice be actualized. The nexus of individual and collective self-determination requires a unity in lively plurality and disagreement. The key to cultivate this emancipatory dynamic is the principle of publicity.

b) The principle of publicity

The concept of the public is a particularly momentous element of Kant's conception of the legal order. Kant introduces this central term of modern political thought at key points of his oeuvre. Elaborating different aspects of the category's meaning,

[87] Cf. Martti Koskenniemi, 'Formalism, Fragmentation, Freedom: Kantian Themes in Today's International Law', *No Foundations* 4 (2007), 7–28.

[88] Cf. John Dewey, *German Philosophy and Politics* (1915), pp. 66–7.

he unfolds and critically reinterprets the complex semantics of the concept. The doctrine of right highlights the major significance of publicity for the legal order. As mentioned above, Kant deviates from the traditional use of the attribute in the legal context: all law in the civil state is called public law. The treatise on peace also stresses and further explicates the decisive role of publicity in the determination of legal rules.

Publicity is put forth as a frame to bind law to the universal will. Empowering this authority, the public mediates two tensions in the foundation of law: reason and popularity, as well as freedom and happiness. In the first place, the condition of publicity makes the formation of rules accessible to everyone's particular perspective. This necessitates taking the views of the people into account. Yet, the public setting in which the popular claims are considered essentially shapes their content. Everyone is pressured to justify and thus reconsider their own stance in the open forum of the public. The need of validation in a universal light pushes the discursive dynamics to the claims of reason. However, as expounded above, reason constrains the discourse not as an alien force. Reason is actualized through this ongoing social exchange.

In the same course, publicity promises to merge the establishment of right actualizing freedom with the political quest for happiness. While acknowledging the accord with public happiness as 'the proper task of politics',[89] Kant also describes politics as 'executing doctrine of right'.[90] He asserts that the principle of publicity can harmonize these seemingly diverging aims. Exposing the determination of law to the light of the public presses for harmony with the concrete needs and desires of the society. At the same time, the effective need of universal approval impels the steady compliance with everyone's rights while pursuing the common welfare. A claim of reason, the doctrine of right suffuses the public intercourse. Indeed, from the public standpoint of the universal will, right and happiness are revealed to be dependent on each other.

Publicity does not merely allow measuring legislation against a preexisting will. Rather, the public constitutes the space to form the required judgment. Indeed, Kant recognizes the public exchange of thoughts as a prerequisite of the 'freedom to *think*'.[91] It is the free encounter with others that allows us to attain a rational standpoint. Publicity enables us to constitute, develop, and enrich our judgment. The community with others also emotionally widens our experience decisively for accurate thought.[92] In this way, the public provides the context to unfold the existential meaning of reason, and to acquire a consciousness enabling individual and collective self-determination. Accordingly, Kant also promotes publicity as the

[89] Kant, 'Toward Perpetual Peace', in *Practical Philosophy*, p. 351 (n. 25).

[90] Kant, 'Toward Perpetual Peace', in *Practical Philosophy*, p. 338 (translation modified) (n. 25).

[91] Kant, 'What Does It Mean to Orient Oneself in Thinking?', in *Religion and Rational Theology*, p. 16 (n. 53).

[92] Cf. Immanuel Kant, *Notes and Fragments: Logic, Metaphysics, Moral Philosophy, Aesthetics*, ed. Paul Guyer, trans. Curtis Bowman, Paul Guyer, and Frederick Rauscher (2005), p. 498, n. 763: 'Everything tastes and pleases better in good company. All of life is amplified in such company. It is indispensable for thinking people.'

trigger of enlightenment. The 'emergence from . . . self-incurred immaturity',[93] he affirms, requires nothing more than the 'freedom to make *public use* of one's reason in all matters'.[94] The universal standpoint of reason is to be sought in the continuous open engagement with others.

Of course, it would be naïve to comprehend publicity as a strict insurance of compliance with the claims of right and universal happiness. Humans err and public discourses are distorted by ideologies and manipulation. The beneficence of publicity seems to presuppose the intellectual independence it is supposed to bring about. Kant's writings prove that he was well aware of this precarious predicament. His account of enlightenment starts with the reluctance and ineptitude of a public used to subjection. First trials of public freedom will fail, evoke resistance, and increase fear. Yet, he holds the confidence that the public use of reason triggers a slow, but determinate tendency toward actual free judgment, 'a true reform in the mode of thinking'.[95] Justifying our views in front of the society, anticipating and hearing diverging perspectives and experiencing the good of a common standpoint pushes our reflection steadily in an emancipatory direction. This enlightenment of judgment, in turn, conduces to the enhancement of the public framework.[96] Once more, Kant puts his trust in a dialectical dynamic. And again, the promoted trust is itself a basis to make the prospect true.

Kant's discovery of publicity has inspired some of the most fruitful readings of Kant in recent political philosophy. Diverse accounts have pointed out the far-reaching consequences of the notion and tracked significant traces of the idea in other parts of Kant's work. Jürgen Habermas exposed Kant's fundamental role for the exploration of the concept in his seminal book on *The Structural Transformation of the Public Sphere*. It is in this context that Habermas, based on a thorough examination of the pertinent texts, revealed the ultimately 'system-exploding consequences' of Kant's corresponding reflections.[97] Publicity shifts from a merely nature-based to a self-constitutive sphere of mediation of politics and morality in the empirical reality of society. Hannah Arendt also highlighted publicity as 'one of the key concepts of Kant's political thinking'.[98] Holding a fairly low opinion of Kant's explicitly political writings,[99] she extrapolated and praised corresponding intuitions in the *Critique of Judgment*, in which she located the rudiments of Kant's missing political philosophy.[100] Arendt's reading revolves around the observation that Kant explicates judgment in this major work not as a mere application of rules, but as a capacity based on the worldly community with others. Kant reveals

[93] Kant, 'An Answer to the Question: What Is Enlightenment?', in *Practical Philosophy*, p. 17 (emphasis omitted) (n. 74).

[94] Kant, 'An Answer to the Question: What Is Enlightenment?', in *Practical Philosophy*, p. 18 (n. 74).

[95] Kant, 'An Answer to the Question: What Is Enlightenment?', in *Practical Philosophy*, p. 18 (translation modified) (n. 74).

[96] Kant, 'An Answer to the Question: What Is Enlightenment?', in *Practical Philosophy*, p. 22 (n. 74).

[97] Habermas, *The Structural Transformation of the Public Sphere*, p. 116 (n. 46).

[98] Arendt, *Lectures on Kant's Political Philosophy*, p. 18 (n. 5).

[99] Arendt, *Lectures on Kant's Political Philosophy*, pp. 7–8 (n. 5).

[100] Cf. Arendt, *Lectures on Kant's Political Philosophy*, p. 9 (n. 5).

the meaning of politics by exposing beyond individual rule-following and physical dependence upon others a distinct sociality springing from the human mind. In a further important yet again very different strand of reception, Christine Korsgaard found the idea of publicity also implied in Kant's moral philosophy. Taking up Wittgenstein's argument of private language she defends the Kantian standpoint with the argument that reasons are inherently public. Thus, universality is implied in the practice of reason-giving because and in so far as they refer to the perspectives of everyone else.[101]

2. Openness of international law

a) *World federation vs. world state*

Kant's dithering with respect to the postulated shape of the world order is especially notorious. Throughout his reflections on international law, he vacillates between the model of a world state and a world federation. It is irritating that despite Kant's systematic genius, the intensive consideration of the topic, and its high significance for both the philosophical system and the cosmopolitan political project he is not clear about this point.

Many efforts have been undertaken to come to terms with this ambiguity. A recent careful examination of the pertinent works assumes a change of opinion behind the seeming contradiction.[102] It is probable, of course, that Kant's political ideas and expectations changed in the course of decades, also with respect to the international realm. Especially the experience of the French Revolution might have impacted his view on the legal development. Yet the oscillation between an actual state and a loose federation on the global level cannot only be observed when comparing writings from different periods. Also within the single writings, the ideal remains consistently vague and ambiguous. In *Idea for a Universal History with a Cosmopolitan Aim*, for example, Kant describes the ideal on few pages as a 'federation of nations' referring to the loose model of the 'Foedus Amphictyonum',[103] and as a 'future large state body'.[104] Other formulations postulate more vaguely 'a united might, and [. . .] the decision according to laws of the united will',[105] and

[101] Christine M. Korsgaard, *The Sources of Normativity* (1996), pp. 131–66; Christine M. Korsgaard, *Self-Constitution: Agency, Identity, and Integrity* (2009), pp. 177–214; Christine M. Korsgaard, interviewed by Herlinde Pauer-Studer, 'Christine M. Korsgaard: Internalism and the Sources of Normativity', in Herlinde Pauer-Studer (ed.), *Constructions of Practical Reason: Interviews on Moral and Political Philosophy* (2003).

[102] Kleingeld, *Kant and Cosmopolitanism*, pp. 40–71 (n. 10).

[103] Kant, 'Idea for a Universal History with a Cosmopolitan Aim', in *Anthropology, History, and Education*, p. 114 (emphasis omitted) (n. 3).

[104] Kant, 'Idea for a Universal History with a Cosmopolitan Aim', in *Anthropology, History, and Education*, p. 118 (n. 3).

[105] Kant, 'Idea for a Universal History with a Cosmopolitan Aim', in *Anthropology, History, and Education*, p. 114 (translation modified) (n. 3).

envisage a condition '*resembling* a civil commonwealth'.[106] The pertinent writings from other periods waver similarly on that point.[107]

Thus, the ambiguity not only reflects a changing mind. Apparently, Kant at no point propounded a clear conclusive vision. The constancy of vague descriptions changing sometimes in the same passage from more unitary to more pluralistic anticipations indicate that Kant exposed this tension deliberately. Neither on the domestic nor on the international level does the idea of the cosmopolitan system provide a ready-made plan for legislation.[108] Its emancipatory potency lies precisely in the dialectical oscillation between contrasting directions.[109]

In principle, reason clearly claims a unitary global order with universal coercive force. 'In accordance with reason there is only one way that states in relation with one another can leave the lawless condition, which involves nothing but war; it is that, like individual human beings, they give up their savage (lawless) freedom, accommodate themselves to public coercive laws, and so form an (always growing) *state of nations* (*civitas gentium*) that would finally encompass all the nations of the earth.'[110] Only a civil state can really end the international state of nature, install globally the rule of the universal will of the people and secure the right of every individual that defines Kant's concept of law.[111] In this respect, the cosmopolitan aim and in particular cosmopolitan law point to an integrated world order, a cosmopolis. In order to be bound by law, states must be subjected to a higher authority. Such an overarching power constitutes an essential conclusive element to the public system of law.[112]

In spite of this conceptual demand, Kant affirms a looser federation. The vigorous defender of reason's claim shows a surprising readiness to adjust the idea in light of the existing political configuration. The federation is 'the *negative* surrogate' that replaces 'the positive *idea of a world republic*' because the peoples 'do not at all want this, thus rejecting *in hypothesi* what is correct *in thesi*'.[113] A global state, he contends, is ruled out by the concept of a 'law of peoples' because this formula presumes peoples and thus states in plural.[114] Kant does not promote the loose arrangement due to its flawlessness. He even denies the actual rule of law in the federation: it 'is of itself already a state of war', only restrained from violence

[106] Kant, 'Idea for a Universal History with a Cosmopolitan Aim', in *Anthropology, History, and Education*, p. 115 (emphasis added) (n. 3).

[107] Cf. Kant, 'On the Common Saying', in *Practical Philosophy*, pp. 307, 309 (n. 52); Kant, 'Toward Perpetual Peace', in *Practical Philosophy*, pp. 326, 328, 336 (n. 25); Kant, 'The Metaphysics of Morals', in *Practical Philosophy*, pp. 487–8, 491 (n. 14).

[108] Cf. Jaspers, 'Kant's "Perpetual Peace"', in *Philosophy and the World*, pp. 113–15 (n. 11).

[109] Cf. Angehrn, 'Kant und die gegenwärtige Geschichtsphilosophie', in *Warum Kant heute?*, pp. 337–9 (n. 11).

[110] Kant, 'Toward Perpetual Peace', in *Practical Philosophy*, p. 328 (n. 25).

[111] Cf. Jürgen Habermas, 'Kant's Idea of Perpetual Peace, with the Benefit of Two Hundred Years' Hindsight', in James Bohman and Matthias Lutz-Bachmann (eds.), *Perpetual Peace: Essays on Kant's Cosmopolitan Ideal* (1997), p. 128.

[112] Cf. Wolfgang Kersting, *Wohlgeordnete Freiheit: Immanuel Kants Rechts- und Staatsphilosophie* (1993), p. 76.

[113] Kant, 'Toward Perpetual Peace', in *Practical Philosophy*, p. 328 (n. 25).

[114] Kant, 'Toward Perpetual Peace', in *Practical Philosophy*, p. 326 (n. 25).

through the federal framework. But this is, Kant argues, still better than 'a universal monarchy' that would extinguish freedom in 'a soulless despotism'.[115]

Belying the prejudice of rationalistic unworldliness, Kant's modifications of the immediate claim show great pragmatic sense. This pragmatism is, however, not a limitation of the appeal to reason; the moderation is immanent to the very idea. Taken as an abstract ideal, the vision of the global state ultimately perverts into its opposite. Ignoring the concrete plurality of peoples, the cosmopolitan state would be a detached institution. Its purported universality would conceal excluded claims. It could not integrate the multiple cultural contexts of human self-realization, promote the diversity implied by individual and collective freedom, and acknowledge the plurality of the popular voice. Lacking the determinacy of a distinct society, it could not unite society in a common project, but only administer social relations as a remote power. The cosmopolitan enterprise, as Kant warns, would turn into exclusionary domination and eventually break up into anarchy.[116]

That is why Kant equates the global state with a despotic monarchy. A republican order seeking equal freedom and the good life of all cannot pass over existing plurality. It must be an expression of the concrete shape and will of the people. Such respect for the genuine claims of the people is implied in the cosmopolitan idea. The basic vision of a global political union is actualized through the continuous inclusion of everyone's perspective. This explains Kant's readiness to modify the initial idea in light of the peoples' rejection of the world state. It is necessitated by the very idea's actualization. As a general, abstract rule—'in thesi' —the idea claims a global state. In its concrete realization—'in hypothesi'—this claim for universality is determined by the regard for the actual will of the peoples.[117] The implications of real universality also warrant Kant's care to uphold the premise of a multiplicity of peoples. The reference to the plurality implied in the concept of a law of peoples is not made out of fixation on the literal meaning of the term, but because it constitutes a fact the pursuit of inclusion must reflect.

True universality cannot be established as an abstract ideal in neglect of plurality. It must concretely involve the other in its diversity. This cannot be accomplished once and for all, but requires an ongoing historical process. Continually, the global order must remain open for new, excluded, unheard claims. In other words: the idea is to be actualized in a practice of infinite approximation. Nonetheless, this pluralistic pursuit must remain connected to the postulate of cosmopolitan union. It is this postulate that pushes for mutual recognition and association with the other, the constant search of the excluded, and the effort to subject all human relations under an ever more stable rule of law. The history of cosmopolitan emancipation is triggered by the idea of a union pointing to plurality and a plurality directing to

[115] Kant, 'Toward Perpetual Peace', in *Practical Philosophy*, p. 336 (translation modified) (n. 25).

[116] Kant, 'Toward Perpetual Peace', in *Practical Philosophy*, p. 336 (n. 25).

[117] Cf. on the meaning of the distinction 'in thesi. . . in hypothesi' Immanuel Kant, *Handschriftlicher Nachlaß: Metaphysik, 2. Theil*, vol. 18, Kant's Gesammelte Schriften, ed. Erich Adickes (1967), n. 5695, pp. 328–9; Immanuel Kant, *Vorlesungen über Metaphysik und Rationaltheologie*, vol. 28, 1, Kant's Gesammelte Schriften, ed. Gerhard Lehmann (1968), p. 407.

unification. Legally, this is not least reflected in the combination of international and cosmopolitan law.

b) Cosmopolitan law

Cosmopolitan law constitutes an essential dimension of the depicted legal order. It forms one of three parts, and it represents—as its designation reveals—in some way the conclusive and most characteristic component of the cosmopolitan system: individual rights on the global level. Kant stresses the indispensability of this portion of the public legal order. He further underlines that it does not only constitute a sphere of philanthropy, but of actual right.[118] Thus, the idea of cosmopolitan law indeed affirms a legal position of the individual beyond the state. This suggests the existence of institutional conditions to enforce rights on that level.

However, the content Kant attributes to this body of law is remarkably restricted: 'The *cosmopolitan law* shall be limited to conditions of universal *hospitality*.'[119] The revolutionary turn to worldwide rights is immediately confined to a weak hospitality claim which Kant explicates as 'the right of a foreigner not to be treated with hostility because he has arrived on the land of another'.[120] He also clarifies that it is 'not the *right to be a guest* [. . .], but the *right to visit*', leaving further rights dependent on contractual agreements.[121] Hence, Kant's cosmopolitan law is far from proclaiming a firm catalogue of human rights or even a world constitution. It only asserts in a rather moral than legal tone a minimal guarantee of peaceful intercourse, and explicitly presumes the ongoing asymmetry of host and visitor. All this implies that—despite the assertion of the legal quality of cosmopolitan law—the global order is conceived as a plurality of states. However, the text is again strikingly ambiguous: in spite of cosmopolitan law's distance from a constitutional setting, Kant asserts that it serves to approach a 'cosmopolitan constitution'. The formulations also alternate between constellations implying multiple peoples and mere interactions among individuals.

The tensions display historicity afresh in a double sense: they reflect the regard for the concrete challenges of Kant's time and expose structurally the historical, system-bursting structure of cosmopolitan law. With the right to visit Kant proclaims a pragmatic path for the radical step of concretely recognizing an original equality and unalienable legal standing of every human being. The precondition for a stranger's rejection that 'this can be done without destroying him'[122] is a demand whose full actualization is—as the current situation at borders throughout the world harrowingly exposes—still wanting. Kant's arguments for limiting the right reveal that the restrictions are primarily motivated by the concern that the right might likely be abused for colonial purposes.[123] The law of hospitality aims

[118] Kant, 'Toward Perpetual Peace', in *Practical Philosophy*, p. 328 (n. 25).
[119] Kant, 'Toward Perpetual Peace', in *Practical Philosophy*, p. 328 (translation modified) (n. 25).
[120] Kant, 'Toward Perpetual Peace', in *Practical Philosophy*, pp. 328–9 (n. 25).
[121] Ibid. [122] Ibid.
[123] Cf. Ingeborg Maus, 'From Nation-State to Global State, or the Decline of Democracy', *Constellations* 13 (2006), 471–2.

at a middle way between cementing privileges 'uti possidetis' and unleashing an exploitative mobility. Slightly, but fundamentally it pierces the walls of separated communities. The enabled intercourse is moderate, but its restricted shape is set up precisely to initiate a subtle dynamic toward the most revolutionary aspiration of a cosmopolitan constitution.

Apart from this mindful attention for given circumstances, the balanced character of the conception has also a structural dimension. Cosmopolitan law is essentially a law of borders.[124] To be sure, it is supposed to ensure a universal legal status of the individual beyond and independent of state borders. Yet this universality cannot simply be provided through a set of rules on the global level. Every distinct legal body, even if it had a worldwide scope, implies by its very determinacy a limit that excludes and conceals claims. Universal recognition beyond borders requires therefore an unending activity of border crossing.

This elucidates why the description of cosmopolitan law is so deeply shaped by the condition of boundaries. This condition is not only evoked through the constellation of separated territories and the asymmetry of host and guest. It is also implied in the ambiguous status of cosmopolitan law between an enforceable law and a moral demand, as well as by its vague content between a narrow 'natural right' and a further reaching reference to contracts and philanthropy.[125] These traits express the genuine claim of cosmopolitan law: it exposes the constant need of every legal order to be opened up for its other, the beyond of its boundaries, for excluded claims that have not yet been perceived. Cosmopolitan law asserts such incessant questioning of the order's limits as a demand *within* law. Qualified as distinctly 'cosmopolitan' and pointing toward a cosmopolitan constitution, this dimension of law promises to trigger the infinite course of global emancipation.

Yet, leading beyond existing orders its force is also eminently precarious. On the one hand, the scope of law is restricted; much care remains dependent upon the existence of philanthropy. But even as far as the claim is construed as law it lacks an enforcing cosmopolitan authority. It can only be backed up institutionally within the legal orders it surpasses. The transcending character is associated with a distinctive weakness. A strange medium between law and morality, a moral excess within law, cosmopolitan right constitutes an incorruptible, yet ever uncertain element of law.

Not least against the background of the tremendous contemporary challenges of migration, different philosophers have emphasized the significance of Kant's cosmopolitan law. Jacques Derrida has examined its logic meticulously in various studies. His considerations centre on the fragile constellation of hospitality implying on the one hand an unconditional and incalculable openness for the other, on the other hand the unequal property, authority, and restricting rules of a home.[126] Derrida acknowledges the importance of qualifying hospitality as a law and points out how

[124] Cf. Benhabib, *Another Cosmopolitanism*, p. 22 (n. 18).
[125] Kant, 'Toward Perpetual Peace', in *Practical Philosophy*, p. 329 (n. 25).
[126] Jacques Derrida, 'HOSTIPITALITY', *Angelaki* 5, (2000), 3–18.

far away we still are from redeeming Kant's claim.[127] Yet, contrasting Kant with Levinas, he also points out the ambivalence of the juridical comprehension: the affirmation of the legal, not merely charitable nature of the claim is bound up with its restriction.[128] Nevertheless, Derrida underscores an 'implosion' in the concept of hospitality that at all times leads beyond set rules.[129] The political Kant puts forward 'is always inadequate to itself'.[130] This inadequacy is particularly present in the cosmopolitan right of hospitality that—oscillating between a limited right and an infinite claim of the other[131]—pushes into a never conclusively attainable time 'to come [à venir]'.[132]

Following Derrida, Seyla Benhabib elaborated further on the peculiar status of cosmopolitan law, developing on this basis her seminal concept of 'democratic iterations'. She particularly highlights the distinct normative quality of cosmopolitan right establishing—on a theoretical basis beyond natural law and legal positivism—a third kind of obligation between moral and juridical claims.[133] Regulating the relations with persons across the boundaries of instituted political communities, cosmopolitan norms claim from beyond polities their juridical actualization within them; 'they create a universe of meaning, values, and social relations that had not existed before by changing the normative constituents and evaluative principles of the world of "objective spirit"'.[134] Thus, they provide external criteria to question and advance the ineluctably limited legal orders.

The concluding, overarching 'cosmopolitan' layer of Kant's legal system pierces the boundaries of orders and provides the individual—ultimate representative of plurality—with a tool to express claims that have not yet been taken into account. One last time, Kant asserts the ideas of a global system, a cosmopolitan order, and an encompassing rule of law. Once again, he portrays this cosmopolitan system of law as the venue of an infinite, incalculable and fragile, yet obstinately hopeful history of emancipation.

V. Conclusion

At the core of Kant's definition of the concept of right lies the claim of universality. Law ought to bring universality into the world. It is this inner claim that implies

[127] Jacques Derrida, 'On Cosmopolitanism', in *On Cosmopolitanism and Forgiveness*, trans. Mark Dooley and Michael Hughes (2001), p. 11.

[128] Jacques Derrida, *Adieu to Emmanuel Levinas*, trans. Pascale-Anne Brault and Michael Naas (1999), pp. 87–101; cf. also Jacques Derrida and Anne Dufourmantelle, *Of Hospitality: Anne Dufourmantelle Invites Jacques Derrida to Respond*, trans. Rachel Bowlby (2000), pp. 69–83.

[129] Derrida, 'HOSTIPITALITY', *Angelaki* 5 (2000), 3–18, at 5 (n. 126).

[130] Derrida, *Adieu to Emmanuel Levinas*, p. 97 (n. 128).

[131] Derrida and Dufourmantelle, *Of Hospitality: Anne Dufourmantelle Invites Jacques Derrida to Respond*, pp. 75–83 (n. 128); cf. also Jacques Derrida, 'The Principle of Hospitality', *Parallax* 11 (2005): pp. 6–9.

[132] Derrida, 'HOSTIPITALITY', *Angelaki* 5 (2000), 3–18, at 14 (n. 126).

[133] Benhabib, *Another Cosmopolitanism*, pp. 20–5 (n. 18).

[134] Benhabib, *Another Cosmopolitanism*, p. 72 (n. 18).

a system of rules, requires their public determination, and points beyond national borders to a cosmopolitan frame. This same claim accounts for the singular structure of the global legal system. As beings endowed with finite reason, we cannot actualize universality once and for all. The idea embodied in the system is an infinite endeavour, pushing us to constantly question and transcend settled orders, opening up the historical tendency towards a utopian future that exceeds our anticipations.

Accordingly, Kant was conscious that neither a philosopher nor a lawyer can conclusively determine the perfect legal system. Its shape has to be sought in the historical course of society. Yet the scholar can record the structure of the idea. This is what Kant's account of the system presents: he reconstructs the underlying demand of reason, the need of common concretization, the emancipatory direction, and the system-exploding openness. In this way, he at the same time asserts the authority of law as it is publicly determined and shows that by its inner logic it ushers beyond itself. While explicating this structure, Kant is committed to the theorist's public role he locates therein. From his distinct historical standpoint, he explores with a pragmatic sense the real utopian perspectives harboured in law.[135] He promotes the confidence in the promise of law and endeavours to excite the public for the modality of future. All these aspects give Kant's conception of the international legal system its irritating shape. They expose the idea of the system as a correlate of freedom. What irritates is, in fact, the emancipatory irritation of law.

Selected Bibliography

Bohman, James and Lutz-Bachmann, Matthias (eds.), *Perpetual Peace: Essays on Kant's Cosmopolitan Ideal* (Cambridge: MIT Press, 1997).

Kersting, Wolfgang, 'Politics, Freedom, and Order: Kant's Political Philosophy', in Paul Guyer (ed.), *The Cambridge Companion to Kant* (Cambridge: Cambridge University Press, 1992), pp. 342–66.

Jaspers, Karl, 'Kant's "Perpetual Peace"', in *Philosophy and the World: Selected Writings and Essays*, trans. E.B. Ashton (Washington DC: Regnery Publishing, 1963), pp. 88–124.

Kleingeld, Pauline, *Kant and Cosmopolitanism: The Philosophical Ideal of World Citizenship* (Cambridge: Cambridge University Press, 2012).

Koskenniemi, Martti, 'Constitutionalism as Mindset: Reflections on Kantian Themes about International Law and Globalization', *Theoretical Inquiries in Law* 8(1) (2007), 9–36.

[135] Cf. on the 'realistically utopian' dimension of Kant's conception Rawls, *The Law of Peoples* (n. 82). Rawls proposes on the basis of Kant's conception an own 'realistic utopia' of the international legal order. Rawls' ahistorical understanding of a 'realistic utopia' seems, however, decidedly less utopian (and thus, Kant might say, less realistic) than the project of his spiritus rector (cf. Rawls, *The Law of Peoples*, pp. 11–23 (n. 82)).

16

Fichte and the Echo of his Internationalist Thinking in Romanticism

Carla De Pascale

I. The Early Fichte as the Heir of the Pacifist-Cosmopolitan Tradition

To gain a general understanding of Fichte's thought, it is important to bear in mind that, at the onset of his intellectual career, he engaged in a full-on conflict with the counter-revolutionary A.W. Rehberg.[1] At that time, Fichte was about to tackle Kant's critical philosophy and had not yet himself embarked on his own research in the field of theoretical philosophy. Already there, Fichte explicitly condemns war as an instrument of the power of sovereigns and as something that not only deceived, but also damaged the populations involved.[2]

Fichte was to follow in the wake of the pacifist-cosmopolitan tradition for several years. In the introduction to the *Grundlage des Naturrechts* (1796/97), his principal work of politico-juridical theory, he specifies the difference to the utopian traits of pre-Kantian politico-juridical philosophy. Kant had already drawn attention to the rationality of his own position– and therefore Fichte himself would do so to an even greater extent. If the Abbé de Saint-Pierre and ultimately Rousseau himself had proved that they considered perpetual peace to be an idea as stimulating as it was unattainable, the achievement of the two German philosophers consisted in demonstrating the necessity of peace, in that it is an idea produced by reason.[3] In 1796, Fichte had already published a review of *Zum ewigen Frieden*,[4] without,

[1] Fichte's *Beitrag* argued against Rehberg's *Untersuchungen über die französische Revolution*. See Johann Gottlieb Fichte, 'Beitrag zur Berichtigung der Urtheile des Publikums über die französischen Revolution', in *Werke 1791-1794* (1964), I, vol. 1, J.-G.-Fichte-Gesamtausgabe der Bayerischen Akademie der Wissenschaften (henceforth Gesamtausgabe); August Wilhelm Rehberg, *Untersuchungen über die französische Revolution* (1793).

[2] Fichte, 'Beitrag', in *Werke 1791-1794* (n. 1), p. 244. See Manfred Buhr and Domenico Losurdo, *Fichte, die französische Revolution und das Ideal vom ewigen Frieden* (1991).

[3] Johann Gottlieb Fichte, 'Grundlage des Naturrechts nach Principien der Wissenschaftslehre' (henceforth *Naturrecht*), in *Werke 1794-1796* (1966), I, vol. 3, Gesamtausgabe, p. 323.

[4] Fichte, '[Rezension:] Zum ewigen Frieden. Ein philosophischer Entwurf von Immanuel Kant', in *Werke 1794-1796* (n. 3), pp. 221–8.

moreover, refraining from specific criticisms. In the introduction to his *Naturrecht,* he returned to Kant's text, albeit pointing out how he himself had arrived at certain conclusions *before* reading Kant.[5]

The influence of Kant is proved by the second appendix to the *Naturrecht*, entitled *Grundriss des Völker-und Weltbürgerrechts*.[6] Kant's legacy is in any case already manifest in the titles of the two parts that make up the appendix, and which put forward once again the content of the second and the third 'definitive article' of Kant's *Zum ewigen Frieden*. Fichte followed a personal trajectory in developing his thoughts on the theme of international relations. This is clearly observable only if we look at the overarching parallel Fichte established between the treatment of the internal law of a state and that of the law regulating relationships between states (the contents of this latter theme being indeed considered as an 'appendix' to the principal part of the work). Within this parallel, furthermore, there are two main foci of analysis: the concept of right, which constitutes the foundation of both approaches, and the role of the state as the exclusive element of mediation both in the (juridical) relationships between the citizens of one particular state, and in those between citizens belonging to different states. This depends on the fact that the concept of law finds its full actuation only within the state. On the other hand, Fichte shows no uncertainty about the fact that the concept of state is an abstract concept; one, in other words, to which we should certainly direct our reasoning, albeit without losing sight of the fact that real relationships do not actually occur between different state institutions, but between the citizens of different states—and in the first instance between citizens of bordering states.[7]

The necessity for law arises when at least two individuals enter into reciprocal contact. This implies, first of all, that they should 'know each other' and then that they 'should recognize each other' in their juridical personalities (Fichte anticipated Hegel in developing the concept of recognition).[8] Fichte now applied the same

[5] Faustino Oncina Coves, 'Para la Paz Perpetua de Kant y el Fundamento del derecho natural de Fichte: encuentros y desencuentros', Δαἰμων, Revista de Filosofía 9 (1994), 223–339; Jean-Christophe Merle, 'La réception du Projet de paix perpétuelle par Fichte: La critique de Kant prisonnier du droit de gens', in Hoke Robinson (ed.), *Proceedings of the Eighth International Kant Congress* (1995), vol. II, part 2, pp. 893–900; Claudio Cesa, 'Recensori di Kant: Fichte e Schlegel', in *Teoria politica*, vol. XI (1995), 33–45.

[6] Johann Gottlieb Fichte, 'Naturrecht', in *Werke 1797-1798* (1970), I, vol. 4, Gesamtausgabe, pp. 151–65; see Carla De Pascale, 'Das Völkerrecht (Zweiter Anhang)', in Jean-Christophe Merle (ed.), *Johann Gottlieb Fichte, Grundlage des Naturrechts*, (2nd edn, 2016), pp. 179–91. On the subject of international relations in Fichte see Richard Schottky, 'Internationale Beziehungen als ethisches und juridisches Problem bei Fichte', in Klaus Hammacher (ed.), *Der transzendentale Gedanke* (1981), pp. 250–77; *Kosmopolitismus und Nationalidee, Fichte-Studien* 2 (1990); both of which contain a bibliography; see also Georges Vlachos, *Fédéralisme et raison d'état dans la pensée internationale de Fichte* (1948).

[7] This gives an indication for a definition of the law of peoples (*Völkerrecht*): 'The state itself is nothing but an abstract conception; only the citizens, as such, are actual persons.' See Johann Gottlieb Fichte, *The Science of Rights*, trans. Adolph Ernst Kroeger (1970), p. 475.

[8] 'The relationship of free beings to each other is thus the relationship of an interaction through intellect and freedom. Neither can recognize the other, if not both recognize each other mutually.' (editor's translation). In German, it reads: 'Das Verhältniß freier Wesen zu einander ist daher das Verhältniß einer Wechselwirkung durch Intelligenz und Freiheit. Keines kann das andere anerkennen, wenn nicht beide sich gegenseitig anerkennen [. . .]'; see Fichte, 'Naturrecht', in *Werke 1794-1796* (n. 3), p. 351; to understand the concept of 'recognition', however, it is necessary to bear in mind all of

mechanism to relationships between states.[9] In this passage, again, the influence of Kant is evident: his reasoning opens with the presentation of two alternative routes for inter-state relationships with a view to a possible fusion, both of which are derived from Kant. The first route envisages the progressive formation of a single world state: a result that is judged by Fichte (as indeed it had been by Kant) to be dangerous rather than desirable, on account of its potentially totalitarian features; the second route envisages a series of successive alliances, initially stipulated between bordering states and progressively expanded towards the ultimate establishment of a single confederation of states.[10] This latter option is preferred by both philosophers.[11] The truly significant element, however, is not merely that he agrees with Kant on this point. Rather, it is the idea, clearly set out by Fichte *before* any other issue is dealt with, that the formation of the state is the effect of a command deriving both from nature and reason (it should also be noted how in this case nature and reason are most certainly not in opposing camps).[12]

Fichte therefore turns his attention right from the start to the relationship between two bordering states and to the first germs of an alliance between them.

the first four paragraphs of the work: see Wolfgang Janke, 'Fichtes Grundlegung des Rechtsgrundes', *Kant-Studien* 82, (1991), 197–218; Michael Kahlo et al. (eds.), *Fichtes Lehre vom Rechtsverhältnis. Die Deduktion der §§ 1-4 der 'Grundlage des Naturrechts' und ihre Stellung in der Rechtsphilosophie* (1992); Ingeborg Schüssler, 'Die Deduktion des Begriffs des Rechts aus Prinzipien der Wissenschaftslehre', *Fichte-Studien* 11 (1997), 23–40; Heikki Ikäheimo, 'Fichte on Recognizing Potential Person', and the relative 'Kommentar' by Carla De Pascale, in Kurt Seelmann and Benno Zabel (eds.), *Autonomie und Normativität* (2014), pp. 44–68. For a comparison between Fichte and Hegel on this theme, see Andreas Wildt, 'Recht und Selbstachtung, im Anschluß an die Anerkennungslehren von Fichte und Hegel', in *Fichtes Lehre vom Rechtsverhältnis*, pp. 127–72 (n. 8). On recognition in Hegel, see Ludwig Siep, *Anerkennung als Prinzip der praktischen Philosophie. Untersuchungen zu Hegels Jenaer Philosophie des Geistes* (1970); Axel Honneth, *Kampf um Anerkennung. Zur moralischen Grammatik sozialer Konflikte* (1994), and also Georg Wilhelm Friedrich Hegel, *Enzyklopädie der philosophischen Wissenschaften im Grundrisse* (1830), §§ 430–5.

[9] § 3 of the *Anhang* states: '[. . .] since the possibility of a legal relation is conditioned, as we have seen, by actual and conscious reciprocal influence.' See Fichte, *The Science of Rights*, p. 474 (n. 7); see also corollary 3) at § 4 (Fichte, 'Naturrecht', in *Werke 1797-1798*, pp. 152, 153 (n. 6)).

[10] See Fichte, 'Naturrecht', in *Werke 1797-1798*, §§ 1, 4 corollary 1), 16) (n. 6).

[11] Kant had dealt with this issue not only in *Zum ewigen Frieden*, but also in *Über den Gemeinspruch*.

[12] See Fichte, *The Science of Rights*, p. 474 (n. 7): 'It is a proof that the state is not an arbitrary invention, but is established by nature and reason.' Here, the complexity of the meaning of the term 'nature' emerges clearly: 'rational nature' is the first meaning; a second meaning of nature refers to the condition in which relationships between men are not regulated by civil law, with the consequent opposition between 'state of nature' and 'civil state'. It is precisely in the idealistic philosophies that the element of continuity between *Naturrecht (nature law)* and *Staatsrecht (constitutional law)*, already part of the contractualistic doctrines of the modern age, is emphasized, as may be observable in the subtitle of Georg Wilhelm Friedrich Hegel's *Grundlinien der Philosophie des Rechts: oder Naturrecht und Staatswissenschaft im Grundrisse*, and even before that in the following assumption by Fichte, *The Science of Rights*, p. 201 (n. 7): 'Hence, *Natural Law* [. . .] between men, is not possible at all except in a commonwealth and under positive laws.' This was repeated even more incisively fifteen years later: law, that is constitutional law ('Recht = Staatsrecht') (Johann Gottlieb Fichte, 'Rechtslehre 1812', in *Nachgelassene Schriften 1812* (2002), II, vol. 13, Gesamtausgabe, p. 200). See also Fichte, 'Rechtslehre 1812', in *Nachgelassene Schriften 1812*, p. 200 (n. 12), with regard to the opposition in the following statements: 'natural law, that is legality beyond the state, does not exist'; nature is understood here as laws of reason, see Fichte, 'Rechtslehre 1812', in *Nachgelassene Schriften 1812*, p. 199 (n. 12); 'Law of nature is a conflict of freedom in infinity', see Fichte, 'Rechtslehre 1812', in *Nachgelassene Schriften 1812*, p. 198 (n. 12).

This is nothing more than one of the many possible forms of contract: without curtailing the autonomy of the juridical system internal to each state, the allied states guarantee their citizens their respective rights of property. They recognize, in other words, the boundaries that delimit their respective territories and their relative resources (they recognize first and foremost the boundaries drawn on the land, but there follows also the recognition of certain rights, such as the right to fish and hunt, navigation and mining rights, etc.).[13]

The alliance Fichte proposes is a sort of intermediate solution, based on the consideration that in relationships between states there is no superior judge capable of performing the role of judge and at the same time that of arbiter, which, in national law, is performed by the sovereign for citizens potentially in conflict with one another.[14] On the other hand, it would be a decidedly risky option to entrust the fate of relationships between states to mere 'natural right'.[15] In the latter case, it would not be possible to take any further steps than a regulation of the 'law of war', analogous to that already present in seventeenth-century treatises. Fichte felt that the modern age, aspiring to a long-lasting peace, required that research of a completely different type should be undertaken.[16] The awareness of such a precarious situation is already detectable in the scarcity of arguments contained in the treaty of alliance between neighbouring states, as well as in the scarcely incisive role assigned to envoys. It stands out even more starkly in the many doubt-filled questions on the plausibility itself of the concept of *just war*,[17] which the later Fichte would again ponder at length.

[13] This is perfectly in line with §§ 18–19 of the part on internal law, see Fichte, 'Naturrecht' in *Werke 1797-1798*, pp. 20–58 (n. 6), that says that the contract on which the birth of a state is founded is in turn founded on a contract—and on the relative concept—of property. This gives important insights into the concept of property in Fichte; it is unique within the German landscape of related doctrines. Fichte insists on identifying property not with the possession of goods, but with the quantity of *activities* carried out by man on raw matter and conducive to its transformation; *labour* is, in this context, the most significant among these actions, of which man is responsible in the first person, becoming the actual owner of its effects. In § 19, mentioned above, Fichte briefly outlines his economic theory, which he later describes in detail in other works. This concept is close to the notion of property elaborated by Locke. See Reinhard Brandt, *Eigentumstheorien von Grotius bis Kant* (1974); Reinhard Brandt, 'John Locke', in Otfried Höffe (ed.), *Von den Vorsokratikern bis David Hume*, vol. 1, Klassiker der Philosophie (1985), pp. 360–77.

[14] This is the main difference with respect to the internal law of the state. See Fichte, 'Naturrecht' in *Werke 1797-1798*, § 17, pp. 5–20 (n. 6). This envisages precisely the capacity on the part of the (future) citizens to conclude a pact with the state, thanks to which both their work and the results deriving from this work may be 'recognized'. These results are their property, for the defence of which another contract, called a 'protection' contract, comes into play.

[15] A similar concern is evident in the concluding paragraphs (§§ 330–40) of Georg Wilhelm Friedrich Hegel, *Grundlinien der Philosophie des Rechts*, vol. 7, Werke in zwanzig Bänden (1970), pp. 499 ff.

[16] This does not mean that Fichte is anything less than scrupulous in dealing with this theme, defining in a very precise manner the ways in which a war should be conducted. In his conception the right to war (*Recht zum Kriege*) depends on, first, a 'Verweigerung der Anerkennung' on the part of the neighbouring state, as the right to recognition is a 'Zwangsrecht' (see Fichte, 'Naturrecht' in *Werke 1794-1796*, § 6, pp. 365–83 (n. 3)), and second, a violation of the previously mentioned contract between two bordering states (see Fichte, 'Naturrecht' in *Werke 1794-1796*, § 12, pp. 410–23 (n. 3)).

[17] Fichte, 'Naturrecht' in *Werke 1794-1796*, § 15, pp. 430–2 (n. 3).

It should also be added that when the right of war is 'valid', it is 'infinite', exactly like any right of coercion—a fact that Kant had been forced to recognize.[18] In theory, this means it is possible never to stop pursuing the objective of destroying an enemy state until the complete submission of its citizens has been obtained.[19] However, as we have already seen, war itself has (or ought to have) its own laws, which Fichte describes with the same degree of precision as that traditionally employed by the treatises specifically dealing with this subject. The first of these laws is the protection of the civilian population, which must remain separate from the belligerent forces engaged on the battlefield. The protection comprises not only the physical safety of the population. Rather, it also extends to the goods they possess, situated in the territory of the state that is about to be conquered. Here, it is in the interest of the conquering state itself to make sure the losses are as few as possible, in view of the fact that the conquered territory is about to become one of its possessions. In any case, the law of war forbids the plundering and destruction of the land.

In the part dealing with internal law, Fichte had displayed extreme pragmatism in observing that, since as a consequence of war any juridical relationship comes to an end, this could not be considered a situation of legality.[20] But the exigencies of epistemic systematics must be obeyed, and therefore Fichte had to yield, as it were, to the cogency of theory in the paragraphs dedicated to the law of war. Yet, he was well aware that theory is destined to remain merely words written on the paper of ponderous juridical treatises with no repercussions on reality. The concrete methods of waging war in his own times (*already* in his own times, if seen from a present-day perspective) had changed into something entirely different, and reached extremes of absolute negativity,[21] which no longer reflected traditional doctrine. Here, it is most visible that Fichte's concept of law oscillates between systematic theory that he considers a situation of legality, and mere pragmatic concerns of order.

The advantages deriving from an alliance initially reside, as Fichte argued, in quantity, which generates strength.[22] Fichte does not actually see it as a question

[18] Immanuel Kant, *Metaphysik der Sitten. Rechtslehre, Gesammelte Schriften, Akademie Ausgabe* (1907 ff), vol. VI, § 60, pp. 349 ff.

[19] Fichte, 'Naturrecht' in *Werke 1794-1796*, § 13, pp. 423–5 (n. 3).

[20] 'War ends every legal relationship [. . .] the condition of war is not a legal condition.' (editor's translation). In German, it reads: 'Im Kriege hört freilich alles Rechtsverhältniß auf [. . .] der Zustand des Kriegs ist auch kein rechtlicher Zustand' (Fichte, 'Naturrecht', in *Werke 1794-1796*, p. 419 (n. 3); see also p. 416 and Fichte, 'Naturrecht', in *Werke 1797-1798*, p. 6 (n. 6)). This statement does not simply echo the assumption already formulated in the review of *Zum ewigen Frieden* (Fichte, '[Rezension:] Zum ewigen Frieden. Ein philosophischer Entwurf von Immanuel Kant', in *Werke 1794-1796* (n. 3), p. 226); there is also the awareness of the complexity of the problems (in theoretical-political terms) inherent in the very formulation of a right that allows the subjection of the citizens of the defeated state. A further case specifies the right to subdue people who are not subjected to a state authority; see Fichte, 'Naturrecht', in *Werke 1794-1796*, § 7, pp. 383–8 (n. 3).

[21] § 14 contains a condemnation of the practice of taking prisoners of war and the consequent exchanges and a condemnation of the weapons that had become in vogue in his times, as well as of snipers. Ultimately it contains the rules that should guarantee the safety of the enemy. Fichte, 'Naturrecht', in *Werke 1797-1798*, pp. 158–9 (n. 6); see also Hegel, *Grundlinien der Philosophie des Rechts*, §§ 338 and 339 (n. 15)).

[22] Fichte, 'Naturrecht', in *Werke 1794-1796*, § 15, pp. 430–2 (n. 3).

of mere strength, but is rather prompted to make this statement by a positive idea of humanity, in which the traits of rationality still prevail, and so a multitude of rational and free men will pursue a greater and better good than that which may be pursued by a single and isolated man.[23] Fichte pointed out, however, that the allied forces may in fact be bent on pursuing what is wrong rather than what is right.[24] It is nevertheless precisely here that the transition from a mere agreement between two states to a wider alliance is outlined, and that an embryonic version of a confederation is set out (its essential characteristic being the *voluntary* participation of the individual member states). In this case, the advantages reside essentially in the fact that, in order to combat the aims of any state that is extraneous to the alliance, a league of nations may proceed to set up its own tribunal[25] and military force,[26] though preferably not in the form of a permanent army, something which had already been opposed by Kant as well.

The progressive extension of the alliance will produce a confederation that will become universal if its ultimate goal is perpetual peace. In addition to this desirable aim, Fichte's reflections here are important as a gauge of the tenability of a *juridical theory* and are in any case of considerable historical interest. Like Kant, he contributed to the German discussion whether a federation was preferred to a unitary state, and if so, what *type* of federation should be set up (*confederation* or *federal state*). There we find an excellent summary of the main 'problem' concerning Fichte's juridical conception, including his idea of inter-state relationships:

> The absolute impossibility of an unjust decision by the confederation has not yet been established. [. . .] Until reason herself appears in person upon earth and assumes judicial power, we shall always have a supreme court, which, being finite, is liable to error or to evil motives. The problem is simply to discover a tribunal from which there is the least likelihood to except this; and such a tribunal is for civil relations the nation, and for the relations of states [and this would be the principle theme of his reflections in the following period], the just described confederation.[27]

The second part of the second appendix, which is dedicated to cosmopolitan right (*Weltbürgerrecht*), consists of very few paragraphs, and pivots on one fundamental concept that in fact constitutes the theoretical presupposition of cosmopolitanism: Cosmopolitan right is the right of man as a 'citizen of the world'. This does not concern rights of a private foreign citizen that spring from a contractual agreement of reciprocal recognition between states. Nor does it concern envoys who are officially sent on a mission. It concerns instead the right of any foreigner. Fichte argues that this man possesses in any case the 'originary' right of every man, which consists in the possibility itself of acquiring rights. It is precisely this right that

[23] Fichte, 'Naturrecht', in *Werke 1794-1796*, p. 400 (n. 3).

[24] Fichte, 'Naturrecht', in *Werke1797-1798*, p. 162 (n. 6). It is precisely here, in § 20, the concluding paragraph of the section dedicated to *Völkerrecht*, that we first come across the expression *ewiger Friede*.

[25] Fichte, 'Naturrecht', in *Werke 1797-1798*, § 17, pp. 5–20 (n. 6).

[26] Fichte, 'Naturrecht', in *Werke 1797-1798*, § 18, pp. 20–4 (n. 6).

[27] Fichte, *The Science of Rights*, p. 488 (n. 7).

makes all other juridical relationships possible.[28] Certain preliminary conditions must subsist: the state in question must be aware of the existence of this foreigner (*blosser Weltbürger*) who intends to 'walk freely on the ground, and to offer a legal relation',[29] but it also has the right to refuse his request (though Fichte does not specify the degree of justifiability). Yet, in any case, it has to defend this foreigner's safety (§ 23).

The cosmopolitan right has a different position in Kant's and Fichte's systems.[30] Nevertheless, both authors are convinced that peace cannot be attained with*out* the state if there is no justice with*in* it: this is the conclusion of Fichte's review of Kant's *Zum ewigen Frieden*, which he states in its final lines. If indeed a difference between the two philosophical constructions can be seen, it is the progressive importance assumed in Fichte's vision by the idea of justice, in the sense not only of the ultimate outcome of a legal system, but also in wider, moral, sense.[31]

[28] Fichte, *The Science of Rights*, p. 490 (n. 7): A few lines above: 'He has that original right of man, which precedes all law-agreements and first makes them possible, namely, *the right that all men must presuppose the possibility of entering into a legal relation with him.*'

[29] Editor's translation.

[30] Carla De Pascale, 'Le droit cosmopolitique comme synthèse du droit', in Jean-Francois Kervégan (ed.), *Raison pratique et normativité chez Kant : Droit, politique et cosmopolitique* (2010), pp. 199–211, argues how highly Kant valued cosmopolitan right, in which solely the origin of peace resides. This is the theme of Kant, *Zum ewigen Frieden*. Consequently, Kant attributed less importance to the organization of the internal law of the state (which revolves entirely around the notion of a 'republican constitution') compared to that of the *jus publicum civitatum* (in which the main actor is the *jus belli*, which must now be set aside) and of the *jus cosmopoliticum*. In the theoretical ordering of his definitive doctrine of law (the later *Rechtslehre* contained in the *Metaphysik der Sitten* (n. 18)), the three arguments correspond to the three constituent elements of juridical synthesis, and cosmopolitan right is the culmination in that it is a law capable of organising peace, beginning with the confederation. As regards Fichte, in his juridical manual, published before and independently of Kant's work, the approach is different and the term *Weltbürgerrecht* refers exclusively to the right of the foreigner who finds himself in the situation that has just been described.

[31] Fichte's attention focused mainly on the internal juridical organization of the State; he was convinced that if the state was built 'according to reason', this would eliminate many causes of conflict between men. Not all causes, first, because although men are rational beings, they are finite, and therefore imperfect; second, because differences in condition and class (*Stand*) are great and most of all, third, because every man judges for himself and therefore men's judgments are all different, but in theory all equally legitimate. Each person's freedom consists precisely in the faculty to judge autonomously and act consequently. For this reason the 'community of free beings', which is in theory guaranteed by law, is in practice constitutively aporetic—as may be gathered by two ideas Fichte wishes to hold firm: man is endowed with an inalienable *Urrecht*; the organization of the state is based on a collection of laws which must be unfailingly valid, which must be passed and implemented by a sovereign power whose force must be inexorable. The republican constitution is founded on these two elements and requires freedom and equality (of everyone before the law, but paying attention to the material conditions of each person's life). While also requiring parliamentary representation, in Fichte's conception (Kant had seen things differently) the republican constitution *does not* foresee the division of powers and instead prescribes the institution of a further power (with an exclusively prohibiting, 'negative' function); this is a sort of constitutional jury whose object is to protect, first, the legality of laws, and second, the legitimacy of the sovereign's actions. If this construction is put into effect and respected, the tasks that fall to state institutions will progressively diminish (until the state itself will tend to extinguish) and all this may, if extended to all men endowed with reason, produce peace; see Hans-Jürgen Verweyen, *Recht und Sittlichkeit in J.G. Fichtes Gesellschaftslehre* (1975); Carla De Pascale, *'Die Vernunft ist praktisch'. Fichtes Ethik und Rechtslehre im System* (2003), pp. 195–254.

In *Der geschloßne Handelsstaat* (1800, hereinafter *Handelsstaat*), Fichte attaches relevance to the theme of inter-state relationships, as well as (and to an even greater extent) to the theme of justice, on which all juridical relationships within a state should be based. In fact, it is precisely the issue of 'justice', a material, substantive and not merely formal justice, with important economic consequences, that serves as one of the foundations for the recommended state intervention in economic matters.[32] The other foundation for state intervention in the economy is, as has been mentioned, the search for an answer to the problem of conflictual relationships between states and, in particular, the search for a positive solution to the threats of war, which in turn is produced by economic causes.

There is a clear distance in perspectives between the *Handelsstaat*, deeply concerned as it is with celebrating the advantages of a commercial closure of the state to everything that lies outside it, and the cosmopolitan perspective which had fuelled Fichte's vision in the preceding decade. This distance would not be bridged in Fichte's later thought. However, notwithstanding the radicalness of the change, one should not think that the theme of peace and the connected issue of cosmopolitanism disappeared from Fichte's theoretical horizon. Nor had he definitively ceased to enquire into solutions to the problems of his times, which he had himself devised in the opening years of the new century, as we shall see in the following section.

Accused of atheism, having toyed with the idea of moving to the University of Mainz (which, following the Treaty of Campoformio, had come under French rule) and finally accused of fomenting unrest among the many students who had presented a petition for his reinstatement at the University of Jena, Fichte finally decided to move to Berlin. Here, after unsuccessfully undertaking the route of a political reformism on the terrain of what we today call the humanities,[33] he decided that he needed to tackle the issue of the disastrous economic state of Prussia, in a period when the mercantile doctrine was being superseded by the emergent doctrine of free trade. While Fichte tackled this issue in an entirely innovative manner, he nevertheless failed to exert any influence whatsoever on the real situation of the country.[34] He dedicated his work to the Minister of

[32] Andreas Verzar, *Das autonome Subjekt und der Vernunftstaat. Eine systematisch-historische Untersuchung zu Fichtes 'Geschlossenem Handelsstaat' von 1800* (1979); Hans Hirsch, 'Fichtes Beitrag zur Planwirtschaft und dessen Verhältnis zu seiner praktischen Philosophie', in Klaus Hammacher (ed.), *Der Transzendentale Gedanke*, (1981), pp. 215–33.

[33] The attempt to influence the Masonic outlook through the important position he had acquired within the Royale-York Lodge of Berlin, and the outline of the reform project he proposed, may be found in a text published in 1802: Johann Gottlieb Fichte, 'Philosophie der Maurerei. Briefe an Konstant', in *Werke 1801-1806* (1991), I, vol. 8, Gesamtausgabe, pp. 407–62.

[34] There have been different interpretations of Fichte's proposal, ranging from a typical expression of the dirigisme of enlightened despotism to heralding a form of state socialism; see e.g. Jürgen Bona Meyer, *Fichte, Lassalle und der Sozialismus* (1878); Marianne Weber, *Fichtes Sozialismus und sein Verhältnis zur Marx'schen Doktrin* (1900).

Finance Karl August von Struensee, who himself had had an important career as a reformer (and who, also in 1800, had published about public economics).[35] What is significant about this dedication is the definition Fichte gives of his subject: an application of the principles of his philosophy of law to economic politics.[36] The proposal was the sketch of a 'state according to reason' capable of promoting perpetual peace[37] and, at the same time, following an economic perspective in contrast to the institutional perspective he had been taken until then.

Despite his clear anti-liberal stance, Fichte adopted Adam Smith's great principle that the wealth of nations consists not in the quantity of gold and silver accumulated, but in value (which is produced by labour). Labour, as we have already mentioned, is the only thing man truly owns. As a consequence, one of the fundamental and inalienable rights of man is that such labour should be guaranteed and suitably remunerated, so that everyone may live decently on the fruits of his own labour. This must be an equal starting condition for all men and the ultimate outcome must also respect such a criterion of equality.[38] The details of this construction are complex. In short, the state organizes the distribution of labour through different work classes and ensures the distribution of goods. It takes entirely (and exclusively) the duty of foreign commerce, until autarchy is reached. Once a national currency has been introduced, and economic balance attained (with an improvement of the quality of life and a reduction in working hours), the closed commercial state will be able to defend its citizens from economic aggression from the outside,[39] in the same way that its institutions defend it from the attacks of its enemies. If the mercantile doctrines had furnished the theoretical justification for commercial wars, the very recent discovery (in Germany) of the free market risked turning the masses into the casualties of a war of pillage and rapine, while the physiocratic doctrine, which had so far been valued by Fichte, was becoming progressively obsolete because of the rapid descent in the scale of values of agriculture compared to manufacturing and commerce.

[35] Karl August von Struensee, *Abhandlungen über wichtige Gegenstände der Staatswirthschaft* (1800).

[36] This is already visible in the subtitle of Johann Gottlieb Fichte, 'Der geschloßne Handelsstat. Ein philosophischer Entwurf als Anhang zur Rechtslehre und Probe einer künftig zu liefernden Politik', in *Werke 1800-1801* (1988), I, vol. 7, Gesamtausgabe, pp. 37–141.

[37] Fichte, 'Der geschloßne Handelsstat', in *Werke 1800-1801*, p. 141 (n. 36); stated again e.g. in Fichte, 'Die Grundzüge des gegenwärtigen Zeitalters', in *Werke 1801-1806*, p. 324 (n. 33).

[38] Fichte, 'Der geschloßne Handelsstat', in *Werke 1800-1801*, pp. 53, 55 (n. 36). Here one sees clearly that the aim was to offer in this text the application, on the economic plane, of the juridical principles set out in his treatise, where one could read: 'The highest and universal end of all free activity is, therefore, that men may be alive. This end each one has, and the guarantee of freedom involves this guarantee. Unless he attains it, freedom and the continued existence of his person will be impossible.' 'To be able to live is the absolute, inalienable property of all men.' (Fichte, *The Science of Rights*, p. 292 (n. 7)). The connection between economic investigation (which had already been carried out in *Der geschloßne Handelsstaat*) and juridical investigation is also highlighted in the *Rechtslehre 1812;* see e.g. Fichte, 'Rechtslehre 1812', in *Nachgelassene Schriften 1812*, p. 288 (n. 12).

[39] 'addiction of conquest' as we find in Fichte, 'Der geschloßne Handelsstat', in *Werke 1800-1801*, p. 118 (n. 36).

II. The Effects Produced on Fichte's Thought by his Reflections on History and by the Historical Problem of Nation-Building

Fichte was not only aware of the doctrine of 'natural boundaries', which had been adopted by the French parliament at the close of 1792, but had also to a certain extent agreed with it.[40] The issue of natural frontiers came once more to the fore when, from 1800 onwards, Fichte found himself working in the political and cultural heart of Prussia, developing a doctrine aimed, on the one hand, at healing the financial situation of a country already much weakened by Napoleon's military campaigns and, on the other hand, at exorcising the risk of future wars. The issue became particularly relevant because it was linked to the commercial closure of the state, which would have benefited from a configuration of the territory that favoured an autarchic economy. The problem of not allowing a defensive war to turn into a war of conquest remained: a position that had formerly been upheld by the French Jacobins and which Fichte would try to maintain (despite the concessions he gradually made to power politics, as for example with his essay *Über Machiavell, als Schriftsteller*). Hence, his renewed condemnation of war in general,[41] and his repeated considerations on and doubts about the so-called *just war*: an alliance among a larger number of states through their unified strength could still defeat an 'unjust state'.[42] Despite all of Fichte's attempts, the certainty of attaining justice was not reached in his later research. He would continue to work on this issue for over a decade, with varying, though always essentially unsuccessful, outcomes.

Another much more urgent issue, however, that of the formation of a national state, was emerging.[43] This historical process had already taken place for the majority of European states, but was still very much in the making for the German territories (although it had *de facto* crumbled, the formal dissolution of the Holy Roman Empire did not take place until 1806). Generally, such a process is prompted in its initial phases by a strong feeling of cohesion among the population, with the additional bolstering of a strong reforming spirit, while the potential charge of aggressive nationalism is reserved for later times. This, at any rate, is reflected in the development of Fichte's thought.

The ethnic and cultural homogeneity of a people, residing in a state with a sufficient size to ensure a good economic organization, is an idea that re-emerges at regular intervals from Fichte's pamphlet on the *Handelsstaat* right up to *Die Grundzüge des gegenwärtigen Zeitalters* (1804/05), his first important work on the philosophy of history. It grew up within a specific literary genre popular throughout

[40] See Fichte, 'Naturrecht', in *Werke 1797-1798*, p. 152 (n. 6).

[41] See the vivid description in Johann Gottlieb Fichte, 'Bestimmung des Menschen', in *Werke 1799-1800* (1981), I, vol. 6, pp. 269 ff.

[42] See Fichte, 'Naturrecht', in *Werke 1797-1798*, p. 160 (n. 6).

[43] See Massimo Mori, *La ragione delle armi. Guerra e conflitto nella filosofia classica tedesca* (1984); Gaetano Rametta (ed.), *Filosofia e guerra nell'età dell'idealismo tedesco* (2003).

Europe (though it originated in France, starting with Voltaire, and developing with Condorcet), to which Kant and German idealism contributed significantly.

That historical development may be determined *a priori*[44] is the fulcrum of Fichte's vision, which subdivides the course of the history of mankind into five fundamental epochs, the fifth and last of which is characterised as an age that has achieved perfection. Its contours are only partially defined, insofar as most utopian constructions have no clear-cut outlines. The aim of historical development is, he believed, to mould all relationships between men on the principles of reason, and therefore of freedom. The precondition for the birth of history is the presence of reason and language, a precondition that is satisfied by the existence, in an unspecified time and in an unspecified place, of an 'originary people' (*Urvolk* or *Normalvolk*).[45] A second precondition is that an encounter/clash should occur between this 'originary people' and its exact theoretical opposite: a savage people led only by the instinct of self-preservation and the drive to satisfy natural needs.[46] From the intermingling of these two peoples, history is engendered—and with it inequality and conflict emerge. In the second age of history, the state comes to life, as a result of the authority exerted through force by the strongest members of the species. In the third age, to which Fichte believed he belonged, those who are subjugated follow the impulse to free themselves of authority. This age is characterised by the complete eclipsing of reason, and therefore by the indifference to virtue. The impulse that prompts a radical transformation, or more precisely an actual spiritual and religious rebirth, lies in the 'concept', a new starting point for the power of science to affirm itself (fourth age). It will only unfold entirely in the following, and final, epoch of history, where the definitive triumph of reason will take place.

In addition to this, however, Fichte carries out an empirical investigation of history, through which he reveals a much less linear progress within each historical epoch; in particular, he vividly illustrates, through actual examples, something which he had already hinted at in his early political writings of 1793/94: historically, the state came into being following acts of violence, and sometimes simply by chance. This overview of actual history, with the aid of some of the theoretical presuppositions briefly outlined above, would constitute the materials out of which Fichte would slightly later construct the *Reden an die deutsche Nation* (1808). For the time being, the *Grundzüge* served to illuminate the deep-seated reasons for so many inter-state conflicts as well as for more or less prolonged periods of peace.

[44] This idea is connected to the concept of 'cosmic plan' (*Weltplan*): Fichte, 'Die Grundzüge', in *Werke 1801-1806*, p. 197 (n. 33).

[45] Where there dominated a primordial form of reason, more specifically described as a 'Vernunftinstinct' ('rational instinct'), which had constituted the distinctive trait of the first age, the age of innocence (that is a condition of absence of self-consciousness, and therefore of will, and for this very reason of freedom).

[46] On the model of the relationship I/not-I, already set out in Johann Gottlieb Fichte, 'Grundlage der gesamten Wissenschaftslehre als Handschrift für seine Zuhörer', in *Werke 1793-1795* (1965), I, vol. 2, Gesamtausgabe, pp. 264 ff, and reformulated as the relationship I/you, the foundation of that doctrine of inter-personality which would also be so important for the construction of the juridical institutions (Fichte, 'Naturrecht', in *Werke 1794-1796*, pp. 340 ff (n. 3)).On the birth of history: Fichte, 'Die Grundzüge', in *Werke 1801-1806*, pp. 329 ff (n. 33).

Christian Europe, for example, constituted a source of stability for this part of the world,[47] while the period in which national states came into being was a time of great conflicts, in which wars of expansion and conquest were also waged against very different people. New entities were also formed through alliances. The recent system of power balance within Europe was itself historically the result of the political guideline followed by different states reciprocally interested in self-containing their respective forces.[48]

A passage from the *Reden* offers a powerful short account of this historical *excursus.* It is a crucial passage for understanding the reasons and the aims of this work. While nothing has changed with respect to the historical and theoretical picture outlined in the *Grundzüge*, very much has changed in respect to the tone with which different aspects are emphasized. Now, for the first time, the role and the destiny of Germany within Europe are exclusively highlighted.[49] The historical reasons for this radical shift in Fichte's thought have often been put forward by scholars: the catastrophic defeat of Prussia at the hands of the French at Jena and Auerstädt had not only definitively confirmed the worst misgivings about that very Napoleon[50] who only a few years before had awakened hopes of freedom, but had also, and more importantly, revealed the inanity of all attempts so far made to reform the state. Once the state has collapsed, the only other possible leverage was the people, who had not yet, however, become a nation. This was the task that was now demanded: to re-awaken and call to arms an entire people and re-found a policy that could bring about a radically new and global educational project, as the old leaders had been defeated and the old institutions had not survived the attack of the enemy.[51] The place of these leaders and governors would in the future be taken by scholars, i.e. intellectuals, to whom Fichte (himself an impecunious intellectual with no pedigree) had entrusted the most important duty of all.[52]

In the years in which Germany, although already involved in the war, had not yet rushed headlong to its ruin, Fichte had strived to combine the patriotism required by the historical moment with his own deep-rooted cosmopolitism, or at least he had wondered whether this was possible.[53] The *Patriotismus und sein*

[47] On Christian States = Republics: Fichte, 'Die Grundzüge', in *Werke 1801-1806*, p. 345 (n. 33).

[48] Fichte, 'Die Grundzüge', in *Werke 1801-1806*, p. 349 (n. 33).

[49] Johann Gottlieb Fichte, 'Reden an die deutsche Nation', in *Werke 1808-1812* (2005), I, vol. 10, Gesamtausgabe, pp. 268 ff: if the balance described above had been respected and preserved, nothing would have happened; instead, the strength of precisely that nation which formed its geographical centre (a nation previously weakened by religious schisms and subdued by foreigners) was undermined; for a better understanding of the epoch, one should read, in parallel, Fichte's important lesson XIV of 'Die Grundzüge', in *Werke 1801-1806*, pp. 353–363 (n. 33).

[50] See Johann Gottlieb Fichte, 'In Beziehung auf den Namenlosen', in *Nachgelassene Schriften 1806-1807* (1994), II, vol. 10, Gesamtausgabe, pp. 83–5.

[51] See Fichte, 'Reden', in *Werke 1808-1812*, p. 203 (n. 49): the contraposition between the state and the people and homeland. See also Richard Schottky, 'Fichtes Nationalstaatsgedanke auf der Grundlage unveröffentlicher Manuskripte von 1807', in *Fichte-Studien* 2, (1990), pp. 111–37; Richard Schottky, 'Fichtes Nations-Begriff 1806–1813. Innenspannung und Entwicklung', in Rudolf Burger, Hans-Dieter Klein, and Wolfgang H. Schrader (eds.), *Gesellschaft, Staat, Nation* (1996), pp. 159–84.

[52] Fichte, 'Reden', in *Werke 1808-1812*, p. 115 (n. 49).

[53] Johann Gottlieb Fichte, 'Patriotismus und sein Gegentheil', in *Nachgelassene Schriften 1805-1807* (1993), II, vol. 9, Gesamtausgabe, pp. 393–445.

Gegentheil (1806–1807) had been devoted precisely to the attempt—fruitless as this may seem to us today—at setting up a relationship of continuity between the two concepts ('Cosmopolitanism is the dominant will that the purpose of existence of mankind is fulfilled in mankind'; 'The patriot wants that the purpose of existence of mankind is fulfilled at first in the nation in which he takes part.').[54]

The doctrine of natural boundaries itself was now subjected to a revision,[55] in line with an even more significant change regarding the question of language. In the *Reden*, Fichte states that men live together not because they find themselves to be within natural boundaries, but because they have for other reasons decided to live together and therefore find that they are protected by natural boundaries. Language homogeneity is the first of these reasons. Fichte had already dealt with language, adding this new subject of study to his constellation of ideas, at the centre of which was social and communicative striving.[56] In the *Reden*, language becomes the most important instrument for the reconstruction of *German* identity: the German people, the heirs of the ancient Germans described by Tacitus, have never abandoned their ancient seats and have preserved their *originary* language. There remained one small step to be taken. There is only a small distance between declaring that the German language is the originary language and declaring that it is the only 'living' language while all other languages are branded as dead. The superiority of the Germans over all other peoples, first and foremost over the French, is thus assured. Finally, the living language is the instrument par excellence for the diffusion of culture, thereby making German culture the supreme expression of culture *tout court*. Within the space of very few pages, a defeated and depressed people who have nothing left to do but obey their conquerors are now spurred on to become the vessel of a new ideal of humanity. Certainly, rhetoric and psychology play their role to the hilt, but this sudden swerve in the argument also indicates an actual condition of extreme difficulty.

As regards German culture, now transformed into *the* culture, this is precisely the issue through which we may measure the distance between this work—born out of the conferences held to boost the morale of the people and urge them to action—and all of Fichte's other works, preceding and following.[57] For example, the passage quoted just above continues thus: 'In our times, this purpose of existence can only be promoted through science'.[58] Science appears as the highest expression of culture, while both science and culture are associated with the idea of freedom. *Kultur*

[54] Editor's translation. In German, it reads: 'Kosmopolitismus ist der herrschende Wille, daß der Zweck des Daseins des Menschengeschlechts im Menschengeschlechte erreicht werde'; 'Der Patriot will, daß der Zweck des Menschengeschlechts zuerst in derjenigen Nation erreicht werde, deren Mitglied er selber ist.' Fichte, 'Patriotismus und sein Gegentheil', in *Nachgelassene Schriften 1805-1807*, pp. 399, 404 (n. 53).

[55] Fichte, 'Reden', in *Werke 1808-1812*, p. 267 (n. 49).

[56] Fichte, 'Von der Sprachfähigkeit und dem Ursprung der Sprache', in *Werke 1794-1796*, pp. 91–127 (n. 3).

[57] See Reinhard Lauth, 'Der letzte Grund von Fichtes Reden an die deutsche Nation', in *Fichte-Studien* 4, (1992), 197–230.

[58] Editor's translation. In German, it reads: 'In unsrer Zeit kann jener Zweck nur von der Wißenschaft aus befördert werden.' Fichte, 'Patriotismus', in *Nachgelassene Schriften 1805-1807*, p. 404 (n. 53).

zur Freiheit is the favoured formula that recurs frequently in Fichte's texts, and not only in the early political writings. It expresses the idea that it is man in his entirety who is the subject and the object of all transformative action, which, in Fichte, sounds simply tautological in that for him all action is in itself a modification. This is certainly not an end in itself, but a movement towards a perfecting of the single man and of the species, which must be carried out in the political as well as in the moral and religious spheres. Although theory requires these three fields to be rigorously distinguished, as each field needs its own particular perspective through which specialised investigation may be conducted, in man, who is a whole, they continually intersect and intermingle. The same occurs in life, which is different from philosophy, though it is always desirable that philosophy should assist life. Culture thus plays a central role in Fichte's philosophy.

It would instead be more interesting to show how even in such a unique work as the *Reden*—in which the pursued aim is felt to be so important as to subvert completely the theoretical foundations that had hitherto seemed indefectible—this concept should once more reappear in the guise of a universal culture, as both the general framework within which national culture places itself and as the aim towards which it tends. The context of this argumentation is the same (*Discourse VIII*) where Fichte hints at a wider examination of the fate of humanity as a whole—otherwise rare in this work.

Next to culture, however, and to an even greater extent next to the pedagogic thrust that pervades the *Reden*, an undeniably prominent position is taken by war, intended as a war of the people, aimed at driving out the foreign invader and conqueror. Fichte had been meditating on this subject for some time, at least since the winds of war had been blowing and increasingly so with the advance of the French armies. His work on Machiavelli proves this even more clearly. Between 1806 and 1807,[59] Fichte assiduously studied the *Discourses*, the *Prince*, the *Art of War*, and the *Florentine Histories*. He was well aware that almost three centuries separated him from Machiavelli and that the Italian writer belonged to a pre-modern world that had now definitively (and fortunately) disappeared. On the other hand, the close of *The Prince*, that is, *An Exhortation to Liberate Italy from the Barbarians*, dedicated to Lorenzo de Medici (and with it the connected issue of national unification), might in those year have awakened in any German reader similar impulses and yearnings of the soul. Intriguingly, among the excerpts from the *Prince* that Fichte translated

[59] In this period, Fichte spent some time at Königsberg (to where the court had moved), having realized it was no longer safe in Berlin. Here, he taught some courses at the university, and here he once again took up and further investigated Pestalozzi's work. Königsberg was also the birthplace of the journal 'Vesta', which in its first issue printed Fichte's essay on Machiavelli, quoted here in the following note. With the arrival of the French, Fichte moved to Copenhagen. On this issue, see Claudio Cesa's entry 'Fichte, Johann Gottlieb', in *Enciclopedia Machiavelliana* (2014), vol. I, pp. 546–50; Albert Elkan, 'Die Entdeckung Machiavellis in Deutschland im 19. Jahrhundert', *Historische Zeitschrift* 119 (1919), 427–58; Douglas Moggach, 'Fichte's engagement with Machiavelli', in *History of political thought* 14/4 (1993), 573–89; Gaetano Rametta, 'Note su Fichte lettore di Machiavelli', in *Filosofia e guerra*, pp. 109–122 (n. 43); Ives Radrizzani (ed.), *Fichte lecteur de Machiavelli* (2006); Marco Rampazzo Bazzan, 'Unter der Konjunktur denken. Fichtes Auseinandersetzung mit Machiavell', *Fichte-Studien* 40 (2012), 87–107.

for the German public, the first to appear was precisely the *Exhortation*. The work also contains a long introductory essay, the last paragraph of which is, not incidentally, entitled 'in how far Machiavelli's politics applies to our times'. It is here that we find observations on inter-state relationships, which had not so far been regulated by law and always remained potentially conflictual, given the universal impulse towards expansion, a herald of later power politics.[60]

Fichte also uses the introduction to put forward his considerations on war. Echoing certain tones which his contemporaries had already sensed in Kant's philosophy of history, these ideas form his new 'power-political' outlook: 'And as the practice of war must not cease, if humankind shall not become limp and corrupted for possible later wars, so we have in Europe, but even more in other parts of the world, enough barbarians which must, in the short or long run, be incorporated with force in the Empire of culture. These fights shall toughen the European youth [...]'.[61] The final page of this section calls for a new, firmer art of government which Fichte depicts as strongly opposed to the political philosophy of the second half of the previous century and which he describes as 'flat, weakly and poor, presenting as its greatest good a form of humanity and libertarianism, and popularity' and finally 'in love with the perpetual peace'.[62]

It is worth remembering at this point that in his introduction Fichte also paid special attention to those passages in the *Art of War* in which Machiavelli rejected the assumption that artillery was the most suitable means of victory on the battlefield. Fichte, as we know, had already suggested as much in the second appendix of the *Grundlage des Naturrechts*, against the generally held view on this subject in his own times. Slightly later, Carl P. G. von Clausewitz expounded his beliefs in a letter published in the same issue of the journal in which Fichte's essay was published, dated 11 January 1809, and entitled *Ein Ungenannter Militär an Fichte*. Von Clausewitz had been prompted to write this piece not only by the subject matter itself (he had been studying Machiavelli for some time), but also by Fichte's urgent

[60] See, in particular, the following passage: in the relationships between the Prince and the other states—unlike what happens in the relationship between the Prince and his peaceful people—'there is neither law nor right, just the law of the powerful [...]' (editor's translation): Johann Gottlieb Fichte, 'Ueber Macchiavell, als Schriftsteller, und Stellen aus seinen Schriften', in *Werke 1806-1807* (1995), I, vol. 9, Gesamtausgabe, pp. 244f. The notes on reading the works of Machiavelli, 'Real Bemerkungen bei Machiavell', may be found in *Nachgelassene Schriften 1806-1807*, pp. 301–69 (n. 50).

[61] Editor's translation. In German, it reads 'Und da gleichwohl die Kriegsübung nicht ausgehen darf, wenn die Menschheit nicht *erschlaffen*, und für den späterhin doch wieder möglichen Krieg *verderben* soll, so haben wir ja noch selbst in Europa, noch mehr aber in den andern Welttheilen, Barbaren genug, welche doch über kurz oder lang, mit Zwang dem Reiche der Kultur werden einverleibt werden müssen. In Kämpfen mit diesen stähle sich die Europäische Jugend [...]' Fichte, 'Ueber Machiavell', in *Werke 1806-1807*, p. 244 (n. 50) (emphasis added).

[62] Editor's translation. In German, it reads: 'gar flach, kränklich, und armselig, darbietend als ihr höchstes Gut eine gewisse Humanität, und Liberalität, und Popularität' and finally 'verliebt in den ewigen Frieden'; Fichte, 'Ueber Machiavell', in *Werke 1806-1807*, p. 245 (n. 50). There are evident elements of self-criticism, which are stated more clearly a couple of lines down: even on the part of some Germans, 'the teachings of human right and of freedom and originary equality of everyone' have been treated with too much importance. Yet, Fichte argues, it is true that these doctrines are 'the eternal and indestructible foundations of societal order', but it is possible neither to establish nor to administer the state *by their means alone* (editor's translations).

exhortation to the experts that they should reconsider the opinions of the great Florentine writer.

When Napoleon's power finally began to wane (after the defeat of his troops in Russia) and when Germany was pushing for the final victory, Fichte returned to his reflections on history, which he now decided to divide simply into two great epochs (the 'old' and the 'new' world), the birth of Christianity functioning as a watershed between the two.[63] Once again he deployed historical investigation for the purpose of determining in what phase of history humanity was *now*. He aimed to establish—at a more restricted, but also at a more concrete level—the exact stage of the struggle against the enemy on German territory, as well as what was being done specifically (or had to be done in the immediate future) in order to inject lifeblood into the nation. This, Fichte argued, was of the highest importance in properly gauging the scope of present action, without naturally losing sight of that final objective: the setting up of a state according to reason.[64] Fichte clearly displays some anxiety that the immediate—but also the ultimate—result of the disappearance of the danger represented by Napoleon would be the return of the old regime.

It is within this framework that we must read the three lessons on the concept of 'real war'.[65] These are no longer merely investigations into whether it is possible to speak of a 'just war' (and indeed in what manner one might do so), but rather into what actually caused the present war, what prospects it had opened up and what conditions were to be satisfied so that a tangible result might be reached. First of all, true war is such when it is a mass war, something completely different from the dynastic wars that had so far been waged generally with the aid of mercenary troops. As a consequence, each man must engage in war *personally*[66] and is perhaps capable of bringing about peace. In recent history, this had briefly seemed possible thanks to France, but all hope had rapidly vanished, one might suggest, on account of the negative spirit of the times. Fichte had previously enlightened his readers on the spiritual condition of the Germans before the war. The French, however, instead of turning such a momentous event as the Revolution into an opportunity to forge for themselves a 'system of thought' in step with the times, and strengthen their spirit through an understanding of the true sense of such concepts as 'liberty' and

[63] Johann Gottlieb Fichte, 'Die Staatslehre, oder über das Verhältniß des Urstaates zum Vernunftreiche', in *Nachgelassene Schriften 1813* (2011), II, vol. 16, Gesamtausgabe, pp. 1–176. See Marco Ivaldo, 'Politik, Geschichte und Religion in der Staatslehre 1813', *Fichte-Studien* 11 (1997) 209–227; Marco Ivaldo, 'Le statut de la Politique dans la Doctrine de l'Etat de 1813', in Jean-Christophe Goddard and Jacinto Rivera de Rosales (eds.), *Fichte et la politique* (2008), pp. 63–80.

[64] As we see from the title of chapter III: Fichte, 'Von der Errichtung des Vernunftreiches', in *Nachgelassene Schriften 1813*, pp. 63 ff (n. 62).

[65] These correspond to chapter II: Fichte, 'Ueber den Begriff des warhaften Krieges. Drei Vorlesungen', in *Nachgelassene Schriften 1813*, pp. 39 ff (n. 63), which closes with some pages of violently anti-French and anti-Napoleonic polemic.

[66] Fichte, 'Die Staatslehre', in *Nachgelassene Schriften 1813*, p. 48 (n. 63). The portrait painted in this work both of the dynastic wars and of the conduct of the governors that decide to undertake them is in no way different from that presented in his first work: Fichte, 'Zurückforderung der Denkfreiheit von den Fürsten Europens, die sie bis herunterdrückten', in *Werke 1791-1794*, pp. 165–92, see e.g. p. 170 (n. 1).

'the reign of law', have chosen to trample on them (led, moreover, by a foreigner who descends from a savage people).[67] What the French lacked, and what indeed (as things stood) the Germans alone might attain, was the awareness of the *moral destiny* of the human race.

This, Fichte argues, is the point from where the German people had once again to begin, and their aim should be to build a new form of state. They had to bear in mind, however, that their state itself, ripped apart as it had been by war, was no longer composed of one stock, but of two, those who possessed property and those who had none. Far from being a coherent set of institutions with a specific and noble purpose, the state was now in fact 'enslaved' by the owners. These *are not* the state, they simply *occupy* the state, and it is for this reason that the state in the modern age has not yet progressed beyond the stage of being a patrimonial institution based on private enterprise. We should therefore not be surprised if selfishness is the true sign of the times. To counter this state of affairs, it is necessary to bring about a regeneration of both the single individual and the multitude who, by following this path, will truly become a people.

III. Fichte as a Master of the Romantics

No investigation of Romanticism can be carried out without acknowledging the difficulty of circumscribing and describing such a phenomenon. Like all other great cultural movements, such as the Enlightenment, Romanticism developed differently and took on different forms in the different geographical areas in which it took root. It is not by chance that I mention the Enlightenment, as the two movements were closely connected, and it may be said that different configurations of the Enlightenment determined different configurations of Romanticism. This was certainly true for Germany: romanticism had visceral ties with the enlightenment, in part as its natural continuation, in part as a conscious reaction against it. Both also shared another characteristic, in that they became aware of their true essence only as they were waning, as their vital charge had diminished.

A similar, though indeed more significant, difficulty may be detected in *political* Romanticism, and a further consideration must be made when reflecting on politics compared to philosophy. The direct antecedent here was no longer so much German Enlightenment as its French and English equivalents.[68] English thought inspired German Romantics and offered them validation, while after some initial enthusiasm they soon took up an attitude of strong antagonism against the *lumières*. When indeed some form of intellectual and spiritual agreement was shown,

[67] Fichte, 'Die Staatslehre', in *Nachgelassene Schriften 1813*, pp. 58 ff (n. 63). To avoid misunderstandings, it must be added that Fichte sees Napoleon as a world-historical individual, harsh, and unaware of mankind's moral destiny, but proud and endowed with an unrelenting willpower and enthusiasm.

[68] Ulrich Scheuner, *Der Beitrag der deutschen Romantik zur politischen Theorie* (1980); Carl Schmitt, *Politische Romantik* (1919).

this was always for the views elaborated by French émigré thinkers, who had long left their country behind.

This picture nevertheless needs some adjustment and correction as regards the role played by the younger Fichte; it was rather on the terrain of philosophy that the earliest and strongest ties were developed. For example, Fichte was not only an inspirer, but also an actual teacher, at Jena, of both Novalis and Friedrich von Schlegel, both of whom (the former in particular) started their course of studies with philosophy. Later, in their early political publications, they showed how close they had remained to their master on some of his favourite themes of investigation.

I am referring here to the first period of Romanticism, generally divided by scholars into successive phases, Jena being the first of these, followed by Heidelberg, then Berlin and finally Vienna.[69] At Jena, where he had just been taken on by the university and had immediately become the rising star of *modern* philosophy, Fichte became the catalyst of a *young* way of thinking (*young* not only because it was developing just then, but also because the renewal and cultural rejuvenation of culture were progressively adopted as its bywords). Apart from the more strictly philosophical themes,[70] Fichte's legacy is perceivable in the 'pacifist' vision set out in Novalis' political writing, first and foremost in *Die Christenheit oder Europa* (1799, published in 1826),[71] but also in *Glaube und Liebe, oder der König und die Königin* (1798).[72] What might more properly be termed the Christian universalism of Novalis has at its root the idea that it is necessary for religion to recover its founding role, reinstating its ancient bond with politics. Incidentally, it was precisely the newly found connection between religion and politics that would come to be the defining character of political Romanticism, most of all in Germany.[73]

It is on the basis of this presupposition that Novalis assigned the duty of building perpetual peace[74] to the Pope, who would have to become first the promoter and then the guarantor of such an initiative. While the steps that were being taken in order to achieve the result of creating a 'state of the states' are not clear—he says nothing of possible alliances between different states—what is certain is that his

[69] Paul Kluckhohn, *Das Ideengut der deutschen Romantik* (1961); Jacques Droz, *Le romantisme allemand et l'état* (1963).

[70] In 1795, Novalis began to engage with Fichte's *Wissenschaftslehre*, writing the notes that would later be published as *Fichte-Studien*. Despite Novalis' well-known predilection for aphorisms and for the publication of fragments, Fichte's influence may also be felt in the project for an 'encyclopedia' entrusted to the *Allgemeines Brouillon* (1798–99), a project that was certainly not unaware of Fichte's plan to build a 'system' of philosophy. See Hannelore Link, 'Zur Fichte-Rezeption in der Frühromantik', in Richard Brinkmann (ed.), *Romantik in Deutschland*, pp. 355–68; Theodor Haering, *Novalisals Philosoph* (1954); on his political philosophy: pp. 444–508.

[71] In Paul Kluckhohn and Richard Samuel (eds.), *Novalis Schriften* (1968), vol. 3, pp. 495–524.

[72] Paul Kluckhohn and Richard Samuel (eds.), *Novalis Schriften* (1965), vol. 2, pp. 485–98, where peace appeared closely connected to the ideal of monarchy (p. 488). See Hans Wolfgang Kuhn, *Die Apokalyptiker und die Politik: Studien zur Staatsphilosophie des Novalis* (1961).

[73] See Carl Schmitt, *Politische Theologie: Vier Kapitel zur Lehre der Souveranität* (1934).

[74] The concept is clearly expressed in the assumption, taken from Kant, that any other form of peace is an illusion, being in actual fact an armistice: *Novalis Schriften*, vol. 3, p. 522 (n. 71).

model was the ancient *Res Publica Christiana*. The three Christian denominations would ultimately reunite under the aegis of the Papacy.

Friedrich Schlegel was to a much greater extent inspired by the ideals of the French Revolution and more interested in the political implications of Fichte's thought. In his essay on the concept of republicanism (1796),[75] he had moved from Kant's text on perpetual peace, though his analysis had centred on an idea of republicanism derived not from Kant, but from antiquity. From here came his ideal of a universal republic united by a lasting peace and composed of a large number of national republics. Many further texts may be quoted in this context, given the vastness of the debate that took place in this period on the theme of peace[76] and war,[77] but as our scope must here be limited to Fichte's *direct* influences we will not follow any further the development of these authors' thoughts. Nor is it possible to examine in any greater depth the maturation of the thought of Friedrich Schlegel. He would later subscribe to the ideal of the Empire, arriving, as other thinkers also did, at a religious universalism, but would finally decide to abandon Prussia and embrace the religious and political creed of Metternich's Vienna. The relationship between Fichte and the exponents of the early Romantic movement could not but slacken as their respective positions took on more clear-cut contours. In the meantime, the polemic against the Enlightenment and against the legacy of ideas of the French revolution had, at the beginning of the new century, progressively abandoned the pacifist ideals. The rediscovery of the role of religion, which had gone hand in hand with the re-evaluation of the Middle Ages, had also brought with it a re-evaluation of wars conducted in the name of religion. An increasingly important role was played by wars waged in the name of national freedom, in the wake of Napoleon's conquests, but also as a result of the recent developments in political thought, which had put centre stage the construction of national unity and in particular the elaboration of the concept of nation. Fichte's future thought would develop, as we have seen, precisely in this direction.

IV. The Influence of Fichte in the Nineteenth and Twentieth Centuries

If, having examined the vision of international relationships that emerges in Fichte's thought and its influence on his early pupils and followers, we wish to look at the further developments and the actual impact of Fichte's thought on later times, we first have to limit carefully the field of investigation. It is crucial to isolate the specific object of investigation against the much wider background of the general

[75] Friedrich von Schlegel, 'Versuch über den Begriff des Republikanismus' in *Kritische Neuausgabe* (1961), vol. 6, ed. Ernst Behler, pp. 11–25.

[76] See Zwi Batscha and Richard Saage (eds.), *Friedensutopien. Kant, Fichte, Schlegel, Görres* (1979).

[77] It may be sufficient here to quote Adam Müller's *Die Elemente der Staatskunst*, 2 vols. (1922), whose opening pages are dedicated precisely to the concept of war, the founding principle of his vision of politics and of the relationships between states.

and enduring presence, over the space of two centuries, of his political philosophy. Fichte's legacy in this field was rather subtle and very far-reaching, its range reflecting the variety of positions he put forward in the various phases of his intellectual production and the many nuances of his complex thought. One would therefore have to start with the Fichtean echoes in the thought of the young exponents of the Hegelian Left, beginning with David Friedrich Strauß, and later in *Vormärz* liberalism (e.g. in Karl von Rotteck) and during the 1848 Revolution,[78] in the socialism of Lassalle, and through Marx and Engels,[79] right down to Lenin. Alternatively, following another route, one might investigate the interpretations of Fichte's thought in the Wilhelmine era down to its rediscovery in the Nazi period; or again, those interpretations which, even as late as the twentieth century, celebrated the democratic Fichte (Reinhard Strecker and Gerhard Leibholz) or the socialist Fichte (from Jean Jaurès to Marianne Weber). Or one might decide to reconstruct the history of the various editions and re-editions of the philosopher's works, as well as their translations into foreign languages, which themselves were prompted by different political and cultural climates. What I instead propose to do here is to delineate briefly the evolution of the interest in Fichte's thought in relation to the themes discussed in my first two sections.

Following the first extremely vocal reactions to his writings of 1793–1794, and the accusations of Jacobinism by the conservative and reactionary milieu of the journal 'Eudämonia', and following the (more or less fierce) ironic attacks on the part of many Romantics (with the exclusion of Friedrich Schlegel) to the *Handelsstaat*, the earliest effects on the institutional plane were produced by Fichte's *Reden an die deutsche Nation*. These were initially and understandably obstructed by the occupying French. Their publication was later prevented by the Prussian authorities for very different reasons. Napoleon had by then disappeared from the scene and the political situation appeared to have stabilised after the Congress of Vienna. In1822, Prussian censorship forbid publication of the *Reden* throughout the national territory, lest the 'republicanism' they advocated should find any followers.

The earliest date in which the *Reden* may be said to have enjoyed actual success was 1862, which was marked by the celebrations of the first centenary of Fichte's birth,[80] while being a period that saw a growing effort towards the achievement of national unity. The most prominent voices in favour of Fichte's philosophy—seen as representing a 'nationalist' strain that German thought had been capable of expressing right from the start of the century—hailed then from the socialist and liberal camps.[81] Such an interpretation hinged on the *Reden*, but also on the

[78] This encouraged a return to Fichte's vision: see Wilhelm Busse, *J.G. Fichte und seine Beziehung zur Gegenwart des deutschen Volkes* (1848).

[79] See Tom Rockmore, *Fichte, Marx and the German Philosophical Tradition* (1980).

[80] With a great number of conferences organised by the Nationalverein: see Claudio Cesa, *Introduzione a Fichte* (1994), pp. 202 ff; Isaac Nakhimovsky, *Perpetual Peace and Commercial Society* (2011).

[81] With Ferdinand Lassalle and E.W. Kalisch, respectively: see Erich H. Fuchs, *Fichtes Spuren in der deutschen Nationalbewegung 1819–1871*, Bayerische Akademie der Wissenschaften, <https://www.academia.edu/11529634/Fichtes_Spuren_in_der_deutschen_Nationalbewegung_1819–1871>; a detailed account of three works by Lassalle which expressly deal with Fichte. Kalisch's text may be

Grundzüge and the *Staatslehre*. Later, just as German unification was taking place, another interpretation (also along these lines, but of much greater complexity) tried to show how there had been, in Fichte's work, an actual merger of the older surviving cosmopolitan spirit with the new sensibility for the value of the national characters of individual peoples.[82]

However, this would not be the prevailing interpretation in the Wilhelmine-Bismarckian era. The lens through which Fichte now came to be interpreted was that of the history of the making of German unification under the guidance of Prussia, with Fichte being viewed as an early champion of Prussian hegemony. This, for example, was the position of Heinrich von Treitschke, who believed the philosopher to have been a forerunner of the ideas that inspired the national-liberal party, including a 'power-political' vision that did not shy away from a celebration of force and war.[83] It was this vision that many historians, beginning with Friedrich Meinecke, considered to be in general responsible for the aberrations of the Nazis and, more specifically, for the rise of the nationalistic interpretation of Fichte in the years between the two World Wars.[84]

In France, in the mid-nineteenth century, Jules Barni, who had studied and translated Kant and subscribed to his cosmopolitan vision, saw Fichte as a genuine interpreter of the ideals of the revolution, 'rejected' by the France of Napoleon. With evident anti-Bonapartist intent, Barni offered his country the first translations of the *Beitrag* and of the *Zurückforderung* (he had been amongst the founders in 1848 of the Democratic Society of Free Thinkers). He inaugurated an interpretative tradition which stretches out as far as Xavier Léon (the author of the most important historiographic work on Fichte in France: *Fichte et son temps*, in three volumes, 1922–1927) and Martial Gueroult, who on the 150th anniversary of the French revolution dedicated an essay specifically to Fichte and the French Revolution.[85]

The strongly nationalistic interpretation prevalent in twentieth-century Germany had, it must be noted, already gradually been forming during and immediately after the First World War, concomitantly with various reprints of Fichte's works, first and foremost his work on Machiavelli. This interpretation had originated, already in Fichte's time, in Friedrich Ludwig Jahn's *Deutsches Volksthum* (1810), and had in time matured into the already-quoted interpretation of Heinrich von Treitschke, who had placed Fichte side by side with Ernst Moritz Arndt, which

found in *1812-1814* (1991), vol. 5, Erich Fuchs (ed.), *Fichte im Gespräch. Berichte der Zeitgenossen*, pp. 33–9.

[82] Johann Huber, *Das Verhältnis der deutschen Philosophie zur nationalen Erhebung* (1871).

[83] Heinrich von Treitschke, 'Fichte und die Nationalidee', in *Deutsche Lebensbilder* (1927), pp. 34–69, part. pp. 35, 53, 54.

[84] The most comprehensive study on this remains Reiner Pesch, *Die Politische Philosophie Fichtes und ihre Rezeption im Nationalsozialismus* (1982), where bibliography relative to the authors I have just mentioned may be found; see especially pp. 103 ff. See also Erich Fuchs, 'Fichte Stammvater des deutschen Nationalismus?', *Fichte-Studien* 35 (2010), pp. 267–384.

[85] Cesa, *Introduzione a Fichte*, pp. 203, 220 (n. 80); Michel Espagne, 'Die Wirkung der Fichte-Rezeption auf das Revolutionverständnis', in *Republik der Menschheit. Französische Revolution und deutsche Philosophie*, eds. Manfred Buhr et al. (1989), pp. 76–103.

was no coincidence; this line of interpretation was further developed by Othmar Spann,[86] Alfred Baeumler and Hans Freyer.[87]

After the Second World War, philosophical studies also followed the impulse towards rebuilding and reconstructing, the object in this case being consciences. This movement was propelled by an ideal (we may even go so far as to call it an ethical) drive. As occurs in such exceptional historical moments, a renewal of interest took place, which was sustained, if not by the aim of objectivity, at least by the need for a better understanding of Fichte.

V. Conclusion

To conclude, we can briefly reflect on the different stages of Fichte's argument that have been presented in this chapter. Fichte developed his international legal thought mostly in close relationship to Kantian cosmopolitanism, preferring like him a confederation of states as the model that could guarantee perpetual peace. In suggesting this construct, he was remarkably influenced by the German constitutional question. Much more than Kant, however, he highlighted the role of the economic relationships within the state as a central determinant for the relationships between states.

What is more, in his further intellectual career, he takes a turn towards observations on the importance of cultural homogeneity, culture and the role of history. These elements put him in line with another tradition of international legal thought, that is Machiavelli and Montesquieu.[88] With a combination of the Kantian systematic structure and these ideas, he became one of the most important thinkers in German Romanticism.

Selected Bibliography

Cesa, Claudio, 'Recensori di Kant: Fichte e Schlegel', *Teoria politica*, vol. XI, Issue 2 (1995), pp. 33–45.

Fichte, Johann Gottlieb, *Gesamtausgabe der Bayerischen Akademie der Wissenschaften*, Reinhard Lauth, Erich Fuchs, Hans Gliwitzky (eds.) (Stuttgart-Bad Cannstatt: Frommann Verlag, 1962–2012).

[Friedrich von Hardenberg], *Novalis Schriften*, Paul Kluckhohn and Richard Samuel (eds.), 5 vols. (Stuttgart: Kohlhammer, 1960ff).

De Pascale, Carla, 'Das Völkerrecht ('Zweiter Anhang')', in Jean-Christophe Merle (ed.), *Fichtes Grundlage des Naturrechts* (Berlin: Akademie Verlag, 2001), pp. 197–210.

[86] The editor of a collection of Fichte's writings on the philosophy of society, including the *Reden an die deutsche Nation*, vol. 15, Die Herdflamme (1928).

[87] Who had worked on a new edition of the *Reden* in 1933, had published in 1936 an essay on Fichte's *Ueber Machiavell, als Schrifsteller* and in 1938 another on Fichte and Machiavelli, in addition to Hans Freyer, 'Johann Gottlieb Fichte', in *Sächsische Lebensbilder*, vol. 2 (1938), pp. 114–31.

[88] See contributions of Volk and Roth-Isigkeit, in this volume.

De Pascale, Carla, 'Le droit cosmopolitique comme synthèse du droit', in Jean-Francois Kervégan (ed.), *Raison pratique et normativité chez Kant : Droit, politique et cosmopolitique* (Lyon: Ecole Normale Supérieure, 2010), pp. 199–211.
Oncina Coves, Faustino, '*Para la Paz Perpetua* de Kant y el *Fundamento del derecho natural* de Fichte: encuentros ydesencuentros', *Δαίμων, Revista de Filosofía*, vol. 9 (1994), 223–339.
Rockmore, Tom and Breazeale, Daniel (eds.), *Fichte, German Idealism and Early Romanticism, Fichte-Studien Supplementa*, vol. 24 (Leiden/Boston: Brill, 2010).
von Schlegel, Friedrich, *Kritische Neuausgabe*, Ernst Behler (ed.) (Paderborn-Wien-München: Schöningh, 1958ff).
Vlachos, Georges, *Fédéralisme et raison d'état dans la pensée internationale de Fichte* (Paris: Editions A. Pedone, 1948).

17

The Plurality of States and the World Order of Reason

On Hegel's Understanding of International Law and Relations

Sergio Dellavalle

By addressing Hegel's conception of international law and relations we come face to face with a paradox. Although Hegel can hardly be seen as a thinker who concentrated his research on international law and relations, he was nevertheless chosen to be the ombudsman of that strand of political and legal thought that pleaded for moving away from the cosmopolitism of the enlightenment era and for endorsing the centrality of the nation state.[1] However, if we consider the question more in depth, we can see that this interpretation of Hegel's political philosophy as one of the theoretical sources of the shift from universalism to particularism at the beginning of the nineteenth century is far from self-evident. Starting, therefore, from a methodological doubt as regards this well-established interpretation, Section I of this chapter presents the main contents of Hegel's conception of international law and relations.[2]

To understand whether the interpretation of Hegel as the leading philosopher of German nationalism and state power is really convincing, I have put his thought, in Section II, within the context of the paradigms of social order that had been developed until his time. The surprising result is that he was no coherent advocate of any of the established paradigms. In other words, while he was surely no cosmopolitan universalist in the sense that was common before him, he did not support the particularism of the classic school either.[3]

[1] Hermann Heller, *Hegel und der nationale Machtstaatsgedanke in Deutschland* (1921); Friedrich Meinecke, *Weltbürgertum und Nationalstaat* (1922), p. 278.

[2] For an overview of Hegel's theory of international law and relations, see also David Boucher, *Political Theories of International Relations* (1998), p. 330; William E. Conklin, *Hegel's Laws* (2008), p. 270.

[3] On Hegel's ambiguity as regards the legacy of the enlightenment, see Norberto Bobbio, *Studi hegeliani* (1981); Steven B. Smith, 'Hegel's Views on War, the State and International Relations', *The American Political Science Review* 77 (1983), 624.

Instead, he can rather be regarded as the philosopher who, as first, paved the way to a new paradigm of order and, thus, also to a new idea of the relation between the state and international law. The final Section III is dedicated to a critical assessment of this hypothesis.

I. Hegel's Theory of International Law and Relations

International law and international relations are rather minor topics in Hegel's work for at least three reasons. Firstly, considerations on the issue appear relatively late in the evolution of his thought. Secondly, even in the works in which it is addressed, little space is dedicated to the subject. Thirdly, Hegel's view on international law and international relations does not show the same richness and variants of approaches that typifies his presentation of other issues of political and legal philosophy.

As regards the first point, it may be quite surprising that either his early texts do not contain any reference to the question, or the references are concentrated on only one topic, namely war, or, lastly, insofar as the first attempts to construe a system of political philosophy require a general overview on all components of the matter, the legal and political relations among states are only seen from a negative perspective. The silence on the topic concerns, in general, all manuscripts from the Bern and Frankfurt period.[4] In contrast to a large part of the political philosophy of the late seventeenth and of the eighteenth century, which always located individuals and states within the broader context of the law of peoples, Hegel's political interest seems to narrow down the horizon to the development of just the single political community. Not by chance, yet: whereas the philosophers of the enlightenment understood the *homo politicus* in terms of his essential, natural, and universal characteristics, building this way the bridge between the *societas civilis*, or the individual commonwealth, and the *jus gentium*, Hegel concentrates his attention on the social conflicts *within* the single political order. As a consequence, the driving force of human evolution is not the aspiration to fully realize an abstract concept of humanity any longer, but the concrete struggle that unfold between individuals and social groups within the most immediate context, namely each single society. Hegel's unprecedented sensibility for social processes and conflicts is thus achieved at the quite not irrelevant cost of a nearly complete blindness for the phenomena of the international realm. Hegel's indifference towards the international dimension is testified—for the last time and in the most systematic way—in his *First Philosophy of Spirit* of 1803–1804.[5] In this second attempt, after the *System of Ethical Life* of 1802–1803, to construe a comprehensive understanding of society, law, and politics, the forms taken in its evolution by the 'spirit' (*Geist*)—Hegel's definition for the expressions of the self-realization of the individual in relation to its conscience,

[4] Respectively, from 1793 to 1796 and from 1797 to 1801.

[5] The *First Philosophy of Spirit* dates back to the period that Hegel spent at the university of Jena, where he stood, first as a *Privatdozent* and then as an extraordinary professor, from 1801 to 1807.

to other individuals, as well as to the social world—pass directly from the struggles within the individual society to the whole of the 'people' (*Volk*) as the highest manifestation of the ethical life.[6]

However, an element coming from the world of international relations—indeed the most disruptive of all, i.e. war—attracted Hegel's attention even before his first lectures in Jena on the *Philosophy of Spirit* in 1803–1804. In fact, his idea concerning war's ethical significance had been already highlighted for the first time a couple of years before, in his script on *The German Constitution* of 1801–1802. His understanding shows already here a content which will be maintained, in its essential form, until the mature works: war is the condition in which 'the strength of the association between all [individuals] and the whole is displayed'.[7] In other words, war is the phenomenon that overcomes the unfettered selfishness of the individuals, making them aware of the superiority of the interests of the community. This interpretation was then resumed and clarified in the essay on *Natural Law* of 1802–1803, where Hegel introduced his definition according to which war is 'the blowing of the wind that preserves the sea from the foulness which would be the result of a prolonged calm'.[8]

Therefore, in Hegel's perspective the realm of international relations is essentially characterized by war. As a result, it is *negative* because it has the fundamental task of *negating the excessive self-reliance of individuals*.[9] The negative interpretation typifies also what can be regarded as the first proper mention of international law and relations that Hegel made in his philosophical system, beyond the usual reference to the meaning of war. Indeed, in his Jena lectures of 1805–1806—also known as the *Third Philosophy of Spirit*—Hegel already refers to many of the features attributed to international law and relations in the later works:

> The relation [between nations] is partly the placid subsistence of individuals independent of one another – [i.e.] sovereignty – [and] partly [their] connection through agreements. These agreements do not, however, have the actuality of a true contract. There is no existent power in them, but rather the 'individual' that is the nation (*Volksindividuum*) is likewise the universal as existing power. [International agreements] must not be regarded, therefore, in the way that civil contracts are. They have no binding force as soon as one of the parties annuls them. This is the eternal deception, in concluding treaties, to obligate oneself and then to let

[6] Georg Wilhelm Friedrich Hegel, *Jenaer Systementwürfe I: Das System der spekulativen Philosophie*, eds. Klaus Düsing and Heinz Kimmerle (1986), p. 217; trans. G.W.F. Hegel, *System of Ethical Life and First Philosophy of Spirit*, eds. H.S. Harris and T.M. Knox (1979).

[7] Georg Wilhelm Friedrich Hegel, 'Die Verfassung Deutschlands', in *Frühe Schriften* (1971), vol. 1, Werke in zwanzig Bänden, pp. 461–581, at p. 462; trans. G.W.F. Hegel, 'The German Constitution', in Laurence Dickey and H.B. Nisbet (eds.), *Political Writings* (1999).

[8] Georg Wilhelm Friedrich Hegel, 'Über die wissenschaftlichen Behandlungsarten des Naturrechts, seine Stelle in der praktischen Philosophie und sein Verhältnis zu den positiven Rechtswissenschaften', in *Jenaer Schriften 1801–1807* (1971), vol. 2, Werke in zwanzig Bänden, pp. 434–530, at 482; trans. G.W.F. Hegel, *Natural Law*, trans. T.M. Knox (1975).

[9] This interpretation is reiterated also in the *System of Ethical Life*, which Hegel wrote shortly after the essay on *Natural Law*. See Georg Wilhelm Friedrich Hegel, 'System der Sittlichkeit', in *Schriften zur Politik und Rechtsphilosophie*, ed. Georg Lasson (2nd edn, 1923), pp. 413–99, at p. 460; trans. G.W.F. Hegel, *System of Ethical Life* (n. 6).

that obligation evaporate. A general confederation of nations (*Volkerverein*) for permanent peace would mean the supremacy of one nation, or it would mean there is only one nation (the individuality of nations suppressed), a universal monarchy.[10]

We find here, thus, the individuality of the state and its sovereignty, the plurality of the international realm, the limited normative force of international treaties, and the criticism against the cosmopolitan project—quite the whole repertoire of Hegel's interpretation of international law and relations in outline. Nevertheless, the role played by them within the system is different. International law and relations do not mark, here, the passage from the individuality of states to a kind of mundane universality—imperfect, indeed, but nonetheless located beyond the selfishness of the single polities. They have just the function—only attributed to war in the earlier works, and now assigned to the specific conditions of interaction that characterize international law and relations as a whole—of making the members of the single polity aware of their shared interests and of their ethical unity. For the first time in the evolution of Hegel's thought, the system draft of 1805–1806 culminates with what he will later call the 'absolute spirit', i.e. with 'art, religion, and science', and not with the constitution of the ethical polity.[11] In contrast to the later works, the universality of the non-material spheres of human experience and knowledge arises here, in an almost abrupt way, from the internal processes of the single polity, without passing through the yet worldly, but nonetheless universal dimension of international law. As a result, international law and relations have just a *negative* sense in systemic perspective since they do not represent a step on the way to the accomplished universality in the realm of the 'absolute spirit', but only serve to maintain and strengthen the selfishness of the individual political community—precisely that selfishness which, albeit highly ethical, has to be overcome, starting by the Jena lectures of 1805–1806, by the artistic, religious, and scientific (lastly philosophical) expressions of human experience and knowledge.

To find a positive meaning of international law and relations in Hegel's system we have to look further on his way to a comprehensive philosophical system. In fact, the stronger became the systematic ambition of the probably most systematic thinker of the whole history of philosophy, the more intense was the need to give a positive interpretation to almost all dimensions of human life, thus also to the unsteady relations among states. In Hegel's mature system, indeed, almost every aspect of human experience—despite its limitedness—embodies a kind of partial truth on the way to the discovery of the absolute idea. Furthermore, Hegel's interest shifted progressively from the analysis of the conditions for the realization of a strong, unitary, and ethical community, to the affirmation of the superior universality of the intellectual spheres of the 'absolute spirit', to which also the incomplete universality of international law could already be seen as a move forward if compared

[10] Georg Wilhelm Friedrich Hegel, *Jenaer Systementwürfe III: Naturphilosophie und Philosophie des Geistes*, ed. Rolf-Peter Horstmann (1987), p. 250; trans. G.W.F. Hegel, *Hegel and the Human Spirit*, trans. Leo Rauch (1983).

[11] Hegel, *Jenaer Systementwürfe III*, p. 253 (n. 10).

to the narrow self-reliance of the single polity. As a result, in his Heidelberg lectures on the *Philosophy of Right* of 1817–1818—the first he held on this subject—[12] still international relations are a kind of state of nature, international law is weak, and war is pandemic among states. Nevertheless, the function of war does not consist any longer in just strengthening the internal cohesion of the state. Quite the opposite, 'in war the self-reliance of a people is exposed to contingency', so that 'the universal world spirit maintains the higher right on the peoples.'[13] The task of war is thus, now, to make the contingency of the assumed self-reliance of the states evident, bringing about the passage from the ethical life of the self-referent political community to a higher stage of the self-realization of the spirit, i.e. to the universality of world history and, then, of art, religion and science. Indeed, 'the self-reliance [of the peoples] is nothing absolute, and can perish; something higher, the spirit of the world, is above it, and the rights of peoples vanish where the spirit of the world appears.'[14] The same concept was then repeated in all lectures held by Hegel on the *Philosophy of Right* as well as in the published book on the *Elements of the Philosophy of Rights*. In the *Encyclopaedia of the Philosophical Sciences* we can find, then, the most lapidary formulation and the evident proof that Hegel had changed his mind as regards the role of war within the whole of the system: 'in the state of war the independence of states is at stake'[15]—and precisely this frailty of the individual communities is what allows the spirit to develop further.

Between the Heidelberg period and Hegel's call to the Berlin university, thus, international law and relations—and even war—found their definitive and *positive* place within the philosophical system, as a necessary step on the way to the higher self-realization of the spirit, between the individuality of state constitution and the universality of world history. On this basis, Hegel developed a more detailed conception of the subject which was first presented in the above-mentioned Heidelberg lecture on the Philosophy of Right of 1817–1818 as well as in two further courses in Berlin in 1818–1819[16] and 1819–1820.[17] It was then published as part of the

[12] Hegel's professorship at the university of Heidelberg—the first full professorship in his career—lasted for just two academic years (1816–1818), coming after the even shorter period as a newspaper editor in Bamberg (1807–1808) and the time as a headmaster of a *Gymnasium* in Nuremberg (1808–1816), and preceding the call to the Berlin university (1818).

[13] Georg Wilhelm Friedrich Hegel, 'Vorlesungen über Naturrecht und Staatswissenschaft. Heidelberg 1817/18. Nachgeschrieben von P. Wannenmann', ed. Claudia Becker et al., in *Vorlesungen: Ausgewählte Nachschriften und Manuskripte*, vol. 1 (1983), p. 254; trans. G.W.F. Hegel, *Lectures on Natural Right and Political Science*, trans. J. Michael Steward and Peter C. Hodgson (1995) [trans. by the author].

[14] Hegel, 'Vorlesungen über Naturrecht und Staatswissenschaft', p. 255 (n. 13) [trans. by the author].

[15] Georg Wilhelm Friedrich Hegel, 'Enzyklopädie der philosophischen Wissenschaften im Grundrisse (1830): Dritter Teil. Die Philosophie des Geistes', ed. Ludwig Boumann (1845), in *Werke in zwanzig Bänden*, vol. 10, p. 346; trans. G.W.F. Hegel, *Philosophy of Mind. Part Three of the Encyclopaedia of the Philosophical sciences*, trans. William Wallace (2007).

[16] Georg Wilhelm Friedrich Hegel, 'Naturrecht und Staatswissenschaft: Nach der Vorlesungsnachschrift von C.G. Homeyer 1818–19', in *Vorlesungen über Rechtsphilosophie 1818–1831*, ed. Karl-Heinz Ilting (1973), vol. 1.

[17] Georg Wilhelm Friedrich Hegel, *Vorlesungen über die Philosophie des Rechts. Berlin 1819–1820: Nachgeschrieben von Johann Rudolf Ringier*, ed. Emil Angehrn et al. (2000).

Elements of the Philosophy of Right (*Grundlinien der Philosophie des Rechts*)—officially printed in 1821, but actually already released in 1820. Two more courses on the Philosophy of Right followed, after this publication, in 1822–1823[18] and 1824–1825,[19] whereas the lecture of 1822–1823 does not contain the usual references to international law and relations. The lecture of 1824–1825 was the last occasion in which Hegel explicitly addressed the issue in depth, while a shorter version of the Philosophy of Right, including a brief presentation of international law and relations, was inserted into the *Encyclopaedia*.[20]

Yet, although international law and relations, starting from the Heidelberg period, had come to have a relevant role to play within the whole structure of the system, the topic still does not seem to attract Hegel's highest interest, which is always more concentrated on what comes before and after it. Indeed, whereas we have detailed analysis of the constitution of the state, as well as of world history, art, religion, and philosophy, the analysis of international law and relations always remains limited to the essential features. As a consequence, in his most important work on political and legal philosophy Hegel dedicated to the issue just twenty, rather short paragraphs—from § 321 to § 340 inclusive.[21] The presentation, here, is divided into two parts: the first one—called 'Sovereignty vis-à-vis Foreign States' (*Souveränität gegen außen*)—is yet inserted into the chapter on the 'Constitution of the State' or 'Internal State Law' (*inneres Staatsrecht*), while the second builds a chapter on its own, with the title 'External State Law' (*äußeres Staatsrecht*), which is located between the chapters on the 'Constitution of the State' and on 'World History' (*Weltgeschichte*).

This two-parts structure characterizes also Hegel's lectures of 1819–1820 and 1824–1825 on the subject, while the two former courses of 1817–1818 and 1818–1819 present the matter in only one section called 'External State Law', omitting thus the part on 'Sovereignty vis-à-vis Foreign States' as a subsection of the 'Internal State Law', and the course of 1822–1823 completely avoids addressing the topic. As regards Hegel's lectures on political philosophy, it has to be kept in mind that we know them from notes and postscripts laid down by students who wrote them according to their own individual criteria, which might have been quite different and are always difficult to be critically assessed. Nonetheless, aside from the lastly marginal structural differences, it is not possible to work out for Hegel's conception on international law and relations—as for other aspects of his political thought—significant divergences, and maybe also some tensions, between the published work

[18] Georg Wilhelm Friedrich Hegel, 'Philosophie des Rechts: Nach der Vorlesungsnachschrift von H.G. Hotho 1822–23' in *Vorlesungen über Rechtsphilosophie 1818–1831*, ed. Karl-Heinz Ilting (1973), vol. 3.

[19] Georg Wilhelm Friedrich Hegel, 'Philosophie des Rechts: Nach der Vorlesungsnachschrift K.G. v. Griesheims 1824–25', in *Vorlesungen über Rechtsphilosophie 1818–1831*, ed. Karl-Heinz Ilting (1973), vol. 4.

[20] See Hegel, 'Vorlesungen über Naturrecht und Staatswissenschaft: Heidelberg 1817–18', p. 255 (n. 13).

[21] Georg Wilhelm Friedrich Hegel, 'Grundlinien der Philosophie des Rechts', in *Werke in zwanzig Bänden*, vol. 7, p. 490; trans. G.W.F. Hegel, *Philosophy of Right*, trans. S.W. Dyde (1896).

and the Heidelberg and Berlin lectures. Rather, it can be maintained that his theory of international law and relations not only takes little place in his works but also that its main tenets remain largely unchanged during the whole Heidelberg and Berlin period, i.e. since it was granted a positive systematic meaning. For that reason, I will analyse the three most important elements of Hegel's theory of international law and relations—namely state sovereignty, the pluralism of international relations, and international law as 'external state law'—relying mostly on the published *Grundlinien* and referring to the lectures only in the few cases when a topic is presented there in more details or in the even fewer cases when a significant divergence can be fleshed out.[22]

1. State sovereignty

One of the most relevant features of Hegel's conception of the state—and surely the most important for his understanding of international law and relations—is the centrality of sovereignty. According to Hegel, the concept of state sovereignty expresses the specificity of the realization of the spirit (*Geist*) within the social and political context. As manifestation of the explicitly *human*—individual as well as interpersonal—dimensions of reality and knowledge, the spirit develops in Hegel's system after the one-sided abstraction of logical thinking and the no less unilateral concreteness of nature. While articulating itself in different shapes—from the psychological components of the subject to law and morality, and from civil society and state to the higher spheres of the absolute knowledge that can be achieved through art, religion, and philosophy—the spirit conciliates thinking and worldliness, abstraction and reality. The first stage of the self-realization of the spirit consists—as always in Hegel's triadic dialectics—in a kind of individual limitedness and self-reliance, in this case in the expressions of the subjective psychology. Beyond the solipsistic dimension which is connatural to the 'subjective spirit' as the manifestation of the psyche, the spirit dives into the concrete and interpersonal world of social and political relations. Also here, once again, the first steps are the most abstract and limited: the 'law' as the only *external* obligation,[23] and 'morality' as the just *internal* duty.[24] The next stages, in which external compulsion is combined with interior commitment, build the spheres of 'ethical life' (*Sittlichkeit*), with 'family',[25] 'civil society',[26] and the 'state' as its apex.[27]

In Hegel's conception, the state is thus 'the spirit which is in the world and realizes itself in the world'.[28] Within the state, freedom materializes as the most accomplished feature of human nature, although not in the sense of the decision-making capacity of the individuals—generally assumed to be the essential epistemic

[22] See e.g. *infra*, n. 89. [23] Hegel, 'Grundlinien', §§ 34 ff, p. 92 (n. 21).
[24] Hegel, 'Grundlinien', §§ 105 ff, p. 203 (n. 21).
[25] Hegel, 'Grundlinien', §§ 158 ff, p. 307 (n. 21).
[26] Hegel, 'Grundlinien', §§ 182 ff, p. 339 (n. 21).
[27] Hegel, 'Grundlinien', §§ 257 ff, p. 398 (n. 21).
[28] Hegel, 'Philosophie des Rechts 1824/25', § 258, p. 632 (n. 19) [trans. by the author].

attribute of free humans by the liberal and democratic political thinking—but as the willingness by the individual to make the largely predetermined values and interests of the community to his/her own. Regardless of the doubts that we can understandingly cast on Hegel's essentially anti-individualistic and lastly illiberal understanding of freedom, it is nevertheless clear, in his perspective, that the state is the highest form that the spirit—as the properly human dimension of the 'idea' (*Idee*) as the whole sum of reality and knowledge—can take in the social and political dimension and, thus, within the horizon of social order. Nonetheless, even in Hegel's view the state is afflicted by a deficit: indeed, since the spirit externalize itself here into the realm of reality, its inherent universality becomes obfuscated by this move—as always happens in Hegel's system when the universality of the idea takes a real shape and must therefore accept compromises with the material dimension of the world. Whereas the universality of the idea hides itself behind the manifold appearances of nature, the universal validity of the spirit forfeits its immediate evidence by its concretization in the plurality of states and constitutions. As a result of the material dimension of the world, in the context of which the unity of the spirit must recede, states form a *pluriverse*, never merging into a *universe*. The realization of the spirit in the world happens, therefore, at the cost of an alienation which can only be removed if the spirit overcomes the plurality of states, thus regaining its explicit and evident universality.

The immediate consequence of the externalization—or alienation—of the spirit into the plurality of the political reality is that the state, in Hegel's view, must have 'individuality'.[29] In the real world, characterized by diversification and plurality, every appearance of the spirit is insofar 'individual' as it refers with priority to itself, whereas the universal rationality of the whole is expressed rather in the form of an 'invisible hand' or—with Hegel's words—as a 'cunning of reason'.[30] Furthermore, depending on the categories of subjectivism which Hegel adopted in his mature works, one of the most important features that make an actor a real 'individual' consists in his/her capacity of acting according to his/her personal preferences and without external constraint. As a result, every 'individual' polity shall act, at least in its self-perception, keeping with priority—if not exclusively—its own interests in mind and thus, as a result of this self-reliant approach to the world, as a 'sovereign'.

Hegel's theory of the state as a sovereign individuality has three effects. The first is that the state has a right to suspend—and eventually also to annihilate—the self-reference and autonomy of its citizens. Concretely, this means that the sovereign polity, in order to establish itself within the conflictful pluriverse of states, is authorized to make use of the private property of its citizens for its own purposes and, under extreme circumstances, even to require from them the sacrifice of their lives.[31] This way, within the overhuman whole of state individuality even the most

[29] Hegel, 'Grundlinien', § 321, p. 490 (n. 21).
[30] Georg Wilhelm Friedrich Hegel, 'Die Vernunft in der Geschichte', in *Vorlesungen über die Philosophie der Weltgeschichte*, ed. Johannes Hoffmeister (1994), vol. 1, p. 105; trans. G.W.F. Hegel, *Lectures on the Philosophy of World History: Introduction, Reason in History*, trans. H.B. Nisbet (1980).
[31] Hegel, 'Grundlinien', § 278, p. 442 (n. 21).

essential interests of the private and concrete individuals are neglected in the name of the establishment of the totality—quite without granting to the citizens an adequate forum to express their justified claims.

The second consequence is that every state is closed in itself towards other polities, so that it stands necessarily *against* them. Every state individuality is indeed—according to Hegel's words—'a singleness which has incorporated these subsistent differences into itself and so is a unit, exclusive of other units'.[32]

The third—and last—effect is that foreign policy is located among the powers of the crown. In fact, since the state is an individual vis-à-vis other states, it has to be represented before them by a single and real individuality, namely the monarch. In particular, Hegel explicitly refers to his power 'to command the armed forces, to conduct foreign affairs through ambassadors & c., to make war and peace, and to conclude treaties of all kinds'.[33]

2. Pluralism in international relations

From the concept of state sovereignty Hegel derives his conception of international relations. In its attitude towards other political communities, every state—as a sovereign and exclusive individuality—is aware 'of one's existence as a unit in sharp distinction from others'.[34] In international relations, states stand against each other as an individual against another individual. This view does not imply, however, that the world of relations among states is affected by a condition of uninterrupted conflicts and struggles. What Hegel wants to flesh out, here, is rather that in the international world the specificity of each single actor has absolute priority—at least from its selfish and individual perspective. The consequence is that no reliable supra-state order can be built, so that tensions as well as their degeneration into war can always be possible. Yet, Hegel's argument starts—unlike Carl Schmitt's—[35] from the essential and idiosyncratic identity of each individual polity, introducing only in a second step the pandemic character of conflict. In other words, the sometimes hostile relationship between political communities is, in Hegel's view, the occasionally inevitable consequence of the affirmation of the single identities[36]—in the absence of a worldwide institutional and legal framework—and not the existential essence of the 'political' from which, in Schmitt's opposite argumentative itinerary, the distinctiveness of a community shall emerge. In fact, the 'political' consists for Hegel primarily in the organization of the ethical life, and not in the struggle for existential self-affirmation.

Therefore, Hegel cannot be regarded as a kind of early supporter of the conception of the friend–enemy dualism as the essence of the 'political'. Nonetheless,

[32] Hegel, 'Grundlinien', § 321, p. 490 (n. 21).

[33] Hegel, 'Grundlinien', § 329, p. 497 (n. 21).

[34] Hegel, 'Grundlinien', § 322, p. 490 (n. 21).

[35] Carl Schmitt, *Der Begriff des Politischen: Text von 1932 mit einem Vorwort und drei Corollarien* (1963); trans. C. Schmitt, *The Concept of the Political*, trans. George Schwab (1976).

[36] Hegel, 'Grundlinien', § 323, p. 491 (n. 21).

we find in his work the thesis that the insistence on the identity of the political community in contraposition to the 'others' as well as, eventually, open conflicts against them may strengthen the internal stability since 'successful wars have checked domestic unrest and consolidated the power of the state at home'.[37] Moreover, an 'ethical moment' is attributed to war[38] insofar as it submits every particularistic and short-termed interest of the individuals—as his/her self-realization, happiness, property, and even life—to the priorities of the long-lasting institutions of ethical life or, even more significant, to the universalistic teleology of history. Towards the state and the spirit of the world, which come to the fore during war, the single individual experiences quite clearly his/her marginality.

Hegel refrains explicitly from the theory of just war.[39] In an international arena in which no supra-state norms are recognized and respected and no international organization has competence and power in case of conflicts, every individual state is lastly judge in its own account. When the principle of the defence of one's own interest suggests to wage war, a *casus belli* will be captiously but easily found. Regardless of whether a breach of treaties is declared or 'an injury to the honour and autonomy of the state,'[40] no independent authority will ever check whether the justification is legitimate. This way, war becomes a rightful instrument for the settlement of disputes between states: 'if states disagree and their particular wills cannot be harmonised, the matter can only be settled by war'.[41] If confronted with the difficult decision between peace and war, those who are in charge of the interests of the polity shall opt for the reason of state, i.e. for the egoistic advantage of the single community,[42] and not for 'a universal thought (the thought of philanthropy)' or for abstract 'universal thoughts supposed to be moral commands'.[43]

As regards the organization of the military, Hegel underlines the necessity of standing armies, whereas he considers compulsory military service inevitable only in times of acute danger.[44] On this point, he remains largely bound to the understanding of warfare of the eighteenth century and seems not to penetrate fully the novelties introduced by the social, ideological, and also military mobilization as a consequence of the Napoleonic wars. Evidently wrong—and fully defying the later developments of history—was then Hegel's prediction according to which wars, as a result of technological progress, would become more humane and less brutal for the individuals, regardless of the persistent danger to life, because of the decrease in importance of hand-to-hand combat.[45]

[37] Hegel, 'Grundlinien', § 324, p. 493 (n. 21).
[38] Hegel, 'Grundlinien', § 324, p. 492 (n. 21).
[39] Hegel, 'Grundlinien', § 334, p. 500 (n. 21).
[40] Ibid.
[41] Ibid.
[42] Hegel, 'Grundlinien', § 336, p. 501 (n. 21).
[43] Hegel, 'Grundlinien', § 337, p. 501 (n. 21).
[44] Hegel, 'Grundlinien', § 326, p. 494 (n. 21).
[45] Hegel, 'Grundlinien', § 328, p. 496 (n. 21).

3. International law as 'external state law'

On the basis of Hegel's understanding of state sovereignty and inter-state relations, international law can only have limited effectivity and a low-level normativity. Because states are thought to be self-reliant, inter-state agreements are always dependent on the selfish will of everyone of them. As a result, treaties are inevitably fragile and, not being rooted in any context of concrete ethical life—which is assumed to be impossible beyond the state—build a system of purely abstract norms. As regards this point, it has to be underlined that in Hegel's view the normative content of a system of norms is always strictly intertwined with its social effectiveness. Therefore, it is at its best in the 'ethical' spheres within the state, while international law, due to its specific uncertainty, is considered to be rather near to a kind of moral duty, or—in Hegel's words—to a pure 'ought-to-be' (*Sollen*).[46] Even the highest principle of international law, namely that treaties have to be respected (*pacta sunt servanda*), is regarded by Hegel as a just formal and lastly empty, if not hypocritical obligation, which is left in the hands of the actual balance of power and of the arbitrary decisions of the individual states.[47]

Despite its limitedness, international law builds nevertheless—even according to Hegel—a normative reality, albeit of a lower rank than the 'ethical life' within the state. The first function that Hegel attributes to the *jus gentium* derives from states' aspiration to recognition: indeed, by signing treaties they mutually acknowledge each other as sovereign entities.[48] Nonetheless, this kind of recognition is just formal and refers only to the external sovereign individuality of states. In other words, it is assumed not to affect the internal constitution, so that the legitimacy of the political order is still a purely internal matter. Yet, Hegel admits an exception: if the internal constitution of a state becomes a threat for other polities, these are allowed to refuse recognition as well as to require that the internal constitution of the threatening state is changed.[49] Hegel points out, moreover, that a recognition according to international law is only possible between states that have overcome the stage of a purely religious identity in favour of a political one, realized in the forms of a largely secular ethical life:[50] although Hegel never underestimates the religious influence during the formation process of the modern society, only an essentially political state with its laical institutions can be a subject of international law.

A further function of international law consists, according to Hegel, in regulating inter-state interests and questions—as well as also low-intensity disputes—albeit only in a provisional and sometimes aleatoric way.[51] Yet, he emphasizes how thin the content of such treaties is if compared with the comprehensiveness of the legal

[46] Hegel, 'Grundlinien', § 330, p. 497 (n. 21).
[47] Hegel, 'Grundlinien', § 333, p. 499 (n. 21).
[48] Hegel, 'Grundlinien', § 331, p. 498 (n. 21).
[49] Ibid., even more explicitly, with reference to the French Republic, in Hegel, 'Vorlesungen über Naturrecht und Staatswissenschaft 1817–18', § 161, p. 251 (n. 13).
[50] Hegel, 'Grundlinien', § 331, p. 499 (n. 21).
[51] Hegel, 'Grundlinien', § 332, p. 499 (n. 21).

system of each individual polity. Lastly, Hegel dedicates, according to tradition, a special attention to the laws of war. Here is his tone—in particular for an author supposed to be a supporter of war as an instrument for conflict solution—surprisingly mild. For instance, he claims—analogously to much criticized Kant—that war should be conducted in a way that does not exclude the possibility of establishing peace again. This condition includes the immunity of legates and the protection of non-military facilities as well as of life and property of civilians.[52] As regards the reasons for the mitigation of violence in war, Hegel refers to the 'customs of nations'[53] as well as, in the lecture of 1824–1825, to the ethical 'family' of European nations.[54] These concepts, however, are hardly substantiated in his system, in which 'ethical life' is reduced only to the institutions of the individual civil societies and states. Rather, they can be understood as the opening of a new perspective which, however, was never really investigated in Hegel's work.

II. Hegel against the Background of the Established Paradigms of Social Order

On the basis of the contents of Hegel's theory of international law and relations the question arises whether it is justified to regard him as the turning point from the cosmopolitan approach of the enlightenment era to the nation- and state-centred understanding of international law that dominated the whole nineteenth century and at least the first half of the twentieth century.[55] To address this topos it is indispensable to consider Hegel in the light of the main strands of political thought that shaped the landscape of Western philosophy until his time, or—with the language of a 'general theory of social order'—[56] in view of what we can call the *established* 'paradigms of order'.

1. Historic paradigms of order

The first assumption of a 'general theory of social order' is that a human community, in order to work properly, needs effective rules that make interaction predictable. In other words, it needs 'order'. Adding then a value-related component, a '*well*-ordered society' is the human community in which rules do not only aim at making interactions foreseeable but also organize social life in a *peaceful* way, allowing for the pursuing of the various interests of all agents involved and, in the most ambitious understandings, even facilitating mutual cooperation.

[52] Hegel, 'Grundlinien', § 338, p. 502 (n. 21).
[53] Hegel, 'Grundlinien', § 339, p. 502 (n. 21).
[54] Hegel, 'Philosophie des Rechts 1824–25', § 339, p. 743 (n. 19).
[55] Sometimes the reference to Hegel seems to become a kind of *topos*. See Christian Tomuschat, 'Wer hat höhere Hoheitsgewalt?', *Humboldt Forum Recht* (1997), pp. 72–5, at p. 73.
[56] For more details, see Sergio Dellavalle, *I paradigmi storici*, vol. 1, Dalla comunità particolare all'ordine universale (2011).

However, even if every society requires rules to function, different rules—and therefore also distinct kinds of 'order'—are conceivable and, in fact, have been elaborated and established during the centuries. I propose to call these different patterns 'paradigms of social order'. In general, a *paradigm* is a set of concepts that serve as the most fundamental theoretical requisites for the use of the theoretical and practical reason with reference to a specific field of knowledge and action and in a certain period of human history. Once assumed this definition, to be a 'paradigm of social order' a set of concepts has to shape the understanding of what are and should be the conditions for a peaceful, mutually advantageous and, in the most favourable situations, even cooperative social interaction within a specific historical context. In doing so, it has to address three main questions regarding the rules that govern society: extension and limits of the rules that ground social order; the ontological foundation of order; and its unitary or polyarchic structure, whereas the polyarchic order may be organized, more precisely, in a multilevel setting or as a plurality of largely self-reliant regimes. Depending on the answers that a set of concepts concerning social order gives to these questions, we have different patterns of order, and thus also distinct 'paradigms'. Being led back to their general paradigms, the theories of order obtain a systematic dimension; in other words, order becomes a system through the application of the paradigmatic approach, i.e. by organizing the rules around a conceptual core.

Three 'paradigms of social order' had consolidated until the beginning of the nineteenth century. All of them maintained that a system of rules, in order to guarantee a peaceful and cooperative society, cannot but be *unitary* in the sense that a plurality of diverging norms, all applying to the same matter and at the same time, has to be seen as a pathology and thus ruled out.[57] Different, though—and even diverging—were the contents of these paradigms as regards extension and ontological foundation of order. Concerning this second point, both most ancient paradigms claimed that order can only be based on a social totality—a *holon*—which has to be considered superior to its members. To the contrary, the most recent paradigm turned the hierarchy between individual and community upside down, thus putting reason, rights, and interests of the former to the centre of society. As regards the extension of order, on the other hand, the division line separates the most ancient paradigm from both later patterns of order: whereas the former conception is particularistic in the sense that order is conceived as possible only within limited and homogeneous societies, both later paradigms accept, at least in principle, the idea that the whole human community can be unified by only *one* universalistic order. In the following I will briefly introduce each one of the paradigms of order

[57] The idea that also a society based on legal pluralism or on a multilevel set of rules can be seen as 'well-ordered' appeared much later, dating back to just a few decades ago. For more details, see Andreas Fischer-Lescano and Gunther Teubner, 'Fragmentierung des Weltrechts: Vernetzung globaler Regimes statt etatistischer Rechtseinheit', in Mathias Albert and Rudolf Stichweh (eds.), *Weltstaat und Weltstaatlichkeit. Beobachtungen globaler politischer Strukturbildung* (2007), p. 37; Matthias Kumm, 'On the Cosmopolitan Turn in Constitutionalism', in Jeffrey L. Dunoff and Joel P. Trachtman (eds.), *Ruling the World? Constitutionalism, International Law, and Global Governance* (2009), p. 258; Nico Krisch, *Beyond Constitutionalism* (2010).

that had been established until the beginning of the nineteenth century, pointing out their main features and exponents in order to design the background for a better understanding of Hegel's theory of international law and relations.

a) Holistic particularism

The most ancient of all Western paradigms of order maintains that order is only possible within limited and rather homogeneous communities, whereas between these social, political, and legal communities only containment of dis-order would be feasible. Furthermore, order must be grounded, here, on an ontological basis in which the whole of the community is clearly assumed to have more value than the single individual or even than the sum of all individuals that make up the community. Due to the first characteristic this pattern of order is *particularistic*, and due to the second it is *holistic*; therefore, I call this first paradigm of order *holistic particularism*.

As far as the first assumption of the paradigm is concerned—namely the limited extension of order—the most essential tenets were already laid down by the historian Thucydides.[58] They can be summarized in three points: first, when no balance of power is given, power prevails over law; second, the law of the strongest corresponds to natural or even divine order; third, no trust in the intervention of a third independent party, a *tertium super partes*, is justified since every party which is ready to intervene will do this on the basis of egoistic interests. These tenets have constituted since then the core of every particularistic—or, according to a second, very common definition, of every *realistic*—conception of international law and relations far beyond Hegel's times, lastly until ours.[59]

More complicated is the question as regards the justification of why a well-ordered, but limited society should be conceived as holistic. The first deep-going foundation of society as a *holon* was delivered by Plato. In his political philosophy, he maintains that the polis has to be established on the principle of 'justice'. In his understanding, however, justice has nothing to do with the distribution of resources, but is the condition in which everyone implements the activity for which he has the most relevant natural predisposition.[60] Thus, a society is 'just' if it is conceived of as an organic body in which every part or member can do his own work, and is 'unjust' if the division of labour is not sufficiently accomplished and there is a somehow inefficient overlapping of activities as well as a general tendency to interfere with occupations and decisions outside the sphere of one's own competencies.

[58] Thucydides, *The Peloponnesian War* (1982), V, n. 84, p. 349.

[59] Quite resorting to epistemological instruments different from Thucydides', these basic elements against the idea of the possibility of a universalistic order can be found again in all neo-realistic conceptions of international law and relations: from Hans Morgenthau, *Politics Among Nations* (1954) and Kenneth Waltz, *Theory of International Politics* (1979), until Jack Goldsmith und Eric Posner, *The Limits of International Law* (2005).

[60] Plato, 'Politeia', in *Werke* (1990), vol. 4, IV, 433b, pp. 322 ff.

Yet, Plato's idea of social homogeneity proved to be far too demanding already during his lifetime. In a period in which the cohesion of the Greek polis was fading away, the individuals could not see the self-identification with the aims of their *politeia* as the one and only purpose of their life any longer.[61] The social cohesion—and, with this, also the law that had to express it—needed to rest on a new fundament, and the author who gave to this question a groundbreaking answer that deeply influenced the political thought for almost two thousand years was Aristotle. In fact, he not only proposed a new definition of 'justice' according to which it is essentially related—in a way that is much nearer to our sensibility—to the principles that guides the distribution of resources and advantages on the basis of reasonable and justifiable criteria,[62] but also located the highest goal of practical life not in the service for the political community, as Plato did, but in what he called the 'theoretical life'.[63] Nevertheless, he maintained—like Plato—the necessity of an organic and holistic understanding of the *politeia*. Yet, why should the members of the political community owe solidarity to each other if their most essential aim consists in living a life characterized by the individual search for the theoretical truth and by its comtemplation? On which fundament can the loyalty to the social group be based? Aristotle's answer is astonishingly plain and intuitively convincing at the same time: because all members of the political community belong to an enlarged family, so that they have to support the community as every good family member is expected to do.[64]

The familistic justification for social order was a huge success in political thought. However, in Modern Ages it degenerated progressively into a mere validation of the absolutistic monarchic power. We see the beginning of this process in the work of Jean Bodin,[65] whereas the defence of the absolutistic monarchic power became then the central issue in John Filmer's *Patriarcha*.[66] Yet, the subordination of the familistic understanding of the holistic order of society to the justification of absolutism marked also its definitive decline. Indeed, as the crowned heads began to tremble in Europe and America and were substituted by republics by the two great revolutions of the late eighteenth century, the sustainers of the particularistic–holistic interpretation of society were once again in search for a new ontological basis for social order. This was—precisely in the period in which Hegel developed his philosophy—the most central issue for all those who still maintained that order can only be achieved within homogeneous communities and not worldwide. Political romanticism—led by Adam Müller as its most significant figure—located the basis for a renewed holism in the idea of the *nation*, understood not primarily

[61] Hegel himself pointed out that Plato's philosophy excluded, in its very essence, the idea of individuality. See Hegel, *Jenaer Systementwürfe III*, p. 240 (n. 10).

[62] Aristotle, 'Nikomachische Ethik', in *Philosophische Schriften* (1995), vol. 3, V, 9, 1134a, p. 114.

[63] Aristotle, 'Nikomachische Ethik', X, 7, 1177a, p. 248 (n. 62).

[64] Aristotle, 'Politik', in *Philosophische Schriften* (1995), vol. 4, I, 2, 1252b, p. 4.

[65] Jean Bodin, *Six livres de la république* (1579).

[66] John Filmer, *Patriarcha, Or the Natural Power of Kings* (1680).

as the community of citizens, but rather as the quasi-natural and in any case pre-political and pre-legal *Gemeinschaft* of the members of the *Volk*.[67]

b) Holistic universalism

The first paradigmatic revolution in the theories of order brought the transition from the idea that order is only possible *within* the particular and homogeneous communities and not *between* them, to the conviction that order is, in principle, extendable to the whole humanity. Yet order, although understood on a cosmopolitan range, was conceived as no less organic and holistic than in the older paradigm: indeed, the community remains also in this paradigm not only genetically but also ontologically and axiologically superior to the individuals as its members; simply, the community is here so widened as to comprehend the whole humankind. The new paradigm of *holistic universalism* was introduced by the Stoic philosophers.[68] The fundamental assumption made by them was that not only the natural but also the social and political world is run by just one universal Logos. From this, a universal Nomos is derived which applies to the whole human community and is regarded as the ultimate basis of any legal system of the single political communities.

It was with its further development by the Christian political theology, however, that the holistic–universalistic conception of order became influent. The Christian theology of the Middle Ages as well as its Catholic prosecution situated the last source of the universality of order not only in God's revelation but also in the capacity of natural reason to attain the most essential elements of the divine law. Concretely, this assumption took different forms. Initially, it was the plea in favour of a universal monarchy, where the worldwide validity of mundane power is justified as the worldly expression of God's universal authority.[69] Later, as this project was abandoned not only by the rulers but also by the thinkers, the idea was developed, in particular by Francisco Suárez, of a highly differentiated and innovative system of laws in which the unity of the *lex divina* is articulated, within a multilevel setting including natural law and the *jus gentium*, as an all-encompassing dome thought to include and justify all legal systems of the single polities beneath it. In this conception, the relations between independent states should be regulated, in order to improve peace and preserve mutual recognition, on the basis of generally accepted principles derived from God's commands.[70] In any case, one element was present throughout the whole history of the Christian and then Catholic theology between the Middle Ages and the early Modern Ages: it was on the universal scope of God's law and on the osmosis between this and natural reason that the project of a worldwide order was grounded.

[67] Adam Müller, *Die Elemente der Staatskunst* (1922), I, IV, pp. 76 ff.

[68] Johannes von Arnim, *Stoicorum veterum fragmenta*, vols. I and III (1903–1905).

[69] The most articulated philosophical justification of the idea of a Christian universal monarchy can be found in Dante Alighieri, 'De Monarchia (1310–1314)', in *Opere minori*, vol. II (1986).

[70] Francisco Suárez, 'De legibus, ac Deo legislatore (1612)', in *Selections from three Works* (1944), in particular books I–III.

From the perspective of the Calvinist theology, on the contrary, the way of the direct derivation of the validity of social order from God's will had been shut down since the possibility of grasping the divine truth by means of reason had been made impossible—according to the Protestant doctrine—by human original sin. Therefore, the legal philosophers influenced by Protestantism had to seek elsewhere the source of the reasons why order should be conceived as universal. They found it by going back to the old Stoic concept of οικέιωσις, namely to the idea that all human beings are bound to each other by a natural tendency to 'sociability'. In particular, the alleged social 'essence' of humans was regarded as the basis for the universal norms of international law. The foundation of international order on the assumption of a universal human 'sociability' was first introduced by Alberico Gentili,[71] further developed by Hugo Grotius,[72] and then taken up by Samuel Pufendorf[73] and Christian Wolff.[74] Thus, while in the Catholic political theology the guarantee for the universality of order was located in the recognition of God's will, in its Protestant counterpart—due to the impossibility of recognizing the divine law by means of natural reason—the same function had to be accomplished by a laical assumption regarding the ontological nature of human beings.

c) Universalistic individualism

The second paradigmatic revolution in the theories of order overturned the former hierarchy between community and individuals: while within the older paradigms the whole of the community was thought to be in any sense superior to the sum of its members, now the centre of social order was put in the rights, interests and rational capacity of the individuals, whereas authority was only justified if it aimed at the protection of individual rights and interests. The revolution from holism to *individualism* was initiated by Thomas Hobbes[75] and then carried forward by the major exponents of modern contractualism, explicitly Locke,[76] Rousseau,[77] and, in particular, Kant.[78]

The question arises, here, on how far the individualistic order of society can reach, i.e. whether it is assumed to stop at the borders of the single polity, or is thought to include, in principle, the whole humanity. On this point, it has

[71] Alberico Gentili, *De jure belli libri tres* [1612] (1933), Liber I, Cap. XV, p. 107.

[72] Hugo Grotius, *De Jure Belli ac Pacis* [1646] (1995), Prolegomena, no. 6, 16, and 17.

[73] Samuel Pufendorf, *De jure naturae et gentium libri octo* [1672] (1995), book II, chs. II, III, VII, and XV; book VIII, ch. VI.

[74] Christian Wolff, *Institutiones juris naturae et gentium* (1750), book IX, chs. I, V, and VI.

[75] Thomas Hobbes, *De Cive* [1642] (1651); Thomas Hobbes, *Leviathan, or the Matter, Form, and Power of a Commonwealth Ecclesiastical and Civil* (1651).

[76] John Locke, *Two Treatises of Government* [1690] (1698).

[77] Jean-Jacques Rousseau, *Du contrat social, ou principes du droit politique* [1762] (1966).

[78] Immanuel Kant, 'Kritik der praktischen Vernunft. Grundlegung zur Metaphysik der Sitten', in *Werkausgabe*, ed. Wilhelm Weischedel (1977), vol. VII, p. 65; Immanuel Kant, 'Zum ewigen Frieden: Ein philosophischer Entwurf', in *Werkausgabe*, vol. XI, p. 204; Immanuel Kant, 'Die Metaphysik der Sitten', in *Werkausgabe*, vol. VIII, p. 429.

to be kept in mind that, at least at the beginning, the contract theory of state—namely the state theory in which the individualistic epistemology took form in political philosophy—was conceived as an instrument for the new foundation of political power and for its legitimation under the conditions of the modern centrality of individuals. In other words, interest in international order was initially marginal and, insofar as international law and relations were addressed, scepticism was the prevailing attitude.[79] Regardless of the early indifference of its exponents towards global order, the individualistic paradigm was cosmopolitan in its essence. Indeed, according to the individualistic paradigm, human beings are regarded as endowed with socially non-situated rights, interests and reason, so that they are considered in principle equal. Moreover, these socially non-situated individuals are seen as the barycentre of the political and legal community. As a result, there is no reason why this community should be shaped along the lines of ethnic, cultural, linguistic, historic or religious identities. In other words, due to its conceptual premises the individualistic paradigm cannot but be universalistic. It was only with Kant, however, that the paradigm came to develop its full potentialities. In particular, Kant introduced a tripartition of public law which contains for the first time, beside the traditional dimensions of 'constitutional law' (*Staatsrecht*) and 'international law' (*Völkerrecht*), also a third sphere—the 'cosmopolitan law' (*weltbürgerliches Recht*)—in which the rights holders are the individuals not as citizens of a specific polity, but simply as human beings involved in a worldwide interaction.[80] Furthermore, universal peace was regarded by Kant not only as a political necessity but also as a moral duty. Nevertheless, when it came to the formulation of a concrete proposal, Kant swung undecided between the 'world republic' (*Weltrepublik*) and the 'confederation of peoples' (*Völkerbund*).[81] The lack of an implementable option did not come by chance: having developed the idea of cosmopolitan order at the price of a radical decontextualization of the individuals, Kant's groundbreaking intuition was lastly doomed to remain abstract.

2. Hegel's position within the traditional paradigms of international order

Against the background of the short description of the different paradigms of order, the question can be addressed to which of them Hegel's philosophy is considered to belong and, therefore, also which role it may have played in the history of the theories of international law and relations.

[79] Hobbes, *Leviathan*, ch. XXX (n. 75); Baruch Spinoza, 'Tractatus theologico-politicus', in *Opera*, ed. Carl Gebhardt (1924), vol. 3, ch. XVI; Baruch Spinoza, 'Tractatus politicus', in *Opera*, vol. 3, ch. III (n. 79); Locke, *Two Treatises*, book II, ch. 2, para. 14 and ch. 16, para. 183 (n. 76).

[80] Kant, 'Zum ewigen Frieden', p. 203 (n. 78).

[81] Kant, 'Zum ewigen Frieden', p. 212 (n. 78); Kant, 'Metaphysik der Sitten', § 54, p. 467 and § 61, p. 474 (n. 78).

a) Hegel's criticism against universalism and cosmopolitanism

Undoubtedly, Hegel rejected both paradigms that endorsed the idea of a cosmopolitan order. As regards the Catholic version of the holistic universalism, it cannot be surprising that Hegel—a rather fervent supporter of the political Protestantism, at least in his mature years—regarded with disbelief, if not even with suspicion, the idea of a *communitas Christiana* under the aegis of the Holy See. In general, he considered this conception as definitively belonging to the past since the transition from the Middle to the Modern Ages and as a consequence of the Reformation.[82]

Yet, even the theory of the existence of a *communitas humana* characterized by the same interests and values, which had been developed by authors deeply influenced by the Protestant theology, was not favourably considered by Hegel either. To detect his position on this point we have only some clues at disposal, but they all indicate, coherently, the same attitude. In his criticism against the project of a worldwide federation,[83] as well as in his rejection of the idea of a peaceful and sociable state of nature,[84] in his almost absolute silence on the theory of a universal *communitas humana*, or, when the silence is broken, in his disregard for Grotius as its most influent advocate—[85] in all these cases Hegel shows no affinity towards the non-religious version of holistic universalism and rather sympathy for the opposite, non-universalistic approach.

Explicit was, on the contrary, Hegel's negative judgment about the strand of universalism that was originated from the individualistic epistemology and social theory, in particular as regards Kant's project for a *Perpetual Peace*. Since 'there is no Praetor to judge between states; at best there may be an arbitrator or a mediator, and even he exercises his functions contingently only,' the perpetual and universal peace treaty proposed by Kant would need the consent of each individual state. This, however, 'in any case would always depend ultimately on a particular sovereign will and for that reason would remain infected with contingency'.[86]

[82] See Hegel's analysis of the transition from the Middle Ages to the Modern Age in his lecture on the philosophy of world history: Georg Wilhelm Friedrich Hegel, *Vorlesungen über die Philosophie der Weltgeschichte. Berlin 1822–23. Nachschriften von Karl Gustav Julius von Griesheim, Heinrich Gustav Hotho und Friedrich Carl Hermann Victor von Kehler*, ed. Karl Heinz Ilting et al. (1996), p. 462; trans. G.W.F. Hegel, *Lectures on the Phiosophy of World History: Volume I. Manuscripts of the Introduction and the Lecture of 1822–1823*, eds. Robert F. Brown and Peter C. Hodgson (2011). On Hegel's political protestantism see Sergio Dellavalle, *Freiheit und Intersubjektivität* (1998), p. 193.

[83] Hegel, 'Vorlesungen über Naturrecht und Staatswissenschaft 1817–18', § 162, p. 253 (n. 13).

[84] Hegel, 'Grundlinien', § 194, p. 350 (n. 21); Hegel, 'Philosophie des Rechts 1822–23', p. 33 (n. 18).

[85] Georg Wilhelm Friedrich Hegel, 'Vorlesungen über die Geschichte der Philosophie', ed. Carl Ludwig Michelet (1833/36), in *Werke in zwanzig Bänden*, vol. 20, p. 224; trans. G.W.F. Hegel, *Lectures on the History of Philosophy*, vol. 3, trans. E.S. Haldane and Frances H. Simson (1995). Hegel's disregard for Grotius is bluntly contrasted by his appraisal of Hobbes' pessimistic understanding of the state of nature as *bellum omnium contra omnes*. See Hegel, 'Vorlesungen über die Geschichte der Philosophie', p. 225 (n. 85).

[86] Hegel, 'Grundlinien', § 333, p. 500 (n. 21).

b) Hegel's case for particularism—and beyond it

While Hegel's refusal of both strands of the universalistic idea of order is hardly questionable, his attitude towards the particularistic-holistic paradigm is—at least at first glance—more debatable. In particular, his open polemics against universalism could suggest his nearness to the opposite approach, namely to holistic particularism. Indeed, we find in his texts both constitutive elements of the first Western paradigm of social order. First, Hegel endorses the organic understanding of the political community;[87] and, second, he interprets international relations as an arena characterized by pandemic conflicts. Thus, both holism and particularism seem to be present at the core of his thought. Nevertheless, even more significant arguments speak against the conclusion that Hegel should be regarded as a backward-oriented philosopher who simply wanted to take up the more traditional forms of holistic particularism, or even as a reformer who aimed at renewing the old paradigm in front of the challenges of the beginning nineteenth century.

As regards the possibility that Hegel just wanted to re-propose old-fashioned versions of holistic particularism, this hypothesis can be easily rejected if we consider the role that the most relevant exponents of the older forms of this paradigm play in his philosophy. For instance, he refers many times in his works to Thucydides as one of the most important historians of all times and as an outstanding figure of the ancient culture, but never as the thinker who laid down the fundaments for the so-called 'realistic' understanding of international relations. In Hegel's thought, indeed, the struggle between states is always overcome by an idealistic teleology of history in which it finds its more profound meaning. Moreover, neither Plato's 'justice' nor Aristotle's 'happiness' are regarded as suitable basis for the order of the political community: reason is for Hegel the only fundament of the polity, whereas an even higher realization of rationality is located beyond the state. Lastly, also Hegel's sovereignty concept is quite different from Bodin's: first, it has no familistic background, and, secondly, it is not assumed to serve primarily dynastic interests or absolutistic political projects.

Yet, if Hegel is not just a backward-oriented thinker, could he be seen as one of those intellectuals who reinvented the paradigm, giving to it a new guise after a two hundred years lasting crisis due to the rising of universalistic rationalism and enlightenment? Three elements are crucial to the re-invention of the paradigm in the light of political romanticism: nationalism, contextualism, and the justification of war.

aa. Beyond nationalism: Hegel's conception of the *Volk*

The re-foundation of holistic particularism at the beginning of the nineteenth century was essentially connected with the idea that the nation—as a group of individuals united by pre-political and pre-legal features like language, history, culture, sometimes religion, and almost always natural kinship, or 'blood'—had to be seen

[87] Hegel, 'Grundlinien', § 269, p. 414 (n. 21).

as the fundament of the state. However, evidences that Hegel made this view to his own are less than rare.[88] In fact, we can find only one reference, in the postscript of a lecture, to the nation as the anthropological fundament of the individuality of the state.[89] This assertion remains, yet, completely isolated in Hegel's work. Moreover, if the role assigned to the nation maybe in one marginal case incidentally positive, it is, in all other passages in which Hegel refers to it, downright negative—which is at least curious for a philosopher who should have been, at least in the view of some influential interpreters, as one of founding fathers of the emerging vision of the nation-state of the nineteenth century. In general and according to the more fundamental tenets of his philosophy, the 'nation' is a social group which is still 'natural', i.e. so close to the original, not to say primitive, forms of interaction that it could not reach the higher stage of a constitutionally organized 'people' (*Volk*).[90] In Hegel's philosophy, the basis of the 'people' organized in a state is not the 'nation' as the pre-political expression of the most elementary and thus 'natural' social interaction, but the 'ethical life' (*Sittlichkeit*). This concept expresses the historically situated and culturally constructed form of an eminently political interaction, which has overcome by far the level of the immediate nearness to nature, or—as we could say more precisely—of an unreflected belongingness. In other words, Hegel's 'people' is not a synonym for 'nation', and it is not something essentially linked to some assumed natural roots. Insofar as it is a concretization of the 'spirit' and of reason, the 'people' is a highly legally and socially structured idea, in which the natural elements—albeit undoubtedly present—are just a remainder of the limits in which the mundane 'spirit', though always longing for higher dimensions of self-realization, is trapped.

bb. Beyond contextualism: World history and the absolute spirit

A second element which characterizes the rebirth of holistic particularism at the beginning of the nineteenth century consists in the contextualization of reason. According to the exponents of romanticism, human interaction cannot be founded in universal reason. Rather, we have many rationalities, rooted in the distinct traditions of the different *Völker*, from which separate and lastly incommensurable communications within the social and political communities develop. Yet, if no universal reason exists, no system of international order endowed with consistent normativity will be possible, so that untamed existential conflicts actually dominate the scene, with just few interruptions through feeble compromises.[91]

[88] Armin von Bogdandy, 'Hegel und der Nationalstaat', *Der Staat* 30, (1991), p. 513.

[89] Hegel, 'Vorlesungen über Naturrecht und Staatswissenschaft 1817/18', § 159, p. 246 (n. 13).

[90] Hegel, 'Enzyklopädie der philosophischen Wissenschaften im Grundrisse (1830). Dritter Teil', § 549, p. 350 (n. 15).

[91] The idea that a kind of global order may exist even without the assumption of a universalistic rationality is quite new and fully unconceivable on the basis of the epistemology that dominated Western thought until the rise of postmodernism. On the conditions of a pluralistic order, see Krisch, *Beyond Constitutionalism* (n. 57).

The idea of international relations as a field dominated by conflicts is surely part of Hegel's conception. But it is not its reason's last word.[92] First, the individual state is nothing but the manifestation of the universal reason in the mundane domain. Secondly, in Hegel's work a dimension arises from the field of international conflicts, and is lastly situated above it, which is far away from the horizon of particularism: it is world history which is, indeed, essentially made of inter-state conflicts, but, on the other hand, also overcomes the one-sidedness of states, making the implementation of universal reason possible.[93] Thus, the universality of human interaction does not take the form, here, of a global community endowed with ontological sociability as well as with shared values and interests, nor is it expressed through a worldwide social contract. Nevertheless, universality is by far not deleted from the horizon: insofar as history is interpreted as a kind of a 'world's court of judgment' and the absolute spirit overrides all dimensions of the political world, universal reason is still present and effective, although in a sphere which is distant—as far as world history is concerned—from the self-reflective behaviour of concrete individualities and, as regards the absolute spirit, even from the social processes in which individuals and groups are involved.

cc. Beyond the existential struggle for survival: Hegel on war

Hegel's understanding of war has been matter of much debate and of some unease among the interpreters who tried not to relegate him to the ranks of the bellicists.[94] The disappointment, indeed, seems to be well-grounded if we consider, for instance, the following passage:

> What is ethical must itself intuit its vitality in its difference, and it must do so here in such a way that the essence of the life standing over against it is posited as alien and to be negatived. [. . .] A difference of this sort is the *enemy* [. . .]. For ethical life this enemy can only be an enemy of the people and itself only a people.[95]

Here, Carl Schmitt's most aggressive statements seem to be anticipated by more than a century. Yet, it would be a mistake to overestimate this assertion: on the whole, Hegel's position is far from making him an advocate of that understanding of war that was—and still is—so beloved among the exponents of the particularistic paradigm of international order (or rather dis-order), namely of an idea that war is the existential struggle for survival between somehow homogeneous communities. If it has to be admitted that war is not condemned by Hegel—which may be disturbing enough for us—it has also to be recognized that, in his texts, it is never just at the service of particularistic and egoistic interests. For the victims it does not make a great difference indeed; for the historical, philosophical, and ethical considerations, however, it does.

[92] Charles Covell, *The Law of Nations in Political Thought* (2009), p. 189.
[93] Hegel, 'Grundlinien', § 340, p. 503 (n. 21).
[94] Shlomo Avineri, *Hegel's Theory of the Modern State* (1972), p. 194.
[95] Hegel, 'System der Sittlichkeit', p. 466 (n. 9).

Four main reasons speak for this interpretation. The first and most important is that in Hegel's mature works war is justified always and alone as an instrument for the realization of the universal 'spirit'. In this sense, war may have the task of strengthening internal cohesion, but—which is lastly much more significant—builds also the gate that leads from the selfishness of the individual states to universal reason.

Secondly, war is not seen as a ruthless struggle for self-affirmation or survival by a people or a nation, but as the event that prevents society from becoming too much accustomed with selfishness and routine.[96] As a result, war has the task to shake up political communities in which a well-established tendency to enjoy a comfortable life may have led to the sheer impossibility to deal with new challenges.[97] The assumption of an inescapable connection between war and social change may be—with some good reasons—quite disturbing to us, but it was a kind of *topos* at Hegel's times. In this sense, war—far from being just an instrument for the self-assertion of a particularistic community—becomes an always painful, but sometimes necessary instrument for a new step forwards in the universalistic progress of humanity towards freedom.

Thirdly, in one of his lectures on the Philosophy of Right Hegel makes a claim that a true supporter of the particularistic understanding of order would never endorse, namely that through international law states recognize each other 'as such [political communities], with which it is possible to live in peace'.[98] In doing so, he assumes that peace is not just—negatively—a condition in which hostilities are temporarily suspended, but rather a positive state of mutual recognition, which is worth aspiring to. Thus, peace describes in Hegel's conception not an absence—i.e. the lack of war—but a presence, namely respect for each other.

Fourthly, the fact that war, for Hegel, cannot be the consequence of unilateral decisionism by the executive power is proved by the role that he attributed to the Estates (*Stände*) within the procedure of the declaration of war.[99]

III. Towards a New Paradigm of Order?

On the basis of the analysis carried out in the former section we can maintain that Hegel was not a supporter of universalism, regardless of what strand of it. However,

[96] Hegel, 'Grundlinien', § 324, p. 493 (n. 21). Here, Hegel repeats the same sentence already used almost twenty years earlier. See Hegel, 'Über die wissenschaftlichen Behandlungsarten des Naturrechts', p. 482 (n. 8).

[97] Hegel's rejection of social stagnation is proved by his rather reserved judgment as regards the Holy Alliance—which is even more surprising if considered in relation to the political condition of his time. See Hegel, 'Philosophie des Rechts 1822–23', p. 835 (n. 18).

[98] Hegel, 'Vorlesungen über Naturrecht und Staatswissenschaft 1817–18', § 161, p. 250 (n. 13).

[99] Hegel, 'Philosophie des Rechts 1824–25', § 329, p. 738 (n. 19). As a result of the role played by the Estates, in England no 'unpopular war can be waged.' However, people's involvement can also have, according to Hegel, negative consequences since it may lead to an uncontrolled and disadvantageous war enthusiasm.

he seems not to defend particularism either, be it in its rather traditional form or in the new nationalist shape. Should this mean that Hegel is laying down the fundament for a new paradigm of order, anticipating a development which would completely unfold much later? By doing so, he would not only conceive order as a 'system'—which emerges clearly from the investigation of the deep connection between his interpretation of international law and relations and the broader context of his philosophy—but this 'system' would also be something new within the horizon of the patterns of social order. Indeed, two elements of a new paradigm are at least outlined in Hegel's philosophy: the polyarchic setting of order, and its dialectic (or even communicative) understanding.

1. The polyarchic setting

For the first time in Western philosophy Hegel realizes a system in which the defence of the individuality and sovereignty of states coexists with a robust idea of universal order. Before him, either the political life was centred on the state and the order of reason beyond the state was denied any serious consideration—like in authors going from Thucydides to Adam Müller, passing through Machiavelli and Bodin—or, vice versa, the *civitas maxima* was seen as the only realization of reason in human society, whereas the state was condemned to have just a second-hand legitimation—like in the Scholastic thought, in Kant and, more than one hundred years after Hegel, also in Kelsen. Even Suárez, who defends—to a certain extent—the individuality of the state, inserts this into a structure that remains, albeit multilevel, strictly hierarchical. And those thinkers—like Grotius and Pufendorf—who limit the basis for global order to general assumptions on natural reason, are confronted, in the end, with the weakness of this fundament.

On the contrary, in Hegel the identity of the state is undeniable and constitutes the basis for the political involvement of the individuals who, this way, are not deprived of their tangible field of political commitment in favour of a distant global community. Otherwise, the idea of global order is extremely robust since it expresses the progress to a higher level of the realization of reason. With his conception, Hegel overcomes both traditional dichotomies of the paradigms of order: indeed, it is at the same time particularistic (since it defends state sovereignty) and universalistic (because it assumes the existence of world order), as well as individualistic (since it underlines the role of individuals) and holistic (because it inserts them into an ethical community with shared values). Moreover, Hegel goes also beyond the usual unitary understanding of order: his system, indeed, enters the field of the post-unitary paradigms insofar as the individual state and global order are linked to each other not primarily through hierarchy—on the whole, global order is superior to the states, but each single state is the master in the field of the mundane realization of reason—but through a dialectic and thus implicitly communicative relation.

The most significant problem, in Hegel's conception, is that, while within the horizon of the single state individuals are aware of the identity of their community as well as of the rationality of its institutions and contribute to its functioning through their actions, the field of global order is almost completely detached from them. As regards global order, what individuals can reach—rather just some of them—is an abstract consciousness about contents and necessity of universal rationality. Yet, they can never contribute consciously to its development since universal rationality—as a result of the 'cunning of reason'—[100] is an object for *ex post* philosophical speculations, not for *ex ante* political projects.

2. On the way to a communicative understanding of social order

In Hegel's thought order is not the result of formal hierarchies or abstract agreements, but of dialectic processes.[101] In this sense, he anticipates some aspects of the *communicative paradigm of order*, which was then systematically developed more than one hundred years later.[102] The key to this role as precursor is to find in the concept of 'spirit' as it is developed in the context of the 'ethical life': the idea of a community of interaction and communication is contoured, here, in a way which is unprecedented in the history of Western philosophy. Concretely, the spirit represents the different forms of interaction and communication that individuals and social groups have with each other, and from which social order arises. Thus, order is neither something given by nature or God, nor the result of abstract epistemic categories; rather, it is the consequence of social interactions, including conflicts that are brought to a solution by the mediation of reason.

Yet, the potentialities of this groundbreaking innovation are limited by two factors, the first of diachronic, the second of synchronic nature. The first limit consists in the subjectivistic turn that Hegel's concept of 'spirit' progressively took in the course of the development of his philosophy.[103] While in the early works the 'spirit' is almost exclusively made by the unfolding of social conflicts, in the later texts these are superseded by an all-encompassing subjectivity which seems to presuppose the final result of order even before intersubjective interactions and conflicts begin. Such a presupposition constrains in a significant way the necessarily open-ended results of genuinely communicative processes.

Secondly, it is surprising that the component of the 'spirit' that is characterized by the development and solution of social conflicts—which entails the whole definition of 'spirit' in the early works and at least a part of it in the later texts—was never applied to the realm of international law and relations. The subjectivistic rule—expressed by a rationality that is detached from the awareness of the involved individualities—remains unchallenged here. This is partially due to the fact that Hegel's

[100] See *supra* n. 30.

[101] Axel Honneth, Kampf um Anerkennung (1992), p. 11; Dellavalle, Freiheit und Intersubjektivität, p. 91 (n. 82).

[102] The communicative paradigm of order is based mainly on the works of Jürgen Habermas. For a general presentation of the topic, see Armin von Bogdandy and Sergio Dellavalle, 'Universalism Renewed. Habermas' Theory of International Order in Light of Competing Paradigms', *German Law Journal* 10 (2009), 1, 5.

[103] See Dellavalle, *Freiheit und Intersubjektivität*, p. 127 (n. 82).

interests in international law and relations arose at the same time as his subjectivistic turn took place. But it seems also that Hegel wanted to keep the dimension of international law and relations completely free from conscious processes of social and political interaction, whereas these always play a certain role—albeit increasingly subordinate—in the sphere of the individual state. In other words, it is not clearly understandable why, while the institutions of the single state are backed by the individual awareness of their rationality, international law and relations not only have weaker institutions but also their rationale, i.e. the realization of universal rationality, should never be accompanied by individual cognition carried out by the concrete subjects involved.[104]

We can find attempts to partially extend Hegel's infra-state concept of 'spirit' also to the inter-state dimension already a few years after his death.[105] However, to fully develop a communicative understanding of international order from Hegel's quite sketchy anticipation two changes had to be introduced. First, the intersubjective dimension of social interaction had to be emancipated from the oppressive burden of the all-encompassing subjectivity with its predetermined ontological truth. Second, also the realm beyond the state had to be interpreted as a field of reflexive social interactions and political projects. More than one and a half centuries after its formulation, Hegel's intuition found application, at last, under completely different epistemological premises. However, just recently his contribution to a polyarchic conception of order has found some recognition.[106] And as regards the anticipation of the communicative paradigm of order, Hegel's role is yet to be properly understood and appreciated.[107]

Selected Bibliography

Avineri, Shlomo, *Hegel's Theory of the Modern State* (London/New York: Cambridge University Press, 1972).

Boucher, David, *Political Theories of International Relations* (Oxford/New York: Oxford University Press, 1998).

Buchwalter, Andrew (ed.), *Hegel and Global Justice* (Dordrecht/Heidelberg: Springer, 2012).

Conklin, William E., *Hegel's Laws* (Stanford: Stanford University Press, 2008).

[104] Individual subjects can have indeed cognition of the rationality of world history; yet, exclusively at a philosophical level and not as long as they are involved, but only afterwards.

[105] See Johannes Fallati, 'Die Genesis der Völkergesellschaft', *Zeitschrift für die gesammte Staatswissenschaft* 1 (1844), p. 558; Adolf Trendelenburg, *Naturrecht auf dem Grunde der Ethik* (1868), p. 564; Heinhard Steiger, 'Völkerrecht und Naturrecht zwischen Christian Wolff und Adolf Lasson', in *Naturrecht im 19. Jahrhundert. Kontinuität – Inhalt – Funktion – Wirkung* (1997), pp. 45–74, at p. 66.

[106] Lydia L. Moland, *Hegel on Political Identity* (2011); Andrew Buchwalter (ed.), *Hegel and Global Justice* (2012); Hans-Martin Jaeger, 'Hegel's Reluctant Realism and the Transnationalisation of Civil Society', *Review of International Studies* 28 (2002), 497.

[107] The first exponents of the communicative paradigm of order—namely Habermas and Apel—rather marginalize or even deny Hegel's influence. To the contrary, authors who further developed the paradigm, in particular Honneth, recognize his contribution, but limit it to the inner-state political dimension.

Heller, Hermann, *Hegel und der nationale Machtstaatsgedanken in Deutschland* (Leipzig/Berlin: Teubner, 1921).

Meinecke, Friedrich, *Weltbürgertum und Nationalstaat* (München/Berlin: Oldenbourg, 1922).

Moland, Lydia L., *Hegel on Political Identity* (Evanston Ill.: Northwestern University Press, 2011).

PART II

PERSPECTIVES ON THE PHILOSOPHY OF INTERNATIONAL LAW

18

What Should International Legal History Become?

Martti Koskenniemi

A student asked me the other day: 'does the historicization of something mean that this something is dead?'. The occasion for the question was produced by the launch of a new volume edited by Miia Halme and Pamela Slotte, *Revisiting the Origins of Human Rights* (Cambridge, 2015). The essays in that book arose from the increased interest since Samuel Moyn's 2010 *Last Utopia,* in trying to understand the origins and intellectual history of the human rights phenomenon.[1] Does this mean that human rights are now dead? The suspicion is not hard to understand. Why tell stories about something instead of engaging in that something? Why look backwards instead of forwards? Histories of, say, revolutions are told only as the bland normality has set in, when former revolutionaries sit down to revisit past struggles, to talk about comrades absent and present, and to reflect on the loss of the revolutionary spirit. If the pull now is to looking backwards, does this mean that the project is over, that nothing is visible ahead, or perhaps that one finds oneself in an unfamiliar place and wants to know: 'how did I get here in the first place?'. When does the need to *understand* or remember overweigh the need to keep going?

I do not think that the need to think historically about something necessarily signals the death of that something. When the need to think about the historical context of the life of Jesus arose at the beginning of the nineteenth century, it raised a profound concern among the believers. Does not the very search for a historical understanding mean that one has lost faith? More worryingly, might not portraying Jesus as a historical figure destroy even the possibility of spontaneous faith? As it turned out, Christianity did not 'die' with the sensational publication of David Strauss' *Das Leben Jesu* in 1835.[2] Of course, many pious Christians were shocked. Strauss was accused as a 'modern Judas'. But the shock wore away, and historical studies of the Bible became gradually a respected part of the theological curriculum everywhere.

[1] Samuel Moyn, *The Last Utopia: Human Rights in History* (2010).
[2] David Friedrich Strauss, *Das Leben Jesu, kritisch bearbeitet* (2 vols., 1839).

But the wish to historicize a set of ideas—human rights, Christianity, international law—is likely to signal some concern, some malaise about the pursuit of those ideas. For instance: how come there has been so little progress recently? The concern would not be about external obstacles; those might lead to a closing of the ranks and an even more determined pursuit of the project. The worry is likely to be internal to the set of ideas themselves. Does the lack of progress result from disagreements between adherents? Might there be something wrong in those ideas? What are they supposed to be, after all? Historicization may signal that all is not right, or at least as it used to be, among the believers. Taking a break is needed. This would be history as therapy.

I suggest the turn to history has to do in part with a sense of international law's present ineffectuality, if not irrelevance, in view of present 'crises', in part from doubts about the international legal 'project' itself. What is that 'project'? If 'fragmentation' signals the collapse of a firm centre in the law, how to choose from the many specializations, the many projects that compete under its name? Is international law a cure to the world's ills—or perhaps (at least in some of its forms) a part of those ills itself? It seems to me that the malaise has to do with the difficulty of understanding the complex relationship between international law and international power. How to have a better grasp on power? Might history illuminate the ways in which law has been used in the past to structure, support, channel, and oppose international power? 'Power' is of course a complex, many-layered notion. So is the concept of the 'international'. I would like to propose that in case international lawyers do feel the urge to have a better grasp of power, then they must develop a more complex and many layered concept of international law itself.

In this chapter I argue that the scope of history of international law ought to be expanded beyond its received sense. If the interest lies in 'power', then it is not a surprise that international lawyers might worry about the state of their field. For history to grasp this worry, it should illuminate the process through which some things come to be understood as belonging to 'international law' while others are relegated to 'domestic' or 'private' law, to 'political economy', or indeed to 'international politics'. A study of international law's relations to international power would need to include an examination of the way such categories, professional fields, and intellectual distinctions are made and remade so as to determine what may seem possible to achieve and what is beyond professional argument and contestation.

I

Much recent writing about international law's past has been inspired by a postcolonial interest.[3] The relationship of law to European empire and expansion—not necessarily identical phenomena—has been subjected to increasing scrutiny. What role did international law and international lawyers play in the creation of formal

[3] The trigger for that work has been Antony Anghie's *Sovereignty, Imperialism and the Making of International Law* (2003).

empire at the close of the nineteenth century? Legal notions such as occupation and conquest as bases of European territorial rule have become fruitful topics of research.[4] Natural law is no longer thought as a uniquely pacifying language but also as a repository of large justifications for war and dispossession.[5] Political and legal historians were always drawn to 'humanitarian intervention' as a particularly intriguing topic. It continues to be such today, while attitudes to the beneficial character of Western humanitarianism have become increasingly ambivalent.[6] Historical treatments of genocide and crimes against humanity have often been concerned to explore the question of apologies, compensations, and the politics (and law) of memory. The development of economic law and the laws surrounding international investment are likewise being treated historically, with special attention to their colonial dimension.[7] On-going re-examination of the interwar period may also be connected with a post-colonial interest—the rise and fall of the mandates system provides a fruitful platform on which to examine the transformations of imperial rule.[8] So does the examination of the strategies of non-European jurists in the early twentieth-century international institutions.[9] New research is also directed to the first decades of the United Nations. Scholars are keen to understand what happened to the early embrace by international institutions of the 'New International Economic Order', including such connected projects as technology transfer to the third world and the distribution of proceeds from the extraction of seabed mineral resources at the law of the sea conference (1974–1982). Where did 'permanent sovereignty to natural resources', UNESCO's 'new international information order' or the commodity agreements once imagined as the centre of international development, disappear?[10]

Much of this new work is fed by present-day concerns; it is history 'of the present'. As the United Nations celebrates its 70th anniversary, many of the organization's declared objectives—the creation of a more just and peaceful world seem no closer than they were in 1945. Global inequality is rising—according to studies carried out by Oxfam and Credit Suisse last year, one per cent of the world population owns more than the remaining 99 per cent combined, and that 69 per cent of that wealth lies in Europe and North America with a share of world population of only 18 per cent.[11] War in the Middle East has led to a refugee problem unforeseen

[4] A recent work is Andrew Fitzmaurice, *Sovereignty, Property and Empire 1500-2000* (2015).

[5] Apart from Anbghie above, see also Richard Tuck, *The Rights of War and Peace. Political Thought and the International Order from Grotius to Kant* (1999).

[6] See e.g. Anne Orford, *International Authority and the Responsibility to Protect* (2011).

[7] Kate Miles, *The Origins of International Investment Law: Empire, Environment and the Safeguarding of Capital* (2013).

[8] A good example would be Susan Pedersen, *The Guardians: The League of Nations and the Crisis of Empire* (2015).

[9] See Arnulf Becker Lorca, *Mestizo International Law: A Global Intellectual History 1842-1933* (2015).

[10] Sundhuya Pahuja, *Decolonising International Law: Development, Economic Growth and the Politics of Universality* (2013); Luis Eslava, Michael Fahkri, and Vasuki Nesiah (eds.), *Bandung, Global History and International Law: Critical Pasts and Pending Futures* (2016).

[11] 'Having it All and Wanting More, Report on Inequality 2015', Oxfam, 19 January 2015, <http://policy-practice.oxfam.org.uk/publications/wealth-having-it-all-and-wanting-more-338125?cid=rdt_

in Europe since the Second World War (though of course massive refugee fluxes have been part of the everyday in the developing world). The collapse of the 'Arab Spring' has fed deadly conflict and authoritarianism across the Middle East and beyond. Both 'terrorism' and obsessive 'anti-terrorism' have made transgressing any international legal rules part of the global everyday. And then there is Trump. The problem is not only that it is hard to say which rules are in force and which are not, but that the very ideological structure of liberal progress that used to provide the foundation for legal polices may have crumbled away. It would be trite to speak of the 'normalization of the exception', the exception was always latent in the law. The more sombre assessment suggests that in fact the decades between the Cold War and the fall of the Twin Towers were the exception and that we are now back in the melancholy normality of inequality and violence.

Whichever way one prefers to think about that last problem, it seems clear that many received ideas about the inexorable march of international progress have shown themselves at least unworkable, if not outright wrong. The international legal project is not faring well. When, to take just one example, did the International Law Commission of the United Nations, assigned to deal with the 'codification and progressive development of international law' and reporting annually to the UN General Assembly, last make a contribution that had any influence on the lives of human beings anywhere? Who will remember the latest maritime delimitation from the International Court of Justice? The World Trade Organization's (1995) Doha round has been stalled for more than a decade and the International Criminal Court (1998) is facing a rebellion from African States tired of being at the receiving end of prosecutions. Even the arguably more significant aspects of recent progress—the human rights system and the rise of international environmental law—seem bogged down undecided about whether to think of themselves in terms of ideology or bureaucratic technology.[12] Syria, Ukraine, the Middle East, and South Sudan . . . the refugee crisis has made the expression of ultra-nationalist, even racist, sentiments part of Western politics. The timescale and even the direction of what international lawyers used to think about progress must be revised. True, there is some advance in the UN's 'millennium goals'. Extreme poverty in the developing countries has dropped in 1990–2015 from 47 to 14 per cent. Today 91 per cent of children in the developing world enjoy primary education, child mortality has been halved, and gender equality is on the rise.[13] But these results can hardly be accredited to international *law*. And how are they compatible with the data on the growth of global inequality? Will the world's new inhabitants become a global underclass to be exploited by the one per cent? The gap between the global economy and local political contestation keeps expanding without expectation that international law might have any influence on either.

havingitall> and 'Global Wealth Report 2015', Credit Suisse, October 2015, p. 6, <https://publications.credit-suisse.com/tasks/render/file/?fileID=F2425415-DCA7-80B8-EAD989AF9341D47E>.

[12] I have argued this in 'The Fate of International Law. Between Technique and Politics', *The Modern Law Review* 70 (2007), 1–32.

[13] United Nations, The Millennium Development Goals Report (2015).

Recent post-colonial histories share the intuition that something about present inequality and violence bears an inheritance of the past. They focus on the many ways in which international law has been implicated in colonialism and imperialism. But I am doubtful about the existence of a single 'tradition' of international law that would have passed through history as an instrument of European predominance and could be indicted as responsible for today's injustice. There is as much reason to be sceptical of that proposition as of histories that used to depict international law as a carrier of liberal and humanitarian progress, a 'Grotian tradition'. The relations between law and international power are much more complex and involve contradictory ideas about what 'international law' or even 'law' is and how it can be used.

II

Expressions such as *jus gentium, droit public de l'Europe, Völkerrecht*, or 'law of nations' emerged at different moments, in different parts of Europe, to give effect to varying concerns and objectives. They do not link together in any single tradition that could be traced, say, to Roman antiquity, Renaissance Italy or the Thirty Years' War. This is not to say that the legal vocabularies of each moment would not feed on each other and express ideas that can be generalized between them. For example, all of them have something to do with mediating the tension between the autonomy of territorial polities and an overarching set of 'international' norms. But how they do this and on which side they fall in that tension is wholly dependent on the context: who is arguing, and for what purpose? The relationship between Rome and its provinces is not the same as that between the Holy Roman Empire and North Italian City States in the fourteenth century—but it is possible to find lawyers using arguments from *jus gentium* on all sides. In the conflict between absolutist France and other Christian powers in the late seventeenth and early eighteenth century all sides were arguing about 'perpetual peace'—but the meaning of such a project could be deciphered only once we knew who was speaking. No doubt there are reasonably stable vocabularies that address issues of international power in a legal idiom—just war, occupation, diplomatic immunity, *mare liberum*. But these words do not emerge from any coherent blueprint—they do not stand for any 'system and order' in the words of this collection. They are vessels that carry the most varied ideas. At least two further points challenge the assumption of a single tradition.

First is that such expressions articulate projects that are always already split against themselves. From the twelfth to the seventeenth century, the expression *jus gentium* has been associated both with immutable natural law rules that bind the princes and their states absolutely as well as with the customary practices that princes and their states have followed.[14] From early on, many jurists, including

[14] For the complexity of '*jus gentium*', see Peter Haggenmacher, *Grotius et la guerre juste* (1983), pp. 311–57; Annabel Brett, *Changes of State: Nature and the Limits of the City in Early Modern Natural Law* (2011), pp. 23–8, 75–89.

Grotius, separated two distinct types of *jus gentium*, one associated with natural law (*jus gentium primaevum*), the other with human (positive) law (*jus gentium secundarium*).[15] By choosing either understanding, it has been possible to support or critique the most varied types of policy. The complexity of the locution *jus gentium*, the difficulty to pin it down with any stable meaning has, in fact, been a frequently expressed concern of system-minded lawyers. But that concern may be misplaced. The very usefulness of that notion may lie in its interminable flexibility, its availability to argue whatever one needs to argue in view of one's academic project or client interest.

Although *jus gentium* cannot be said to stand for any definite political project, any power in itself, it is of course possible to trace the ways in which it has *actually* been used in particular situations—what interests has it supported, what has been invoked against? The same can be said about international legal naturalism of the 'classical' type. At only a few years' distance from each other, the Protestant refugee in England, Alberico Gentili and the Spanish Jesuit Francisco Suárez wrote about the law of nations in utterly different ways. Gentili forged a theory of the just war that opened a wide door for England to use pre-emptive force in support of the rebellion in Netherlands so as to combat possible intervention by Spain.[16] Composing his text in a scholar's chamber in Coimbra, Suárez suggested that the requirement imposed by James I on his Catholic subjects to swear an oath of allegiance was unlawful and justified the collective intervention of Christian princes. It is possible to see a tradition of peace and justice in the writings of both Gentili and Suárez. But this must be a tradition that is so open-ended as to be empty of substantive significance outside the specific context of sixteenth and early seventeenth century imperial-religious strife.

A number of new studies have sought to contextualize Grotius as a Dutch patriot, a moderate activist in the Protestant cause and a legal counsel to the Dutch East India Company (VOC). His legal writings become understandable once we situate them in the context of those projects—for instance his oscillation between support to the principles of *mare liberum* in respect to the Portuguese empire in the East Indies and monopoly trading rights with local rulers in his negotiations with the English.[17] This is not to point to anything dubious in his character but to show the very flexible nature of the law that enables jurists to defend contrasting positions in view of the interests of their clients—which is, of course, what jurists are professionally trained to do. Again, instead of there being a 'tradition of *mare liberum*' carried within international law, there has been a vocabulary that has allowed arguing both *mare liberum* and *mare clausum*. The best histories have demonstrated how lawyers

[15] Hugo Grotius, *Commentary on the Law of Prize and Booty*, ed. and with an Introduction by Martine Julia van Ittersum (2006 [1604–6]), *Prolegomena*, p. 45.

[16] Alberico Gentili, *De iure belli libri tres* (1933 [1612]), ch. XIV, pp. 61–6; Francieco Suárez, *Defensa de la fe catolica y apostolica contra los errores del anglicanismo* (1970 [1613]), ch. 23, pp. 333–40.

[17] See e.g. Arthur Weststejin, 'Love Alone is not Enough: Treaties in 17th Century Dutch Colonial Expansion', in Saliha Belmessous (ed.), *Empire by Treaty: Negotiating European Expansion 1600-1900* (2015), p. 35.

have argued those cases, and what it has been necessary to believe in order to think one or other argument as the more plausible one.

I am also thinking of Emer de Vattel's ingenious insertion of what he called 'voluntary law' between 'necessary' natural law and 'conventional law', the positive treaty law dependent on the will of the prince(s). When Vattel wrote that 'voluntary law' was natural law but not quite as immutable and powerful as 'necessary law' but not dependent on the changing will of the sovereign, either, he opened another way for lawyers to argue on the basis of will and a non-will related standard as situations might require: 'will' against binding rule and the other way around. Instead of a 'doctrine', what becomes visible is an argumentative move that tells much about law as technique but little of its substantive orientations.[18] Again, Vattel's natural law was not part of any substantive tradition of war or peace, statehood, or the international order. It was all of that at the same time, offering for later jurists an argumentative toolbox—a diplomatic casuistry, Ian Hunter has written—on which they could freely draw.[19]

But the second and more important point about the purported 'tradition' of *jus gentium, droit public de l'Europe*, law of nations, and our 'public' international law lies in the 'conflict of the faculties' that has always surrounded those notions and framed their field of applicability. For the early modern advocates of *jus gentium* it was clear that the way the world was organized, and how it should be governed was determined by theology. Early civil lawyers of the fourteenth century such as Bartolus of Saxoferrato or his student Baldus of Ubaldis, for example, were concerned over the rise of territorial *regna* across in northern Italy and the old Frankish realm. They saw this as an effect of the retreat of the empire and the re-emergence of an old *jus gentium* that had provided for the 'division of *dominia*' in the first place. And yet they were clear that however the novel situation was to be understood, deference was to be paid to canon law, the only really universal law, and that denying the emperor's status as '*dominus mundi*' would be heretical. To think of the history of *jus gentium* without reference to Aquinas' *Summa theologiae,* for example, would be impossible. To read it in abstraction of the concerns of conscience that inspired the *Summa* would be a sure way to missing its point. Why, for instance, did *jus gentium* exist both in the part that deals with 'law' and the part that deals with the virtue of 'justice'?[20] Because it was insufficient just to 'apply the law'; this must be done with the view to reaching a good outcome.

For the Spanish scholastics, Grotius and most natural lawyers until way into the eighteenth century, the Bible remained the highest legal source and Christian moral theology the most authoritative language for understanding the international world. As Grotius put the matter in the opening paragraph of *De jure praedae*: 'What God has shown to be His Will that is law.'[21] And yet we do not access

[18] Emer de Vattel, *The Law of Nations* (2008 [1758]), pp. 75–8.

[19] Ian Hunter, 'Law, War and Casuistry in Vattel's Ius Gentium', *Parergon* 28 (2011), 87–104.

[20] Compare Aquinas ST I-II Q 95A 4 (resp) and II-II Q 57 A 3 in R.W. Dyson (ed.), *Political Writings* (2007), pp. 135, 163–4.

[21] Grotius, *Commentary on the Law of Prize and Booty*, Ch II (19).

to Grotius' religious feelings and need to bear in mind that elsewhere he wrote of a natural reason operating at some distance from revelation. And then again during a short period between the end of the seventeenth and beginning of the eighteenth century,ambitious jurists at German enlightenment universities such as Halle and Göttingen used a basically secular natural law to consolidate the monarchies they served, before they transformed it into a technology of government that imagined itself as a Policy-science (*Polizeiwissenschaft*) and a *Staatskunst,* oriented towards empirical and comparative studies of the resources of rival states.[22]

From early eighteenth century onwards, the attention of rulers, diplomats, and jurists interested in international affairs has been on the discovery and application of the rules of statecraft that would enable the state to maintain and augment its power in relationship to its rivals. This was more specifically the ambition of men such as Gabriel Bonnot de Mably whose *Droit public de l'Europe* (1746, 1757) hoped to inaugurate a science of negotiations that would teach statesmen and diplomats to identify their 'real', long-term interests that would allow them to ignore their momentary passions and so devise policies advantageous to the nation as a whole. The 'public law of Europe' was indebted to a combination of the Machiavellian diplomatic tradition with the emerging science of political economy. The law of nations would be wise policy, and wise policy consisted of calculations of the resources available for the state and how either to maintain the balance of power or to tilt it in an advantageous direction.[23]

In Britain at the same time, the most ambitious natural lawyers, many of them from Scotland, were contemplating the principles through which what they would call commercial societies would prosper in an increasingly tough world of economic competition. A key part of their natural law was a conjectural history that saw all development, including legal development, directed through predetermined stages towards a society where free trade would lay the conditions for increasing welfare everywhere.[24] Although some of them subscribed to the idea of peace through commerce, others were not equally optimistic; intense debates were waged about the pros and cons of the possession of colonies and the conditions of colonial trade. It is no doubt symptomatic that having published his *Theory of Moral Sentiments* to great acclaim in 1759, Adam Smith declared that he would now produce a legal theory to match the psychological insights of his sentimental morality—but that once he moved to Glasgow to give the famous lectures of jurisprudence, the outcome was not a theory of *law* but of the *Wealth of Nations* (1776).

[22] Martti Koskenniemi, 'Transformations of Natural Law: Germany 1648-1815', in Anne Orford and Florian Hoffmann (eds.), *Oxford Handbook of International Legal Theory* (2016), pp. 59–81.

[23] See further, Martti Koskenniemi, 'The Public Law of Europe: Reflections on a French 18th Century Debate', in Helena Lindemann et al. (eds.), *Erzählungen vom Konstitutionalismus* (2012), pp. 43–73.

[24] See Adam Smith, *Lectures on Jurisprudence*, eds. R.L. Meek, D.D. Rahael, and P. Stein (1978), LJ(A), pp. 14–16 and the discussion in Peter Stein, *Legal Evolution: The Story of an Idea* (1980), pp. 23–50.

The variants of natural and public law that preoccupied European jurists in the eighteenth century did not survive to the nineteenth. The science of statecraft and the calculative approach to foreign policy soon gave impetus for the establishment of alternative vocabularies, namely those of political economy or 'diplomatic science'. Instead of jurists, it soon became clear that European rulers needed economists and experts in diplomacy—in due course of 'political science'—to counsel them on wise policy. Chairs of natural law at German universities were turned into chairs of policy-science, political economy or *Nationalökonomie*. What was left of 'natural law' became, not least under the powerful attacks waged by Immanuel Kant and the Kantians on the old 'Wolffian' natural law, 'legal philosophy', ostracized into the margins of the law faculty from where it would have no influence on policy whatsoever. It would be only towards the last third of the nineteenth century that activist liberal lawyers would resuscitate 'international law' as the platform of a meaningful engagement with policy-makers and diplomats.[25]

The world as we know it is not the product of a continuous tradition of 'international law' not least because there is *no such tradition*. I have above tried to show that the various legal vocabularies through which jurists have addressed the 'international' world are internally indeterminate and speak of things that we would not today call 'law' at all (virtue, faith, skilful management of state resources, diplomatic strategy, the creation of a international market for enterprising merchants, etc.). And even as 'law' does intervene in setting out the way in which resources in the world should be allocated and exchanged, and how international 'development' is to be conceived, this would not be 'public international law' as we now understand that expression but the 'private law' regulating the possession and transfer of property rights.

III

It was clear for the theologians and jurists contemplating the rise of the European states-system that the justification of the exercise of power therein would be a complex matter. At the beginning, everyone agreed, only God has power over humans. God was *Dominus* while humans were originally free and equal among themselves. However, according to both civil and canon law, and as elaborated in countless scholastic tracts on 'justice and law' from the thirteenth to the seventeenth centuries, humans would soon divide things between themselves, establishing territorial polities and proceeding from common to private property.[26] Alongside the power of the ruler as *dominium jurisdictionis*, there emerged the power of the owner as *dominium proprietatis*. As was clear for the late medieval and early

[25] Martti Koskenniemi, *The Gentle Civilizer of Nations: The Rise and Fall of International Law 1870-1960* (2001).

[26] For this narrative, see the still unsurpassed Marie-France Renoux-Zagamé, *Origines théologiques du concept moderne de propriété* (1987).

modern publicists contemplating these two forms of human power, much about the nature of the polity depended on how their relationship was conceived. Did the prince have the power to tax, or to expropriate the owner, and under what conditions?[27] Absolutism contained one set of answers to that question—but after the eighteenth century those answers were hardly plausible. With John Locke, Adam Smith, and the French Revolution, the view became predominant in Europe that private property was not only the most important of individual rights but that, properly conceived, it was also the most important element in the legal system of a prosperous—thus powerful—nation.

Historians of international law are keen to reflect, for example, on the views of the Spanish Dominican Francisco de Vitoria on the lawfulness of the Spanish conquest of the Indies in the sixteenth century. His famous *relectiones* raised issues of just war and the powers of dominion that became standard *topoi* of a whole literature moving freely between moral theology and law. Much less attention is given, however, to the massive discussion on the principles having to do with the expansion of commerce in Europe and beyond that was triggered by the import of silver from the American colonies. The most significant contribution, of the 'Salamanca school' was, arguably, the discussion of principles of property and contract that would fit the new commercially oriented world while still seeking to balance the requirements of this new morality (and law) with Christian ethics.[28]

The writings of the Salamancans on private law and commerce were accompanied by the consolidation in Europe of a *jus commune* that was inspired by civil and canon law and integrated to a greater or lesser extent the local laws of European provinces. The right of private property was a central aspect of that common law. In the seventeenth and eighteenth centuries writings on *lex mercatoria* brought to light the formation of a reasonably uniform set of rules to govern international trade on the basis of private property and contract. This did not take place through treaties between sovereigns. It emerged as a result of spontaneous developments more or less everywhere in Europe and the colonies in response to economic and commercial pressures. Governments debated the costs and benefits of monopolies and worried over their inability to control interests and currency rates in a way that made them increasingly vulnerable to the fluctuations of international commerce. One after another Western European states would carry out agricultural reforms leading to the privatization of common lands and drawing large populations into great manufacturing centres. By the eighteenth century, it was held evident that the power of a nation lies in the resources it has available to itself, this being a

[27] For a useful introduction, see Kenneth Pennigton, *The Prince and the Law, 1200-1600: Sovereignty and Rights in the Western Legal Tradition* (1993).

[28] I have argued this in 'International Law and Empire: The Real Spanish Contribution', *University of Toronto Law Journal* 61 (2011), 1–36. See now also Wim Decock, *Theologians and Contract Law: The Moral Transformation of the Ius Commune (c. 1500-1650)* (2013).

function of its positive trade balance: it needed to produce and sell more cheaply than its rivals.[29]

The massive codifications of civil law across Europe, the professionalization of law and legal education, the rise of constitutionalism, the heritage of the *jus commune*—all these offered a legal foundation for the 'European century' which, with all its conflicts and contradictions, ensured that 'civilization' and 'modernity' would equal what was going on in the continent and, increasingly, also the United States. The differences between civil and common law systems, between the laws of European north and south were real but nevertheless only variations of a common theme. That these laws would be applicable to Europeans also *outside* Europe would be guaranteed by complex extraterritoriality arrangements and, increasingly, by the direct subordination of non-European territory under European rule.

Of course, 'law' has been crucial in the production of European statehood and the welfare of its populations. It also played an important role in the expansion of European influence outside the continent and in the formation of the colonial relationship between Europeans and others. Some of that law has been articulated in terms of sovereign statehood, the principles of constitutionalism, good administration, and fundamental rights. A specific 'colonial law' also developed in the latter half of the nineteenth century. But most laws influencing the ways of international power consolidated the principles of private property and contract, the organization of the family, and the conditions of work (including slavery). A history that pays no attention to the latter cannot fulfil the ambition to illuminate law's involvement in how international power has been structured, supported, channelled, and opposed.

IV

A history motivated in the way suggested should give up exclusive focus on states, sovereignty, formal diplomacy, great questions of war and peace. No doubt, a state-centric view haunts the imagination of jurists preoccupied with the 'international'. This applies also to the post-colonial critics of empire. As long as focus is on states, matters of great importance are left out of sight. I wrote earlier that late medieval and early modern jurists were clear that human power is of two types—*dominium jurisdictionis* and *dominium proprietatis*, 'sovereignty' and 'property' for short. They were clear that property was about power between humans, namely the power to exclude others, and often terribly uncertain on how to justify this. Some of the earliest commentators regarded private property an effect of the sin of avarice. Others saw some benefit in the practice of buying and selling but stressed the dangers that doing this professionally posed for one's soul.[30] It is useful to note that much of these debates took

[29] See Istvan Hont, *Jealousy of Trade: International Competition and the Nation-State in Historical Perspective* (2005).

[30] See Janet Coleman, 'Propery and Poverty', in James H. Burns (ed.), *The Cambridge History of Medieval Political Thought c. 350-c. 145* (1988), pp. 607–48.

place under the assumption that private property was *jus gentium*—that is, it was an 'international' law though instead of being decreed by natural law but merely 'permitted' by it.[31]

In due course the idea emerged that property was justified by the labour that one had put into producing a thing—the 'workmanship model' of property that John Locke drew from the biblical creation narrative.[32] This was of course wholly insufficient for justifying the kinds of large properties that had come to accumulate for example through the activities of the Caroline Company of which Locke was one of the secretaries and a shareholder. The systems of banking and credit that upheld the process of accumulation—of great concern to contemporaries—find little space in standard international law histories. Nor is there much attention to how the company could have property rights on slaves that were working in the colony for its proprietors' benefit. Such property right was unquestionably valid under prevailing assumptions and extended throughout the North American colonies and the Caribbean as an immensely important aspect of legal power. And yet, that power largely escapes standard histories of international law. Worse, the concentration of many international legal histories on the process of *abolition* of slavery while staying silent on the *operation of slavery as an international legal system* is surely a massive distortion of the relations of law and power. About 12.5 million Africans embarked from Africa as slaves in 1501–1866.[33] How was the slave contract made with the African trader? What about the conditions of sale at the American end? That discussion of the American slave codes or the French *Code Noir* are no part of regular international legal histories is striking evidence of the narrowness with which 'international law' has been conceived and may perhaps explain some of the malaise of the perceived irrelevance of the field.

A standard work in the history of international legal ideas would mention Machiavelli and Hobbes but neither Antoine de Montchrétien nor Adam Smith.[34] Such a work would dwell extensively on the Spanish conquest of the Indies but say little about the carriage of silver from Potosi to Seville, and remain positively silent about its contribution to oiling the wheels of global commerce (to borrow an expression of François Braudel). Such a work would describe in detail Grotius' views about the just war but rarely mention that he regarded the Dutch East India Company as *both* a private company and representative of the United Provinces. It would make mention of Emer de Vattel's *Droit des gens* but not of the view of Christian Thomasius (and many other German eighteenth-century natural lawyers) that the *jus gentium* was neither law (*justum*) nor morality (*honestum*) but rules of diplomatic courtesy (*decorum*).[35] An international legal history would also rarely

[31] Brian Tierney, *Liberty and Law: The Idea of Permissive Natural Law, 1100-1800* (2014).

[32] James Tully, *A Discourse on Property: John Locke and His Adversaries* (1980), pp. 8–9, 35–45.

[33] Herbert S. Klein, *The Atlantic Slave Trade* (2nd edn, 2010), pp. 214–15.

[34] The paragraphs below follow my 'Expanding Histories of International Law', *American Journal of Legal History* 56 (2016), 104–12.

[35] Christian Thomasius, *Grundlehren des Natur- und Völkerrechts* (2003 [1709]) Book I, Ch. 5 § 70 and generally 65–81 (105–8).

include an analysis of the charters under which private companies and individual proprietors would rule Britain's thirteen colonies in North America. Nor would it pay much attention to the seventeenth-century uses of the vocabulary of *jus gentium* in Britain to uphold the royal prerogative against common law institutions.

A basic history of international law might treat the East India Company's rule over much of the Indian peninsula from 1757 as an aberration—while it was merely the most conspicuous case of basic forms of English and early French colonial expansion. And it would have nothing to say about the development and use of instruments such as the letter of credit and letter of exchange as they were transformed from facilitators of trade fairs into building blocks of a wholly global banking system by the end of the eighteenth century. Studies of *lex mercatoria* might make reference to a series of judgments by Lord Mansfield in the 1770s that gave legal effect to bills of exchange in violation of the common law doctrine of consideration.[36] But histories of international law have so far failed to notice that the autonomy international mercantile law, recognized in those judgments as *jus gentium*, would become a crucial instrument in the policy of 'jealousy of trade' that would be regarded as a key element of the eighteenth century European foreign policy. Virtually no attention has been given to the French efforts during the Seven Years' War (1756–1763) to codify a policy of 'balance of trade'—and objections by naturalists such as J. H. G. Justi according to which this would violate the 'natural freedom' of economic relations.[37]

In other words, while international legal histories have meticulously traced the legal trajectories of the foreign policy of states, they have paid much less attention—virtually no attention—to the private law relations that undergird and support state action that become visible only once analysis penetrates beyond what takes place in diplomatic chancelleries. The Spanish maintained a formidable imperial presence in the Indies, striving to rule its provinces directly through viceroys and royal *cedulas* issued through the Council of the Indies. However, in reality, the *encomenderos* governed the provinces quite independently from the centre, and royal legislation was frequently left unimplemented. The government lacked funds needed to set up an effective government over the territories. Borrowing from an international banking system where interest rates could not be domestically manipulated resulted in a series of bankruptcies that sometimes paralyzed the central government. Now the legal operations carried out with the help of new financial instruments arguably overweighed in importance any formal legislation. The fact was not lost on Spanish jurists themselves, whose treatises on commerce or monetary policy have often been seen as the first in-depth treatments of a global financial system.[38] And yet, neither the new practices nor their articulation in the legal works of Martin de Azpilcueta or Diego de Covarrubias have been given much attention in the histories of international law. The works of the theologian Vitoria on the Indies and on just war have of

[36] Pillans v. Van Mierop, 5 Geo B.R. 1663, 1669 (1765).

[37] Johann H.G. Justi, *Die Chimäre des Gleichgewichts der Handlung und Schiffahrt* (1759).

[38] See e.g. Tomás de Mercado, *Suma de tratos y contratos* (1975 [1553]).

course been examined in great detail—unlike his extensive commentaries on the rights of property and contract that sought to drive a compromise between the orthodox Aristotelian–Thomist suspicion of mercantile culture and the realities of an expanding commercial system.[39]

International lawyers have been interested in the vicissitudes of sovereignty. Even when their interest has been inspired by a critical attitude, they have not given up the view that sovereignty is the concept around which legal histories, and hence their criticisms, should revolve. They have therefore focused on the emergence of independent 'states' and the extent of the sovereign rights states have claimed vis-à-vis each other. They have traced the forms of diplomatic interaction and concentrated on war and treaty-making as privileged instances of international authority. They have set aside any wider interest in the relations of contract and property that support state policies, the development of instruments for long-distance trade and finance that make not only trade but also the actions of the sovereign in the 'international' space possible. As a consequence they have, with few exceptions, largely failed to notice the great shift in the seventeenth and eighteenth centuries that accounted for the 'jealousy of trade' becoming a principal aspect of the struggle of international power and a standard of measurement of alternative policies.[40] While histories of international law feel at home discussing proposals for perpetual peace by theologians or philosophers such as the Abbé de Saint-Pierre or Immanuel Kant, not much attention has been given to parallel ideas among writers in 'political economy' such as Giovanni Botero or Charles Davenant.

Of course there are exceptions and deviations from the pattern. Some have focused attention to the role of *private* international law in addressing 'some of the biggest problems the law faces today [including] the character of sovereignty [and] the nature of legitimacy in situations of political conflict'.[41] Collective works on international legal history sometimes include essays on *lex mercatoria* or state debts. Moreover, recent works in private international law have sometimes read the relevant materials through the lenses of international politics or the organization of global trade.[42] But owing to the often intransgressible boundary between public and private law, these have been scarce. The prejudice that public law has to do with matters by their nature 'political', while private law deals with non-political and 'only technical' matters, is strong. Trade law straddles the private–public boundary, but so far little has been done towards producing credible, non-teleological histories of economic law (that is to say, histories that would not start with Adam Smith or look towards free trade as the inevitable product of a

[39] See further my 'The Political Theology of Trade Law: the Scholastic Contribution', in Ulrich Fastenrath et al. (eds.), *From Bilateralism to Community Interest: Essays in Honour of Judge Bruno Simma* (2011), pp. 90–112.

[40] On this theme, see Istvan Hont, *Jealousy of Trade: International Competition and the Nation-State in Historical Perspective* (2005).

[41] Karen Knop, Ralf Michaels, and Annelise Riles, 'Foreword' to 'Transdiclipinary Conflict of Laws', *Law & Contemp. Prob.* 71 (2008), 16.

[42] Alex Mills, *The Confluence of Public and Private International Law* (2009).

progressive history), especially from the perspective of reading economic decision-making within a state from the perspective of its overall political strategy.[43]

Not much historical work has been undertaken to examine the role of property regimes for constitutional law or international policy.[44] There is of course a huge amount of writing on 'mercantilism' (although it is now orthodox to doubt the appropriateness of that word to describe the myriad of economic writings that appeared in Europe between the late sixteenth and late eighteenth centuries), but that scholarship rarely examines the legal instruments or institutions that govern trade policy. The relevant literature at the time made much of the role merchants played in enhancing the power of the state. Malynes, for example, insisted in 1629 that 'of the six members of all the governments of monarchies and common-weales, [the merchants] are the principal instruments to increase or decrease the wealth thereof'.[45] Even as they often discussed about the pros and cons of trade agreements, there is little international law commentary on them.

V

The way we think about the history of international law is part of the 'system and order' we see in the international world. It directs and limits our scope of vision and determines what, for us, seems important and unimportant, what items are worthy of study and what may be left aside, perhaps for others to develop or study. In this chapter I have suggested that in case the ambition of international legal history is to grasp the role of law in supporting, channelling, and opposing power, then it is insufficient to focus on public law and the interactions of formal states. Attention should be directed to the ways in which the international order as a whole has been structured so as to distribute spiritual and material values in the world. In what ways does it help to produce and reproduce the conditions of living that exist in different parts of the world? Very often the answers to such questions are not immediately visible on the surface of things. In that case, attention must be directed to the *background rules* that choose among different actors those who will be authoritative, picks from the facts of social behaviour those that are 'relevant', and singles out from the mass of events and occurrences in the world those that qualify as 'legal problems' worthy of the time and energy of international lawyers. In studying past law it would be important to penetrate the surface of the legal '*parole*' so as to make visible the 'system and order' that conditions the production of legal thought and practice. Among those background rules is the distinction between sovereignty and

[43] An important opening in the Anglophone world in this respect is Thomas Poole, *Reason of State: Law, Prerogative and Empire* (2015).

[44] An interesting exception is Olivier Beaud, 'Constitution, Ownership and Human Rights', in Kelly L. Grotke and Markus J. Prutsch (eds.), *Constitutionalism, Legitimacy and Power: Nineteenth-Century Experiences* (2014), pp. 127–38 (largely denying that 'capitalist' property rights greatly influenced the French constitution).

[45] Gerard Malynes, *Consuetodo vel lex mercatoria, or The Antient Law-Merchant* (1629), p. 62.

property, or 'public law' and 'private law'. This suggests that relations between public power and citizens on the one hand and between private subjects on the other are somehow very different. This assumption plays a hugely important role in structuring the way lawyers but also other people think about the world. It makes us believe that the power embedded in legislation is wholly different from the power expressed in contract; it suggests that it would be a mistake to equate debates in a national parliament to those at a shareholder meeting of a large company; it labels certain transactions as 'corruption' while regarding other as merely 'marketing'. Overall, it suggests that there is a realm of distribution that should be called 'politics' while another ought to be understood as 'the economy' and that very different accountability rules ought to be applied to them.

The production of such distinctions is a feat of what could be called the *legal imagination* and at its best, the history of international law could illuminate how that imagination has worked it the past—how, for example, it has produced and keeps reproducing the distinction of the 'public' and the 'private', including (public) international law and the (private) moves of property and contract across the world. By showing how such a distinction has emerged, by historicizing it, it may be possible to think of it as just a contingent aspect of our world, something to be reflected on its merits. If it is not a historical 'necessity', then why should we have it? What does it *do* in the world, and to us? The work of disenchantment might be further enhanced if it were possible to show that the distinction is actually much more unstable than we think, that in fact, the two—public and private—depend and rely on each other in a myriad of ways. Such a history of international law could demonstrate, for example, that behind every sovereign, there is some set of relations of property that help to sustain it, provide it with resources and determine its direction. Or conversely, it could be shown that every significant property relies on state power and state institutions, from legislation to military force, that provide the conditions where it may thrive. If the separation of the two—public and private, sovereignty and property—is merely a contingent and unstable aspect of the law, then it would be natural to examine its consequences by reference to alternative ways to think about how power might be organized. At the outset of this chapter, I noted the tremendous intensification of global inequality. Might that in some way be the outcome of the distinction? If it is, and if the inequality itself is something lawyers should deal with, perhaps the resources of the *legal imagination* that once produced that distinction could be enlisted to throw a critical eye on it. Perhaps it could be possible to think differently about the institutional choices through which law affects the distribution of resources in the world. Perhaps, for example, we could learn to think of operations in the 'private realm' as equally 'political' as those in the public realm. Perhaps there is no great difference between being coerced by the police and by a labour contract. Perhaps it is possible to see both virtuous behaviour and Mafioso arrangements across the board.

If the history of international law has the ambition to become a history of how law has enabled, channelled, and opposed international power, then it should not be confined by settled distinctions but take the formation of those distinctions as its object, and enquire into their consequences. This necessitates focusing from express discourses to the background rules and assumptions, and demonstrating both their contingency and their empirical effects. This may require setting aside some conventional truths about how law operates in its relationship with power. And it would require some imagination. Fortunately, this is a resource to which past lawyers possess no monopoly.

19

State Theory, State Order, State System—Jus Gentium and the Constitution of Public Power

Nehal Bhuta

The historicity of international law as a system and an order is, in many ways, the historicity of the state, its concept, and its theory. In this chapter I argue that how we theorize the state carries with it strong consequences for how we 'see' the state and how we 'do' the state.[1] It also necessarily carries implications for whatever kind of political and legal order we understand to lie 'beyond' or 'between' state orders and for the sinews that bind them together.

Since at least the seventeenth century, as recognizably modern states came to 'occupy Europe and lay siege to an entire world,'[2] various state concepts have been constitutive organizing ideas for law and legitimacy in international society. Claims concerning the rightful and proper internal ordering of states and the constitution of state power (*jus publicum, droit politique*),[3] have consistently stood in *some kind* of relationship to claims about the constitution of international law, rightful membership in international society, and the meaning and nature of sovereignty in international order.[4] Rightful membership in international society after 1815 was understood as resting upon the proper constitution and composition of individual states,[5] not the least because internal ordering was considered directly related

[1] On 'seeing' the state and 'doing' the state, see: Joel Migdal and Klaus Schlichte, 'Rethinking the State', in Klaus Schlichte (ed.), *The Dynamics of States: The Formation and Crises of State Domination* (2005), pp. 1–23.

[2] Richard Tuck, *Philosophy and Government 1572-1651* (1993), pp. 91–4.

[3] Martin Loughlin, *Foundations of Public Law* (2010), pp. 40–4.

[4] See in particular the concise and subtle account by Andrew Hurrell, *On Global Order: Power, Values, and the Constitution of International Society* (2008). Hurrell observes, for example, that the difference between pluralism and solidarism as contemporary (ideal-typical) visions of global order implies profoundly different visions of the state. In the case of solidarism, 'the relationship between different understandings of what is meant by the term "state"... become far more consequential for international law and for the practices of international society: the state as the embodiment of a nation or people; the state as a territorially bounded polity; the state as an organizational unit, administering society, and extracting resources from it.' (ibid. at p. 66). See also ibid. pp. 114–17, noting that descriptively and normatively, the rise of complex governance beyond the state 'involve[s] a very different view of the state ... [giving] ontological primacy to individuals and groups within the state: what states are and how they act is based on the character of state-society relations.'

[5] Ian Clark, *Legitimacy in International Society* (2005).

to an expectation of *rightful conduct* in respect of other states. The relationship between (internal) 'right ordering' and (external) 'rightful conduct' was perhaps most clearly expressed in the nineteenth-century concept of the standard of civilization. Uncivilized political societies, whose internal ordering (for racial, religious, or historical reasons) did not correspond to the legal and ethical principles characteristic of civilized societies, did not qualify for plenary membership of the family of states nor for complete sovereign rights, because they were constitutionally incapable of reciprocating the lawful conduct of full members of international society.[6] Ian Clark notes from a contemporary standpoint that 'many of the key issues that exercised policy makers since the 1990s—such as humanitarian intervention, democracy promotion ... post-conflict reconstruction, [rogue states] and regime change—are all at base symptomatic'[7] of a shifting conception of rightful membership; that is, of legitimate statehood. The closely related claims about 'revolutions in sovereignty' are 'actually about the proper form and function of the state, which hitherto have been expressed through the medium of doctrines of sovereignty.'[8]

Every concept of sovereignty, it would seem, presupposes a concept of the state, and every state concept achieves determinacy within a state theory.

In the first part of this chapter I develop this contention by arguing that state concepts and state theories are performative: they partially constitute the object that they describe, and become means through which the state order is justified, materialized, and indeed organized. As such, state theory and state concept are indispensable to any actually existing state order, and have strong determinative consequences for the intellectual construction of international law as a legal order and system of relations between and across state orders. In the second and third parts of this chapter, I try to demonstrate the organizing force of state concepts on the conceptualization of the nature of the order of international law, and also the way in which *jus naturae et jus gentium* became essential to the theorization and reproduction of the distinctive kind of public power we associate with the modern state concept.

I. State Theory and State Concept

As a historically determinate theoretical phenomenon, 'state theory' refers to a family of mostly German theoretical and political writings from the nineteenth century: *Staatslehre* or *Staatsrechtslehre* (State Theory or State Law Theory).[9] The central problematic of this theoretical constellation was how to characterize the

[6] Jennifer Pitts, 'Boundaries of Victorian International Law', in Duncan Bell (ed.), *Victorian Visions of Global Order - Empire and International Relations in Nineteenth Century Political Thought* (2007), pp. 67–88.

[7] Clark, *Legitimacy in International Society*, p. 160 (n. 5). [8] Ibid.

[9] Michael Stolleis, *Public Law in Germany, 1800-1914* (2001). Duncan Kelly, *The State of the Political: Conceptions of Politics and the State in the Thought of Max Weber, Carl Schmitt and Franz Neumann* (2003).

fundamental nature of the state and how to theorize the sources of state power and authority. A closely related—perhaps even generative—question, concerned the source of the political order embodied in the state, and whether that order was productive of or parasitic upon legal order. The problem of how to identify the bearer of sovereignty within the state, which preoccupied German constitutional law after 1815, was a problem endowed by the various princes' decision to grant constitutions to their territories, seemingly binding themselves to a law and state structure that originated in their own will and in the absence of any successful revolutions in German territories. The resulting dualism of prince and people—somewhat reminiscent of the Middle Ages' dispute concerning the 'holder' of sovereign power—was sought to be resolved through theories of state and state law.

The theoretical answers given to such questions as 'what is the nature of the state?' and 'who is the bearer of the sovereignty of the state?' ranged from an idea of the state as an organism or person (Bluntschli), to Gierke's emphasis on Germanic *Genossenschaft* as the true source of national law's binding qualities, to Stahl's attribution of state personality to the real person of the monarch.[10] The *theoretical* answers generally had significant *practical* consequences: at stake in such conceptual contestations over the state and its essence was the real conflict between contending political forces organized around the poles of ruler sovereignty (monarchical government) and popular sovereignty (parliamentarism), as well as the consequences of the social transformation that characterized nineteenth-century Germany—the dissolution of the traditional authority of estate-based orders, the social emancipation of the individuals, and the free movement and ownership of capital.[11]

The intellectual ferment over state theory was thus a ferment over the intellectual foundations of the modern state and the basis upon which its sovereign power was generated, authorized, and wielded. As such, it was intimately connected with arguments about the nature of public law and of public authority as exercised through and under law.[12] Where one stood on such state-theoretical questions carried strong implications for what kind of domestic *and* supranational legal and political orders were conceivable and considered realizable. Thus, in state theory treatises of the second half of the nineteenth century, international law appears as a subdivision of state theory,[13] while in the D'Alembert

[10] For an overview of these theories, see Kelly, *The State of the Political* (n. 9) and also Ernst-Wolfgang Böckenforde, *State, Society and Liberty: Studies in Political Theory and Constitutional Law*, trans. J.A. Underwood (1991), chs. 1–4.

[11] Böckenforde, *State, Society and Liberty*, pp. 82–3 (n 10). Comparably, Laborde notes that a renewed interest in state theory in early-twentieth century France reflected a 'deep sense of crisis' that stemmed from the increased demands placed on the state in the form of social and economic intervention, and challenges to its political legitimacy from the left and the right. This turn to state theory led to 'new conceptual problematics which . . . focused on the relation between the social fabric and political authority'. Cécile Laborde, 'Pluralism, Syndicalism and Corporatism: Léon Duguit and the Crisis of the State (1900–1925)', *History of European Ideas* 22(3) (1996), 227–44, 224.

[12] Martin Loughlin, 'In Defence of Staatslehre', *Der Staat*, 48(1) (2009), 1–27. Duncan Kelly, 'Egon Zweig and the Intellectual History of Constituent Power', in Kelly L. Grotke and Markus J. Prutsch (eds.), *Constitutionalism, Legitimacy, and Power* (2014), pp. 332–50.

[13] See e.g. Johann Caspar Bluntschli, *The Theory of the State* (1885), pp. 13–15.

and Diderot's *Encyclopédie, droit des gens* is described as one of two branches of public law.[14]

To argue about the state and its essential nature (or lack of it) is to make claims about the foundations of its coercive authority; it is also to make an argument about law's authority as it relates to these foundations. If we step back from the historical context of *Staatslehre* and its disputations, we might recognize that the types of questions and problematiques that characterized 'state theory' as a specific theoretical tradition continue to preoccupy us today. There is undoubtedly a pervasive sense that we inhabit, and reflect upon, a world in which state-centred thinking and *staatliche* concepts have lost purchase, and in which fundamental legal-political categories and vocabularies appear to have been decisively untethered from the concrete historical circumstances that gave birth to them (democracy, the rule of law, constitutionalism, administrative law, solidarity, public authority, to name a few). But despite—or perhaps, precisely because of, the ever-louder exhortation to think ourselves 'beyond the state', we are also living through a period in which some of the animating questions of state theory are being disinterred, re-examined and renovated. The statist (or, *staatliche*) presuppositions of our inherited political and legal vocabularies are being subjected to profound scrutiny, whether with a view to demonstrating their severability from plausible theoretical accounts of concepts such as democracy and constitutional order, or, in order to underline the deep conceptual puzzles generated by attempting to coherently articulate a concept like 'global law'.[15]

But another global field of intellectual and practical endeavour has also brought essential questions of state theory to the fore: state-building. Beginning in the last years of the Cold War, international organizations, coalitions of sovereign states, and non-government organizations have engaged in lengthy and intensive attempts to re-found durable and effective political orders in the aftermath of civil conflict or foreign intervention, usually under the auspices of United Nations-mandated peacemaking and peacekeeping initiatives,[16] and more dramatically after foreign interventions (Kosovo, Iraq). The result is a new techno-practical discourse of state-ness, in which the state is understood as (partly or predominantly) a *technical achievement*, amenable to a variety of programmes of intentional institutional design, therapeutic political techniques (such as transitional justice) and expert

[14] Denis Diderot and Jean d'Alembert (eds.), *L'Encyclopédie ou Dictionnaire Raisonné Des Sciences Des Arts et des metiers*, 5 vol. (1969) [1751]. Robert Morrissey and Glenn Roe (eds.), *University of Chicago: ARTFL Encyclopédie Project* (Spring 2016 edn), available at <http://artflsrv02.uchicago.edu/cgi-bin/extras/encpageturn.pl?V5/ENC_5-127.jpeg>.

[15] For recent examples: Hans Lindahl, *Fault Lines of Globalization: Legal Order and the Politics of A-Legality* (2013). See also Neil Walker, *Intimations of Global Law* (2015). Alexander Somek, *The Cosmopolitan Constitution* (2014).

[16] For the vast literature see, Roland Paris, *At War's End: Building Peace after Civil Conflict* (2004). Simon Chesterman, *You, the People: The United Nations, Transitional Administration, and State-Building* (2005). Gregory H. Fox, *Humanitarian Occupation* (2008). Lise Morjé Howard, *UN Peacekeeping in Civil Wars* (2007). Roland Paris and Timothy D. Sisk (eds.), *The Dilemmas of Statebuilding: Confronting the Contradictions of Postwar Peace Operations* (2009). Francis Fukuyama, *State-Building: Governance and World Order in the 21st Century* (2004).

knowledge claims about how to generate 'state strength' and combat 'state weakness'.[17] The seemingly obvious relationship[18] between weak states and the threat of transnational non-state terrorism has accelerated and deepened this tendency, with a strong interest in being able to claim to understand the 'drivers' of state-fragility in order better to intervene so as to contain them and the security risks they intimate. This technical-functional terminology of state-ness has even started to penetrate the categories of international law governing state sovereignty, with an accelerating willingness to accept the idea that weak states of a certain kind (those 'unable or unwilling' to control non-state terrorist groups on their territory) may be subject to the lawful use of military force against them, through tactics such as drone strikes.[19]

In both its theoretical and technical registers, our contemporary reflection on the state returns us to such questions as: what is a state? How is a state founded? How does it vindicate its claim rightfully to coerce a population and control the territory? How are political, social, and economic power generated and concentrated into an apparatus of government? What is the relationship between legal norms (and normativity generally) and factual power of the kind that the state must both generate and rest upon?

The activity of answering questions such as these in relation to a phenomenon such as 'the state' can reasonably called 'theory', but it is a kind of theorizing not easily amenable to clear-cut distinctions between Is and Ought, Fact and Value, or the Descriptive and the Normative. At the time of its emergence as a distinct and distinguishable term towards the end of the sixteenth century,[20] 'the state' was at once a descriptive and prescriptive concept articulated and argued for in order to represent a contemporary reality in a way that 'help[ed] particular people understand and define, and thus begin to deal with, certain problems.'[21] A state-concept is at once a theory-dependent notion, and a reality-shaping theoretical instrument, as Geuss elucidates:

In interesting cases, like 'the state,' introducing the 'concept' requires one to get people not merely to use a certain word, but also to entertain a certain kind of theory, which has a strong 'normative' component. You don't 'have' the concept of the state unless you have the

[17] See, inter alia, James Dobbins and others, *The Beginner's Guide to Nation-Building* (2007). See also the vast synthesis of these kinds of arguments achieved by the World Bank's World Development Report of 2011: World Bank, *Conflict, Security and Development* (2011). For a reading of this discourse, see Nehal Bhuta, 'Against State-Building', *Constellations* 15 (2008), 517–42; Nehal Bhuta, 'Governmentalizing Sovereignty: Indexes of State Fragility and the Calculability of Political Order', in Kevin Davis, Angelina Fisher, Benedict Kingsbury, and Sally Engle Merry (eds.), *Governance by Indicators: Global Power Through Quantification and Rankings* (2012).

[18] In fact, the relationship is not self-evident once one starts to try to identify the attributes of the concept of state weakness and relate it to specific security risks: see Stewart Patrick, 'Weak States and Global Threats: Fact or Fiction?', *The Washington Quarterly*, 29(2) (2006), 27–53; Edward Newman, 'Weak States, State Failure, and Terrorism', *Terrorism and Political Violence* 19(4) (2007), 463–88.

[19] See the dispassionate but generally supportive argument of Theresa Reinold, *State Weakness, Irregular Warfare, and the Right to Self-Defense Post-9/11* (2011). See also Christian J. Tams, 'The Use of Force against Terrorists', *European Journal of International Law* 20(2) (2009), 359–97.

[20] Quentin Skinner, 'A Genealogy of the Modern State', *Proceedings of the British Academy* (2008), pp. 325–70.

[21] Raymond Geuss, *Philosophy and Real Politics* (2008), pp. 43–4.

idea of a freestanding form of *authority*. And the idea of authority requires some appeal to notions like 'ought' or 'should.'... Characteristically, the concept 'the state' is introduced *together with* a theory about the nature and source of the authority which the abstract entity so named is supposed to have. In the early modern period this was usually some version of the social contract theory. Of course, once the state actually gets established as a distinct and massive social reality that cannot be ignored, one can come to reflect that the purported sources of its 'authority' are deficient ... When they were introduced, concepts like 'the state' did not exactly mirror any fully pre-existing reality, because using these concepts represented as much an aspiration as a description. It is also the case that merely *using* the concepts did not *by itself*, without the assistance of real social forces that actually act in history, bring any state into existence; neither concepts nor theories realize themselves. Nevertheless inventing this new concept, in this case by transforming the meaning of existing terms such as *status/estat/stato*, could be an important contribution to clarifying an obscure situation and to guiding action directed at institutional change. Having the 'concept' (... including the various theory-fragments that were associated with it) meant that one saw certain problems clearly ..., and it also meant that one had a solution, or at any rate a suggestion for a solution that one could try to put to work...[22]

Geuss observes that one of the consequences of a (successful) conceptual innovation such as the concept of 'the state' is that 'when such innovations work, they imprint themselves upon the world ... Conceptual innovation ... is a complicated process in which descriptive, analytic, normative, and aspirational elements are intricately intertwined.... Conceptual innovations often "stick", escape our control and become part of reality itself. [Once invented,] the idea of the "state" can come into contact with real social forces with unforeseeable results. The "tool" develops a life of its own, and can become an inextricable part of the fabric of life itself.'[23]

Theoretical claims about what the state is, how it is formed, stabilized, and justified, do not only describe, they also (where successful) generate schemata of interpretation that orient action, spur attempts to realize certain designs, and underwrite certain kinds of abstentions or interventions.[24] To theorize the state at certain junctures and in the crucible of certain great epochal shifts, is to engage in an effort to interpret *and* change the world by endeavouring to shift the schemata of intelligibility and reference that orient thought, judgment, and action. Foucault captures pellucidly this movement between the 'conceptual' and the 'real' in the European state theories of the early seventeenth century:

It would be absurd to say that the set of institutions we call the state date from this period of 1580 to 1650 ... After all, big armies had already emerged ... Taxation was established before this, and justice even earlier.... But what is important ... and what is at any rate a

[22] Ibid., pp. 44–6. [23] Ibid., pp. 47–9.

[24] Unsurprisingly, Skinner maintains a similar view about how theorization is—in the right context—a form of action: 'Our concepts form part of what we bring to the world in our efforts to make sense of it. The shifting conceptualizations to which this process gives rise constitute the very stuff of ideological debate ... Koselleck and I both assume that we need to treat our normative concepts less as statements about the world than as tools and weapons of ideological debate.' Quentin Skinner, 'Retrospect: Studying Rhetoric and Conceptual Change', in *Visions of Politics* (2002), pp. 176–7.

real, specific, and incompressible historical phenomenon is the moment this something, the state, really *entered into reflected practice*.[25] . . . What is a king? What is a sovereign? What is a magistrate? What is a constituted body? What is a law? What is a territory? . . . All these things began to be thought of as elements of the state. The state is therefore a schema of intelligibility for a whole set of already established institutions, a whole set of given realities . . . *The state is therefore the principle of intelligibility of what is, but equally of what must be; one understands what the state is in order to be more successful in making it exist in reality*.[26]

A state theory is (or, under the right conditions of felicity,[27] at least could be) 'performative'. A performative utterance, in Austin's famous definition, is one which does (performs) the act or is a constitutive part of the action, rather than one which describes an action (constative) or demands or exhorts it.[28] The 'conditions of felicity' for even a simple performative utterance (such as naming a ship) to be complete are demanding.[29] But the concept of performativity has been extended in recent social theory to attempt to grasp the ways in which theoretical action (concepts, models, causal claims, normative contentions) can not only have empirical effects by becoming a reason for action, but also become a constitutive part of the world that they diagnose and describe. In this sense of performative, theories or models 'contribute toward enacting the realities they describe'.[30] The modalities of theoretical performativity could be numerous.[31] A model or theory posits a world, in order to gain purchase upon a reality that (at least in the first instance) confronts it. The action of theorizing takes an ambiguous and obscure reality and endeavours to articulate it as a connected order of facts, concepts and so forth. Articulation implies description but exceeds it, bringing new properties into being by composing elements and stabilizing compositions and relations between composites.[32] If the composition 'catches on' and becomes assimilated into thought, argument, or as a rule informing practice and judgment, the theoretical action (conceptual innovation, in Geuss's terms) has described reality but also transformed it. The path to such a 'catching on' may be surprising and indirect, and will always be the result of

[25] Michel Foucault, *Security, Territory, Population*, Michel Senellart, François Ewald, and Alessandro Fontana (eds.), (2009), p. 247.

[26] Ibid., pp. 286–7 (n. 25).

[27] Pierre Bourdieu, *Language and Symbolic Power*, John Thompson (ed.), trans. Gino Raymond and Matthew Adamson (7th edn, 1999), p. 73, for a gloss on John L. Austin, *How to Do Things with Words: Second Edition*, James O. Urmson and Marina Sbisà (eds.) (1975), p. 8, pp. 14–15.

[28] e.g. 'By the power invested in me by the state of New York, I pronounce you husband and wife.' This is a performative utterance that marries a man and a woman, it does not describe (Jane and John got married) or exhort (Jane and John should really get married). Austin, *How to Do Things with Words*, p. 6 (n. 27).

[29] Austin, *How to Do Things with Words*, p. 23 (n. 27).

[30] Michel Callon, 'What Does It Mean to Say That Economics Is Performative?', in Donald A. Mackenzie, Fabian Muniesa, and Lucia Siu (eds.), *Do Economists Make Markets? On the Performativity of Economics* (2007), p. 315.

[31] See Donald Mackenzie, 'Is Economics Performative? Option Theory and the Construction of Derivatives Markets', *Journal of the History of Economic Thought* 28(1) (2006), 29–55.

[32] Emmanuel Didier, 'Do Statistics Perform the Economy?', in Donald A. MacKenzie, Fabian Muniesa, and Lucia Siu (eds.), *Do Economists Make Markets?: On the Performativity of Economics* (2007), pp. 305–6.

the human and technological mediators acting in contexts. For example, conceiving of human agency as a rational faculty equivalent to a relationship of dominium over property—as the late Scholastics did—was not an ex nihilo theoretical innovation.[33] But it was an arduous recomposition of Thomist and Dominican thought that paved the way for a transformational new theory of state power—a theoretical innovation indispensable to the architecture of legal order (natural and civil) more generally. Such a theory of human agency became the presupposition for a theory of public power and of legal obligation, that was *concretely enacted and contested* through real actions—as assertions of authority, defenses of right, and above all through violence and coercion within and between human communities.

It is important to note here that to contend that state theories are performative does not imply that theories are magical words, acting on reality merely by articulating it. Neither concepts nor theories realize themselves, no matter how brilliant and comprehensive.[34] Rather it is to maintain that under contingent but determinate historical conditions which we can at least partially grasp, (some) state concepts and state theories become constitutive of how we enact the state and, in the last instance, how we (attempt to) create, authorize, maintain, and reinforce (or disqualify) political orders. To reiterate Foucault's summation in his lectures on *Security, Territory, Population*, 'one understands what the state is in order to be more successful in making it exist in reality'.

II. External State Law's Ontology of Stateness

It is perhaps a cliché of the twentieth century historiography of international law to decry its statist orientation, its reification of state-will, and its understanding of the order of international law as constituted through the free will of its privileged subject, the state. As Jouannet demonstrates, such a characterization of international law as a system of states, or an 'anarchical society' of self-contained state orders bound together solely through contractual or consensual ties, takes shape not contemporaneous with the Treaties of Westphalia, but in the last decade of the eighteenth century and first two decades of the nineteenth century—in particular after the Congress of Vienna.[35]

[33] See, with the most subtlety, Annabel S. Brett, *Changes of State: Nature and the Limits of the City in Early Modern Natural Law* (2011), ch. 2.

[34] Skinner, 'A Genealogy of the Modern State', pp. 348–54 (n. 20). Skinner observes that Hobbes' theoretical genius was to provide clear and decisive arguments for overturning previous state theories which conceived of the state as *either* inhering in the body of the people or in the person of the monarch, and proposing instead the state as an artificial person and persona ficta that stood distinct from the actual multitude and the person of the ruler. But this had 'little immediate impact on English political debate' (p. 348), being adopted more quickly in Germany by Pufendorf and in Switzerland by Vattel before being embraced in English political thought in the mid-eighteenth century.

[35] Emmanuelle Jouannet, *The Liberal-Welfarist Law of Nations: A History of International Law*, trans. Christopher Sutcliffe (2012), ch. 10.

The 'truly foundational status'[36] acquired by the notion of the will of the state in the nineteenth century presupposed a plurality of autonomous state orders that held legal and political supremacy over a particular population and territory, and which were internally constituted in a manner which refracted these historical, spatial, and geographic particularities of a people (nation) and place (territory).[37] As much as such a vision of order appeared to rest only upon formal legal bonds expressly agreed between a diversity of free-standing state orders, each with their distinctive political, religious, and economic institutions—i.e. a plurality of demoi and ethoi—it simultaneously presupposed a substantive and thickly prescriptive state-concept as a condition of possibility for membership in the 'family' of sovereign states endowed with the capacity for such juridical relationships. The status of a state as both legal and moral subject rested upon a strong ontology of the sources of its unity, boundedness, and agency—as a nation, a bearer of a culture, and a participant (or potential participant) in a universal civilization that included a high degree of commonality in the legal and political foundations of the state and its internal organization.[38]

With such an ontology, the law of nations became a regionally-derived law of civilizational membership bound to a philosophy of history and state-theory rooted in eighteenth and nineteenth century Europe and its concepts of law, property, public power, and private right.[39] Interference in the 'interior' or 'reserved domain' of states corresponding to *this* (spatially-delimited) cohort of political and legal orders was strictly prohibited and the absoluteness of their rights as states consecrated. But political orders that did not bear the hallmarks of such state-ness were not equally protected from intervention and indeed were not bearers of the plenary rights held by civilized states. Those political orders—such as late Qing China and late Tokugawa Japan—that found themselves demoted to bearers of partial and limited state-ness within a universal legal order of hierarchical inequality, reacted in part by seeking to appropriate and reproduce within their territories the very state-concepts and techniques of state science that were identified with full membership in the order of sovereign states.[40]

[36] Jouannet, *The Liberal-Welfarist Law of Nations*, p. 119 (n. 35).

[37] See e.g. the chapters concerning Hegel and Fichte in this volume.

[38] See Carl Schmitt, *The Nomos of the Earth in the International Law of the Jus Publicum Europaeum* (2006), pp. 185–209. Allen W. Wood (ed.), *Hegel: Elements of the Philosophy of Right* (1991), § 339: 'The European nations form a family with respect to the universal principle of their legislation, customs, and culture.'

[39] See, rather iconically, James Lorimer, *The Institutes of the Law of Nations; a Treatise of the Jural Relations of Separate Political Communities* (1883), Vol 1, pp. 93–113. But similar conclusions can be drawn from any leading nineteenth-century international law treatise. See the various sources discussed in Jouannet, *The Liberal-Welfarist Law of Nations,* ch. 11 (n. 35).

[40] Tong Lam, 'Policing the Imperial Nation: Sovereignty, International Law, and the Civilizing Mission in Late Qing China', *Comparative Studies in Society and History* 52(4) (2010), 881–908. Lam writes (887) of the establishment of a national police force (including a mandatory curriculum on the law of nations) in 1901:

The boundary condition for international law as a system of right *inter gentes* was not anarchy (a global disorder of self-contained orders) but the reification of a specific set of historical conditions (the three-centuries long emergence of the European state through religious civil war, absolutist monarchy, and national revolution) into a performative ideal of stateness. Under this ideal of stateness, the order of nineteenth century international law was liberal in as much as states are understood as *particular individual wills* relating to one another as independent entities and each pursuing their particular welfare.[41] *Outside* this spatial–civilizational zone of liberal relations, the order of international law was asymmetrical and conditional. Other political and legal orders were not nullities, nor were they immediately subordinated to civilized states. Rather, they enjoyed at best only conditional reciprocity and existed within a zone of surveillance and incipient tutelage, potentially requiring intervention in order to ensure the universal norms and conduct demanded by states conforming to this ideal type.[42] The order of international law was an association of states conducting themselves liberally inter se, and licensing the exercise of their coercive authority over other, 'un-state', political and legal orders in a manner similar to a community regulating its minors or its deviants. A key aspect of this nineteenth century state-concept—the idea of the state as an independent and individual will, unlimited in its freedom except through the will of other states or its self-imposed legal obligations—would persist well into the twentieth century, even as the underpinnings of nineteenth century state theory died a slow and turbulent death under assault from within (the critique of the metaphysical theory of the state)[43] and without (Japan's rise to civilized power status and the emergence of anti-colonial movements).[44] In a dialectical irony that Hegel would not have failed to notice, the true universalization of sovereign statehood in the mid-twentieth century would be the result of the insistence by colonized and subjugated peoples to their own status as nations with particular, concrete existences, that are equally entitled to absolute respect for their independence and internal affairs.

> [I]n order to defend its territorial rights the Qing had to display certain competencies in governing its population within a bounded territory using the latest political technologies. . . . [T]hese new technologies were employed as more than just a performance of modernity; they also enabled the state to reconceptualize and remake its people by transforming them from imperial subjects into national citizens, as was required by the proposed constitutional state. The preoccupation with these two concerns became the underlying impetus for the formation of the Qing's national police, coordinated by the central government using a statewide standard.

[41] Here the formulation is taken from Allen Wood (ed.), *Hegel: Elements of the Philosophy of Right*, §§ 336–40 (n. 38). At § 337, Hegel captures the logic of such an inter-state order concisely: 'The immediate existence of the state as the ethical substance, i.e. its right, is directly embodied not in abstract but in concrete existence and only this concrete existence, rather than any universal thoughts which are held to be moral commandments, can be the principle of its action and behaviour.'

[42] See e.g. Davide Rodogno, *Against Massacre: Humanitarian Interventions in the Ottoman Empire, 1815-1914* (2015), pp. 49–62.

[43] See e.g. Leonard T. Hobhouse, *The Metaphysical Theory of the State: A Criticism* (1918). See also, David Runciman, *Pluralism and the Personality of the State* (Rev edn, 2005), chs. 6–9.

[44] See Jörg Fisch, *The Right of Self-Determination of Peoples: The Domestication of an Illusion*, trans. Anita Mage (2015), ch. 12.

III. Early Modern Jus Gentium's Constitution of Public Power

But as Jouannet has trenchantly contended, this nineteenth century topos of international law as external state law belied its descent from an earlier architecture of legal norms, in which the ontology of state was not yet so self-confidently (and self-servingly) aligned with a stable, idealized, European model of legal and political order.[45] Early modern jus gentium was reconstructed not so much as the handmaiden of the emergent society of states, but as its mid-wife, articulating a juridical foundation for the *constitution* of the state and public power that did not itself derive from the state legal order, but from a natural legal order that was at once immanent and transcendent.[46] The early modern law of nature and of nations (*c.* 1500 – *c.* 1700) was an intellectual outgrowth of a period in which order—natural and civil, moral and political—was both an urgent practical problem and a profound intellectual challenge. At the heart of the intellectual problem was precisely the relationship between a natural order of reason, liberty and right, and a civil order of human artifice that supervenes natural liberty and authorizes coercion in the name of civil power and authority.

It is trite, but worth repeating, that the three-hundred year gestation and birth of the modern state form (*c.* 1300–*c.* 1600) had as both pre-cursor and by-product, the destruction of the medieval political and legal order. More immediately, the urgent crises confronting European political actors and European political thought in the seventeenth century were crises of political and social order and of political and social authority, haunted by severe crises in the inherited frameworks for knowledge and judgment. From our sociologically disenchanted present, the extraordinary consecutive impacts of renaissance, reformation, counter-reformation, and the ensuing 100 years of religious and civil war, on the horizon of late medieval thought and action can only be partially grasped. Late medieval Europe was of course far from static, and indeed had already been deeply punctuated since 1300 by the periodic and bitter conflicts that raged between Emperor and Papacy,[47] and between universal authorities and the emerging territorially organized kingdoms and city-states.[48] The recovery and revival of Roman law as an instrument of rule and means of centralizing authority against the vestigial particularities of feudal order, the flourishing of urban commercial centres and expansion of trade, and innovation in military organization from the fourteenth century, all generated sources of destabilization and new modes of social and political organization.[49]

45 Jouannet, *The Liberal-Welfarist Law of Nations*, chs. 2 and 7 (n. 35).

46 John N. Figgis, *Political Thought: From Gerson to Grotius 1414-1625, Seven Studies* (1960).

47 See e.g. Quentin Skinner, *The Foundations of Modern Political Thought, Vol. 2: The Age of Reformation* (1978), pp. 1–40. See also, Figgis, *Political Thought*, p. 8 (n. 46). Figgis notes that 'the substitution of civil for eccelesiastical power can be traced to the claims of the civil power in the controversies of the eleventh and the twelfth centuries.'

48 Figgis, *Political Thought*, Lectures I–IV (n. 46); Joseph Canning, *Ideas of Power in the Late Middle Ages, 1296-1417* (2014).

49 Marc Bloch and Geoffrey Koziol, *Feudal Society* (2014). Harald Kleinschmidt, *Understanding the Middle Ages: The Transformation of Ideas and Attitudes in the Medieval World* (2008). Jimmy H. Burns (ed.), *The Cambridge History of Medieval Political Thought c.350-c.1450* (1991).

Nonetheless, despite considerable conflict and disputation, late medieval society, 'still thought of itself as one society [. . .] [This sense of unity] eludes precise and satisfactory statement [. . .] but [. . .] a belief in the actual unity of Christendom, however variously felt and expressed, was a fundamental condition of all medieval political thought and activity.'[50] Mattingly points out that while the res publica Christiana never amounted to a functioning legal or political administration, it achieved 'something like a common body of law'[51] through the long and far-from coordinated labour of jurists trained in the universities of Paris, Bologna, Orleans, or Naples, and working assiduously in the service of the Church, the Empire, or one of the nascent territorial Kingdoms. Canon law, civil law, and custom, but above all a common legalism born of a society 'by nature universalist and founded on spiritual things',[52] led 'men to think of themselves as living in one society under the rule of a common law'.[53] The public law of Christendom may have been interminably contested in its sources and interpretation, with the canonist maintaining that jus naturale and jus gentium derived from moral rules implanted by God in the hearts of mankind, and the civilian looking to those Roman law rules considered reflective of the common reason and common consent of a universal human community of nations. But the divisions belied the extent to which the high Middle Ages witnessed the emergence of a deep and rich common language of political thought occurring through the medium of legal science—a jus commune: 'civilians and canonists built up a rational differentiated jurisprudence which constituted a characteristic way of looking at the world, . . . a "true philosophy" (vera philosophia) whose priests they were.'[54]

It is commonly remarked that the medieval view of law presupposed an ontological derivation of valid legal obligation from a divinely established order of being: 'central to the mentality of the medieval layman was the identification of existing positive law with the divine order'.[55] The legacy of Thomist thought's attempted synthesis of revelation (scripture), reason (Aristotelian philosophy), and legal rules (civilian and canon law), was to validate human reason as a means of identifying and deriving binding obligation. Reason partook *in the order of being* and thus provided an innate, God-given means of understanding the consecrated order maintained by eternal and divine law. Natural law could be rationally reconstructed through the medium of reason, but the ground of its validity was not its rationality, rather its status as a partial emanation of the divine order.[56] Law commands

[50] Garrett Mattingly, *Renaissance Diplomacy* (2009), p. 16.

[51] Mattingly, *Renaissance Diplomacy*, p. 18 (n. 50). See also Joseph Canning, *A History of Medieval Political Thought: 300-1450* (2nd edn, 2005), pp. 65–6, pp. 114–18.

[52] Marc Bloch and Geoffrey Koziol, *Feudal Society* (2014), p. 80.

[53] Mattingly, *Renaissance Diplomacy* (2009), p. 23 (n. 50).

[54] Canning, *A History of Medieval Political Thought*, p. 114 (n. 51). Peter Stein, *Roman Law in European History* (1999), pp. 65–6. Stein describes how 'Roman civil law became, together with canon law and theology, part of a common Christian learned culture shared by those who occupy positions of authority.'

[55] Otto Brunner, *Land and Lordship: Structures of Governance in Medieval Austria*, trans. by Howard Kaminsky and James Van Horn Melton (1992), p. 117.

[56] Merio Scattola, 'Models in the History of Natural Law', *Ius Commune - Zeitschrift für Europaïsche Rechtsgeschicte* 28 (2001), 91–159, at 108. Thomas Aquinas, *The Summa Theologica of St. Thomas*

rightly because it is a measure of reason, and reason commands rightly because it is a measure of a natural order that binds us objectively as derived immediately from divine and eternal order.[57] Law is in reason alone, as Aquinas would put it, but in the medieval order reason 'cannot be its own light; in order to perform its work it needs a higher source of illumination . . . "Nisi credideritis, non intelligetis." '[58]

The political order and its law were bound to the eternal order by natural law; civil authority was a derivative of the authority of natural law, discerned by reason. As one might imagine, great uncertainty remained as to what natural law required, leaving much room to argue about the extent and nature of duties of obedience and sources of right. Local customary law, canon law, civil law, and feudal contracts could each, in the right hands and under the right conditions, vie to be an emanation of some natural legal obligation—or, indeed, be demoted as mere human artifice subject to a higher law. Hence, the presumptive completeness and objectivity of the orders of divine, eternal and natural law, were not falsified by the fact of human conflict over their meaning—the finitude of human understanding implied that only partial knowledge of the totality was concretely possible and disagreement inevitable.[59] Indeed, by extension, no human, political, and legal order could ever be absolute, as there persisted alongside and above the laws of a political community an 'independent set of rules, eternal and independent of the will of the king, and [which] can be used as a standard to measure the rightness of justice of a government'.[60] Law issued from the will of the ruler, but where the will of the ruler did not comport with reason, it was not law but sin and might *in extremis* be disobeyed.[61] The 'lawful state' of the medieval political order did not readily admit open revolt against a ruler;[62] after all, the status quo—to the extent that it was an order at all—demanded obedience as reflecting the eternal authority of a higher order of law, and divine law prohibited disobedience and sedition. But the possibility of

Aquinas, trans. Fathers of the English Dominican Provinc (1981), 1.2, q.90.I: 'Law is a certain rule and measure . . . First, as in that which measures and rules, and since this is a characteristic of reason, in this way law is in reason alone . . . Reason has its power of moving from the will . . . but in order that the will has the reason of law in those things that it commands, it is necessary that it be informed by some reason.'

[57] Aquinas, *The Summa Theologica of St. Thomas Aquinas*, pp. 114–18 (n. 56).

[58] Scattola, 'Models in the History of Natural Law', p. 95 (n. 56).

[59] Ernst Cassirer, *The Myth of the State* (1961), p. 107: 'Medieval philosophy could easily account for all the inherent and necessary defects of the social order . . . The *corpus morale et politicum* was at the same time a *corpus mysticum*. In spite of the differences and opposition between its parts there was, as Thomas Aquinas said, an *ordinatio ad unum* and the different and conflicting forces were directed to a common end. This *principum unitatis* was never forgotten. The totality of mankind appeared as a single state founded and monarchically governed by God himself and every partial unity, ecclesiastic or secular, derived its right from this primeval unity.'

[60] Scattola, 'Models in the History of Natural Law', p. 110 (n. 56). Cassirer, *The Myth of the State*, p. 104 (n. 59): 'It follows that no political power can ever be absolute. It is always bound to the laws of justice. These laws are irrevocable and inviolable because they express the divine order itself, the will of the supreme law giver.'

[61] Carl Joachim Friedrich, *The Philosophy of Law in Historical Perspective* (2nd edn, 1963), pp. 42f.

[62] Canning, *A History of Medieval Political Thought*, p. 130 (n. 51).

resistance in the name of a superior order of right could not be excluded, and indeed was intermittently confirmed as a caution to rulers.[63]

It is at the denouement of the century-long collapse of this lawful ontology of political order and civil obligation, that we ought to situate the specificity of early modern jus gentium and jus naturale discourses. A recognizably modern theory of sovereignty—sovereign power as *summa potestas* and *plenitudo potestatis* and markedly distinguished by *non-dependence* (perfection, self-sufficiency) on the authority of universal powers—begins to emerge, although even in Bodin the strong legacy of the medieval 'lawful' state theory is visible through his cautious attitude towards the maintenance of fundamental norms of the ancient constitution.[64] With the advent of the reformation, the germ of resistance theory inhering in the Thomistic system of thought flowered into bitter religious civil wars in France, the Low Countries, and the Holy Roman Empire and communal confessional violence, with rights of resistance invoked by both confessions to oppose rulers whose sectarian affiliation was understood to threaten the very salvation of the communities they ruled. Rivalries between territorial rulers supplemented and fuelled confessional conflict and enlarged the conflict across Northern Europe and into Italy.[65] While the Thirty Years War (1618–1648) is commonly identified as window of epochal transition, medieval Europe's sense of unity had been gravely and irrevocably damaged by a confessionalization that began in 1521 and only intensified after the 1555 Peace of Augsburg.[66]

The beginnings of the uncoupling of theology from political thought had preceded the reformation by perhaps one century,[67] but it is within the same two decades as Luther's apocryphal nailing of his ninety-five theses to the church door in Wittenburg, that the first use of reason of state (*ragione degli Stati*) appears in Guicciardini's *Del reggimento di Firenze* to describe the distinctive expedient measures (*poco cristiana e poco umana*) that may be validly and prudently relied upon to preserve a political regime against its enemies; Machiavelli's *The Prince* was of course already in circulation, with its advice to Princes on the arts and techniques by which they can maintain their *stato*.[68] Political order was no longer—as it so clearly was in Dante's *De Monarchia*—a partial expression of an eternal order of being, an *ordinatio ad unum* with a common presupposition of faith and authority. Various attempts to revive the ideal of universal monarchy as an actually-existing

[63] See e.g. John of Salisbury, *John of Salisbury: Policraticus*, ed. Cary J. Nederman (1990).

[64] See Daniel Lee, '"Office Is a Thing Borrowed" Jean Bodin on Offices and Seigneurial Government', *Political Theory* 41(3) (2013), 409–40.

[65] Ronald G. Asch, *The Thirty Years War: The Holy Roman Empire and Europe, 1618-48* (1997), ch. 1.

[66] See Stephen Toulmin, *Cosmopolis: The Hidden Agenda of Modernity* (1992).

[67] Maurizio Viroli, *From Politics to Reason of State: The Acquisition and Transformation of the Language of Politics 1250-1600* (2005). Skinner, *The Foundations of Modern Political Thought*, Vol. 2, Part II (n. 47).

[68] *Stato* here means the power structure of a political order or a dominant regime. See, Nicolai Rubinstein, 'Notes on the Word Stato in Florence before Machiavelli', in J.G. Rowe and W.H. Stockdale (eds.), *Florilegium Historiale: Essays Presented to Wallace K. Ferguson* (1971), pp. 313–26. See also the contribution by Roth-Isigkeit in this volume.

unified order of justice and law (such as Botero's *Ragione di Stato* or Campanella's *Aformisi Politici*) were short-lived, declining rapidly after the final defeat of Spanish ambitions to maintain its rule in the Low Countries in 1609.

The sources of power and authority in a legal-political order could no longer be directly extra-mundane, and certainly not naturally ordered in any ontological way. Rather, in a discernably modern manner, the foundation of political order becomes widely theorized as in some manner *immanent* to the specific human society generating that order, and equally immanent and this-worldly are the ultimate ends of such order: security, civil peace, prosperity.

Paradoxically, the religious and political theory of the Lutheran reformation would only accelerate this process, transferring to the civil power most of the prerogatives claimed by the Church in order to advance to 'destruction of the Church and its hold on an extraterritorial public opinion'.[69] The Church as *congregatio fidelium* in Lutheran doctrine, was ruled solely by Christ, whose powers were entirely spiritual. The Godly Prince ruled in order to keep civil peace between sinful men, and to protect and maintain his subjects in peace and plenty so that they can achieve the destiny ordained for each of them by God.[70] The unity of the civil order was in this sense perfect, rendering the *persona ficta* of the Church an association entirely subordinate to the complete authority of the sovereign power. In this way,

> Luther dealt the *civitas dei* of the Middle Ages a death blow. He gave to the territorial magnates the last thing they needed to make their power into an autocracy, and to rule out all effective interference from above ... The [protestant] Church helped maintain and vivify the principle of territorialization as in Protestant countries it was a national organization ... The supremacy of the common law of the land over everyone within its borders, including the Clergy, triumphed universally with the Reformation ... [71]

Of course, the exact mechanism of the immanent generation of order varied widely across streams of political thought, and in its most sophisticated forms (such as the mid-sixteenth century Dominican and Jesuit thought), the foundation of civil order began in a theory of human agency that took divinely-given natural law and legalistically conceived natural right, as the modular building blocks for the awesome edifice of sovereign power.[72] But the relationship between the order of nature and natural law, and the political and legal order of the human civitas, could no longer be the hierarchical one conceived of by high medieval Thomism; consistent with the dissolution of a strong and substantive homology of order between the divine, natural and human, the function of nature and natural law as a warrant for the authority of civil order becomes a

[69] Figgis, *Political Thought*, p. 45 (n. 46). Skinner, *The Foundations of Modern Political Thought*, Vol 2, pp. 14–19 (n. 47).

[70] Skinner, *The Foundations of Modern Political Thought*, pp. 14–15 (n. 47).

[71] Figgis, *Political Thought*, pp. 49–50 (n. 46).

[72] Brett, *Changes of State*, p. 62 (n. 33): 'The construction of human beings as free coincides with the construction of the subject of law. Government by law works by commanding choice, and it demands a subject capable of choice.'

problem to be solved rather than a solution to the problem of authority. As Brett summarizes:

Common to all the different types of what is considered 'civil philosophy' in this period . . . [is the key question of] how to construct a unity out of the natural plurality and diversity of individuals [and protect it from dissolution.] . . . Nature and natural law, seen as a set of substantive rules of action which form an unchanging baseline of moral rectitude, generate precisely the threat to the legal autonomy or integrity of the city that civil philosophy strove to avoid.[73]

By the sixteenth century, natural law and natural right were no longer an emanation of divine law but were either established by an act of divine will (the voluntarist thesis of natural law as *commanded* by God but discerned and interpreted by human reason) or a set of rules immanent in the (divinely created) order of nature—including human nature—to be identified and applied as fundamental norms of human co-existence in any kind of society. On either kind of argument, the state (*civitas* or *societa perfecta*) was a more perfect order of human relations because of its achievement of a supreme unity, enabling it to realize imperative conditions of human flourishing, such as peace, security and justice under civil law.[74] The unity of religion and religious law in Europe was no longer possible. At best, after the Peace of Augsburg, religious unity within a territorial entity might have been achieved by expulsion or massacre of the religious minority, but within a generation the French *Politiques* would recognize that even unity in religion could be sacrificed to preserve the unity of the state.

Jus naturale and jus gentium provided a fertile, even inexhaustible, reservoir of arguments and authorities for the sixteenth-century re-articulation of public power as constituted through comprehensive unity of a political community, or as in some way inherent in the very nature of such an order.[75] The profoundly legalistic ethos that was a legacy of both feudalism and the medieval revival of Roman law as a source of authority, made legal argument indispensable to the justification of political rule:[76] argument from the mere fact of political power or from an abstract theory of the state was not unknown but nonetheless remained scandalous until well into the seventeenth century,[77] implying as it did a foundation for law and politics derived exclusively from *utilitas* and human will. But the concept of public

[73] Annabel Brett, 'Natural Right and Civil Community: The Civil Philosophy of Hugo Grotius', *The Historical Journal* 45(1) (2002), 31–51.

[74] See e.g. Hugo Grotius, *Commentary on the Law of Prize and Booty*, ed. Martine Julia van Ittersum (2006), pp. 34–47. Grotius's position is very close to Suarez's, indicating the relative insignificance (by the end of the sixteenth century at least) of the sectarian identity of the theorist on this matter.

[75] Or as Gierke puts it in, Otto Gierke, *Natural Law and the Theory of Society 1500-1800*, trans. Ernest Barker, (1957), p. 35: 'The Natural Law Theory of the State . . . served as a pioneer in preparing the transformation of human life. It forged intellectual arms for the struggle of new social forces; it disseminated ideas which, long before they even approached realization, found admittance into the thought of influential circles and became, in that way, the objects of practical effect.'

[76] Gierke, *Natural Law and the Theory of Society*, p. 36 (n 75); Figgis, *Political Thought*, pp. 99–100 (n. 46).

[77] See e.g. the reception of Hobbes: Jon Parkin, *Taming the Leviathan: The Reception of the Political and Religious Ideas of Thomas Hobbes in England 1640-1700* (2007).

power which we still readily associate with the modern state—a reservoir of public right which is indivisible and supreme in relation to any other kind of right and unified in one person or organ—[78] rests upon the transformation of ideas of private (or individual) legal right into means of generating an abstract and homogeneous ideal of public power. Distinctive to this post-medieval conception of public power was its quality as comprehensive and plenary. In contrast to the medieval notion of sovereignty as a *priority* of right or power of final decision in respect of a specific relationship,[79] the early modern concept of sovereignty came to 'denote the relationship of the state to everything within itself . . . From the quality of being simply the highest authority, there is deduced the whole of that absolute omnipotence which the modern state demands for itself.'[80]

But neither theology nor historical lineage could provide adequate warrant for such an awesome power over men and things, for this conception of public power insisted that all other corpora and collegia (the Church, the estates) derived their existence and legal rights only mediately from the public power of the state, the only true *societas perfecta*.[81] Both this theory of the state, *and its actualization*, implied an epoch-making destruction and reabsorption of feudal right, urban liberties, and *ständisch* privilege. The natural individual, outside civil society and the commonwealth, has by virtue of natural law the right of disposition over his own will ('equivalent to ownership over property')[82] and can establish authority over himself and others through pacts creating a unified and permanent body that wields *summum potestas*.

> Political authority was the product of a fusion of *so many individual authorities*, whether total or limited on certain points. Community was an aggregate, a mere union of the wills and powers . . .
>
> . . . The only legal method of bringing community into existence was the free act of individual wills.[83]

The abstract, purified natural individual—acting in order to defend and expand essential common objects such as peace, security and the possibility of mundane justice—unites his will with others through a contract which establishes a common power authorized to suborn the will of any individual member in pursuit of the purposes for which the commonwealth was formed. Depending on the theorist,

[78] Dieter Grimm, *Sovereignty: The Origin and Future of a Political and Legal Concept* (2015), p. 32.

[79] Grimm, *Sovereignty*, pp. 14, 17 (n. 78).

[80] Gierke, *Natural Law and the Theory of Society*, p. 41 (n. 75).

[81] Gierke, *Natural Law and the Theory of Society*, p. 69 (n. 75). Althusius's account is of course a contemporary counterpoint to this tendency, but it assumes the organic and durable unity of associations that come together to form consociations of associations at a larger scale. As such, it is indebted to a certain spirit of the medieval world. See Gierke, *Natural Law and the Theory of Society*, pp. 51–2 (n. 75), complaining that Althusius was never able to make a 'personified popular community into a real state personality which served as the active effective bearer of the will of the Commonwealth'.

[82] Grotius, *Commentary on the Law of Prize and Booty*, p. 34 (n. 74), citing Vázquez, although this understanding of dominium over will as the basis of human agency and subjective right is widely argued in different ways from 1500. See Brett, 'Natural Right and Civil Community', chs. 3–4 (n. 73).

[83] Gierke, *Natural Law and the Theory of Society*, pp. 106–7 (n. 75).

the limits of the state's power would be found either in the specific contracts of association and rulership establishing sovereign power (Grotius),[84] or in the fundamental *raison d'être* of such an association ('reason of state') established by natural law (Pufendorf and Suarez, in different ways),[85] or through a final and irrevocable alienation of any decision over such purposes to the sovereign himself (Hobbes, Spinoza, Rousseau).[86] Irrespective of any particular author's position within this topos of argumentation, what can be said to unite modern natural law (and its derivation, jus gentium)[87] is its

close connection to the idea of the state as an exercise of sovereignty . . . On the one hand, an important part of the natural law was intended to explain the origin and the existence of every commonwealth; and on the other hand, sovereignty was regarded as the basic condition for enforcing natural rules.[88]

An implication of this skeptical and post-skeptical argument for the foundations of political and legal order is an almost anthropological and historicist attitude to discerning the modalities by which commonwealths can be created, across history and across civilizations. The attempt to reduce the foundations of human political communities to the striving to realize the essential objects of human co-existence and human well-being, as well as the effort to assert non-sectarian origins for binding legal obligations, generated a relatively thin ontology of stateness. The formal model of the transfer of authority from individuals in a state of nature to sovereign power, was not dependent on a prior ratification of the civilizational capacity of natural man—all humans presumptively held such a juridical capacity, in as much as they possessed natural reason, and the important question was whether historical and contemporary evidence demonstrated the existence of legal and political order that could be attributed to an underlying pact (and, if one wished to intervene on behalf of a people against their sovereign, one ought to know the terms of that pact to ensure that one is acting in support of a bona fide legal right inhering in the people). It should be observed immediately that this historicist and ontologically relatively thin understanding of the foundations of state power and sovereign power, was not per se incompatible with aggressive and ultimately imperial violence

[84] See the contribution by Kadelbach in this volume.

[85] On Jesuit reason of state thinking see: Harro Hopfl, 'Orthodoxy and Reason of State', *History of Political Thought* 23(2) (2002), 211–37. On Pufendorf and Suárez, see the contributions by Fiorillo and Schaffner in this volume.

[86] See the contributions by Heller and Altwicker in this volume.

[87] In the classical division between Gaius and Ulpian, jus gentium is understood either as part of natural law (and thus as part of natural reason), or as a body of human customary law applicable directly between members of different *gentes* not otherwise governing directly by civil law—and thus standing alongside the jus naturale. The division would become highly controversial in Christian Europe, because of the priority accorded to natural law obligations (emanating from divine law) over laws originating only in human custom; to the extent that the latter were not derived from or licensed by natural law, they may be either invalid or subject to non-enforcement when confronted with a natural legal obligation.

[88] Scattola, 'Models in the History of Natural Law', p. 99 (n. 56). See also Chris Thornhill, 'Natural Law, State Formation and the Foundations of Social Theory', *Journal of Classical Sociology* 13(2) (2013), 197–221.

by European states against non-European states.[89] Indeed, the presumption of a universal juridical legal order derived from jus naturale rules—rooted as a practical matter in Roman law—that could be directly enforced by sovereigns against each other, or even by individuals in a state of nature (such as the high seas) against other public powers, licensed much warfare and land appropriation against non-European political communities. But what is perhaps noteworthy for our purposes is that this violence did not require a general claim of civilizational superiority through which non-European legal and political orders were disqualified from being public powers at all.[90]

The rules of natural law and jus gentium, as applied directly to the commonwealth acting as an individual vis-a-vis other natural or fictive persons in a state of nature, would thus provide the juridical framework for the regulation of relations beyond the *civitas*. In this, as Figgis notes, jus naturae et jus gentium became simultaneously 'the foundations of both international law and modern politics', and a 'residuum which the medieval world passed on to its successor'.[91] The perplexity of this legacy for the modern state concept is that it at once consecrated and underwrote the idealization *and* materialization of the state—with its legal omnipotence and unity and destruction of all competing universal powers—even as it bound the state concept to some substantive purpose: the common good, peace, security, a legal order of justice. The distinction between utility (*utilitas*) and *honestum*, so essential to the division between the temporal and sacred ends of human existence in Christian thought, could be maintained only by asserting a higher unity of *humanitas* that establishes a natural legal and social bond between commonwealths—a *societas gentium* in which the original unity of the human community survived in the form of the juridical order of natural law. But the judgment of utility remained in the hands of each sovereign power, a conclusion driven by the very theory of natural right that underpinned the argument for the necessity and rightness of the state. Differentiating between the state as a means to the common good, and the state as an end in itself, challenged even the casuistic and argumentative brilliance of Grotius: the good of the individual depends in the last instance on the prosperity and safety of the common good, private interest must yield to public interest; and the common good is interpreted as the good of the unit, as determined by the bearer of sovereign power.[92] The substance accorded to purpose of the state within this state-concept is ultimately that which conduces to the flourishing of the

[89] See Hugo Grotius, *The Rights of War and Peace*, ed. Richard Tuck (2005); Martti Koskenniemi, 'Empire and International Law: The Real Spanish Contribution', *University of Toronto Law Journal* 61(1) (2011), 1–36; Martti Koskenniemi, 'International Law and the Emergence of Mercantile Capitalism: Grotius to Smith', in Pierre-Marie Dupuy and Vincent Chetail (eds.), *The Roots of International Law / Les Fondements Du Droit International* (2013), pp. 1–37; Anthony Pagden, *The Burdens of Empire: 1539 to the Present* (2015).

[90] Jouannet records instances where the concept of 'civilization' is doubted as a foundation for the application of the jus gentium by late seventeenth century writers: Jouannet, *The Liberal-Welfarist Law of Nations*, pp. 88–9 (n. 35).

[91] Figgis, *Political Thought*, p. 141 (n. 46).

[92] See Grotius, *Commentary on the Law of Prize and Booty*, pp. 34–41 (n. 74).

state and its population, concretized only in and through the historical development of the state, its population and its economy. Over the seventeenth century the universal principles of jus naturae et jus gentium are invoked increasingly as part of the science of the state, as rules ordering *both* relations *inter gentes and* prescribing modes of governing populations and territories as *gutepolizei*.[93] In its internal dimension, the law of nations and of nature becomes an instrument of state- and nation-building, licensing the further intensification and concentration of state power for the purposes of creating and maintaining a legal, political, and economic order that enhances the welfare of the prince, territory and people.[94]

IV. Conclusion

By the time we reach the end of the eighteenth century, we are but a short conceptual distance from the characterization of the modern state as the first and last ground of political and ethical value, and the understanding of the authority of the state as unconditional and as a final reservoir for the state's capacity to create and preserve legal and political order. The very success of state-building in Europe would tend to destroy any possibility of maintaining a distinction between *utilitas* and *honestum* in the idea of the common good to which the concept of the state was bound. It would also finally banish the residual idea of a universal legal unity of humanity, and create the conditions for modern nationalism.[95] The law of nature and the law of nations would pass into the external public law of states, in no small part due to the consolidation of the modern form of state power that early modern jus naturale had done so much to help construct.

[93] See e.g. Keith Tribe, *Governing Economy: The Reformation of German Economic Discourse, 1750-1840* (1988), chs. 1–5.

[94] See the chapters on Wolff and Vattel in this volume, which discuss the expressly mercantilist dimensions of their treatises on the law of nations.

[95] As Oakeshott points out, it is state-building that ultimately created the conditions for modern ideals of nationhood: the prince's pastoral power authorized deeper administration of social life by sovereign power, and paved the way for the insinuation of sovereign authority into all aspects of the *bildung* of a population. The result was the possibility of generating a 'sentiment of solidarity' and the endowment of 'some semblance of substantive unity' among a territorial peoples through the promotion of linguistic, cultural, or religious homogeneity, 'or, in the parlance of later times, to make them a "nation"'. Michael Oakeshott, 'On the Character of the Modern European State', in *On Human Conduct* (1991), p. 279.

20

Spatial Perceptions, Juridical Practices, and Early International Legal Thought around 1500

From Tordesillas to Saragossa

Thomas Duve

I. Cartographic and Spatial Revolutions and International Legal Thought around 1500

In many accounts of the history of international law, European developments around 1500 are considered pivotal for the formation of international legal thought. Wilhelm Grewe dates the beginning of the European state system and international law to 1494 and according to Randall Lesaffer, the years around 1500 brought about a change in the conceptualization and implementation of war, which in turn significantly expanded the scope of the legal doctrine. Similarly, editors of this volume regard Niccolò Machiavelli as one of the first authors to have put forth the idea, as early as in the first decades of the sixteenth century, that international legal thought be translated into positive law between European states.[1]

At the same time, the decades around 1500—the era of 'proto' or early modern globalization—also hold particular historical significance for having witnessed the emergence of the first global cultural and political systems in tandem with, and in

[1] Wilhelm G. Grewe, *The Epochs of International Law* (trans. and rev. by Michael Byers, 2000), p. 13; Randall Lesaffer, 'Peace Treaties and the Formation of International Law', in Bardo Fassbender and Anne Peters (eds.), *The Oxford Handbook of the History of International Law* (2012), pp. 71–94, at p. 76. On the history of international law around 1500 especially regarding the Iberian empires see also: Randall Lesaffer, 'Charles V, Monarchia Universalis and the Law of Nations (1515-1530)', *Tijdschrift voor Rechtsgeschiedenis = The Legal History Review* 71(1–2) (2003) 79–124; Alfred P. Rubin, 'International Law in the age of Columbus', *Netherlands International Law Review* 39 (1992) 5–35; Jörg Fisch, *Die europäische Expansion und das Völkerrecht. Die Auseinandersetzungen um den Status der überseeischen Gebiete vom 15. Jh. bis zur Gegenwart* (1984). On the beginnings of what he calls an 'Indian system of international law' for the Americas see Ricardo Zorraquín Becú, 'El Sistema Internacional Indiano', in Ricardo Zorraquín Becú (ed.), *Estudios de Historia del Derecho I* (1988), pp. 163–266. For a perspective which emphasizes the continuity of early modern international legal thought with medieval tradition see with further references James Muldoon, 'Rights, Property, and the Creation of International Law', in James Muldoon (ed.), *Bridging the Medieval-Modern Divide: Medieval Themes in the World of the Reformation* (2013), pp. 175–204.

response to, the European overseas expansion. Notwithstanding the overwhelming importance of the reformation movements, wars of succession, and territorial disputes in constituting European modernity, from a global-historical perspective, broader, oceanic categories, such as the 'Atlantic world', 'Atlantic system', and 'Atlantic law', have helped us to better understand the formation of the modern world. However, the growth of a space that was first an 'Iberian Atlantic' was the result of the search for riches in the Pacific—a drive that would eventually become the catalyst for attempts to 'Europeanize the World' in east and west. Over the ensuing five centuries, European powers would seek to impose their cultural systems on non-Europeans along the shores of both Oceans.[2] The colonial structures of international law dating back to this period have been object of intense discussion during the last decades.[3] At times, these debates unconsciously perpetuated colonial epistemic structures by a historically uninformed postcolonial repetition of the account of a 'Northwestern Europeanization'.[4]

This already indicates that European expeditions into the New World significantly impacted not just the non-European peoples, for their relevance for early-modern Europeans was considerable. Historians have shown the extent to which not only the arts, culture, and the sciences, but also early-modern state building mechanisms and foundational doctrines of European legal thought, like 'sovereignty', were shaped by imperial forays and interactions.[5] Important innovations in

[2] See on the 'Atlantic perspective' Nicholas Canny and Philip Morgan, 'Introduction: The Making and Unmaking of an Atlantic World', in Nicholas Canny and Philip Morgan (eds.), *The Oxford Handbook of the Atlantic World: 1450-1850* (2011); Joan-Pau Rubiés, 'The Worlds of Europeans, Africans, and Americans, *c.* 1490', in Nicholas Canny and Philip Morgan (eds.), *The Oxford Handbook of the Atlantic World: 1450-1850* (2011); Lauren Benton, 'Atlantic Law: Transformations of a Regional Legal Regime', in Nicholas Canny and Philip Morgan (eds.), *The Oxford Handbook of the Atlantic World: 1450-1850* (2011); Stuart B. Schwartz, 'The Iberian Atlantic to 1650', in Nicholas Canny and Philip Morgan (eds.), *The Oxford Handbook of the Atlantic World: 1450-1850* (2011). For early modern—'first' or 'proto'—globalization see Serge Gruzinski, *Les Quatre Parties du monde. Histoire d'une mondialisation* (2004); Serge Gruzinski, *The Eagle and the Dragon: Globalization and European Dreams of Conquest in China and America in the Sixteenth Century* (2014); Felipe Fernández-Armesto, *1492. The Year Our World Began* (2009). On the 'Europeanization of the world' see the polemical text of John M. Headley, *The Europeanization of the World: On the Origins of Human Rights and Democracy* (2008).

[3] See on this Martti Koskenniemi, 'Vitoria and Us: Thoughts on Critical Histories of International Law', *Rechtsgeschichte - Legal History* 22 (2014), 119–138; Bardo Fassbender and Anne Peters, 'Introduction: Towards A Global History Of International Law', in Bardo Fassbender and Anne Peters (eds.), *The Oxford Handbook of the History of International Law* (2012), pp. 1–24; Arnulf Becker Lorca, 'Eurocentrism in the History of International Law', in Bardo Fassbender and Anne Peters (eds.), *The Oxford Handbook of the History of International Law* (2012), pp. 1034–57; Antony Anghie, *Imperialism, Sovereignty and the Making of International Law* (2005).

[4] On the necessity to abandon the narrative of a 'Northwestern Europeanization' see Jorge Cañizares-Esguerra and Benjamin Breen, 'Hybrid Atlantics: Future Directions for the History of the Atlantic World', *History Compass* 11(8) (2013), 597–609.

[5] See e.g. from recent literature Arndt Brendecke, *Imperium und Empirie: Funktionen des Wissens in der spanischen Kolonialherrschaft* (2009); Harold J. Cook, *Matters of Exchange: Commerce, Medicine and Science in the Age of Empire* (2007); Lauren Benton, *A Search for Sovereignty: Law and Geography in European Empires, 1400-1900* (2010); Helge Wendt and Jürgen Renn, 'Knowledge and Science in Current Discussions of Globalization', in Jürgen Renn (ed.), *The Globalization of Knowledge in History* (2012), pp. 45–72.

what is being called 'European' legal thought, like the normative reflection stemming from the School of Salamanca, are unimaginable without imperial encounters with Non-Europeans.[6]

In this context, study of the History of Knowledge has dedicated growing attention to the stunning advances made in the fields of geography, astronomy, geodetic measurement, and cartography especially in sixteenth century. Since Henri Lefebvre's seminal *La Production de l'espace* (1974), which raised the hypothesis that at the dawn of the sixteenth century a common spatial code had come to serve as the organizing principle for Western European culture, scholars have begun to discuss the 'rationalization of space' and its implications for global power structures. Not least 'America' was seen as a space which was 'invented', produced historically, through the interaction of culturally contingent expectations and interests with observed geographical phenomena, embodied in the technique of mapping.[7] In a related move, research on historical cartography identified a 'cartographic revolution' in the fifteenth and sixteenth centuries, which was intimately connected to the reception of Ptolemaic *Geography* in the last decades of the fifteenth century. The printing press allowed mapmakers to reproduce and distribute their maps in large numbers, so that by 1500 there were already approximately 60,000 individual maps in circulation within Europe. By 1600 this number had risen to 1.3 million.[8] Scientific communication between experts and exchange of information became much easier. As a result, the decades around 1500 saw the emergence of what has been called the '*first coherent, and rationally cumulative pictures of the world since antiquity*' and opened a century of radical transformation of our knowledge about the shape and size of the world.[9]

Again, European expansion has been decisive for this process. Caravels travelling across the oceans, loaded with spices, gifts, and prizes, but also with nautical and astronomical instruments, became the laboratories of the early-modern 'cosmographers', who embarked on exploratory voyages and collaborated with navigators and statesmen in the search for seaways, longitudes, and latitudes. Commercial development, missionary impetus, and territorial expansion went hand in hand with creation of scientific knowledge. Around 1500, the Iberian crowns played a key role in this. As early modern Iberian empires built on this knowledge, an official—or

[6] See for further references Thomas Duve, 'Von der Europäischen Rechtsgeschichte zu einer Rechtsgeschichte Europas in globalhistorischer Perspektive', *Rechtsgeschichte - Legal History* 20 (2012), 18–71; Thomas Duve, 'Katholisches Kirchenrecht und Moraltheologie im 16. Jahrhundert: Eine globale normative Ordnung im Schatten schwacher Staatlichkeit', in Stefan Kadelbach and Kaus Günther (eds.), *Recht ohne Staat?. Zur Normativität nichtstaatlicher Rechtsetzung* (2011), pp. 147–74.

[7] See for further references to O'Gormann, Mignolo and others Ricardo Padrón, *The Spacious Word: Cartography, Literature, and Empire in Early Modern Spain* (2004), esp pp. 12ff.

[8] Jerry Brotton, *A History of the World in Twelve Maps* (2012), p. 158.

[9] David Woodward, 'Maps and the Rationalization of Geographic Space', in Jay A. Levenson (ed.), *Circa 1492: Art in the Age of Exploration* (1991), pp. 83–8, at p. 85. For a broader picture see the contributions in David Woodward (ed.), *The History of Cartography. Cartography in the European Renaissance*, vol. 3/1 (2007); James R. Akerman, 'Introduction', in James R. Akerman (ed.), *The Imperial Map: Cartography and the Mastery of Empire* (2009), pp. 1–9; Jerry Brotton, *Trading Territories. Mapping the Early Modern World* (1998); Brotton, *A History* (n. 8).

even 'juridical'—cartography emerged, a 'secret science' that was closely linked to political and state interests.[10]

This cumulative knowledge, as some authors emphasize, marked the beginning of a new form of rationality that would lay the foundations for modernity and pave the way for imagining physical spaces, new territories, and blank spaces on the map—a 'positive emptiness'.[11] For some observers, the resulting 'rationalization of space' is intimately connected with the emergence of what has been termed the 'cartographic state'. According to them, the ever-evolving technical knowledge did not only determine European politics, but helped European powers to deploy an array of techniques to integrate non-European territories and peoples into their empires. Political and legal imperialism, the 'rise of the West', became possible due to technical knowledge. The '*geometric division of space* [...] *made it possible for as yet unknown places to be claimed, so long as they fall within the geometric division proposed by the map*'.[12]

These—popular, yet not undisputed—diagnostics find a parallel in a not less contested, yet also influential account of the history of international law, namely, Carl Schmitt's analysis of sixteenth century's 'spatial revolution' and its 'global linear thinking', which he developed in his *Nomos of the Earth*. Schmitt had anticipated the notion of rationalization of space as well as its centrality in shaping international legal thought as early as 1950, when he described the beginning of what he calls the *Jus publicum Europaeum*:

> No sooner had the contours of the earth emerged as a real globe—not just sensed as myth, but apprehensible as fact and measureable as space—then there arose a wholly new and hitherto unimaginable problem: the spatial ordering of the earth in terms of international law. The new global image, resulting from the circumnavigation of the earth and the great discoveries of the 15th and 16th centuries, required a new spatial order. Thus began the epoch of modern international law that lasted until the 20th century.[13]

[10] From the vast bibliography on these issues see María M. Portuondo, *Secret Science. Spanish Cosmography and the New World* (2009); David Buisseret (ed.), *Monarchs, Ministers, and Maps: The Emergence of Cartography as a Tool of Government in Early Modern Europe* (1992); Padrón, *The Spacious Word* (n. 7); Alison Sandman, 'Spanish Nautical Cartography in the Renaissance', in David Woodward (ed.), *The History of Cartography: Cartography in the European Renaissance* (2007), pp. 1095–1142; Antonio Sánchez Martínez, *La espada, la cruz y el Padrón (Soberanía, fe y representación cartográfica en el mundo ibérico bajo la Monarquía Hispánica), 1503-1598* (2013); Antonio Sánchez Martínez, 'An Official Image of the World for the Hispanic Monarchy: The Padrón Real of the Casa de la Contratación in Seville, 1508-1606', *Nuncius* 29 (2014) 389–438; Antonio T. Reguera Rodríguez, *Los geógrafos del rey*, III (2010); Felipe Fernández-Armesto, 'Maps and Exploration in the Sixteenth and Early Seventeenth Centuries', in David Woodward (ed.), *The History of Cartography: Cartography in the European Renaissance* (2007), pp. 738–70; Richard L. Kagan and Benjamin Schmidt, 'Maps and the Early Modern State: Official Cartography', in David Woodward (ed.), *The History of Cartography: Cartography in the European Renaissance* (2007), pp. 661–79; Ricardo Cerezo Martínez, *La cartografía náutica española en los siglos XIV, XV y XVI* (1994).

[11] Padrón, *The Spacious Word*, esp. pp. 35ff. (n. 7).

[12] Jordan Branch, *The Cartographic State: Maps, Territory and the Origins of Sovereignty* (2014), p. 59. From a legal historical point of view, see the critique of Benton, *A Search for Sovereignty*, esp. pp. 10ff. (n. 5).

[13] Carl Schmitt, *The Nomos of the Earth in the International Law of the Jus Publicum Europaeum, trans. and introduced by G.L. Ulmen* (2003), p. 86.

For Schmitt, who presented his thesis as a legal-historical piece with a normative drift in the tradition of German Historical School, a new spatial perception had allowed Europe to cultivate a functioning system of controlled aggression and violence in Europe, whose tragic end he mourned in writing the *Nomos*.

Interestingly, both discourses—the more recent formulations of 'cartographic revolution' and 'rationalization of space' as well as Schmitt's earlier 'spatial revolution' and 'global linear thinking'—have a common historical reference point. The centrepiece of the account is twofold: on the one hand, the 1494 Treaty of Tordesillas, drawn between the two Iberian powers, Castile and Portugal, and on the other, the Bulls issued by Pope Alexander VI dating back to 1493, which gifted the King of Castile all lands discovered and yet to be discovered in the New World. And just as Schmitt locates the beginning of the new 'global linear thinking' in the lines of demarcation drawn in the Papal Bulls and the said Treaty, recent scholarship on the history of international relations has tended to view Tordesillas as the main impetus for the 'politicization of the globe'. The Treaty '*stands as maybe the first genuine example of how the political boundary originates in a map or rather, in a carto-scientific representation of space which, in consequence, plays a performative role in shaping the world*'.[14] In a similar vein, for experts in the history of cartography like Jerry Brotton, Tordesillas is '*one of the earliest and most hubristic acts of European global imperial geography* [. . .] *The world was divided in half by two European kingdoms, using a map to announce their global ambitions*'.[15]

Even if one considers Schmitt's historical account in *Nomos of the Earth* pure ideology, his ideas have had a significant impact on the classical narrative of the history of international law in seminal works, such as those of Wilhelm Grewe. The growing interest in Schmitt's ideas, especially in Anglo-American scholarship, highlights the links between spatial perceptions and the formation of international legal thought.[16] The same applies to the strong statements made on the role the rationalization of space played in the formation of the international system.[17] Is it

[14] Jeppe Strandsbjerg, *Territory, Globalisation and International Relations: The Cartographic Reality of Space* (2010), p. 94.

[15] Brotton, *A History*, pp. 186–7 (n. 8).

[16] On the influence of Schmitt in Grewe see Bardo Fassbender, 'Stories of War and Peace On Writing the History of International Law in the "Third Reich" and After', *European Journal of International Law* 13(2) (2002), 479–512; on the reception of Schmitt's *Nomos* in the Anglo-American world and on the status of the text as political theology Martti Koskenniemi, 'International Law as Political Theology: How to Read *Nomos der Erde*?', *Constellations* 11(4) (2004), 492–511. For a critical survey see also the contributions in Stephen Legg (ed.), *Spatiality, Sovereignty and Carl Schmitt: Geographies of the Nomos* (2011). For some authors, especially in more popular works, Schmitt has even become the main reference when dealing with the demarcation line, see e.g. Joyce E. Chaplin, *Round about the Earth: Circumnavigation from Magellan to Orbit* (2012), p. 11, n. 11.

[17] The question of the links between scientific and practical knowledge about space, the objects in which this knowledge materialized, and the formation of legal thought is starting to attract growing attention in general legal historiography as well as in intellectual history. See as a first important contribution from the 1980s Antonio M. Hesphana, 'El espacio político', in Antonio M. Hesphana (ed.), *La gracia del derecho. Economía de la cultura en la edad moderna* (1993), pp. 85–122. More recently Benton, *A Search for Sovereignty* (n. 5) and the contributions in *Rechtsgeschichte – Legal History* 23 (2015), especially Massimo Meccarelli, 'The Assumed Space: Pre-reflective Spatiality and Doctrinal Configurations in Juridical Experience', *Rechtsgeschichte - Legal History* 23 (2015), 241–52; see also Massimo Meccarelli and Julia Solla Sastre (eds.), *Spatial and Temporal Dimensions for Legal History:*

true, one wonders, that the 'spatial revolution' and the new strain of 'global linear thinking' were responsible for the emergence of the first international legal order around 1500?

The aim of this chapter, thus, is to take a closer look at notions of the 'spatial revolution', 'global linear thinking', and 'cartographic revolution', as well as their impact on the emergence of system and order in international legal thought around 1500. Therefore, I will reconstruct some aspects[18] of the practice of early modern treaty-making, with special attention to the demarcation lines drawn between the two Iberian monarchies during the era of Tordesillas,[19] starting with the 1479 Treaty of Alcáçovas[20] (II.). After this, I will extend the survey to the Treaty of Saragossa, signed in 1529, often seen as a direct consequence and extension of the Treaty of Tordesillas. Although less famous, it has been increasingly considered not only as a '*watershed in the political history*

Research Experiences and Itineraries (2016). On the need to integrate History of Science and Intellectual History see John Tresch, 'Cosmologies Materialized: History of Science and History of Ideas', in Darrin M. McMahon and Samuel Moyn (eds.), *Rethinking Modern European Intellectual History* (2014), pp. 153–72. On History of Knowledge and History of Law Jürgen Renn, 'The Globalization of Knowledge in History and its Normative Challenges', *Rechtsgeschichte - Legal History* 22 (2014), 52–60.

[18] I will not be able to discuss the complex problem of the juridical status of the territories which were allocated to the crowns by the demarcation lines. Despite of the many generalizing statements which indicate the contrary, it should, however, be clear that drawing demarcation lines did in no case mean granting absolute dominion over these territories; this would be an anachronism for this period, and an underestimation of the variety of functions the delimitation of spheres of influence could fulfil.

[19] There is 'endless bibliography' on Tordesillas, as Tamar Herzog, *Frontiers of Possesion: Spain and Portugal in Europe and the Americas* (2015) writes in her study before giving a good selection of references. From a legal historical perspective, fundamental reference points for any further discussion of the Papal Bulls and the subsequent Treaties are: Alfonso García-Gallo, 'Las bulas de Alejandro VI y el ordenamiento jurídico de la expansión portuguesa y castellana en África e Indias', *Anuario de Historia del Derecho Español* 27–28 (1957–1958), 461–829; Paulino Castañeda Delgado, *La teocracia pontifical en las controversias sobre el Nuevo Mundo*, ed. Instituto de Investigaciones Jurídicas (1996); Antonio Rumeu de Armas, *El Tratado de Tordesillas: Rivalidad hispano-lusa por el dominio de océanos y continentes* (1992). Important contributions have been published on the occasion of the anniversary of Tordesillas in 1994, see especially: Luis Antonio Ribot García, Adolfo Carrasco Martínez, and Luís Adão da Fonseca (eds.), *El Tratado de Tordesillas y su época: Congreso internacional de historia, 3 vols.* (1995); José Manuel García and Angel Sodano (eds.), *O Tratado de Tordesillas e a política papal face à expansão Iberíca*, Comemorações do V Centenário do Tratado de Tordesilhas na Santa Sé (1994); Jesús Varela Marcos, 'La cartografía del segundo viaje de Colón y su decisiva influencia en el Tratado de Tordesillas', in Jesús Varela Marcos (ed.), *El Tratado de Tordesillas en la cartografía histórica* (1994), pp. 85–108. See also the earlier collections: Seminario de historia de America (ed.), *El tratado de Tordesillas y su proyección: Vol. I*, Jornadas Americanistas (1973); Armando Cortesão and Avelino Teixeira da Mota (eds.), *Portugaliae Monumenta Cartographica* (1987).

[20] The relevant sources for this period are accessible in different collections: Wilhelm G. Grewe, *Fontes Historiae Iuris Gentium: Sources Relating to the History of the Law of Nations*, 2 (1988) collects texts taken from different publications. The English translations are taken from Frances Gardiner Davenport (ed.), *European Treaties Bearing on the History of the United States and its Dependencies*, Vol. 1 (2012). Some further documents concerning Spain and Portugal are printed in Primitivo Mariño, *Tratados Internacionales de España: Carlos V*, Vol. I (1978) and in the collections by Martín Fernández de Navarette: *Colección de documentos inéditos relativos al descubrimiento*, [. . .] (1864, reprint 1964); Martín Fernández de Navarette, *Colección de los Viajes y Descubrimientos* [. . .] (1825–1837, reprint 1945).The Papal Bulls are cited after Josef Metzler, *America Pontificia: Primi saeculi evangelizationis 1493-1592, vol. 1-2, Collectanea Archivi Vaticani 27/1, 27/2* (1991).

of early modern Europe', but as a '*turning point in the political apprehension of the importance of geography in defining the contours of the early modern world*'[21] (III.). In fact, it is only a joint perspective on the Treaties of Tordesillas and of Saragossa which can show the impressive transformation of spatial perceptions in the first decades of the sixteenth century. In the thirty-five years between these Treaties, new spatial perceptions, generated not least by new media for visualizing geographic knowledge, had an enormous impact on international legal thought. Notwithstanding these remarkable developments, the demarcation lines drawn in these years seem less 'revolutionary' than when presented by Schmitt and others (IV.).

II. From Alcáçovas to Tordesillas

1. Drawing the lines of demarcation from the east to west: The Treaty of Alcáçovas

The Treaty of Tordesillas must be situated in the fifteenth century context of the aggressive maritime expansion undertaken by the Iberian powers, in particular, in reference to the plans initiated by Henry the Navigator, the third son of King John I.[22] In light of the fall of Constantinople in 1453 and the threat of the strong position the Ottoman Empire had consolidated, the Iberian powers became more attentive to the Atlantic, to areas extending far beyond the immediate coastlines of the Iberian Peninsula. During the course of latter half of the fifteenth century, both powers sought to expand their reach to the East, in an effort to gain access to the riches of Asia without crossing the Mediterranean. It was this effort to extend their reach beyond the border of the Strait of Gibraltar that lends deeper meaning to the famous motto '*Plus ultra*'.[23]

The several conflicts that ensued between Spain and Portugal—in the 1470s, before and after Isabella and Ferdinand had ascended the throne in 1474—were

[21] Brotton, *Trading Territories*, p. 150 (n. 9).

[22] See for general introductions into this historical period, especially regarding the Iberian powers the bibliography in n. 2 as well as John Huxtable Elliot, *Empires of the Atlantic World: Britain and Spain in America, 1492–1830* (2006); A.R. Disney, *A History of Portugal and the Portuguese Empire, Volumen 2 The Portuguese Empire*, 2 vols. (2009); Giuseppe Marcocci, *L'invenzione di un impero: Politica e cultura nel mondo portoghese (1450-1600)* (2011); Hugh Thomas, *Rivers of Gold: The Rise of the Spanish Empire* (2010); Ana María Carabias Torres (ed.), *Las relaciones entre Portugal y Castilla, en la época de los descubrimientos y la expansión colonial, ponencias presentadas al congreso Hispano-Portugués celebrado en Salamanca, 1992*, Acta salmanticensia, Estudios históricos y geográficos (1994); for a specific account of the European explorations and their context see Felipe Fernández-Armesto, 'Exploration and Navigation', in Hamish Scott (ed.), *The Oxford Handbook of Early Modern European History, 1350-1750: Volume II: Cultures and Power* (2015), pp. 173–99.

[23] See on this Ricardo Padrón, 'Mapping Plus Ultra: Cartography, Space, and Hispanic Modernity', *Representations* 79 (2002), 28–60; Antonio Sánchez Martínez, 'Los Artífices del Plus Ultra: Pilotos, Carógrafos y Cosmógrafos en la casa de la contratación de Sevilla durante el siglo XVI', *Hispania* 236 (2010), 607–32.

resolved through the Treaty of Alcáçovas, which was signed on 4 September 1479, and ratified by the Catholic monarchs in Toledo in 1480.[24] In the Treaty, the parties agreed to draw a line of demarcation at the Canary Islands and to grant all land south of it to Portugal. In compensation, Portugal agreed to recognize the Castilian dominion over the Canaries and the legitimacy of the Catholic monarch's succession to the throne. With that, both parties had in effect confirmed previous acquisitions based on traditional rationales for acquiring titles of dominion, like discovery and appropriation, contingency to one's own territory, or missionizing in territories under Muslim dominion. Following the medieval practice, the parties sought Papal confirmation for their agreement, which was granted through *Aeterni Regis*, a Papal Bull issued by Sixtus IV on 21 June 1481. *Aeterni Regis* represented the culmination of the first phase of European Atlantic expansion based on the theocratic doctrine that bore the seal of Papal approval through Papal Bulls.[25]

Notably, the Treaty and its subsequent ratification introduced a practice of drawing a line dividing the waters, in this case, from east to west, in order to confirm the rights over already existing possessions, and to demarcate the spheres of influence and rights of free navigation and possessions for future discoveries. The imaginary line would run through the Canary Islands and separate spheres which were basically well known. The maps used for navigating close to the coastline were already relatively reliable, and the Portolan charts contained the information needed for making a precise determination of the vessel's position in relation to the Canary Islands. The demarcation line was a line of latitude, which was easy to measure even in those days. Given that several expeditions had already pushed south during the days of Henry the Navigator, and had reached the Senegalese coast in the 1460s, considerable knowledge had already been accumulated on areas to the south of the line. Although the Cape of Good Hope was first rounded in 1488 by Bartolomeu Dias, mid-fifteenth-century maps, for instance, the famous map of Fra Mauro, reveal that a general idea of the African continent and its coastline already prevailed.[26] Thus, in Alcáçovas a demarcation line was drawn using established techniques that followed the portolan logic, which involved conceiving and organizing space on the sea between coastlines and known islands.

24 See for a general description Alberto de la Hera Pérez-Cuesta, 'La primera división del océano entre Portugal y Castilla', in Luis Antonio Ribot García, Adolfo Carrasco Martínez, and Luís Adão da Fonseca (eds.), *El Tratado de Tordesillas y su época* (1995), pp. 1051–70; Rumeu de Armas, *El Tratado de Tordesillas*, pp. 61ff. (n. 19); Sánchez Martínez, *La Espada* (n. 10). The text of the Treaty in Grewe, *Fontes Historiae Iuris Gentium,* I, 683–90 = D XIII, 3b (n. 20).

25 See for the text Grewe, *Fontes Historiae Iuris Gentium*, I, 649–53 = D XI 4f. (n. 20); on this Hera Pérez-Cuesta, 'La primera división', pp. 1051–70 (n. 24).

26 See on this Inácio Guerreiro, 'Ciencia e cartografia: a imagem do mundo físico em Portugal em finais do séc. XV', in Luis Antonio Ribot García, Adolfo Carrasco Martínez, and Luís Adão da Fonseca (eds.), *El Tratado de Tordesillas y su época* (1995), pp. 943–58.

2. The demarcation line from pole to pole: the Bulls of Pope Alexander VI

The discovery of the first Caribbean islands during the voyages of Christopher Columbus and the measures taken by the Catholic kings in response dramatically changed the situation.

In their attempt to secure exclusive rights over the new territories once Columbus returned in March 1493, the Catholic monarchs enlisted the support of Pope Alexander VI. Within a few months, the Pope issued a total of five Bulls that granted the Spaniards a series of rights over the Indies (the so-called *Bulas Alejandrinas*). *Inter Cetera*, the first bull dated 3 May 1493, granted them the islands and lands discovered and to be discovered, sailing westward towards the Indies.[27] A second bull, dated 4 May 1493, which was almost a verbatim copy and also called *Inter Cetera*, established a demarcation line that extended 100 leagues to the west of the Azores and the Cape Verde islands in the north-south direction.[28] This granted the Catholic monarchs ownership over all lands discovered and yet to be discovered, as well as monopoly over navigation, in the Atlantic to the west of the demarcation line, while awarding the Portuguese dominion over the sea to the east of the line, right up to the African coast, except over the Canary Islands. As for territories that had been discovered, the third Papal Bull, *Eximiae devotionis*, dated 3 May 1493, granted the Catholic monarchs the same privileges as those accorded to Portugal.[29] *Piis Fidelium* of 25 June 1493, recognized the right of the Spanish crown to have a stake in the evangelization of the 'heathens' in the newly discovered territories, for which purpose extraordinary powers were granted to the missionaries[30]. *Dudum siquidem*, issued on 26 September 1493, granted the monarchs of Castile lands discovered by them to the east, south, and west of India that were not under the actual temporal dominion of another Christian ruler.[31]

The historical circumstances, under which these Bulls were issued, as well as their juridical interpretation, are highly contested and cannot be fully explicated here.[32] The Spanish legal historian, Alfonso García Gallo, convincingly argued in 1957–1958 that the five Bulls, modelled on previous concessions granted to the Portuguese kings (*Romanus Pontifex*, 1455; *Inter caetera*, 1456; *Aeterni Regis*, 1481), were intended to grant sovereignty over territories yet to be discovered as well as over lands already discovered, and established a monopoly over navigation, trade, and future discovery that excluded the participation of nations other than the Iberian powers. In this respect, the Bulls signified a clear shift from previous concessions given to the Portuguese some decades ago. Whereas *Romanus Pontifex* (1455) of

[27] Metzler, *America Pontificia*, I, n. 1, pp. 71–5 (n. 20).

[28] Metzler, *America Pontificia*, I, n. 3, pp. 79–83 (n. 20).

[29] Metzler, *America Pontificia*, I, n. 2, pp. 76–8 (n. 20).

[30] Metzler, *America Pontificia*, I, n. 4, pp. 83–6 (n. 20).

[31] Metzler, *America Pontificia*, I, n. 5, pp. 87–9 (n. 20).

[32] On the Papal Bulls see fundamental García-Gallo, 'Las bulas', pp. 461–829 (n. 19); for a summary of the discussion Castañeda Delgado, *La teocracia*, pp. 321ff. (n. 19); Rumeu de Armas, *El Tratado de Tordesillas*, pp. 115ff. (n. 19).

Nicolaus V had granted nearly exclusive rights to the Portuguese to navigate *usque ad Indos*, this was no longer the case. Now, the Atlantic had to be divided between the two Iberian powers. Moreover, *Dudum siquidem* granted Castile wide-ranging rights over the whole Indies. Power relations between the two crowns seemed to have been turned around. But the way the Pope acted was quite traditional.

Can the same be said of the way the demarcation lines were drawn? Looking more closely at the way the line was determined suggests that the *modus operandi* was not so different from what had been done before either. There are a lot of clues that practical observations of the explorers, and not the precise measurement of longitude, an impossible task then, nor an imaginary line through unknown spaces, formed the basis for drawing the demarcation line.[33]

The first evidence stems from legal documents issued to Columbus, dated 28 May 1493, in which the Catholic kings confirm the *Capitulaciones de Santa Fé* of 17 April 1492 and accord Columbus the title of *Almyrante*, of the Ocean, '*which belongs to us and which starts at a line which we have ordered to be drawn and which runs from the islands of the Azores to the Cape Verde islands, from North to South, from Pole to Pole; so that everything which is beyond this line towards the Occident, is ours and belongs to us.*'[34] Although the text is said to be a transcription of the earlier title from 1492, the reference to a '*line which we have ordered to be drawn*' was not a part of the original document, suggesting that the line drawn in the Papal Bulls had been based on the recommendations of the monarchs after Columbus return.[35] In addition, it is possible to conclude that it was the same Columbus who may have advised the monarchs to insert the line between the poles into the Papal Bulls.[36] In a later letter to Columbus, dated 3 September 1493, the Catholic kings refer to '*the line that you said should be part of the Papal bull*'.[37] This is in accordance with the fact that the distance of 100 leagues had appeared in Columbus' observation of an important change in navigational conditions at that height in relation to the magnetic declination,[38] which suggested the possibility of a precise determination

[33] On the method employed by Columbus and his geographical knowledge see G.E. Nunn, *Geographical Conceptions of Columbus: A Critical Consideration of Four Problems* (1924), esp. pp. 13ff.

[34] *Confirmación del título dado á Cristóbal Colón* [. . .], in Martín Fernandez de Navarrete, *Colección de los viages y descubrimientos que hicieron por mar los Españoles* [. . .], vol. II (1945), n. 41, pp. 73–9, at p. 77: '[. . .] del dicho mar Océano, que es nuestro, que comienza por una raya ó linea que Nos habemos fecho marcar que pasa dedsde las isalas de los Azores [. . .]'. The *Capitulaciones* are transcribed in Martín Fernandez de Navarrete, *Colección de los viages*, vol. II (1945), pp. 18–21.

[35] See on this Ricardo Cerezo Martínez, 'El meridiano y el antimeridiano de Tordesillas en la geografía, la náutica y la cartografía', *Revista de Indias* 54 (1994), 509–42; Castañeda Delgado, *La teocracia*, pp. 349ff. (n. 19).

[36] See on this already H. Vander Linden, 'Alexander VI. and the Demarcation of the Maritime and Colonial Domains of Spain and Portugal, 1493-1494', *The American Historical Review* 22 (1916), 1–20, with references to earlier discussions.

[37] *Carta mensager de los Reyes* [. . .], in Fernandez de Navarrete, *Colección de los viages*, vol. II, n. 71, pp. 131–3, at p. 132 (n. 34): '[. . .] *abajo fasta la raya que vos dijistes que debia venir en la Bula del Papa* [. . .]'.

[38] At least this can be read in his report on the third voyage, referring to an experience he had had previously. See on this Martín Fernandez de Navarrete, *Colección de los Viages y Descubrimientos* [. . .], vol. I (1945), p. 371. See on this point Varela Marcos, 'La cartografía', pp. 85–108 (n. 19) based on citations from the *Libro Copiador*, Antonio Rumeu de Armas, *Libro copiador de Cristóbal Colón: correspondencia*

of the longitude through magnetic measurement. Taking these pieces together, and notwithstanding the fact that Columbus' obviously had studied Ptolemy,[39] the line drawn in Tordesillas was to an important extent based on observations made by Columbus at sea. The line indicated in the Papal Bulls blended the astronomical and geodesic knowledge that Columbus and others had acquired with observations during their voyages. Even as it followed established patterns of fixing spheres of influence, there was a 90° shift from the line drawn in the Treaty of Alcáçovas. However, as a line measured from a fixed reference point, like islands, it still responded to a cognitive pattern rooted in contemporary cartography which organized space measured as distance on sea.

3. Negotiating the line drawn in the Papal Bulls: The Treaty of Tordesillas

In light of the new developments, King John II of Portugal was convinced that the Treaty of Alcáçovas had been breached. He sought direct negotiations with the Catholic monarchs for a new agreement. The negotiations that eventually led to the Treaties of Tordesillas had begun.

The interests of both sides were clear. The Portuguese king had reasons to be wary due to a tense relationship with the pope and also due to the close ties between the Catholic monarchs and Pope Alexander VI, who was heavily indebted to them and relied on their protection to realize his own political goals in the kingdom of Naples. Portugal, on the other hand, was responsible for securing the seaway to the East, via the African coastline, which was important as the Catholic monarchs had left no doubt about their plans to expand to the Atlantic along a route that would lead them to India. On 26 September 1493, only a few months after having returned to Europe, Columbus set off on a new expedition, with a fleet of seventeen ships and the order of the Catholic kings to send back a map as soon as possible.

Castile was in a better position now than it ever had been before, for Castilians believed they had found a way to Asia without having to cross the line drawn in the Treaty of Alcáçovas, and the terms of *Dudum siquidem* clearly favoured them as well. Notwithstanding this, they also feared a new military conflict with Portugal. Although they had just signed the Treaty of Barcelona with France (1493), the situation in the north and along the coastlines remained unstable, and a loss of influence in Naples as well as the threat of Turkish expeditions from the Mediterranean

inédita con los Reyes Católicos sobre los viajes a América (1989). The authenticity of these documents is still contested, see Fernández-Armesto, 'Maps and Exploration', pp. 738–70, at p. 748 (n. 10).

[39] On Columbus' reading of Ptolemy see Carmen Manso Porto, 'Cristóbal Colón y el incunable de la cosmografía de Ptolomeo de la Real Academia de Historia', in Jesús Varela Marcos (ed.), *Cristóbal Colón, su tiempo y sus reflejos: 'Actas del Congreso Internacional V Centenario de la muerte del Almirante', celebrado en Valladolid, del 15 al 19 de mayo de 2006*, Vol. II (2006), pp. 369–81. On the reception of Ptolemy more generally see Patrick Gautier Dalché, 'The Reception of Ptolemy's *Geography* (End of the Fourteenth to Beginning of the Sixteenth Century)', in David Woodward (ed.), *The History of Cartography: Cartography in the European Renaissance* (2007), pp. 285–364; Brotton, *A History*, pp. 162ff. (n. 8).

could not be easily averted. They agreed to new diplomatic talks between envoys and ambassadors for which purpose a technical committee would accompany them. Contacts established during the last months of 1493 paved the way for a new round of negotiations at Medina de Campo in March, which continued until 8 May 1494, when they moved to Tordesillas. Negotiations also referenced the new cartographic material that Columbus had sent to the Catholic kings from his second voyage.[40] The Portuguese, on the other hand, referred to a map drawn by Pêro da Covilhã, which was based on Ptolemaic calculations, and the famous map of Fra Mauro.

On 7 June 1494, two treaties were signed in Tordesillas—one is the famous Treaty of Tordesillas,[41] under which the parties agreed to establish a demarcation line in the Atlantic that modified the previous lines established in earlier treaties, such as the Treaty of Alcáçovas (1479) and in several Papal Bulls previously issued to the Portuguese kings and the Spanish monarchs in 1493. The demarcation line was defined as a '[. . .] boundary or straight line [. . .] drawn north and south, from pole to pole, on the said ocean from the Arctic to the Antarctic pole'.[42] The agreement stipulated that this line be drawn 'straight, as aforesaid, at a distance of three hundred and seventy leagues west of the Cape Verde Islands, being calculated by degrees, or by any other manner as may be considered the best and readiest [. . .]'. All lands already discovered 'or to be found and discovered hereafter' should 'belong' to the respective kings. Hence, all islands and lands to be discovered to the west of the aforementioned line would belong to the Spanish crown and those to the east to the Portuguese crown. In the end, the Treaty had essentially moved the line 270 leagues west of the position specified in the earlier Papal Bulls. The new line was measured from one fixed point (not two, as in the Papal Bulls) and ran straight from north to south.

Speculating about the reasons for this shift,[43] some argue that Castile hoped to gain in the Pacific what it had lost in the Atlantic.[44] This, however, is quite improbable, as we will see later. Others simply interpret it as an agreement that served to maintain peace in the Iberian Peninsula. Scholars also discuss the Treaty's impact on the Papal Bulls and the respective parties, especially whether the two crowns had actually requested the Bulls at a prior date.[45] However, juridical concerns seemed

[40] Varela Marcos, 'La cartografía', pp. 85–108 (n. 19); Cerezo Martínez, 'El meridiano', pp. 509–42 (n. 35); Sánchez Martínez, *La espada*, pp. 97ff. (n. 10).

[41] The Treaty was accompanied by a lesser-known second document, signed and ratified on the same dates and at the same places, sometimes referred to as '(Second) Treaty of Tordesillas'. The purpose of this agreement was to clarify the limits of the Portuguese and Spanish territories of the African coast. See on this Rumeu de Armas, *El Tratado de Tordesillas*, pp. 99ff. (n. 19).

[42] Grewe, *Fontes Historiae Iuris Gentium*, II, 110–116 = n. 11 (n. 20).

[43] Marta Milagros del Vas Mingo, 'Las bulas alejandrinas y la fijación de los límites a la navegación en el Atlántico', in Luis Antonio Ribot García, Adolfo Carrasco Martínez, and Luís Adão da Fonseca (eds.), *El Tratado de Tordesillas y su época* (1995), pp. 1071–90.

[44] See e.g. Christoph Auffarth, 'Neue Welt und Neue Zeit - Weltkarten und Säkularisierung in der Frühen Neuzeit', in Dürr Renate (ed.), *Expansionen in der Frühen Neuzeit* (2005), pp. 43–68, at p. 56.

[45] Castañeda Delgado, *La teocracia* (n. 19); Pedro Borges Morán, 'La anómala ratificación pontificia del Tratado de Tordesillas (1494-1506)', in Jesús María Usunáriz Garayoa (ed.), *Historia y Humanismo: Estudios en honor del profesor Dr. D. Valentín Vázquez de Prada* (2000), pp. 317–29.

not to worry the kings too much, as they let more than ten years go by, until 24 January 1506, when Pope Julius II issued *Ea Quae* to confirm the agreement at the request of the Portuguese king.[46]

4. Fixing the demarcation line: a voyage that never happened

Still, one important practical problem needed to be solved.[47] As there was no common standard for measuring longitude,[48] the Treaty foresaw a particular mechanism to agree on how to mark and honour this line. The parties agreed that the line would be established more accurately within a period not exceeding ten months from the date of the signing of the Treaty. The plan was to send out one or two caravels with pilots, astronomers, and sailors, who would swap ships with those of the other kingdom. The caravels would meet at Gran Canaria, where they would set sail for the Cape Verde islands and continue their joint voyage up to the 370-league limit,

> so that they may jointly study and examine to better advantage the sea, courses, winds, and the degrees of the sun or of north latitude, and lay out the leagues aforesaid, in order that, in determining the line and boundary, all sent and empowered by both the said parties in the said vessels, shall jointly concur.

Once it was reached, such a 'point will constitute the place and mark for measuring degrees of the sun or of north latitude either by daily runs measured in leagues, or in any other manner that shall mutually be deemed better'. As it was impossible to mark this point on open sea, the parties had to find a way to establish and safeguard it. They might have hoped to find an island close to this point. If not, the line had at least to be clearly indicated in their maps:

> And when this line has been determined as above said, those sent by each of the aforesaid parties [. . .] shall draw up a writing concerning it and affix thereto their signatures. And when determined by the mutual consent of all of them, this line shall be considered a perpetual mark and bound, in such wise that the said parties, or either of them, or their future successors, shall be unable to deny it, or erase or remove it, at any time or in any manner whatsoever.[49]

In summary, the Treaty did not simply use the Ptolemaic grid and partitioned the world into two in order to establish the new demarcation line. On the contrary, the new line constituted a shift with respect to the conceptualization of the lines

[46] Metzler, *America Pontificia*, I, n. 10, pp. 100–2 (n. 20).

[47] See on the following Luis Mendonça de Albuquerque, 'O Tratado de Tordesilhas e as dificultades tecnicas da sua aplicação rigorosa', in Seminario de Historia de América (ed.), *El Tratado de Tordesillas y su Proyección: Segundas Jornadas Americanistas: Primer Coloquio Luso-Español de Historia Ultramarina* (1973), pp. 119–36; Cerezo Martínez, 'El meridiano', pp. 509–42, at pp. 523ff. (n. 35).

[48] Mariano Esteban Piñeiro, 'Elio Antonio Nebrija y la búsqueda de patrones universales de medidas', in Luis Antonio Ribot García, Adolfo Carrasco Martínez, and Luis Adão da Fonseca (eds.), *El tratado de Tordesillas y su época* (1995), pp. 569–82; Ana María Carabias Torres, 'La medida del espacio en el Renacimiento: La aportación de la Universidad de Salamanca', *Cuadernos de historia de España* 76 (2000), 185–202.

[49] Grewe, *Fontes Historiae Iuris Gentium*, II, 110–16, n. 10, quote at 113 (n. 20).

previously established. Now, it ran in lesser known parts of the sea, so that its concrete position needed to be empirically verified, 'measured in leagues, or in any other manner that shall mutually be deemed better'. In addition to this, both sides assumed that the circumference of the world was much smaller than it effectively was, and no one imagined at this moment that the line drawn would divide a whole continent in two.

III. From Tordesillas to Saragossa

1. The line drawn in Tordesillas and the dominion over the Moluccas

The joint voyage foreseen in the Treaty of Tordesillas never took place. No map as stipulated in the Treaty was produced. This is a revealing fact. Despite growing tension due to some minor conflicts, during the first years after Tordesillas, there was no immediate need for clarification of the exact position of the line drawn.

The situation clearly changed at the beginning of sixteenth century, not least through the discovery of Brazil in 1500. The reason, however, that drew the parties back to the negotiation table was not the need to further define the line in the Atlantic, but, rather, to discuss the vexing issue of dominion over the Moluccas, modern-day Malaysia. The desire to gain access to the treasures these legendary Islands in the Pacific harboured had once been the driving force for Columbus' voyages and inspired most of the explorations undertaken in the first decades of sixteenth century. The intense activities of both powers in this Pacific area led to a series of diplomatic conflicts that were resolved through the Treaty of Saragossa in 1529. The Treaty established a demarcation line in the Pacific, running between the poles from north to south that would separate their respective spheres of influence and give exclusive rights over territories already under their dominion, or those yet to be discovered.[50] As recently with this demarcation line, the line drawn in Tordesillas was completed, for some authors the Treaty of Saragossa was of an unprecedented significance. For

> the western European empires of first Portugal and Castile, then Holland and England, the act of drawing a line, first on a map, then on a terrestrial globe, and laying claim to places that their putative imperial lords never visited, set a precedent that would be followed through the centuries, and shape so much European colonial policy across the globe over the subsequent 500 years.[51]

In the context of negotiating the demarcation line, as well as in diplomatic exchanges preceding the Treaty of Saragossa, at least since the second decade of sixteenth

[50] See on this Treaty the overview in Leoncio Cabrero, 'El empeño de las Molucas y los tratados de Zaragoza: cambios, modificaciones y coincidencias entre el no ratificado y el ratificado', in Luis Antonio Ribot García, Adolfo Carrasco Martínez, and Luís Adão da Fonseca (eds.), *El Tratado de Tordesillas y su época* (1995), pp. 1091–132. The text in Grewe, *Fontes Historiae Iuris Gentium*, II, 117–34, n. 12 (n. 20).

[51] Brotton, *A History*, p. 217 (n. 8).

century, both sides seemed to have taken it for granted that the Moluccas would belong to the crown that could prove that the Islands lay within 'its' demarcation line, and that this line was related to the line drawn in Tordesillas. This is somewhat astonishing, as the Treaty of Tordesillas '*said nothing about where that line, or "half-meridian", would fall if it were extended into a full meridian, a circle encompassing the whole globe by way of the two poles*'.[52] Although many scholars have proclaimed that in Tordesillas the world was partitioned in two,[53] geographical knowledge in 1494 '*could literally not encompass the entire globe as, prior to the Portuguese voyages, nothing was known with any degree of accuracy of the geographical coordinates of the Indian ocean*'.[54] Neither had the Castilian king's cosmographer Jaime Ferrer, in charge of working out the details for the crown, mentioned a line in the Pacific. He had sent a '*forma mundi*' to the Catholic kings, which showed, as he writes, '*the two hemispheres: . . . our Arctic and the opposite Antarctic*', which clearly indicates that he had only the Atlantic in mind.[55] In the same vein, the confirmation of the Treaty of Tordesillas issued by Pope Julius II in his bull *Ea Quae* of 1506 only speaks of *one* singular ocean: *per dictum mare navigare et insulas novas perquirere et capere.*[56]

So why did the parties assume—from a certain moment at the beginning of sixteenth century—that a demarcation line in the Pacific already existed? Why did they accept that the line drawn in Tordesillas had an effect on the Pacific, if in Tordesillas there was no reference to the antemeridian or the Pacific whatsoever? The only explanation to these questions which, as far as I can see, has never been raised, is that at some moment in time, surely after signing the Treaty of Tordesillas and before the signing of the Treaty of Saragossa, something happened which convinced all interested parties that the line established in Tordesillas was meant to be extended to the other hemisphere and form a circle with the meridian. But what was it that had happened?

2. Uniting kingdoms, exploring the globe

A brief look at the historical context of these negotiations may be necessary to answer this question. In the thirty-five years between the signing of the Treaty of Tordesillas and the Treaty of Saragossa, Europe experienced the Reformation movements and a

52 Ricardo Padrón, 'A Sea of Denial: The Early Modern Spanish Invention of the Pacific Rim', *Hispanic Review* (2009), pp. 1–27, at p. 11.

53 Even experts like Brotton, *A History*, p. 187 (n. 8).

54 Brotton, *Trading Territories*, p. 120 (n. 9). See also Rumeau de Armas, *El Tratado de Tordesillas*, pp. 207ff. (n. 19).

55 Cerezo Martínez, 'El meridiano', pp. 509–42, at pp. 523ff. (n. 35). In the same vein Ramón Ezquerra Abadía, 'La idea del antimeridiano', in Avelino Teixeira da Mota (ed.), *A viagem de Fernão de Magalhães e a questão das Molucas: actas do II Colóquio Luso-Espanhol de História Ultramarina* (1975), pp. 1–26, at pp. 7–8, although he points out that there might have been a first 'allusion at a hypothetical antimeridian'. For the text see *Letra feta als molt Catholichs Reis* [. . .], dated 27 January 1495: '[. . .] y ansi envio con un hombre mio [. . .] una forma mundi en figura extensa en que podran ver los dos hemisferios: conviene saber, el nuestro Artico y el opósito Antártico [. . .], in Fernandez de Navarrete, *Colección de los viajes*, vol. II, n. 68, pp. 119–28, at p. 120 (n. 34).

56 Metzler, *America Pontificia*, I, n. 10, pp. 100–2, at p. 101 (n. 20).

media revolution, new power balances, and not least a change of the guard. Charles I had ascended the throne in 1516 as the King of Aragon and Castile along with his mother and in 1519, he inherited the Habsburg monarchy. In Portugal, Juan III succeeded his father Manuel, who had died in 1521. Most importantly for the relations between the two monarchies, in 1524 the crowns agreed upon the marriage between Catherine of Castile, the sister of Emperor Charles, and King John III of Portugal. Two years later, in 1526, Emperor Charles married the *Infanta* Isabel of Portugal, the sister of the King John III.

The cross-marriages carried important consequences for the relations of the two kingdoms and their overseas policy. After Tordesillas, both crowns had pursued intense exploratory activities in both directions, to the east and the west. With the discovery of the seaway around the Cape of Good Hope, the Portuguese crown attempted to monopolize the spice trade with the Pacific Islands and aggressively sought to reach the Moluccas. The goal each shared was to annex the so-called Spice Islands, with their legendary riches, into proprietary spheres of influence. Their commercial interest was to experience immense growth during the first decades of sixteenth century, especially through explorations and discoveries in the West. Explorers sent out to the West had reached the Brazilian coast in 1500 and established settlements in the Indian Ocean. In 1511, the Portuguese explorer, Alonso de Albuquerque, reached the Moluccas, and later captured the city of Malacca. Some also headed to China. The first European ambassadors arrived in Canton in 1517. During the same period, Amerigo Vespucci's expeditions confirmed that Columbus' voyages had led to a whole new continent lying between Europe and the East Indies, and not to India. In 1513, Vasco Nuñez de Balboa crossed the Isthmus of Panama and reached the Pacific by land. After failed first attempts in 1517, Hernán Cortes in 1519 began the *conquista* of what would soon be called New Spain. In 1519, the Portuguese-born Ferdinand Magellan, now serving the Castilian crown, embarked on his voyage in search of the westward sea route to the Pacific. Part of his fleet reached the Moluccas in 1521 and returned to Castile in 1522, albeit without its commander and led instead by his companion Juan Sebstián de Elcano. The significance of this voyage has been enormous. '*If the Magellan/Elcano expedition had made the globe into a real object, a global stage on which humans actually did something, it also made plans for global empire real, more than metaphors.*'[57]

All this activity was accompanied by the intense efforts of both crowns to augment their knowledge about the world. In 1505 and 1508, the Castilian king, Fernando, gathered experts in the *Juntas* in Toro and Burgos to discuss ways of finding a new route to the Spice Islands.[58] They agreed on creating the new function of a *piloto mayor* in the nucleus of what later became the Council of the Indies. This *Casa de Contratación* was slated to be that place in the Spanish empire where

[57] Chaplin, *Round about the Earth*, pp. 38–9 (n. 16). See for the general historical context the bibliography cited in (n. 2).

[58] See on this Sánchez Martínez, *La Espada* (n. 10); Ezquerra Abadía, 'La idea del antimeridiano', pp. 1–26 (n. 55).

cosmographical, nautical, and cartographic knowledge would be centralized. It hosted the *Padrón Real*, a map where all available geographical and geodetic information was incorporated.[59] Similarly, the Portuguese crown had already in 1500 established a *Casa da Índia* and had made enormous progress in cartography.[60] Cartography served the crown's interests in both Iberian empires, not least when the quest for the Moluccas intensified.[61]

3. Cutting the world 'like an orange': the antimeridian appears

It may have been due to this interest in and not least the institutionalization of cosmographical knowledge that the notion of the 'antimeridian' appeared on the stage of history of international law.[62] The first clues that the meridian drawn in Tordesillas was considered to have an effect on the Pacific appear in documents from the beginning of the second decade of sixteenth century. After receiving the news of the occupation of Malacca by Albuquerque in 1511, King Fernando sent out a Spanish expedition under the command of Juan Díaz de Solis. The *capitulación* given to Solis, dated 27 May 1512, clearly described as a goal of this voyage to clarify the demarcation line in the Pacific, and to take possession of what belonged to the Castilian crown, especially the Moluccas 'which falls within our demarcation line'. Solis was also ordered to be careful in drawing adequately and justly the demarcation line, assumed to fall in the middle of what is today Sri Lanka, because it was the explicit intention not to violate the agreements with the Portuguese.[63] After his voyage had been suspended, in 1514 Solis was sent again to make discoveries '*por las espaldas de Castilla de oro*'—which meant on the other

[59] Mariano Cuesta Domingo, 'Tradición y progreso en la cartografía de la Casa de la Contratación', in Mariano Cuesta Domingo and Alfredo Surroca Carrascosa (eds.), *Cartografía Hispánica: Imagen de un Mundo en Crecimiento, 1503-1810* (2010), pp. 21–45; Sánchez Martínez, '*An Official Image*' (n. 10).

[60] See Brotton, *Trading Territories*, pp. 46ff. (n. 9); an overview also in David Turnbull, 'Cartography and Science in Early Modern Europe: Mapping the Construction of Knowledge Spaces', *Imago Mundi* 48 (1996), 5–24; Maria F. Alegria, Suzanne Daveau, João Carlos Garcia, Francesc Relaño (eds.), *História da Cartografia Portuguesa, séculos XV a XVII* (2012); Cortesão and Teixeira da Mota, *Portugaliae Monumenta Cartographica* (n. 19).

[61] Antonio Sánchez Martínez, 'De la 'cartografía oficial' a la 'cartografía jurídica': la querella de las Molucas reconsiderada, 1479-1529', *Nuevo Mundo Mundos Nuevos* [*En ligne*] (2009); Brendecke, *Imperium und Empirie*, pp. 109ff. (n. 5); Reguera Rodríguez, *Los geógrafos del rey* (n. 10).

[62] Ana María Barrero García, 'Las juntas y las conversaciones castellano-portuguesas en los años posteriores al Tratado', in Luis Antonio Ribot García, Adolfo Carrasco Martínez, and Luís Adão da Fonseca (eds.), *El Tratado de Tordesillas y su época* (1995), pp. 1365–86; Mariano Cuesta Domingo, 'La fijación de la línea - de Tordesillas - en el Extremo Oriente', in Luis Antonio Ribot García, Adolfo Carrasco Martínez, and Luis Adão da Fonseca (eds.), *El Tratado de Tordesillas y su época* (1995), pp. 1483–1518; María Lourdes Díaz-Trechuelo López Spínola, 'Consecuencias y problemas derivados del Tratado de Tordesillas en la expansión oriental', in Luis Antonio Ribot García, Adolfo Carrasco Martíne, and Luís Adão da Fonseca (eds.), *El Tratado de Tordesillas y su época* (1995), pp. 519–40; Cerezo Martínez, 'El meridiano', pp. 509–42 (n. 35); Ezquerra Abadía, 'La idea del antimeridiano', pp. 1–26 (n. 55); Sandman, 'Spanish Nautical', pp. 1095–1142, esp. p. 1111 (n. 10).

[63] The *capitulación* is transcribed in José Toribio Medina, *Juan Díaz de Solis. Estudio Histórico*, 2 (1897), n. 22, pp. 58–69, esp. pp. 64–6.

side of the Americas, with the same idea of clarifying the demarcation.[64] There is further evidence that Magellan, who had participated in the occupation of Malacca in 1511, was convinced that if the Treaty of Tordesillas were applied to the Pacific, the Moluccas would lie within the sphere allocated to the Castilian crown, an opinion he expressed in the same years.[65] Uncertainty about whether the line could be stretched to the other hemisphere to form the antimeridian—or the fear that this would happen—might also have been the reason for why King Emmanuel of Portugal had approached Pope Leo X with the supplication to renew the concessions granted to the Portuguese crown in previous Bulls, assuring it the rights to the whole Pacific. The Pope had accomplished just that in the bull, *Praecelsae Devotionis*, of 3 November 1514 not by mentioning the previous Papal Bulls that had been issued by Pope Alexander VI in 1493, but, instead, by referring to the earlier concessions granted to the Portuguese, including the Treaty of Alcáçovas.[66]

Over the years, the line drawn in Tordesillas seemed to denote with greater clarity, at least for the Castilian side, a meridian, which would be extended beyond the poles into the other hemisphere to form the antimeridian. In the *capitulación* with Magellan, signed in Valladolid on 22 March 1518, the goal of the explorations was described as being to 'discover what has not yet been discovered [. . .] within our limits and demarcation, within the dominions which are ours in the Ocean, within the limits of our demarcation, Islands and *tierra firme* and rich spices', separating this from what was within the demarcated territories of the Portuguese king.[67] Theoretical writings supported that viewpoint. The *Suma de Geographia q[ue] trata de todas las partidas [et] provincias del mundo: en especial de las indias* [. . .], published in 1519 in Salamanca, a centre for cosmographic debates, put forth a clear statement for the Spanish territories in parts of the Pacific, due to a 'border' ('*limite*').[68] Frequently cited in this context is the statement of a Castilian crown official, Alonso de Zuazo, who in 1518 wrote to the emperor from his new post in Santo Domingo, Hispaniola, informing him that it was common knowledge ('*Sábese*') that Pope Alexander's concession had rendered the world divided '*like an orange*'. In the same letter, the recently appointed judge, and ambitious *protegée* of Cardenal Cisneros, pointed out that Portugal had many territories in the Pacific that belonged to the

[64] In the *asiento* dated 24 November 1514, they stipulate that he should go 1,700 leagues from the tip of the Americas towards the Pacific, without touching upon what belongs to the Portuguese, see Martín Fernández de Navarette, *Colección de los viajes y descubrimientos que hicieron por mar los Españoles*, vol. III (1945), n. 35, pp. 147–9; n. 36, pp. 149–50, at p. 147 and similarily p. 149.

[65] See on this Brotton, *Trading Territories*, p. 125 (n. 9), citing the chronicler's Bartolomé Leonardo de Argensolas, *Conquista de las Islas Malucas*. See also Ezquerra Abadía, 'La idea del antimeridiano', pp. 1–26, pp. 12ff. (n. 55).

[66] The Bull is transcribed in Gardiner Davenport, *European Treaties*, n. 12, pp. 112–17 (n. 20).

[67] See *Capitulacion y asiento que SS. MM. mandaron tomar con Magallanes y Falero sobre el decubrimiento de las islas de la especería* [. . .], 22 March 1518, in Martín Fernández de Navarette, *Colección de los viajes y descubrimientos que hicieron por mar los Españoles*, IV (1946), n. 3, pp. 109–13, at p. 109.

[68] Martín Fernández de Enciso, *Suma de Geographia* (1519), cited after the edición facsimilar, por José Ibáñez Cerdá, *Colección Joyas Bibliográficas* (1948), p. 25: 'Y pasado de Melaca docientas leguas se acaba el límite de lo del Rey de Portugal: y al fin deste limite está la boca del Ganges [. . .]'. See on Encisco's work more extensively Padrón, *The Spacious Word*, pp. 84ff. (n. 7).

king, '*at least according to the world map which Amerigo, who has been around this area, ordered to be printed, which has a round form and which the señor Infante has in his room*'.[69]

4. Cosmography, cartography and the production of law

Alonso de Zuazo's remark shows that if by 1518 the antimeridian had already become a legal argument this may have been not least due to the visualization of cosmographic knowledge. It seems reasonable to assume that visualizing the world not as a flat map, but with a spherical projection in a round map, as might have been part of the decoration of the Castilian *Infante's* room, might have been important for understanding the line drawn in Tordesillas as a meridian which had to have effect on the other side of the globe.[70]

In fact, two decades after the signing of the Treaty of Tordesillas, the image of the world had undergone a radical change, and the dynamic production of world maps ensured that the size and shape of the earth was being visualized differently than in the days of Tordesillas.[71] Now, world maps, spherical projections, or globes, were produced at many sides, not least in the centres of cosmographical knowledge in Castile and Portugal. These maps did not only empower their owners '*in making a series of claims to both worldly, and other-wordly authority*',[72] they also provided practical information, defined provisional fields of economic exploration, and not least, they demonstrated that it was possible and necessary for the meridian drawn in Tordesillas to be stretched to the other hemisphere as an antimeridian in order to form a full circle.

The first map to be painted for the Spanish crown showing a meridian is attributed to Juan de la Cosa, dating from 1500.[73] It shows a line called *linia meridionalis*,

[69] See *Carta del licenciado Alonso de Zuazo a Carlos I* [. . .], 22 January 1518, in Joaquín Pacheco, Francisco de Cárdenas, and Luis Torres de Mendoza (eds.), *Colección de documentos inéditos relativos al descubrimiento, conquista y organización de las antiguas posesiones españolas de América y Oceanía* (1864, reprint 1964), pp. 292–8, at p. 296. Ezquerra Abadía, 'La idea del antimeridiano', pp. 1–26, at p. 13 (n. 55), suggests, without further explanations, that the map could be the Waldseemüller World Map.

[70] This shows that Magellan might not have been thinking so much '*outside the geographical mentality of his time*', as Brotton, *A History*, p. 194 (n. 8) emphasized, and that at this moment princes and diplomats did not continue 'to envisage the world on a flat map, with no real sense of the connection between the earth's western and eastern hemispheres'. However, it confirms that 'beginning to imagine the world as a global continuum' was quite recent these days and clearly related to spatial perceptions shaped by the visualization of space in objects like maps or globes.

[71] See for an overview on the history of cartography Fernández-Armesto, 'Maps and Exploration', pp. 738–70 (n. 10); Sandman, 'Spanish Nautical', pp. 1095–1142 (n. 10); Maria Fernanda Alegria, Suzanne Daveau, João Carlos Garcia, and Francesco Relaño, 'Portuguese Cartography in the Renaissance', in David Woodward (ed.), *The History of Cartography: Cartography in the European Renaissance* (2007), pp. 975–1068; David Buisseret, 'Spanish Colonial Cartography, 1450–1700', in David Woodward (ed.), *The History of Cartography: Cartography in the European Renaissance* (2007), pp. 1143–71; Portuondo, *Secret Science*, pp. 33ff. (n. 10); Sánchez Martínez, '*An Official Image*' (n. 10); Cerezo Martínez, *La cartografía* (n. 10); on Antonio de Nebríjas teaching on the longitude of Tordesillas see Carabias Torres, 'La medida del espacio', pp. 185–202 (n. 48).

[72] Brotton, *Trading Territories*, p. 23 (n. 9).

[73] Jesús Varela Marcos, *Juan de la Cosa: la Cartografía Histórica de los Descubrimientos Españoles* (2011). See also Sánchez Martínez, *La espada*, pp. 62ff. (n. 10).

which in all probability was the line drawn in Tordesillas that ran through the Atlantic, without touching American soil.[74] The distance between Europe and America is still clearly underestimated, as was common at that time. After Pedro Alvares Cabral's expedition had reached the Brazilian coast in 1500, the precise location of the line gained practical importance. The famous Cantino planisphere—see Plate I—was drawn after the return of the expedition in 1502 and based on the information brought back from this voyage, probably as a copy of the official map held in the *Armazém da Guiné e Indias* in Lisbon.[75] This planisphere is considered the oldest map in existence, undisputedly with latitudes determined by using the astronomical method.[76] And although the circumference of the earth is again underestimated, the line of Tordesillas is clearly marked and runs through Brazil.[77] It was, however, still a flat map which avoided answering—or even raising—the question where the meridian of Tordesillas would fall if it ran right round the globe.

An increasing number of maps followed, drawn not least by Portuguese cartographers: the Pirî Reis Map of the Atlantic (1503), the Map of the Atlantic by Pedro Reines (circa 1504), and the Nautical Planisphere of Nicolò Caverio (1505).[78] Also Martin Waldseemüller's famous World Map and the gores for constructing globes also appeared in these years, 1507, published together with the *Cosmographiae introduction*.[79] One year later, in 1508, for the first time, a flat map depicted the globe in its entirety.[80] Some years later, cartographers of both kingdoms drew world maps which clearly depict the world divided by a meridian and an antimeridian.[81] A 1519 drawing attributed to Antonio de Holanda, part of the so-called *Miller Atlas*, made for the Portuguese king, clearly shows that the line drawn in Tordesillas had an effect on the Pacific;[82] the whole world shown on the map is the hemisphere belonging to the Portuguese king, and that included the Moluccas—see Plate II.

[74] Hugo O'Donnell and Duque de Estrada, 'La Carta de Juan de la Cosa, primera presentación cartográfica del Tratado de Tordesillas', in Luis Antonio Ribot García, Adolfo Carrasco Martínez, and Luís Adão da Fonseca (eds.), *El Tratado de Tordesillas y su época* (1995), pp. 1231–44.

[75] Mendonça de Albuquerque, 'O Tratado de Tordesilhas', pp. 119–36 (n. 47). See on the Cantino planisphere Brotton, *A History*, pp. 190ff. (n. 9); Sánchez Martínez, *La Espada*, pp. 81ff. (n. 10).

[76] Joaquim Alves Gaspar, 'From the Portolan Chart to the Latitude Chart: The Silent Cartographic Revolution', *Comité français de Cartographie* 216 (2013), 67–77.

[77] Fernando Lourenço Fernandes, *O planisfério de Cantino e o Brasil: Uma introdução à cartologia política dos descobrimentos e o Atlântico Sul* (2003).

[78] Luisa Martín-Meras Verdejo, 'The Exploration and Geopolitical Stakes of Iberian Cartography, 15th and 16th centuries', in Catherine Hofmann, Hélène Richard, and Emmanuelle Vagnon (eds.), *The Golden Age of Maritime Maps: When Europe Discovered the World* (2013), pp. 110–125; Henrique Ferreira Botelho, ed., *Quatro séculos de imagens da Cartografia portuguesa = Four centuries of images from Portuguese Cartograph* (2nd edn, 1999).

[79] See on Waldseemüller and his World Map Brotton, *A History*, pp. 146ff. (n. 8).

[80] See on this Padrón, 'A Sea of Denial', pp. 1–27, at p. 12.

[81] One of the first—or perhaps the very first—is the map of Jorge Reinel, drawn *c.* 1519 for the preparation of the voyage of Magellan, which was lost in the Second World War. See on this Henriette Ozanne, 'La découverte cartographique des Moluques', in Monique Pelletier (ed.), *Géographie du monde au Moyen Âge et à la Renaissance* (1989), pp. 217–28. See also Ezquerra Abadía, 'La idea del antimeridiano', pp. 1–26 (n. 55).

[82] Mappemonde circulaire représentant l'hémisphère portugais - Atlas Miller: Œuvre de Lopo Homem [Pedro et Jorge Reinel, António de Holanda], [Portugal], 1519. Manuscrit enluminé sur vélin, 41.5 x 59 cm et 61 x 118 cm. BnF, département des Cartes et Plans, CPL GE D-26179 (RES),

Some years later, the nautical planisphere known as Salviatis Map, most probably a copy of the *Padrón Real*, the official map held in the Spanish *Consejo de Indias* of circa 1525, clearly shows the Atlantic and the open Pacific, with the meridian of Tordesillas and an antimeridian, but it situates the Moluccas in the Spanish territory. This already shows that now, both sides staked their claims over the Moluccas based on geographical findings, instruments, and cartographic proofs. 'Official cartography', it has been said, was transformed into 'juridical cartography'.[83] Since then, the objects which embodied geographical knowledge, like maps and globes, became an indispensable tool for diplomats and a representation of their aspirations. Some historians even assign them the status of 'legal authority'.[84] Even if one might not agree with these wide ranging conclusions, it seems clear that there is a relation between the enormous changes in the knowledge of the world, its visualization, the appearance of the anti-meridian, and the new interpretation of the Treaty of Tordesillas between 1494 and the second decade of sixteenth century.

5. Settling the dispute: the Junta de Badajoz y Elvas and the Treaty of Saragossa

After the return of Magellan's expedition, intense negotiations took place between the two kings through letters and ambassadors,[85] resulting in the *Asiento de Vitoria*, which was signed on 19 February 1524. In this agreement, the crowns agreed to send two expert committees—astronomers, pilots, cosmographers, mathematicians—to discuss the line of demarcation in the Pacific.[86] On 1 March 1524, both committees met at the border between Castile (Badajoz) and Portugal (Elvas). Renowned expert emissaries for both crowns like Lopo Homen, Diogo Ribeiro, and Diogo Lopes de Sequira participated, bringing along their charts, instruments, and globes, but were unable to reach any agreement.[87] The presence of the objects clearly determined the negotiations, and the failure of the *Junta* must be seen as a consequence not least of still lacking scientific standards.

f. 1 © Bibliothèque nationale de France, online: <http://expositions.bnf.fr/marine/grand/ge-d-26179_01-2.htm>. See on this Sánchez Martínez, *La espada*, pp. 104ff. (n. 10).

[83] Sánchez Martínez, 'De la 'cartografía oficial' (n. 61); Sánchez Martínez, '*An Official Image*' (n. 10).

[84] Brotton, *A History*, p. 201 (n. 8).

[85] See e.g. the *Instrucción que dió el rey al Dr. Cabrero y al Protonotario Barroso sus embajadores para tratar con el rey de Portugal sobre la capitulación del año 1494*, in Fernández de Navarette, *Colección de los viajes IV*, n. 29, pp. 274–7 (n. 67).

[86] See Sánchez Martínez, *La Espada*, pp. 114ff. (n. 10). For the text of the agreement see Mariño, *Tratados internacionales*, n. 15, pp. 113–24 (n. 20). English translation in Gardiner Davenport, *European Treaties*, vol. I, n. 16, pp. 169–98 (n. 20).

[87] Brotton, *A History*, pp. 201ff. (n. 8); Cuesta Domingo, 'La fijación', pp. 1483–1518 (n. 62), Artur Teodoro de Matos, 'As reunioes e as conversaçoes castelhano-portuguesas nos anos posteriores ao Tratado de Tordesilhas', in Luis Antonio Ribot García, Adolfo Carrasco Martínez, and Luís Adão da Fonseca (eds.), *El Tratado de Tordesillas y su época* (1995), pp. 1355–1641; Díaz-Trechuelo López Spínola, 'As reunioes', pp. 1519–1540 (n. 62); Barrero García, 'As reunioes', pp. 1365–86 (n. 62); Rumeu de Armas, *El Tratado de Tordesillas*, pp. 221ff. (n. 19).

Under the changed circumstances, in large part owing to the closer ties between the Portuguese and Castilian Crown, following the crossed marriages of 1524 and 1526, the crowns started to prepare a settlement of the dispute through the Treaty of Saragossa. In the making of the final Treaty of Saragossa of 22 April 1529 which was signed by the representatives of King Charles I of Spain and King John III of Portugal, participants of the Junta de Badajoz y Elva had collaborated. The map of Diego Ribeiro had been particularly important for determining the specifics, and both parties relied heavily on their interpretations of Ptolemy, and the results of the measurements made by their expeditions.[88] The concluding agreement took a surprising turn, in that the treaty was but a contract of sale, with a repurchase agreement (*retrovendendo*) incorporated into it, indicating that the King of Castile would sell

> from this day and for all time, to the said King of Portugal [. . .] all rights, actions, dominions, ownerships, and possessions, or quasi possessions, and all rights of navigation, traffic, and trade in any manner whatsoever that the said Emperor and King of Castile declares that he holds and could hold howsoever and in whatsoever manner in the said Moluccas [. . .].

The demarcation line they then drew served, primarily, to clarify what had been sold:

> . . . in order to ascertain what islands, places, lands, seas, and their rights and jurisdiction, are sold henceforth and forever by the said Emperor and King of Castile, by this contract under the aforesaid condition, to the said King of Portugal, a line must be determined from pole to pole, that is to say, from North to South, by a semi-circular extending northeast by east nineteen degrees from the Moluccas [. . .].

This line should be drawn on two charts to be made according to the model chart held in the *Casa de la Contratación*, the *Padrón Real*, drawn by Diego Ribeiro.

However, both parties seemed unwilling to definitively cede positions claimed on the basis of the demarcation line drawn according to cosmographical criteria close to where they had assumed the antimeridian would run. While the King of Castile had the right to 'cancel the contract', the King of Portugal also reserved for himself the right to 'prove his right to the ownership' of the Moluccas, and appointed an expert commission to that end. The appointment stipulated that these experts

> shall consult, covenant, and agree upon the manner of asserting the right of said proprietorship pursuant to said Treaty and contract made between the said Catholic sovereigns, Don Fernando and Doña Isabella, and the said King, Dom John II, of Portugal. In case the said Emperor and King of Castile be judged to have the right of said proprietorship, such sentence shall not be executed nor used until the said Emperor and King of Castile [. . .] shall first have actually returned all the said 350,000 ducats, which by virtue of this contract should have been given. . .

[88] Brotton, *Trading Territories*, pp. 135ff. (n. 9); Sánchez Martínez, '*De la "cartografía oficial"*' (n. 61).

and vice versa.[89] A pragmatic solution was contracted between two dynasties that decided to strengthen their ties, eventually even uniting the crowns under one hereditary line through cross-marriages.

This might already show that contrary to common perception, the Treaty of Saragossa did not partition the world or simply draw a line through unknown territories, when in fact all it did was settle a dispute that arose owing to the year-long race to explore and occupy territories in the area that had motivated European overseas expansion since its beginnings in the fifteenth century.[90] Obviously, both sides claimed their rights over the dominions in the Pacific, but they did not do so exclusively drawing on this title. For the purpose of this chapter, however, it seems clear that it was precisely the inability of early modern cosmographers to determine the exact position of the Malacca islands which motivated the treaty.

IV. Conclusion

What can this survey of the legal practice of drawing demarcation lines between 1479 and 1529 tell us about system and order in international law, especially the importance of changing spatial perceptions and their impact on the formation of international legal thought? Obviously, the results of a brief survey—constrained by time and space—can only be limited. However, the following aspects deserve to be highlighted.

(1) Important advances in cartography and changing spatial perceptions around 1500 clearly impacted international legal thought. In fact, within two decades of its signing, the Treaty of Tordesillas was being interpreted very differently. Even if at the moment the Treaty was signed no consideration was given to extending the demarcation line to the Pacific, twenty years later, the interpretation was adapted to new knowledge. Due to new insights about the shape and size of the world that had materialized in world maps and globes, between c. 1502 and c. 1512 the antimeridian drawn using the meridian of Tordesillas seems to have been recognized as a legitimate means of delimitating spheres between the two crowns in both hemispheres. New knowledge about the world, embodied in maps with a spherical projection, and globes, had produced a legal argument. It also had changed the way frontiers were negotiated between the two crowns.

(2) Notwithstanding the said importance of this growing knowledge and its impact on law, drawing demarcation lines around 1500 has to be understood as a blending of traditional practices, empirical observations, and new

[89] The translation follows Gardiner Davenport, *European Treaties*, pp. 187–9 (n. 20).

[90] Obviously, this interpretation is far more sober than the usual affirmations, see for example Chaplin, *Round about the Earth*, p. 41 (n. 16): 'The line's imprecision mattered less than its global pretension: it was the first civil boundary drawn *around* the whole Earth, a breathtaking imperial claim to the world, premised on the ability to go around it.'

scientific knowledge. As is the case with the legal historical interpretation of the treaties,[91] which could not be dealt with extensively here, and as emphasized in recent historiography on early sixteenth-century cartography,[92] continuity with previous medieval thought and practices should not be underrated. In the Papal Bulls and the Treaty of Tordesillas, the demarcation line drawn in Alcáçovas in 1479 was changed, shifted, and fixed according to the interests of the parties. The space in which these lines were drawn was neither unknown nor considered blank space. The line drawn in Alcáçovas as well as the 100-league-line of the Papal Bulls and the 370-league-line of Tordesillas were drawn from fixed and known points. They responded at least in part to observations made on sea and some of them were suggested by Columbus himself. The Treaty of Saragossa finally established a demarcation line in an area absolutely not unknown. By the time the Treaty was signed in 1529, the histories of conquest, subjection of peoples, discoveries, and appropriation of islands and cities had already been under way for over fifteen years. No doubt, geodetic measurements were important for locating the antimeridian and influenced the negotiations. But as the agreement to send out a joint voyage to the 370-leagues-line in Tordesillas as well as the failing negotiations at the *Junta* of Bajadoz and Elvas thirty years later demonstrated, there was no scientific knowledge sufficient to fix a line simply by drawing on cosmographic knowledge. Many maps used were still based on Ptolemy's 1,300-year-old map projections, '*reproducing many of the Greek geographer's errors, and adhering to a geocentric view of the universe that would only be challenged with the publication of Copernicus's* On the Revolution of the Celestial Spheres *in 1543*'—as Jerry Brotton emphasizes '*hardly signs of a challenging modernity*'.[93] What has been called a 'rationalization of space' thus was a complex, slow process that built upon tradition, and existing practices and went in hand with explorations and experimental knowledge-creation by measurements.[94]

(3) In the light of what has been said up to this point, Carl Schmitt's far ranging diagnosis of the spatial revolution and the emergence of global linear thinking seems to lack historical foundation. Without taking previous practices into account, as in other fields a 'frustrating lack of detail and textual specificity to his arguments', he created a teleological and political-theological

[91] See Muldoon, 'Bridging the Medieval-Modern Divide', pp. 175–204 (n. 1) with further references. From a doctrinal point of view, García-Gallo, 'Las bulas', pp. 461–829 (n. 19); Hera Pérez-Cuesta, 'La primera división', pp. 1051–70 (n. 24) also emphasize that the Papal Bulls and the subsequent treaties have to be interpreted from their medieval origins.

[92] Padrón, *The Spacious Word*, p. 69 (n. 7); Brotton, *A History*, p. 182 (n. 8), regarding the Waldseemüller map of 1507.

[93] Brotton, *A History*, p. 154 (n. 8).

[94] In a similar vein, looking at later developments, Benton, *A Search for Sovereignty* emphasizes: 'The same treaty that appears to represent the extra-European world as an object of European imperial rule instead shows the ways it stimulated a fluid geographic discourse and open-ended legal politics', p. 23 (n. 5).

interpretation of the history of international legal thought.[95] Schmitt 'recognized (and celebrated)' the dependence of the entire European state system upon colonialism and imperialism and rightly emphasized that modern territorial politics emerged as a consequence of the conquest of the New World.[96] However, the function of his historical interpretation, explicitly posed in line with Savignian historical jurisprudence, was to base his tragic vision on the rise and fall of his *Jus publicum Europaeum*.[97] One should read his account as what it is: a piece of political philosophy, a normative statement, drawing on a very small historical basis.

(4) Finally, the case study presented here might illustrate that considering the changing knowledge about space can be an important element for writing the history of international law. Taking changing spatial perceptions into account, being attentive to the objects which embody this knowledge and shape spatial imagination, and integrating the insights drawn from history of knowledge into praxeological perspectives might help to improve our legal historical interpretation about how international normative orders emerge. Despite the understandable temptation to reduce complex historical processes to suggestive 'revolutions', the challenge legal historical research is facing precisely consists in the opposite: in understanding the elements and mechanisms, the ideas as well as the material dimension which jointly determine the complex and gradual transformations of (international) legal orders.

[95] Stuart Elden, 'Reading Schmitt Geopolitically. Nomos, Territory and Großraum', in Stephen Legg (ed.), *Spatiality, Sovereignty and Carl Schmitt: Geographies of the Nomos* (2011), pp. 91–105, at p. 97. Michael Heffernan, 'Mapping Schmitt', in Stephen Legg (ed.), *Spatiality, Sovereignty and Carl Schmitt: Geographies of the Nomos* (2011), pp. 234–43; Koskenniemi, 'International Law', pp. 492–511 (n. 16). For a critique of the concept from a legal historical point of view see briefly Benton, *A Search for Sovereignty*, pp. 282–3 (n. 5).

[96] Stephen Legg and Alexander Vasudevan, 'Introduction: Geographies of the Nomos', in Stephen Legg (ed.), *Spatiality, Sovereignty and Carl Schmitt: Geographies of the Nomos* (2011), pp. 1–23, at p. 3; Elden, 'Reading Schmitt', pp. 91–105, at p. 96 (n. 95). A critique of Schmitt's ideas also in Fisch, *Die europäische Expansion* (n. 1).

[97] See on this and the term also Armin von Bogdandy and Stephan Hinghofer-Szalkay, 'Das etwas unheimliche Ius Publicum Europaeum: Begriffsgeschichtliche Analysen im Spannungsfeld von europäischem Rechtsraum, droit public de l'Europe und Carl Schmitt', *Zeitschrift für ausländisches öffentliches Recht und Völkerrecht (ZaöRV)* 73/2 (2013), 209–48, at 236ff.

21

The Disorder of Economy? The First *Relectio de Indis* in a Theological Perspective

Mónica García-Salmones Rovira

Christophe Grellard locates the nominalist debate that took place at the end of the Middle Ages within the process of evolution towards a secularist society. In his helpful interpretation of Certeau's thesis about the possibility of contrasting form and content in a history of doctrine and a sociology of practice, Grellard describes how the enunciation of faith became increasingly disassociated from the demands of action. A 'relativization of the social value of belief' occurred 'that allows the progressive secularization of society'. According to both these authors, a movement started towards dispensing with the practices that should have accompanied doctrinal content. While content and dogma remained, these practices vanished on the basis of an order subject to different constraints than those proposed by faith. 'It is this that allows the substitution of a code by another: we move from a theological code, in which theology supports the whole of the social structures to a political and economic code.'[1]

On the basis of an analysis of the theology of Francisco de Vitoria (1483–1546) and a review of his famous *Relectio de Indis*, this chapter nuances the previous argument that a new secular world of politics and economy arose at the end of the Middle Ages, in which the practice of Christian faith became unwelcome. For one thing, although their humanist sympathies meant that they did not favour imperialist conquest per se, it was theologians, rather than economists or politicians, who responded positively to the macro-economic enterprise aspect of the colonization of America. Adherents to the late scholastic tradition, such as Vitoria, cemented the work of rationalization and secularization of the communication between peoples (from there Vitoria's already traditional title of founder of international law).[2]

[1] Christophe Grellard, *De la certitude volontaire: débats nominalistes sur la foi à la fin du Moyen Âge* (2014), pp. 13–15, at p. 14 (author translation; unless otherwise stated all translations are the author's); Michel de Certeau, 'The Formality of Practices: From Religious Systems to the Ethics of Enlightenment (the Seventeenth and Eighteenth Centuries)' in *The Writing of History*, trans. Tom Conley (1988), pp. 147–205.

[2] Joseph Barthélemy, 'François de Vitoria', in *Les fondateurs du droit international: F. de Vitoria, A. Gentilis, F. Suarez, Grotius, Zouch, Pufendorf, Bynkershoek, Wolf, Wattel, de Martens; leurs œuvres, leurs*

The Disorder of Economy? The first Relectio de Indis *in a Theological Perspective.* Mónica García-Salmones.

Moreover, they did so as theologians. The fact that between the internal perspective of the moral and virtuous individual and the external needs of an expanding economy of exchange the moral theologians of Salamanca appeared to have been drawn to choose the latter is particularly visible in Vitoria's *De Indis*, which continues to astonish the reader due to its remarkable novelty and independence of contemporary theory.[3] Despite its avowedly Thomistic approach to many doctrinal points, the Salamanca School avoided the tension that would have arisen if Aquinas's theory of moral virtue had been applied to its members' thinking on economic and political matters. It seems that the Salamanca School developed an economic theory and employed a type of moral theory that reflect one another.

The moral economy that flourished in Salamanca during the sixteenth and seventeenth centuries has been the object of a great deal of study.[4] The influence exerted by these theologians has recently been emphasized in the argument that the Salamanca School developed a special moral theory for merchants, enabling them to establish in the long run an international system of commerce that was out of the reach of the prince and based on the key concepts of *dominium* and *jus gentium*.[5]

The activities of the scholastic theologians of Salamanca also coincided with a general engagement with law on the part of moral theologians, similar to what canon lawyers had been doing during the course of at least three centuries. Decock thinks that that was a 'jurisdiction over man that has now disappeared'.[6] My intuition is that back then and now the key question continues to revolve around the freedom of conscience and the government of conduct.[7]

Furthermore, in the face of the new situations, new territorial discoveries and new challenges to imperial authority that arose in the sixteenth and seventeenth centuries, a massive extension of the rules of natural law as moral law can be ascertained.

doctrines, ouvrage collectif (1904), pp. 1–36; James Brown Scott, *The Spanish Origins of International Law: Francisco de Vitoria and His Law of Nations* (1934).

[3] This attitude is also articulated through the development of the theory of the providential function of commerce. For this argument, see Ileana M. Porras, 'The Doctrine of the Providential Function of Commerce in International Law: Idealizing Trade' in Martti Koskenniemi, Mónica García-Salmones, and Paolo Amorosa (eds.), *International Law and Religion: Historical and Contemporary Perspectives* (forthcoming).

[4] Among others, see Raúl González Fabre, *Justicia en el Mercado: La Fundamentación de la ética del mercado según Francisco de Vitoria* (1998); José Barrientos García, *Repertorio de Moral Económica (1536-1670): La Escuela de Salamanca y su proyección* (2011); Domenec Mele, 'Early Business Ethics in Spain: The Salamanca School (1526-1614)', *Journal of Business Ethics* 22 (1999), 175–89; Juan Manuel Elegido, 'The Just Price: Three Insights from the Salamanca School', *Journal of Business Ethics* 90 (2009), 29–46.

[5] Martti Koskenniemi, 'Empire and International Law: The Real Spanish Contribution', *University of Toronto Law Journal* 61 (2011), 1–36.

[6] He also refers to a 'juristic notion of conscience': Wim Decock, *Theologians and Contract Law: The Moral Transformation of the jus Commune (c. 1500-1650)* (2013), at p. 21 and p. 27.

[7] The charge that priests and casuists have governed conduct is a common topos in some histories of conscience. For an insightful argument on the governing of conduct in the post-Reformation era and Locke's own techniques in that regard, see James Tully, 'Governing Conduct' in Edmund Leites (ed.), *Conscience and Casuistry in Early Modern Europe* (2002), pp. 12–70. Foucault also addressed this issue in Michel Foucault, 'Truth and Subjectivity', 20.1.1980, <http://www.lib.berkeley.edu/MRC/foucault/howison.html>.

At the outset, the question may candidly be asked as to why, when new events occur, would one need *new* moral theories, if naturally the terms of moral action—that is to say, the means to decide what was morally right—may be found within human nature. Arguably only the labouring of reason about the new cases would have sufficed.[8] Or to put it in Christian terms, would the Decalogue not suffice?

Francisco de Vitoria's answer in *De Indis* about the morality of the *Conquista*, although it fits squarely within doctrinal elaborations of natural law, is far from typical of casuistic doctrines provoked by moral uncertainty. Vitoria, in fact, works with casuistic theology, for instance in his commentary on the *Summa Theologia*, and frames his answer in *De Indis* as a case of conscience, admonishing the listener to act either '*per rationem probabilem*' or '*per auctoritatem sapientum*'.[9] However, in *De Indis* he does not theorize in the abstract, as is the case in the inherently paradoxical casuistic literature.[10] Rather, Vitoria responds to the specific question of whether one should consider what was happening in the New World to be legitimate or not, and thus act accordingly. Moreover, notwithstanding his setting the facts of the real situation before his audience, the manner in which Vitoria studied the actual event in relation to the moral and cosmological order is simply unorthodox. It is not possible to recognize in Vitoria, a Christian theologian, the dichotomy of order built upon the individual being and upon the universal order, both being dependent on each other. The conclusion at which he arrived, and his very reasoning, shows that despite the presentation of the problem as a moral question of conscience the activity of inquiry undertaken by the Salamancan theologian was not driven by a concern for order in the Augustinian sense.[11]

[8] See e.g. Stefan Kadelbach, in this volume p. 147, stating the opinion of Grotius: '"Natural law" including the first principles of nature (*prima naturae*), the "first duty" to take care of oneself (I 2, 1.1), can be ascertained by virtue of human reason, since a sense of what complies with it and what does not is part of the human condition (Pr. 9, 23, 39).'

[9] Francisco de Vitoria, 'De Indis recenter inventis. Relectio prior, in *De Indis et de Ivre Belli Reflections*, ed. Ernest Nys, Herbert Francis Wright editor of the Latin text (1917), at p. 220. On probabilism, see Rudolf Schüssler, 'On the Anatomy of Probabilism', in Kraye and Saarinen (eds.), *Moral Philosophy on the Threshold of Modernity* (2005), pp. 91–113, at pp. 97, 101, and 106.

[10] See generally, the commentary on questions pp. 57–66, 'On Justice' by Vitoria, who concentrates on the casuistic element already present in Aquinas, and magnifies it. One example among a multitude is about a poor man who is in debt to a rich man. Paying the debt will cause immense harm to the former and cause him to lose his own social status. After considering the different previous opinions, Vitoria concluded that he has to pay and asserted that that question appears often in confession. Vicente Beltrán de Heredia, *Comentarios del maestro Francisco de Vitoria, O.P. a la Secunda secundae de Santo Tomás*, vol. 3, De Justitia (qq. 57/66) (1934), pp. 172–3.

[11] Augustine, *Die Ordnung*, trans. Carl Johann Perl (1966); on the dichotomy of order: 'Man erkennt bei Augustin eine 'Dichotomie der Ordnung' in eine individuelle, dem Einzelwesen inhäriendere (*ordo cuique proprius*) und eine allgemeine, das All umfassende (*ordo universitatis*): Die eine muss man befolgen, einhalten und bewahren (cf. *sequi ac tenere*), die andere will entdeckt und erkannt werden (cf. *vel videre vel pandere*). Beides bedingt einander nach augustinischer Auffassung', Jörg Trelenberg, *Augustins Schrift 'De ordine'* (2009), quote at p. 36, pp. 39–40; see also Therese Fuhrer, 'Tage und Nächte in Cassiciacum. Die Antimanichäische Theodizee in Augustins Dialog De Ordine', in Wolfgang Sonntagbauer and Johannes Klopf (eds.), *Wolfgang Speyer zum 80. Geburtstag*, Supplementband XVI *Grazar Beiträge. Zeitschrift für die klassische Altertumwissenschaft* (2013), pp. 41–57. Although he defines much of his ethical and legal discussion by reference to Augustine's writings, it is now thought that Vitoria, unlike Melchor Cano and Domingo de Soto, had not read Augustine's *The City of God*

This chapter explores three avenues: Vitoria's theology, his understanding of the dispensation of natural law, and the actual text of *De Indis*. Its aim is to acquire further insight into this influential text and its relationship with the doctrinal history of the discipline of international law, as well as into the moral theology of the Salamancan theologians in general. An analysis of the ideas that Vitoria poured into his influential work will also help to assess the argument that in the late Middle Ages a new world order focused on economic issues that a new economic morality adjudicated upon. Rather than in economy, the chapter seeks in a specific style of doing theology and in its partial resurgence as natural law the reasons for disorder, for that division between faith and practice and for the fragmentation between reason and moral decision.

I. Vitoria's Theology for International Law

Francisco de Vitoria was a theologian.[12] An important part of his official tasks was to train future confessors and much of his work makes sense within that historical context.[13] However, in order to appraise his theology properly it is necessary to see him as an intellectual of the first rank. He was a Doctor of the University of Paris, and thus an elite member of the Church.[14] Later Vitoria became a professor at the University of Salamanca, which at that time was the Spanish Empire's principal centre of learning, of an Empire on which, in his time, the sun never set.[15] Furthermore, and not the least in importance among his achievements, Vitoria was founder of his own theological school. Moreover, he consistently introduced himself as a theologian doing theology, as opposed to an advisor to a prince on political matters, and in his writing he never deviated from theological commentary. Therefore, the crucial question is that of what type of theology he, and consequently the School of Salamanca, developed.

closely or even in its entirety: see Mary Keys, 'Religion, Empire and Law among Nations in *The City of God* – From the Salamanca School to Augustine and Back Again' (n. 3).

[12] For a comprehensive study of Vitoria's legal work in this volume, see the contribution by Bunge in this volume.

[13] See n.10. Koskenniemi also notes that a contextual reading of Vitoria 'would highlight that his lectures on the Indians or on just war were composed in the context of teaching future clerics on the management of the sacrament of penance', Martti Koskenniemi, 'Histories of International Law: Significance and Problems for a Critical View', *Temple International and Comparative Law Journal* 27 (2013), 215–40, at 227.

[14] Statistics collated by Farge about theologians who graduated from the University of Paris between 1500 and 1543 suggest this idea. Vitoria is among the twelve most prolific theologians, among the four most re-edited (sixty-one, the others are Josse Clichtove, 210; Guillaume Pepin, eighty-two; and Pierre Dore, fifty-two) and together with Jean Aleaume, Jacques Almain, Josse Clichtove, and John Mair forms a group of five theologians that account for 75 per cent of all the later editions/impressions in scholastic theology. See James K. Farge, *Orthodoxy and Reform in Early Reformation France: The Faculty of Theology of Paris, 1500-1543* (1985), pp. 100–4.

[15] The saying that in the Spanish Empire 'the sun never set' was apparently written in the 1520s by Fray Francisco de Ugalde, see e.g. in Jean-Benoit Nadeau and Julie Barlow, *The Story of Spanish* (2013), p. 172.

An overview of current theological commentary shows that the theology of the Salamanca School, and in particular that of Vitoria, receives a generally positive appraisal.[16] The latter is considered to be the 'father of a new theological style' who did not shy away from 'drinking from the waters of humanism', understood theology as a dynamic and 'open science' and engaged in an actualization of politics. This was reflected in the fact that Vitoria had 'contact with the reality of the concrete, taking distance from the universalities that were considered more proper of medieval thought'.[17] In sum, the founder of the Salamanca School managed to combine 'humanist demands together with dogmatic, ecclesiological, and Christian spirituality', producing a syncretism of humanism and Thomism. His theology combined the 'Mystery of God' with a 'historical sense'. The result was a 'practical fertility' which possessed a 'vital and anthropological orientation', and constituted, in a nutshell, a 'modernization of theology'.[18] This new theology was humanist but not Erasmian, although it fought against the '*verbosismo*' and 'abstractism' so derided by Northern humanists.[19] The renowned historian of theology Melquiades Andrés Cano thought that the greatest originality of the theology practised in the universities of Salamanca and Alcalá derived from the bringing together of philosophical realism and nominalism, articulated in a theology that cares for each person.[20]

Vicente Muñoz Delgado also thought that Vitoria followed the inclination of the Parisian Nominalists towards practical theology and that it is in this area in which Vitoria's fame is well deserved. He also regarded this as a sign that Vitoria adopted Aquinas's theology and not his philosophy. More critical than other commentators, this Professor of Logic and the Philosophy of Sciences at the University of Salamanca for around forty years during the twentieth century took the view that the return of the Salamanca School to Thomistic theology had occurred without benefitting from the advances in science and logic that had taken place between the thirteenth and the sixteenth centuries. Vitoria did not adapt Aquinas to the new *imago mundi*.[21] Teófilo Urdánoz also pinpointed an excessively intense nominalist

[16] Among many others: 'Así nació una fecunda generación teológica de buscadores incansables de la verdad: la generación de Vitoria, Domingo de Soto, Andrés Vega', Melquiades Andrés, 'Facultades de teología, planes de estudio y proyecto de hombre', *Scripta theologica* 12 (1980), 161–9, at p. 164.

[17] Miguel Anxo Pena González, 'La "Escuela de Salamanca": un intento de delimitación del concepto', in Angel Poncela González (ed.), *Escuela de Salamanca. Filosofía y Humanismo ante el Mundo Moderno* (2015), pp. 83–129, pp. 91–2.

[18] Juan Belda Plans, 'Teología práctica y Escuela de Salamanca del s. XVI', *Cuadernos Salmantinos de Filosofía* 30 (2003), 461–89, at 468.

[19] Juan Manuel Villanueva Fernández, 'Erasmismo o teología española del siglo XVI?' in Ruth Fine and Santiago López Navia (eds.), *Cervantes y las religiones* (2008), pp. 301–26. In Spain, the decadent scholastic characterized by strong dialectic aspects that belongs to the historical context of Vitoria was derisively labelled 'teología verbosista', see Juan Belda Plans, *La Escuela de Salamanca y la renovación de la teología en el siglo XVI* (2000), at p. 44.

[20] Andrés Cano, 'Facultades de teología, planes de estudio y proyecto de hombre', at 164–5 (n. 16).

[21] Vicente Muñoz Delgado, *Lógica, ciencia y humanismo en la renovación teológica de Vitoria y Cano* (1980), at p. 49. For instance, he notes that in neither of his *Relectiones de Indis* does Vitoria offer any commentary on the great significance of Colon's discovery for European science, which he interprets as a 'divorce between theology and science', at p. 47.

influence.[22] Other theologians of the twentieth century castigated the theology of the Salamanca School for developing 'a lifeless rationalism' and for professing a 'theology of conclusions'.[23] In spite of the references I have only found a passing mention to the School of Salamanca in Henri de Lubac's *Le Mystère du Surnaturel*.[24] However, it is true that in that text the French theologian provided a forceful critique of an entire tradition of interpretation of Aquinas. Lubac regarded this as erroneous and as establishing a division between 'pure nature' and 'the supernatural' that he also viewed Cajetan, Domingo de Soto, and Francisco Suárez as pursuing.[25] As we will see, one should also include Vitoria in Lubac's list.

Adding to the scholarly debate among theologians as to where the Salamanca School stands in the history of theology, several characteristics attract atention in those texts that are of special interest for international law. This chapter focuses on Vitoria's commentaries on the *Prima Secundae* 'On Law', questions 90–108, his commentaries on the *Secunda Secundae*, questions on 'Justice', and the first *Relectio de Indis*.

For a theologian who wanted to be involved in all human affairs Vitoria worked with a surprisingly pessimistic anthropology, in which the will was not inclined to natural law and natural law was *not inserted* in nature, despite the natural inclination to judge what is right.[26] The objectivism of the Salamanca School to which Richard Tuck refers in his classic work on natural rights,[27] and which he ascribes partly to their Thomism, seems to me to be more related to the firm guidance that is demanded of natural law within the context of a negative anthropological vision

[22] On the basis of a too 'human', in the sense of secular, approach in Vitoria's *Relection on Increase and Diminution of Charity*. Rovira Gaspar, in turn rejects this critique: see María del Carmen Rovira Gaspar, 'La influencia del nominalismo en el pensamiento de Francisco de Vitoria', in Virginia Aspe Armella and María Idoya Zorroza (eds.), *Francisco de Vitoria en la Escuela de Salamanca y su proyección en Nueva España* (2014), pp. 61–71.

[23] On this allegation and the reference to L. Charlier and Henri de Lubac's *Le Mystère du Surnaturel*, see Luis Martinez Fernández, *Sacra doctrina y progreso dogmático en los 'Reportata' inéditos de Juan de Guevara: Dentro del Marco de la Escuela de Salamanca* (1967), at p. 98; also Belda Plans, *La Escuela de Salamanca y la renovación de la teología en el siglo XVI*, pp. 353–4 (n. 19). Mártinez argues against the critique: see pp. 203–20, and also Belda, pp. 353–60.

[24] Henri de Lubac, *Le Mystère du Surnaturel* (1965).

[25] This distinction between the natural and the spiritual man is also identified by Prodi as Cajetan's 'true renovation' of Aquinas's system: Paolo Prodi, *Eine Geschichte der Gerechtigkeit. Vom Recht Gottes zum modernen Rechtstaat*, trans. Annette Seemam (2005), at p. 146. It appears that the debate continues on the basis of two positions that I have only cursively ascertained: on the one side, Lawrence Feingold's apology for Cajetan, in Lawrence Feingold, *The Natural Desire to See God According to St Thomas and his Interpreters* (2010); and on the other, John Milbank attacks that apology as 'palaelothic neo-Thomism' in John Milbank, *The Suspended Middle: Henri de Lubac and the Debate Concerning the Supernatural* (2005).

[26] Aquinas's 'natural law is to be found not in will but in reason' amounts in Vitoria to natural law being located in reason and not in the will 'because the will is not inclined to natural law. But it is proved that it is inclined to the contrary.' Francisco de Vitoria, *De legibus* (2010), at p. 91; the second point; 'Non ergo dicitur lex naturalis quia insit nobis a natura, nam pueri non habent legem naturalem nec habitum, sed quia ex inclinatione naturae iudicamus quae recta sunt, non quod insit qualitas a natura.' Vitoria, *De legibus*, q. 94, *de lege naturali*, at p. 122. Brett also notes this: see Annabel S. Brett, *Changes of State: Nature and the Limits of the City in Early Modern Natural Law* (2001), at p. 12.

[27] See Richard Tuck, *Natural Rights Theories* (1981), at p. 48.

of human beings. Furthermore, Vitoria displayed a clear focus on moral theology and had a tendency to make theory of the concrete case, as Belda has aptly decribed it.[28] The ubiquity that Vitoria sought for the discipline of theology and the activity of the theologian favoured these attitudes. He regarded all matters as being open to theological reflection, as he argued in the introduction to *De Indis* and repeated often in his works.[29]

Vitoria rarely speaks about truth. His theory of knowledge with direct influence in the theory of practical reason seems to be more influenced by nominalism than by Aquinas.[30] For the latter, human beings *participate* in God's cognition and *that* is the science of theology, while it is highly improbable that Vitoria considered theology a science in the classical sense.[31] Aquinas also viewed the light of natural reason that illuminates the first speculative and practical principles as participating in the eternal law.[32] Vitoria's case is intriguing because he often referred to the light of reason but his theory of knowledge did not evince a theory of participation.

As noted above, several of the features of Vitoria's theology appeared in the work of the Parisian Nominalists, and notably in that of Jean Gerson (1363–1429). Vitoria is usually connected with him due to the adoption by the Salamancan theologian of Gerson's notion of *jus*.[33] It is that notion of *jus* as a subjective right and Gerson's ideas on conciliarism that have prompted historians of political theory to revisit his work in the last few decades. The French theologian is viewed today

[28] Belda Plans, 'Teología práctica y Escuela de Salamanca del s. XVI' (n. 19).

[29] 'sacra theologia non habet limites, quia non est homo qui in ea proficere non potest'. From the prologue to the commentary on the *Prima Pars, Summa Theologia*, quoted in Simona Langella, '"Apuntes" sobre el concepto de teología en Francisco de Vitoria', *Cuadernos Salmantinos de Filosofía* 30 (2003), 277–90; also 'El oficio del teólogo es tan vasto, que ningún argumento, ninguna disputa, ninguna materia, parecen ajenos as su profesión', Francisco de Vitoria, 'De la potestad civil', in Luis Getino (ed.), *Derecho natural y de gentes*, trans. with an introduction Eduardo de Hinojosa (1946), at p. 114; for comment on the historical context of this attitude, see Wim Decock, *Theologians and Contract Law*, pp. 21–104 (n. 6).

[30] A good synthesis of Aquinas's practical reason can be found in Michael Baur, 'Law and Natural Law', and Thomas M. Osborne, Jr, 'Practical Reasoning' in Brian Davies and Eleonore Stump (eds.), *The Oxford Handbook of Aquinas* (2012), pp. 238–54, pp. 276–86.

[31] Martinez Fernández painstakingly attempted to demonstrate that he did: see Martinez Fernández, *Sacra doctrina y progreso dogmático en los 'Reportata' inéditos de Juan de Guevara*, pp. 203–20 (n. 23).

[32] Sancti Thomaes de Aquino, *Quaestiones disputatae de veritate*, q. 14, <http://www.corpusthomisticum.org>; John I. Jenkins, *Knowledge and Faith in Thomas Aquinas* (1997); John Finnis, *Natural Law and Natural Rights* (2011), pp. 398–402; Steven P. Marrone, 'Scotus at Paris on the Criteria for Scientific Knowledge', in Stephen F. Brown, Thomas Dewender, and Theo Kobusch (eds.), *Philosophical Debates at Paris in the Early Fourteenth Century* (2009), pp. 383–400; *Aristotle's Posterior Analytics*, ed. and trans. E.S. Bouchier, B.A. (1901); Mark D. Jordan, 'Theology as Speculative and Practical in Thomas Aquinas', in Reijo Työrinoja, Anja Inkeri Lehtinen, and Dagfinn Føllesdal (eds.), *Knowledge and the Sciences in Medieval Philosophy*, vol. 3, 55 *Annals of the Finnish Society for Missiology and Ecumenics* (1990), 430–9; 'And because this active force (the agent intellect) is a certain participation in the intellectual light of separated substances, the Philosopher compares it to a state and to light; which would not be an appropriate way of describing it if it were itself a separate substance.' *Aristotle's De Anima in the Version of William Moerbeke and the Commentary of St. Thomas Aquinas*, trans. Kenelm Foster and Silvester Humphries, introduction by Ivo Thomas (1951), at p. 430.

[33] See q. 62, art. 1, On Restitution, Vitoria, *Comentarios a la Secunda Secundae de Santo Tomás*, at p. 64. Among others, see Tuck, *Natural Rights* (n. 27) and Annabel Brett, *Liberty Rights, and Nature: Individual Rights in Later Scholastic Thought* (2003).

as one of those responsible for the advent of practical theology.[34] His theological method, again similarly to Vitoria's, is described as a theology 'closer to living experience'.[35] Gerson also developed 'an agenda for the theologian', proposing reforms in the study of theology to his mentor Pierre d'Ailly (1351–1420) and the elimination of *useless* teachings, such as those related to definitions of God and of the Trinity. In the same vein, Gerson emphasized moral theology, suggesting that not only the first book of the Sentences by Peter Lombard would be lectured on, but also the second, third, and fourth books, which are devoted to questions of morals and Christian ethics.[36] As a director of consciences he is thought to have coined the term 'moral certainty'.[37] Gerson, who was perhaps a mystic,[38] combined his distrust about the judgments of reason, with the certainty that faith gives 'because only God is immobile, and constant and stable truth and a sure light'.[39]

Richard Tuck has identified the confluence of Gerson's theology with his theory about rights 'in the belief that man's relationship to the world is conceptually the same as God's,' and in the manner that for Gerson God's and man's *dominium* are comparable. Furthermore, Tuck also describes the fact that man's free will 'matched' with the arbitrary freedom of God's will and stated that the covenant that Gerson saw existing between God and man brought about rights for both sides.[40] Together with his influential definition of *jus*, Gerson produced a concept of natural *dominium* as a power or faculty that helped to explain how the unjust may have *dominium* over the just, or why *dominium* continued in mortal sin.[41]

The twist that Vitoria added to Tuck's accurate depiction of *dominium* in Gerson, as a division of rights between God and humanity, was that of placing greater emphasis on the *enjoyment or on using* the 'right and *dominium*' that God, 'out of

[34] Alf Härdelin, 'Jean Gerson ou la théologie pratique en France et en Suède', in Olle Ferm and Per Förnegård, in cooperation with Huges Engel, Aällskapet Runica, and Mediaevalia (eds.), *Regards sur la France du Moyen Âge* Mélanges offerts à Gunnel Engwall (2009), pp. 276–97, at p. 281.

[35] Brian Patrick McGuire, 'Jean Gerson and the Renewal of Scholastic Discourse 1400-1415', in Joseph Canning, Edmund King, and Martial Staub (eds.), *Knowledge, Discipline and Power in the Middle Ages: Essays in Honour of David Luscombe* (2011), pp. 129–44, at p. 129.

[36] Both points in McGuire, 'Jean Gerson and the Renewal of Scholastic Discourse 1400-1415', at p. 131, pp. 142–4.

[37] Rudolf Schlüsser, 'Jean Gerson, Moral Certainty and the Renaissance of Ancient Scepticism', *Renaissance Studies* 23 (2009), 445–62.

[38] Brian Patrick McGuire, *Jean Gerson and the Last Medieval Reform* (2005), pp. 350–2.

[39] 'that there is no judgment of the right reason that is firm and obligatory, unless it is fixed (*stabiliatur*) by the first law and light'. 'De vita spirituale animae', in *Oeuvres complètes [de] Jean Gerson*, intro., texte et notes par Mgr Glorieux, vol. III, ed. Palémon Glorieux (1960–1973) at p. 137. On the value that Gerson attached to Saint Bonaventura's *Journey to God's Mind*, that constituted his favourite reading for thirty years, see Inos Biffi, 'San Bonaventura e la sapienza Cristiana', in Inos Biffi and Constante Marabelli (eds.), *La Nuova Razionalità*, XIII Secolo (2005), pp. 531–96, at p. 554.

[40] 'quo pacto concipi posset absque juris et dominii alicujus collatione apud creaturam cui donatur quoniam recta ratio dictat ut illud sit debitum et suum creaturae quod deus eidem conferre voluerit.' Gerson,'De vita spirituale animae' at p. 145 (n. 39). Tuck, *Natural Rights*, at p. 30 (n. 27).

[41] 'Ex his etiam patet dissolutio illus difficultatis quae multos turbat an injustus possit juste dominari et an ex quocumpque peccato mortali perdatur continuo dominium; similiter quomodo apud religiosos maneat et quomodo non maneat dominum supra res communes.' Gerson, 'De vita spirituale animae', at p. 145 (n. 39).

pure liberality' gave to men.[42] Perhaps more clearly than in other texts, in respect of his commentary on the first article of question 62, *Secunda secundae*, one can speak of a theology of possession in Vitoria. To ascertain whether Vitoria belonged to a theological tradition that possibly reacted against an overly spiritualist conception of how Christians related to the world or, less gloriously, whether he developed a theology for a mercantile empire, requires a more intense engagement with his sources.[43] However, the fact is that the utilitarian aspect of his writings pops up in different ways—sometimes in a subtle manner, often quite explicitly.[44]

II. Natural Good and Dispensation of Natural Law

In keeping with his entire *oeuvre*, notes by his students constitute the commentaries by Vitoria to the *Prima Secundae* on Law, questions 90–108.[45] Examination of a recent edition of those texts reveals that Vitoria comments on the text in his capacity as a theologian and is almost entirely preoccupied with theological problems. Thus the majority of the text deals solely with divine law, in its expressions of natural law, positive divine law, or ecclesiastical divine law.

The question of 'whether the effect of law is to make men morally good' was one of the few instances in which Vitoria refers to human law. He distinguished between virtue on the one hand and the good that is *useful* or *delectable* on the other, and the conclusion of his analysis was that the human legislator also must make citizens morally good.[46] His discussion in *De legibus* shows that Vitoria employed an understanding of the 'natural good' as useful and pleasant, and which amounts

[42] '*Non est potestas nisi a Deo* (Rom. 13.1). Non est dubium. Ergo non haberem dominium mei nisi ipse dedisset mihi, quia nullum potest esse dominium, quomodocumque capiatur dominium nisi a Deo. Et quod dictum est, omnis potestas a Domino Deo est, potest dici de quocumque dominio. Fuit ipse proprietarius omnium. An ergo dederit hominibus aliquod dominium rei.' In the subsequent discussion of the objections, Vitoria's conclusion is that '[Deus] jus et dominium omnium dedit hominibus', 'homo habet dominium omnium rerum', *Comentarios del maestro Francisco de Vitoria, O.P. a la Secunda secundae de Santo Tomás*, at pp. 69, 71, 73 (n. 10).

[43] The second argument in Martti Koskenniemi, 'The Political Theology of Trade Law: The Scholastic Contribution', in Ulrich Fastenrath, Rudolf Geiger, Daniel-Erasmus Khan, Andreas Paulus, Sabine von Schorlemer, and Christoph Vedde (eds.), *From Bilateralism to Community Interest: Essays in Honor of Bruno Simma* (2011), pp. 90–112.

[44] That one of the main principles in Vitoria's manner of theorizing is 'utility' has been observed by others. See e.g. recently Campagna: 'Wird Hobbes in seinem Leviathan sagen, dass es nicht die Wahrheit sondern die Autorität ist, die ein Gesetz zum Gesetz, also zur verbindlichen Norm macht (*auctoritas, non veritas facit legem*), so könnte man Vitorias Ansicht mit folgender Formel darstellen: *utilitas, non sola iustitia facit legem*.' Norbert Campagna, *Francisco de Vitoria: Leben und Werk. Zur Kompetenz der Theologie in politischen und juridischen Fragen* (2010), at p. 75.

[45] One very comprehensive commentary among the numerous made in relation to the contextual history of the University of Salamanca is that done by Barrientos García, *Repertorio de Moral Económica (1536-1670)*, pp. 19–122.

[46] 'Item probatur. Quia respublica ipsa habet auctoritatem inducendi homines ad virtutem, cum habeat ad inducendum ad bonum utile et delectabile, quae sunt minora bona.' Vitoria, *De legibus*, at p. 114 (n. 26).

to keeping oneself from destitution and indigence in the form of material poverty or the loneliness of living like beasts.[47]

Against the background of his concern for natural law and reason stands the fact that by using the terms 'natural good' and 'moral good' Vitoria designated two different realities.[48] This can also be seen in the subtle difference between his definition of natural law and that of Aquinas. Aquinas stated that natural law is that to which a human being is inclined by nature, and *among those things* is acting according to reason.[49] The theologian of Salamanca considered that natural law does not form part of nature, because children do not have it. But he regarded it as natural because from a natural inclination we judge what is right.[50] Vitoria associated 'natural good' with the physical and affective needs of human beings and 'moral good' with reason and natural law. Once this methodological principle is grasped one ascertains that it radically transforms Vitoria's endorsements of Aristotle's and Aquinas's teachings, which are present in almost every page of his writings. Clearly, Vitoria did not theorize about natural law to the same level of complexity as evinced by the writings of Aquinas, who produced an almost impossible balance, both ontologically dependent on the eternal law and autonomous from it.[51] To be sure, wherever Aquinas's natural law is discussed there is scope for debate.[52] But it is clear that Aquinas's system melts away without the foundation of the eternal law, while Vitoria's does not: the 'sensitive nature' would remain.[53]

[47] For instance, when he is adducing the argument against it: 'Quia finis regis idem est sicut finis civitatis et reipublicae, cuius finis est; quia unus homo non sufficit sibi soli, ideo non degunt in monte sicut ferae, quia unus indiget multis et non potest omnia. Unde non posset homo vivere solus, sed indigent adiuvari invicem. Videtur ergo quod civitas non est congragata per bonum morale, sed propter istam indigentiam. Sed idem est finis civitatis et legislatoris. Ergo finis et intentio legislatoris non est inducere homines ad bonum morale, sed ad bonum naturale, et ad cavendum illam indigentiam.' Q. 92, Vitoria, *De legibus,* at p. 110 (n. 26). See also 'Sed si leges nihil aliud faciunt quam commodum naturale, quare qui resisteret regi ressiteret dei ordinationi?', at p. 115.

[48] 'sed de civile est dubium, utrum intentio regis debeat esse quod faciat bonos, an divites, an incolumes', Vitoria, *De legibus,* at p. 110 (n 26).

[49] Thomae de Aquino, *Summa theologiae*, Iª-IIae q. 94 a. 4 co. This can be found at <http://www.corpusthomisticum.org/iopera.html>.

[50] 'Non ergo dicitur lex naturalis quia insit nobis a natura, nam pueri non habent legem naturalem nec habitum, sed quia ex inclinatione naturae iudicamus quae recta sunt, non quod insit qualitas a natura.', q. 94, de lege naturali, lec. 123, Vitoria, *De legibus,* at p. 122 (n. 26). The classic discussion of the difference also in Daniel Deckers, *Gerechtigkeit und Recht. Eine historische-kritische Untersuchung der Gerechtigkeitslehre des Francisco de Vitoria (1483-1546)* (1991), pp. 111–19.

[51] However, Deckers refers also to 'die Komplexität, aber auch die mangelnde Stringenz der vitorianischen Theorie des *lex naturalis*' insofar that Vitoria wanted to endorse the incompatible positions of, on the one hand, the *moderni* (the nominalists and Scotus, I assume) and their emphasis in the *potentia absoluta* of God, and, on the other, of teleological conceptions of epistemology and natural law. Deckers, *Gerechtigkeit und Recht*, pp. 123–4 (n. 50).

[52] For a treatment of the topic, see Denis J.M. Bradley, *Aquinas on the Twofold Human Good* (1997); and Jan A. Aertsen, *Medieval Philosophy as Transcendental Thought: From Philip the Chancellor (c. 1225) to Francisco Suárez* (2012), at pp. 264–6, and ch. 6 generally. This question was the subject of several interpretations (Jacques Maritain, Etienne Gilson, Cornelio Fabro) during the twentieth century. For a helpful review of the positions involved, see Joseph Owens, 'Aquinas on Knowing Existence', *The Review of Metaphysics* 29 (1976), 670–90.

[53] Aquinas's argument in this regard is most conspicuous in *Prima Secunda*, q. 106, a. 1 co, and ad 1, on the New Law or the Law of the Gospel that Aquinas considered to be inserted in our hearts (lex nova est indita homini).The opposite extreme can be found in Vitoria's *Reflection on Homicide*: 'What

Deckers saw in that dualism of the Salamancan theologian an anthropology that has its roots in ancient philosophy, but is not Christian.[54] It seems defensible to view the issue as being entangled, above anything, within a history of theology, and as having further ramifications. The latter includes the separation between the *finis naturalis* and the *finis supernaturalis*, and the distinction between the man of nature (*in puribus naturalibus*) who does not desire God and, interestingly, the man of natural law and grace (*cum virtutibus infuses*) who does. Vitoria, for one, placed prudence partly within the sensitive nature.[55] In the end it does not come as a surprise that the 'state of nature' has a place in the system of the of Salamanca's theologian.[56] But Vitoria's conception of two natures is a source of theoretical and pragmatic conundrums, such as that the desire of man '*in puribus naturalibus*', since it is

remains now is that we answer in some way the arguments on the other side. In doing this, we must first remember that human beings are composed of two natures: rational and sensitive. The Apostle [Paul], in *Romans* 12 calls these "the interior and the exterior man". This is not to be understood in such a way that the soul itself is the interior man or the rational nature while the body is the sensitive nature. Rather the whole man according to the spirit is the interior man, and the same man according to the flesh is the exterior man and the sensitive nature. Secondly, we should note that because man is man precisely inasmuch as he is rational and not inasmuch as he is sensitive: the inclination of a man precisely as such is the inclination of a man inasmuch as he is a man, namely, the inclination of will and intellect, and not the inclination of the sensitive part, which is not the inclination of man, or not insofar as he is man, but only to a certain extent and not simply as such.' Francisco de Vitoria, *Reflection on Homicide and Commentary on Summa theologiae IIa – IIae q. 64*, trans. and introduction John P. Doyle (1997), at p. 69. Vitoria also stood at the opposite pole to the naturalist anthropology of Albert the Great who espoused a theory of penetration of reason in the entire human being, soul, body, and senses: see, for this, Georg Wieland, *Zwischen Natur und Vernunft. Alberts des Großen Begriff vom Menschen* (Lectio Albertina 2) (1999).

[54] See Deckers, *Gerechtigkeit und Recht*, at pp. 117–18 (n. 50).

[55] On this point, in Vitoria's critique of Scotus's statement that God is the natural end of human being, see the following: 'Ad argumentum ergo principale nego quod Deus est finis naturalis hominis'; also 'Secundo negatur quod homo desideret naturaliter videre Deum, sed tamen conceditur quod appetitus est inquietus usque dum Deum videamus.' Both quotes are from the manuscripts of Vitoria's commentary on the *Summa* in Langella, '"Apuntes" sobre el concepto de teología en Francisco de Vitoria', at 284, 287. See Gerson, 'quod homo qui subsistit ex duplici substantia, una spirituali, aeterna divinάque, alia corporali et mortali, duplicem habet finem, unum supernaturalem, alium naturalem, qui humanus potest dici seu politicus et civilis': Gerson, 'De vita spiritual animae' at 133. Gilby mentions how Aquinas had noted that 'the notion of the "political" or "civil"' is taken by Aristotle and the jurists in different senses; 'to a social philosopher the meaning is more comprehensive, since he sees laws which are the bond of political association stemming from moral imperatives rather than the regulations men make for themselves.' Thomas Gilby O.P. 'Introduction' to *Summa Theologiae*, vol. 28 (Ia2ae. 90–97) *Law and Political Theory*, trans. and intro. Thomas Gilby (1966), at p. xxii. Interestingly this suggests that Aristotle is more comprehensive with his notion of 'the political' than the theologian Gerson. For Vitoria on prudence, see *Comentarios del maestro Francisco de Vitoria, O.P. a la Secunda secundae de Santo Tomás*, qq. 45–55, 348–88.

[56] 'Contra quos S. Thomas dicit quod saepissime oportet uti rationibus ad multa quae, dato in auctoritate divina fundetur, tamen non possunt per illam immediate probari. Et hoc probat optime quia gratia nihil derogat naturae: ergo aliquando est utendum rationibus, sicut uteabantur in statu naturae.' Langella, '"Apuntes" sobre el concepto de teología en Francisco de Vitoria', at p. 288. This stands in contrast to other theologians such as Albert the Great, who explicitly denied that there was ever a 'state of nature'. For instance, in his first commentary on *Nichomachean Ethics* Albert clarifies that Cicero's 'natural man' never existed, but his was only a manner of speaking '*ex hypothesi*': 'Et similiter dicendum est ad tertium de silvestribus hominibus, quod habent ordinem naturalem, si tamen ponuntur esse; non enim videtur, quod homines umquam silvestres fuerunt; Tullius autem loquitur ex hipothesi.' Alberti Magni, *Super ethica*, vol. 1, ed. Wilhelm Kübel (1968–1972), p. 17.1.

not spiritual, appears to lie outside the scope of evil.[57] This makes one wonder how to *know* to what lengths natural needs might extend.

That predicaments arise with regard to boundaries within this conception of separated 'sensitive nature' and 'rational nature' in parallel with a 'natural good', as *utiles* or *delectabiles*, separate from the 'moral good', is plain in Vitoria's discussion of the dispensability of natural law on article 8 of question 100: 'whether the articles of the Decalogue are dispensable'. The Dominican connected article 8 with two other instances, one located earlier and the other later in the text. Previously, in question 94, article 5, on 'whether the natural law can be changed or altered', Vitoria had explicitly directed the reader to question 100, since Aquinas understood the Decalogue to be an expression of natural law.[58] Next, Vitoria linked article 8 substantially with his remarkable solution in question 105, article 2: 'Whether the Judicial precepts were suitably framed as to the relations of one people with another' by touching again upon the issue of dispensation of the law.

In the commentary on the question about the dispensability of the precepts of the Decalogue, Vitoria starts by expounding Aquinas's teaching in the *Summa*, which left little room for ambiguity. Since 'the precepts of the Decalogue embody the actual intention of the lawgiver, God', Aquinas concluded that 'they admit of no dispensation whatever'.[59] Vitoria's personal commentary would revolve around the opinions of William of Ockham and Pierre d'Ally, John Duns Scotus, and Durandus of Saint Pourçain and was an opportunity to display his theological skills. Notoriously, Ockham and d'Ally considered that God could make a dispensation of any precepts of the Decalogue and even command human beings to hate Him with merit.[60] Vitoria firmly denied the truth of this position.

Scotus's intermediary position was regarded as 'probable'.[61] God could not exempt anyone from the precepts of the first table, related to piety towards God, but He could do so with those of the second table that were about relations between human beings. For Scotus, in Vitoria's reading, everything that God operated *ad extra* He wanted in a contingent manner. He wanted homicide to be a sin, but He could have wanted otherwise, and in fact He had relaxed these precepts occasionally—for instance when He ordered Abraham to kill his son Isaac.[62] But

[57] Or at least only 'per accidens est malum aliquando. Sed ista inclinatio non est absoluta hominis ut homo est, sed secundum quid ut animal est.' Commentary Summa Theologia, IIa-IIae, q.26.a.3.n.2, quoted in Deckers, *Gerechtigkeit und Recht*, at p. 119 (n. 50).

[58] Vitoria, *De legibus*, Question 100, Art. 1, at p. 191 (n. 26).

[59] *St Thomas Summa Theologiae, vol. 29. (Ia2ae. 98–105), The Old Law,* q. 100, art. 8, translated with an introduction and notes by David Bourke and Arthur Littledale (2006), at pp. 91–3. Aquinas elaborated further on this issue in *De malo* q. 3, but it is not possible to discuss it here.

[60] An analysis of this idea can be found in John Kilcullen, 'Natural Law and Will in Ockham', in Knud Haakonssen and Udo Thiel (eds.), *History of Philosophy Yearbook* vol. 1 (1993).

[61] Together with that of Aquinas, which is 'the most probable', Vitoria, *De legibus*, at p. 206 (n. 26).

[62] 'Item Deus dispensavit aliquando in adulterio, furto et homicidio. Primo cum Abraham quod occideret Isaac innocentem. Non fuit mutata res, sed lex.' at p. 202. Vitoria adopted the question of the deaths of innocents for his *Relectio de iure belli*: 'Per accidens autem etiam scienter aliquando licet interficere innocentes, puta cum oppugnatur arx aut civitas iuste, in qua tamen constat esse multos innocentes nec possunt machinae solvi vel alia telva vel ignis aedificiis subici quin etiam opprimantur innocentes sicut nocentes', Francisco de Vitoria, *Relectio de iure Belli of Paz dinámica. Escuela española*

Vitoria countered this opinion, with Durandus's terminist argument that if it were licit to take someone's goods, then terminologically they would no longer belong to anyone but be commonly held. Thus that act would not amount to theft, and a similar argument held true for homicide, adultery, and other sins.[63]

Vitoria's novel approach to resolving the contradictions between Aquinas and Scotus was to introduce the distinction of the two perfections of the 'omnipotent God': the lord and the legislator.[64] That was a sign that he was using what has been called Ockhamist theology, with its characteristic methodology of employing the notion of an 'omnipotent God' in order to know what was or was not necessary in the created world and therefore, in this case, which natural law could be the object of dispensation.[65] Acting not as legislator but as lord over human lives and created goods God could order Abraham to kill the innocent without relaxing the law. 'If I had a similar right over the life of a man as over the life of a horse, could I not kill him with impunity, even though I am not a legislator?' asked the theologian.[66] Moreover, God the lord could give anyone a woman—anything, in fact—*without relaxing the law*, as God did, when He ordered the prophet Oseas to take a woman without marrying her and he would take the woman 'with more right than if he were to marry her'.[67]

Continuing with the issue of dispensation in the third occurrence in *De legibus*, Vitoria asked in question 105, article 2 whether a prince could re-enact an ancient law in order to govern the city. The difficulty here was that some of the laws in question went against natural law, covering such matters as the promotion of polygamy, the killing of the innocent and so on. The first reply of the Salamancan theologian was

de la paz, primera generación, 1526–1560, L. Pereña, V. Abril, C. Baciero, A. García, and F. Maseda (1981), at p. 166.

[63] Vitoria, *De legibus*, pp. 200–2 (n. 26). Vitoria often had recourse to terminist argumentation. Colish observes that the 'central conviction uniting late medieval terminists was the view that the only grammatical contexts in which supposited terms are meaningful are full propositions'. Marcia L. Colish, *Medieval Foundations of the Western Intellectual Tradition, 400-1400* (1997), pp. 302–15.

[64] 'Pro solutione nota quod Deus omnipotens duo habet. Primum quos est dominus omnium; secundum, quod est legislator. Et haenc sunt distincta. Ex inconsideratione horum mult erraverunt in his argumentis. Hoc supposito, opportet videre quod potest Deus facere inquantum dominus, etiamsi non esset legislator; ut si Pater esset dominus solum, et Filius legislator, Pater posset dare mihi omnia bona mundi, quamvis mihi prohiberet Filius ne furarer. Et non esset dispensatio quando Pater dare omnia bona mundi.' Vitoria, *De legibus*, at p. 204 (n. 26).

[65] The emphasis on logic, the denial of the status of knowledge or science both to speculative and practical theology, together with the introduction of the 'potentia absoluta' as a methodological principle applied in order to know what is or is not necessary in the created world are core elements of what Biard calls 'Ockhamist theology'. See Joël Biard, 'Guglielmo di Ockham e la teologia', in Inos Biffi and Constante Marabelli (eds.), *Figure del Pensiero Medievale: La Via Moderna – XIV e inizi del XV secolo* (2010), pp. 1–59, at p. 57. On the fact that *potentia absoluta* was a much discussed issue in Ockham's time, see Eugenio Randi, 'Ockham, John XXII and the Absolute Power of God', 46 *Franciscan Studies, William of Ockham (1285-1347) Commemorative Issue* (1986), 205–16.

[66] 'Ideo ego dico, si ego haberem tamtum jus super vitam hominis sicut super vitam equi mei, nonne possem occidere impune, etiamsi non essem legislator? (. . .) Dico ergo quod nulla fuit dispensatio, quia Deus usus est non auctoritate legislatoris, sed domini. Nec cum Samsone fuit dispensatio, sed fecit sicut fortis vir ut occideret multos inspiratus a Deo.' Vitoria, *De legibus*, at p. 206 (n. 26).

[67] 'Immo meliori iure accedebat ad illam quam si contraxisset cum ea.' Vitoria, *De legibus*, at p. 204 (n. 26).

that only God could do that, but not man. However, this reply gave rise to a problem of incapability for the worldly prince. *The prince sometimes needed to enact laws that were useful but not in accordance with natural law*. However, since the prince could not revoke natural law, Vitoria advanced the possible objection that might be made to the effect that 'if this is true, it follows that the prince has not sufficient authority to enact useful laws (*leges utile*) in the government of the political community'.[68]

Thus Vitoria's answer was as follows:

> That is why the second proposition is: *What is contrary to natural law cannot be always and universally beneficial for the political community*. In this manner, the authority of the king that cannot make a dispensation of natural law is not diminished in the least. Moreover, the political community cannot subsist without natural law that was instituted for its benefit; in this sense what is contrary to natural law cannot be universally useful for the political community. However, in a concrete case, at a certain moment and for a particular nation that which is contrary to natural law can be useful.[69]

This response is in my view ambiguous. It presents as fact drawn from experience that natural law and utility as *good* might disagree, but with the caveat that they can do so not as a rule but occasionally. However, Vitoria's answer is consistent, inevitable, and, in a sense, representative of the dissonances creeping into a theology that divided human nature into two. Taking into account Vitoria's theology of the concrete case it is illustrative of the manner in which he solved, or rather *left open* the question of a moral dilemma around the years 1533 to 1534, during which he commented for the first time on the *Prima Secunda*.[70] A matter that is obviously contrary to natural law, but which may in a concrete case also be useful to the political community, and is not allowed to become the rule, reveals itself as neither the trigger of a moral dilemma nor a sin, but a theological positive institution—a 'dispensation of natural law' that God can accomplish. What did that mean to the prince? Vitoria stopped short of answering that question. In my view Campagna reads too much into this passage when he writes that 'here he (Vitoria) distinguishes between the punctual and useful violation and the damage that would occur due to the general violation, with the result that the punctual violation also ought not to be allowed'.[71] Some years later Vitoria would approach the moral dilemma with a real situation in mind.

[68] 'Sed dicetis, si hoc est verum, sequitur quod princeps non habet sufficientem auctoritatem condendi leges utiles ad regimen reipublicae.' Vitoria, *De legibus*, at p. 264 (n. 26).

[69] Vitoria continues: 'ut patet de pluritate uxorum, quae est contra jus naturale, tum propter concordiam familiae et educationem liberorum, tum quia unus non potest bene sufficere pluribus uxoribus. Item interficere innocentes non potest esse universaliter utile reipublicae, *sed bene pro tempore*, qui illi amalechitae erant impii et inimici Dei, et Deus volebat omnino eos delere ut nec semen eorum remaneret.' Vitoria, *De legibus*, p. 264 (n. 26). (Footnotes omitted, emphasis added.)

[70] 'Immanuel Kant's denial that duties can conflict and John Stuart Mill's claim in *Utilitarianism* that moral conflicts can be solved by appeals to the notion of utility are perhaps the best-known examples from modern philosophy of the rejection of the existence of moral dilemmas.' M.V. Dougherty, *Moral Dilemmas in Medieval Thought: From Gratian to Aquinas* (2011), at p. 117. The text published by Langella, Barrientos García, and García Castillo is the first commentary on the *Prima Secunda*, for the years 1533–1534, Simona Langella, 'Estudio Introductorio', in *De legibus*, at p. 27 (n. 26).

[71] Campagna, *Francisco de Vitoria*, pp. 77–9 (n. 44).

III. De Indis

Stiening has wondered why Vitoria generated a special problem for theology out of the legal-political debate revolving around the Indians. Since the Salamancan theologian had frequently asserted that civil laws were binding in conscience, also in his commentary on the *Summa*, the recourse to theology, his turning towards that discipline for the whole issue, was so to speak superfluous.[72] From the outset, Vitoria's theological *De Indis* dovetails with the argument of this chapter that Vitoria had a style of doing theology that tended to include any morally relevant issue as being within the competence of the theologian.[73] This methodological approach, in which any issue can become theology, can be usefully compared with an author closer to our time. In a similar manner to that in which Carl Schmitt stated that any matter could be political, Vitoria argued that practically any matter could be theological and therefore fall within the remit of the moral theologian. Schmitt's well-known theoretical frame for his definition of the political is the capacity for distinguishing between friend and enemy:

Every religious, moral, economic, ethical or other antithesis transforms into a political one if it is sufficiently strong to group human beings effectively according to friend and enemy.[74]

Although there is no such elaborate treatment of the criteria for 'the theological' in Vitoria's work, he came close to articulating his scientific criteria, which he introduced as an expert's statement, in *De Indis*. In his commentary on the *Prima Pars*, Vitoria used an argument of benefit, presumably for the soul: 'sacred theology has not limits, because there is no man that cannot benefit from it'.[75] At the beginning of the *Relectio de Indis* he was more specific, stating that:

[I]n matters which concern salvation there is *an obligation* to believe those whom the Church has appointed as teachers, and in cases of doubt their verdict is law. Just as a judge in a court law is obliged to pass sentence according to the evidence presented, so in the court

[72] Gideon Stiening, 'Nach göttlichen oder menschlichen Gesetzen? Zum Verhältnis von Theologie und Philosophie in *De Indis*', in Norbert Brieskorn, Gideon Stiening (eds.), *Francisco de Vitorias De Indis in interdisziplinäre Perspektive* (2011), p. 3, pp. 123–51, at p. 131.

[73] Vitoria simply offers a theological justification for that theologization. The affair of the Indians was in his view a matter of divine law. Since it was impossible to find any valid positive law on the question, jurists were 'not sufficiently versed to define the question': Vitoria, 'De Indis recenter inventis', at p. 222 (n. 9). In the words of Andrés Martín, Vitoria 'was not a moralist and a jurist' and, one should add, an economist, 'in spite of being a theologian but as a result of being theologian': Melquiades Andrés Martín, *La teología española en el s. XVI*, vol. 2 (1977) at p. 358. See also the commentary by Langella, ' "Apuntes" sobre el concepto de teología en Vitoria' (n. 29); and Campagna, *Francisco de Vitoria*, pp. 35–49 (n. 44).

[74] Carl Schmitt, *The Concept of the Political*, trans. and ed. Georg Schwab (2007), p. 37.

[75] Quoted in Langella, ' "Apuntes" sobre el concepto de teología en Vitoria', at p. 279 (n. 29). The dates of the commentary of the Prima Pars are 1531–1533 and 1539–1540, see Augusto Sarmiento, 'Lecturas inéditas de F. De Vitoria: bases para la edición crítica', *Scripta Theologica* 12 (1980/82), 575–92, at 582

of conscience every man must decide not according to his own inclination, but *by logical argument or the authority of the learned.*[76]

Not altogether surprisingly, the criteria for the theological appears in the space where we are dealing with 'matters which concern salvation'. But where Schmitt found 'the political' in the existential and thus unalienable decision to judge whether the other was one's enemy or friend, it was characteristic of Vitoria that he thought that the decision of 'the theological' was transferable. The text in which he stated as much may be translated in painfully literal fashion:

Since a question *de foro conscientiae* is raised, it concerns the priests, that is, the Church, to lay down the rule.[77]

The Latin expression *de foro conscientiae* retains the sense of locality and thus, in an interesting way, of the jurisdiction that Vitoria was reclaiming. He established it in contradistinction to matters *de foro contentioso.*[78] Methodologically, therefore, beyond the substantial matters strictly belonging to the province of theologians, Vitoria's idea in *De Indis* was that if any matter was raised or could be raised with regard to conscience and salvation there was an issue for the theologian. This chimes with his argument for an all-encompassing discipline of theology and, historically, with the manner in which Imperial Spain had been vacillating over its plans of *Conquista* due to a troubled conscience.[79] Only now the ultimate foundation of knowledge is not in terms of theology but of the theologian.

[76] Translation in English from Anthony Padgen and Jeremy Lawrance, *Vitoria: Political Writings* (1991), pp. 233–92, pp. 235–6 (emphasis added).

[77] 'Nec satis scio an unquam ad disputationem et determinationem huius quaestionis vocati fuerint theologi digni, qui audiri de tanta re possent. Et cum agatur de foro conscientiae, hoc spectat ad sacerdotes, i.e. ad Ecclesiam, diffinire.' Vitoria, 'De Indis recenter inventis', at p. 222 (n. 9). *Diffinire* is defined as 'to lay down a rule', in the *Oxford Latin Dictionary* (1982). Other definitions mentioned there include: ordain, bound, fix, limit, restrict, confine. Campagna notes that Vitoria doubted both the competence of jurists and that of the other theologians that had dealt with the question. Vitoria, 'De Indis recenter inventis', at p. 222 (n. 9); Campagna, *Francisco de Vitoria,* at p. 174 (n. 44).

[78] On the history of these plurality of fora, see Prodi, *Una storia della giustizia: Dal pluralismo deo fori al moderno dualismo tra conscienza.* I have used the German translation, which loses the idea of the *fora* in the title; Prodi, *Eine Geschichte der Gerechtigkeit: Vom Recht Gottes zum modernen Rechtstaat* (n. 25). For an explanation of the implications of the differences of *fora* in circumstances of *dominium,* see Jörg A. Tellkamp, 'Vitorias Weg zu den legitimen Titeln der Eroberung Amerikas', in Kirstin Bunge, Anselm Spindler, and Andreas Wagner (eds.), *Die Normativität des Rechts bei Francisco de Vitoria* (2011), pp. 147–70. Half a century later, Alberico Gentili's theory on the question was that no one but God judged the conscience; theologians interpreted God's commands but jurists acquired a much greater role in helping to interpret anything that was juridical, so that, in fact, they ought to be interpreters on matters of the second table of the Decalogue: see Giovanni Minnucci, 'Foro della coscienza e foro esterno nel pensiero giuridico della prima età moderna', in Gerhard Dilcher and Diego Quaglioni (eds.), *Gli inizi del diritto pubblico, 3 Verso la costruzione del diritto pubblico tra medioevo e modernità* (2009), pp. 55–86.

[79] To mention only one example, as late as 3 July 1549—that is, ten years after the *Relectio de Indis* was given—the Council of the Indies advised the King to prohibit the granting of permission for new expeditions due to the great dangers involved for 'the bodies of the Indians' and 'the King's conscience'. Accordingly, the Council concluded that a new meeting of theologians and jurists had to take place in order to discuss 'how conquests may be conducted justly and with security of conscience'. The Council

Vitoria's standpoint was remarkable in that it involved wresting authority from the Church and giving it to the expert theologian.[80] At any rate the idea that an external source could adjudicate over one's salvation in a concrete case did not sit well with the official doctrine of the Catholic Church at that or any other time. A century earlier John de Capistrano (1386–1456), in his *Speculum Conscientiae*, had identified personal communication with God as the last resort to obtain wisdom when suffering doubts of conscience. Wisdom was to be asked for personally from God, above the counsel of the experts (*peritiores*), and even above the authority of the Church.[81] The issue, after all, was that of recognizing truth.[82] Here more than anywhere the distance between Vitoria and Aquinas is clear. The latter thought that prudence always assists the practical intellect in perplexing situations.[83] Against Capistrano and Aquinas, Vitoria gracelessly 'forced a theologisation'—to use Stiening's words—of the political and moral question revolving around the conquest of the Indies, only to envelope it in the voluntarist discussion over what criteria should be applied in cases of moral uncertainty.[84] It is probably not necessary to produce a history of theology as a science in order to note that when Vitoria referred solely to rationalist arguments and to authority ('*per rationem probabilem*' or '*per auctoritatem sapientum*') as the basis for deciding on matters of conscience, he was partaking of the logicism and the theory of knowledge characteristic, again,

thus prepared the way for the well-known debate involving Bartolomé de las Casas and Juan Ginés de Sepúlveda. See Lewis Hanke, *The Spanish Struggle for Justice in the Conquest of America* (1949), pp. 115–32, at p. 116.

[80] Vitoria is here reinterpreting a tradition that defends an elitist conception of theologians as bearers of a *lumen medium,* between the common light of faith and the light of glory. This tradition goes back at least to Henry of Ghent. See for this, Marialucrezia Leone, 'Moral Philosophy of Henry of Ghent', in Gordon A. Wilson (ed.), *A Companion to Henry of Ghent* (2011), pp. 275–314.

[81] Capistrano declared the hierarchy to be applied when deciding on the basis of an erroneous conscience. Firstly, following Aquinas, one had to listen to one's conscience, even though it is erroneous. Next, one needed to try to overcome error: 'Ratione autem ipsius conscientiae, erronea conscientiae ligat vinculo conscientiae ad faciendum quod dictat, nec tamen est simpliciter perplexus, quia potest et debet deponere talem erroneam conscientiam. Et ideo simpliciter & proprius & magis ligatur ad deponendum eam quàm ad faciendum secundum eam. & si de illa per se nesciat iudicare, debet peritiores consulere, & saltem recurrere ad ecclesiam si non posset aliter declarari. Et quod auctoritas ecclesiae roborat & declarat, idinconcussè ab omnibus catholicis est servandum, ut in capitu. firmiter, extra de summa Tinitate (sic), & fide catholi & in capitulo debitum, & in c. maiores, extra de baptis. & eius effec. *Et si tandem omne sibi consilioum deficeret humanum, debet se per orationem ad Deum convertere, iuxta illud Iac. 1. Si quis autem vestrum indiget sapientia, postulet eam a Deo, qui dat omnibus affluenter, & non improperat, & dabitur ei: postulet autem in fide, nihil hesitans.*' *Speculum Conscientiae. Tractatu universi Iuris, duce et auspice Gregorio XIII Pontifice Maximo in unum congesti* I (Venice, 1584), pp. 323, 73, at p. 328 (emphasis added). Vitoria's standpoint also glossed over the evolution that occurred in the Middle Ages towards less juridification and more subjectivization in matters of conscience, Marie-Dominique Chenu, *L'éveil de la conscience dans la civilisation médiévale* (1969), especially pp. 1–32. In language typical of the 1960s, Chenu speaks of the 'rights of conscience', at p. 29.

[82] Compare with the interpretation of Capistrano by Prodi, *Eine Geschichte der Gerechtigkeit,* pp. 142–7 (n. 25).

[83] See M.V. Dougherty, *Moral Dilemmas in Medieval Thought* (2013), pp. 112–44 (n. 70). For a comparison between Aquinas and voluntarist discussions of moral uncertainty, see Ilkka Kantola, *Probability and Moral Uncertainty in Late Medieval and Early Modern Times* (1994).

[84] Stiening, 'Nach göttlichen oder menschlichen Gesetzen?', at p. 148 (n. 72).

of Ockhamist theology.[85] In the face of that distrust as to the possibility of reaching truth through the illumination of practical reason, or, in other words, as to every human being's existential union with God, Vitoria's yearning for authority is linked to a characteristic and unbending fidelity to the Catholic Church.[86]

To sum up, Vitoria's formula of the 'theological' was a decision founded on external authority which can be put in parallel with Schmitt's existential decision in 'the political'. Viewed in this particular light of the 'theological', Vitoria's expert judgment in *De Indis* contains some interesting nuances.

De Indis was not the result of smooth reportage of the facts of the case. In fact, a misrepresentation of reality in the description of the nature of the relations between Spaniards and Indians is its most striking feature. The turning point of the text is most intense in the justification of the first just title by which the Indians 'passed under the rule of the Spaniards':

> Amongst all nations it is considered inhuman to treat strangers and travellers badly without some special cause, humane and dutiful to behave hospitably to strangers. (. . .) [i] t would not be lawful for the French to prohibit Spaniards from travelling or even living in France, or vice versa, so long as it caused no sort of harm to themselves; therefore it is not lawful for the barbarians either.[87]

This depiction of the Indians during the Spanish Conquista as equal members of a universal society has given rise to an array of conflicting interpretations and continues to puzzle any reader that approaches the text today. Much of the Spanish and North American commentary during the twentieth century simply ignored the problematic aspects of Vitoria's presentation of facts and highlighted his humanist argumentation. More recent and critical comments have involved a range of interpretations. Some view it as anti-imperialism—the empire in denial—founded on the threat that the empire, as the Salamancan theologians understood it, posed to the true nature of the civil community. Others have considered it a description of over-inclusive imperialism, and thus cynicism, or have thought of it, more moderately, as a 'familiar irony'.[88]

[85] See Biard: 'So an "Ockhamist theology" was born, in which the essential perhaps passed into the background, and the explosion of theology as a scientific discipline occurred to facilitate the diversified use of reason in examining multiple questions and judgments that could be relevant to human salvation.' Biard, 'Guglielmo di Ockham e la teologia', p. 59 (n. 65).

[86] Distrust in the potential for reason to attain the truth or know God is among the features that Garcia-Villoslada detected in the Parisian nominalist professors, teachers of Vitoria, Ricardo G. Villoslada, *La Universidad de Paris durante los estudios de Francisco de Vitoria O.P. (1507-1522)* (1938), pp. 73–92; but see p. 92.

[87] Vitoria, *Political Writings*, at p. 278 (n. 76). The second redaction of the *Relectio,* considered by Luciano Pereña the most significant for Vitoria's new proposal is entirely written in this *spirit of misrepresentation of facts*, see 'Hipótesis de Francisco de Vitoria: jus naturalis societatis et communicationis. Primera versión del ms de Palencia, in Luciano Pereña (ed.), *Escuela de Salamanca: Carta Magna de los Indios – Fuentes Constitucionales 1534-1609* (1988), pp. 50–5. The views of Pereña in Luciano Pereña, 'Proyecto de reconversión colonial', in the same, pp. 3–32, at 11–12.

[88] James Brown Scott, *The Spanish Origins of International Law: Francisco de Vitoria and His Law of Nations* (1934); Anthony Pagden, *Lords of All the World: Ideologies of Empire in Spain, Britain and France, 1500-1800* (1995); Annabel Brett, *Changes of State*; Antony Anghie, *Imperialism, Sovereignty and the Making of International Law* (2007). A certain 'Vitorian utopia' is present in the literature in

Arguably Vitoria's theory of 'the theological' about the *dominium* of conscience by experts-theologians offers a further key to unravel that paradox or irony. We have already seen that Vitoria's theory of law envisages the possibility of conflict between natural law and situations of utility. However, he did not use that argument in order to justify legal claims in relation to actions undertaken by the Spanish in the New World. On the contrary, Vitoria became famous for showing, creatively to be sure, that such claims were nothing other than an *expression* of natural law in the form of *jus gentium* 'which either is or derives from natural law'. The *jus peregrinandi,* the *jus negotiandi,* and *as a consequence of those two*, also the *jus evangelisandi*, were interpretations of natural law that the founder of the Salamanca School of theology produced in a spirit of innovation.[89]

In his apparent misreading of events Vitoria does not describe the processes of conquest and colonization as such, while the reader is left in no doubt that he knows the facts. Instead, he chose to depict the entire adventure as a commercial and evangelical enterprise sanctioned by natural law. By couching the benefits for the Spanish in terms of natural rights the message conveyed by the expert's judgment was that *in this case utility and reason* or, in other words, nature and natural law, need not be in opposition to one another. That Vitoria intended a rectification of the colonial policy is a general interpretation of the *Relectio de Indis*. Luciano Pereña called it 'el proyecto de reconversion colonial'.[90] However, without carrying out a critical assessment of Vitoria's utopian depiction of the facts of the case, the normativity of the utilitarian ideology of the new theory is lost. Therefore, I would suggest that Vitoria's *Relectio de Indis* ought to be read not as a justification of a fait accompli (the conquest) but as an ethical-normative orientation for the future. If 'all this business of the barbarians'[91] were to be conducted in the manner in which he described it, it would be a manifestation of natural law and, as a consequence, it would be done according to justice.

Another important insight to be gained from that reading of *De Indis* is that its utopianism prevents the unfolding of the moral dilemma. In this case an evolution towards the reasoning used in the commentary on the *Summa* q. 105, a. 2 has occurred. In the latter, placing utility in opposition to natural law provided an occasion on which God could make a dispensation of natural law. Based on the authority of the expert, such opposition became both an expression and an interpretation

the sense of going beyond reality, transcending it in order to produce something more favourable to the Indians. Notably so, Redondo's doctoral dissertation, which Luciano Pereña directed: see María Lourdes Redondo Redondo, *Utopia Vitoriana y Realidad Indiana* (1991) <http://biblioteca.ucm.es/tesis/19911996/H/2/AH2008601.pdf>.

89 'patet ex predictis, quia si habent jus peregrinandi et negotiandi apud illos, ergo possunt docere veritatem volentes audire'. Vitoria, 'De Indis recenter inventis', at p. 262 (n. 9).

90 See, Luciano Pereña, 'Proyecto de reconversión colonial', in *Escuela de Salamanca. Carta Magna de los Indios.* Also, on the occasion of the 450th anniversary of the *Relectio*, Francisco de Vitoria, *Relectio de Indis – Carta magna de los indios: 450 aniversario, 1539-1989,* essays by L. Pereña, trans. C. Baciero, corrections by F. Maseda, Corpus Hispanorum de Pacis (1989). Vitoria's letter to Fray Miguel de Arcos (1534) seems to be an early condemnation of the open violence and thieving involved in the Conquista, in *Escuela de Salamanca. Carta Magna de los Indios,* pp. 37–40.

91 Vitoria, *Political Writings*, p. 237 (n. 76).

of natural law. In this process, natural law underwent a dramatic transformation. Firstly, the theologian turned a decision of conscience into positive law, as natural law, which goes against the very nature of an act of conscience.[92] Furthermore, an expansion of the discipline of theology thereby occurred. Secondly, the (theoretically possible) dispensation of natural law was internalized and transformed into an interpretation of it. The other possible moral routes—immorality and moral dilemma—disappeared. That all this was happening at the expense of order, which the individual must discover and preserve by means of a moral decision, was without a doubt the downside of this incredibly creative moment.[93]

This analysis of *De Indis* also teaches us something important about the theory of sources in international law with regard to the activity of experts. Namely, that experts are today and have always been an important source of international law. The key point of experts is that they are independent individuals and entities, who are not members of a government, and who are considered to have authority due to their expertise in some field.[94] To my knowledge Vitoria was the first to remove natural subjective rights from their original environments of individuals' moral theology and canon law and transplant them into an encounter between peoples.[95] There is no reason to doubt that he knew that he was creating new law by doing that.[96] Arguably, experts are needed because they help governments or groups of people to make determinations of law in circumstances where tough or contested moral and political decisions are required. This is exactly what made *De Indis* a classic. But experts' judgments are neither objective nor sources of truth. Depending on our political inclinations we might agree or disagree with them. A historiography of *De Indis* suffices to demonstrate that.[97] Nevertheless, experts are facilitators of law in a world that has despaired of ever reaching truth. Thanks to them, thanks to Vitoria, making new law has become possible in the history of international law.

[92] For instance, Aquinas regarded the act of conscience as a personal judgment in God's presence and not a norm: 'The act of conscience that something must be done is nothing other than a judgment that it would be against God's will not to do it (habere conscientiam de re aliqua facienda, nihil aliud est quam aestimare quod faciam contra Deum, nisi illud faciat).' Quote from Dougherty, *Moral Dilemmas in Medieval Thought*, at p. 154 (n. 70). As to the positivization of natural law, I see it occurring much earlier than Habermas affirmed (with the bourgeois revolution) and not as constitutional law, but, paradoxically as natural law. See Jürgen Habermas, *Theory and Practice*, John Viertel trans. (1974), ch. 2.

[93] See n. 11. [94] Jan Klabbers, *International Law* (2013), at p. 37.

[95] Brian Tierney's in-depth study seems to imply the same: Brian Tierney, *The Idea of Natural Rights: Studies on Natural Rights, Natural Law and Church Law, 1150-1625* (1997), generally and at p. 252.

[96] Compare with Skinner, who referred to the description of Vitoria as the founder of the modern concept of international law due to his ideas on *jus gentium*'s precepts created by the authority of everyone, although this would not be the way 'he would have recognised himself'. My discussion here deals purely with natural law. Quentin Skinner, *The Foundations of Modern Political Thought, Volume 2: The Age of Reformation* (2004), at p. 154.

[97] See Martti Koskenniemi, 'Vitoria and Us: Thoughts on Critical Histories of International Law', *Rechtsgeschichte - Legal History* 22 (2014), 119–38.

IV. Conclusions

In his ambitious theological programme, which aimed to make sense of the world he inhabited, Vitoria was an innovator. As a consequence of the implementation of that programme he theologized his world. However, Vitoria developed a theology that was unorthodox. As we have seen on the occasion of the first lecture on the Indians, his practice of theologizing questions amounted to subjecting them to the authority of the theologian, extracting them from their true existential space and integrating them into his own utilitarian theory about the natural human being and the world. Putting aside the need for existential decision, natural law became, in the hands of the so-called founder of international law, and subsequent international lawyers, a virtual realm with endless possibilities for positive determinations about what would be the sensible thing to do. In an important sense a new system of natural law was created, while order, as described by the classic theologians, collapsed. David Kennedy has recently called a similar phenomenon 'experts' creative moments of destruction'.[98] Whether the economy of free trade of the Spanish Empire—and the Dutch, British, and other empires—caused this or was the motive for it, the fact that European society was permeated by a practical theology not primarily directed to God's love deserves further consideration.

[98] David Kennedy, *A World of Struggle: How Power, Law and Expertise Shape Global Political Economy* (2016), p. 28.

22

Power and Law as Ordering Devices in the System of International Relations

Gunther Hellmann

The title of this chapter is meant to speak to the overarching theme of this volume* while at the same time irritating established language games in International Law (IL) and International Relations (IR).[1] This irritation is potentially productive because it may help in sensitizing readers early on for the fact that concepts such as power, law, system, and order have a central place in the disciplinary discourses of both fields while being loaded with different meanings both within each of them and—in terms of dominating disciplinary narratives—across the disciplinary dividing lines between IL and IR. As a matter of fact, as I try to argue in some detail, the placements which these key concepts are usually accorded in the theoretical vocabularies and discourses of IL and IR have specific functions in describing what the central disciplinary problematiques of IL and IR presumably are—and possibly even help to explain why both have 'evolved as parallel yet carefully quarantined fields of inquiry'.[2] To be sure, the designation of disciplinary boundaries, the construction of disciplinary histories, and the representation of disciplinary discourses are as much an expression of intellectual contention as are disciplinary debates about proper understandings of key concepts. Yet these disciplining exercises are also potentially fruitful in the sense of reexamining what we do in our respective fields and how these scholarly practices can be justified—or how they might be changed.

* I am grateful to Friedrich Kratochwil and the editors, especially Stefan Kadelbach, for comments and to Daniel Fehrmann for research assistance.

[1] I am here following a convention which is shared in the academic disciplines of 'International Relations' (IR) and 'International Law' (IL) in differentiating between discipline and subject matter where the academic discipline is usually capitalized whereas the actual subject matter of the field (i.e. 'international relations') is designated in lower case. For IL, see David Armstrong, 'Introduction', in David Armstrong (ed.), *The Routledge Handbook of International Law* (2009), pp. 1–9, at 1.

[2] Chris Reus-Smit, 'Introduction', in Chris Reus-Smit (ed.), *The Politics of International Law* (2004), pp. 1–13, at 1. For a critique of this separation into two disciplinary fields see Friedrich Kratochwil, *Rules, Norms and Decisions: On the Conditions of Practical and Legal Reasoning in International Relations and Domestic Affairs* (1991), pp. 1–6.

When the editors of this volume justify their take at the history of international legal thought in terms of a focus on the key concepts 'system' and 'order' with a certain bias—a bias *against* anarchy, or a normative commitment to system and order[3] they are placing themselves in a specific reading of disciplinary traditions in IL while at the same time offering a narrative of what one of the key problematiques of IL actually is (or should be). By the same token (and with the aim of offering one possible description as to how to separate IL and IR in a disciplinary perspective from an IR point of view) I will venture to argue that IR—as it has been practised as an emerging scholarly discipline which ever more clearly located itself in a 'social science' tradition[4] as the twentieth century progressed—has cultivated a bias *towards* anarchy besides a 'normative' commitment to the 'empirical'.[5] Only recently have core disciplinary discourses started to move beyond anarchy while rediscovering normativity or (re-)emphasizing the internal connections between normative and empirical (i.e. 'causal') theorizing.[6]

Of course, this thesis needs to be elaborated—not least because the concepts 'anarchy', 'normativity', and 'empirical' have their own (different) meanings in different theoretical vocabularies. In what follows I hope to be able to show how this thesis can be substantiated in discussing the significance which 'power' and 'law'—as key concepts—have been accorded in IL and IR in describing and explaining the emergence, maintenance, and transformation of international order. Care has to be taken in both conceptualizing and interpreting power, law, system, order, anarchy, normativity, and the empirical because of their multiple uses in specific contexts. The definitional approach to concept formation which is still widespread in IR is a major hindrance in that regard because it wrongly assumes that 'defining' a concept with other words in one or a few sentences suffices to explain its meaning. Yet the history of mankind and language has amply shown that this definitional approach commits what Wittgenstein called the 'mistake' of 'nominalists': 'Nominalists make the mistake of interpreting all words as *names*, and so of not really describing their use, but only, so to speak, giving a paper draft on such a description.'[7] Naming, in other words, is just one function in our ways of using words. To *understand* means

[3] See the contribution by Kadelbach, Kleinlein, and Roth-Isigkeit in this volume, pp. 7–11.

[4] Stanley Hoffmann, 'An American Social Science: International Relations', *Daedalus* 106 (1977), 41–60.

[5] For a description of IR's development from an IL perspective see Martti Koskenniemi, *The Gentle Civilizer of Nations: The Rise and Fall of International Law* (2004), esp. chs. 3 and 6; see also Martti Koskenniemi, 'Law, Teleology and International Relations: An Essay in Counterdisciplinarity', *International Relations* 26 (2012), 3–34. See also Kratochwil, *Rules, Norms and Decisions*, pp. 45–68 (n. 2) and Friedrich Kratochwil, *The Status of Law in World Society: Meditations on the Role and Rule of Law* (2014), pp. 26–49.

[6] A thorough and broad critique of disciplinary preoccupations with theoretical problems which are derived from a fixation on anarchy in IR, including a review of the respective literature is provided by Benjamin Herborth, *Challenging Anarchy? Outlines of a Critical Theory of World Society* (2014).

[7] Ludwig Wittgenstein, *Philosophical Investigations*, trans. G.E.M. Anscombe (1958), § 383, emphasis in the original.

that one is grasping the different ways of using words in different contexts and in performing different functions.[8]

Therefore, the irritations which may arise from combining concepts such as system, order, power, and law in unusual ways, as in the title of this chapter, may actually help in sharpening our awareness for what Thomas Kuhn pointed to when he discussed the difference between the limits of translation of 'incommensurable' paradigms and the possibility *and* necessity of 'language learning' when we encounter novel concepts or theoretical vocabularies.[9] Language learning requires 'that one must go native', i.e. aim at 'becoming bilingual' based on the assumption that 'anything that can be said in one language can, with sufficient imagination and effort, be understood by a speaker of another'.[10]

Given the limitations of space the challenge in subsequent sections will be to show how the different uses of the key concepts mentioned above can be sufficiently explained in order to be understood in the context of an overarching argument about power and law as ordering devices in disciplinary discourses, here mainly in IR. Section I starts out by explaining how a different understanding of 'system' and 'order' in IR fits in with the cultivation of a bias towards anarchy and a fixation on the 'empirical' at the expense of normativity. In Section II, I illustrate on the basis of three prominent themes in IR scholarship how a causal and instrumental understanding of both power and law has shaped disciplinary ways of theorizing order.

I. System, Order, and Anarchy

In order to understand how the relationship between power and law is conceptualized in IR it is useful to place this relationship in the context of the two key concepts around which this volume has been organized—precisely because 'system' and 'order' are of central importance in both IL and IR while carrying a somewhat different meaning and fulfilling a different disciplinary function which relates, among others, to how the relationship between power and law is conceived.

To start with the concept of 'system', the broad notions of completeness, wholeness, coherence, unity, and stability which the editors associate with this term in their introductory chapter[11] is of equal importance in IR discourses as well. Yet in

[8] Gerald Gaus, *Political Concepts and Political Theories* (2000), pp. 7–23; John G. Gunnell, *Political Theory and Social Science: Cutting Against the Grain* (2011), pp. 129–54.

[9] For Kuhn paradigms or, more generally, 'theories' are incommensurable in the sense that translation—taken to be 'a quasimechanical activity governed in full by a manual that specifies, as a function of context, which string in one language may, *salva veritate*, be substituted for a given string in the other'—is insufficient to fully transport the meaning of theorizing in one language into another language. Yet this does not mean that understanding via 'language learning' is equally impossible. See Thomas S. Kuhn, 'Dubbing and Redubbing: The Vulnerability of Rigid Designation', in C. Wade Savage (ed.), *Scientific Theories* (1990), pp. 298–318, at p. 299, emphasis in original.

[10] The first quote is from Thomas S. Kuhn, *The Structure of Scientific Revolutions* (1996 [1962], 3rd edn), p. 204, the others from Kuhn, p. 300 (n. 9).

[11] Kadelbach, Kleinlein, and Roth-Isigkeit in this volume, pp. 7–9.

IR these notions of wholeness and coherence are usually not associated with a complex and differentiated system of law or legal thought but rather with a fairly sparse understanding of an international (political) system made up of states interacting in an anarchic environment.

To be sure, the 'social' dimension of international politics which has been emphasized as a critical element in any form of systemic theorizing of international politics by 'classical realism', the 'English School', and IR 'social constructivists' has always allowed for some 'causal weight' of norms and rules as ordering devices. Even Hans Morgenthau, the realist most associated with the notion that the main driver of world politics was the 'aspiration' or 'lust for power' granted that 'international law, international morality, and world public opinion' provided for the only other 'normative limitations' upon the struggle for power besides the balance of power.[12] Yet in the process of IR highlighting its profile as a social 'science' in the second half of the twentieth century where positivism and empiricism as philosophies of science predominated, normativity was increasingly sidelined as an element in, not to mention an integral part of, theorizing international politics.

Kenneth Waltz, undoubtedly the most influential theorist in IR in the last few decades, pushed this preference for 'parsimonious' theory building to the extreme. In his view a proper theory of international politics had to be 'systemic' in the sense of avoiding the 'reductionism' which, in his view, much of the theorizing about international politics had exhibited up until the 1970s. Reductionist theories, in Waltz's view, committed an error by trying to causally explain systems-wide effects with reference to individuals and/or states.[13] Yet 'international politics' as a systemic process was qualitatively different from 'foreign policy'. Moreover, since he took his clues for conceptualizing 'theory' from 'the natural sciences' and 'some of the social sciences, especially economics'[14] his 'systemic theory' was explicitly sparse, thereby cherishing 'parsimony' as an epistemological virtue. Given that 'system' was conceived as consisting of 'interacting units' and 'a structure (...) that makes it possible to think of the units as forming a set as distinct from a mere collection' the theory could limit itself to only three causal 'variables' with the potential of producing systemic effects: states (as 'like units'), anarchy (as prevailing 'ordering principle'), and the 'distribution of (material) capabilities' ('power') among states.[15] Norms and rules, not to mention international law had no place whatsoever in this systemic approach.

Alexander Wendt, probably the IR theorist most influential in the discipline next to Waltz, was sympathetic overall with Waltz's systemic approach. However, in his understanding international politics had to be conceived as social relations which, in turn, implied that norms and rules had to be constitutive of any systemic theorizing. Yet even here the primary focus was on processes of political interaction and only derivatively on international law. Waltz's structural constant (anarchy) was

[12] Hans J. Morgenthau, *Politics among Nations: The Struggle for Power and Peace* (1948), pp. 8–9, 36.
[13] Kenneth Waltz, *Theory of International Politics* (1979), pp. 18–37, 60–78.
[14] Ibid., p. 6. [15] Ibid., pp. 40, 79–101.

dynamized and international law even accorded a systematic place as 'a key part of the deep structure' of international politics.[16] However, law figured primarily as an unspecified background condition for (and outflow of) political interactions among states which developed and transformed patterns of social relationships characterized by enmity and amity in the context of three overarching (and potentially transformative) 'cultures of anarchy' for which the political philosophies of Thomas Hobbes ('enmity'), John Locke ('rivalry'), and Immanuel Kant ('friendship') were mobilized as place holders.[17]

This appropriation of some of the differentiated *systems* of thoughts of philosophers dealt with in detail in this volume is telling for IR as a discipline because it illustrates another dimension of systemic and systematic theorizing of power and law in IR. Political and legal thinkers in the tradition of Western political thought are referred to as sources of distinct bodies of thought which may be (re-)claimed for particular purposes in the pursuit of alternative ways of theorizing the whole (or essence) of international politics. Yet this is done primarily as short-cuts for a limited set of three or four 'cultures of anarchy', 'theories' along 'paradigmatic' lines[18] (such as 'realism', 'idealism' / 'liberalism', 'constructivism', or 'Marxism') or 'traditions of thought'[19] which are then linked with these key figures—mainly Machiavelli, Hobbes, Grotius, Locke, and Kant. This manner of organizing the discipline in what Hedley Bull called the spectrum of 'competing traditions' or 'theories' in IR reflecting 'the nature of international politics and a set of prescriptions about international conduct'[20] serves at least three functions: it authoritatively grounds disciplinary practice, it establishes (or at least claims) some historical lineage, and it sets IR apart from other disciplines (such as philosophy, political theory, and law) which lay claim to these thinkers as well. In the end, the differentiated systems of thought of political and legal scholars are reduced to some presumed essence which helps in sorting conceivable systemic patterns of international politics.

International law figures differently in these systemic projects but in terms of its ordering effects it is always trumped by politics and power. Even Hedley Bull, the influential IR theorist who, besides Hans Morgenthau, engaged the tradition of political and legal thought most thoroughly and sympathetically, warned of committing the 'error' to look at international law 'as if (it) were to be assessed only in relation to the function it has of binding states together, and not also in relation to its function as an instrument of state interest and as a vehicle of transnational purposes'.[21]

This takes us to a closer examination of the second interpretative key of this volume, the concept of 'order'.[22] Again, Hedley Bull and the 'English School' exhibit

[16] Alexander Wendt, *Social Theory of International Politics* (1999), p. 280.

[17] Ibid., pp. 246–312.

[18] Yosef Lapid, 'The Third Debate: On the Prospects of International Theory in a Post-Positivist Era', *International Studies Quarterly* 33 (1989), 235–54, at 239–41.

[19] Hedley Bull, *The Anarchical Society: A Study of Order in World Politics* (2002 [1977]), pp. 23–6.

[20] Ibid., p. 23. [21] Ibid., p. 49.

[22] Kadelbach, Kleinlein, and Roth-Isigkeit in this volume, p. 9.

the closest affinity with the tradition of legal theorizing which associates order, as the editors put it in the introduction, with stability as a desired outcome.[23] For Bull 'order' is associated (in a factual sense) with things being 'related to one another according to some pattern'. Yet at the same time this relationship can be called orderly only if it also serves (in a normative sense) some larger purpose.[24] 'World order' thus stands for broad 'patterns or dispositions of human activity' which serve the purpose of 'sustain(ing) the elementary or primary goals of social life among mankind as a whole' whereas 'international order' is only concerned with those patterns of activity that sustain the 'primary goals of the society of states'.[25] In other words, orders emerge from the interplay of certain forces where intentionality is difficult to pinpoint but they are also created as the result of some human agency in purposefully steering social relations.

This second definitional dimension is crucial for two reasons. First, 'disorder', Bull's antonym for 'order' is largely synonymous with anarchy and lawlessness in a Hobbesian tradition.[26] It mainly refers to patterns of activity which undermine or openly violate rules-based social life,[27] and becomes meaningful only against this understanding of the term 'order'. Second, and more importantly, the purposive connotation of the concept of 'order' is largely absent in most of IR's theorizing. Here an 'order' is simply an 'arrangement' of component parts (and in this sense synonymous with 'system' or, as in Waltz's case, also with 'structure'). How the key components and processes that make up an international system are 'arranged' or 'ordered' is of central importance for these IR theories. For the broad (and very influential) 'rationalist' versions of 'realist' and 'liberal' theory in IR it is also sufficient.[28] 'Anarchy' in this view is not to be associated with 'disorder' or lawlessness. Rather it is merely an 'ordering principle' in the sense of taking the absence of an overarching authority beyond states to enforce international rules, especially as far as the domestication of violence is concerned, as an expression of how the international system is arranged (or 'ordered'). Patterns and dispositions of states' activities can be observed and theorized without assuming that purposive steering takes place. In this regard Waltz and other IR rationalists explicitly follow the economic reasoning of a 'theory of the market': '(P)atterns emerge and endure without anyone arranging the parts to form patterns or striving to maintain them. The acts and the relations

[23] As to the widespread understanding of 'order' as a basic social phenomenon see also the close affinity between Bull, *Anarchical Society*, pp. 3–8 (n. 19), and the editors' example of Menasse's novel *Wings of Stone*: Kadelbach, Kleinlein, and Roth-Isigkeit, in this volume, pp. 15–16.

[24] Bull, *Anarchical Society*, pp. 3–4 (n. 19). [25] Ibid., pp. 19, 8.

[26] Ibid., pp. 23–6, 44–8; see also the contribution by Heller in this volume. This association of 'anarchy' with disorder is largely shared by Morgenthau; see Morgenthau, *Politics Among Nations*, pp. 138, 310–11, and 431 (n. 12).

[27] Bull, *Anarchical Society*, pp. xxxii, 3–4, 91, and 181 (n. 19).

[28] In IR discourse 'rationalism' is often combined with certain versions of 'realism' and 'liberalism' in order to highlight utility-maximization as a key assumption of a methodological-individualist outlook. See James Fearon and Alexander Wendt, 'Rationalism v. Constructivism: A Skeptical View', in Walter Carlsnaes, Thomas Risse, and Beth Simmons (eds.), *Handbook of International Relations* (2002), pp. 52–72.

of parties may be regulated through the accommodations they mutually make. Order may prevail without an orderer.'[29]

This rationalist take of 'order' obviously collides with approaches which explicitly emphasize the 'social' nature of international politics without, however, basing it (as Bull does and how Hobbes has often been read) on a dualism of 'order' *versus* 'disorder'. Roughly these approaches come in two versions, a systemic and an actor-based understanding. Alexander Wendt's 'constructivism' represents the most prominent 'states systemic-centric'[30] perspective which conceives of 'political order' in general not only in the classical Hobbesian view of 'getting people to work together toward mutually beneficial ends like reducing violence' but which, in addition, sees a 'sociological' problem of order in the challenge of 'creating stable patterns of behavior, whether cooperative *or* conflictual.' This is based on the postulate that while the regularities and patterns which we observe in nature or markets may be driven by material forces or assumptions of rational utility-maximization, social relationships, and patterns 'are determined primarily by shared ideas that enable us to predict each other's behavior'.[31] In other words, where Bull often associates various forms of conflict with disorder,[32] *patterns* of 'conflictual' encounter may be thought of as being an expression of order if they enable us to build stable expectations as to how others will act in social encounters. Wendt further elaborates this by conceiving of his three 'cultures of anarchy'.[33]

Besides the systemic approach to a social understanding of international political order, IR theorizing has always known actor-based approaches, i.e. forms of theorizing which causally link order (largely synonymous with 'stability') as an outcome of international politics with the intentions and policies of major powers. In the more limited realist versions states are normally attributed certain motivations to pursue 'status quo' policies or 'revisionist' ('revolutionary' or 'imperialistic') policies based on their satisfaction or dissatisfaction with their own position in a given political order.[34] These approaches often side with Bull's understanding of disorder when political strategies such as revisionism are linked with effects on political order. There are, however, also 'liberal' actor-based approaches which conceive of order-building as an exercise analogous to constitution-making. Here order is still defined systemically in terms of '"governing" arrangements among a group of states'.[35] However, these arrangements are visibly shaped by some powerful actor (where 'power (is) turned into order').[36] In other words, these orders are intentionally

[29] Waltz, *Theory of International Politics*, pp. 71–2, 77 (n. 13). For a critique of this '"scientification" of international political theory' by Waltzian neorealism, including a detailed critique of (partially intentional) 'misreadings' of Morgenthau and the political tradition, especially Hobbes and Rousseau, see Hartmut Behr, *A History of International Political Theory: Ontologies of the International* (2010), pp. 197–225.

[30] Wendt, *Social Theory of International Politics*, p. 257 (n. 16).

[31] All quotes ibid., p. 251 (emphasis in original).

[32] Bull, *Anarchical Society*, pp. 55, 90–1, 145–7, 181, 201 (n. 19).

[33] Wendt, *Social Theory of International Politics*, pp. 246–312 (n. 16).

[34] Morgenthau, *Politics Among Nations*, pp. 129–33 (n. 12); Henry A. Kissinger, *A World Restored* (1964), pp. 1–6, 145–7; John J. Mearsheimer, *The Tragedy of Great Power Politics* (2001), ch. 2.

[35] G. John Ikenberry, *After Victory: Institutions, Strategic Restraint, and the Rebuilding of Order after Major Wars* (2001), p. 23.

[36] Ibid., p. xiii.

designed, they do not merely result from systemic processes or mechanisms. As John Ikenberry, among others, has shown, it is particularly after great wars that the victors are provided with huge opportunities to create new rules and institutions.[37]

To sum up, 'system' and 'order' are as central to the dictionary of IR's theoretical vocabulary as they are to IL. Here and there they are also used synonymously—and synonymy is certainly not limited to the description of polarity constellations as, for instance, in John Mearsheimer's thesis that 'a multipolar system has more potential conflict situations than does a bipolar order'.[38] Discipline-specific differences in usage are, however, clearly discernible too—and especially in a historical perspective as IL and IR have more clearly demarcated the contours of disciplinary border lines over the past century. This is less visible as far as 'system' is concerned. Here notions of wholeness are equally applied in IR and IL to an arrangement which is (largely) made up of states as key units of (legal and/or political) analysis. Moreover, alternative forms of systemic theorizing from sociology or the natural sciences have left traces in both IL and IR.[39] However, the dynamics and processes which hold these arrangements together and endow them with their specific 'systemic' character are conceived of differently at the cores of both disciplines.

The normativity of law is obviously at the centre of IL as a subject matter. However, it also shapes a certain form of scholarly reasoning which is distinct from styles and methods of reasoning (or 'theorizing') in IR. 'International law may be a university discipline, but it is above all a rhetorical practice', as Martti Koskenniemi put it, approvingly quoting Friedrich Kratochwil that 'what makes rules "legal" is their *principled use* in application'.[40] In contrast, international—or, better: inter-state—political systems have increasingly been conceptualized in the evolving discipline of IR as being shaped by a notion of 'anarchy' which fundamentally changed the meaning of the term as it had been understood by legal and political theorists from Hobbes to Kant. Anarchy as an 'ordering principle' was drained of almost all the dreadful normative connotations which were associated with it not only in the legal and political philosophical tradition but also in much of IR scholarship up until the first half of the twentieth century.[41] Even the harshest of 'offensive realists' haste to emphasize today that even though 'the international system is anarchic

[37] Ibid. [38] Mearsheimer, *Tragedy of Great Power Politics* (n. 34).

[39] For discussions of Luhmann in IR theorizing see Mathias Albert and Lena Hilkermeier, *Observing International Relations: Niklas Luhmann and World Politics* (2004). The influence of systems theory from the natural sciences and cybernetics is most clearly visible in Waltz, *Theory of International Politics*, esp. pp. 38–59 (n. 13).

[40] Koskenniemi, 'Law, Teleology and International Relations', p. 20 (n. 5). Friedrich Kratochwil, 'Legal Theory and International Law', in David Armstrong (ed.), *Routledge Handbook of International Law*, (2009), pp. 55–67, at p. 58, emphasis in the original. On law 'as a "style" of reasoning' see also Kratochwil, *Rules, Norms, Decisions*, pp. 205–10 (n. 2).

[41] Brian Schmidt has shown that at least two meanings prevailed in the first half of the twentieth century. World War I was widely interpreted in the emerging discipline as having been the consequence of an 'orthodox juristic theory of the state' and a form of international anarchy which emphasized the absence of an overarching sovereign. Yet there was also a literature focusing on decolonization which was widely construed as an anarchic process where 'uncivilized' peoples would fall into lawlessness, chaos, and disorder when colonial powers withdrew. See Brian C. Schmidt, *The Political Discourse of Anarchy: A Disciplinary History of International Relations* (1988), pp. 123–87.

(this) does not mean that it is chaotic or riven by disorder.' What is more: 'By itself (. . .) the realist notion of *anarchy has nothing to do with conflict*; it is an ordering principle, which says that the system comprises independent states that have no central authority above them.'[42]

International anarchy in this sense highlighted a fundamental difference to 'domestic hierarchy'. Moreover, by postulating anarchy as a form of *order* which was both *factually obvious* and *central* as an organizing principle of the international political system it became the disciplinary anchor around which IR as an emerging 'social science'[43] could be profiled against other disciplines. The contrast to IL stands out in particular because IL remains committed, in its self-descriptions, to 'a teleological project' aiming at 'an international community ruled by law' and, thus, is decidedly 'not a social science'.[44]

As will be discussed in more detail in the next section this difference is important because 'power' and 'law' as ordering devices or mechanisms figure differently in the main discourses in both disciplines even if they may be conceptualized in similar fashion. Moreover, this difference may also help to understand why much of IR theorizing about the place of power on the one hand and 'norms' and 'rules' (as the preferred concepts in IR discourse compared to what is widely conceived as too narrow a notion of 'law') on the other hand remains fixated on stark dualisms of 'theory' versus 'practice', 'theory' versus 'the empirical' (or, for that matter, 'real' things that may be observable or 'non-observable'[45]) or all of the latter (the 'is') versus 'the normative' (the 'ought').

II. Power, Law, and Order

Concept formation is 'the limit of the empirical'[46] and, thus, a central part of 'theorizing'—taken here in a Gadamerian sense of 'seeing what is'.[47] In this understanding

[42] Mearsheimer, *Tragedy of Great Power Politics*, p. 30 (n. 34), emphasis added. On Mearsheimer and 'offensive realism' see also Glenn H. Snyder, 'Mearsheimer's World: Offensive Realism and the Struggle for Security', *International Security* 27 (2002), 149–73.

[43] For an argument which traces the shift from practical reasoning based on normative concerns to causal argumentation all the way back to Hobbes see also Martti Koskenniemi, *From Apology to Utopia. The Structure of International Legal Argument* (2nd edn, 2006), pp. 79–82.

[44] Koskenniemi, 'Law, Teleology and International Relations', pp. 14, 20 (n. 5).

[45] The 'scientific realist' vocabulary which leads to sentences such as 'states and the states system are real (ontology) and knowable (epistemology), despite being unobservable' has been introduced to IR mainly by Alexander Wendt. For his discussion of 'empirics', 'empirical research' and how this relates to 'real' things, irrespective of whether these are 'observable' or 'unobservable' see Wendt, *Social Theory of International Politics*, pp. 47–64(n. 16). For a critique see John G. Gunnell, 'Social Scientific Inquiry and Meta-theoretical Fantasy: The Case of International Relations', *Review of International Studies* 37 (2011), 1447–69.

[46] Ludwig Wittgenstein, *Remarks on the Foundations of Mathematics* (1978), p. 29.

[47] Theory, Gadamer recalls, derives from the Greek *theoria*, which means 'observing'. 'It does not mean a mere 'seeing' that (. . .) stores up information.' Rather, it is 'a way of comporting oneself, a position and condition. It is 'being present' in the lovely double sense that means that the person is not only present but completely present.' Hans-Georg Gadamer, *Praise of Theory*, trans. Chris Dawson (1999), p. 31.

theorizing 'power' and 'law' implies first and foremost to grasp how these concepts are used in the context of broader vocabularies.[48] As has been argued in the previous section, one of the key differences between IL and IR as academic disciplines can be located in disciplinary purpose ('teleological project' versus 'social science'). In this section I will argue that this difference in purpose translates into specific understandings and uses of 'power' and associated concepts in a core IR vocabulary on the one hand and 'law' as a secondary concept in the disciplinary vocabulary of IR on the other hand. Most importantly, in IR 'power is all too often understood in simple contradistinction to law'.[49] This attitude, I will argue, has been nourished by a gradual shift over the last century in the self-understanding of the discipline from one which had grown out of its deep roots in history, law, and philosophy into a particular brand of social science.[50] To the extent that it has defined itself as a social science this has sharpened its preference for theorizing the overarching state *system* primarily via generalizing explanation. In contrast, to the extent that IL is practiced as a 'teleological project' it has focused on theorizing generalized *and* individualized foreign policy practices via legal argument.

Power is ubiquitous in politics, be it 'international' or 'domestic'. This ubiquity, unsurprisingly, has also left its mark in a plethora of historically contingent and (necessarily) essentially contested conceptualizations.[51] Notions of power which almost naturally merge the two Latin sources of meaning of 'potestas' and 'potentia' with justice/legitimate rule[52] or which stand, even more abstractly, purely for a polity, a form of government or some 'political order', have been largely sidelined in IR, especially in those 'rationalist' approaches which have increasingly become dominant in the course of turning IR into an 'American social science'. Instead power came to be largely associated with 'capacities'—such as 'control over resources' and 'control over outcomes'—with which states as key agents were endowed. In the systemic conceptualization of an 'anarchical order' which pervaded the discipline any potential ordering authority (polity) at the level above the state dropped out and thus perfectly combined with an almost exclusive focus on the possession of 'material resources' and their use in affecting preferred outcomes.[53] The key question of

[48] 'Vocabulary' here is taken to refer to that linguistic net of words and concepts which forms the most basic point of reference for the creation of meaning. See Richard Rorty, *Irony, Contingency and Solidarity* (1998), pp. 3–22. See also Robert B. Brandom, 'Vocabularies of Pragmatism: Synthesizing Naturalism and Historicism', in Robert B. Brandom (ed.), *Rorty and his Critics* (2000), pp. 156–90.

[49] Andrew Hurrell, *On Global Order: Power, Values, and the Constitution of International Society* (2007), p. 13.

[50] Brian C. Schmidt, 'On the History and Historiography of International Relations', in Carlsnaes, Risse, and Simmons (eds.), pp. 3–22, at pp. 5–6 (n. 28).

[51] For a contemporary overview see Keith Dowding, *Encyclopedia of Power* (2011). A broad-ranging conceptual history is provided by Karl-Georg Faber, Karl-Heinz Ilting, and Christian Meier, 'Macht, Gewalt', in *Geschichtliche Grundbegriffe*, Vol. 3, ed. Reinhart Koselleck (1982), pp. 817–935. See also Walter Bryce Gallie, 'Essentially Contested Concepts', *Proceedings of the Aristotelian Society* 56 (1956) 167–98.

[52] Faber, Ilting, and Meier, 'Macht, Gewalt', pp. 818–19 (n. 51).

[53] See also Stefano Guzzini, *Power, Realism and Constructivism* (2013).

how order is maintained in a system without an orderer, thus boiled down to the question of identifying those factors which presumably 'explain' (causally) what had been set up as the major 'puzzle' in the first place.

This is obviously not the only use of 'power' in IR—especially if one conceives of power broadly as 'the production, in and through social relations, of effects that shape the capacities of actors to determine their circumstances and fate'.[54] Yet even a comprehensive 'taxonomy' which results from such a broad definition cannot disguise the fact that power figures most prominently in IR as a 'variable' in *causal* explanation. Even those theories or 'paradigms' which were set up in opposition to realism—such as 'neoliberal institutionalism ', 'liberalism', or 'constructivism'[55]—have primarily 'attempted to demonstrate their theoretical salience by demonstrating how 'power' variables are *not causally consequential* in their explanation of empirical outcomes'.[56] Against this background it is not surprising that (international) 'law' is treated as just another possible variable (or *ordering device*) in accounting for 'outcomes' in international politics—which is obviously at odds with the understanding and uses of law in IL.

In the following I will highlight a few persistent themes in IR scholarship which illustrate how a causal and instrumental understanding of both power and law has shaped disciplinary ways of theorizing order. Much more briefly I will contrast these understandings with ways of theorizing power and law in international legal thought.

1. Balance of power theory

If 'anarchy' is one of the core ideas in theorizing order in international politics the concept of 'balance of power' is the corresponding conceptual tool to theorize ordering mechanisms or devices to provide for 'stability within a system composed of a number of autonomous forces'.[57] The origins of the 'balance of power' concept date back to a time when 'inter-national' politics was not yet associated with a 'Westphalian' state system. As a matter of fact, what is known today as the balance of power 'theory'[58] was encapsulated by the idea of counterbalancing hegemony and a system of checks and balances as it was reflected in the work of historians and political theorists who described and analysed the relations that existed among the Italian city states in the fifteenth and sixteenth centuries. Since then the concept has experienced different mythical, metaphorical, and/or analytical uses in different

[54] Michael Barnett and Raymond Duvall, 'Power in International Politics', *International Organization* 59 (2005), 39–75, at 42; see also Guzzini, *Power, Realism and Constructivism*, pp. 1–12 (n. 53).

[55] See the respective overview chapters: Arthur A. Stein ('Neoliberal Institutionalism' pp. 201–21); Andrew Moravcsik ('The New Liberalism', pp. 234–54); and Ian Hurd ('Constructivism', pp. 298–316) in Christian Reus-Smit and Duncan Snidal (eds.), *The Oxford Handbook of International Relations* (2008).

[56] Barnett and Duvall, 'Power in International Politics', p. 40 (n. 54), emphasis added.

[57] Morgenthau, *Politics Among Nations*, p. 125 (n. 12).

[58] See Waltz, *Theory of International Politics*, p. 117 (n. 13): 'If there is any distinctively political theory of international politics, balance-of-power is it.'

disciplines.[59] In IR the metaphorical association of the balance of power with scales, a *just* equilibrium and a system of mutual restraints which was clearly present in the sixteenth and seventeenth centuries[60] steadily gave way in succeeding centuries to an understanding which increasingly focused on the measurability of power (in terms of 'capabilities') thereby depriving the balance of power concept of its previous, almost natural, connection between an equitable distribution of power on the one hand and a form of stability on the other hand which was also considered to be legitimate.

This nexus between a certain distribution of power and stability on the one hand and legitimacy (including a limited role for international law) on the other hand was still present in the writings of Hans Morgenthau.[61] For subsequent 'neorealists', such as Kenneth Waltz, and 'neoclassical realists',[62] however, it lost whatever limited role it might have had due to a particular way of practicing 'social science'. In this understanding scientific inquiry had to be subjected to certain 'rigid' criteria, tests, and processes in order to count as 'valid'. Accordingly debates surrounding the balance of power during the past few decades have largely centred on the social scientific prerequisites for actually stating what a particular balance of power theory entailed as a 'theory',[63] how one would demonstrate the value, 'explanatory power' or 'falsifiability' of such a theory,[64] what was required to properly 'operationalize variables'[65] and/or how one accurately 'measured power' and whatever balance might have been present or absent in a particular historical phase or constellation.[66]

[59] Richard Little, *The Balance of Power in International Relations: Metaphors, Myths and Models* (2007); Michael Sheehan, *The Balance of Power: History and Theory* (1996). See also Robert R. Sullivan, 'Machiavelli's Balance of Power Theory', *Social Science Quarterly* 54 (1973), 258–70 and the contribution by Roth-Isigkeit on Machiavelli in this volume. On the shifting meaning of the notion of 'balance of power' in the history international law and IL see Alfred Vagts and Detlev F. Vagts, 'The Balance of Power in International Law: A History of an Idea', *The American Journal of International Law* 73 (1979), 555–80.

[60] Bull, *Anarchical Society*, pp. 31–6 (n. 19); Little, *Balance of Power*, pp. 67–8 (n. 59). On the balance of power as a system of restraint in a 'republican security theory' on the one hand and political practice in the 'natural "republic" of Europe' see also Daniel H. Deudney, *Bounding Power: Republican Security Theory from the Polis to the Global Village* (2007), pp. 136–60.

[61] Morgenthau, *Politics Among Nations*, pp. 125–66 (n. 12) and Felix Rösch, 'Pouvoir, Puissance, and Politics: Hans Morgenthau's Dualistic Concept of Power?', *Review of International Studies* 40 (2014), 349–65. On the nexus between the balance of power and international law in Morgenthau's thought see also Koskenniemi, *Gentle Civilizer*, pp. 457–9 and 471–2 (n. 5).

[62] Steven E. Lobell, Norrin M. Ripsman, and Jeffrey W. Taliaferro, *Neoclassical Realism, the State, and Foreign Policy* (2009).

[63] Waltz, *Theory of International Politics*, pp. 116–28 (n. 13); John A. Vasquez and Colin Elman (eds.), *Realism and the Balancing of Power: A New Debate* (2003); T.V. Paul, James J. Wirtz, and Michel Fortmann, *Balance of Power: Theory and Practice in the 21st Century* (2004).

[64] John A. Vasquez, 'The Realist Paradigm and Degenerative versus Progressive Research Programs: An Appraisal of Neotraditional Research on Waltz's Balancing Proposition', *The American Political Science Review* 91 (1997), 899–912 and Kenneth H. Waltz, 'Evaluating Theories', *The American Political Science Review* 91 (1997), 913–17; see also Douglas Lemke, 'Great Powers in the Post-Cold War World: A Power Transition Perspective', in Paul, Wirtz, and Fortmann, pp. 52–75 (n. 63).

[65] Randall L. Schweller, *Deadly Imbalances: Tripolarity and Hitler's Strategy of World Conquest* (1998), ch. 1.

[66] William C. Wohlforth, 'Measuring Power—and the Power of Theories', in Vasquez and Elman, pp. 250–79 (n. 63); Stuart J. Kaufman, Richard Little, and William C. Wohlforth, *The Balance of Power in World History* (2007), pp. 25–6; William C. Wohlforth et al., 'Testing Balance-of-Power Theory in

To what extent a particular configuration of the balance of power was an expression of order or disorder, stability or instability—not to mention a normative yardstick formulated in a vocabulary of justice or injustice[67]—was no longer of central importance. Moreover, the application of one of the most widespread standards of this type of social science, the evaluation of a balance of power *theory* based on its *predictive* value, quickly revealed to what extent it had almost degenerated into an empty signifier.[68]

In any case, irrespective of whether the balance of power figured as 'dependent variable' or as 'independent variable' in IR scholarship the causal weight of legitimacy or international law in producing or preventing some form of order had completely dropped out of the picture as a potential additional or possibly even competing causal factor during the past decades. In contrast, legal scholarship continued to look at the idea or principle of the balance of power as one factor, among others, in the production of order besides law.[69]

2. Democratic peace theory

Whereas the 'balance of power' has been one of the key reference points of 'realist' theorizing in IR the so-called 'democratic peace' theory has in many ways fulfilled a similar anchoring function in 'liberal' and 'constructivist' theorizing, i.e. those 'paradigmatic' orientations in IR with the strongest inclination to accord 'norms' or 'law' a major place in ordering international relations. Articles by Michael Doyle from the 1980s in particular are usually cited as having generated renewed interest in Kant as a proponent of a 'liberal' or 'democratic peace' *theory*. In contrast to some of his more statistically inclined colleagues who concentrated on causal links between democratic regime type and peace,[70] Doyle invested some effort in addition in actually reconstructing Kant's argument why world peace may not only be an appealing moral ideal but also a realistic political goal.[71] Rather than focusing

World History', *European Journal of International Relations* 13 (2007), 155–85; and Mette Eilstrup-Sangiovanni, 'The End of Balance-of-Power Theory? A Comment on Wohlforth et al.: Testing Balance-of-Power Theory in World History', *European Journal of International Relations* 15 (2009), 347–80.

67 For detailed examples from legal scholarship see Vagts and Vagts, 'The Balance of Power in International Law: A History of an Idea' (n. 59).

68 Waltz was explicit early on that the 'predictions' of his balance of power theory were 'indeterminate. Because only a loosely defined and inconstant condition of balance is predicted, it is difficult to say that any given distribution of power falsifies the theory'; Waltz, *Theory of International Politics*, p. 124 (n. 13). He merely wanted to 'predict that, willy nilly, balances will form over time'; Waltz, 'Evaluating Theories', p. 915 (n. 64). See also John A. Vasquez, 'The New Debate on Balancing Power. A Reply to my Critics', in Vasquez and Elman, pp. 87–113 (n. 63) as well as the other chapters in this volume for major controversies surrounding proper definitions, measures and adequate empirical observations that either strengthened or weakened ('falsified') balance of power theory.

69 Koskenniemi, *From Apology to Utopia*, pp. 148–51 (n. 43).

70 Lewis F. Richardson, *The Statistics of Deadly Quarrels* (1960); and Rudolph J. Rummel, *War, Power, Peace* (1979) (also available as *Understanding Conflict and War, Vol. 4* at <https://www.hawaii.edu/powerkills/NOTE13.HTM>, last accessed 8 February 2017).

71 Michael W. Doyle, 'Kant, Liberal Legacies, and Foreign Affairs: Parts 1 and 2', *Philosophy and Public Affairs* 12 (1983), 205–35 and 323–53, reprinted in Michael W. Doyle, *Liberal Peace: Selected Essays* (2012), pp. 13–60.

on single dimensions of state institutions and conduct or international interaction as sources of peace—as E.H. Carr did in grounding the 'utopian background' of the 'Twenty Year's Crisis', among others, solely in Kant's conviction that 'there would be no wars under a republican form of government'[72] or as Morgenthau did when he focused exclusively on Kant's argument that 'the commercial spirit cannot coexist with war'[73]—Doyle provided a detailed reconstruction of a multidimensional causal argument about the connections between domestic republican government (or 'constitutional law'), international law and cosmopolitan law ('which permits the 'spirit of commerce' sooner or later to take hold of every nation') on the one hand and peace on the other. 'No one of these constitutional, international or cosmopolitan sources is alone *sufficient*, but together (and only where together) they *plausibly connect* the characteristics of liberal polities and economies with sustained liberal peace.'[74]

To what extent any of these *causal* readings are doing justice to Kant's *Perpetual Peace* has been a matter of debate for some time.[75] Among political theorists and philosophers there has always been a tendency to emphasize the extent to which 'Kant's idea' or 'proposal'[76] marked a 'regulative idea'[77] or 'realistic utopia'.[78] In IR the so-called 'democratic' or 'Kantian peace' research programme[79] has instead focused largely on a much more narrow reading of how one may causally explain what was even claimed to be an 'empirical law'[80] according to which democracies do not fight each other. In contrast to a reading of Kant which emphasizes (at a minimum) the mutual constitution of the restraining force of republican government, international law, cosmopolitan law, and peace, the overwhelming majority of IR 'liberal' inquiries into the 'Kantian peace' treats any form of law as a peripheral causal 'variable' at best. Only the (domestic) rule of law plays a somewhat more

72 Edward H. Carr, *The Twenty Year's Crisis, 1919-1939: An Introduction to the Study of International Relations* (1964), p. 25.

73 Morgenthau, *Politics Among Nations*, p. 310 (n. 12).

74 Doyle, 'Kant, Liberal Legacies, and Foreign Affairs: Parts 1 and 2', pp. 26–9 (n. 71), last quote on p. 29, emphasis added. See also the contribution by Vischer on Kant in this volume.

75 Eric S. Easley, *The War over Perpetual Peace: An Exploration into the History of a Foundational International Relations Text* (2004). For a detailed critique of Doyle's reading of Kant see also Tomas Baum, 'A Quest for Inspiration in the Liberal Peace Paradigm: Back to Bentham?', *European Journal of International Relations* 14 (2008), 431–53.

76 Jürgen Habermas, 'Kant's Idea of Perpetual Peace, with the Benefit of Two Hundred Years' Hindsight', in Ciaran Cronin and Pablo De Greiff (eds.), *Habermas: The Inclusion of the Other: Studies in Political Theory* (1998), pp. 165–201, at pp. 166, 179.

77 Martti Koskenniemi, 'Formalism, Fragmentation, Freedom: Kantian Themes in Today's International Law', *No Foundations: Journal of Extreme Legal Positivism* 4 (2007), 7–28, at 22; Robert B. Loudon, 'Cosmopolitical Unity: The Final Destiny of the Human Species', in Alix Cohen (ed.), *Kant's Lectures on Anthropology: A Critical Guide* (2014), pp. 211–29, at p. 228.

78 James Bohman, 'Beyond the Democratic Peace: An Instrumental Justification of Transnational Democracy', *Journal of Social Philosophy* 37 (2006), 127–38, at 128.

79 For an overview see Steve Chan, 'Programmatic Research on the Democratic Peace', in Robert A. Denemark (ed.), *The International Studies Encyclopedia* (2010).

80 Jack S. Levy, 'Domestic Politics in War', in Robert I. Rotberg and Theodore K. Rabb (eds.), *The Origin and Prevention of Major Wars* (1989), p. 88.

visible role[81]—but even here it mostly shows up as a component part of highly aggregated and complex 'variables' such as 'democracy'[82] (sometimes split up into 'normative' and 'structural' dimensions)[83] or 'liberal ideas'.[84] 'International organization' as one of three variables in a prominent 'triangular' explanation of mutually reinforcing factors which produce peace comes closest to a systemic variable that entails legal or normative constraints.[85] In sum, even in cases where 'power' plays only a marginal role in explaining a certain state of 'order' (as in liberal IR theorizing of 'war' and 'peace') 'law' figures only indirectly in accounting for it.

3. Regime theory

The reference in the previous paragraph to 'international organizations' as a possible variable in accounting for certain configurations of international order at the intersection of power and law nicely serves as segue into a final illustration of how IR conceptualizes and theorizes order. Theorizing 'international organization(s)' in the context of 'regime theory'[86] is an interesting example in the context of our discussion because it is situated somewhere 'between' forms of theorizing order which either focus exclusively on power (as 'balance of power' theory) or largely sideline it (as 'democratic peace' theory). Moreover, it also exhibits a particular understanding of 'norms' which illustrates some fundamental disciplinary differences between IR (as a 'social science') and IL (as a 'teleological project' and 'rhetorical practice').

Historically the subject matter of 'international organization' was viewed not so much as a subfield of IR 'as practically the core of the discipline'.[87] What is more, in the field's self-description 'the dominant viewpoint' had for a long time been 'the viewpoint of international law and organization' where the underlying 'conception of scholarship' was said to be 'to discover the goals and objectives toward which international society ought to be tending'.[88] In the course of gradually positioning

[81] Vesna Danilovic and Joe Clare, 'The Kantian Liberal Peace (Revisited)', *American Journal of Political Science* 51 (2007), 397–414.

[82] Tarak Barkawi and Mark Laffey, 'The Imperial Peace: Democracy, Force and Globalization', *European Journal of International Affairs* 5 (1999), 403–34, at 405–10.

[83] Zeev Maoz and Bruce M. Russett, 'Normative and Structural Causes of Democratic Peace, 1946–1986', *American Political Science Review* 87 (1993), 624–38.

[84] John M. Owen, 'How Liberalism Produces Democratic Peace', *International Security* 19 (1994), 87–125, at 93–104. For a discussion of the different, sometimes even contradictory meanings of 'liberalism' and 'democracy' see Seyla Benhabib et al., 'The Untidy World of Liberal Democracies', in *The Democratic Disconnect: Citizenship and Accountability in the Transatlantic Community* (2013), pp. 7–19.

[85] Bruce M. Russett and John R. Oneal, *Triangulating Peace: Democracy, Interdependence, and International Organizations* (2001).

[86] For overviews and discussions of conceptual distinctions in IR of concepts such as 'international organization/s', 'institutions', and 'regimes' see Christer Jönsson, 'Theoretical Approaches to International Organization', in Robert A. Denemark (eds.), *The International Studies Encyclopedia* (2010), and Benjamin Meiches and Raymond Hopkins, 'Regime Theory', in Robert A. Denemark (ed.), *The International Studies Encyclopedia* (2010).

[87] J. Martin Rochester, 'The Rise and Fall of International Organization as a Field of Study', *International Organization* 40 (1986), 777–813, at 780.

[88] Kenneth W. Thompson, 'The Study of International Politics: A Survey of Trends and Developments', *Review of Politics* 14 (1952), 433–6, at 436.

itself as a social 'science' IR increasingly turned against these traditions in favour of more 'rigorous' 'theory'. One outflow of this shift was the research programme on 'international cooperation' and 'international regimes' which took shape against the diagnostic of an increasingly 'interdependent' world where the maintenance of order could no longer be fashioned by states alone.[89] Building on a Lakatosian rhetoric of a 'progressive' problem shift the new research programme was said to keep the realist core's 'fundamental insights about world politics and state action' but 'adapt' it.[90] Where realists treated international regimes and institutions as mere instruments of state action[91] 'neoliberal institutionalists' allowed for cooperation to 'emerge' even 'under anarchy'[92] if certain conditions prevailed. Among others 'international regimes'—defined as 'sets of implicit or explicit principles, norms, rules, and decision-making procedures around which actors' expectations converge in a given area of international relations—were seen as possibly affecting state behavior and international outcomes as 'intervening variables'.[93]

For the purposes of our discussion this research programme is particularly interesting because it prominently employed a legal vocabulary ('rules', 'norms' etc.) in such a way that the *causal* effects of norms on taming power competition might be studied and the limits of pure power-based approaches be shown. Yet the actual *uses* of this vocabulary illustrated precisely where the differences between IL and IR lie: 'Norms' and 'rules' are not only treated as causal variables but as problem-solving devices. This implies that the states which employ these devices are conceptualized as having existed prior to the regimes which they create, maintain or ignore. In other words, regimes are treated as the result of a utilitarian (i.e. rationalist and individualist) calculus of pre-existing states without any regard to the underlying normative contexts in which they themselves are embedded.[94] More importantly still, from a sociological point of view the way in which 'norms' are conceptualized misconstrues their function in social action. As Kratochwil and Ruggie have pointed out early on, a one-sided fixation on norms as 'causes' does not do justice to central dimensions of the operation of norms and rules in social interaction. 'Norms may "guide" behavior, they may "inspire" behavior, they may "rationalize" or "justify" behavior, they may express "mutual expectations" about behavior, or they may be ignored. But they do not effect cause in the sense that a bullet through

[89] Robert O. Keohane and Joseph S. Nye, *Power and Interdependence: World Politics in Transition* (1977); Robert O. Keohane, *After Hegemony: Cooperation and Discord in World Political Economy* (1984).

[90] Robert O. Keohane, 'Theory of World Politics. Structural Realism and Beyond', in Robert O. Keohane (ed.), *Neorealism and its Critics* (1986), pp. 158–203, at pp. 159–61.

[91] John J. Mearsheimer, 'The False Promise of International Institutions', *International Security* 19 (1994), 5–49.

[92] Kenneth A. Oye, 'Explaining Cooperation Under Anarchy. Hypotheses and Strategies', in Kenneth A. Oye (ed.), *Cooperation Under Anarchy* (1986), pp. 1–24, at pp. 1–2.

[93] Stephen D. Krasner, 'Structural Causes and Regime Consequences: Regimes as Intervening Variables', in Stephen D. Krasner (ed.), *International Regimes* (1983), pp. 1–21, at p. 2.

[94] Richard K. Ashley, 'The Poverty of Neorealism', *International Organization* 38 (1984), 225–86, at 243–4, and Andreas Hasenclever, Peter Mayer, and Volker Rittberger, *Theories of International Regimes* (1997), pp. 158–60.

the heart causes death or an uncontrolled surge in the money supply causes price inflation.'[95]

These and similar functions of norms had been of key interest at times when 'political science' was still defined as a practical discipline where 'prudence rather than theoretical knowledge' was cherished and when scholarly inquiry did not yet have to 'satisfy the epistemological ideal'.[96] To the extent that IR was now practiced as social 'science' these practical (and by necessity normative) dimensions of social action were not only beyond its self-imposed methodological means but also beyond its interest.

III. Conclusion

In IR the whole of the relations between, and interactions among, states are customarily labeled 'international system'. At first sight it is irritating, however, to speak of a 'system of International Relations' where reference is made to the academic discipline rather than its subject matter. Still, as mentioned earlier, the epistemic dimension of the meaning of 'system' (as it has been introduced in this volume) does entail those disciplining functions which the editors identify—i.e. systems being man-made, representing the exercise of theorizing itself and describing how a system of thought integrates different phenomena under one or more guiding ideas.[97]

To the extent that IR can be meaningfully described as a system in this sense it had over the past century gradually become a discipline which almost celebrated 'anarchy' as a unique identity-generating idea and disciplinary anchoring concept on the one hand and an 'ordering principle' with regard to the subject of the discipline on the other hand. The confluence of a particular brand of regularity-fixated social 'science' and a spreading acceptance of 'non-reductionist' systemic theorizing meant that *systemic processes* (as they are reflected in the debates about the balance of power, the democratic peace, and international regimes) largely marginalized key social *practices* in the international realm (such as the practices of 'foreign policy' and 'diplomacy') because they obviously entailed contingencies of human agency which were deemed essentially 'untheorizable'—at least in the standard ('positivist') epistemological understanding of regularity and generalizability.

As a result, those forms of practical reasoning and judgment which still formed a disciplinary link between international legal and political thought before the twentieth century were either marginalized or relegated to the practice of providing 'policy recommendations' which supposedly followed almost naturally from observed regularities. Yet given the achievements of IR as an academic discipline the 'system of International Relations' seems to have succeeded in establishing the sort

[95] Friedrich Kratochwil and John G. Ruggie, 'International Organization: A State of the Art on an Art of the State', *International Organization* 40 (1986), 753–75, at 767.

[96] See the discussion of IR and IL 'inter-disciplinarity' in Kratochwil, *The Status of Law in World Society*, pp. 26–49, at p. 27 (n. 5).

[97] Kadelbach, Kleinlein, and Roth-Isigkeit, in this volume, pp. 7–9.

of 'equilibrium' or 'stability' among the different 'autonomous forces' within the discipline—to hark back to Morgenthau's description of the 'balance of power'[98]—which is a precondition for disciplinary survival. This 'equilibrium' may yet provide room for alternative forms of theorizing order which reconnect to some of the disregarded forms of practical reasoning—and thereby reconnect in novel ways with international legal thought.

[98] Morgenthau, *Politics Among Nations* (n. 12).

23

Universalism and Particularism

A Dichotomy to Read Theories on International Order

Armin von Bogdandy and Sergio Dellavalle

I. Introduction

There is, as this book shows, an enormous wealth of diverse theories (or systems) on what today is understood as international order. Systematizing them (i.e. ordering by reflected criteria) can provide for better understanding and making that wealth more productive, in particular by comparative and dialectic thinking. This contribution* is to show the potential of the paradigms of universalism and particularism in this respect.

Systematizing should follow relevant questions. We do so by three sets of contemporary issues on how to understand international order: common interests, individual rights, and authority. The first concerns the relationships between polities. Is the idea that the international order binds them together in the pursuit of the common good meaningful, or is the idea of a common good meaningful only with respect to an individual polity? Or, to give another example, should a decision by international courts be understood, today, as being taken only in the name of the states contesting in the proceeding, or rather in the name of some larger community? The second set concerns the treatment of individuals: does international law contain universal standards on how individuals are to be treated, no matter by what authority? If so, are those standards to be broadly or narrowly construed? And do they amount to true rights that individuals enjoy? How do such rights relate to the rights of nationals? The third set of issues concerns the organization of power: should the international order be backed up by international bodies with universal outlook, as institutions of global governance for a global community or even cosmopolitan citizenship? If so, what are the possible resources of authority of such institutions, and of their legitimacy? How do they relate to the nation and the state?

* We thank Leonie Vierck for editing this text.

These longstanding questions have been treated by many great texts. We purport that most texts can be systematized by the thrust of how they address the three guiding sets of issues. This in turn can help to develop answers for the contemporary concerns. The systematization occurs by a distinction between two fundamental approaches to these questions - approaches which we define as paradigms: particularism on the one hand; universalism on the other.[1] The authors who can be seen as universalists tend to assume the idea of global common goods meaningful, advocate individual rights no matter what, and support international institutions to advance those ends. Particularists, by contrast, tends to be skeptical and even negative on all these issues. We think that systematizing the various answers with the respective arguments along these two paradigms is a path to insight and advancement. This, however, requires first reflecting on the two concepts (Section II.). Then, we apply them not only—quite cursorily - to frame the attitudes of some of the authors presented in this volume with regard to the questions related to the possible extension of the 'well-ordered society', but also—in some more details—to detect the presence of the dichotomy in twentieth-century theories (Section III.). Our outlook shows, finally, how some strands of contemporary thinking try to overcome the dichotomous character of the distinction, and how the dichotomy remains nevertheless useful (Section IV.).

II. Universalism and Particularism—The Meaning, Value, and Limits of a Dichotomy

1. Particularism and universalism as paradigms of order

Particularistic theories see little common normativity beyond polities and conflict as the default condition. Three ontological assertions are important for theories to be classified as *particularistic*: that any polity exists in a primarily conflictual relation to other polities; that any normative order beyond polities is irremediably precarious; that a viable polity needs to be strongly integrated. By contrast, universalistic positions assert common principles among all humans, and, on that basis, are more positive about the possibility of public order on a transnational and eventually global scale. Universalist thinking does not deny conflict as essential to human interaction. But it usually holds that such conflicts can and should be peacefully processed according to those common principles.

[1] We build on earlier common texts: Armin von Bogdandy, Sergio Dellavalle, 'Parochialism, Cosmopolitanism, and the Paradigms of International Law', in Mortimer N.S. Sellers (ed.), *Parochialism, Cosmopolitanism, and the Foundations of International Law* (2012), pp. 40ff.; Armin von Bogdandy and Sergio Dellavalle, 'Universalism Renewed. Habermas' Theory of International Order in Light of Competing Paradigms', *German Law Journal* 10(1) (2009), 5. For a detailed account: Sergio Dellavalle, *Dalla comunità particolare all'ordine universale. Vol. I: I paradigmi storici* (2011), pp. 2ff.; Dellavalle, 'The Plurality of States and the World Order of Reason: On Hegel's Understanding of International Law and Relations' (see Chapter 17 in this volume).

We present these two understandings as paradigms. As a paradigm we see a set of foundational concepts which shape the use of theoretical and practical reason when applied, within a specific historical context, to a particular matter of knowledge and field of action. Against the background of this general definition, 'paradigms of social order' are those paradigms that refer to the conditions for a peaceful and generally advantageous social interaction. Among the questions that every paradigm of order has to address is the feasible extension of social order. More concretely, we can conceive of order by assuming that peaceful and cooperative interaction can only be achieved within the boundaries of limited and rather homogeneous communities, whereas beyond them order is inherently precarious. International law, at its core, is then more about limiting disorder. Universalist thinking, by contrast, holds that peaceful and cooperative interaction are in principle possible at a transnational and even worldwide level. The sets of concepts that respectively form the fundament of the two understandings of order are the paradigms at the core of our analysis: particularism as the paradigm which assumes the inherent limitation of the extension of order; and universalism as the paradigm which posits the idea of a global well-ordered society as a principle of understanding and action.

The extension of order is not the only question that can—or rather must—be addressed by a paradigm of social order. Further essential components are the ontological basis for a well-ordered society, as well as its unitary or pluralist structure. As regards the first issue, a well-ordered society can be based on the priority of the community and of its alleged interests; or, instead, it can give preference to rights and liberties of the individuals. In the first case, order has a *holistic* character; in the second, by contrast, it is *individualistic*. As a result, insofar as paradigms of order combine claims as regards both the extension and the ontological basis for a well-ordered society, particularism can be holistic, if it prioritizes the benefit of the community; or individualistic, if it favours the interests of the community members. On the other hand, we have a variant of universalism as well, which relies on the assumption of a worldwide community of humankind; and another one, which refers to the universalization of individual interests and rationality.

However, the theories of the past mostly seem a bit simplistic to us today. We will explain this with a transition from unitary to post-unitary conceptions of order. This transition has introduced—as we will sketch towards the end of this contribution—significant changes into the overall landscape of the paradigms of order. For now, we only note, for the purpose of a conceptual clarification at the beginning of our analysis, that particularism and universalism are kinds of 'limited' paradigms of order, in the sense that they are conceptually derived from restraining the analysis of the paradigms of order to only *one* of their features, namely to the question of the extension of a well-ordered society, and to the most relevant among the possible answers that can be given to it.

Before we move on to justify our proposal to conceive of the relation between particularism and universalism as a dichotomy, one more element should be stressed as regards our use of the concept of 'paradigm'. In fact, we apply the 'paradigms' of 'particularism' and 'universalism' to theories the authors of which, in the most cases, give to these concepts only a quite marginal role, or do not employ them at all. In other words, qualifying a theory as being universalistic or particularistic is a choice—specifically, *our* choice—very often not supported by a self-qualification by the author to be found in the analysed text or theory. It would be wrong, however, to conclude that the conceptual framework used to analyse the object is just an arbitrary creation of the observer to systematize the materials of the research from a perspective which arises essentially from her or his interests, being thus rather alien to the main thrust of the theories themselves. To the contrary, we claim that our paradigms, though they do not mirror the texts in all their richness, grasp an important *inherent* aspect of them, helping not only to organize our thinking in light of contemporary issues, but also to better locate the authors in the history of legal and political ideas and to understand how ideas have developed in the past.

2. On the functions and status of the dichotomy

In our analysis, we arrange the two paradigms of particularism and universalism as a dichotomy. Dichotomies are heuristic instruments, as dualisms are a standard tool in modern European thinking. They are used to provide for understanding, orientation and evaluation, insofar as they help to structure a field of theories with their arguments.

Dichotomies can have several uses. There is a possible classificatory use, according to which a theory is either the one or the other; the attention being fixed on, precisely, classification. That helps in providing a first structure. Dichotomies can, however, also support comparison, providing for a scale, a continuum, usually between two extreme theories (e.g. Machiavelli v. Kant, Kelsen v. Schmitt). In this case, it helps to order the many shades of grey, as is the case with most of the theories presented in this book. Not least, dichotomies are an essential elements of dialectic thinking which aims at overcoming the dichotomy, knowing that each overcoming is likely to produce a new dichotomy. This is a constructive use which aims at developing an original idea from using elements from theories reconstructed in this light. Much of the theory developed in our days seems to be heading there. In any event, such ordering helps telling a history of political thought: reading past theories in the light of these two opposing paradigms allows for a richer interpretation than the presupposition of linear progress.

A dichotomy has, therefore, at least three different dimensions—the classificatory, the comparative, and the constructive—which are generally difficult to be kept clearly distinct. We use the epistemological instrument by including all three dimensions into our considerations. Moreover, we maintain also that the concepts of particularism and universalism imply each other—and this in a twofold sense: first, because the definition of the one concept is only possible if we have an idea of what is the opposite; and second, since in almost every expression of particularism lies a piece of universalism, be it even so small, and vice versa. Let us clarify this with an example. We can imagine the opposite concepts of a dichotomy as the two ends of a rope, which is tightened between them. The rope represents the continuity that binds the two extremes. On this rope are situated, more or less near to one end—and, thus, to one concept of the dichotomy—the different theories on international law and the thinkers who stand as their authors. But does this construction mean that there is no break in continuity on the line that binds particularism and universalism? Not precisely. In fact, we can assume that there is a kind of red knot on the rope, which divides the rather universalistic from the essentially particularistic theories. The red knot, specifically, is marked by different answers—the one given by the theories on the right side of the red knot; the other by those on the left side—to two distinct questions:

a) first, can the well-ordered society expand in principle to a cosmopolitan reach or not? No matter how subtle the nuances may be, all theories of international law—as we will try to demonstrate in the next section—can be read as giving an unequivocal answer to this most fundamental question at the basis of the dichotomy.
b) And, second, from where does the legitimation to shape the rules of the well-ordered society and to interpret them come from? Is the source to be located in the individual community and in its institutions, or in something which is situated beyond it?

Most interestingly, the divide turns out to be positioned in the same spot for both questions, so that we have only one red knot, or break in continuity. And this is precisely the point where the difference lies between the two core concepts at the basis of our inquiry.

As we already anticipated before, dichotomies are not self-evident, since they are usually not used by the texts to which they are applied. Moreover, dichotomies are often not neutral.[2] The dichotomy at hand provides a fine example: this dichotomy, though not the terminology, saw the light of the day with an ideological purpose in the interwar years.[3] It was set up, as the 'realists' vs. 'idealists', to discredit a number of authors on how to understand and evolve the interwar order. The proponents of what we see as particularistic positions were successful in that: it seems evident that on international order a 'realist' appears to be more trustworthy than an unduly normative 'idealist'.[4]

There are more caveats to observe. The use as a classificatory instruments tends to guide attention to theories which are laying out uncompromisingly one of the poles is a clever way to academic fame. Some of the success of Machiavelli's *Prince*, Carl Schmitt's *Concept of the Political* and certainly much of that of Eric Posner's and Jack Goldsmith's *Limits of International Law* can be explained by that.

[2] Karl Acham, *Philosophie der Sozialwissenschaften* (1983), p. 45.

[3] E.H. Carr, *The Twenty Years' Crisis: An Introduction to the Study of International Relations* (1940); Jens Steffek and Leonie Holthaus (eds.), *Jenseits der Anarchie: Weltordnungsentwürfe im frühen 20. Jahrhundert* (2014).

[4] For a detailed analysis of how 'realists' misrepresented 'idealists', see Andreas Osiander, 'Missionare oder Analytiker? Versuch einer Neubewertung der "idealistischen" Schule in der Lehre von den Internationalen Beziehungen', in Steffek and Holthaus (n. 3), p. 25.

The dichotomy *universalism* and *particularism* is not to be applied directly to international law, but to academic texts[5] on international order. Such texts are the actual object of this contribution. Yet, insofar as legal theories read either instruments of international law or their judicial interpretations as examples of 'particularism' or of 'universalism', the paradigms can also be employed—although indirectly—to legal instruments and their judicial interpretation. Even within the horizon of this restraint, a consciousness of the fluidity and contingency of those great intellectual movements is required. A critical perspective seems all the more adequate in our time, during which stable intellectual dominants have been put into question.[6] Thus, the traditional set of conceptual instruments, much of it developed by the authors presented in this book, seems to be unable to adequately grasp phenomena of growing legalization on a transnational and global scale. This crisis of normal science may suggest the probability of a coming change of paradigms;[7] others even perceive this as the nearing end of systems thought as such.[8] This touches immediately on the question of particularism and universalism as guiding ideas for the general theme of this volume: the question of the adequate theory (system) building on order in international law. European theories developed until the nineteenth century are hard to apply to today's age of globalization.

Though the basic orientations of universalism and particularism are worlds apart, they depend on each other, which is why they form a dichotomy. Their respective meaning flows from their inner reference to each other. Arguments that designate a European classics of international law as universalistic or particularistic respectively stand in an indivisible relation with elements of the contrary position. Particularity without reference to universality is almost meaningless. Equally, universality only gains its content of meaning from the existence of particularities. The philosophical critique of metaphysics in the twentieth century has laid bare the roots and the contingency of such thinking and raised the question whether this dualist perspective already contains in itself a value judgment against multitude, variety, and plurality. Whatever one takes from this, that critique confirms that the dichotomy of universalism and particularism flows from prior basic orientations and that they contain a value judgment.

If the theories become more nuanced, the dichotomy does not necessarily lose explanatory potential. In light of theoretical relatedness and penetration, they may prove to be of epistemological use.[9] Certainly, their role is changing: instead of bringing about systematic division, they serve to connect contrary concepts, and by doing so they may contribute to further theoretical development substantially.[10]

5 'Systems', in the logic of the title of this book.

6 Sergio Dellavalle, 'Beyond Particularism: Remarks on Some Recent Approaches to the Idea of a Universal Political and Legal Order', *European Journal of International Law* 21(3) (2010), 765–88, pp. 766 and 786.

7 Thomas S. Kuhn, *The Structure of Scientific Revolutions* (3rd edn, 2008).

8 Jean-Francois Lyotard, *La condition postmoderne: rapport sur le savoir* (1979).

9 Heinz Heimsoeth, *Die sechs großen Themen der abendländischen Metaphysik* (4th edn, 1958), p. 38.

10 Niklas Luhmann, *Macht* (1975), p. 43.

Thus, the value judgment in favour of a dualist description of the world leads to a simplifying structure, in which the mutually referring pair of concepts generates a high theoretical productivity. However, the relation of mutual reference needs to be contextualized, ranging from an almost total negation of the contrary position (as with Machiavelli), up to the conscious adaptation to elements of the contrary position, as in many cases of contemporary theories, in particular pluralism. Contemporary theory has developed much mutual permeation and enrichment.

To end, the very idea that there is a field of international law that can be brought into a system by whatever kind of thought flows from a specific and probably culturally contingent historical tradition of western metaphysics, an idea put into question in important parts of contemporary theory in favour of pure plurality.[11] At this point, we maintain that our *conceptual* dichotomy for systematizing a theoretical field is informed by a *normative* decision in favour of a coherent legal system in the first place.

III. Applying the Dichotomy

1. Applying the dichotomy to the classics

We have compared the concept of particularism and universalism, in a metaphorical sense, to the poles of a rope straightened between them, with the different theories—and their authors—located at some point at a certain distance to the extremes. The picture illustrates that—except for the few theories that represent the perfect and uncompromising realization of one of the paradigms—most of them contain elements of both conceptions. This insights flows from the detailed analyses in the first part of this volume. We will not restate their outcomes. Nevertheless, a few examples can be useful for a better understanding of the question. Whereas Machiavelli appears to be the undisputed embodiment of particularism and its philosophical champion, no other author is so unequivocal. Bodin, another beacon of particularism, grounds his idea of political order on the particularistic concept of sovereignty, but recognizes the relevance of divine and natural law, the two pillars of universalism in Western thought. The second framer of modern sovereignty, Hobbes, though mostly concentrated on the way to legitimate properly the particular Commonwealth, has an unquestionably universal understanding of the individual as a holder of rights, interests and reason. And Rousseau, who shares his predominant interest in domestic politics with Hobbes, is not indifferent to the question of order beyond the individual polity, as testified by his commentary to the peace project of the Abbé de Saint-Pierre.[12]

On the side of the thinkers considered as committed universalists, things are also more nuanced than we could assume at first glance. Beginning with Vitoria

[11] See the contribution of Koskenniemi in this volume.

[12] Jean Jacques Rousseau, 'Jugement sur la paix perpétuelle' (1755), in Jean-Jacques Rousseau, *Collection complète des œuvres*, vol. XII (1782–1789), pp. 40ff.

and moving on to Suárez, Gentili, and Grotius, until Pufendorf and Wolff, all authors involved with the creation of a modern law of nations articulate their conceptions of order by resorting preeminently to the universal framework of natural law. However, they are all well aware—each of them in his own way—of the significance of parochial power. Indeed, Vitoria rejects as first among the great Christian philosophers the universal claim not only of the Emperor but also of the Pope;[13] Suárez acknowledges the specificity of the *leges civiles* within the horizon of natural law;[14] and though both Gentili and Grotius ground the laws of war on the fundament of a universal community of humankind, the first justifies preemptive war,[15] and the second admits that 'the laws of each state consult the utility of that state'.[16] Furthermore, while Pufendorf largely identifies the fundamental tenets of natural law with the principles of the law of nations,[17] nevertheless the most essential force that shapes natural law—as well as the law of nations—in his understanding, namely the need for social cooperation as a result of individual weakness,[18] is first realized within the limited range of the individual community, and not on a worldwide scale.[19] Lastly, Christian Wolff maintains that the *civitas maxima* is an organic whole which unites all nations on the basis of the universal natural law,[20] but justifies the right of a nation to wage war in order to defend its entitlements and interests.[21]

As a result, the black-and-white picture that was suggested by the application of the dichotomy between particularism and universalism seems to fade away, turning into innumerable shades of grey. Is thus the dichotomy useless, at best, or even a misleading conceptual instrument for the mapping of the modern Western body of thought on what we understand today as international law? Not really. Regardless of the many nuances and of the importance of highlighting them, we specified above that in the continuum that binds—and separates—particularism and universalism a dividing point can be identified, and that this 'red knot' distinguishes the two camps on the basis of two criteria: the possibility of a cosmopolitan order, and the source of the legitimacy of social, political and legal order. And indeed, if we apply these criteria to the authors, two factions can be separated clearly. Starting in the particularistic camp with Bodin, it is surely true that he recognizes the relevance of natural and divine law, but it is also indubitable that, first, the interpretation of that law lies only in the hands of the individual sovereign, so that an order beyond the borders of the single state is made at least unlikely and precarious, if not downright

[13] Francisco de Vitoria, 'Relectio prior de Indis recenter inventis' (1538–1539), in Walter Schätze (ed.), Francisco de Vitoria *De Indis recenter inventis et de jure belli Hispanorum in Barbaros* (1952), pp. 48ff.

[14] Francisco Suarez, 'De legibus, ac Deo legislatore' (1612), in Francisco Suarez, *Selections from Three Works*, Book III (1944), pp. 196ff.

[15] Alberico Gentili, *De jure belli libri tres* (1612), Book I (1933), Chapt. XIV, pp. 101ff.

[16] Hugo Grotius, *De jure belli ac pacis* (English trans: *The Rights of Law and Peace*, ed. Richard Tuck) (2005), 1749.

[17] Samuel Pufendorf, *De jure naturae et gentium libri octo* (1672), Book VIII (1995), chs. VIff.

[18] Ibid., Book II, chs. IIff. [19] Ibid., Book VII, chs. Iff.

[20] Christian Wolff, *Institutiones juris naturae et gentium*, Book IX (1750), ch. I, § V.

[21] Ibid., Book IX, ch. VII.

impossible. Second, the particularistic power of the sovereign is the unique source for the legitimacy of social, political and legal order. Changing sides, although all supporters of universalistic order acknowledge to some extent the individuality of the single polities, the reason for the legitimacy of order is located either in the law of God and nature, or in the general sociability of humans—both unequivocally cosmopolitan in scope and essence. As a result, cosmopolitan order is not only possible and desirable, but also the only legitimate order per se, so that the social, political and legal orders of the single polities, to be fully legitimate, are to be established within the context of the purposes of the higher universalistic order.

A special case is the position of contractualists like Hobbes, Rousseau, and Kant. At first, indeed, the contract theory of state was created in order to identify a new source of legitimacy for the public power of the single political community. However, since this source has been located in the individuals—and these individuals were conceived of not as members of a culturally embedded community, but as abstract holders of rights, interests and reason—no convincing justification could be found why the legitimate order should stop at the borders of the single polity. If individuals can justify the establishment of domestic public power by means of a contract, why should they not bind themselves—by means of a contract too—to shape a cosmopolitan legal community of humanity, under the only condition that all human beings are seen as equal and rational in a worldwide perspective? This is the reason why contractualism started as a theory of sovereignty with Hobbes, and ended—with Kant—as the most powerful advocacy for universalism in the modern history of philosophy. Kant was also the first thinker to introduce a tripartition of public law in domestic, international, and cosmopolitan law.[22] His failure to conceive of sovereignty as shared, however, proved to be an insuperable obstacle for the transition from a groundbreaking intuition to an unequivocal and feasible proposal.

The outcome of this short overview shows that there are good reasons to maintain that the dichotomy of particularism and universalism is perfectly applicable to the outstanding philosophies on international system and order between the beginning of the sixteenth and the end of eighteenth century. The dichotomy also provides a valuable instrument for a better understanding of how these authors have addressed one of the most fundamental questions related to social, political and legal order.

At the end of the golden era of the modern philosophy of international law, Hegel was then the first thinker to pave the way for a new paradigm beyond the dichotomy, in which the identity of the polity and universal reason are reconceptualized under an explicitly multilayered idea of order. But, before we explore the new intellectual landscape beyond the dichotomy, we shall first concentrate on whether the distinction between particularism and universalism can still be helpful for the analysis of twentieth century theories.

[22] Immanuel Kant, 'Zum ewigen Frieden: Ein philosophischer Entwurf', in Immanuel Kant, *Werkausgabe* (1977), Wilhelm Weischedel (ed.), vol. XI, p. 203.

2. Particularism in 20th-century theories: Carl Schmitt and beyond

As Machiavelli was the champion of particularism in Modern Ages' philosophy, Carl Schmitt has been its twentieth-century embodiment, in particular in his 1932 text on 'The Concept of the Political'. In this milestone of *particularism*, Schmitt introduces numerous innovations; in particular, he stylizes it and brings it into an era where interdependence becomes a major topic. Schmitt makes the core points of particularism with supreme vigor. In particular, he posits the readiness to sustain a war with another state as the vanishing point for its conceptual construction.[23] This concept is highly consequential insofar as it requests all law to be framed and practiced in this light, be it international law, or, and that is the focus of 'The Concept of the Political', domestic public law.

The development of his concept starts with the famous very first sentence of the book: the concept of the state presupposes the concept of the political. The text presents the state as an institution that only frames political relationships, rather than enabling them, as would a state-centred, conventional understanding. The political relationship is distinguished from other types of relationship in a modal way: it is defined as the most intensive of all modes of human relationship. It is the relationship in which the other is either friend or enemy in a confrontation which includes his or her legal and legitimate annihilation.

It is crucial to Schmitt's train of thought that the state is but one form of relationship, because this allows to depict it as a huge civilizing achievement. The state is the institution that overcomes deadly conflict on the inside and civilizes it on the outside. Inside, it succeeds in overcoming a possibly deadly conflict by creating political unity, i.e. strong leadership over a homogeneous people. The true political, i.e. possibly deadly conflict, is confined to the relationship with other states. Nevertheless, even on the outside, the institutional form of the state is grand, not because it overcomes conflict, but because it channels and civilizes it. The state provides the most civilized form of inevitable, and even desirable violence.

Probably the most important supportive argument is epistemological. Schmitt claims in 'The Concept of the Political', as in many other writings,[24] that true insight requires thinking from the exception. As he sets out, deadly struggle is not occurring all the time. However, it is a possibility from which, because of its seriousness, everything needs to be conceived. Under these premises, the political relationship, or deep enmity, is the default condition of human relations. As in Hobbes, it is ever present as long as there is no common legal order backed up by strong common institutions. True order is by necessity concrete order in this sense, a kiss of death to international law.[25] In this brute world, order is predicated on another

[23] For a step by step analysis of the core passages see the contributions in Reinhard Mehring (ed.), *Carl Schmitt: Der Begriff des Politischen. Ein kooperativer Kommentar* (2003).

[24] The core text is Carl Schmitt, *Politische Theologie: Vier Kapitel zur Lehre von der Souveränität* (1922), p. 13.

[25] For a recent application, showing its potential, Nehal Bhuta, 'The Frontiers of Extraterritoriality: Human Rights as Global Law', in Nehal Bhuta (ed.), *The Frontiers of Human Rights* (2016), pp. 1–20.

truth proclaimed as self-evident: the protector, and only the protector, is obeyed. This gives a key to purport international law's insurmountable weakness.

Schmitt's concept of the state presupposes a plurality of states. This presupposition is assumed as a fact, but Schmitt adds grounds which strongly militate against any attempt for overcoming such conflictual plurality. The very possibility of a state is predicated on the conflictual relationship with another state. According to the logic of protection and obedience, order would vanish if protection became superfluous. The plurality provides for social integration because of the external threat, and hence the viability of states.

The plurality of states has normative value also because it allows for different forms of concrete life. This is another kernel of particularistic thought. Indeed, Schmitt gives only one rational argument for why to fight: 'Each participant is in a position to judge whether the adversary intends to negate his opponent's way of life and therefore must be repulsed or fought in order to preserve one's own form of existence'.[26] The background for this is Schmitt's concept of the people, which surfaces rarely in 'The Concept of the Political', but underlies his approach. Schmitt provides a bellicose take on otherness.

Conceiving the state through the international is highly consequential for domestic as well as for international law. Schmitt radicalizes and stylizes a conventional holding of foreign policy hawks, namely of the primacy of foreign policy. This primacy of the international is highly consequential for the way a state should be set-up internally, contrasting liberal ideas of parliamentary democracy.[27] Schmitt also advocates a strictly anti-individualistic construction of the law. Fundamental or human rights should not stand at the core of public law. Rather, the very point of political community and public law is the power to order an individual into mortal combat.[28]

Schmitt challenges today's mainstream understanding of international law in almost all respects. It lays the ground for different doctrinal constructions, different evaluations, a different historical reconstruction, and, indeed, for a different discipline. The very concept of international law is questioned, and thereby the identity of the discipline as such.

Firstly, for Schmitt *international law* is a misleading terminology as *international* suggests some independence from states. Such authority is impossible: accordingly organizations such as the League of Nations are rather instruments of the foreign policy of some states, not truly international organizations. What the conventional understanding depicts as international law appears in 'The Concept of the Political' as external relations law.

Secondly, the conventional international law focus is too narrow to understand order between states. The distinction between *Landesrecht* and *Völkerrecht*, domestic law and international law is, for Schmitt, a mere façade. He defines the field as

[26] Carl Schmitt, *The Concept of the Political* (1995), p. 27.

[27] On the debates of his time see the contributions in Christoph Gusy (ed.), *Demokratisches Denken in der Weimarer Republik* (2000).

[28] Schmitt, *Concept of the Political* (n. 26), p. 46.

jus gentium, later he speaks of *jus publicum europaeum*. This field embraces not only international law, but also common constitutional standards and a common regime of property protection, i.e. transnational economic law. Schmitt's *jus publicum europaeum* gives much attention to such common European constitutional standards as well as to a common economic constitution before the First World War.[29] Accordingly, the narrow field of international law simply misses the core point for understanding order between states. This point resonates strongly with a current attempt to reconsider the very cut of a history of international law.[30]

Schmitt challenges furthermore the conventional narrative of progress in international law, in particular with respect to innovations introduced after the two world wars as progress. Schmitt presents the *jus gentium* in 1914 as the peak of civilization and the greatest human achievement because it civilizes war. This civilizatory achievement got lost after World War I. Schmitt militates against much what contemporary international law hails as epochal progress. The *jus ad bellum* stands at the core of international law. Overcoming that doctrine constituted no less than the demise of classical international law.[31] Along these lines, accepting the authority of an institution such as the UN-Security Council threatens statehood,[32] a provision such as Article 2 No 4 CUN is fanciful with respect to true states, while weak states have no right to exist.

This bears important implications on how to think the international order today. Much of its core terminology comes out to be confusing, if not misleading or outright ideological. This is not limited to the very concept 'international', but also applies to many other core concepts such as 'humanity', 'universalism', 'progress'. Schmitt reads much of it as a façade for US hegemony, and posits 'demasking' as a central task of legal thought.

Schmitt remains in this book short on the topic of how to establish order. Schmitt's most famous proposal of how to respond to the challenge was to devise large-range order, modelled on what he understood as the US hegemony in the Americas. He envisaged a large-scale order for Europe under German rule.[33] He came up with this original brand of imperialism in the early 1940s, i.e. after having penned 'The Concept of the Political', 'Raum und Großraum im Völkerrecht' (1940),[34] and 'Völkerrechtliche Großraumordnung' (1941).[35] The hegemons should guarantee the order within their respective spheres of influence, which would be in the hand

[29] Carl Schmitt, *Der Nomos der Erde im Völkerrecht des Jus Publicum Europaeum* (1997), p. 182.

[30] Martti Koskenniemi, 'What Should International Legal History Become?', in this volume.

[31] Carl Schmitt, *Ex Captivitate Salus: Erfahrungen der Zeit 1945/47* (1950), p. 71; *Der Nomos der Erde im Völkerrecht des Jus Publicum Europaeum* (n. 29).

[32] Schmitt, *Concept of the Political* (n. 26), p. 49.

[33] Proposing political institutions for broader spaces is not original to Schmitt, see Andreas Osiander, 'Missionare oder Analytiker? Versuch einer Neubewertung der "idealistischen" Schule in der Lehre von den internationalen Beziehungen', in Jens Steffek and Leonie Holthaus (n. 3), p. 25. Schmitt gives the proposal, however, the usual Schmittian spill, alongside the logic of his concept of the political.

[34] In Carl Schmitt, *Staat, Großraum, Nomos* (1995), pp. 234ff.

[35] Carl Schmitt, *Völkerrechtliche Großraumordnung mit Interventionsverbot für raumfremde Mächte* (1941), reprinted in Carl Schmitt, *Staat, Großraum, Nomos* (n. 34), pp. 269ff.

of an ethnically and ideologically homogeneous group organized within a nation state as the heart of the *Großraum*. Between the spheres of influence the principle of non-intervention should rule, and international law between these powers should maintain its 'classical' form. In Schmitt's conception, the community based on pre-reflexive homogeneity assumes continental proportions due to a more comprehensive definition of the possible reasons for cohesion.

Carl Schmitt's contribution may be unique in the history of contemporary political thought, in particular because of his uncompromising radicalism. He was, however, by no means isolated in some of his most decisive assumptions, so that we can conclude that particularism—far from being an idea of the past—is still present and influential. Four distinctive characteristics of particularism have been resumed—generally, with great success—in the recent debate: a) the centrality of sovereignty; b) the cultural embeddedness of political identity; c) the search for selfish outcomes as the only rational behavior; d) the exclusion of the 'other' as the condition for the survival of one's own community.

a) From *sovereignty* as a core tenet of particularism, two assertions are derived: first, that the unity of the law is intrinsically related to a sovereign public power;[36] and, second, that public law has to maintain an incontestable primacy over all other legal domains in order to guarantee the hierarchical coherence of the whole legal system. According to Martin Loughlin as one of the most prominent advocates of particularistic sovereignty within the contemporary legal theory, sovereign public power—and, therefore, public law as well – express the political will of an autonomous entity that constitutes itself precisely through this act.[37] In other words, the public sphere—organized by the system of norms of public law—has its origin in the apodictic assertion of will made by a sovereign social actor, firmly rooted in the factual terrain of power.[38] No precondition such as the cultural or ethnic identity of the nation is here required to the political act of will; the only indispensable requisite is that the act of will has to be free, i.e. independent from any other source of power.[39]

b) The second tenet of particularism, which influences today's theories, is the *national rootedness of political identity*. According to this element, developed among others by German constitutionalists like Josef Isensee, Paul Kirchhof, and Dieter Grimm, only the unity of the legal system, grounded on the primacy of the national constitution, can guarantee the rule of law and a high standard of legitimacy, both of which would be lost in the context of a cosmopolitan turn of constitutionalism.[40] More concretely, the unity of the law[41] is based on the unity of public power[42]—and this, for its part, can only be the result of

[36] Martin Loughlin, *Foundations of Public Law* (2010), p. 50.

[37] Ibid., pp. 208, 221, 228, and 231. [38] Ibid., p. 216. [39] Ibid., p. 209.

[40] Dieter Grimm, *The Constitution in the Process of Denationalization*, Constellations 12 (2005), 447.

[41] Josef Isensee, 'Staat und Verfassung', in Josef Isensee and Paul Kirchhof (eds.), *Handbuch des Staatsrechts der Bundesrepublik Deutschland. Band I: Grundlagen von Staat und Verfassung* (1987), pp. 591, 619.

[42] Ibid., 620.

the national unity of the people (*Volk*).[43] The search for a fundament for the unity of the *Volk* introduces, then, a distinction between two variants of this strand. On the one hand, some authors identify this fundament—according to Isensee's words—with 'geographic and geopolitical situation, historic origin and experience, cultural specificity, economic necessities of the people, natural and political conditions.'[44] All these elements are expressions of a pre-political state of facts, of a quasi-natural condition of the *Volk*, on which political and legal institutions are built. They constitute the *Volk*, thus, as a 'community of destiny',[45] before and beyond any individual decision or preference.[46] On the other hand, a second variant—represented, in particular, by Dieter Grimm—locates the basis for the unique character of a *Volk* and its law rather in the common language spoken by all members of the people.[47] Only the existence of a shared language—according to Grimm—enables the members of the political community to legitimate the institutions of public power as well as their decisions.[48]

c) Another feature of particularistic thinking relies on an understanding of rational choice according to which only *egoistic behaviour*, insofar as it aims at maximizing individual payoffs, can be regarded as rational. Slightly more than a decade ago, Jack L. Goldsmith and Eric A. Posner have applied this rather short-term-oriented conception of rational choice to legal theory in order to assert the normative limits of international law.[49] According to their interpretation, since we cannot know precisely what are the preferences of other polities or what their next actions are going to be, individuals will act rationally—i.e. will enhance their selfish outcomes—only if the polity does not bind itself to strict supra-state rules, or if it does so just in the case that these rules are evidently at the service of its immediate interests. Neither customary international law nor treaty law would build a reliable normative framework of shared and effective rules. As a result, states should comply with international law only insofar as this compliance coincides with their immediate and egoistic interests, so that the legal framework of relations among political communities is left with a very modest normative consistency.

d) The fourth—and last—main characteristic of particularism refers to the definition of the identity of one's own political community as strictly related to the *contraposition to some kind of 'otherness'*. Samuel P. Huntington develops this foundational tenet of particularism in his analysis of the political state of mind of the US society at the dawn of the twenty-first century. Given the premise that the individual political community, in order to maintain its strength and vitality, must build on its cultural and

[43] Ibid., 634. [44] Ibid. [45] Ibid.

[46] Paul Kirchhof, 'Der deutsche Staat im Prozess der europäischen Integration', in Isensee and Kirchhof (eds.), *Handbuch des Staatsrechts der Bundesrepublik Deutschland* (n. 42), p. 869.

[47] Dieter Grimm, 'Braucht Europa eine Verfasssung?', *JuristenZeitung* 50 (1995), p. 581.

[48] Ibid., p. 588.

[49] Jack L. Goldsmith and Eric A. Posner, *The Limits of International Law* (2005).

religious heritage,[50] he claims that the definition of the essential principles of the social and political life of the community are largely depending on the identification of a counterpart,[51] or even of an enemy.[52] As a consequence, America—but the same claim could be made for every other polity—has to assert itself in the international arena as the expression of specific values, which are the result of long-term historical processes.[53] Furthermore, as far as the internal dimension is involved, no allegedly self-reliant 'otherness' should be accepted as a component of the domestic society. Insofar as immigration is allowed and even welcomed, the new fellow citizens have to take on the basic elements of the leading culture of the country, namely the language, the work ethic, the individualism and the respect for the rule of law which are assumed to be typical for the traditional Anglo-Protestant majority.[54]

2. Radicalizing and concretizing universalism: Kelsen and the constitutionalization of international law

If Carl Schmitt is the most visible example of particularism among legal scholars in the last century, this same role, but on the universalistic side, is taken by Hans Kelsen. Kelsen's plea for universalism is built on his analysis of the contraposition between dualism and monism.[55] His starting point is what he maintains to be a paradox: paradoxical indeed is the claim put forward by the supporters of nationalism, according to which a nation state pretends to be sovereign though acknowledging the validity of international law. In fact—Kelsen argues—the condition of sovereignty is realized when no power needs to be recognized, factually and normatively, as situated above oneself, so that the own capability of acting is not limited.[56] Yet, international law—if taken seriously—imposes precisely such a limitation.[57] For that reason, either the nation state is not sovereign, or international law has little, if any, normative quality.

Kelsen presents three possible ways for resolving the paradox—the first one basing on a dualistic interpretation of the legal system, the second and third ones on a monistic view. The dualistic solution assumes that two different legal systems—the national and the international—coexist, the first one providing rules for the domestic realm, the second for the relations between states. According to this perspective, each system has its own basis of legitimacy and is unchallenged in its area of

[50] Samuel P. Huntington, *Who Are We? The Challenges to America's National Identity* (2004), pp. 19ff., 337ff.

[51] Ibid., pp. 24ff.

[52] Ibid., pp. 258ff., 357ff.

[53] Ibid., pp. 362ff.

[54] Ibid., pp. 131ff., 178ff.

[55] Hans Kelsen, *Reine Rechtslehre. Einleitung in die rechtswissenschaftliche Problematik* (1934), p. 140.

[56] Hans Kelsen, *Das Problem der Souveränität und die Theorie des Völkerrechts* (1920, reprint 1981), p. 12.

[57] Ibid., p. 40.

competence.[58] The problem, in Kelsen's view, is that in this case we would possibly have two diverging norms, derived from two different legal systems, both effective and legitimate, which simultaneously apply to the same matter. Kelsen refuses this possibility and points out that the simultaneous validity of two diverging norms leads to a contradiction which would jeopardize the normative quality of the entire legal system.[59] Therefore, in his approach, the existence of a plurality of norms—that means: the presence of more than one rule applicable at the same time to the same legal field—is completely inacceptable: a pathology of disorder that should be avoided, or, if already present, healed as soon as possible.

The second and the third solution are both grounded on a monistic conception of the legal system, i.e. on the assumption that domestic and international law have one and the same foundation for validity and legitimacy. The difference is that in the first case domestic public law prevails over international law, whilst in the second international law is placed at the top of the pyramid of legal norms. In accordance with the first definition of monism, international law is conceived of as a part of domestic public law, or, as it has been described, as 'external state law'.[60] Therefore, it is among the competences of the sovereign individual state to specify the scope of international legal norms. The curious—and, according to Kelsen, even quite absurd—consequence of this modus operandi is that, given the fact that we have a large number of individual states, if international law is depending for the specification of its normative range on sovereign decisions taken by each of those single states, we will also have as many different international law orders as we have sovereign states; that means, lastly, that no binding international law would exist. A further circumstance would be no less absurd: since international law norms provide for the mutual recognition of states as equal actors in the international arena, exactly this mutual acknowledgment, which is fundamental for the very functioning of the international order, should rely upon the free and arbitrary will of each individual states. The result would be that the recognition of every state as equal actor of international law would lie in the hands of every other single state, as well as that each individual state would decide on the international recognition of all other states—a confusing condition, which is illogical and would destabilize international relations.[61]

The only solution of the problem would thus consist, if we follow Kelsen and accept his conceptual presuppositions, in the preference for the monistic structure of the entire legal order, but turned upside down as against the former option, i.e. with international law at the apex of the pyramid and domestic public law as the executor of the fundamental principles and norms of international law within a limited territory, towards a specific group of individuals—the citizens of the state—and within the range of competences attributed to the state by international norms.[62]

[58] Ibid., p. 102.
[59] Hans Kelsen, *General Theory of Law and State* (1945, reprint 1949), p. 363.
[60] Kelsen, *Reine Rechtslehre* (n. 55), p. 140.
[61] Ibid., p. 142.
[62] Ibid., p. 149; Hans Kelsen, *Peace through Law* (1944), p. 35.

Kelsen admits explicitly that such a construction of the legal system would mark the end of any serious pretension of sovereignty by the single states.[63]

Few doubts, if any, can be raised on the cosmopolitan scope of Kelsen's idea of international order. Rather, his position marks a twofold radicalization of previous understandings of universalism. Kelsen's first step on the way to a quite uncompromising version of the *civitas maxima* is related to the limitation of the role of individual states to mere executors of what is allowed by international law—a restriction which is not only radical but downright unprecedented in the history of political thought at least since Machiavelli. In fact, the formal legitimacy of the single states as recognized and empowered agents within the international legal arena is exclusively derived from the *Grundnorm* of international law, which is at the same time the hierarchically highest legal source, and the epistemologically most essential foundation of the global legal order. As a result, also the scope of the legitimate action of the individual states turns out to be significantly curbed. The second step of Kelsen's radicalization of universalism consists in his exclusively *legal* conception of cosmopolitan order. The conviction that world order—if it has ever to be concretized—will be essentially a legal one had been already expressed by Kant.[64] Nonetheless, Kant maintained that, if this legal order should be established, important political problems concerning primarily the transfer of sovereignty by individual states have to be settled.[65] Thus, given that the order is to be based on a legal framework, the cosmopolitan legal system needs—according to Kant—a strong and steady political support. The political dimension, by contrast, is largely ignored by Kelsen. This is true, first, for the domestic dimension, since the state, in Kelsen's understanding, is nothing more than the system of public law.[66] And, insofar as an order beyond the borders of the state is feasible, this cannot but be a legal order as well.[67]

Kelsen's intellectual courage and originality are unquestionable. Nevertheless, his radicalization of universalism—in particular, his marginalization of the role of nation states—did not find many supporters. Rather, most of the authors who resumed universalism after Kelsen were concerned with the attempt to reconcile the idea of cosmopolitan order with a more realistic view of what individual states *can* actually do as well as with the legitimacy basis of their actions. A most significant contribution to a further development of a well-balanced universalism has been delivered by the theory of the constitutionalization of international law.[68] States are still regarded, here, as the most important actors of international law,

[63] Kelsen, *Reine Rechtslehre* (n. 55), pp. 142 and 153.

[64] Immanuel Kant, 'Über den Gemeinspruch: Das mag in der Theorie richtig sein, taugt aber nicht für die Praxis' (1793), in Kant, *Werkausgabe*, Bd. XI (n. 22), pp. 125, 169ff.

[65] Kant, *Zum ewigen Frieden* (n. 22), p. 212; Immanuel Kant, *Die Metaphysik der Sitten* (1797), in Kant, *Werkausgabe*, Bd. VIII ('Rechtslehre') (n. 22), § 61, 474.

[66] Kelsen, *Reine Rechtslehre* (n. 55), pp. 116ff.

[67] Kelsen, *Peace through Law* (n. 62).

[68] Stefan Kadelbach and Thomas Kleinlein, *Überstaatliches Verfassungsrecht, Archiv des Völkerrechts* 44(3) (2006), 235; Jan Klabbers, Anne Peters, and Geir Ulfstein (eds.), *The Constitutionalization of International Law* (2009); Thomas Kleinlein, *Konstitutionalisierung im Völkerrecht* (2012).

although—contrary to what the pre-Kelsenian tradition of international law scholarship claimed—further subjects have also to be recognized as autonomous agents, such as supra-state institutions, international organizations, courts, and, last but not least, individuals and NGOs. The consequent limitation of state sovereignty confirms the commitment of the theory of the constitutionalization of international law to the most essential tenet of universalism, namely the priority of international law over the self-reliant interests of the nation states. Yet, while Kelsen's idea of a worldwide order is based on a strictly monistic legal framework, global constitutionalists rather presuppose that an essentially multifaceted international legal community frames and directs political power in the light of common values and a common good.

IV. Beyond the Dichotomy

The dichotomy of particularism and universalism allows to map the landscape of the theories of international order by distinguishing between those theories which back the perspective of a somehow institutionalized cosmopolitan legal community, and those which deny such possibility. Some approaches are radical enough to fit easily into the dichotomy; some other are more at the edge of the field. But most of them—with only few exceptions, Hegel for instance—can be described within the horizon of the dichotomous perspective. Yet, both particularism and universalism—if understood as a dichotomy—show a mirror-inverted deficit. In fact, universalistic theories shape the framework for the creation of a legal and political order that include the whole humankind, but at the cost of a certain indifference towards the precious identities of the individual communities; and, vice versa, particularistic authors made a strong case for singular identities, but often forgot that these can thrive only within a broader context of peaceful interaction and inclusion.

Therefore, we can conclude that the overcoming of the one-sidedness of the approaches can be reasonably seen as a desirable intellectual task. Nevertheless, no significant author of the founding era of international law made it to his main proposal—even not Hegel, who only introduced some clues, albeit highly interesting, of a post-dichotomous order. The reason is that, in order to conceive of an alternative in which the advantages of both the universalistic and the particularistic position could be adequately integrated, a deep-going paradigmatic revolution was needed. This is a quite recent and still ongoing phenomenon, which involves what we have described as the third element of a paradigm of order—along with the claims concerning the extension of order and its ontological basis—namely the assertion about the unitary or non-unitary character of a well-ordered society. Regardless of whether they were particularistic or universalistic, social, political, and legal theories were characterized, until just a few decades ago, by a *unitary* idea of order. This means that the institutional structure and a body of norms was considered 'well-ordered' only if organized as a coherent and hierarchical unity, as a pyramid in which conflicts between different institutions and norms had to be resolved by defining which institution or norm, respectively, has priority over the conflicting one. According to the traditional conception, both the particularistic individual community and the cosmopolitan *civitas maxima* were, thus, unitary and hierarchical. Instead, the paradigmatic revolution from a unitary to a post-unitary idea of order has paved the way for an understanding in which a well-ordered society can also be conceived of as a polyarchic and horizontally interconnected structure that reminds more of a network than of a pyramid. In this social, political and legal configuration of interrelated decision-makers, conflicts of institutions and norms are not a dangerous threat to order; rather, they can be operationalized in discursive procedures aiming at reaching a shared objective and not at establishing—or re-establishing—hierarchy. As a result, order can be universal and particular at the same time, insofar as it extends far beyond the borders of the single community, but recognizes the inescapability and value of the sub-universal institutionalizations of order. Three approaches can be singled out in this still unfolding process.

1. Systems theory

Systems theory eschews any reference to an overarching rationality that, starting from the transcendental capacities of the individuals, would encompass all forms of social interaction. Contrary to any form of traditional universalism, no universal reason—subjective or intersubjective—is here envisaged, either at the descriptive or at the prescriptive level.[69] To the contrary, system theory maintains that many rationalities can be observed by the social scientist, each of them characterizing the specific way of functioning of one social subsystem. According to systems theory, there are no extra-systemic rational processes. However, different rational processes within the manifold functional subsystems of society guarantee that these subsystems deliver the performances for which they have developed and that are necessary for the continuity and the further improvement—in the sense of higher efficiency—of the whole society.

Under these premises, also the legal system—as a social subsystem itself—is characterized by its specific rationality. Moreover, because the function of the law consists in stabilizing the normative expectations of the actors of social interactions,[70] and since these social expectations derive from a large number of social subsystems in which functionally specified social interactions occur, the existence of a plurality of social subsystems corresponds to a fragmentation of the legal system.[71] Put differently, insofar as the law has the function to guarantee the internal order of different social subsystems, the law itself loses its unity and develops distinct legal subsystems, each of them characterized by the

[69] Niklas Luhmann, *Soziale Systeme. Grundriß einer allgemeinen Theorie* (1984); Niklas Luhmann, *Das Recht der Gesellschaft* (1993); Niklas Luhmann, *Die Gesellschaft der Gesellschaft* (1997).

[70] Luhmann, *Das Recht der Gesellschaft*, p. 131.

[71] Gunther Teubner, *'Global Bukowina': Legal Pluralism in the World Society'*, in G. Teubner (ed.), *Global Law Without a State* (1997), p. 3.

rationality, expressed in legal terms, that underlies the implementation of the subsystemic functions.[72]

Systems theory can be read as considering the fragmentation of society into subsystems and the fragmentation of the law into legal regimes not only as facts but also as developments to be welcomed insofar as they enhance the functional efficiency of social performances. In doing so, it recognizes the importance of the particularistic dimension of social interaction. Nonetheless, the particularistic subsystems do not reply national borders; to the contrary, they tend to unfold at a global scale. Social subsystems, thus, also overcome traditional parochialism in a way that incorporates, though in a quite peculiar form, some traditional elements of universalism.

2. Postmodernism

Relying on the de-construction of the modern idea of unity as the best realization of a rational order, *postmodernism* has pointed out too, in an even more uncompromising fashion, the inherent pluralism of contemporary society and of its legal order.[73] From the postmodern perspective, no social structure or legal regime can claim to embody the principles of a superior rationality. Rather, every form of social interaction and every legal order, and system, are products of narrations that have their *raison d'être*—not less than any other narration—in the historical conditions in which they happen to occur. As a result, diversity itself is a value, with the consequence that any attempt by supra-ordered norms to force hierarchy on the manifold plurality of social interactions is condemned as a suffocation of what is a normatively desirable opportunity to unfold the freedom of individuals and social groups.

The theory of social and legal pluralism differs clearly from the unitary conceptions of order, be they universalistic or particularistic. In fact, it acknowledges the multifaceted dimension of the social and legal phenomenon as it has developed in the contemporary world, without trying to impose on it an overarching system of rules either at the national or at the international level. The favourable assessment of the multifaceted unfolding of social and legal *orders* takes the relevance of specific—and, thus, particularistic—issues adequately into account. Since from the point of view of postmodern social and legal pluralism no universal standard of rationality can be convincingly established, every social narration has to be considered as rational as any other, and the social and legal rules that give predictability to the interactions that unfold within the societal context of a narration should be recognized as being on an equal footing as any other system of rules. On the other hand, the characterizing features of a specific system of rules are never

[72] Andreas Fischer-Lescano and Gunther Teubner, 'Fragmentierung des Weltrechts: Vernetzung globaler Regimes statt etatistischer Rechtseinheit', in Mathias Albert and Rudolf Stichweh (eds.), *Weltstaat und Weltstaatlichkeit. Beobachtungen globaler politischer Strukturbildung* (2007), p. 37.

[73] Paul Schiff Berman, *Global Legal Pluralism* (2012); Miguel Poiares Maduro, *Three Claims of Constitutional Pluralism*, accessed 1 September 2016, available at <https://cosmopolis.wzb.eu/content/programs/conkey_Maduro_Three-Claims-of-Pluralism.pdf;>; Nico Krisch, *Beyond Constitutionalism* (2010).

necessarily related with a territory or a population, so that social and legal orders can expand transnationally, with the result of involving different territories and populations. As in systems theory, hence, the acknowledgement of a certain form of particularism goes along with an undeniable post-parochial understanding of order. However, the postmodern approach to a post-unitary conception of order is also distinguished from systems theory insofar as it eschews to endorse the idea of a precisely determined criterion for the distinction between rational and non-rational. Concretely—and in contrast to systems theory—social and legal pluralism gives up the strictly binary code in interpreting legal communication, in favour of a more nuanced attention to 'graduation'.[74]

3. Discourse theory

According to the fundamental assumption of the *communicative paradigm*,[75] society is made of a plurality of interactions, each of them characterized by a specific aim that influences decisively the discursive contents of the interaction. Although manifold in its essence, social communication—and the rationality that is embedded in it—are neither exclusively functional, as in systems theory, nor are they spelled out in a plurality of incommensurable forms as in postmodern thinking. Rather, the communicative rationality—right from the understanding of communication here presupposed—has always a normative core. The normative core of communicative rationality consists in the assumption that discursive communication can achieve its goal only if all those involved mutually presuppose that: a) from an *objective* perspective, the assertions are *true* (in the sense that the propositions are referred to real situations or facts); b) from a *subjective* perspective, the speakers act *truthfully* (in the sense that they are committed to fair-minded purposes and are sincerely persuaded that their assertions meet the conditions for truth); and c) from an *intersubjective* perspective, the speakers interact according to the principles of *rightness* (in the sense that they accept that their assertions have to meet the criteria for a general and mutual acknowledgement by all participants in the communication).[76] Precisely this normative essence, based on the general principle of mutual recognition, is what makes communicative rationality universal and justifies the claim that the communicative paradigm represents a sort of renewal of universalism, now fully aware of the undeniable value of the sub-universal orders as well as of their autonomous and irreducible legitimacy.

As regards the legal order, communicative rationality paves the way to a conception in which the particular articulation of legal order is recognized, but in a quite

[74] Krisch, *Beyond Constitutionalism*, p. 305.

[75] Karl-Otto Apel, *Transformation der Philosophie* (1973); Karl-Otto Apel, *Diskurs und Verantwortung* (1990); Jürgen Habermas, *Theorie des kommunikativen Handelns* (1981); Jürgen Habermas, *Moralbewußtsein und kommunikatives Handeln* (1983).

[76] See Habermas, *Vorstudien und Ergänzungen zur Theorie des kommunikativen Handelns* (1984), p. 598; Jürgen Habermas, *Nachmetaphysisches Denken* (1988), pp. 73, 105, 123; Jürgen Habermas, *Wahrheit und Rechtfertigung* (2004), p. 110.

different way than in the approaches described before. Plurality is here embedded into an overarching structure, held together by the display of communicative reason as a counterpart of systemic rationality—a counterpart that is operating not only from outside the social subsystems but also inside each of them.[77] Two characteristics stick out. Firstly, the communicative understanding of legal order overcomes the hierarchical notion of the legal order which was typical for the traditional conception, but maintains a normative ranking between the different levels. The normative quality of the norm, however, is not justified here by the level of 'hard power' of which the authority vested with the task to impose this norm over other rules can dispose, but rather by the more or less high inclusivity of the range of validity of the norm. In this sense, international law has the highest normative quality, albeit endowed with relatively little authoritative and compelling 'hard power'. Secondly, the recognition of legal differentiation and diversity as a matter of fact and as a desirable outlook does not correspond, from the standpoint of the communicative paradigm, to a value-free, horizontal pluralism like in the perspective of postmodern criticism. Instead, the fundamental values—conveyed through the communicative reason—pervade all subsystems and all levels of the legal system. As a result, the normative centre of the legal order is held by the principle of democratic legitimation and definition of common interests and values, whereby the democratically legitimated public order maintains a normative superiority over private law subsystems.

As a post-unitary, non-hierarchical and non-pyramidal whole, the communicative paradigm supports constitutionalism beyond the borders of the nation state,[78] the cosmopolitan dimension of which, due to its acknowledgment of diversity, is quite different from the old ideas of the 'world state' or of the *civitas maxima*. Indeed, the political interactions within the single polity, the inter-state relations, and the supra-state norms and institutions are interpreted as distinct kinds of interaction which must be acknowledged in their mutual inter-dependence, but also in their autonomy.[79] This way, the communicative paradigm supports a robust epistemological foundation of a multilevel understanding of public law.

At the domestic level, state public law regulates the interactions between citizens of each single political community as well as between these citizens and the domestic institutions. The theory of communicative reason demands that decisions are taken through deliberative processes based on the reflexive involvement of the citizens. At the international level, public international law addresses the relations

[77] Jürgen Habermas, *Faktizität und Geltung* (1992); Jürgen Habermas, *Der gespaltene Westen* (2004); Jürgen Habermas, 'Eine politische Verfassung für die pluralistische Weltgesellschaft?', *Kritische Justiz* 38 (2005), 222.

[78] Mattias Kumm, 'On the Cosmopolitan Turn in Constitutionalism: On the Relationship between Constitutionalism in and beyond the State', in Jeffrey L. Dunoff and Joel P. Trachtman (eds.), *Ruling the World?* (2009), pp. 258, 265.

[79] Jürgen Habermas, *Der gespaltene Westen* (2004); Habermas, *Eine politische Verfassung für eine pluralistische Weltgesellschaft* (n. 78); Jürgen Habermas, *Zur Verfassung Europas* (2011), pp. 43ff.; Jürgen Habermas, 'Democracy in Europe: Why the Development of the EU into a Transnational Democracy Is Necessary and How It Is Possible', *European Law Journal* 21(4) (2015), 546.

between citizens of different states mediated through their states; therefore, the focus is on relations between states. Lastly, the third level of public law is made by the cosmopolitan law as the public law that shapes direct interactions between individuals from different states as well as between individuals and the states of which they are not citizens.

4. And yet

On the basis of this short overview, one can conclude that current strands of the theories on international, supranational and transnational law are on the road to leaving the dichotomy of universalism and particularism. Should one derive from this state of facts that universalism and particularism are obsolete categories? Have they lost definitively their epistemological and heuristic value? We claim that such conclusion cannot convince for at least three main reasons. Firstly, while some innovative conceptions look forwards to post-dichotomous rearrangements of domestic and international order, many other authors are still to be located within the traditional categories. Secondly, even if the theories presented in this section overcome the dichotomy of universalism and particularism, this does not imply that these categories fully belong to the past. To the contrary, they are still instruments for the understanding of the contrasting interpretations of domestic and international order. System theory, postmodern pluralism, and communicative paradigm may be located beyond the dichotomy, but they propose different mixtures of the inherent value of some parochial tenets and the impetus towards a global well-ordered society. As a result, they maintain in their conceptual constructs implicit and often even explicit references to both particularism and universalism. Thirdly, the categories of universalism and particularism are not only descriptive, but also normative. They help to shape preferences as regards the extension of order and the sources of its legitimacy, enabling to substantiate options by a well-founded interpretation of the old and new scholarship. Even if some strands of contemporary universalism do not deny the reasonableness of at least some tenets of particularism any longer, seeking a more balanced approach than in the older theories, they maintain nevertheless the conviction—a genuinely normative conviction, indeed—that the well-ordered society can expand to include in principle the whole humankind. And everyone who shares this conviction will further read these theoretical proposals as the continuation of the old idea that striving for a world of peace and solidarity represents not only a distant hope, but a moral obligation.

Some Brief Conclusions

Pierre-Marie Dupuy

The international legal system established in 1945 can be seen, in its very design, as an incarnation of western rationalism. Like that rationalism, it implicitly embodies a certain ideology of progress. In terms of its philosophical underpinnings, it would seem to be heir to the philosophy of the Enlightenment and the *Aufklärung* despite the fact that a number of its most influential advocates came from countries closer to Anglo-Saxon utilitarianism than to Kantian constitutionalism. This immediately poses a question therefore: could this set of norms claim in the long term to be truly universal in scope.

I. Space and Time

Despite the ideological neutrality traditionally professed by the proponents of legal positivism, contemporary international law is founded on a particular western tradition. That tradition is itself based on the belief that subordinating the conduct of states to communal laws, recognized by all as valid and legitimate, will progressively bring about a gradual move away from if not ultimately a renunciation of any recourse to force. Kant seems to be its most inspired prophet in that regard, in particular in his essay *Perpetual Peace* which seeks precisely to lay the foundations of a true legal cosmopolitanism, propounded in the name of all peoples. Kant remains moreover one of the crucial inspirations behind a shift away from metaphysics, in particular in terms of his philosophy of knowledge. Nevertheless, the project for perpetual peace he inspires, itself has a messianic dimension. We will find it again in the Charter of the United Nations: that instrument, proclaimed in the name of 'the peoples of the United Nations determined to save succeeding generations from the scourge of war . . . and to reaffirm faith in fundamental human rights, in the dignity and worth of the human person . . .,' presents itself as a promise. It is an ideal purpose assigned to the community of peoples, implicitly founded on the sediments laid down in the collective conscience by a particular tradition, one which is primarily Christian but also discernible in other monotheistic systems.

At the same time, the text adopted in San Francisco in 1945 took the risk of claiming to be valid *here and now*, that is to say, from entry into force of the communal law which the Charter of the United Nations represents, ideally affirmed as a universal constitution in the Kantian sense updated in that regard by Habermas.

There is therefore in any event a tension and a temporal contradiction between the law and the promise or, to put it another way, between the time needed to bring the project to fruition and the immediacy it claims.

There is only one direction to be found in that timescale. Time's arrow has only one target, the progress of humanity. There is no going back, much less any eternal recurrence. As in Hegel or Marx, who in certain regards follow on from Kant here, in the Charter of the United Nations history has one sense, that is to say, both one meaning and one direction. There may be times when it is stopped, different stages, but no regression. This text proposed in 1945 to be adopted collectively by all states, thus contains a particular philosophy of history which should be taken, if not to full term, at least towards completion. The rationale behind this wish not to stop but to stabilize history by subjecting it permanently to the reign of reason has much to do with the horror, albeit in the beginning partly underestimated, of the Holocaust. Never again. We cannot go backwards without the risk that the unthinkable which nevertheless came true will happen again. This promise is therefore also founded on a turning back, turning back barbarism, which the Second World War had just shown could reach previously unparalleled dimensions, even in one of the countries which had contributed most to western humanist philosophy.

Behind the dense rhetorical screen deployed in the Preamble to the UN Charter, the ulterior motives were, of course, many and difficult to reconcile. Beyond apparent agreement on the big principles, the communist world, too, was thinking of progress, although progress through the dictatorship of the proletariat, itself a long way from both liberal democracy and respect for the Rule of Law, identified in its continental Europe version by the notion of the 'Rechtsstaat' or 'Etat de droit'. Be that as it may, the, communist, Soviet Union despite everything shared the same world as the West in so far as it drew part of its ideology from Hegel via Marx. For the Soviet Union, too, history was a series of successive phases aimed at improving humanity's lot. There was no fundamental rupture in that regard, then, between East and West, both of which cherished the ideology of progress. The 'Cold War' would therefore be fought between two antagonistic notions of the routes leading to the progress of humanity.

A 'directional predication', to borrow an expression from Alain Badiou, the UN Charter not only announced a new era but affirmed a rupture, a new departure in the history of peoples and their states at the same time as it enshrined a universal dimension of the human person (prefiguring the emergence of humanity as a subject of international law, which appeared gradually from the 1970s). It is in that aspect that we must look for its constitutive value which would lead Habermas to conclude that it is constitutional, a term admissible only when used metaphorically.

II. Questioning and Regression

There are many who from the outset have thought, as Jean-Jacques Rousseau himself, who ultimately had little faith in human perfectibility, would no doubt have done, that the project enshrined in the UN Charter was merely an unattainable ideal. Nevertheless, in the first decades, the myth of progress applied to the law if not always to international relations, could more or less give the impression that it was working. Admittedly, the Cold War brought back tensions, but at the same time it kept out of direct conflicts, at least among the permanent members of the Security Council. The Security Council, it must be said, remained paralysed, but it was in certain, especially normative, respects, beneficially replaced by the dramatic rise of the General Assembly taken as a World Forum, at least until the mid-1980s. The 'outlawry of war' movement had crumbled, but official recognition by all parties of the fundamental legitimacy of the principle of the renunciation of force in international relations, enshrined in Article 2.4 of the UN Charter, nevertheless remained in place. The right of the 'international community as a whole' took over from claims for the 'right to development', the new incarnation of the right of peoples. There was a growing impression, then, at least after the Cuban missile crisis (1963), that albeit not ruling out all danger of war, the UN Charter, supplemented by the United Nations Declaration on Principles of International Law concerning Friendly Relations and Cooperation among States (1970), gave all parties a renewed basis for 'peaceful coexistence' and even more 'cardinal' and 'intransgressible' principles, as the International Court of Justice would call them in 1986 and ten years later. This remains true even though some seem to be under the illusion that this 'community', for all it is indeed a legal fiction, which functions rather effectively but only in formally legal terms, has itself already become a long standing political reality.

III. Back to the Turning Back

The ideological inspiration behind contemporary international law from the time of its founding text adopted in San Francisco in 1945 has been given its full force by the fact that for a while now it has been perceived in all its fragility. With Daesh and the other rehashings of radical Islam we are back in the age, which we believed had been consigned to history, of militant obscurantism. Be off with you! Using theology to signal both its anchorage in the past and its diminishing horizon, it resolutely turns its back on the Enlightenment. It has brought back not only metaphysics but theocracy and sets up the 'Caliphate' as its model with a cry of 'long live Death', like the Francoist general Millan-Astray back in the Spanish Civil War. Explicitly set on repudiating any democratic ideal, radical Islamism systematically rejects any reference to 'human rights', asserting in particular that women can legitimately be reduced to a radically subordinate status. It resolutely destroys the vestiges of any ancient civilizations liable to illustrate the heritage boasted of by 'infidels'. Man does not exist in his own right but only as a subject literally in submission to the religion of a Book, itself seen in this context without any interpretive distance, the Koran being written without the slightest ambiguity in the language of God and as dictated by God.

That is not the only instance of regression, however, and it would be very wrong to believe that the attacks against the edifice of the UN Charter come only from a perverted element of the Muslim East. Another threat is coming from some of its founding fathers themselves. Permanent members of the Security Council, taking their inspiration from the unfortunate precedent set by the United States at the time of its intervention in Iraq in 2003 if not even from the military intervention of some NATO countries in Kosovo, back in 1999 may be reputed to take a somewhat flexible interpretation of some of the most fundamental principles of positive international law. This time, however, those states are no longer really looking to either the vocabulary or the norms of current international law to justify their actions. Hanna Arendt believed she could say that man had freed himself from both nature and history. History is nevertheless resurfacing to justify a rupture with the universality of modern international law, a universality partially recast, however, by the advent of the universality of the human person as a reference, which has emerged to compete with the reference of respect for state sovereignty.

IV. A Precarious International Constitutionalism

A rather muddled way of analysing the current situation might be to see it as a questioning, on a large scale, of the sway the post-war victorious powers have held over international law. However, that way of seeing things, whilst it may at a push apply to the adherents of Islamic fundamentalism as replacing the myth of the Marxist revolution, is completely inapplicable to the behaviour of the United States in 2003 or other permanent members of the Security Council. The loss of any common reference undermines the explicit universality of the message put out by the UN Charter, as a historical project at risk of being reduced to a precarious collective contract.

By the same token, the 'constitutionalist' effort of 1945 dear to Habermas is revealed in all its precariousness. It saw itself as the product of a collective desire to rationalize international relations. Yet was it, as the short-lived product of an exceptional moment, ultimately based on an illusion—the illusion that peoples could stop history by bringing it once and for all under the reign of reason as Kant was already inviting them to do in his essay on *Perpetual Peace*?

History, however, never stops, but it often falters. The desire to institutionalize the subjective reign of reason would appear to have proved, if not futile, at least in part naive. If we wanted to make almost the same observation this time from the standpoint of Schopenhauer's dualism, we would say that the Charter, which is by definition part of the world of *representation*, was an invitation to an illusory attempt to stem the tide of the *will*, that is to say, from Schopenhauer's point of view, of the spontaneous will to live, the irrational chaos of which the persistence of war and hatred of the other is undoubtedly the least spasmodic manifestation.

One of the collateral victims of this shift is likely to be the reference to 'humanity' as affirmed in the early 1970s as a holder of rights and the organizing spirit behind a significant amount of the international law of the last seventy years. It is surely no accident that the deluded warriors of the so-called Islamic State seek to signify their difference precisely by committing 'crimes against humanity'. They signal their power by mocking that portion of humanity which each of their victims carries inside and stake out their territory with severed heads.

V. Competing Notions of Universality

The first, Kantian, notion of universality is that in the UN Charter, as already pointed out above, based on the idea that there are truly universal values of which the rights of the person and the pursuit of perpetual peace other than in the grave are the most tangible sign. This is the universality of the declarations of human rights, from 1776 to 1948, and emerged to complete the idea that the *state of nature* must be able, despite the nature of the State, to yield before the communal law.

Alongside this, although much older, since it goes back to Descartes, we also have the universality asserted by scientific and technical discourse, which believes itself by definition to apply to everyone, in any latitude and in any age. It has thereby come to replace regional mythologies, each of which, going beyond often common themes, confirms the identity of the specific culture from which it came. Those individual cultures are as a result reduced by the sweeping proclamations of universalism (and very much despite them) to being merely picturesque, as that is 'the misery of others'. The assertion of cultural diversity advocated by UNESCO therefore perhaps hides in that regard, although against its wishes, an attempt to balance out that technicist universalization.

The world of technology, in Heidegger's sense, leads ultimately both to the abolition of Kant's categorical imperatives and to an affirmation of the Nietzschean will to power which ultimately has no other purpose than its own expansion. Both those movements have therefore come to us from eighteenth-century Europe in so far as the rationalist Europe of the Enlightenment believed simultaneously in progress, in the attainment of human happiness as the ultimate aim and in the advance of science and technology which is the means of achieving it (the dream of the Voltairian Third Republic petit bourgeois par excellence) but could not see that, by placing its faith solely in reason as inherited from the Cartesian *cogito*, it also gave rise to the inexorable 'disenchantment of the world' already denounced by Max Weber.

VI. Globalization

The globalization progressively coming to the fore at the end of the twentieth century seems therefore to be revealing that the cosmopolitan purpose proposed by the UN Charter is incapable of arresting the loss of meaning engendered by the technological age, articulating the drive for growth as an end in itself, increased productivity as a perpetual objective, a perpetual obsession with short-term profitability and competition as the ultimate possible horizon. At that breakneck pace, mankind, seeing itself quite clearly as the impecunious 'master and possessor of nature' is jeopardizing a planet which has become unbreathable and headed for the sterility of silent springs.

The regression we are currently witnessing appears therefore to be, at a deeper level, an increasingly clear manifestation of that 'universal loss of meaning' of which Heidegger and the Frankfurt School had both announced its emergence and deplored its expansion.

At a stroke, the geostrategic or cultural causes which had been invoked previously, far from losing their force as explanations, can be seen precisely as the indirect effects of a shift in history of a quite different magnitude, beginning in western Europe several centuries ago, with the *Discourse on Method*.... The brutal regression embodied in Islamic barbarism would in that respect in fact be related to technicist savagery, just as destructive of the human environment, in the broadest sense, as of the values which underpin it. In the same way that Heidegger himself, misguided genius as he was, believed he had found in Nazism a return to the meaning of history, radical Islamism is in the present age an archaic attempt to compensate for the loss of a meaning it believes it can find in blind faith in a primitive god, Allah becoming confused with Baal. The technicist and productivist globalization triumphing in the capitalist world, by corroding the very values which allowed it to exist, is thus contributing indirectly to the return of a summary divinity suitable for those marginalized by capitalism. Is the eternal recurrence not always, ultimately, the eternal recurrence of barbarism?

VII. Towards a Programme to Combat Regression?

To devise a programme of action attempting to rein in the degradation of an international legal system established seventy years ago is beyond the scope of these brief conclusions.

As optimism and hope remain a moral duty, we can nevertheless advance the opinion that a necessary first step is to reread the authors whose works have been analysed here, since, as already said, their successive contributions, going beyond their differences if not to say their divergences, helped lay down the ideological bedrock on which the normative framework of that system was built. We must therefore stress the importance of an approach inspired by Antonio Cassese consisting of reconciling realism and utopia. We must at the same time be aware of the constraints imposed by the persistent inertia of sovereignties whilst inviting all peoples to harmonize their visions of the future in pursuit of common aims which are constantly being reformulated. Utopia is only reprehensible when it is a substitute for action, not when it inspires it.

The pursuit of peace and the renunciation of recourse to force today still constitute a crucial direction of travel. In order to give the UN Charter back its messianic dimension, however, we now have to add to it the, inherently universal, cause of safeguarding and restoring the health of the planet. As the Stockholm Declaration on the human environment had already said, 'we only have one Earth', and it has today been degraded to such a degree that it can only be restored to health with a gigantic collective effort of universal cooperation, the framework and programme for which were successfully laid out by the Paris Agreement on protection of the global climate, adopted in December 2015. The formalism which is all too often unthinkingly levelled against the law should therefore be seen on the contrary as a means of clarifying the targets incumbent upon all the components of an international community comprising, besides the States, the various participants in international civil society, because, from now on, upholding the law is quite clearly too important to leave to the diplomats. It is, also, through invocation of a well-tempered Utopia that mercantile globalization will encounter competition from a cosmopolitan solidarity intended to reinvest it with meaning whilst upholding universal respect for the Other.

Index

The manufacturer's authorised representative in the EU for product safety is Oxford University Press España S.A. of El Parque Empresarial San Fernando de Henares, Avenida de Castilla, 2 - 28830 Madrid (www.oup.es/en or product.safety@oup.com). OUP España S.A. also acts as importer into Spain of products made by the manufacturer.
Printed and bound by CPI Group (UK) Ltd, Croydon, CR0 4YY
14/09/2026
02216284-0010